S0-CTI-695

CORPORATE FINANCE

ELVIN F. DONALDSON

PROFESSOR OF FINANCE
COLLEGE OF COMMERCE AND ADMINISTRATION
THE OHIO STATE UNIVERSITY

THE RONALD PRESS COMPANY · NEW YORK

9

Library of Congress Catalog Card Number: 57–6815
PRINTED IN THE UNITED STATES OF AMERICA

To

MY WIFE

PREFACE

This book offers a complete survey of the principles underlying the financial practices and the financial management of the modern business corporation. The book is designed primarily for the undergraduate course in corporation or business finance as that course is taught in schools and colleges of business and in departments of economics. Much of the material will be of interest, also, to those engaged in the financial management of business organizations as well as to those who desire an understanding of corporate securities and the basic financial practices of the corporation.

The plan for the book developed out of many years of teaching and from close association with the financial management of business firms. It is hoped the reader will find a salient feature of the book to be the combination of the basic principles and practical aspects in a unified whole. No effort was spared to produce a book that is at once complete and also easy both to read and to assimilate.

In writing the book, a studied attempt was made to incorporate a background of the best current legal and accounting thought relating to the financial policies of corporations. The important area of taxation and its impact on the corporation and corporation owners is thoroughly explored and reflects this approach. The vital subject of depreciation also embodies this approach, as do all the chapters dealing with securities. The use of depreciation allowances as a source of funds for expansion is discussed, and the section on working capital contains ample treatment of both short and intermediate-term financing.

Review questions will be found at the end of each chapter. In addition, several problems—modified situational or case analyses—relating to and integrated with the text are included with each chapter. This material has been purposely designed to stimulate student interest in thinking through problem situations requiring in their solution the application of basic principles.

The author is indebted to many people for their help and constructive criticisms in connection with the preparation of this book. Gratitude is expressed particularly to H. E. Hoagland, Professor Emeritus of Finance at The Ohio State University; and to my colleague, John K. Pfahl, who read the entire manuscript and offered invaluable suggestions for its improvement. Thanks are due, also, to Mrs. John K. Pfahl and to Mrs. William Bischoff for their painstaking work in typing the original manuscript. And for her help in reading the proof, for her patience and understanding throughout the writing of this book, a special debt of gratitude is owed Kathryn, my wife.

Elvin F. Donaldson

Columbus, Ohio
January, 1957

CONTENTS

Part I

FORMS OF BUSINESS ORGANIZATIONS

Part II

CORPORATE SECURITIES

Part III

PROMOTION AND FINANCING THROUGH SECURITIES

Part IV

WORKING CAPITAL

Part V

ADMINISTRATION OF INCOME

Part VI

EXPANSION AND COMBINATION

Part VII

READJUSTMENT, REORGANIZATION, RECEIVERSHIP, AND DISSOLUTION

TABLES

Part I

FORMS OF BUSINESS ORGANIZATIONS

Chapter 1

THE NATURE OF CORPORATE FINANCE

INTRODUCTION. We in the United States live in a corporate world. We depend upon business corporations for our food and clothing, for light and heat, for transportation, for communications, and for many other things. We should know something about this form of business organization that plays so vital a role in our everyday life. And the activities of these corporations which relate to finance are tremendously important. Without adequate financial management corporations would be unable to fulfill their functions.

To the novice *corporate finance* might seem a dry, uninteresting subject involving an infinite variety of modern complexities understood only by a "Philadelphia lawyer," and practiced by men who go about in black shoes and with long, solemn faces. Or to some it might, perhaps, bring to mind a more glamorous picture of making fabulous fortunes in stocks and bonds in the half-century-old building at the corner of Broad and Wall in New York—the New York Stock Exchange. Those who are acquainted with the subject only through a reading of the financial history of the Roaring Twenties, and the crash of 1929, are apt to have a distorted idea of the field, with an overemphasis on strange practices, such as manipulation and deception, bull and bear pools, marginal trading, and gambling that leads even to suicide.

THE FIELD OF BUSINESS. The history of the United States could well be written from the viewpoint of the development of its business. Aside from governmental employees, practically all of those gainfully employed in the United States are working in a business of some kind. In times past businessmen "learned the ropes" by practicing, but today the business leaders of the future are trained in schools of commerce and business throughout the country. Many see the need for higher business education in the graduate schools. Some companies now send their promising executives to special schools that offer Executive Development programs.

Finance is an important subject in all forms of business organizations, and to companies and individuals engaged in the various types of business. Most of what is said in this book will have general application to the different kinds of business undertakings. In most instances we will not be concerned with the peculiar problems of businesses that are subject to special laws and regulations, such as railroads, public utilities, and financial corporations. At the outset it will be useful to classify types of businesses.

Various agencies classify businesses in different ways. In stock market parlance we speak of (1) railroads, (2) public utilities, (3) financial concerns, and (4) industrials. The fourth group includes all types of companies which do not come under one of the other three headings. In some instances all businesses are classified into two broad groups, (1) industrial and (2) commercial. The former consists of manufacturing companies and the extractive industries (mining and quarrying), and the latter of all other types of business concerns. Tables 1 and 2, which show the number of business firms in the United States, and the national income by industrial origin, illustrate the classification followed by the U.S. Department of Commerce.

TABLE 1

BUSINESS FIRMS IN THE UNITED STATES BY MAJOR INDUSTRY

Industry	*Number in Thousands*
Mining and quarrying	37.9
Manufacturing	328.2
Contract construction	433.8
Transportation, communications, and other public utilities	185.7
Wholesale trade	284.8
Retail trade	1,864.1
Finance, insurance, and real estate	338.0
Service industries	739.8
Total	4,212.3

SOURCE: *Survey of Current Business,* U.S. Department of Commerce, Office of Business Economics, January, 1954. The data are for June 30, 1953.

LAW AND BUSINESS. Laws are always necessary, but especially in the society in which we live. As business has developed and become more and more complex by creating corporate enterprises, the impact of laws is felt to an increasing extent. A study of corporate finance would be impossible without delving into the law. From the formation of a business organization through all its life, including its dissolution, the procedures must strictly follow the law. Security

TABLE 2
NATIONAL INCOME IN THE UNITED STATES IN 1955 BY INDUSTRIAL ORIGIN

Industry	*In Billions of Dollars*
Mining	5.8
Agriculture, forestry, and fisheries	15.8
Manufacturing	101.8
Contract construction	16.2
Transportation	15.5
Communications and other public utilities	11.7
Wholesale and retail trades	55.5
Finance, insurance, and real estate	29.4
Service industries	31.6
Total	283.3

SOURCE: *Survey of Current Business,* U.S. Department of Commerce, Office of Business Economics, February, 1956, p. 13.

sales, rights of the stockholders and bondholders, powers and liabilities of the officers and directors, the declaration and payment of dividends, etc., are all governed by the law. There are three types of law: (1) common law, (2) statutory law, and (3) administrative law.

Common law. Common law represents the prevailing legal opinions and attitudes of the people as laid down by the judges in court decisions. It is an elastic system of law which can apply to an infinite variety of circumstances. It represents the thinking of many learned individuals over a long period of time. Where there are no statutes dealing with a particular situation, the common law is applicable. Each state has its own court decisions, and therefore its own common law. Generally speaking, the common law of the various states is about the same, but there are some differences.

Certain forms of business organizations, such as the individual proprietorship and the general partnership (in some states), which will be discussed later, are formed merely by contract among the members and are therefore referred to as common-law forms of organizations.

In former times in England when an individual thought that the common law was too rigid and did not give him relief, he sometimes appealed to the king for justice. The king eventually was compelled to refer these actions to the chancellor. This developed into the chancery courts. Today in this country we refer to such courts as *equity courts,* and the actions brought in these courts are called *equity* actions. Certain types of actions will be brought in *equity,* whereas others will be brought in the *law* courts. An injunction to prevent the occurrence of a wrongdoing, for example, would be brought in equity, but a suit for damages in a contract action would be brought in law. In most instances in the United States the same court hears both legal and equitable actions. The term *equity* is sometimes used synonymously with *justice.* In some instances the term is used to refer to "ownership," such as the stockholder's *equity* in the corporation, or *equity* securities.

Statutory law. The common law has certain weaknesses. It is slow to develop and therefore is inadequate for the rapidly changing economic and social systems. In some instances conflicting decisions on the same issue have been handed down by different judges. The legislatures of the various states and Congress have therefore enacted *statutory* law to supersede the common law in certain fields, or to apply in situations in which there was no common law. In some instances the statutes merely codify the existing common law, or clarify it. Statutory law represents a less elastic but more definite system than the common law. In the event of conflict between the common law and the statutes, the latter will prevail, unless they are declared unconstitutional. The corporation and certain types of partnerships, which will be discussed later, are formed under statutory law.

Administrative law. Out of some statutes has developed what has come to be known as *administrative law.* Administrative bodies or commissions are sometimes set up by the state legislatures or by Congress to carry out some specific statute or statutes. For example, the Federal Trade Commission administers the antitrust laws, and the Internal Revenue Service administers the federal income tax laws. These bodies will adopt rules and regulations governing the procedure for carrying out the statutes or passing on certain actions which may or may not be taken under the particular statutes. The rulings of the commissions have the force of law, until or unless the parties affected appeal to courts and get a contrary ruling. In most instances the rulings of the commissions will not be appealed, and when they are, it is probable that they will be upheld. It is thus apparent that these administrative commissions, which are executive in character, assume or take on powers that are really legislative or judicial in nature. As business develops it is becoming more and more subject to regulation by various types of commissions.

Importance of finance

PLACE OF FINANCE IN BUSINESS. The primary purpose of most businesses is to make a profit for their owners. To do this over a long period of time it is essential that a product or service be produced or profitably sold that will be purchased by other producers or by the consuming public. All the various departments or functions of a business concern are of importance in attaining that final objective.

The functions of a business, particularly an industrial concern, are oftentimes divided into only two broad groups, (1) production, and (2) distribution (selling). Included in these are the detailed functions, such as accounting, advertising, financing, purchasing, research, etc. The task of management is to administer the various departments or functions of the business. Every act of management relates directly or indirectly to one or more of the various departments of a business.

The importance of good management cannot be overstressed. With proper management the problems of all the departments will be solved, and without it a business cannot be a success for any extended period of time. It should be appreciated, however, that production management, financial management, sales management, etc., are all a part of "management."

A business may have good production and sales departments, but it may be doomed to failure if it has been financed improperly at the time of its establishment. Or, the improper use of bank or trade credit may result in failure. The unwise purchase of equipment or inventories might prove to be disastrous. Improper control of expenses may shoot costs up to the point where failure is inevitable. The inability to float a bond or stock issue at a particular time may result in complete failure. And in general, the inability to meet debts as they come due will force any company to the wall. The point should be stressed that all of these are *financial management* problems.

Accounting is indispensable and very closely related to financial management. The financial results of operations are recorded in the accounting books, and from these books are taken the data with which financial decisions are made. A good accounting system properly administered is essential to efficient financial management. In the section of the book dealing with the determination of income, depreciation, dividend policy, undistributed profits, and surplus reserves, we will be utilizing accounting methods. An elementary knowledge of accounting is of value to a student studying corporate finance, but the accounting phases of finance discussed in this book are not so technical that the uninitiated would be unable to grasp the meaning of what is being said.

There are several reasons why financial management does not attract the attention of the average person as much as some of the other functions of business. One reason is that there are ordinarily not many people involved in performing the financing function of a typical business concern, and the other is that in the great majority of businesses there is no "finance" department. The accounting and credit departments carry on detailed and routine operations of a financial character, and the purchasing department is entrusted with the spending of considerable amounts of money, but these departments are ordinarily not directly responsible for the financial management of a company.

In an individual proprietorship the owner is the financial manager. In a partnership or small corporation one of the owners or perhaps all of them take on the financial function. In some instances part of the work is done by a treasurer, secretary, bookkeeper, or credit manager. Financial management becomes more involved as the size of the business increases, just as it is usually the case with the other business functions. In a large corporation the board of directors is charged with the responsibility of policy making. In some instances a "finance committee" of the board, which may act between board meetings, determines financial policies, which policies are usually adopted by the entire board at its next regular meeting.

The chairman of the board of directors, when active in the affairs of a corporation, may devote a considerable amount of time to financial matters. The chief executive officer appointed by the board is the president of the company. In some companies, or at certain times in any company, the president will be directly occupied with financial management. The chief financial officer of the corporation, also appointed by the board of directors, is commonly the treasurer. In some instances a vice-president in charge of finance will be the principal financial officer of the company. In some companies the controller (sometimes spelled "comptroller," but pronounced the same), or auditor, is charged with some financial management. In some instances all of these officers get together to formulate financial policies, which are recommended to the board of directors. A budget committee, which may be composed of some or all of these officers, may be appointed to aid in the determination of financial policies. In some companies this is a committee of the board.

The financial management of a company may thus be carried on by various officers or committees within the company. The financial policies adopted by those in charge reach out and affect every department of the company.

Corporate Finance Defined. As used in academic circles, the word *finance* is applied to courses in both *public finance* and *private finance.* Public finance has to do with the procurement, administration, and spending of money by governmental bodies—local, state, and national. Many years ago the subject of public finance was of greater importance in the United States than that of private finance, because the government was an important supplier of capital for banks, public utilities, and railroads. With the development of the country, the accumulation of savings, and the rise of the modern corporation, private citizens took over the role of supplying capital for the development of business. Beginning with the depression of the early 1930's, and continuing through and after World War II, the federal government got back into the financial picture. Huge amounts of federal money have been poured into private business by the Reconstruction Finance Corporation, an instrumentality of the government. Public housing projects and financial aid to farmers have taken millions of dollars of the taxpayer's money. With the huge government debt hanging over our heads and the continuation of the trend toward greater governmental intervention in business, the subject of public finance will long continue to be of vital importance in our lives.

In this book, however, we will not be concerned with public finance. Our interest lies in the field of *private finance.* Generally speaking, private finance covers the activities of raising and managing money by business concerns. Some erroneously believe that the subject of private finance is confined solely to the financing of privately *owned* businesses or "close corporations." This latter term is sometimes used to distinguish these types of businesses from those whose stock is widely owned by a large number of stockholders. The term "*publicly owned* corporations" is often used to apply to these corporations. Thus, the financing of both *privately* owned and *publicly* owned businesses properly comes under the heading of *private finance.*

Contents

Scope of the Book. The use of this book in college work accounts for its contents and the order in which the various subjects are taken up. The following briefly indicates what we will be discussing.

1. *Forms of business organizations.* Our primary interest lies in the corporation and its methods of financing, as the title of the book would indicate. A brief discussion of the noncorporate forms

of business organizations, however, will be taken up before the corporation is studied. The noncorporate forms of organizations in the United States greatly exceed the number of corporations, and thus our study of private finance would be very incomplete unless we gave some attention to them. The financing of these businesses is important but not so intricate as in the case of the corporation. Their capital must come from relatively few owners, trade creditors, banks, and from the reinvestment of earnings. Little discussion is needed for an understanding of these sources of capital. Corporations obtain capital from banks and from the plowing back of earnings, but a considerable amount of their money comes from the sale of securities. An understanding of the various types of these securities calls for a rather lengthy discussion. Furthermore, the problems connected with the administration of corporate funds are much more complex than those encountered in the other forms of organizations. The types of noncorporate forms of business organizations which will be discussed in this book are as follows:

Individual proprietorship
General partnership
Limited partnership
Partnership association
Mining partnership
Joint venture
Joint stock company
Massachusetts trust

Immediately following the above will be a discussion of the organization and control of the corporation. Since we will be concerned mainly with the financial policies of corporations, it is advisable that we first consider the nature of the corporate form of organization. Included under this head will be the following: the development of corporation laws; types of corporations; attributes of the corporation; selecting state of organization; state taxes; incorporation procedure; nature of the charter and bylaws; transacting business in foreign states; federal corporate income tax; stockholders' rights; methods of stockholder voting; and powers, duties, and liabilities of corporate directors and officers.

2. *Corporate securities.* One of the most important parts of a book on corporation finance is that dealing with corporate securities. Before we can decide upon the proper kind of securities to sell in order to raise capital, it is necessary that we have a clear understanding of the nature of the various kinds of securities. In this section we will discuss the following: nature of corporate stock,

transfer of stock, stockholders' rights to dividends, liability of stockholders, treasury stock, reacquisition of stock by corporations, par and no-par stock, determination of book value and market value, common stock, guaranteed stock, prior-lien stock, deferred stock, debenture stock, nature of preferred stock and the specific rights of preferred shareholders as compared with common shareholders.

The remaining section on securities will be devoted to a discussion of bonds. Included in this will be the following: the nature of bonds as compared with stocks, computing bond yields, relationship between interest rates and bond prices, registered and coupon bonds, redemption and call features, bond trustees, the bond indenture, reasons for selling bonds, effect of leverage, classifications of bonds, types of mortgage bonds, open- and closed-end bond issues, after-acquired-property clause, collateral trust bonds, equipment obligations, land trust certificates, leasehold mortgage bonds, unsecured bonds, assumed and guaranteed bonds, joint bonds, receivers' and trustees' certificates, debenture bonds, income bonds, participating bonds, convertible securities, stock purchase warrants and options, bond retirement, and sinking fund and serial bonds.

3. *Financing through sale of securities.* After having considered the different types of securities, we will turn to the promotion of businesses and the problems related to raising funds through the sale of long-term financial instruments. We will consider the promoter, the problems relating to capitalizing a corporation, determination of the capital structure, types of security buyers, sale of securities to various types of buyers including employees, customers, and the corporation's own shareholders, investment banking, and the regulation of the issuance of securities under the Securities Act of 1933.

Although corporations receive their money from the primary distribution of securities, the secondary market for securities created by the over-the-counter market and the national securities exchanges are of considerable importance in the field of finance, and these organized markets make it easier for a company to sell additional issues of securities. Brief mention will be made of the over-the-counter market, and a more complete discussion will be given of the national securities exchanges, particularly the New York Stock Exchange. Regulation of the exchanges and the over-the-counter market, effected by the Securities Exchange Act of 1934, and the Securities and Exchange Commission will be briefly discussed. This will be followed by a discussion of the mechanics of buying and selling listed stocks. Included are the types of orders, buying on margin, dealing in odd lots, short selling, brokers' commissions, transfer taxes, and secondary distribution and special offerings.

4. *Working capital.* Although the typical course in corporation finance is concerned primarily with the raising of money through the issuance of the long-term instruments of stocks and bonds, treatment must also be given to the methods of raising money from short-term sources, and the problems related to working capital. In this connection we will discuss the following: nature of working capital, kinds of working capital, inventory turnover, inventory valuation, discounts, receivables turnover, budgets, working capital ratios, sources of working capital, commercial-paper houses, finance companies, and factoring.

5. *Administration of income.* This section will deal with the problems relating to the internal financial administration of income. Included will be the following: determination of the net income; depreciation, obsolescence, and depletion; retained income, surplus, surplus reserves; and dividend policies and the various kinds of dividends.

6. *Expansion and combination.* After discussing the organization and financing of corporations and the problems dealing with working capital and internal financial control, the next logical subject to consider is the expansion and combination of businesses. The first chapter of this section deals with the methods and types of expansion and the financial problems connected with them. This is followed by a discussion of the legality of combinations and the various forms of combination which have been used by businesses. Included are the following: gentlemen's agreements, pools, trusts, communities of interest, interlocking directorates, leases, trade associations, purchase of assets, mergers, consolidations, and holding companies.

The last chapter in this section deals with investment companies or, as they are sometimes called, "investment trusts." It is the belief of the author that due to the nature and importance of investment companies today, they should be discussed in a book dealing with corporate finance. Although there is a considerable difference between the objectives of holding companies and investment companies, there are some similarities, and perhaps a discussion of the two types of companies in the same section of the book is warranted.

7. *Recapitalization, readjustment, failure, compromises, receivership, reorganization under equity courts and the Bankruptcy Act, dissolution, liquidation, and bankruptcy.* These are the procedures

that will be discussed in the final part of the book. Recapitalization of one type or another is often carried out by a solvent and successful company. In other instances a recapitalization or readjustment results from failure or threatened failure of a company. The last phase of the life of a business is failure, and this subject warrants some discussion. Consideration of the causes of failure may be of value in that it may lead to the prevention of some failures in the future. Following failure, various courses of action may be taken by companies depending upon the circumstances present and the seriousness of the failure. The following procedures will be briefly discussed: compromise settlements, equity receiverships and reorganizations, reorganization under the Bankruptcy Act, dissolution, liquidation, and bankruptcy.

Questions

1. List the various types of businesses. Do you think that the federal government should have been listed as a type of business? Why or why not?
2. Indicate reasons why agriculture and the professions should be considered businesses. Why should they not be so considered?
3. List and explain briefly the various kinds of law. Do these same kinds of laws affect you as an individual? Explain.
4. Which is more important in an industrial concern, production or distribution?
5. Indicate the relative importance of financial management in a large corporation.
6. State specifically who is charged with the responsibility of financial management in large business concerns.
7. Do you believe that more job offerings would be available in production or distribution than in "finance"? If so, how do you account for it? Would this be a reason why you might not want to follow finance as a career? Explain.
8. Distinguish between public and private finance. Is the study of the financial phases of publicly owned corporations considered private finance?
9. Indicate the various ways in which a person might benefit from taking a course in corporate finance.
10. Indicate the importance of accounting and law in the study of corporate finance.

Problems

1. Look up the books (not over twelve) in your library which deal with the general subject of corporate finance, and list the following for each book: (a) Titles, (b) Authors, (c) Author's connections, (d) Date of publication of most recent edition.
2. Ascertain from the financial manuals in your library the titles of officers in the following corporations who you believe would have an important part in the financial management of their particular companies: (a) Federated Department Stores, (b) General Motors, (c) Pennsylvania Railroad, (d) U.S. Steel.

Chapter 2

INDIVIDUAL PROPRIETORSHIP AND GENERAL PARTNERSHIP

INDIVIDUAL PROPRIETORSHIP, PARTNERSHIP, AND CORPORATION COMPARED. In this and the following chapter we will be concerned with the noncorporate forms of business organizations. In the chapter following these the corporation as a form of organization will be discussed. At the outset of this chapter, however, the extent of use of the corporate form will be discussed along with the individual proprietorship and the partnership, in order that the relative importance of these three forms of business enterprises may be understood. Later in the chapter the income tax status of the corporation will be discussed, again in order that a comparison may be made with the other importation forms of organizations.

RELATIVE IMPORTANCE IN THE UNITED STATES. The figures used in this comparison are not recent, but they are the latest available from the U.S. Department of Commerce. Partial information from the Internal Revenue Service indicates that the relative importance of the various forms of organizations at the present time is not much different from the percentages shown here.[1]

At the time of the study there were approximately 4,200,000 business firms in the United States (agriculture and the professions excluded). Of these, slightly over 69 per cent were individual proprietorships, 18 per cent were partnerships, about 11 per cent were corporations, and a little less than 2 per cent operated under some other form of organization. Perhaps these data might be better comprehended if we say that generally speaking two out of every three businesses are formed as individual proprietorships, one out of every five is a partnership, and one out of every ten is a cor-

[1] *Survey of Current Business,* U.S. Department of Commerce, Office of Business Economics, April, 1955, p. 16.

poration. Table 3 shows the relative importance of the various forms of organizations in the various industries in the United States.

TABLE 3

PER CENT DISTRIBUTION OF FIRMS IN THE UNITED STATES BY FORM OF ORGANIZATION AND INDUSTRY

Industry	*Individual Proprietorship*	*Partnership*	*Corporation*	*Others*	*All Forms*
Mining and quarrying	52.8	21.4	23.5	2.3	100
Manufacturing	45.3	23.6	29.4	1.8	100
Contract construction	78.2	15.5	6.2	.1	100
Transportation, communications and other public utilities	76.8	7.5	12.3	3.3	100
Wholesale trade	44.6	25.5	27.9	2.0	100
Retail trade	72.5	20.5	6.1	.9	100
Finance, insurance, and real estate	54.3	14.3	22.2	9.2	100
Service industries	81.4	13.6	4.4	.6	100
All industries	69.5	18.0	10.7	1.8	100

SOURCE: *Survey of Current Business,* U.S. Department of Commerce, Office of Business Economics, June, 1951, p. 10. The data in this study were as of March 31, 1947. The latest material available is contained in the *Survey of Current Business,* for April, 1955, which shows the breakdown only between corporations, and noncorporate forms of organizations lumped together, as of January 1, 1955. This study revealed that corporations then comprised approximately 13.5 per cent of the total number of business firms instead of 10.7 as was the case in the study published in 1951.

It will be noted that over half of the firms in the various industries, except manufacturing and wholesaling, are operated under the individual proprietorship form of organization. But even in the excepted two groups the individual proprietorship is used much more frequently than either the partnership or the corporation. Expressed in general terms, about three fourths of all firms in the construction, public utility, retail, and service industries are individual proprietorships. With the exception of public utilities, this might have been expected. Although all the railroads and electric light and power, gas, and water companies are incorporated, the relatively large number of proprietorships results from the fact that in the transportation group there are many small trucking firms in business.

Although the individual proprietorship is by far the most numerous form of organization, in terms of employment and the volume of business the corporation is the most important in most of the industries. Corporations account for about three fourths of the national income and employment in the country (agriculture and the professions excluded).[2] Even in the retail trade, where only about one in each sixteen firms is incorporated, slightly more than 40 per cent of the national income from retailing comes from corporations.

Table 4 shows the total number of nonagricultural corporate and noncorporate business firms (professional services excluded) in the United States as of January 1, for the years 1950–1955. Data on the breakdown of the noncorporate forms of organizations are not available for these years.

TABLE 4

Number of Business Firms in Operation in the United States on January 1, 1950–55, Classified According to Form of Organization

(Number in Thousands)

	Total		*Corporate*		*Noncorporate*	
Year	*Number*	*Per Cent*	*Number*	*Per Cent*	*Number*	*Per Cent*
1950	4,009	100	495	13.5	3,514	86.5
1951	4,067	100	516	12.7	3,551	87.3
1952	4,121	100	526	12.8	3,595	87.2
1953	4,179	100	539	12.9	3,640	87.1
1954	4,185	100	551	13.2	3,634	86.8
1955*	4,182	100	564	13.5	3,618	86.5

* Based on incomplete data.

Source: Betty C. Churchill, "Business Population by Legal Form of Organization," *Survey of Current Business*, U.S. Department of Commerce, Office of Business Economics, April, 1955, p. 15.

The individual proprietorship

Nature of the Individual Proprietorship. The oldest, simplest, and most commonly used form of organization is the *individual proprietorship*. It is sometimes called the *individual enterprise* or *entrepreneurship*, *sole proprietorship*, or merely, the *proprietorship*. The business is owned, managed, and controlled by a single person. For legal purposes there is really no distinction between the proprietor and the proprietorship. The business property is held in the name of the proprietor, suits are brought by and against him, and contracts are made in his name.

The individual proprietorship is the most easily formed of the various forms of organization. In fact, there are no formalities connected with its creation. If a person starts a business by himself,

[2] *Survey of Current Business*, U.S. Department of Commerce, Office of Business Economics, April, 1955.

and takes no steps to start another form of organization, the law will say that he has an individual proprietorship. No organization papers need be drawn up, nor are there any organization taxes and fees to be paid. If the business operated is such that special licenses must be obtained, such as the sale of tobacco or drugs, for example, then the proprietor must conform in the same way as any other form of organization.

The federal income tax must always be reckoned with in the formation of any type of organization. In the case of the individual proprietorship the tax laws do not distinguish between the proprietor and the proprietorship. The business income is reported on the individual's income tax form, and this is true regardless of whether or not any of the income is withdrawn from the business. The example given later in the chapter of the taxation of a general partnership will apply equally to the individual proprietorship.

One of the most important disadvantages of this form of organization from the viewpoint of the proprietor is that of unlimited liability. If the business assets are insufficient to satisfy the firm creditors, they may proceed against the individual's personal property. Thus, the proprietor subjects all his personal property to the risks of his business. Property which is held in his wife's name, however, cannot be attached, provided the title to such property was not transferred to her in anticipation of action by the creditors.

Although the corporation overshadows the individual proprietorship in terms of wage earners and value of product, nevertheless the individual proprietorship is still the most commonly used form of business organization in the United States. It leads by a wide margin in the professions and in agriculture. Other strongholds of this form of organization are in retailing, service establishments, construction, small trucking concerns, and real estate firms.

The general partnership

NATURE OF THE GENERAL PARTNERSHIP. The *general partnership* may be defined as an association of two or more persons carrying on as co-owners a legal business for profit. It is referred to as a common-law form of organization, although at the present time most of the states have statutes relating to it. In thirty-two of the states and in Alaska the Uniform General Partnership Act has been adopted. These include the leading commercial and industrial states. In most of the others, special statutes cover certain phases of partnership activity.

The general partnership is based on a contract between two or more persons. It is advisable that the contract be in writing and signed by the partners, but it may be oral, or even implied. When written articles of partnership are drawn up, it is advisable that adequate provisions relating to the following be included:

1. Name of the partnership
2. Names of the partners
3. Nature of the business to be conducted
4. Capital contribution of each of the partners
5. Method to be followed in dividing profits and losses
6. Agency powers of the partners
7. Procedure for admitting new partners
8. Procedure for partners withdrawing from the firm
9. Amount, if any, of salaries, or interest on investment, to be paid to the partners
10. Procedure to be followed, and how assets should be distributed upon dissolution

Legal Status. For business purposes the partnership is looked upon as a firm or company. At law, however, it is not treated as a legal entity. In contrast to the partnership, the corporation is considered a legal entity, with a life separate and apart from that of the individuals who own it. When suits are brought by or against the partnership, they are at common law brought in the names of the partners. In some states statutes have been adopted giving the partnership power to sue and be sued in its own name. According to the Uniform Partnership Act, real estate may be held in the partnership name. At common law personal property could be held in the firm name, and ordinary contracts could be made in the company name. This, of course, is also true under the Uniform Partnership Act. The fact that the partnership is not considered to be a legal entity is of special importance in relation to taxation, which will be discussed later.

Agency Power of Partners. In the absence of agreement to the contrary, each partner has full authority to enter into *ordinary business* contracts for the firm. Such contracts bind the other partners just the same as if they had made the contracts themselves. Partners, however, cannot bind their partners on personal contracts. Any agreements in the articles of partnership restricting or limiting the contractual rights of a partner are not effective as against innocent third parties such as firm creditors. The other partners, however, have a legal claim against a partner for losses sustained by them as a result of the particular partner's breaking his agreement.

Unless otherwise provided in the articles, each partner has one vote in connection with the internal management of the firm, regardless of the amount of his capital contribution. For *extraordinary* matters, such as taking a new partner, amending the articles, changing the firm name, selling all the assets, etc., unanimous consent of all the partners is necessary.

PARTNERSHIP NAME. Unless the statutes of the state provide otherwise, the partnership may adopt any name it desires. Thus, it may contain the name of one or more of the partners, or it may not contain any of their names. The statutes of some of the states provide that if the firm name does not contain the names of the partners, the partnership must file with the proper county or state officials the name of the firm and the names of the partners.

Some people think, mistakenly, that whenever the word *company* is included in the name of a business, the concern is incorporated. It is true that the various states require that the word *company, corporation, incorporated,* or their abbreviations appear in a corporate name, but it does not follow that a partnership cannot use the word *company*. Partnerships are sometimes advised against the use of the word *company* since some people may believe that the firm is incorporated. This may result in more difficulty in obtaining credit, since it may be thought that the owners have limited liability.

If a business firm, including a partnership, adopts a name which is so similar to that of another firm previously formed that material confusion results, certain legal actions may follow. The first firm to use the name may bring an injunction action to restrain the continued use of the name on the part of the other company, or it may sue for damages, or for part of the profits of the newer firm.

NATURE OF PARTNERS' LIABILITY. One of the principal disadvantages of the partnership form of organization is the liability of the various partners for debts or wrongdoings on the part of their partners or themselves. It was pointed out above that in an individual proprietorship the owner has unlimited liability. In other words, the liability of the owner is not limited to the assets of the business. Partners in a general partnership likewise have unlimited liability. But in a partnership this is more severe than in an individual proprietorship, since a partner is not only unlimitedly liable for debts which he himself contracts, but is also liable without limit for those contracted for the firm by his partners. This grows out of the fact which was explained above, that each partner is considered an agent of the firm and can bind it and the partners on all matters concerned with the business.

The liability of a partnership is spoken of as a *joint* or *joint and several liability*. In a technical sense, partners are said to be liable *jointly and severally* for torts (wrongdoings) committed by their partners. Thus, if one partner in the course of ordinary business operations injures a person, action may be had against all the partners or any of the partners. In respect to business debts, partners are said to be *jointly* liable. That is, action is brought against all the partners. But having done this and obtained judgment against all the partners, a creditor may proceed to collect against any or all the partners. Thus, in final analysis, this may also result in a *several* liability.

From what has been said, it is evident that a particular partner may lose all his personal property as a result of a partnership debt contracted by one of his partners. A question of law arises when it comes to deciding the respective rights of personal and partnership creditors in respect to personal and partnership property.

Partners are never liable for the personal debts contracted by their partners. Personal creditors may, however, proceed against the partnership assets to collect a personal debt of one of the partners, but the most they could obtain would be that particular partner's equity in the partnership. According to the court decisions and statutes in some of the states, however, before such creditors could collect from the partnership assets there must be an accounting with the firm creditors. In other words, the firm creditors would have to be paid first.

A partnership creditor could, after having received judgment against the partners, come against either the partnership assets or the personal assets of any or all the partners. A different situation exists when the two classes of creditors file their actions at the same time, or when the business is being dissolved under court authority, or is bankrupt. Then the court will allow the personal creditors prior right against the personal assets of the respective partners, and the firm creditors prior right against the partnership assets. In the event that the creditors are not fully satisfied from such assets they may then proceed against the other class of assets (provided there are any left). This is referred to as the *rule of marshaling of assets*. But, as stated above, the right of personal creditors is limited to the particular partner's equity in the firm assets.

If one partner is unable to stand his pro rata share of a partnership debt or loss, such loss must be borne by the other partners according to their profit-and-loss-sharing ratio. When one partner is forced to stand more than his pro rata share of a loss, he has what is called a *right of contribution* against the other partner or partners for their pro rata share.

Unless otherwise provided, profits and losses are divided equally by the partners. If they so desire, they can provide in the articles of partnership that profits be divided according to capital contribution, or in any other agreed ratio. It should be kept in mind that partnership creditors can hold any or all the partners liable for the debts regardless of the profit-and-loss-sharing ratio.

The foregoing can perhaps best be understood by an example. Assume that three partners enter in a general partnership and agree to share profits and losses equally. After several years of unsuccessful operation the business is dissolved under court authority. Neither the partnership nor the personal creditors had previously received judgment against the partners. No profits or losses have been divided among the partners. Partnership debts existed in the amount of $6,000. Upon court sale of the partnership property the assets bring only $3,000. The original contributions to the partnership capital, and the personal assets and personal debts of the partners are as follows:

	Adams	*Brown*	*Clark*
Partnership capital	$6,000	$8,000	$10,000
Personal assets	$5,000	$5,000	$15,000
Personal debts	$1,000	$8,000	$ 1,000

Let us now proceed to determine how settlement would be made. Since this is a dissolution under court authority, with neither class of creditors having prior judgment, the court will allow the partnership creditors first claim against the firm assets, and the personal creditors first claim against the personal assets.

Thus, the $3,000 from the firm assets would be applied toward the partnership debts of $6,000. This leaves a deficiency of $3,000. The personal creditors would then be paid from the personal assets. This would leave Adams $4,000 in assets, Brown would still owe $3,000, and Clark would have assets of $14,000 left.

The next step is to determine the amount of the profit or loss. Since the business started out with a capital of $24,000 and lost all of this and still owed $3,000, the total loss of the business amounted to $27,000. Since the losses are to be borne equally, each of the partners should stand a loss of $9,000. If this could be done then Adams should put in an additional $3,000, Brown should contribute

$1,000, and Clark should get back $1,000. Such a settlement would provide the $3,000 to pay the deficiency to the firm creditors. After paying off his personal creditors, Adams has $4,000 left, so he could contribute the $3,000 which he owes. But Brown used all his personal assets and still owes his personal creditors $3,000. Since Adams and Clark stood losses equally, they will have to stand Brown's $1,000 partnership deficiency equally. Thus, Adams will have to contribute an additional $500, and Clark will get back $500 instead of $1,000. The $3,500 collected from Adams will thus pay the firm creditors their $3,000, and Clark will get $500. Adams and Clark will then each have a *right of contribution* against Brown for $500.

If Brown later comes into possession of property the partners could come against him for the amount owed. The personal-deficiency-judgment creditors of Brown, however, would have to be satisfied first before the partners could satisfy their claim.

The above indicates the final settlement. As a practical matter, the firm creditors may have proceeded against Clark for the entire deficiency of $3,000. If this had been done, Clark would have a right against Adams for $3,500, and against Brown for $500. (If Brown had $1,000 in personal property left, Clark would go against him for $1,000 and against Adams for $3,000.)

Sharing of Profits. It was stated above that in the absence of agreement otherwise, profits and losses are shared equally by the partners. In the above example settlement was illustrated when a loss was experienced. We will now illustrate how settlement will be made when there is a profit. Let us assume that after all the business debts were paid the partnership ended up with $51,000. Since they started out with a capital of $24,000, it follows that the business made a profit of the difference between these two figures, or $27,000.

Unless provision to the contrary was made, this profit would be divided equally among the partners. Thus, each partner would receive a profit of $9,000. Then the original capital investment of the partners would be returned. Thus, settlement would be made as follows:

	Adams	*Brown*	*Clark*	*Total*
Original Capital	$ 6,000	$ 8,000	$10,000	$24,000
Share of Profits	9,000	9,000	9,000	27,000
Total	$15,000	$17,000	$19,000	$51,000

Status of Partners' Loans to Business. When a partnership is in need of additional money, some or all the partners may add to their capital contribution, or they may lend money to the firm. Such loans may or may not draw interest, depending upon the agreement. In event of dissolution of the business the firm creditors, sometimes called *outside* creditors, must be paid in full before the partners' loans (called *inside* creditors) are paid. After these business creditors are paid off, the partners' loans must be paid before there can be any distribution of profits or return of capital.

LIABILITY OF OUTGOING PARTNERS. If a partner withdraws from the business, he retains full liability for all debts existing at the time of his withdrawal. This holds true even if the remaining partners have agreed with him to assume his share of the debts. If such an agreement is made and the withdrawing partner is forced to stand some of the debts, he may have recourse against the other partners. The withdrawing partner can be assured of relief from existing debts only by agreement with the creditors themselves.

May the withdrawing partner be held liable for debts contracted by the partnership after his withdrawal? That all depends. If the proper procedure is not followed the withdrawing partner may be held liable by creditors who thought that he was still a partner. What the withdrawing partner should do is to notify existing creditors, or those with whom the firm has done business in the past, of his withdrawal from the business. It is a good idea to get the names of the creditors before withdrawing, otherwise the remaining partners may refuse to open the books. But this gives no notice to other persons who have known of his presence in the firm. To take care of these possible future creditors, a public notice of withdrawal should be inserted in a newspaper in general circulation in the community.

LIABILITY OF INCOMING PARTNERS. According to common law, if a new partner enters an existing partnership he is not liable for the debts that are on the books at the time he comes into the firm. In those states which have adopted the Uniform Partnership Act, however, he is liable for existing debts, but the law provides that this liability can be satisfied only from his interest in the partnership. If an incoming partner agrees with the partners to stand a pro rata share of existing debts, then as far as the partners are concerned he could be held to his agreement.

PARTNERSHIP LACKS STABILITY. The legal doctrine of *delectus personae* applies to the general partnership. This means that each partner has a right to choose the partners with whom he wishes to engage in business. At common law any change in the personal composition of the partnership will legally terminate it. Thus, the withdrawal of any partner, or the admission of a new partner will legally dissolve the old partnership, although from a practical standpoint a new partnership will begin the next moment. Although the old partnership may be dissolved, the partners, of course, remain liable for the debts owed.

Death, bankruptcy, or insanity of any of the partners will likewise terminate the partnership. The executor, trustee in bankruptcy, or guardian, as the case may be, can compel the remaining partners to account to him for the particular partner's equity in the business. In order to do this it may be necessary to dissolve the firm. It follows from this that the wife of a deceased partner does not step into her husband's shoes as a member of the partnership. She, however, could compel the remaining partners to account to her for her husband's interest in the firm.

General partnerships are sometimes formed also for a definite period of time. Where this is the case, then the termination of this period would dissolve the partnership. The Uniform Partnership Act, as adopted in a number of the states, provides that the sale by a partner of his interest in a general partnership does not of itself dissolve the partnership. The assignee, however, would not become a partner unless the other partners wanted to admit him to the firm. If not admitted, he has no right to interfere with the management of the partnership nor is he permitted to inspect the books, but he does have the assignor's rights to any profits, and in event of dissolution he is entitled to the assignor's interest.

From what has just been said it is apparent that as a practical matter partners cannot sell their interests to others without the consent of the other partners. This shortcoming causes some people to hesitate to invest money in a general partnership. In contrast to this form of organization, shares of stock in a corporation, which evidence ownership in the organization, can be freely transferred without the consent of the corporation or its other stockholders.

PROVISIONS FOR STABILITY. Liquidation sometimes results from the death of a partner because of the inability of the remaining partners to buy out his interest. An increasing use is being made of partnership life insurance for this purpose. Each partner takes out life insurance for an amount up to the value of his interest in the firm. The other partners are made the beneficiaries of the policies. Upon the death of a partner the remaining partners will get the necessary cash to buy out the deceased partner's interest or to pay part or all of the firm debts, or the proceeds may be used in part for both purposes.

Another arrangement that is being used by many partnerships is the *buy-and-sell agreement*. Each partner agrees in writing that upon his death the remaining partner (assuming two partners) may buy out his interest at a stipulated price. This agreement is properly signed by both partners and each retains a copy. This settles the disposition of the partner's interest in the firm upon his death. Furthermore, it establishes the value of his interest. Partnership life insurance, as described above, may enable the surviving partner to buy the deceased partner's interest from his estate or from his heirs. Another advantage of the buy-and-sell agreement is that the valuation of the partners' interests specified in the agreement is usually accepted as the value of the interest for purposes of the inheritance and federal estate taxes. The provisions of the buy-and-sell agreement will take precedence over any stipulations made in a will.

Where a partner wants to be sure that his family will take over his interest in a business, it is desirable to incorporate. Part of the stock may be transferred to the wife or children before the owner's death. This will lessen the amount of the inheritance and estate taxes. Upon the death of the owner, the life of the corporation would not be affected, and the heirs of the deceased owner would inherit his remaining shares and thus become owners of his entire former interest.

TAXATION OF THE GENERAL PARTNERSHIP. With taxes high, and with the prospects for continuing high taxes for the foreseeable future, the question of tax status of any form of business organization is an important one. Like the individual proprietorship, the general partnership does not have to pay any organization tax, or any annual franchise tax. In this respect it has an advantage over the corporate form of organization.

At first glance the general partnership might appear to have an advantage over the corporation in respect to the federal income tax. The latter has to pay the corporation income tax, but the general partnership is not subject to this tax. (However, the partnership must file a tax form.) In addition, any dividends paid by the corporation are subject to the personal income tax (after giving effect to the dividend exclusion and credit), in the hands of the recipient stockholder.

In the case of the general partnership each partner annually reports his share of the partnership profits on his personal income tax form, regardless of whether or not any of the profits are withdrawn from the business. A partner may or may not enjoy an advantage over a stockholder in a corporation, depending upon the particular circumstances.

If practically all the business profits are going to be paid out to the owners every year, from the income tax standpoint, the partnership would be preferred over the corporation. If, however, a substantial part of the earnings are going to be retained in the business, the owners of a partnership might find it difficult to secure the necessary amount of cash to pay their income taxes. If the business was incorporated, the earnings for that year would be subject to the corporate income tax and this would, of course, be paid from the corporate earnings. The part not paid out, however, would not be subject to the personal income tax.

Another consideration relates to the size of the individual's income. If an individual's personal income is relatively large for a particular year, his share of the partnership profits would be subject to a high tax rate, and as mentioned above, this tax would have to be paid regardless of whether the profits were withdrawn from the business. If the business was incorporated and relatively small so that the particular individuals had control over the dividend policy, they might refrain from paying any dividends in those years in which their personal incomes were large. During these years, then, only the corporate income tax would have to be paid. In those years in which their personal incomes were small, and their incomes subject to the lower tax rates, they could distribute the corporate accumulated earnings to themselves in the form of dividends. The combination of the corporate tax and the personal tax on the dividends might in this case be smaller than what they would have had to pay each year if the business had been formed as a partnership. A word of caution, however, should be injected here. If a corporation retains earnings beyond the reasonable needs of the business, such earnings may be subject to an additional tax.[3]

In most instances, however, particularly in the case of small businesses, the partnership form of organization enjoys a tax advantage over the corporation. Thus, unless there is some other reason why the corporate form should be used, such as to secure limited liability, or to secure capital, etc., it is not recommended.

According to the Internal Revenue Code of 1954, certain partnerships (as well as other noncorporate forms of organizations) may

[3] In any year in which a corporation retains earnings "beyond the reasonable needs of business," it may be taxed 27½ per cent on the first $100,000 of "unreasonably retained" earnings plus 38½ per cent on any excess over that amount. Up to $100,000 of total accumulated earnings, however, is exempt. Sections 531–537, Revenue Act of 1954, as amended in 1958.

elect to be taxed as a corporation. To make such election the business must not have over fifty members, and it must be one in which capital is a material income-producing factor (this would include most manufacturing and mercantile firms), or in which the income is derived from trading as a principal or from brokerage commissions. This provision of the law would benefit those firms which wish to retain a substantial part of the earnings, and for which the corporate tax rate would be less than the personal tax rate. Subsequent withdrawals of earnings from the business will be subject to the personal income tax the same as corporate dividends. Having elected to be taxed as a corporation, the business cannot switch back to its former tax status unless there is a substantial change in the ownership.[4]

TAXATION OF PARTNERSHIPS AND CORPORATIONS COMPARED. A better understanding of the relative tax burdens of partnerships and corporations can perhaps best be had by an example. We will, of course, assume that the partnership has not elected to be taxed as a corporation. Although tax rates are changed frequently, we will use definite rates—those applicable for the year 1956. If these rates are changed, the reader can substitute the existing rates.

We will assume that Mr. Adams and Mr. Brown have capital investments in a business of $100,000 and $500,000 respectively. The 1956 net income of the business before owners' salaries and taxes was $70,000. Each owner by agreement is entitled to an annual salary of $5,000. Aside from salaries and business income, Adams had taxable personal income of $5,000, and Brown had $245,000. Both are married and each has one dependent child, and take the "standard deduction" of $1,000. We will assume that the wives have no income, and that each files a joint personal income tax return. We will assume that the owners share profits according to their capital investment. To bring out the desired points, we will assume that in Case A, none of the business profits are withdrawn by the owners, and in Case B, that all of the available profits are distributed. We will proceed to determine how much in federal income taxes would be paid in Case A and Case B if the business was operated as (1) a general partnership, and (2) a corporation.

If business operated as a partnership

By agreement each partner takes a salary of $5,000. Subtracting total salaries of $10,000 from the business profits of $70,000 leaves $60,000 profits. Adams is entitled to one sixth of this, or $10,000,

[4] Effective 1958, certain corporations with 10 or fewer stockholders may elect to be taxed as a general partnership.

and Brown is entitled to five sixths, or $50,000. In a general partnership each partner must report his share of the business income on his personal income tax return *regardless of whether or not it is withdrawn from the business.* Therefore, the taxes paid in Case A and Case B would be the same.

The income tax for each partner would be computed as follows:

	Adams	*Brown*
Salary	$ 5,000	$ 5,000
Other personal income	5,000	245,000
Share of business profits	10,000	50,000
Adjusted gross income	$20,000	$300,000
Less: Deductions	1,000	1,000
	$19,000	$299,000
Less: Exemptions (3 × $600)	1,800	1,800
Taxable income	$17,200	$297,200
Taxes due on this income	$ 4,328	$221,148

In computing the taxes, if the partnership profits are considered to be the top part of the individual's income, it is found that the highest rate which is applied to Adam's share is 34 per cent, and the highest rate applied to Brown's share is 89 per cent. Considering Case A, when no business profits except salaries are distributed, it might be difficult for Adams to pay personal income taxes of $4,328, when his total cash income was only $10,000. If no salaries were withdrawn, the situation would, of course, be still worse. Since the taxes have already been paid on the partnership income, however, no further taxes would be paid in the future if the partners withdraw some or all of these profits from the business. Thus, taxes on the partnership income are paid only once, at the time the income is earned by the business, and it is a personal income tax only that is paid.

If business operated as a corporation

Case A, No Dividends Paid

Net corporate income before salaries	$70,000
Less: Salaries	10,000
Taxable net income	$60,000
Taxes on first $25,000 @ 30 per cent	$ 7,500
Taxes on balance of $35,000 @ 52 per cent	18,200
Total corporate taxes	$25,700

After paying the taxes of $25,700, a balance of $34,300 would be retained in the business. No personal tax would be paid on this unless sometime in the future it was distributed as dividends to the owners. The personal tax for Adams would be only $1,504 (computed on an adjusted net income [before deductions and exemptions] of $10,000), and Brown's personal tax would be $176,648 (computed on an adjusted net income of $250,000). But since these two people are the sole owners of the corporation, the corporate tax in effect comes out of their pockets. Since the partners share profits in the ratio of one sixth, and five sixths, we will assume that the corporate tax burden is felt in this same ratio. Therefore, of the total corporate tax of $25,700, Adams stands $4,283 (to nearest dollar), and Brown stands $21,417. Adding this to the personal tax paid in Case A, the total tax burden would be $5,787 for Adams, and $198,065 for Brown. Comparing this with Case A for the partnership, it is seen that the tax burden for Adams would be more in the case of the corporation, but less for Brown. Again, the point should be stressed that if any of the retained corporate profits are distributed as dividends in the future, such dividends would be subject to the personal income tax.

CASE B, ALL CORPORATE PROFITS (AFTER TAXES) DISTRIBUTED AS DIVIDENDS

	Adams	*Brown*
Dividends received (1/6, and 5/6 of $34,300)	$ 5,717	$ 28,583
Less: Dividend exclusion	50	50
Dividends reported	$ 5,667	$ 28,533
Salary	5,000	5,000
Other personal income	5,000	245,000
Total	$15,667	$278,533
Less: Deductions and exemptions	2,800	2,800
	$12,867	$275,733
Taxes on this income	$ 2,980	$202,043
Less: Dividend credit (4% of reported dividends)	227	1,141
Personal taxes due	$ 2,753	$200,902

In Case B, for the corporation it is obvious that part of the business income is taxed twice. The corporate tax comes out first, and then the remaining part of the income which is paid in dividends, less the dividend exclusion and dividend credit, is subject to the personal income tax. Again since Adams and Brown own the corporation, they feel the effect of the corporate tax. To get the true tax burden we should add their respective shares of the corporate tax and their personal taxes.

	Adams	*Brown*
Share of corporate tax	$4,283	$ 21,417
Personal tax	2,753	200,902
Total tax burden	$7,036	$222,319

Comparing the above computed tax burden with the amount of taxes that would be paid if the business was operated as a partnership, it is seen that the tax burden for Adams is considerably more operating as a corporation, and only slightly more for Brown. If it is intended that the business profits should be distributed each year to the owners, the partnership would be the preferred form of organization, *from a tax standpoint.* There may be other reasons, which will be discussed in Chapter 4, why they may still prefer the corporate form of organization. If profits are not to be distributed, or only a small portion of them paid out, people in the high tax bracket, such as Brown, might prefer the corporate form of organization in order to escape the high personal taxes that would have to be paid if the business were operated as a partnership. Furthermore, with the corporate form of organization, owners might retain the profits in the business until years in which their other income was small, and then pay themselves dividends—which would be taxed at lower rates because of the smaller total income of the shareholder. People with large incomes prefer to "take their profit" through a long-term capital gain by selling the stock, rather than receiving dividends, since the maximum tax on a long-term capital gain is only 25 per cent.

The individual proprietorship is taxed in the same way as the general partnership, so the above example would apply with equal force if we were comparing the relative advantages of the individual proprietorship and the corporation.

Use of the Partnership Form of Organization. The general partnership, like the individual proprietorship, is often used in the case of retail and wholesale establishments, small manufacturing concerns, and the professions. Practically all the states prohibit the use of the corporate form of organization by professional business. Thus, if a particular professional business is to be carried on by more than one individual, the partnership form of organization will be used. The states have their own decisions, or opinions of the attorneys general, as to what constitutes professional business. Generally speaking, medicine, dentistry, and law are, of course, considered professional business.

The partnership form of organization is used also by many stock brokerage and investment banking firms. The rules of the New

York Stock Exchange prior to 1953 provided that memberships could not be held by corporations. A brokerage firm that owned a seat on the Exchange therefore had to use the individual proprietorship form of organization, the general partnership, or the limited partnership.

ADVANTAGES AND DISADVANTAGES. Some of the advantages and disadvantages of the general partnership form of organization have been mentioned previously. The following include these, and, in addition, contain some other points which are more or less self-explanatory.

Advantages.

1. It is easy to organize.
2. It pays less taxes than the corporation.
3. Generally speaking, it is free from government control.
4. The unlimited liability of all the partners aids in obtaining credit.
5. The personal element is present to a larger degree than in the case of the corporation.
6. It can engage in any lawful business.
7. It can transact business in other states without qualifying and paying special taxes.

Disadvantages.

1. All the partners have unlimited liability for the firm's debts.
2. It lacks stability.
3. It is sometimes difficult to secure harmony among the partners.
4. It is difficult to sell a partnership interest.
5. It is difficult to secure long-term capital.

Questions

1. Indicate specifically how the income of the various forms of organization discussed in this chapter is taxed under the federal income tax laws.
2. Indicate the factors which might determine which of the forms of organizations discussed in this chapter would be used in a particular instance.
3. State the advantages and disadvantages of each of the forms of organizations covered in this chapter.
4. Explain in detail the nature of the liability of partners in a general partnership.
5. Explain the nature of the liability of incoming and outgoing partners in a general partnership.
6. In which industry do the individual proprietorships comprise the highest percentage of total firms? How do you account for this?
7. In which industry does the corporation comprise the highest percentage of total firms? How do you account for this?

8. What are the different names that may be applied to the individual proprietorship?

9. May the word *company* be included in the name of a general partnership? Is there any reason why it should not be used? Explain.

10. Indicate the possible advantages and disadvantages of two partners having a "buy and sell" agreement with each other to become effective upon their deaths.

Problems

1. Brady, Vanderbilt, and Morgan invested $10,000, $12,000, and $14,000, respectively, in a business enterprise. After several years of unsuccessful operation, the firm was forced to quit business. At the time of dissolution the firm assets were worth only $7,000, whereas business creditors' claims amounted to $10,000. The firm members had personal property and personal debts of the following amounts:

	Brady	*Vanderbilt*	*Morgan*
Personal property	$4,000	$5,000	$10,000
Personal debts	0	6,000	2,000

The firm creditors and the personal creditors filed their actions at the same time. There was no agreement made among the parties for the division of profits and losses. Indicate how final settlement would be made if the business had been operated as a general partnership.

2. Adams and Brown have been in a general partnership for the past five years. Brown sells out his interest to Clay for $5,000, and the business continues with Adams and Clay as general partners. Indicate the nature of the liability, if any, of both Brown and Clay for debts existing at the time of the transfer of interest and for debts contracted after the transfer.

Chapter 3

OTHER NONCORPORATE FORMS OF BUSINESS ORGANIZATIONS

Other forms relatively unimportant

The individual proprietorship, general partnership, and corporation are by far the most important forms of business organizations, from the standpoint of numbers, employment, and their contribution to the national income. Our treatment would be incomplete, however, if we did not consider these other forms of noncorporate organizations.

Limited partnership
Mining partnership
Joint venture
Partnership association
Joint stock company
Massachusetts trust

The limited partnership

How Formed. In all businesses that are formed by contract among the members, such as the general partnership, the owners are subject to unlimited liability for the firm debts. Thus, it can be said that all common-law forms of business organizations (with the possible exception of the Massachusetts trust) have unlimited liability.

The only way a business can secure limited liability is to organize under statutes which specifically provide for it. As the name would imply, the *limited partnership* has, to a certain extent, limited liability. Thus, it is evident that it can be formed only under statutory law. Almost all of the states have statutes permitting the organization of the limited partnership. The Uniform Limited Partnership Act has been adopted in thirty-four states, and in Alaska, and Hawaii. This form of organization was introduced into France from

Italy. Its first appearance in the United States was in Louisiana, where the French law governed in early times.

The laws of the particular state must be strictly adhered to in the creation of this form of organization. The usual method of formation is to file articles or certificates of limited partnership with a county official. No organization tax other than filing fees must be paid. There is also no annual franchise tax. For federal income tax purposes it is treated the same as a general partnership.

NATURE OF THE LIMITED PARTNERSHIP. Such a partnership must contain one or more *general* partners, who have the ordinary unlimited liability as in a general partnership, and one or more *limited,* or *special,* partners whose liability is limited to their contribution to the firm capital.

A limited partner is entitled (1) to full information in regard to the business, (2) to inspect the books of the firm, (3) to have the firm dissolved according to the agreement or by court decree, and (4) to a share of the profits or other compensation provided for, and in event of dissolution, to a return of his contribution (after his share, if any, of firm debts are paid). According to the statutes in some of the states, if no specific time of termination of the business is stated, the limited partner can demand back his contribution after six months' notice. If he is to share in the debts, then these would have to be paid, or sufficient assets retained to pay his share of the debts, before his capital is returned. The limited partner, of course, is not liable for any more than his stipulated contribution to the firm capital.

The limited partner, however, is not permitted to exercise any managerial rights. If he does so, or if he acts as an agent for the firm, or if his name is used in the firm name, or if he allows his name to be used in any way in connection with the business without clearly indicating the nature of his position, he can be held for full unlimited liability. Limited partnership statutes which do not follow the Uniform Limited Partnership Act are construed strictly, and any departure from them will, according to the statutes and court decisions, make the limited partnership a general one, with full liability of the limited partners. In those states which have the Uniform law, however, only substantial compliance with the law is all that is necessary, and the limited status will be respected unless the limited partner induces creditors to think that he is a general partner.

The statutes require that the limited partnership file a certificate in the proper office of the county where formed, and some of them provide that a certified copy of this certificate must be filed in every county in which the firm has a place of business. Outside the state of formation the limited partnership may be looked upon as a general partnership. Particularly would this be the case if the state in question had no laws permitting this form of organization. If the other state has such laws, then it is generally necessary for the limited partnership to file its certificate in the manner provided by the statutes of that state. Otherwise it may be construed to be a general partnership.

The limited partner is entitled to profits according to the agreement contained in the certificate. In the event of dissolution he is generally entitled to his profits and return of his contribution before the other general partners receive anything. The agreement controls the sharing of any losses. He may share his pro rata portion of losses up to the amount of his contribution, or it may be provided that losses are to be stood only by the general partners. The death, insanity, or withdrawal of a general partner will dissolve the firm unless the surviving general partners continue it according to the original agreement, or consent to continuing it.

LIMITED PARTNER'S INTEREST IS ASSIGNABLE. The interest of a limited partner may be assigned without disrupting the life of the firm. Unless otherwise provided, however, the assignee would not have the right to business information, or to inspect the books, but he would have the assignor's right to profits and to his proper share of the contribution upon dissolution. However, if the certificate so provides, or if all the remaining partners agree, the assignee will be a substituted limited partner with all the rights, powers, restrictions, and liabilities of the assignor. The assignor, however, would remain liable for any share of debts for which he was liable, within the limits of his contribution.

Death of the limited partner does not terminate the business. The legal representative of the deceased limited partner would have all of the latter's rights for the purpose of settling the estate, together with such power as the deceased had to make his assignee a substituted limited partner.

LIMITED PARTNER MAY ALSO BE GENERAL PARTNER. The Uniform Limited Partnership Act and the limited-partnership statutes of some of the states provide that the limited partner may also be a general partner. The statutes provide that such a partner shall have all the rights, powers, and liabilities of a general partner, except that in respect to his contribution he shall have the rights against the other members that any limited partner has. Such an arrangement is sometimes made in anticipation of death, so that the administrator or executor of the deceased limited-general partner may continue the latter's status as a limited partner with respect to his contribution for purposes of settling the affairs of the deceased partner, or transferring his limited partnership interest to someone else in accordance with the terms of the agreement.

Use of the Limited Partnership. The limited partnership fits the situation where a person wishes to have an interest in a partnership without the unlimited liability. This might be an old general partner who wishes to retire from active participation. Or it might be a wealthy person who does not want to subject his personal fortune to the risks of a general partnership. In some instances the widow of a deceased general partner would be acceptable as a limited partner, but not as a general one. Limited liability could, of course, be secured through the incorporation of the business, but this may not be acceptable because of the corporate taxes. The limited partnership offers at least part of the advantage of the corporation, without its disadvantages.

In some instances where limited liability was desired, it was impossible to incorporate the business. Before 1953, this applied to brokerage firms which were members of the New York Stock Exchange. As has been stated before, members of the Exchange could not be corporations prior to 1953. Many brokerage firms are limited partnerships.

Generally speaking, if limited liability is imperative and incorporation possible, it is safer to use the corporate form than this statutory partnership, for reasons stated above. Furthermore, the limited partnership statutes have not been adjudicated by court decisions to the same extent as have corporation statutes.

The mining partnership

Reason for Origin. The mining partnership is not widely used. Certain shortcomings of the general partnership resulted in the development of this special type of partnership for the working of a mine or the drilling for oil. Success in a mining operation often depends upon continuous operations in order that water should not flood the mine.

Nature of the Mining Partnership. The partners in a mining partnership are "tenants in common" in respect to the business property, and partners with respect to the profits. It follows from this that one partner could sell his interest in the property without the consent of the others. The transfer of a partnership interest or the death or bankruptcy of a partner does not terminate the business. In some instances the property is owned by only one of the persons, but the working of the property is carried on by the mining partnership. In some cases the interest of a partner is represented by certificates of stock. Where two or more persons own and operate a mining claim, and do not take formal steps to organize in another way, the mining partnership will result from operation of law. The parties, however, may formally organize the mining partnership.

The partners do not have the general agency possessed by members of a general partnership. Otherwise one might imagine the turmoil that could result if an irresponsible individual bought out the interests of one or more of the partners. In many instances only one of the partners acts as manager. He (or they) has only the authority that is given to him, or is customary in the business. The other partners are liable for any debts properly contracted by the manager.

As would be expected, the common law on these partnerships has evolved in those states where mining and oil developments have been carried on. In some of the western states, including Idaho, Montana, and Nevada, statutes relating to the mining partnership have been enacted.

The joint venture

NATURE OF THE JOINT VENTURE. This type of partnership is formed to carry on a single or temporary undertaking. It is often called the "joint adventure," and in some instances is spoken of as a "syndicate," or "deal." Many years ago when the hazards of ocean shipping were greater than at the present time, the joint venture was often used in connection with the transportation of a cargo to some distant port. Today it is perhaps most commonly used in connection with the underwriting and sale of securities from the issuing corporation to the public.[1]

The legal nature of this form of organization can best be described by contrasting it with the general partnership. The duration of the joint venture is limited to the period stated in the agreement. The various owners, or partners, give up their general agency power, and concentrate the management of the undertaking in an elected manager. The latter is paid a salary or commission and the remaining profits are distributed to the owners according to their

[1] See Chapter 18 for a discussion of syndicates.

agreement. The owners possess the unlimited liability of a general partnership, but, of course, the severity of this is lessened by the fact that the partners do not have general agency power to bind the other members.

Modern Uses. It was mentioned above that the joint venture is commonly used by investment bankers in the underwriting and sale of corporate securities. Another modern use of this arrangement is made by contracting firms in the building of relatively large projects. One contractor or contracting firm may not have sufficient capital or equipment to bid on or to complete some construction job. Or, the company may not care to take on the entire risk of the project. The contractor may therefore ask one or more other contractors to "go in with him" on the project. A joint venture is thus formed. This modern use differs somewhat from the original type of joint venture in that one or more of the members may be incorporated companies.

Care is taken to avoid making it appear that the joint venture is an "association," because the latter would be subject to the federal corporate income tax. Representatives of the various contractors or firms involved serve as a committee in the building of the project. Each of these, however, speaks for his own company, rather than for the combined firms. This is done because one or more of the firms will probably be corporations, and the boards of directors of corporations cannot delegate their authority to someone else. Henry Kaiser formed a joint venture in 1931, composed of eight companies, to build the Boulder Dam. The Toronto, Canada, subway, which was completed in 1953, was largely built by a joint venture consisting of three United States companies and one Canadian company, formed by the Arthur A. Johnson Corporation of New York, in 1949.[2]

The partnership association

How Formed. *The partnership association,* which is also called the "limited partnership association," is formed in a manner similar to that of the limited partnership. Articles, signed by at least three persons, are filed in the county in which the business is organized. It can be formed only where the statutes permit it. Only four states, Michigan, New Jersey, Ohio, and Pennsylvania authorize its formation. In Ohio, the organization's life cannot exceed twenty years, and it can be formed for any purpose except banking or dealing in real estate. In some of these states it is taxed like the corporation,

[2] "Joint Venturing Pays Off," *Business Week,* June 26, 1954, p. 175.

while in others it merely pays a filing fee. The latter is the case in Ohio. Under the federal income tax laws it is taxed the same as a corporation.

NATURE OF THE PARTNERSHIP ASSOCIATION. The laws prescribe that there must be at least three members in the organization. In Ohio the maximum number is twenty-five. The interest of each owner is represented by shares. These shares are transferable only with the consent of the members. If a person buys the shares of one of the members, he must be elected to membership by a majority of the members in number and value of their shares, before he is recognized as a member. If he should not be acceptable to the others, the organization would be compelled to buy his shares. If agreement on the value of the shares cannot be reached, the court will appoint appraisers to determine a fair price for the shares. Real estate is held in the firm name, and suits are brought by and against the association in the firm name.

Management of the company is vested in a board of managers or directors elected by the members. The statutes usually provide that there must be at least three managers. In some instances a maximum of five is specified. The board of managers may elect officers to carry out the policies set by them. Debts may be contracted only by one or more of the managers. Any contract involving a liability exceeding $500 must be in writing and signed by at least two managers in order to bind the firm; otherwise only the contracting manager is liable for the debt.

All the partners, or shareholders, in the partnership association have *limited* liability. That means that after they have paid for their shares in full, they will not be liable to firm creditors for any additional amount. In this respect the association is similar to the corporation. The statutes of some of the states prescribe that the word "Limited" appear in the title of the firm. This is to put the firm creditors on notice that the firm has limited liability. Where the reader sees this word in the title of a business, however, he should not conclude that the firm is a partnership association. In England and Canada the word "Limited" must appear in the title of corporations, in a manner similar to the requirement of "Corporation," or "Incorporated" in the name of a corporation formed in the United States. A few of our states, however, permit "Limited" in the name of corporations.

In order to enjoy this limited liability it is necessary for the members to adhere strictly to the statutes. Any deviation from them may render them fully liable as general partners for the firm debts.

Furthermore, outside the state of its formation, the organization is usually looked upon as a general partnership. In some states, however, if it registers like a foreign corporation and pays similar taxes, the limited-liability feature will be respected.

Use of the Partnership Association. This form of organization is one that the student will encounter more frequently in textbooks than in actual business practice. As has been stated heretofore, it can be formed in only a few of the states. Besides, its use even in these states is rare. Although it usually does not have to pay a tax to be formed, as does the corporation, it must pay the federal corporate income tax. The possibility of unlimited liability because of failure to conform to some provision of the law, or of operation outside the state of its formation, restricts its use. Furthermore, there have been very few court decisions to test the statutes relating to it. The fact that the shares are not transferable without consent is another drawback to this type of organization.

The joint stock company

Background. Historians trace the roots of the joint stock company back to medieval Italy in connection with the management of the public debts of the city-states. In England the large stock companies got started in the sixteenth and seventeenth centuries when the great trading and colonizing companies, such as the East India Company, the South Seas Company, and the Hudson's Bay Company, were first formed.

Many of the English joint stock companies reached monopoly size and carried on financial practices which were not in the public interest. This resulted in the registration and regulation of the companies, and constituted the beginnings of the English corporation law. In fact, the English business corporation grew out of the old joint stock companies. In English writings corporations are even today sometimes referred to as joint stock companies.

Although the joint stock companies were of some importance in the United States during colonial times, by the time there was need for a form of organization to carry on large-scale business, we had laws permitting the formation of corporations. A classical example of the joint stock company in the United States is the Adams Express Company, which is no longer engaged in the express business, but is now an investment company, sometimes called "investment trust."[3] Nevertheless, it is still operating under the joint stock company form of organization.

3 See Chapter 32 for a discussion of investment companies.

Reasons for Origin. As is true of other forms of business organizations, the joint stock company originated because there was a need for it. The individual proprietorship and the general partnership could not obtain sufficient capital to carry on large-scale trading business. The introduction of the steam engine and the specialization of labor made large-scale business enterprises imperative in order to secure the advantage of decreasing costs.

The size of the individual proprietorship is limited to the amount of capital possessed by the owner. Larger business units can be formed through the use of the general partnership, but the general agency power of the partners, coupled with the unlimited liability, restricts its usefulness considerably. Furthermore, this type of organization lacks stability and permanence. Another drawback is that the owners cannot transfer their interests to other parties without the consent of their partners.

Nature of the Joint Stock Company. The joint stock company is really a type of partnership. Like the general partnership, it is a common-law form of organization. It is created by agreement among the members or owners. New York, and several other states, however, have statutes relating to its formation and operation.

Ownership in a joint stock company is represented by shares of stock. By agreement among the members, these shares are made freely transferable. Any purchaser of the shares is accepted as a member. The owners, by their agreement, give up their agency powers, and concentrate the management of the company in an elected board of managers or directors. The latter have the right to appoint the executive officers to carry out their policies. This free transferability of the shares and the restriction on the agency power of the owners enable the company to secure more capital than could be obtained by the general partnership. Thus, the shares are similar to corporate stock. The joint stock company has continuous life like a corporation, unless the agreement limits it.

One shortcoming of the general partnership is present in the joint stock company—*unlimited liability*. Due to the restriction on the agency power of the owners, however, this does not constitute such a serious drawback as is the case with the general partnership. In many instances, the contract forms used by the joint stock company contain a stipulation that the creditors can look only to the firm property for the satisfaction of their claims. In some states, however, it is doubtful if the courts would respect such a clause. The shareholder's liability applies to those debts which were contracted while he was a member.

In most of the states the company does not have to pay an organization fee or an annual franchise tax. It follows from this that it may go into the various states and operate without paying any taxes except those which must be paid by individuals. The joint stock company, however, must pay the same federal income tax as a corporation. Thus, it is subject to one of the most important disadvantages of the corporation. But it lacks the very important advantage of the corporation—limited liability. This accounts for the fact that the joint stock company is not, relatively speaking, an important form of business organization in the United States today.

ADVANTAGES AND DISADVANTAGES. Following is a summary of the advantages and disadvantages of the joint stock company. In some instances the comparison is with the general partnership, and in other cases with the corporation.

Advantages.

1. It is easy and inexpensive to form.
2. In most of the states it is not subject to special taxes when it operates as a foreign company.
3. Money may be raised by the sale of stock.
4. Its stock is easily transferred.
5. Its management is concentrated in an elected board of managers.
6. It has continuous life.
7. In most of the states it does not have to file reports, like a corporation.

Disadvantages.

1. Its shareholders have unlimited liability.
2. Its shares are difficult to sell to some people because of the unlimited liability.
3. It is subject to the federal corporate income tax.

Types of trust arrangements

VARIOUS TYPES OF TRUSTS. A *trust* is a legal device whereby a person, or persons, called the *creator, trustor,* or *grantor,* turns over property in trust to a *trustee* or *trustees* (commonly a bank or trust company) to be held and managed by them for the benefit of the *beneficiaries* (also called the *cestui que trust,* or *cestuis que trustent).* The creator and beneficiary may be the same party.

A trust cannot be made perpetual. The statutes of the various states prescribe the maximum duration and the procedure to be followed to renew the trust. In most states the trust is limited in duration to "two lives in being plus twenty-one years and nine months." This means that the life of a trust can extend over a period of twenty-one years and nine months after the death of two persons named in the trust agreement at the time of its creation. There are various types of trusts set up for many different purposes. We will briefly describe the more important types before taking up the Massachusetts trust.

LIVING TRUST. When a person during his lifetime turns over property to trustees to be administered for a specified time and then given back to the person creating the trust, or to another designated beneficiary, the arrangement is called a *living trust.* This may be set up by an actor or actress, or a prize-fighter, whose earnings may fluctuate greatly or may even cease entirely. In some instances people who have an appreciable amount of money and are too busy to manage their investments set up this kind of trust. Most people are not good investors and might, if they have sufficient money, profit from this type of trust. One of the disadvantages of such an arrangement, of course, is that the trustee must be paid for his services.

TESTAMENTARY TRUST. The *testamentary trust* is one which is provided for by a person in his will and which becomes effective upon his death. In some instances, it is provided that the income from the trust investments shall go to one person for his lifetime, called the *life tenant,* and upon his death the property will go to another person, called the *remainderman.*

INVESTMENT TRUST. An *investment trust* is a type of company which invests its money in stocks or bonds, or both, of other companies. By purchasing a share of stock in an investment trust a person gets broader diversification and probably better management than if he handled his own investment program directly. These companies are now more commonly referred to as "investment companies," "investment funds," or "mutual funds." They will be discussed in Chapter 32.

VOTING TRUST. In order to secure continuity of management for a designated period of time, a corporation may deposit part or all of its stock with a trust company, and sell instead *voting trust certificates* to the public. This type of arrangement is called a *voting trust.* This is often used by a reorganized company which desires to continue a particular management until the company has had opportunity to get back on its feet.

The trustees vote the corporate stock and receive any dividends paid on it. Such dividends are then redistributed to the holders of the certificates.

The voting trust certificates are freely transferable in the market, but of course such transfer does not affect the voting right of the corporate stock which is held by the trustees. Voting trusts were not recognized by the common law; statutes in the leading states authorize them, but limit the life to from two to ten years. Provision is sometimes made, however, for a renewal for a like period. Upon termination of the trust, the voting trust certificates are taken up and the corporate stock is given to the certificate holders.

The situation in such a trust is different from that found in the Massachusetts trust, or the holding company. The trustees of the former hold the corporate stock for voting purposes only; they cannot sell the stock or otherwise dispose of it, and are holding the stock for a limited period of time. In the case of the Massachusetts trust, the holding company, or the investment company, the trustees or directors can at any time sell any stock owned by the company. Another distinction may also be made: a "voting trust" applies to the situation where the stock of only *one* company is held by the trustees; the Massachusetts trust, holding company, investment company, or other type of corporation holds, or may hold, the stock of a number of corporations.

COMBINATIONS FORMED BY TRUST DEVICE. In the latter part of the last century some combinations, such as the Standard Oil Trust, were effected through the use of the trust device, by having the shareholders of a number of companies turn their stock over to a group of trustees and receive, in return, trust certificates. The trustees holding the controlling stock in the various companies controlled the election of directors and thus the policies of the various companies. This was really a type of voting trust, but the latter term is usually used where the stock of only one corporation is held, as was described above.

This type of arrangement was not looked upon with favor by the courts. In the first place, objection was made to the trust device since it placed a restriction on the transferability of the corporate stock, a right which should be possessed by a property holder. The other objection was on monopoly grounds. The purpose of the combination was to control the operations of separate, competing concerns. By holding the dominating interest in these companies, the trustees could restrict output, limit territories, set prices, etc. The common law would not allow the enforcement of agreements which were in restraint of trade, and the statutes of many of the states declared them illegal. Finally, the federal government, by the enactment of the Sherman Anti-Trust Act of 1890, made such combinations illegal.

Because of the early use of the voting trust arrangement to effect a combination in restraint of trade, the early monopolies came to be known as "trusts." Even today many people, including writers, use the terms "trust" and "monopoly" interchangeably. When we talk about antitrust legislation, what we really mean is "antimonopoly" legislation. One of the reasons why the various types of trust arrangements were discussed above before taking up the Massachusetts trust was to enable the reader to see that there are many legal uses to which the trust device can be put. The list was not intended to be exhaustive. Many financial institutions are formed as "trust companies." Whenever a corporation issues a mortgage bond issue, it turns the legal title to the property over to a trust company as security for the loan.

The Massachusetts trust

Reason for Origin. The Massachusetts trust is created by the application of trust principles to a business undertaking. Instead of this title, it is sometimes referred to by the following names: *business trust, common-law trust,* and *business association formed under a deed of trust.*

The title used here for this form of organization suggests some connection with the Commonwealth of Massachusetts. This is the case, but the organization may be formed in the various states. It has been more widely developed in Massachusetts than in any other state, and also the laws pertaining to it have been better developed there than in the other states.

Until 1912, the laws of Massachusetts prohibited the corporation from holding real estate for investment purposes. This prohibition grew out of the fear that had existed many centuries ago against the holding of real estate in perpetuity by the Church. In former times many people, upon their death, left their property to the Church or to monasteries. These were types of corporations which had perpetual life. The state became afraid that after a period of time the Church would, by the ownership of the land, become more powerful than the state itself, and that it might overthrow the state. This found expression in the English Statute of Mortmain in 1279, which attempted to prevent the holding of real estate by perpetual bodies.

Since a corporation could not at the time be formed to deal in real estate, it meant that people wishing to engage in this form of business could not secure limited liability. To do so the lawyers thereupon created a form of business organization based on the trust principle. As implied above, since 1912 Massachusetts has permitted the formation of real-estate corporations. So, the original reason for the organization of the Massachusetts trust is no longer present, but nevertheless it continues to be used to some extent, for reasons which will be given later.

FORMATION OF THE MASSACHUSETTS TRUST. Like any other, this trust is formed by drawing up a deed or declaration of trust which places legal title to the property in a board of trustees. This is a purely voluntary agreement, although in Massachusetts it must be filed with the state. The owners of the business, the beneficiaries, receive transferable trust certificates. These are sometimes called "certificates of beneficial interest," or merely "shares." For all practical purposes, they are looked upon in about the way that shares of stock in a corporation are. By the terms of the agreement, subsequent share purchasers become parties to the agreement, the same as the original owners.

The management of the business is placed in the hands of the board of trustees, who can appoint officers to carry out the policies set by them. In practical analysis the trustees run the business in the same way as the board of directors operate a corporation.

The life of the firm is stated in the trust agreement. It cannot be made perpetual. Mention of the limitation of life was made when we were discussing trusts in general.

LIABILITY OF THE SHAREHOLDERS. An important consideration in connection with the Massachusetts trust is the liability of the beneficiaries, or in other words, the shareholders. Regarding this, a flat statement cannot be made which would hold good in all the states, but the following would be applicable to Massachusetts and some of the other states.

If the trust is properly set up, and if the trustees are the real managers of the business and cannot be removed during their terms of office, except for cause, the courts will say that the shareholders have limited liability—the same as shareholders in a corporation. The agreement should state that neither the trustees nor the beneficiaries shall have any personal liability for legitimate business debts, and that a statement to this effect should be made by the trustees in all contracts made by the business.

When the trustees are appointed for life, or for the duration of the trust, the courts are more likely to say that the shareholders have limited liability than when they are elected annually by the shareholders. Even when the trustees are elected at stated intervals, the shareholders may be able to secure limited liability by stipulations in the firm contracts referred to above, saying that the creditors can look only to the firm assets for the satisfaction of their claims. In some of the states the shareholders will have unlimited liability regardless of how the organization is operated.

Some states look upon the Massachusetts trust as a general partnership and thus say that the shareholders' liability is unlimited. Others recognize its status as a true trust, as in the case of Massachusetts. Some treat it as a corporation, which would mean that it would have to register in the state the same as corporations. Some states appear to ignore the Massachusetts trust or at least do not give it any status.

In Massachusetts, Oklahoma, Rhode Island, and Wisconsin, shareholders will have limited liability if the trust is properly formed and operated. Among the states which would probably give unlimited liability to the shareholders are Florida, Indiana, Kansas, Texas, and Washington.

TAXATION. When the Massachusetts trust was first formed it did not have to pay an organization tax, annual franchise tax, or income tax. The result was that many businesses that could be incorporated adopted the trust form of organization instead of the corporate form in order to lessen taxes. In 1916, however, Massachusetts imposed an annual tax on the shares of trusts. In this state they also have to pay filing fees for their trust deeds in all cities in which they transact business. Since 1922, New York has required the Massachusetts trust to pay the same annual franchise tax that is paid by corporations. In states having income taxes it is usually taxed the same as a corporation. Some states require the trust formed in other states to pay the same foreign taxes as are required of corporations. Since 1918, the Massachusetts trust has been required to pay the same federal income tax as is paid by a corporation.

USE OF THE MASSACHUSETTS TRUST. In Massachusetts a number of public utility holding companies make use of the trust. There is a specific reason for this. According to the statutes of the Commonwealth (technically Massachusetts is a "commonwealth" rather than a "state"), any public utility will be dissolved if a foreign corporation (one formed outside the state), which controls a majority of the utility's stock, issues securities based upon this stock. To prevent the utility's stock from falling into the hands of such a foreign corporation, the stock is held by a Massachusetts trust formed for that purpose.[4]

Many of the investment trusts or companies organized in Massachusetts use the Massachusetts-trust structure. These are fairly certain of their status as trusts within the state, and they do not have to operate outside it. The taxes they pay are less than would be if they were incorporated. Furthermore, they need not have annual meetings, which are required of corporations. In passing, it should be noted that an investment trust does not necessarily use the Massachusetts-trust arrangement. The phrase "investment trust" relates to the kind of business and not the form of organization used. Many of these investment trusts, or investment companies, use the corporate form.

The following are prominent examples of Massachusetts trusts: American Optical Company, Eastern Gas and Fuel Associates, International Hydro-Electric System, Massachusetts Investors Trust, and the New England Gas & Electric Association.

Despite the tax advantage that the Massachusetts trust may have over the corporation, this form of organization is not recommended in those instances where limited liability is imperative, and where the corporate form can be used. There are few statutes relating to the trust. Some states do not have court decisions interpreting their status within their particular jurisdiction. In other states where there are decisions, they are somewhat vague as to their attitude toward the trust. In some instances, the cases are contradictory. Even where they are relatively clear, there is no assurance that the judges or a higher court will not reverse the decisions.

Advantages and Disadvantages. Most of the advantages and disadvantages of the Massachusetts trust have been discussed heretofore. The following will therefore be more or less of a summary. In some instances, the points relate to a comparison with the general partnership, and in others they relate to the corporation.

Advantages of the Massachusetts trust.

1. It is easy and inexpensive to form.
2. The state taxes are usually less than those paid by a corporation.
3. Its shares are transferable without consent.
4. It can secure a relatively large amount of capital.

[4] Harry G. Guthmann and Herbert E. Dougall, *Corporate Financial Policy* (3d ed.; Englewood Cliffs, N. J.: Prentice-Hall, Inc., 1955), p. 36.

5. It has continuity of management.
6. It has stability for the period for which it is formed.
7. In some respects it possesses greater flexibility in relation to management and issuance of securities than does the corporation.
8. The shareholders have limited liability in some of the states if the trust is properly formed and operated.
9. Aside from the payment of certain taxes and fees, it possesses greater freedom from government control than does the corporation.
10. It has an advantage over the corporation with respect to taxes and reports when transacting business in some foreign states.
11. Annual meetings need not be held.
12. It may be a better form of organization to be used in Massachusetts than the corporation in certain instances of public utility companies.

Disadvantages of the Massachusetts trust.

1. Its legal status is not well understood or defined in some of the states. It is governed by court decisions which are usually less certain than statutes.
2. The shareholders have unlimited liability in some of the states, an uncertain position in some jurisdictions, and unlimited liability in all the states if the organization is not properly formed and operated.
3. Its life is limited to the period stated in the trust agreement.
4. The shareholders do not have the degree of control over the trustees that the shareholders may have over the directors of a corporation.
5. In some states it is taxed about the same as a corporation.
6. It is subject to the federal income tax the same as a corporation.
7. In some instances, it is relatively difficult to sell its shares because of its uncertain status, or because the public is not as well acquainted with this type of organization as with the corporation.

Questions

1. Distinguish between the limited partnership and the partnership association.
2. Indicate the nature of the liability of partners in a limited partnership and a partnership association in states other than the state of their formation.
3. Indicate the circumstances under which you would recommend the limited partnership. Indicate the same for the partnership association.
4. Indicate the nature of the agency powers of partners in the general partnership, the limited partnership, and the partnership association.
5. Contrast the mining partnership with the general partnership.
6. Contrast the joint venture with the general partnership.
7. Contrast the joint stock company with the general partnership.

8. Do you think that the joint stock company is more similar to a general partnership or to a corporation? Explain.

9. Assume that you own some shares in a joint stock company at the time a debt is contracted. Later you sell the stock and the company subsequently fails and the assets are insufficient to satisfy the debts, including the one contracted while you owned the shares. Would you or the purchaser of your shares be liable for the particular debt?

10. Are the joint stock company and the Massachusetts trust subject to the federal corporate income tax?

11. Can a business trust have perpetual life? A charitable trust?

12. What is meant by a "testamentary trust"?

13. (a) Indicate the reason for the origin of the Massachusetts trust. (b) Is this reason still applicable? Explain.

14. What other titles are used for the Massachusetts trust.

15. Indicate the nature of the agency powers and liability of shareholders of a Massachusetts trust.

Problems

1. Indicate how final settlement would be made if the business in Problem 1, Chapter 2, was a: (a) Limited partnership with Brady being the limited partner, (b) Limited partnership association, (c) Joint stock company, (d) Massachusetts trust.

2. The Massachusetts Investors Trust and the Adams Express Company are both investment companies. Look up these companies in the financial manuals, such as Moody's or Standard & Poor's, and report the following in regard to the companies: (a) Legal nature of the form of organization, (b) Possible reason for the adoption of the form of organization, (c) Name of the policy-making body in each company, (d) Titles of the leading executive officers of each company.

Chapter 4

THE CORPORATION

Introduction. Thus far we have briefly considered the forms of organizations other than the corporation. As has already been stated, many of these forms of organizations are relatively unimportant in the United States today. Nevertheless, it has been advisable to discuss them for their historical value, and also to bring out better the relative advantages and disadvantages of incorporation. The rest of the book will be devoted to corporations. The problems of the individual proprietorship and the partnership are comparatively simple; merely starting in business results in their formation. Their capital must be supplied by the owner or owners, who are few in number. In addition, some of them can secure a limited amount of capital from banks and trade creditors.

On the contrary, the corporation is a relatively complex form of organization. Everything about it appears as a mystery to the uninformed. The raising of capital for large corporations calls for the sale of various types of stocks and bonds. Complicated problems arise in connection with the administration of income, dividends, expansion, consolidation, and reorganization.

History

Evolution of the Corporation. Today we think of the corporation as being a large private business undertaking with many stockholders. But this type is a rather recent development. Authorities disagree as to whether the corporation can exist before it is created by a sovereign power. If we assume that a group of people acting together as a corporate body creates a corporation, then we could say that corporations existed at the time of the Roman Empire. These, however, were not private business undertakings. They were the religious societies, military groups, trade groups, and towns. Later in England such groups acted as corporate bodies. No stock was issued.

If we assume that the corporation must be created by a sovereign power, then we would recognize the churches and monasteries, which were formed by the pope, as being the first corporations. The counterpart in civil life was the granting of royal charters by the king in England. These were first granted to ecclesiastical bodies, municipalities, and trade guilds, and later to the large trading and colonizing companies.

Development of General Incorporating Laws. Until about the middle of the nineteenth century the large business undertakings, such as the trading companies, were formed as joint stock companies. In some instances they received royal charters. But the king used his right to form corporations very sparingly, and people started applying to Parliament for special charters. Then in 1844, Parliament enacted the "Joint Stock Companies Registration Act," commonly called the "Companies Act of 1844." This was a statutory body of law providing for the incorporation of companies, and started the general incorporating laws of England. This Act did not provide for limitation of liability. In 1855, however, an amendment was made which provided for limited liability if it was so stated in the deed of settlement (charter), and provided that the name of such organization should contain the word "Limited."

Corporation Laws in the United States. Prior to the Revolutionary War there were few corporations in the colonies. Those that were here were formed either by royal charter or by special charter from Parliament. After our independence the state legislatures started granting special charters. This was a slow method and in many instances became the subject of political patronage.

The next step was the enactment by the state legislature of a body of law providing for the incorporation of companies under a standard code. It was no longer necessary for the legislature to act separately on each application for incorporation. The first general incorporation act (although limited in its application) in the United States was enacted by New York in 1811. This act antedated the first English general incorporating law by thirty-three years.

The United States incorporation law is different from that in England. In England only one corporation act exists, but here we have separate laws for each of the various states. This makes the study of corporation law in the United States confusing and difficult. Since the federal government has only the powers granted to it in the Constitution, it can form corporations only to carry out these powers. Thus it is the states and not the federal government that have the right to form railroad, public utility, and ordinary business corporations. In recent years the federal government has been exerting an increasing influence over corporations through its power to tax and to regulate interstate commerce and through its war powers; and there has been some agitation for the federal government to either charter or license corporations which are engaged in interstate commerce.

Types of corporations

VARIOUS CLASSIFICATIONS OF CORPORATIONS. Most of us are aware of different types of corporations, but if we attempted to classify them we might encounter difficulty. This results in part from the fact that there are different ways of grouping them. Various methods of classification are:

I. *According to who forms them:*
   A. Public—formed by government
   B. Private—formed by private persons

II. *According to profit:*
   A. Profit
   B. Nonprofit

III. *According to stock:*
   A. Stock
   B. Nonstock

IV. *According to field of enterprise:*
   A. Ordinary business corporations—manufacturing, merchandising, trading, commercial, services, etc.
   B. Public utilities—electric, gas, water, communications, etc.
   C. Railroads
   D. Financial

V. *According to operations:*
   A. Operating company
   B. Holding company
   C. Combined operating and holding

VI. *According to where incorporated:*
   A. Domestic—formed in the state
   B. Foreign—formed outside the state

The detailed chart on page 54 may better illustrate a classification of the various types.

OUR INTEREST IN PRIVATE CORPORATIONS. As indicated above, corporations can be divided into two large groups—public and private. Public corporations are those formed by the government. These include cities and incorporated towns and villages, municipal

Classification of Corporations

- I. PRIVATE
  - 1. With capital stock (Profit)
    - a. Manufacturing
    - b. Merchandising or trading
    - c. Extractive—mining, quarrying, oil, timber
    - d. Agricultural
    - e. Construction
    - f. Personal services—advertising, consulting, etc.
    - g. General services — hotels, cleaners, amusements, etc.
    - h. Real estate
    - i. Financial—banking, insurance, investment, securities
    - j. Public utilities — electric, gas, water, transportation, communications
    - k. Holding companies
    - l. Miscellaneous
  - 2. With or without capital stock
    - a. Mutual companies
    - b. Co-operatives
  - 3. Without capital stock (Nonprofit)
    - a. Educational
    - b. Religious
    - c. Social
    - d. Charitable
    - e. Trade associations
- II. PUBLIC
  - 1. Municipal Incorporated cities and towns
  - 2. Government-owned water and power companies, Tennessee Valley Authority, etc. (Some public corporations issue stock.)

Figure 1. The classification of corporations.

water or electric companies, and those formed by the federal government, such as the Federal Deposit Insurance Corporation. In some instances these are chartered directly by the federal government, such as national banks, or federal savings and loan associations, but in other cases they may be chartered in one of the states;

this was true of the old Reconstruction Finance Corporation (RFC), which was incorporated in Delaware. The activities of public corporations, particularly those created by the federal government, are increasing in importance, but in a book of this kind they are usually not discussed.

Private corporations are formed by individuals rather than by government. The words "publicly owned" and "privately owned" are sometimes used in connection with corporations in a different way from that expressed above. Some would refer to a corporation whose stock is closely held by a few persons (a close corporation), such as the Ford Motor Company prior to 1956, as a *privately owned* corporation, and such companies as the General Motors Corporation, whose stock is widely held, as a *publicly owned* corporation.

PROFIT AND STOCK. Corporations which are formed for the purpose of making a profit practically always issue stock, and nonprofit corporations commonly do not issue stock. We will discuss in this book only the stock-issuing corporation which is formed for profit.

ORDINARY BUSINESS CORPORATIONS. In our first outline profit corporations which issue stock were grouped into four classes—public utilities, railroads, financial, and ordinary business corporations. The latter is a large group into which belong all the business corporations that do not fall into one of the other three classes.

Most of our discussion will apply to all of these four types of corporations, but in most instances the emphasis will be on the ordinary business corporation, such as a manufacturing, merchandising, trading, commercial, or mining company. The states have special laws which apply to public utilities, railroads, and financial institutions, and it is not our purpose in this book to go into details about these laws. In some instances, however, we will refer to certain public-utility or railroad financial practices.

Attributes of the corporation

DEFINITION. Perhaps a description of what a corporation is serves to explain its nature better than a definition. If a definition is desired, the following will suffice. A *corporation* is an artificial, or legalistic, person chartered by the state to perform the purposes stated in its charter. The definition most commonly found in books is the one written by Chief Justice John Marshall in the famous Dartmouth College case in 1819, as follows:

A corporation is an artificial being, invisible, intangible, and existing only in contemplation of the law. Being the mere creature of law, it possesses only those properties which the charter of its creation confers upon it, either expressly, or as incidental to its very existence. These are such as are supposed best calculated to effect the object for which it was created. Among the most important are immortality, and, if the expression may be allowed, individuality; properties, by which a perpetual succession of many persons are considered as the same, and may act as a single individual. They enable a corporation to manage its own affairs, and to hold property without the perplexing intricacies, the hazardous and endless necessity, of perpetual conveyances for the purpose of transmitting it from hand to hand. It is chiefly for the purpose of clothing bodies of men, in succession, with these qualities and capacities, that corporations were invented, and are in use. By these means, a perpetual succession of individuals are capable of acting for the promotion of the particular object, like one immortal being.[1]

LEGAL ENTITY. As we see from the above quotation, the corporation itself is looked upon as a legal being, or *legal entity,* which has an existence and life separate and apart from that of the individuals who own it. Property is held in the corporate name, and suit is brought by and against the corporation. It can even sue its members, and its members can also sue the corporation. Death of a stockholder, or of all the stockholders, does not have any legal effect on the life of the corporation. This point is well appreciated by the person who incorporates his estate so that the property turned over to the corporation will not be subject to the inheritance and estate taxes upon his death.

PERMANENT LIFE. We have already noted that at common law the death, bankruptcy, insanity, or withdrawal of a partner from a general partnership terminates the life of the organization. None of these things affects the life of the corporation. In most states such life is perpetual, or is made so in the charter. All the stockholders could die or transfer their stock to others, and still the life of the corporation would go on. This permanency of life is of considerable advantage to a business organization. Contracts may be made for the next hundred years or so, and bonds are issued which in some instances do not mature for several centuries. From a practical standpoint, however, it is realized that despite the permanency of life given by law, a corporation may terminate within a short time after its organization due to financial difficulties.

TRANSFERABILITY OF SHARES. Corporate shareholders can sell their shares to anyone at any time without affecting the life of the organization. No consent to the transfer is necessary. Any lawful

[1] *The Trustees of Dartmouth College v. Woodward,* 4 Wheat. (U.S.) 518, 636 (1819).

owner of the shares is recognized as a stockholder in the corporation. This is in considerable contrast to the transfer of a person's interest in a general partnership.

The ease of acquiring and disposing of corporate shares results in a greater number of people buying more shares than would otherwise be the case. The stock exchanges and the over-the-counter market organization are of considerable help in buying and selling stock. The ease and speed of selling, however, sometimes works to the disadvantage of a person who decides to sell out at a time which later events show to be the low point. The increased marketability, however, usually results in a higher price. Although the purchaser pays more, he likewise gets more when he sells.

LIMITED LIABILITY. One of the most important features of the corporation is *limited liability*. By this is meant that after the purchaser has paid the full par value, or stated value in the case of no-par stock, for his shares, he cannot be held liable for any further amount either to the corporation or to its creditors. Once this amount has been paid in to the issuing corporation, a subsequent purchaser would not be liable on the stock regardless of what he paid for it. The limited liability feature is further discussed in Chapter 6.

The corporation is the only type of organization that offers limited liability to all its members in all the states. The law on this point is clear and well understood. It would be inconceivable to even think of business organizations of the size we find in the United States today if it were not for this liability benefit. A single enterprise can collect billions of dollars from people all over the world. It would be impossible to get this amount of capital from such distances if the organization could not give its owners limited liability. Buyers know that they can lose all they put into corporate stock, but they also know that neither the corporation nor its creditors can take action against them, regardless of the financial condition of the company. This knowledge results in a more receptive mind toward the purchase of stocks. We are here speaking of buying stock outright. Those who buy on margin (borrowing money to pay for part of the stock) may lose more than they originally put up, but even here they know the limit of their possible losses.

REPRESENTATIVE MANAGEMENT. It was pointed out earlier that each partner in a general partnership had general agency powers to bind all the other partners on all regular matters of business. People would hesitate to enter a business firm which was composed of many owners who could render them liable for any business debts contracted. By making corporate stock subject to limited liability, part of the disadvantage of investing money in a business in which debts can be contracted by others was removed. But corporations on the average have more owners than do partnerships. It would be an impossible situation if each of several hundred thousand stockholders in a corporation had the power to contract debts for the organization—even though the shareholders did have limited liability.

Representative management is a necessity for large corporations. According to the statutes, stockholders do not have any agency powers to contract for the company. They, however, do have the right to elect a board of directors to whom management is delegated. The directors in turn are given the right to appoint officers to carry out the policies adopted by them.

In many instances a particular class of stock, such as preferred stock, may be deprived even of the right to elect directors. Even where all the stock is voting, the average stockholder's vote in the large corporation means little or nothing because of the huge number of shares that are outstanding. Furthermore, when the average stockholder votes, it is usually by proxy.

Selecting state of incorporation

Incorporation Where Business Is Transacted. In most instances a corporation is organized in the state in which it operates. This is particularly true if all the business is to be carried on in that state. If incorporated in another state, the corporation would have to pay taxes and fees in that state, and would besides have to pay a foreign corporation tax in the state in which it operated. The foreign tax would in most instances be as much as the taxes it would have to pay if incorporated there in the first place. Although there are large corporations which transact business in many states, the average smaller firm usually incorporates locally.

When the company is going to operate in a number of states, or when its nature is such that it could locate in one state about as well as another (which would be the situation in the case of a holding company or investment company), then it would be advantageous to compare the laws and select the state that would best serve its purposes. Following are some of the factors that would be considered.

State Taxes. In many instances the amount of taxes due determines the state selected. The most important taxes are:

1. *Incorporation tax.* All the states require a corporation to pay an incorporation tax at the time of organization. In most of the states the amount of the tax varies according to the amount of the authorized capital stock. In Arizona all corporations pay a flat filing fee of $25, but the publication and other fees run the total cost up to approximately $95, regardless of the size of the corporation. In a number of the states the tax is one tenth of one per cent of the capital stock; in some it is ten cents per share. In the case of no-par stock, some states consider it to have a par value of $100 per share for tax purposes, and in other states it is taxed a specified amount per share. In some instances the tax for a no-par stock is less than that paid for a $100 par share. In most of the leading incorporating states the tax per share is gradually reduced on the higher brackets of capitalization. The minimum incorporation tax in the various states ranges from $5 to $50. (In addition there are usually filing fees.)

In Delaware, which is one of the leading incorporating states, the organization tax is as follows:

A. For par stock corporations

Tax per $100 of par	*Capitalization*
1¢	Up to $2,000,000
½¢	Over $2,000,000 to $20,000,000
⅕¢	Over $20,000,000

B. For no-par stock corporations

Tax per share	*Capitalization (shares)*
½¢	Up to 20,000
¼¢	20,001 to 2,000,000
⅕¢	2,000,000 and up

The tax rates stated above, for both the par and no-par stock, apply to the shares within the given bracket. In other words, a corporation capitalizing with 100,000 no-par shares would pay a tax of ½¢ per share on the first 20,000 shares, and ¼¢ per share on the remaining 80,000 shares.

Aside from a few states, such as Arizona, the leading incorporating states of Delaware, Maryland, and New Jersey have lower organization taxes than other states, particularly for the larger corporations. Small filing fees must also be paid.

Although the amount of the tax may be considerable, particularly for large corporations, percentagewise it is not a heavy burden. Also it is paid only once, unless the authorized capital stock is increased. For this reason, the other taxes, particularly the annual franchise tax, are of more importance.

2. *Annual franchise tax.* In a few states, including the Dakotas and Nevada, there is no annual franchise tax. The rest of the states have either this tax or an annual income tax, or both.

The annual franchise tax is usually based on the authorized capital stock, the issued capital stock, or the book value of the stock. In some states the tax is based only on that part of the capital stock which is employed in the state, as measured by the proportion of its property located there, and of its business transacted within the state.

The annual franchise tax in Delaware is based on the authorized stock capitalization, and is as follows:

Total Tax	*Authorized Shares*
$5.50	Up to 250
$11.00	250 to 1,000
$22.00	1,001 to 3,000
$27.50	3,001 to 5,000
$55.00	5,001 to 10,000
$27.50	For each additional 10,000 or fraction thereof

Of the states having franchise taxes, the leading incorporating states of Delaware, Maryland, and New Jersey are among those having the lowest taxes. In Pennsylvania, which has the highest, the tax is $5 for each $1,000 of capitalization. This, however, is based on only the amount of the stock represented by the assets which are employed in the state. In addition, Pennsylvania has a 5-per-cent tax on the corporate income which is allocated to Pennsylvania. The minimum annual franchise fee varies among the states from $5 to $25.

3. *State income tax.* Several states have a corporate income tax. Though in some instances this takes the place of the annual franchise, other states have both taxes. The following have corporate income taxes: California, Connecticut, District of Columbia, Massachusetts, New York, Pennsylvania, and Wisconsin. In some states the income tax is based on the business done in the state, but others base it on the total profits of the corporation regardless of where they were earned.

One advantage of the income tax over the franchise tax is that the amount of tax varies with the profits, and therefore with the ability to pay. It would follow from this, however, that the amount of the tax would be uncertain from year to year.

4. *Property taxes.* The amount of the real and personal property taxes varies among states, and among counties and towns. A

company may locate its place of business in a certain state for lower property taxes. It may then incorporate in that state.

Where personal-property tax rates vary according to city or county, companies with large holdings of personal property, such as holding companies, will often establish their "principal office" in a small town in order to lessen their taxes. Thus the Standard Oil Company (New Jersey), for example, maintains its principal office in Flemington, New Jersey, rather than Newark or Jersey City. They pay a lawyer an annual fee for acting as their resident agent.

Restrictions Imposed by Laws. Where a choice of incorporating states is possible, promoters also consider a number of other factors in selecting the state in which to incorporate. In general they consider the various restrictions which are placed on the formation and operation of the corporation. Other things being equal, they will favor the states which have liberal business laws. Such factors include:

1. Qualifications of incorporators and directors
2. Nature of the liability of stockholders, directors, and officers
3. Whether no-par stock, nonvoting stock, or classified stock is permitted
4. Restrictions, if any, on the amount of bonds that can be issued
5. Whether stockholders' and directors' meetings must be held within the state
6. Relative ease of amending the charter
7. Purposes for which a corporation may be formed

Whether Statutes Have Been Tested. Some states have lenient corporation laws, but promoters hesitate to incorporate in these states, because there have been too few court decisions in the jurisdiction to interpret or test the laws. They prefer a state with a long record of decisions.

Some states by their statutes and court decisions have shown that they want to favor or encourage the formation of corporations and the carrying on of business. The industrialized states are generally of this type. Some of the agricultural states on the other hand have not always taken this attitude, and in some instances it would be difficult to predict what the future attitude of some of the states might be. The reputation of the state should be taken into consideration when selecting an incorporating state.

Incorporation procedure

INCORPORATORS. Usually a lawyer handles the organization routine in forming a corporation. But the articles or certificate of incorporation must be signed by, usually, at least three *incorporators.* Legally, it is they who form the corporation. At common law the only qualifications for incorporators were that they be natural persons and have the capacity to contract. Some of the states require that one or a majority of them be citizens of the United States, and residents of the particular state. Some states require that the incorporators subscribe to stock in the articles of incorporation. Upon the state's acceptance of the articles, the incorporators then become the first stockholders.

In many instances the incorporators are mere "dummies"—disinterested parties who have the necessary qualifications and are used as a matter of convenience.

THE CHARTER. In order to be formed, a corporation must be granted a *charter* by the state. The people wishing to incorporate fill out or have filled out a form usually called *articles of incorporation, certificate of incorporation,* or *articles of association.* After acceptance by the state, this becomes the charter of the corporation. In a technical sense, the charter includes not only the articles, but the state statutes and all higher law. For convenience, however, we will use the term "articles of incorporation" or "certificate of incorporation" interchangeably with "charter."

The charter is looked upon as a contract between the state and the corporation, and between the corporation and its stockholders. It follows from this that any change that is made in the charter will have to be made with the consent of both the state and the stockholders. The usual contents of the articles or certificate of incorporation are as follows:

Name. Since the corporation is a legalistic person it must have a name. The statutes of the various states require that the name be stated in the articles, and that it contain the words, "Corporation," "Incorporated," "Company," or abbreviations of them. Some states require either these words or others such as "Association," "Syndicate," or "Limited." It must be written in English letters, although it may be a foreign name. The word "Bank," "Trust Company," etc., cannot be used unless it actually is a bank or a trust company.

The state will not approve any name too similar to the name of a corporation previously formed there, or a foreign corporation registered in the state, except with the written consent of the other corporation. If it later develops that the name is so similar that material confusion results, the fact that the state approved the name is no defense. If the name of a firm is infringed upon so that material confusion results, proper legal actions may be brought against the offending firm.

Location of principal office. The city or town where the "principal office" is located must be stated in the articles. Some states require the street address as well. It is thus known where to reach the corporation in event of suit, or in sending out tax notices. This "principal office" that is required in the state may not be the place where the corporation transacts its business. Since the low tax rate on personal property often dictates the choice of some small community, a law firm or trust company may serve as the office of hundreds of corporations.

Purpose. An important part of any charter is the *purpose clause.* A common-law organization can carry on any kind of lawful business. A corporation, on the other hand, comes into being with only the powers which are granted to it in the charter. It is therefore advisable to use care in drawing up the purpose clause. Lawyers have form books which contain standard purpose clauses for almost any kind of business operation. In addition to the expressed powers granted in the charter, a corporation has the power to do things that are implied or incidental to the stated purpose.

If a corporation performs acts beyond the stated purpose, or beyond its implied or incidental powers, these are called *ultra vires* acts. Formerly the law said that a corporation lacked the capacity to perform such acts, but more modern law recognizes the power of a corporation to perform them, and any objection will be from the standpoint of the corporation's lack of authority to perform them. Only interested parties, such as the stockholders or the state, have the right to object to the performance of an *ultra vires* act.

Capital stock. The total number of shares authorized for issuance is stated in the charter. If these have a par value, the amount of it is indicated; if there is no par value, this must be made clear. In some instances the "stated value" of the no-par stock is shown. If the stock is classified, this too must be specified, as must any preferences, limitations, or restrictions on any class of stock.

Some of the states place a minimum on the amount of the authorized stock of $500 to $2,000. Although some of the others do not set a minimum, they require that a certain amount, such as $500, or

$1,000, must be paid in before the corporation can transact business. None of the states places a maximum on the amount of stock that can be issued. Some, however, limit the amount of preferred in relation to the common stock.

Duration. Many of the states require that the corporation's duration be stated in the charter. Usually life can be perpetual, but a few states place a limitation of 20 to 100 years. The maximum life permitted is generally stated in the charter. Where the life is limited to a designated number of years, charter renewals are easily obtained. In some states, such as Ohio, if there is no specific statement otherwise, life is assumed to be perpetual.

Other provisions. Ohio and various other states specify that the minimum amount of capital which will be paid in before the corporation transacts business must be stated in the charter. The minimum permitted in Ohio is $500. If business is transacted before this amount has been paid in, the directors can be held personally liable on any debts contracted up to this amount.

In New York the certificate of incorporation must also contain the number of directors, and the names of directors who are going to serve until the first annual stockholders' meeting.

Certain states permit "special charter provisions." These define or limit the exercise of authority of the corporation or the directors, officers, or stockholders.

In addition to the articles, a number of the states require that the corporation also file a form designating the agent to accept *service of process* (notice of suit).

THE BYLAWS. Bylaws are the rules or regulations governing the internal operation and management of the corporation. They are subordinate to the charter, so that in case of a conflict between the two the charter provisions will prevail. The bylaws are usually drawn up by a lawyer before the corporation is formed, and then the stockholders in their first meeting accept them. The directors may also draw up bylaws relating to their own sphere of activity. These must not conflict with those adopted by the stockholders.

In some states such as Ohio, the term "bylaws" applies to the rules adopted by the directors, and the term "regulations" (or, "code of regulations") is used for those adopted by the stockholders. When the term "bylaws" is used in this book it will apply to the rules adopted by the stockholders, unless otherwise indicated.

Since the bylaws relate to the internal affairs of the corporation, they may be amended by the same body that adopted them. Consent of the state is not necessary as it is in the case of the charter, unless the state statutes require it, which they do in some states for financial institutions.

The bylaws contain provisions relating to the following:

Stockholders' meetings. For these, bylaws provide for:

1. Time, place, and purpose of the annual meeting; notice of meeting
2. Special meetings; call and notice of meeting
3. What constitutes a quorum at the meeting
4. Method of voting the stock; proxy and cumulative voting
5. Inspectors of election
6. Order of business

Directors and directors' meetings. The bylaws adopted by the stockholders may adequately cover the directors' meeting. If separate bylaws are adopted by the directors, the detail will be stated there. The following relate to the directors:

1. Number
2. Qualifications
3. Term of office
4. Classification
5. Filling vacancies
6. Powers and restrictions on powers
7. Meetings: regular and special, call and notice, quorum, officers of meeting, order of business
8. Compensation, if any

Committees of the board. The bylaws of the larger corporations usually provide for the appointment of committees of the board to assist the board. An executive committee and a finance committee are often appointed. The duties, responsibilities, etc., of the committees are stated.

Officers. The board of directors is given the power to appoint officers to carry out the policies adopted by them. The following detail is usually included in the bylaws:

1. Officers to be appointed
2. Qualifications
3. Term of office
4. Powers and duties
5. Salaries

Stock. The following are specified in the bylaws relating to stock:

1. Form of the stock certificate
2. Transfers of stock

3. Lost and stolen certificates
4. Transfer agent and registrar
5. Inspection of the stock records

Finances and dividends. The details covering these items are as follows:

1. Fiscal
2. Reserves
3. Bank accounts
4. Signature on checks and notes
5. Dividend dates, stockholders entitled to dividends

Miscellaneous. In addition to the above, the bylaws may contain provisions relating to the following: Form of the corporate seal, inspections of the financial records, surety bonds required of officers, and signatures required on contracts.

Amendment. The bylaws usually end with provisions pertaining to how and by whom they may be amended.

Organization Meetings. To complete the formation of the corporation it is necessary to have the organization meetings. These consist of the first meeting of the stockholders and the first meeting of the board of directors. Actually, these meetings may never be held. The lawyer may write up the minutes and have the stockholders and directors sign them.

Transacting business in other states

Right to Carry on Interstate Commerce. The federal government, through its Constitution, has been given the power to regulate *interstate* commerce. A state therefore cannot tax a corporation formed in another state or prevent it from carrying on trade in the state as long as the business is interstate in nature. The mail order business is a good example of this.

But a state can require a foreign corporation (one formed outside the state) to pay taxes and meet its other requirements if the business is *intrastate* in nature. The opening up of a store in the state is one illustration of intrastate commerce. A corporation's charter usually gives it the right to transact business both within and outside the state. This means only that as far as the state of organization is concerned, the corporation has the power to transact business in the other states. A state's authority, however, extends only to its own boundaries, and therefore it is up to the other states to give the corporation the right to enter their jurisdiction.

Qualification in Foreign State. Before a corporation can lawfully transact intrastate commerce within a foreign state, it must *qualify* as a foreign corporation there—that is, follow the corporation laws of that state.

Corporations formed in a particular state (domestic corporations) must file their articles and pay their taxes and fees in that state. It is therefore only fair to the state's own corporations that they require the same on the part of a foreign corporation that is transacting business within the state. In order to qualify in a foreign state a corporation must usually:

1. File a copy of its articles of incorporation, financial statements, and whatever other papers are required.
2. Pay filing fees, and a tax similar to the organization tax.
3. Appoint an agent to receive service of process (suit).
4. Pay a tax similar to the annual franchise fee, and whatever other taxes are levied by the state.

Penalties for Noncompliance. Qualification would probably not be entered upon unless penalties were inflicted in event of noncompliance. The states vary somewhat in regard to these penalties, but the following are the basic types:

Fines against the corporation. According to the statutes of most of the states, a foreign corporation will be subject to a fine if it transacts intrastate commerce business before qualification. The amount of these fines varies from $10 to $10,000. In some instances the fines can be levied for each offense, and in some states the corporation can be fined a stated amount for each day or each month in which it transacts business before qualification.

Fines against officers and agents. A number of the states have statutes which specify fines against the officers or agents who transact the business. The officers whose duty it was to qualify the corporation are also sometimes fined. The amount of the fine varies among the states from $10 to $2,000. In some states the penalty can be levied for each business transaction. Although they are on the books, such fines are rarely applied, and where they are, the trend is toward leniency.

Imprisonment of officer or agent. Ten of the states provide in their statutes for jail sentences for officers and agents of a corporation that transacts intrastate commerce business before qualifying. The jail term varies among the states from thirty days to six months. This penalty, however, is rarely applied.

Personal liability for debts. The statutes of eight of the states provide that the officers or agents who transact business before qualification can be held personally liable for the corporation's debts. A few of the states extend this personal liability also to the stockholders.

Contracts unenforceable. One of the most common types of penalty in the various states is that of declaring unenforceable any contracts made by an unqualified foreign corporation. This may be very severe in many instances. A corporation may sell a large quantity of goods in a foreign state, and then if the bill is not paid, it finds itself denied the use of the state courts in attempting to collect.

The states which have this type of penalty can be divided into two classes. One class takes the attitude that although the foreign corporation may not sue as long as it is not qualified, it may, after the transaction of business has occurred, qualify and then sue. The other states hold that if an act is wrong when done, later qualification will not enable the corporation to sue. Although the unqualified corporation cannot sue, the other party to the contract can always sue the corporation.

Contracts void. Nine of the states have a more severe penalty than saying the contracts of an unqualified foreign corporation are unenforceable. The statutes of these states provide that the contracts are void—that is, void on behalf of the foreign corporation, but enforceable against it. In these states later qualification would not enable the corporation to sue on any contracts made prior to qualification.

Interstate vs. Intrastate Commerce. We have indicated what must be done in order to qualify in a foreign state. The penalties for noncompliance have also been stated. A real problem oftentimes arises when we try to distinguish between *interstate* and *intrastate* commerce.

Interstate commerce is that which takes place between two states, while intrastate commerce takes place within a particular state. If part of the transaction is interstate in nature, but part is intrastate, the courts will look upon the entire act as being intrastate. The courts oftentimes used the phrase "doing business" to indicate intrastate commerce.

In addition to determining whether or not a particular act constitutes doing business within the state in order to know whether qualification is necessary, there are two other reasons why this is important: (1) to determine whether the penalities are applicable, and (2) to determine whether the corporation is subject to *service of process* in the state. A word of explanation about the latter will be given.

If a corporation is transacting only interstate commerce between its own state and the foreign state, it is not subject to suit in the foreign state. In other words, it cannot be served with summons, or process. But if it is transacting intrastate commerce within the foreign state, then it is subject to service of process in that state and can be sued there.

A study of legal cases involving the question as to whether an act is interstate or intrastate appears to show some conflict among the states and even within a particular one. Some cases arose over the application of the penalties, and some of them on the question whether the company was subject to service of process in the state. Usually a corporation does not have to do as much in the state in order to be held to be doing business for the purpose of service as it does for the purpose of determining whether it is subject to the penalties. In many instances, however, it appears that the court rules the same acts interstate or intrastate regardless of the reason for the origin of the case. The types of transaction listed below would probably be held the same regardless of whether the case arose with respect to the application of penalties or service of process.

INTERSTATE COMMERCE. The following acts on the part of a foreign corporation are usually held to constitute interstate commerce.

1. Solicitation of orders by traveling salesmen subject to approval at the home office from which the goods are shipped to the purchaser
2. Maintenance of a sales office to facilitate the solicitation of orders of the kind stated above
3. Keeping samples in the state which are never sold
4. Collection for goods sold in interstate commerce
5. Consignment sales
6. Purchasing in the state subject to approval of the home office
7. Installation of a complex product that requires the services of an expert from the factory
8. A single or isolated act, unless it appears to be the first of a series of acts, or unless prohibited by statutes

INTRASTATE COMMERCE. Many courts say that in order to be doing business (intrastate) there must be some permanency or continuity in the corporation's business operations. The following acts would usually be held to be intrastate commerce:

1. Completion of contracts in the state
2. The sale of samples kept in state
3. Selling goods after they have come to rest in the state
4. Maintenance of warehouse within the state where goods are sold and delivered
5. Maintenance of principal office
6. Maintenance of a store in the state
7. Making adjustments in the state without being subject to approval of the home office
8. The installation of simple products
9. Construction work
10. Isolated act if it appears to be the first of a series of acts, or if prohibited by statutes

Meeting the Requirements. Many corporations that are now transacting intrastate commerce within foreign states, and are thus running the risk of the penalties, could in many instances change the nature of the business to interstate by making slight changes. For example, if the salesmen can accept the orders in a foreign state, a clause could be printed in the contract form making them subject to approval at the home office. Warehouses could be given up and a new system of distribution effected.

Where it is imperative that business be carried on in the state, a small corporation could be organized to operate within the state as a domestic corporation. Interstate sales could be made to it by the foreign parent company. The taxes for the small subsidiary would probably be less than the qualification taxes of the large foreign corporation. In some states, such as Texas, for example, if the officers and directors of the two corporations are the same they might hold this to be a subterfuge and tax the subsidiary the same as the parent corporation.

In most instances the state officials do not go about looking for foreign corporations for the purpose of levying fines. The situation comes to light commonly when a bill is not paid and the foreign corporation attempts to sue a resident of the foreign state. In most instances people pay their honest debts, and therefore some corporations feel that it is cheaper to run the risk of not being able to collect on some debt than to pay the foreign corporation taxes and fees.

Many corporations are illegally doing intrastate-commerce business in foreign states simply because they do not know that qualification is necessary.

Advantages and disadvantages of the corporation

ADVANTAGES.

1. Limited liability of shareholders
2. Large amounts of capital may be secured
3. Ease with which the stock may be transferred
4. Perpetual life in most of the states
5. Considered a legal entity
6. The owners lack general agency powers; management is concentrated in a small group.

DISADVANTAGES.

1. Relatively difficult to form
2. State taxes, fees, and reports
3. Heavy federal income tax
4. Cost and trouble involved in transacting business in states other than the state of its creation
5. Stockholders have little voice in the management of the business.
6. Possibility that the officers and directors may not always work for the best interests of the stockholders

Questions

1. Trace briefly the development of corporation laws.

2. Indicate six different ways of classifying corporations.

3. List the advantages and disadvantages of the corporation as compared with the general partnership.

4. List the factors which may have an influence on the selection of the state of incorporation. Which of these usually decides the issue?

5. List the items that appear in the articles or certificate of incorporation.

6. (a) What are the requirements and restrictions in regard to the corporate name? (b) If one corporation infringes on the name of another corporation, what action may be had by the latter?

7. (a) What is meant by *ultra vires* acts? (b) What is the attitude of the laws in regard to *ultra vires* acts?

8. Distinguish between the charter and the bylaws of a corporation.

9. What is meant by a foreign corporation? Is this the same as an alien corporation?

10. Indicate the nature of the right, if any, of a corporation to carry on business beyond the boundaries of the state in which it is incorporated.

11. What must a corporation do in order to "qualify" in a foreign state?

12. What penalties may be inflicted against an unqualified foreign corporation for the transaction of business within the various states?

13. Indicate whether the following acts on the part of an unqualified foreign corporation are interstate or intrastate commerce: (a) Completion of contracts, (b) Consignment sales, (c) Maintenance of an office, (d) Maintenance of a warehouse, (e) Purchasing, (f) Installation, (g) Isolated acts.

14. If a corporation finds out that it is transacting intrastate commerce business in a foreign state, what might it do to make its business transactions legal without qualifying as a foreign corporation?

15. Explain what is meant when it is said that corporate shareholders are subject to double taxation. (Reference to federal income taxes.)

Problems

1. Mr. Davis and Mr. Williams invested $200,000 and $600,000 respectively in a business. The net profit of the business for the current year before partners' salaries and federal income taxes was $100,000. Each draws an annual salary of $10,000 from the business. Aside from salaries and business profits, Mr. Davis had personal income for the year of $10,000, and Mr. Williams had personal income of $200,000. Each of the owners had a wife who had no income and one dependent child. Assume that each took the "standard deduction" and filed a joint income tax return. The net profits of the business after salaries and taxes are shared by the owners according to their capital contributions. Assume that in Case A none of the business profits are distributed to the owners, and in Case B that all of the profits after taxes are distributed. Assume the tax laws and rates to be those for the current year. (a) Compute the amount of the personal income taxes that will be paid by Mr. Davis and Mr. Williams in both Case A and Case B, if the business is operated as a general partnership. (b) Compute the amount of the federal corporate income tax and the personal tax that will be paid by Mr. Davis and Mr. Williams in both Case A and Case B, if the business is operated as a corporation. (c) From a tax viewpoint, which of the two forms of organization stated above would you recommend to Mr. Davis and to Mr. Williams? Explain.

2. Assume that a corporation pays dividends equivalent to 100 per cent of its earnings after taxes, and that both the corporation income and the shareholders' dividends are taxed at the highest bracket applicable. Indicate how much of each dollar of corporate earnings before taxes is paid in federal corporate and personal income taxes for shareholders (joint filing assumed) who have the following taxable incomes after deductions, exemptions, and dividend exclusion. (Disregard the "dividend credit" provided for in the Internal Revenue Code.) (a) $5,000, (b) $10,000, (c) $50,000, (d) $100,000, (e) $500,000.

Chapter 5

CORPORATE MANAGEMENT

The stockholders

Stockholders Play Minor Role. The average stockholder in our large corporations takes little or no part in the management of the business. A certain percentage of them send in their proxies and the proxy committee elects the board of directors. The board, in theory at least, adopts the corporate policies and appoints the executive officers. If the stockholder becomes dissatisfied with the management of the firm, he will probably register his disgust by selling his stock. The average stockholder is interested directly in the prospect for an appreciation in price of his stock, or in the dividends.

Recent years, however, have witnessed an increasing number of instances in which displeased shareholders have taken steps to oust the management. This results in proxy fights with the corporate management in an attempt to secure the support of the shareholders, such as that during 1954–1955, when Robert R. Young was successful in ousting William White from the presidency of the New York Central.

Despite the relatively unimportant place which the average stockholder occupies in corporate management, he has certain rights which, if not respected, will give him a legal claim to redress.

Stockholders' Rights. Stockholders' rights can be divided into two classes, (1) general rights, and (2) collective rights. The general rights are those which accrue to him individually by virtue of being a stockholder, such as the right to a stock certificate, and the right to transfer his stock. The collective rights are those which the stockholders as a body possess, such as the right to elect the board of directors. In our discussion we will not distinguish between these two groups of rights.

In many instances if a stockholder's right is not respected by the corporate management, he does nothing about it. Perhaps this is the most practical course to follow. A stockholder owning relatively few shares can do little or nothing if the management does not respect his rights. If attempts are made to take advantage of certain rights, the management may use legal obstacles and the stockholder will cease his efforts, for fighting corporate managements costs more money than the average stockholder possesses. Delaying tactics are often used which may cause the stockholder to give up in disgust. The management can use the corporation's money (really the stockholders') to hire its counsel, but the stockholder has to pay for his out of his own pocket.

However, management is placed in control of the corporation and is charged with the responsibility of looking after the interests of the stockholders as a group—not of a single stockholder. Sometimes the interests of the two are not the same.

Following is a list of the rights of stockholders. A brief discussion of rights needing further elaboration follows the listing.

1. To receive a certificate or certificates representing the number of fully paid shares held
2. To transfer this stock at any time
3. To be notified of meetings and to vote at these meetings, either in person or by proxy
4. To receive dividends when and if declared by the board of directors
5. To share in new issues of stock subject to the restrictions stated below
6. To share in the assets upon dissolution
7. To inspect the corporate books subject to the limitations stated below
8. To elect the board of directors
9. To vote upon amendments to the charter, bylaws, and for dissolution, sale of the assets, merger or consolidation of the corporation

VOTING RIGHTS OF STOCKHOLDERS. Theoretically, it might be said that the stockholders, through their right to elect the board of directors, control the corporation. This, however, would be true only in the case of very small corporations, where a relatively large percentage of the stock is held by one or a few individuals. As the size of the company increases, the average stockholder owns a smaller percentage of the total stock, he is less acquainted with the business, and he has little knowledge of the personal qualifications of the directorial candidates. In corporate giants, once a board of directors is in power it can through the proxy system perpetuate itself in office. Even so, it takes the collective vote of a specified percentage of the shareholders or their proxies to elect the directors.

At common law each stockholder had one vote on each matter that came before the meeting regardless of the number of shares he possessed. This was a carry-over from the partnership and the early corporation. We now look upon the corporation as a collection of capital, rather than a collection of individuals, and the statutes in the various states now give the stockholder the right to cast one vote for each share unless otherwise qualified or restricted.

Cumulative Voting. In the election of directors a stockholder has the right to cast one vote per share for each vacancy to be filled. Thus, if a person had ten shares and there were five directors to be elected, he could cast ten votes for each of five candidates. The criticism of this kind of voting, which is called *straight* voting, is that a faction controlling one more than half the total shares could elect all the directors, and the other faction which had only one less than half the shares would be unable to elect any of the directors. For example, if there were 100 shares of stock voting at the meeting, and five directors to be elected, the faction holding 51 shares could cast 51 votes for each of their five candidates, while the faction holding 49 shares could cast only 49 votes for each of their five candidates. The result is that the bare majority would fill all the vacancies on the board.

In order to overcome the shortcomings of the above, the statutes (or constitution) of a number of the states now provide that the stockholders may *cumulate* their votes. Under this system of voting for the directors a shareholder is given as many votes per share as there are directors to be elected. Of course, this is no more votes than he had under straight voting. But under *cumulative* voting the stockholder can concentrate these total votes on as few candidates as he wishes.

To refer to the above example, if a faction held 49 shares, it would, when there are five vacancies to be filled, have a right to cast a total of 245 votes (5 times 49). These 245 votes could be concentrated on two of the minority's candidates, thus giving each one 122 votes. To prevent them from being elected the majority would have to cast at least 122 or 123 votes for at least four candidates, since the five receiving the highest number of votes would be elected. But the majority has only 255 votes (5 times 51). If it concentrated these votes on four of its candidates, each would receive only 63 votes. Thus the minority would be certain of getting in at least two of its candidates.

If, in the above example, the minority cumulated its votes but the majority did not, the minority could elect four of the five directors. With its 245 votes, the minority could cast 61 votes for each of four candidates. If the majority did not vote cumulatively, it would cast only 51 votes for each of five candidates. The statutes usually require that stockholders notify the company a specified number of hours ahead of the meeting if they are going to cumulate their votes. This puts the other stockholders on guard, and they likewise can cumulate their votes. In the above example, the majority should concentrate its votes on three of its candidates, casting 85 votes for each, in order to insure getting a majority of the board.

A formula can be used to determine the exact number of shares necessary to elect a given number of directors, as follows:

$$\frac{\text{Total number of shares voting} \times \text{Number of directors desired}}{\text{Total number of directors to be elected} + 1} + 1 = \text{Number of shares necessary}$$

In using the formula any fractional part of one in the answer is dropped. Referring again to the example used above, if a person wants to know how many shares he needs to own in order to be sure of electing one person, or himself, to the board of directors, he could ascertain the number by substituting in the formula, as follows:

$$\frac{100 \times 1}{5 + 1} + 1 = 17\tfrac{2}{3}, \text{ or } 17$$

We can prove the result just obtained. If a person had 17 shares he could cast a total of 85 votes (5 times 17) for one director. In order for this candidate not to be elected it would be necessary for the other shareholders to cast at least 85 or 86 votes for five directors. But the other shareholders have only 83 shares, and therefore could cast only 83 votes for each of five directors. If we take a number less than 17, say 16, for example, we find that this would not be sufficient. With 16 shares a person could cast a total of 80 votes for one candidate. The remaining shareholders, however, would have 84 shares, and therefore could cast 84 votes for each of five candidates, and thus elect all of them.

The formula can also be used, of course, to determine how many directors to concentrate on when a given number of shares is held. If a person held 35 shares and wanted to vote in such manner as to be sure of electing the largest number of directors possible, he could determine this by letting x represent the unknown quantity in the formula.

$$\frac{100 \times x}{5+1} + 1 = 35$$

$$\frac{100x}{6} = 34$$

$$x = 2$$

Thus, the person holding 35 shares should cast 87 votes for each of two candidates and they would be sure of being elected.

In the formula it should be noted that it is the total number of shares actually voting which is used, and not the total number of voting shares the corporation has outstanding. A person may have less than half the total number of voting shares outstanding, but if that represents more than half of the shares that are present at the meeting and voting, he would have control of the meeting.

At common law a stockholder could not cumulate his votes, but thirty-eight of the states and Hawaii now have constitutional provisions or statutes relating to it. These are of two types: (1) those that specify that shareholders shall have the right to cumulate their votes (this right cannot be taken away from them by the corporation), and (2) those that give the shareholders the right only if it is so provided in the articles or certificate of incorporation or in the bylaws. In twenty-one of the states and Hawaii, cumulative voting is mandatory if the stockholder wishes to do so.[1] These include the important incorporating states of Illinois, Pennsylvania, Ohio, and Michigan. The others are Arizona, Arkansas, California, Idaho, Kansas, Kentucky, Mississippi, Missouri, Montana, Nebraska, North Carolina, North Dakota, South Carolina, South Dakota, Washington, West Virginia, and Wyoming.[2] Cumulative voting is permissive if included in the articles or bylaws in seventeen of the states, which include the favorite incorporating states of Delaware, New Jersey, and New York. The others are Colorado, Florida, Indiana, Louisiana, Maine, Maryland, Minnesota, Nevada, New Mexico, Oklahoma, Rhode Island, Tennessee, Utah, and Virginia.[3]

[1] C. M. Williams, *Cumulative Voting for Directors,* Graduate School of Business Administration, Harvard University, Cambridge, 1951. For articles on the subject and on the staggering of directors' terms in connection with the fight for control of Montgomery Ward by Louis Wolfson in 1955, see *Business Week,* Feb. 12, 1955, pp. 80–84, and April 23, 1955, pp. 60–61.

[2] Williams, *op. cit.,* p. 8.

[3] *Ibid.,* p. 9.

(Ten of the states have no constitutional provisions or statutes authorizing cumulative voting.)

When such voting is followed there should be only one ballot for the election of all the directors. The ones receiving the highest number of votes, or in other words, a plurality, are elected, regardless of whether or not this represents a majority of the votes. If separate ballots were taken to fill each vacancy on the board, it would defeat the purpose of cumulative voting, as the majority could always cast more votes than the minority. If a tie results, however, additional ballots should be taken.

It should be noted that cumulative voting is used only in the election of directors.

Proxy Voting. At common law a shareholder had to be present at the meeting in order to cast his votes, but the statutes of the various states now permit him to vote by *proxy*. The term "proxy" applies to both the written authorization and the person or committee to whom it is sent. In the case of our large corporations which have hundreds of thousands of stockholders scattered throughout the country it would be impossible to ever secure a quorum at a meeting if proxy voting were not permitted.

A proxy can be revoked at any time prior to the time when it is voted, unless it is coupled with an interest. An example of the latter is one in which a shareholder puts his stock up as collateral for a loan and gives the lender his proxy.

It is the custom for large corporations to send out notices of the stockholders' meetings and to enclose a proxy form for the shareholder to fill out, giving several of the corporate officers, who constitute the *proxy committee*, the right to vote the stock. The Securities and Exchange Commission has adopted rules and regulations relating to the solicitation of proxies on all registered securities. These require the corporation to give the shareholders a considerable amount of detailed information, such as: the principal occupation and number of shares held by each director, and all remuneration received from the corporation and its subsidiaries, of members of the board of directors and the three highest paid officers receiving more than $30,000 a year. If the shareholder has a right to cumulate his votes this also must be stated. Financial reports for the latest fiscal year must also be furnished. Where a vote is to be taken on some proposal other than the election of directors, space must be provided for the shareholder to record his vote.

Class Voting. Corporations can qualify or limit the voting rights of stockholders by appropriate provisions in the charter and bylaws.

This becomes part of the contract under which people purchase the stock. One of these changes from the ordinary procedure is to provide that the stock will vote as a class.

Some corporations issue their stock under a contract which specifies that the preferred stock voting as a group or class shall be entitled to elect a designated number of directors, and the common stock as a group shall be entitled to elect a specified number of directors. This method insures representation on the board of directors for the preferred stock even though the number of shares of preferred outstanding is much less than the number of common shares. An example of class voting can be illustrated with the $1.50 cumulative convertible $25 par preferred stock of Mid-West Refineries, Inc. The contract provides that the preferred shall vote equally with the common, one vote per share, but it is further provided that:

> if total assets (excluding goodwill, deferred charges, and prepaid items) after deducting total liabilities other than contingent liabilities, on two successive quarterly financial statements, shall be less than 133 per cent of the aggregate par value of the preferred stock outstanding, and/or if four quarterly dividends on the preferred stock are in arrears, the preferred stock as a class shall be entitled to elect a majority of the board of directors until the assets over liabilities, as stated, exceed 133 per cent of the par value of the preferred stock, and if four quarterly dividends shall have been in arrears, all arrears of dividends shall have been declared and paid or funds set aside therefor.

FRACTIONAL AND MULTIPLE VOTES. When there is more than one class of stock, it is occasionally provided that the stock of one class shall be entitled to only a fraction of one vote per share, or that it shall be entitled to a specified number of votes per share.

NONVOTING STOCK. Many corporations make their preferred stock *nonvoting*. Such stock, however, sometimes by virtue of statutes or charter provision, has what amounts to a *vetoing* power, in that it is given the right to vote on specified matters such as the creation of a bonded indebtedness, issuance of additional preferred stock, consolidation, merger, or dissolution of the company. Nonvoting preferred stock is often given *contingent* voting power. An example of this is a case in which it is given the right to vote (as a class or otherwise) if the dividends on it are in arrears for a stated number of quarterly periods.

Some companies have *classified* common stock outstanding. One class of the common may vote, and the other class may be made nonvoting. People have not objected to the issuance of a nonvoting preferred stock, since the purchaser is often looked upon as at least a semi-investor, and is willing to sacrifice the voting right for a preference as to dividends. But the nonvoting common stock was not so well received. Traditionally it is the common stockholders who bear the greatest risk and who have the right to elect the board of directors. Since 1926, the New York Stock Exchange has refused to list a nonvoting common stock. Under the Public Utility Holding Company Act, the Securities and Exchange Commission may not permit the sale of a registered public utility common stock unless it has at least equal voting rights with any other securities of the company. The Federal Bankruptcy Act requires that the reorganization plan of a company include a provision prohibiting the issuance of a nonvoting common stock.

OTHER METHODS OF CONTINUING CONTROL. There are additional ways in which a board of directors may perpetuate itself in office. Some of these have been mentioned before but are listed below in summary form.

Minority interest often controlling. It usually does not take 51 per cent of even the voting stock of a corporation in order to get control. If a faction held only 40 per cent of the total voting stock, but all of it was fully represented at a meeting at which there was only 75 per cent of the total stock represented, this 40 per cent would obviously be the controlling interest.

When a majority vote is required to pass a measure at a meeting, it is usually taken to mean a majority of the votes cast, assuming a quorum to be present. If 100 per cent of the stock was represented at the meeting, but only 75 per cent of it voted, the faction holding 40 per cent of the stock could carry a measure.

When a majority of the stock is widely scattered in the hands of many stockholders, none of whom own an appreciable amount, the votes may also be scattered over many candidates for directors, with the result that a concentrated minority may be able to control. Cumulative voting may be used in this way by the minority in order to get control. There is also the probability that some of the votes of this unorganized majority will fall to the candidates or proposals of the controlling minority interest.

If we carry the point just made one step further, we will arrive at the situation we see in our large corporations today. The management holds a small minority of the total stock (or even a negligible amount), but by working together and collecting the proxies of the scattered majority, they end up with a majority of the votes.

Failure to elect new directors. According to common law and the statutes in the various states, failure to elect new directors results in the old ones continuing. In some instances management fails to call a meeting or send out notices of the annual meeting, in order to accomplish this objective. The failure to send notices, however, is contrary to the statutes of many of the states.

Sometimes, where not prohibited by statutes, the charter or bylaws may specify that a two-thirds or three-fourths vote of the entire outstanding stock is necessary to elect the directors. It may be impossible to get that amount of the stock represented at the meeting, or, if it is represented, to secure that percentage vote. This would result in the original board's continuing in office.

Holding company. A *holding company* which owns a majority or all the voting stock of another company can control the latter company. Whoever has control of the holding company can therefore control the subsidiary companies. The holding company is discussed in Chapter 31.

Voting trust. Control is sometimes effected through the use of the *voting trust.* In this setup the stock is held by a group of trustees for a specified number of years. This was described in Chapter 3.

Good management. A method of perpetuating the management which might be so obvious as to be overlooked, is for the management to be so efficient that the company enjoys good earnings and pays liberal dividends. Such managers are usually re-elected.

Staggered terms for directors. When the terms of office of the board of directors are staggered, it is sometimes referred to as *classification* of the board. For example, the charter or bylaws may call for a board of nine persons. Upon organization of the company, three directors would be elected for one-year terms each, three for two-year terms, and three for three-year terms; each year thereafter three directors would be elected for three-year terms each. This prevents a complete turnover of the board in any one year. In many nonprofit corporations the directors' terms are staggered in order to provide for continuity in management. Some profit corporations' boards also are staggered, but the legality of it where cumulative voting is practiced, and the wisdom of it for profit corporations, are subject to some question, which will be discussed in following paragraphs. Those acquiring controlling stock interests in a corporation may be compelled to wait several years before they can get control of the board of directors.

STAGGERED TERMS CLASH WITH CUMULATIVE VOTING. The Supreme Court of Illinois in 1955 ruled that the Illinois statute providing for the staggering of directors' terms was unconstitutional because it conflicted with the cumulative voting rights of stockholders which is provided for in the state constitution.[4] This arose out of the case brought by Louis Wolfson in his fight for control of Montgomery Ward. This company had a board consisting of nine members, but under the staggered system, only three were to be elected at the 1955 meeting. Wolfson contended that Sewell Avery, the president of the company, would still control the entire board even if Wolfson secured sufficient shares to elect a majority of the three directors to be elected at that meeting. The points brought out by the court are included in the following discussion.

The constitutional provisions or statutes giving shareholders the right to cumulate their votes were enacted for the purpose of enabling minority shareholders to receive representation on the board of directors. If a board consists of nine members and all of them are elected each year for one-year terms, under cumulative voting it would take only 11 per cent of the voting stock to elect one director. Two directors could be elected with 21 per cent of the stock, etc. And if 51 per cent of the stock was owned or controlled, a total of five, or a majority of the entire board, could be elected. But if the terms of the directors were staggered and only three were elected each year, 11 per cent, or 21 per cent, of the stock would not elect even one director. With the control of 51 per cent of the stock, only two of the three directors could be elected the first year. The second year two more could be elected. But these four directors would be outnumbered by the other five directors who had previously been elected. It would not be until the third year that the controlling shareholder group could get control of the board of directors.

As a result of the court decision, Montgomery Ward put the entire slate of nine directors up for election at the 1955 meeting. Mr. Wolfson, by cumulative voting, succeeded in electing three of the nine members.

The Supreme Court of Ohio, however, in 1956, held that classification of the board could be used despite the fact that shareholders had the right to cumulate their votes.[5] The Ohio statutes provide that shareholders may cumulate their votes and that this right may not be restricted or qualified by the articles or code of regulations. They further state that the articles or code may provide for classification of the board of directors. The shareholders of the Winous Company, at their January 18, 1954, meeting, voted to amend the code of regulations to provide that of the three-man board, one

[4] *Wolfson v. Avery et al.*, 126 N.E.2d 701 (1955).

[5] *Humphrys v. Winous Co.*, 165 Ohio State 45, 133 N.E.(2d) 780 (1956).

should be elected each year for a three-year term. Humphrys, who controlled approximately 40 per cent of the stock of the company, brought action contending that the amendment to the code of regulations was invalid because it nullified the cumulative voting right conferred by the statute. The court, however, held that the statute confers upon shareholders only a right to vote cumulatively and does not insure minority representation on the board.[6]

The legal status of staggered terms for directors in other states which provide for cumulative voting has not been adjudicated.

Pre-emptive Right of Stockholders. We started out this chapter by listing the rights of stockholders. Thus far we have been concerned with the voting rights. Another right is to share in new issues of stock in the same proportion that his old stock represents to the total stock. This is known as the *pre-emptive right*. This enables the stockholder to maintain his degree of control in the company and his equity in the surplus. This being the case, the right would accrue to only those stockholders whose stock is voting or participating in dividends (entitled to dividends beyond a stated rate), or in assets upon dissolution. The pre-emptive right would not be applicable in the following instances: (1) Sale of nonvoting, nonparticipating preferred stock; (2) Sale of original issue before control had been established; (3) Sale of treasury stock (stock originally issued and then later reacquired by the corporation), and (4) Exchange of stock for property other than cash. This right will be more fully explained in Chapter 17.

Inspection of the Books. The stockholders are the owners of the corporation. Since they elect the directors to carry on the business it is only proper that the stockholders should have the right to examine the corporate records. At common law the shareholders have the right to examine the records at a reasonable time and place and for a proper purpose. They cannot demand the right of inspection to gratify mere idle curiosity, for speculative purposes, or for purposes hostile to the best interests of the corporation and its other stockholders.

The common-law right of inspection applies to all the corporate records. This would include the bylaws and regulations, stock books, financial or account books, and the minutes of the stockholders' and directors' meetings. A proper purpose must always be

[6] It is obvious from this decision that a minority interest, regardless of size, might never be able to elect any directors. In 1955, however, the Ohio statutes were amended to provide that where classified boards are established, there must be at least three directors in each class (126 Ohio Laws, H70, effective October 11, 1955).

present before right of examination has to be given; if the right is demanded because of suspected fraud or mismanagement, very good proof would have to be submitted.

Statutes or constitutional provisions in some of the states confirm, limit, or enlarge the right of examination. In some instances the statutes specify that the stockholders shall have the right to examine the stock books, but say nothing about the right to examine the other records. Where this is done, the stockholders still have their common-law right to examine the other records. The right given by statute may make it more absolute. If no qualifications are made relative to the statutory right of examination of the stock books, then the stockholder might have to show more cause for attempting to exercise his common-law right of examining the account books than in his demand to inspect the stock books. In New York the statutes provide that a stockholder in order to examine the records must have been a stockholder of record for at least six months, or he must hold at least five per cent of the outstanding stock.

This right to examine the corporate records is seldom exercised. Most stockholders do not have enough interest in the management of the company to want to examine the records. If they are dissatisfied with the way things are going they usually sell their stock. If a stockholder applied for the right to inspect the records, he would probably be refused by the management. To attempt to enforce his legal right would probably take more time and money than the average stockholder would want to devote to the cause.

When a stockholder applies for examination of the records the management probably has a right to be suspicious. The person may be a crank, or one who takes his position as a stockholder a little too seriously. Oftentimes the purpose of wanting the examination is contrary to the best interests of the corporation and its other stockholders, and therefore the management should turn down the request.

When statutes specify inspection rights, they often provide penalties for wrongfully refusing to permit the examination. In some instances the statutes provide that the financial statements must be sent to stockholders upon request, and if the officials do not comply with the request they are subject to a fine of a specified amount for each day of default.

The right to examine the corporate records carries with it the right to take along an attorney, accountant, or stenographer to aid in the examination.

The directors

Board of Directors. In a small corporation the stockholders and the directors may be the same persons, but in the case of the large corporations with hundreds of thousands of stockholders, the management must be concentrated in the hands of a relatively small number of people. Despite any shortcoming that may be stated relative to the delegation of management, it would be inconceivable even to think of a situation in which hundreds of thousands of persons could directly manage a business.

The statutes in most of the states prescribe that there shall be at least three directors, and do not place a limitation on the number. The term of office is usually stated to be one year, or until their successors are elected. When *classification* of the board is carried out, the term is longer than one year.

Qualifications of the Directors. At common law the only qualifications for directors are that they be natural persons and have the capacity to contract. The statutes in some of the states require that they be shareholders, and from one to a majority of them citizens of the United States, or residents of the state.

In addition to the common-law and statutory qualifications, the directors should, of course, possess such special abilities as are required in the particular situation. A large stock interest in the company does not necessarily qualify a person for the director's job, but of course that helps him to get elected. Other things being equal, stock ownership is usually advisable because the director might take a greater interest in the business.

Powers of the Board of Directors. The management of the corporation is to be exercised not by the stockholders or the officers, but by the board of directors. Whatever power is granted to the corporation in its charter is really the power of the board. This power is not to be exercised by a single director, or by the various directors acting separately, but only by the board acting as a body in meeting.

It is the power and duty of the board to do all things necessary and proper in carrying on the purposes of the corporation. But it does not have the right to take extraordinary actions without the approval of the stockholders, or to do things which were not properly authorized in the charter. More specifically, the board has the power to do the following:

1. Formulate policies to carry out the purposes for which the corporation was formed

2. Appoint executive officers to carry out these policies
3. Appoint committees of the board to act in the intervals between board meetings
4. Adopt bylaws for their own convenience, which, however, cannot be inconsistent with those adopted by the shareholders
5. Declare dividends from appropriate sources
6. Inspect all the corporate records
7. Ratify important contracts
8. Adopt or approve budgets
9. Adopt or approve financing plans, expansion plans, etc.
10. Initiate proposals to amend the bylaws and charter

BOARD COMMITTEES. The board of directors has the power to appoint committees from the board. Small corporations usually do not have such committees. Larger ones often have an *executive committee,* and sometimes one other, such as a *finance committee,* or *sales committee.*

The executive committee is ordinarily composed of directors who are also active officers in the corporation and therefore are convenient in the event that decisions must be made in the intervals between board meetings. Generally speaking, the executive committee has the power to make the same kind of decisions as the board itself on all ordinary matters, but they cannot act on extraordinary matters, such as the declaration of dividends, expansion, etc., which require the action of the entire board. In order that no question may be raised in regard to the action taken by the committees, it is common practice for the board in its next meeting to approve the actions taken by the committees.

LIABILITIES OF DIRECTORS. A considerable amount of power and responsibility is entrusted to the board of directors. The shareholders may have millions and even billions of dollars invested in the corporation. A director occupies a position of trust. The law takes the attitude that a fiduciary relationship exists between him and the corporation and between him and the shareholders as a body. Such a relationship demands a high degree of care and prudence on the part of the directors. This being the case, it is only natural to expect that the law would provide penalties against the directors for failure to live up to this trust. Certain penalties or liabilities are imposed upon them by common law, and the statutes have added to it. Directors can be held liable for the following:

1. Losses resulting from fraudulent acts
2. Losses resulting from illegal acts, or those which are *ultra vires* (beyond the corporation's powers)

3. Losses resulting from negligence
4. Losses resulting from willful mismanagement, or mismanagement resulting from negligence
5. The payment of dividends from unauthorized sources
6. Wrongfully refusing stockholders the right to examine the corporate records
7. Failure to make required reports
8. Signing statements or reports known to be false
9. Causing or permitting entries in the corporate books which are known to be false
10. Making transfers of property for the purpose of preferring or defrauding creditors when the corporation is insolvent
11. Conversion, embezzlement, larceny, and misapplication of the corporate property
12. Certain acts specified in the Securities Act of 1933, and the Securities Exchange Act of 1934. (These Acts are discussed in Chapters 18 and 19.) Among the more important of these are the following:
    (a) False statements of material facts, or omission to state material facts in the registration statement
    (b) Failure to report, or incorrect reporting, of amount of stock held
    (c) Profit made by the purchase or sale of company stock within a period of less than six months. (Action must be instigated by the corporation or stockholders to recover this profit.)
    (d) The Securities Acts also prohibit the directors from making short sales or manipulating of the company stock, and solicitation of company proxies except as provided in the Act.

Avoidance of Liability. A director should accept his position only if he feels qualified, and can devote the necessary amount of time to the job. He should attend the directors' meetings regularly, and faithfully discharge his duties. Occasional absence from the meetings is permissive, but continued willful absence may result in liability for negligence for some acts committed or omitted by the board.

If certain actions are taken by the board which a particular director believes are wrong, he should see to it that a record is made in the minutes indicating his disapproval. When he is absent from meetings, it is advisable for him to read over the minutes and have his disapproval recorded on any questionable action.

An attempt is sometimes made to relieve the directors from liability for certain acts by a statement to this effect in the articles of incorporation. Examples of this would include provisions of the following type: that the directors will not be liable for profits made on transactions with the corporation; that they will not be liable in any way for contracts made with other corporations in which they are directors or shareholders; that loans may be made by the corporation to its directors or officers. If an act of a director would make him liable, probably most courts would hold him still liable despite the presence of such clauses in the articles.

The officers

OFFICERS REQUIRED. The statutes of most of the states provide that the board of directors shall appoint or elect a *president, secretary,* and *treasurer.* They may also provide for vice-presidents, and assistant secretaries and treasurers. The articles or bylaws may provide for additional officers such as *general manager* or *comptroller.*

Such appointees or electees are called "officers" or "executive officers." Some confusion may exist when the term "officer" is used because it is not known whether reference is made to the executive officers or the directors. The latter are sometimes called "officers" but they are not executive officers. The directors can act only through meetings, but the executive officers have individual duties assigned to them. Both are referred to as agents of the corporation. In addition to the directors and executive officers, there may be other agents, such as a sales manager, or a purchasing agent. These agents and the officers are employees of the corporation, but in contrast the directors as such are not considered employees.

QUALIFICATIONS FOR OFFICERS. Some state statutes provide that part or all the corporate executive officers shall be stockholders. Some specify that the president shall be a member of the board of directors. Also, the articles or bylaws may state additional qualifications.

As a practical matter it is realized that the officers should have the necessary experience or fitness to carry out their duties.

POWERS AND DUTIES OF THE OFFICERS. The powers of the officers are stated in the statutes, the bylaws, and in some instances, in the charter of the corporation. The board of directors may also grant certain powers to them. In addition, the officers have incidental, apparent, and inherent powers. Since officers are agents they, like other agents, have the *incidental* power to do those things which are necessary. *Apparent* powers are those which the officers have by virtue of the corporation's holding out to innocent third parties that they have the power to perform certain acts. An *inherent* power is one that an officer has by virtue of the nature of his office. For all practical purposes there is not much difference between an "incidental" power and an "inherent" power. Their nature can best be understood by briefly stating the powers of each of the executive officers.

President. The president is the chief executive officer of the corporation. Although he along with the other officers is appointed by the board of directors, the president has authority over the other officers. The statutes of some of the states require that he sign or countersign the stock certificates and other corporate instruments. He presides at the stockholders' meetings, and in event that there is no board chairman, at the directors' meetings—the latter is considered an inherent power. In some instances the office of president and chairman of the board is vested in the same person.

Courts are more and more taking the attitude that the president has the power to do any act which the board of directors could authorize or ratify. In fact, in most corporations the president, or some other executive officer, takes the initiative, formulates policies and carries them out, and later has the board of directors ratify the acts. In many instances, of course, the president recommends policies to the board, gets its approval, and then executes them.

The statutes of some states provide for an office of *chairman of the board of directors.* Even in the absence of such statutes this could be done in the bylaws. Sometimes the question is raised whether the president or the chairman of the board is the more important officer of the corporation. No definite answer can be given to this question since it depends upon the particular company and the personalities of the individuals. Since the board, in theory at least, formulates the policies for the officers to carry out, the chairman of the board could be the more important. He presides at the board meeting and might be able to sway the directors to his way of thinking. Furthermore, his vote would be the deciding one in event of a tie. In many corporations the board chairman is undoubtedly the more important officer.

When the board merely approves what the officers do, the board chairman would not be so important. In a number of corporations, the office of chairman is more or less an honorary title which is given to a retiring president. In this way he may still be kept on the payroll. In many instances, however, the president may be too old to engage actively in the everyday activities of the management; but he may be the most valuable man possible for the post of chairman.

In some organizations, such as trade associations, the operating head is commonly called "secretary" or "executive secretary," and the title of "president" is more or less honorary, and is given to one of the active members. The managing head of many savings and loan associations is called "secretary" or "executive secretary," or "executive vice-president."

Vice-president. About all that need be said about the vice-president is that he takes over the president's powers and duties in event of absence, incapacity, or death of the president. Other than that, he has no inherent duties by virtue of his office. If there are first and second vice-presidents, etc., the former would take over if the president was incapacitated, and the second would carry on in the event that something happened to his immediate superior.

In some corporations an employee of the corporation, such as the sales manager, might be given the title of "vice-president in charge of sales." Or the manager of one of the plants or of a company division, such as the export department, might be given the title of vice-president. In some instances these titles are handed out rather freely in order to impress the public, or the particular employee himself. This is particularly true in the case of banks and other financial institutions.

Secretary. The secretary does not have an inherent power to act for or bind the corporation. The board of directors, however, may assign him such specific powers. The usual duties of the secretary as prescribed by statutes and bylaws are: to keep minutes of the stockholders' and directors' meetings, have custody of the corporate seal, sign stock certificates, documents and reports to stockholders and the state, give notice of meetings, and keep the stock books. In the larger corporations the actual details of these duties are handled by other employees, though the responsibility is the secretary's.

An assistant secretary would act in the absence of the secretary. In some companies this title is more or less window dressing.

Treasurer. In brief, the usual power or duty of the treasurer is custody of the corporate funds. His duties or part of them may be found in the statutes, but they are commonly listed in the bylaws. Unless specifically authorized to do so, the treasurer cannot bind the corporation on contracts, but some courts have held that by virtue of his office he could execute corporate notes. The usual powers or duties of the treasurer are as follows: to take care of all the funds and securities; deposit money in banks approved by the boards of directors; indorse checks and other financial instruments received; sign notes, checks, and drafts; supervise the company's financial books; prepare the financial and tax reports; and advise the board of directors on dividends, financial plans, and budgets.

In large firms the treasurer may be in charge of all of these items, but the actual work would be carried on by subordinates. Sometimes the office of "secretary-treasurer" is given to one person. The assistant treasurer would carry out the functions of the treasurer in his absence. This title too is often given for its prestige value.

Other officers. Besides the officers listed above, some corporations have additional ones. An increasing number of firms have a *controller* (same as "comptroller"). His duties are set forth in the bylaws. Practice varies considerably as to the nature of his duties. In some instances he is chosen by the board of directors; in other cases the executive committee of the board may appoint him. In some corporations he is hired by the president or other executive officer, and has the same rank as a department head. The duties of the controller vary widely among companies, but generally speaking, he takes over many of the treasurer's duties. Quite commonly he is in charge of the company's financial books and the budget.

Many corporations have an *auditor.* He may be the chief accounting officer of the corporation, but in some cases he is independent of the accounting department and checks on the records, and reports directly to the treasurer or the president. When there is no controller, he often carries on the work of one. Where there are both of these officers the auditor sometimes reports to the controller. In the case of ordinary business corporations the auditor is usually only an employee and not an executive officer of the company.

Some companies, particularly manufacturing firms with several plants or locations, have an officer who is called the *general manager.* The statutes do not provide for this office, so when it exists, it would be specified in the bylaws. For the particular plant or division, the general manager may be the most important company employee. He is usually looked upon as an important department or divisional head, rather than an officer. Sometimes the title of general manager is given to the president.

Liability of Officers. The law looks upon the executive officers as occupying a fiduciary relation to the corporation and to the shareholders as a group, in a manner similar to that of the directors. Some courts have even held the executive officers, who received salaries and were active in the business, to a higher degree of diligence than the directors, who were serving gratuitously. Because of the similar trust position, the liabilities of the executive officers are practically the same as stated for the directors above, so they will not be repeated here.

The liabilities imposed on the officers by the Securities Act and the Securities and Exchange Act are the same except that the liability for incorrect statements or omissions of material facts in the registration statement applies to only the officers who signed the statement. Liability is imposed on the officers for not properly reporting their stock holdings. They are not permitted to sell the stock short, or to engage in its manipulation. They, as well as the directors, must report all their purchases and sales of the company stock to the Securities and Exchange Commission. Any profit made on company stock owned for a period of less than six months can be recovered by suit by the corporation or by its stockholders.

Questions

1. List the rights that are possessed by corporate shareholders.

2. At common law how many votes did a shareholder possess? Has this been changed by the statutes? Explain.

3. (a) Is cumulative voting permitted at common law? (b) Do the statutes of the various states give shareholders the right to cumulate their votes, or do they merely permit it if so specified in the articles of incorporation? (c) What is the purpose of cumulative voting? (d) Give an example of cumulative voting. (e) Is cumulative voting used for any purpose other than the election of directors? (f) When cumulative voting is followed, how many ballots can be taken in the election of directors? Explain. (g) Do you believe cumulative voting should be permitted in all corporations? Explain.

4. (a) Is proxy voting permitted at common law? (b) What objections might be raised to proxy voting? If proxy voting were prohibited would this overcome the objections?

5. Explain what is meant by class voting and why it is sometimes provided for.

6. Indicate the various ways in which control of a corporation may be obtained without the ownership of a majority of the stock.

7. What is meant by the pre-emptive right of shareholders?

8. (a) Indicate the nature of the common-law right of a shareholder to inspect the books of his corporation. (b) How have the statutes of some of the states modified this right? (c) Of what practical value is this right? Explain fully.

9. (a) Indicate the common-law and statutory qualifications for corporate directors. (b) What is meant by classification of the board of directors? Why is it sometimes done? Is classification of the board legal when cumulative voting is followed? Explain. (c) List the powers possessed by the board of directors. (d) How may a director avoid many of the liabilities which the law imposes on directors?

10. (a) Distinguish between the directors and the officers of a corporation. (b) Who is the most important officer in a corporation?

Problems

1. Look up the statutes of your state in regard to the following: (a) Right of shareholders to inspect the corporate books. (b) Is cumulative voting permitted? If so, must it be so provided in the articles of incorporation? Must notice of intention to cumulate votes be given to the corporation? (c) Whether classified stock is permitted, (d) Whether a voting trust is permitted, and if so, the maximum duration, (e) Restrictions, if any, on shareholders' pre-emptive rights, (f) Number and qualifications of directors, and whether classification of the board is permitted.

2. Assume that the Standard Corporation has 1,000 shares of voting stock outstanding but only a total of 700 shares are represented at the meeting called for the purpose of electing a board of three directors. Each share has one vote for each director to be elected. How many shares would you have to own or control in order to insure the election of yourself to the board if: (a) Straight voting is followed? (b) Cumulative voting is followed?

3. If 1,000 shares vote cumulatively at a meeting called to elect five directors, what is the maximum number of directors that you could be sure of electing if you owned or controlled 280 shares?

Part II

CORPORATE SECURITIES

Chapter 6

CORPORATE STOCK

Nature of Corporate Stock. In an unincorporated organization, such as the general partnership, there is no such thing as "stock." The respective partners own a fractional part of the business, which can be ascertained by looking at the articles of partnership or the financial books of account. No certificates are issued to represent this interest in the business.

The stock of a corporation is divided into units called shares. These may have a par value, for example $100, or there may be no nominal dollar value assigned to them. The latter is called no-par stock and will be discussed later in the chapter.

Stock itself is invisible—no one has ever seen it. What we see is the certificate which evidences the stock. When a person buys stock he merely buys a bundle of legal rights, such as the right to vote the stock, to receive dividends, to share in the assets upon dissolution, etc. These legal rights of the stockholders were discussed in the preceding chapter. Many people think that corporate stock possesses some mysterious power which will make them rich; this despite the fact that most people lose money when it comes to buying stock. There is nothing inherent in stock which will enable it to earn dividends or to advance in price in the market. This would depend, as a rule, on the success of the corporation's business. In order to raise millions of dollars from hundreds of thousands of people it is absolutely necessary that the ownership of the corporation be divided into a large number of shares with a small denomination each.

Authorized, Issued, and Outstanding Stock. When talking about the capital stock of a corporation, confusion sometimes exists because the reference may be to authorized, issued, or outstanding stock.

The *authorized* stock is that amount which the corporation is permitted in its charter to issue. At the time of organization it merely represents a permit on the part of the state. No money may have been paid on the stock, and in fact, maybe the stock certificates are not even printed. To increase the authorized stock calls for action on the part of the stockholders and the state, since the charter is a contract between these parties.

That part of the authorized stock which has been subscribed to by the shareholders and accepted by the corporation or sold to the stockholders is called the *issued stock*. This remains issued until canceled by appropriate action on the part of the corporation.

Outstanding stock is that part of the issued stock which is in the hands of the stockholders. If the corporation reacquires part of its stock this is called *treasury stock*. As long as this remains treasury stock and is not canceled by the corporation, it is still included in the issued stock, but it is not included in the outstanding stock. Thus all outstanding stock is issued stock, but not all issued stock must be outstanding.

Capital Stock. The term *capital stock* is commonly used to refer to the aggregate of the corporate stock. When *preferred stock* is issued, the other class of stock is called *common stock*. But when only one type of stock is issued it is commonly called *capital stock* on the books of the company and in the balance sheet.

Capital. There are various meanings of the word *capital*. The economist defines it as wealth used for further production. This may be satisfactory for his purposes, but it is a little too indefinite for us.

In legal works the terms "capital" and "capital stock" are commonly used synonymously. In other words, lawyers and judges often say that the capital of a corporation is the aggregate of the par value of the stock, or the stated value in the case of no-par stock. This meaning can be illustrated by the legal rule that dividends cannot be paid from *capital*. It is realized, of course, that dividends are never paid from the capital stock. (A dividend in stock is paid from the surplus and increases the amount of the capital stock). What is meant is that dividends cannot be paid when the effect of payment would be to reduce the net assets to a figure below the capital stock. On the financial statements of banks we commonly see the use of the term "capital" in the net-worth section of the balance sheet instead of "capital stock." Since the term "capital stock" is well understood, while the term "capital" has different meanings to different individuals, it is suggested that when referring to the aggregate of the stock, we use the term "capital stock" rather than "capital."

The other common, perhaps most common, use of the term "capital" is to apply it to the total assets of the corporation. This is the use which is here recommended. Perhaps most businessmen when they hear the term believe that it refers to the assets. One question we might raise here is whether the intangible assets such as good will, patent rights, etc., should be included in the capital. For simplicity's sake, we can assume that all the assets are included. Again, when referring to the assets it is suggested that we call them that instead of using the term "capital." In that way the meaning will be clear.

Stock certificates and stock transfer

STOCK CERTIFICATES. The ownership of stock is evidenced by a *stock certificate*. Most people look upon this as the stock. It is of practical importance to distinguish between the stock and the certificate because if a person loses a stock certificate or it is destroyed, he has not lost the stock. A new certificate will be issued if he puts up an indemnity bond with the company to protect it if the old certificate turns up in the hands of an innocent purchaser for value.

The following are contained on the face of a stock certificate: name of company and state of incorporation; serial number of the certificate; number of shares represented; in case of par stock, the par value; name of the registered owner; date of issue; signature of the appropriate corporate officers; seal of the corporation; signatures of the transfer agent and registrar.

One certificate can represent one share or a number of shares. Since 100 shares is the smallest unit of trading for most stocks on the floor of the New York Stock Exchange, most of the certificates transferred there are for this number. On the reverse side of the stock certificate is the form to be completed when the stock is transferred.

TRANSFER OF STOCK. Since the certificate evidences the stock, when a shareholder wishes to sell or transfer his stock he must transfer the certificate by signing the assignment form on the reverse side, having the signature witnessed, and inserting the proper date. It is not necessary to write in the name of the buyer, nor of the person to whom one gives power of attorney to transfer the stock.

The issuing corporation looks to the stockholder of record as the owner of the shares. Stock is properly transferred on the books of the company by someone who is authorized to do so by the regis-

For value received, ______________________________
hereby sell, assign and transfer unto ______________________________
______________________________ ( ) shares of the
______________________________ Capital Stock represented
by the within certificate and do hereby irrevocably constitute and appoint
______________________________ attorney
to transfer said stock on the books of the within named Company with full power of substitution in the premises.

Date ______________________ 19____

____

In presence of:

____

____

Figure 2. Stock assignment form on reverse side of stock certificate.

tered owner. The transfer agent of the issuing company inserts his name in the blank space left by the owner.

If only part of the shares represented by the certificate are being transferred, the number being sold can be inserted in the appropriate space. The transferee's name would be inserted or a letter to the agent would instruct him to transfer over the given number of shares to the transferee. A certificate would be made out to him for the appropriate number of shares and a new certificate would be sent to the transferor for the number of shares being retained by him.

Many large companies appoint a trust company as their transfer agent. Such a company handles all the details in connection with the issue and transfer of the stock. It may also appoint another trust company as registrar. The latter checks on the transfer agent and prevents an overissue of stock. The New York Stock Exchange requires that all companies whose stock is listed must maintain a transfer agent and a registrar in the financial district of New York. These are commonly trust companies. The registrar cannot be the issuing company or the transfer agent.

All stock sold on the New York Stock Exchange must be transferred in that city. A company may maintain transfer offices also in other cities. Some companies that have their stock listed on both the New York Stock Exchange and the Midwest Stock Exchange (located in Chicago) maintain transfer agents in both cities.

If a stock certificate is placed with a bank as collateral for a loan, it is advisable not to sign the form on the reverse side of the certificate, because after the loan is paid off and the certificate returned to the owner, it would bear his indorsement and a finder or thief could pass good title to it. Instead the owner should execute a separate assignment form, called a *stock power of attorney,* and attach this to the certificate.

STOCKHOLDER ENTITLED TO DIVIDENDS. When directors declare dividends they make them payable to stockholders *of record* several days or weeks in the future, and the dividend is paid several weeks or a month after the record date. A typical example would be as follows. The directors meet January 15, and declare the dividend to stockholders of record February 1, with the dividend payable February 15.

When stock is sold about the same time as the record date, the question may be raised whether the seller or the buyer gets the dividends. Stock sold "regular way" on the New York Stock Exchange calls for delivery on the fourth full business day following the sale. Unless otherwise specified by the Exchange, the stock will sell *ex-dividend* three full business days before the record date (if the record date falls on Saturday or a holiday, the stock will sell ex-dividend four full business days before the record date). When a stock sells "ex-dividend" it means that the seller, rather than the buyer, will be entitled to the dividend. In the example above where the record date was February 1, the stock would sell ex-dividend on January 29 (January has 31 days). The stock would sell *cum-dividend* through January 28. This means that the buyer would be entitled to the dividend.

If a person bought the stock prior to the ex-dividend date, but did not get it transferred to his name by the record date, the company would pay the dividend to the stockholder of record, which would be the seller, but the buyer could demand that the seller turn over to him the amount of the dividend. If the stock was purchased through a broker, the latter will secure the amount of the dividend from the seller's broker and credit the buyer with it.

This procedure results in the dividend going to the person who is entitled to it. The seller has his money tied up in the company and is therefore entitled to receive the dividend. If the buyer acquires the stock a few days before the ex-dividend date and gets it transferred to his name by the record date, he will get the dividend. But the stock would have been selling cum-dividend, and the buyer would have paid a price that included the dividend.

If the market in general is rather stable, a good investment stock will sell off on the ex-dividend date by approximately the amount of the dividend. For example, if American Telephone and Telegraph stock would be selling for $180.00 the day before the ex-dividend date, it would sell for about $177.75 (the company is currently paying a quarterly dividend of $2.25) on the ex-dividend date, assuming there were no other factors present which would make the stock sell for more or less than this.

If the board of directors declare a dividend without specifying the record date, then the dividend will be payable to stockholders of record the day the dividend is declared.

Stockholder Entitled to Vote. In the past it was a common practice of corporations to close their stock transfer books some days in advance of a meeting in order that a list of the stockholders entitled to vote at the meeting could be obtained. Although some still do this, the larger corporations now usually provide that the stockholders of record of a particular hour on a given day in advance of the meeting are those entitled to vote.

Some states, such as New York, require that if a person buys stock after the record date but before the meeting date, the seller must upon demand turn over a proxy to the buyer.

Liability of Stockholders. If a person has not paid for his stock in full, he is subject to calls by the directors for the unpaid amount. In the event that a corporation is insolvent, creditors may come against the stockholders for the amount owned.

If partly paid stock is transferred, the question arises as to whether the transferor or the transferee is liable for the unpaid amount. It is difficult to generalize on this point because of differences in state laws and in the circumstances. In most of the states the transferee would be liable for calls made on the stock after the transfer, if he took the stock knowing that it was not fully paid. In some states, however, the transferor is liable to those who became creditors prior to the transfer.

It is common practice now not to issue the stock certificate until the stock is fully paid. The stock certificate usually states that the stock is "fully paid and non-assessable." If an innocent purchaser for value acquired such a certificate, he would not be liable for any assessments on the stock. In this event the liability would either be lost or would be retained by the seller, depending upon the state law, when the call was made, and when the debt was incurred. In some states the innocent purchaser for value would have no liability even if the certificate were not marked "fully paid."

Once the full amount of the stock has been paid to the issuing corporation, a purchaser of the stock in the market has no liability on it regardless of the price he pays.

The Uniform Stock Transfer Act, which has been adopted in all the states and the District of Columbia, gives stock certificates the same negotiable qualities that the Uniform Negotiable Instruments Act gives to negotiable instruments. This means that if a certificate has been properly indorsed, an innocent purchaser for value acquires good title despite the fact that it may have been lost or stolen. If a stock certificate is lost or stolen, the company and its transfer agent should be notified immediately. If the certificate had been indorsed, the loser may still have title to it unless it is held by an innocent purchaser for value. But if the registered owner's name is forged on the certificate, title still remains in him, even against an innocent purchaser for value.

TREASURY STOCK. This is uncanceled stock which a corporation has issued and then subsequently reacquired through purchase or gift. Such stock does not vote, nor does it receive dividends. If the treasury stock is canceled or reissued, it ceases to be treasury stock.

One reason (more common in the past than now) for the origin of treasury stock was to circumvent the liability on par value stock. Promoters usually have a greater abundance of ideas, property rights, options, patent rights, etc., than they do of cash. Many concerns have been able to exchange the corporate stock for fixed assets, property rights, and services. Then they would attempt to sell stock in order to get working capital, and find that the stock would not bring its par value in the market. The laws of the states either prohibited the sale of the stock below its par value, or if it was permitted, the buyer would be liable for the difference between what he paid and the par value. The possibility of this liability might result in the refusal of people to buy the stock.

Anticipating the above difficulty, the organizers of the corporation would be very liberal in the amount of stock which they would exchange to themselves for the property they turn over to the corporation. For example, three partners might turn over to the corporation a mine, or patent rights, conservatively valued at $50,000, for stock with a total par value of $100,000. Many types of property destined for business use are difficult to value. The law in most states provides that in the absence of fraud the valuation placed on property by the directors is conclusive. And fraud is difficult to prove. So the board of directors, which is composed of the partners, places a value of $100,000 on the property which is exchanged for the stock. This makes the stock fully paid.

Then the partners, or shareholders, each donate back to the corporation $10,000, or a total of $30,000, of the stock. This is now treasury stock. It was fully paid as far as the law is concerned when the property was received for it. So it can be sold for any price, or even given away, without any liability attaching to it. Some people may pay $75, for example, for a $100 par share of stock, because they thought they were getting a bargain. This may enable the corporation to get the important working capital of $22,500. The organizers would not be harmed by giving the stock up to the corporation. They still have a total of $70,000 in stock for properties really worth only $50,000. And without the working capital, the properties might not be worth even $50,000. The use of no-par stock, which is discussed later in the chapter, eliminates to some extent the necessity for stock watering of the type just mentioned.

Treasury stock is sometimes used to secure working capital without this overvaluation of properties at the time of promotion. A corporation may run into financial difficulties because of a recession or depression. The value of its inventories declines, many accounts are uncollectible, but still the corporation is liable for 100 per cent of its liabilities. The company's stock may be selling far below its par value in the market, so that the sale of new stock to get cash is out of the question. If it is a close corporation, all the shareholders may donate back to the corporation the same percentage of their stock. Or, one or several of the large stockholders may feel that they would fare better by giving back some of their stock to enable the corporation to secure working capital.

The stock does not have to be given back to be treasury stock. In fact, corporations sometimes buy back their stock. As long as it is not canceled, it is considered treasury stock. Such stock is included in the *issued* stock, but of course it is not *outstanding*.

When treasury stock is acquired, accountants usually recommend that it be shown on the balance sheet as a deduction from the outstanding stock. Since the other balance sheet items are not affected by the donation of the stock back to the corporation, it is necessary to credit a donated surplus account with the same amount as is subtracted from the capital stock. If the treasury stock is sold for less than the amount that was credited to the surplus account, the surplus will have to be charged or debited with the difference.

Many corporations carry treasury stock as an asset on their balance sheets. It is true that it may be sold for cash, but it is usually recommended that it be not listed on the asset side of the balance sheet.

Reasons for Reacquiring Stock. There are various reasons why a corporation might reacquire part of its issued stock. In some instances the purpose will be to resell it. In other cases it is done for cancellation. Other reasons are:

To provide working capital. This was the reason explained above in connection with treasury stock.

For debt owed by stockholders. A corporation sometimes sells its stock on the installment plan. In the event the stockholder is unable to pay for the stock, he may be compelled to forfeit it to the corporation.

Sale to officers and employees. Many corporations have a plan of selling stock to officers and employees at a price below the existing market price. In some instances the stock sold is unissued stock, but in other cases it is stock which the corporation has acquired in the market. If the stock is being sold below the par value, the question of liability would arise in case the stock were unissued stock; but if it were treasury stock, it could be sold as fully paid stock regardless of the price which was paid for it. The corporation may take advantage of low market prices which exist from time to time to acquire the stock.

Redundant cash. At certain times a corporation may find that it has cash on hand which is not needed in the immediate future. The current dividend rate may be rather high at the time, but the corporation may be unable to obtain a high return from investments. Despite these conditions, the market price of the stock may be reasonable. Perhaps the best investment for the corporate funds at this time would be to purchase back part of its stock.

To reduce future dividend requirement. This point is similar to the preceding one. In fact, one of the reasons a corporation may use its surplus cash to buy back its stock is in order to reduce the cash that will be needed in the future to pay the regular dividend rate.

To eliminate burdensome requirements. A corporation may have outstanding a type of stock, such as a cumulative and participating preferred stock (to be discussed in the following chapter), which may prove burdensome, particularly at a time when earnings are low. When the stock is selling for a reasonable price in the market and the corporation has surplus cash, it may buy back the stock and thus eliminate the burdensome features. In this way the common stockholders will benefit both in lean and prosperous years.

Market support. When a corporation's stock is slipping in the market, it may feel that it would be to the best interests of both the corporation and its stockholders to go into the market and buy up part of the stock in order to stabilize the price. Before doing this a corporation should look into the legal question of whether or not it has the right to buy the stock for this purpose. It is not in furtherance of the purpose for which the corporation was formed, nor would it be to the best interests of the shareholders to buy back the stock at one price and be forced to sell it at a lower price.

WAYS OF REACQUIRING THE STOCK. Following are the various ways in which a corporation may acquire back its stock.

Forfeiture from stockholder for debt. This was mentioned above in connection with the reasons for acquisition.

Donation of treasury stock. This also was discussed above.

Purchase from individual stockholders. A corporation will sometimes negotiate with individual stockholders for the purchase of part or all of their stock. Those approached usually hold a large block of stock. But occasionally a corporation will attempt to purchase from persons who hold one or a few shares, in order to reduce the cost of sending out annual reports. The advantage of purchasing directly from individual stockholders is that the corporation will thus not force the market price of the stock up by its purchases.

Purchase in the open market. In some instances the corporation will go into the open market and purchase its stock. The disadvantage of this method is that the corporation by bidding for the stock will tend to push up the price it will have to pay. Sometimes they will have a broker gradually buy up the stock in such a way that the extra demand will not increase the price appreciably.

Stock tenders. Another method used to reacquire stock is for the issuing corporation to advertise for *tenders* of its stock. The corporation agrees to pay not over a specified price per share for a given number of shares or for a specified amount of money available for the purchase. A time limitation is placed on the tenders. The stockholder sets the price which he will accept, commonly the maximum price set by the corporation. Some stockholders, however, will specify a lower price in order to insure better a sale. In the event that more shares are offered than the corporation can purchase, those offering the lowest price will be taken up first.

LEGAL RIGHT OF CORPORATION TO REACQUIRE SHARES. There is no legal objection to a corporation's acquiring treasury stock through donation by the shareholders. But when it comes to purchasing or canceling the stock, the corporation should be careful to follow legal requirements.

Stock can be canceled only by statutory authority. The board of directors usually initiates the cancellation. Statutes usually require a vote of either a majority or two thirds of the shares to effect the reduction in the stock. Since a cancellation involves an amendment to the charter, the procedure for amending should be followed. This requires assent on the part of the state also.

When a corporation buys back its stock there may be two parties harmed—the stockholders and the creditors. Stockholders may be injured because part of the corporation's funds are being removed from the business, and furthermore, the corporation may pay too high a price for the stock. In addition, the proportionate ownership and control of the corporation may be changed by purchasing the stock from only part of the shareholders, or purchasing it from all, but not in proportion to the amount of stock held by each. If the repurchase is permitted, the corporation should see to it that purchase from fewer than all the shareholders, or other than in proportion to the total amount of stock held by each, is permitted. The statutes of the leading commercial states do permit purchase in the market and from individual stockholders, but care should be taken to see that the statutes are followed.

A more serious objection relates to the possible impairment of creditors' rights. The stockholders are the owners of the business, and they collectively, as the corporation, owe the creditors. If the company had the unrestricted right to buy back its stock, it is conceivable that all of the corporate assets might be used to retire the stock and the creditors would be left with nothing.

There is in law what is known as the *trust fund theory*. According to this, the capital stock of a corporation is a trust fund for the benefit of creditors. This title is a misnomer for several reasons. In the first place the capital stock is not a "fund." And in the second place, if it were, it would not be a *trust* fund. What is meant by the law is that the corporation cannot use its assets to reduce voluntarily the net assets (assets less liabilities) below the capital stock figure. The reasoning behind this is that when extending credit, the creditors look to the balance sheet and see a definite amount opposite the caption "Capital Stock," and they thereupon grant credit to the company on the faith that net assets at least equivalent to this amount will be retained in the business for the security of the debt. It is true that operating losses may reduce the net assets below this figure, but the corporation should not voluntarily reduce it by such actions as paying dividends or buying back part of the stock and canceling it.

When the reduction of stock is permitted, the statutes either expressly or by implication provide that such reduction could not be made if it would impair the ability of the corporation to meet its debts. In a number of the states the statutes specifically provide that the reduction can be made only from the "surplus" (meaning from assets equivalent to the amount shown in the surplus account), or that it cannot be made from "capital" (meaning net assets represented by the capital stock account). These are, of course, two ways of stating the same thing.

Par and no-par stock

PAR VALUE STOCK. The early English corporation had par values of various amounts, and some of the corporations formed here during colonial times issued stock with par values ranging up to several hundred dollars. There are a few isolated early cases in the United States of corporations issuing a type of no-par stock under special statutes. But most stock issued by corporations in the United States prior to 1912 had a par value of $100 per share.

Since stock represented a fractional ownership of the corporate property or the corporation, it seems only natural that a fixed dollar amount, or "par value" should be assigned to a share. A par value of "$100" was a convenient figure to use. It was also customary in former times to sell par stock at its par value. Thus, the purchaser or prospective purchaser looked upon the aggregate par value of his shares as the value of his equity in the business.

PAR VALUE AS A MEASURE OF LIABILITY. The aggregate of the par value of a corporation's shares is ordinarily the figure at which the capital stock is carried in the balance sheet of the issuing corporation. If a person buys a share of stock from the issuing corporation for less than par, he can be held liable for the difference between what he paid and the par value. Thus, the par value has served as a measure of liability for the shareholders. The statutes in most states require that the total par value be paid to the corporation before the stock certificate may be issued.

Before passing, however, we should not overlook this exception to the above. According to common-law decisions in a number of the states, if a corporation has tried to sell its stock at par but is unable to do so, and if the money is needed to keep from failing, and not for expansion purposes, the corporation may sell its par stock at the best price obtainable and no liability will be attached to it even if it is sold below par. This common-law rule has been written into the statutes in some of the states.

Disadvantages of Par Value. Some of the disadvantages of par stock will be discussed since it was because of these that no-par stock laws were enacted.

Difficulty in obtaining equity capital. When a corporation is in need of additional funds, its stock may be selling in the market for less than its par value. But the corporation either cannot legally sell additional stock below par, or if it is legal, the public will not buy the stock because of the possible future liability. No one will pay par for new stock when he can buy the same old stock in the market at a discount.

Narrow market. Generally speaking, the lower the selling price of a stock, the wider the market. Other things being equal, a corporation can sell stock at $50 a share to more people than if the price were $100. The wider market enables the company to get more money in relation to the dividend rate which has been paid or which is expected on the stock. If the state law requires a par value of $100, which was usual in the past, it thus narrows the potential market and makes financing charges higher.

Today, however, par values as high as $100 are common only among railroads. Rarely do we find public utilities or industrials with par values so high. On the New York Stock Exchange the most common par value among industrials is $1 per share, and the next most popular par is $5.

Difficulty in obtaining paid-in surplus. In many instances corporate promoters would like to put part of the consideration received from the stock in the surplus account and thus start out with what might be thought of as a good showing. To do this would necessitate selling the par stock at a premium, which might be difficult to do.

Status of bonus stock. In some instances corporations want to give common stock as a bonus in connection with the sale of preferred stock or bonds. Sometimes employees or management are given some of the company's stock. If this is unissued par stock, and nothing is obtained for it, the person to whom it is given might be held liable for the par value, unless the statutes specifically authorize the practice.

Par value is misleading. When a share of stock carries a par value many people believe that the stock is worth that amount, or was originally worth that amount, or will some time in the future be worth that amount. To this extent the par label is misleading. A stock is rarely worth its par value even at the time it is sold. Much of the corporate property is overvalued, large amounts may be paid for promotional services, and the common is often handed out rather freely to facilitate the formation of the corporation. Even if the stock is worth its par value at the time it is sold, operating losses or profits may alter the situation so much that there may be absolutely no relation between the par of a stock and its actual value.

Adoption of No-Par Stock Laws. Because of some of the shortcomings stated above there was agitation for the adoption of laws that would permit a corporation to issue stock which did not possess a par value. New York, in 1912, was the first state to enact such legislation, and since then all the states, except Nebraska,[1] have adopted statutes which permit the issuance of no-par, as well as par, stock. Certain types of corporations, such as banks, trust companies, insurance companies, and savings and loan associations, however, are not permitted to use no-par stock in a number of the states.

Probably about one third or less of the stocks listed on the national exchanges are no-par. In 1950, about 25 per cent of the railroad common stocks and about 40 per cent of the industrials listed on the New York Stock Exchange were no-par shares.[2] In January, 1951, 34 per cent of all common stocks on the New York Stock Exchange were no-par.[3] In a sample study of 72 preferred stocks of all types of industries including utilities issued during 1946–1950, however, only 18 per cent were no-par.[4]

At the same time the states were enacting no-par statutes, many of them changed their laws to permit stock with a par of any amount, or of any amount from $1 up to $100 per share. Some of the disadvantages of $100 par stock have been overcome by the adoption of a low par value.

[1] Not only must all stocks have a par value in Nebraska, but it is required that all the stock of the same corporation must have the same par value per share. Registered public utility holding companies are not permitted to issue no-par stock without SEC approval.

[2] George L. Leffler, *The Stock Market* (New York: The Ronald Press Co., 1951), p. 15; see also p. 16 of the Second Edition, 1957.

[3] William H. Husband and James C. Dockeray, *Modern Corporation Finance* (3d ed.; Homewood, Illinois: Richard D. Irwin, Inc., 1952), p. 73.

[4] Donald A. Fergusson, "Recent Developments in Preferred Stock Financing," *The Journal of Finance*, September, 1952, p. 452.

Stated Value of No-Par Stock. The statutes of some states provide that the no-par stock shall have a *stated value.* This is an arbitary value that is assigned to the stock and is found either in the charter or as a resolution in the minutes of the directors' meeting. Where a stated value is contained in the charter, it is similar to a par value, except that this stated value may not appear on the stock certificate.

In most instances the stated value is determined from time to time by the board of directors. To the extent that a shareholder knows the stated value, if he buys the stock at less than this price, he may be held liable for the difference between what he paid and the stated value. As a practical matter, however, the directors always set a stated value at or below the sale price of the stock.

In other states there is no necessity to establish a stated value. This is more truly no-par stock than when a stated value must be set. The directors merely determine from time to time the price at which new issues of the stock are to be sold. In some states the stated value, or all the consideration received from such stock, must be carried to the capital stock account, but in others part of the consideration may be put in a surplus account, provided a statement to this effect was made at the time the stock was sold.

Advantages of No-Par Stock. Most of the advantages of no-par stock are obviously the same as the disadvantages of par-value stock stated above, so the advantages will merely be listed.

1. Capital may be easier to obtain from the sale of the stock since there is no requirement that a par amount be obtained.
2. There is little chance that stockholder liability will exist after the subscription price has been paid.
3. A wider market may be obtained for the stock than if a relatively high-valued par stock is sold.
4. It may be easier to acquire a paid-in surplus from the sale of the stock than if par stock is used.
5. There is less likelihood that any liability will attach to bonus stock.
6. There is less chance that the investing public will be misled as to the actual value of the stock.

Tax Disadvantage of No-Par Stock. Practically the only disadvantage of no-par stock relates to taxation. In some of the states the organization tax on each no-par share is the same as the tax on each $100 of par value. No-par stock is almost invariably sold for less than $100 a share, so that a larger percentage of the sales price goes to the state. In other words, if one corporation sold its no-par share for $10, and another corporation sold a $10 par stock at the same price, the no-par corporation would have to pay ten times as much in taxes per share as the par stock corporation.

Another tax that may be felt more by no-par stock corporations is the annual franchise tax for domestic and foreign corporations. In some of the states which base this tax on the authorized or the issued stock, it is assumed that each no-par share has a value of $100, or some fixed amount ranging from $10 to $100. This would be a greater burden than the organization tax, since it must be paid each year.

The federal stock-issue tax is also usually higher for a no-par stock corporation. On par stock the tax is 11 cents of each $100 of par or fraction thereof. On no-par stock it is 11 cents for each share, unless the actual value is in excess of $100 per share, in which case the tax is 11 cents on each $100 of actual value or fraction of it for each certificate issued, or unless the actual value is less than $100, in which case the tax is 3 cents on each $20 of actual value or fraction for each certificate. Like the organization tax, the stock issue tax is paid only once—on the original issue of the stock. Effective January 1, 1959, the stock issue tax will be 10 cents on each $100 (or fraction thereof in excess of $50) of the actual value of the shares without regard to whether the stock is par or no par.

The federal stock transfer tax is usually more on no-par shares. This tax is paid by the seller on all transfers after the original issue. The tax is 5 cents per $100 par or fraction thereof and 5 cents for each no-par share selling below $20; if the stock is selling for $20 or more the tax is 6 cents for each $100 par or fraction thereof and 6 cents for each no-par share. Let us assume that a person sells 100 shares of a $10 par stock and 100 shares of no-par stock, each at $10 a share. In the case of the par stock, he would be selling a total par value of $1,000. The tax would be 5 cents on each $100 of par, or a total of $.50. But he would pay 5 cents on each no-par share, or a total of $5.00. The same money value was involved in both transactions but the tax on the no-par shares would be ten times the amount paid on the par stock. (Tax changed; see p. 454.)

Other stock values

Book Value. The book value of stock is the amount shown on the financial books as represented by the assets less the liabilities. Another way of saying this is that the book value is represented by the amount shown in the net-worth section of the balance sheet.

Where there is only one class of stock the book value per share would be calculated by dividing the net worth of the corporation by the number of shares outstanding. Many companies do not place a value on their intangible assets such as good will, patents, and franchises, so their value would not be reflected in the book value. Where these are valued in the balance sheet, the financial services usually subtract them from the net worth in obtaining the book value. They then commonly refer to book value as the "tangible-asset value" or "net tangible-asset value." When "book value" is referred to it is not always known whether the intangibles have been deducted. The conservative way is to deduct them.

When there is both preferred and common stock outstanding the calculation of the book value is a little more involved. To calculate the book value per share of the *preferred* stock one would divide the total net worth (less intangible assets) by the number of preferred shares. As a practical matter, the book value of the preferred means little or nothing, particularly since all of the net assets, including those represented by the common stock, are assigned to the preferred stock. If there is more than one class of preferred outstanding, the book value of each class is calculated by subtracting from the net worth (less intangible assets) the par value (or equivalent) of each class senior to the one under consideration.

The book value of the *common* is calculated by subtracting the preferred stock from the net worth (less intangible assets). To get the book value per share this figure would be divided by the number of common shares. This raises the question as to what figure would be used in subtracting the preferred stock. In many instances subtracting the preferred at its par value would be satisfactory. If there are any accumulated dividends on the preferred stock, these should be added to their par value before subtracting.

If the par value of the preferred, however, has little relation to the worth of the stock, another figure should be used. For example, a preferred stock with a nominal par value of $1 per share may have been sold for $100 a share. The stock may be entitled to $105 and accrued dividends in event of involuntary liquidation, and $110 and accrued dividends in the event that it is voluntary, and it may be callable by the company at $120 a share. The dividend rate specified on the stock may be $6 a share. A book value of the common derived by subtracting the preferred at par would be very misleading, to say the least. Some of the financial services use the involuntary liquidation price, and it is suggested that the reader use this figure. Any accrued dividends would be added.

To illustrate the computation of book value of stock we will assume that the preferred stock in the balance sheet below is entitled to $105 a share plus accrued dividends in the event of involuntary liquidation. We will assume that one year's dividends of 6 per cent have accrued on the stock. Two methods of arriving at the book value will be illustrated.

BALANCE SHEET
The Standard Corporation
As of December 31, 1956

Assets		*Liabilities*	
Current assets	$2,220,000	Current liabilities	$ 500,000
Good will	1,000,000	Bonds	2,000,000
Fixed assets	15,000,000	Preferred stock ($100 par)	2,000,000
		Common stock ($100 par)	10,000,000
		Surplus	3,720,000
Total	$18,220,000	Total	$18,220,000

CALCULATION OF BOOK VALUE

Total Assets		$18,220,000
Less:		
Good will	$1,000,000	
Current liabilities	500,000	
Bonds	2,000,000	3,500,000
Net tangible assets (book value of preferred)		$14,720,000

$14,720,000 divided by 20,000 equals $736, book value per share of the preferred stock.

Net tangible assets		$14,720,000
20,000 preferred shares @ $105	$2,100,000	
6% accrued dividend	120,000	2,220,000
Book value of common stock		$12,500,000

$12,500,000 divided by 100,000 equals $125, book value per share of the common stock.

Alternative method:

Net worth (preferred and common stock and surplus)	$15,720,000
Less:	
Good will	1,000,000
Book value of preferred stock	$14,720,000
Less: Preferred @ $105 plus accrued dividend	2,220,000
Book value of common stock	$12,500,000

$12,500,000 divided by 100,000 equals $125, book value per share of the common stock.

In the past considerable importance was attached to the book value of a company's stock but in recent years it has been given little attention. This is undoubtedly the right attitude for several reasons. In the first place, assets might be carried on the books at a figure far different from the cost. At the time of organization the assets are usually inflated. Later the book figure may be cut down considerably below cost less depreciation in order to be conservative, or to reduce depreciation charges, and thereby increase the net earnings.

Even if the assets are carried at their cost, there is not necessarily any relationship between the book value of the stock and the market value. Some companies acquire assets in appreciable amounts at a time when prices are high. Others purchase them when prices are low. But the earning power of a given asset would be the same regardless of whether it was acquired at a high or at a low price. Furthermore, operating losses or profits retained in the business would either lower or increase the value of the company's assets.

The most important reason why the book value does not indicate the real worth of a stock is that the worth depends upon anticipated future earnings. Two companies may have identical book values for their stock, but one of them may have such better management and location that it can earn considerably more and pay larger dividends than the other company. The anticipated earning power and dividend payments are the factors that determine the stock's real value.

Before buying a common stock it might be at least of some interest to look at the book value, but in most cases not much importance should be attached to it. In analyzing an investment company, however, particularly an open-end company (investment companies are discussed in Chapter 32), the book value of the stock is of importance. The shares of closed-end investment companies tend to sell somewhat near the book value. In the case of open-end firms the book value is calculated daily and the stock can be purchased at this value plus a slight premium. It can be sold back to the issuing company at its book value.

Current-Asset Value. It may be of some importance to calculate the *current-asset value* of a stock. When only common stock is outstanding this is found by subtracting from the current assets *all* the liabilities. The current-asset value per share could then be found, of course, by dividing by the number of shares outstanding. If preferred stock is outstanding, the same procedure as described above is followed. This is really another type of book value, being the current-asset book value of the stock.

Book values are an attempt to determine the liquidating value of the stock. If fixed assets are sold at a forced sale, they usually bring only a small percentage of the book value. The current assets bring a much higher figure. The cash and perhaps the securities would, of course, yield 100 per cent. The current-asset value of a stock might truly represent the liquidating value better than the book value including fixed assets as calculated above.

There are times when the aggregate market value of a stock may be less than its current-asset value. This does not necessarily mean that the stock would be a good buy. In fact, if this situation exists it indicates that the stock is not desired by speculators and investors. The reason is probably that the future prospect is for lower earnings and lower dividends.

Market Value. The easiest of all values to determine is the market value of a stock. For stocks which are listed on the leading stock exchanges, the last sale price or closing price fairly well indicates the market value. If there were no sales for several hours before the market closed, the "bid-and-ask" prices would show the worth of the stock at the time the market closes.

If the listed stock is inactive, a stock broker will get the bid-and-ask prices without charge. In the case of unlisted stocks, or as they are commonly called, the *over-the-counter* stocks, a stock broker can usually secure bid-and-ask prices.

The market value of stocks of companies that have a heavy investment in fixed properties, such as railroads and steel companies, is usually much lower than the book value. On the other hand the market value of the stock of airplane manufacturing companies, or automobile firms may on occasion be several times the book value.

The market price of a stock is a resultant of the forces of supply and demand. People want to buy stocks either for the dividends, or for the anticipated appreciation in the price of the stock, or both. These result from the future earnings of the company. Therefore, as was stated before, the future earning power of the company has more influence on the market price of a company's stock than any other single factor. But no one knows definitely what the future earnings of any company will be. A number of factors, including the new orders being obtained, the prospect for future orders, etc., are used to guess at the probable future earnings. The past and present earnings and the trend of the income are used in attempting to predict the future earnings.

The *price-earnings* ratio is a convenient formula used by many to determine whether they think the market price is high or low in relation to present earnings per share. This ratio expresses how many times its earnings a share is selling in the market. The *earnings per share* is not the dividends the stockholder gets, but rather it is the net profit (after taxes) of the company divided by the number of shares outstanding. If a company is earning $10 a share on its stock, and the stock is selling in the market for $100, the stock would be said to be selling for 10 times its earnings ($100 divided by $10). If a nonparticipating preferred stock is outstanding, the preferred dividend is subtracted from the net earnings to get the earnings on the common stock.

Some years ago there was a rule of thumb that an industrial common stock should sell for something around 10 times earnings. The reasoning behind the 10-times ratio was this. Many companies paid out in dividends approximately 60 per cent of their earnings. If the company earned $10 a share it would pay out $6 a share in dividends. It was thought that a person should earn approximately 6 per cent on his investment. If he would get $6 a share dividends, then he should pay about $100 for the stock in order to get a 6 per cent return on his money. Thus, a price of 10 times earnings was paid for the stock.

In times of stock market booms, people sometimes will pay 25 or 40 times the earnings per share, but ordinarily this would be too high. Somewhere in the neighborhood of 10 to 12 times should be more or less normal. Probably 15 or 20 should be considered the maximum.

Too much importance should not be attached to the price-earnings ratio. If the stock is selling at three or four times earnings a person might think it to be a good buy. On the other hand he may refuse to buy a stock at 25 times earnings. But if a stock is selling for only four times earnings it is an indication that the future prospects for the company are not bright. Conversely a 25-times ratio would indicate that people are discounting the prospect for favorable future earnings. One of the shortcomings of the price-earnings ratio is that it compares present stock prices with past or present earnings. Stock prices at any one time reflect the prospective *future* earnings.

REAL VALUE. We sometimes hear people say that a particular stock is selling at more, or less, than its real value. What do we mean by *real value*? In the case of a listed stock the market value commonly goes up and down in the course of a day, week, month, or year. In times of prosperity stock prices soar to extreme heights, and then when the depression hits they fall to excessive depths. The prices appear to go too far in each direction and then correct themselves and go too far in the opposite direction. They are as much overpriced at the peak as they are underpriced at the bottom of a depression.

The book value or the earnings per share of a stock will not change much, if at all, in a day's time, but the price of the stock may fluctuate violently due to technical factors, such as an overbought or oversold market. The real or intrinsic worth of the stock may not have changed at all. This is one of the reasons why it is said that the market price of a stock does not necessarily indicate the real value. Also, in some instances something which will favorably affect the stock in the future is not generally known and therefore its real worth may be more than it is selling for in the market.

There are many types of property which have a real value to us far in excess of the price we could get if we sold the property. But when it comes to stocks, it is difficult to escape the conclusion that a stock is worth what you can get for it. In other words, generally the market price reflects the real value.

Types of stock

COMMON STOCK. The *common* stockholders are the residual claimants of the corporation. When there are other classes of stock outstanding, the common shareholders are the last ones to receive dividends, and are usually the last ones to receive the assets in event of dissolution. If only one class of stock is outstanding it is necessarily common stock, although many corporations call it "capital stock" on the balance sheet. (All kinds of stock are included in "capital stock.") In England common shares are referred to as *ordinary shares*. In a few instances *ordinary stock* has been issued by companies in the United States.[5]

In 1890, the Great Northern Railway Co. reacquired all of its common stock, leaving only the preferred stock outstanding.[6] Although titled preferred stock, this really became common stock, since it was not preferred over any other stock. Due in part to the misunderstanding, the company finally on July 2, 1954, reclassified the preferred as no-par common, and issued the shareholders two new common shares for each old preferred share.

When preferred stock is issued it is commonly limited to a specified dividend, and is usually nonvoting. It is the holders of the

[5] The Alabama Great Southern Railroad Co. (controlled by the Southern Railway Co.) has an issue of *ordinary stock* outstanding, which is listed on the American Stock Exchange. It is preceded by an issue of $3 cumulative preferred stock which participates equally share for share with the ordinary stock in any dividends after the ordinary has received $3 per share in any one year.

[6] In 1898, the preferred was designated as $6 noncumulative preferred, and in 1935, it was changed from $100 par to no-par through a share for share exchange.

common stock, or their proxies, who control the corporations. When earnings are large the common stand to gain more than the preferred. Thus the common stock usually fluctuates more in the market than does the preferred.

There has grown up in recent years what is known as the *common-stock theory of investment.* This theory embraces the idea that a well selected and diversified list of common stocks held over a long period of years will turn out better than a similar investment in preferred stocks or bonds. Corporations usually pay out only part of their earnings in the form of dividends, and the balance is plowed back into the business. This increases the equity of the common stockholders and gives the company an increased investment which will increase earnings still further in the future.

As the population grows and people develop a higher standard of living, more and more goods will be sold, and thus the earnings will be further increased. Since the government spending grows as a result of wars and preparation for wars, the national debt increases, and prices go higher and higher. Investment in bonds, savings accounts, insurance and annuities are relatively less attractive. Common stock is looked upon as a hedge against inflation. As prices rise, the worth of the corporate property increases. Earnings and dividends also usually increase with inflation. In view of these conditions several states in recent years have changed their laws to permit life insurance companies and trustees to invest a certain percentage of their assets in common stock.

Despite all these factors which argue for the purchase of common stock, the average person will probably continue to lose money on them. The ordinary individual does not have the necessary background, experience and temperament to enable him to select successfully the companies that will probably turn out well in the future. Even if he is possessed of these qualities, it is still exceedingly difficult properly to determine just when to buy the stock and when to sell it. Most people buy their stocks high and sell them low, and that will probably continue in the future.

Preferred Stock. This is preferred over the common with respect to dividends, and usually with respect to assets upon dissolution. It is generally limited to the stated dividend rate, and is commonly nonvoting. As a class it is considered less speculative than the common, and is usually purchased more by the investor or semi-investor as distinguished from the speculator. In England preferred shares are called *preference shares.* Preferred stock will be discussed in some detail in the following chapter.

Classified Stock. This is usually designated as Class A and Class B stock. The A stock is preferred over the B in respect to dividends, but usually the A stock does not possess the right to vote, or at least does not vote as long as dividends are being paid on it. In some instances the dividend is *cumulative* (cumulation is discussed in the following chapter), but in other cases it is noncumulative. In some cases after the A stock has received its specified dividend and a liberal dividend has been paid to the B, the A stock may be *participating*, i.e., it is allowed to participate with the B stock in any additional dividends declared. The A stock is also generally preferred over the B in respect to assets upon dissolution, and often is made *callable* by the company. Both classes are usually no-par stocks.

If a company has no preferred stock outstanding, the Class A is really a preferred stock. Even if there is a preferred issue out, the Class A may be considered a junior type of preferred. The restrictions on the use of classified common stock were mentioned in the preceding chapter. An example of classified stock is the Class A $1 par stock of the Curtiss-Wright Corporation. This stock is entitled to a $2 noncumulative dividend before anything can be paid to the common stock. The A stock, however, is entitled to the same voting rights as the common (one vote per share) and the same liquidation rights. It is convertible into one share of common, and is callable at $40.

Guaranteed Stock. This is a stock the dividends on which have been guaranteed by another company. It commonly arises in railroad consolidation where Company A leases the lines of Company B, and as one of the provisions of the lease, A guarantees the dividends on B's stock. This could be either common or preferred stock.

If the dividends on the guaranteed stock are not paid, the shareholders have a claim against the guaranteeing company the same as any other unsecured creditor. Since the principal amount of stock does not represent a debt, they would have no claim against the guaranteeing company with respect to the principal amount. If the latter should fail and be unable to pay anything, the stockholders would have no claim against the issuing company in respect to dividends or principal. In other words, they are just ordinary stockholders so far as the issuing company is concerned.

Preferred stock without a guaranty is sometimes called guaranteed stock. This is incorrect, since a company cannot guarantee the dividends on its own stock.

TABLE 5

SELECTED LIST OF GUARANTEED RAILROAD STOCKS

Stock	*Par Value*	*Guaranteed by*
Allegheny & Western Ry. 6%	$100	Baltimore & Ohio R.R.
Bessemer & Lake Erie R.R. 6% Pfd.	50	Carnegie-Illinois Steel Co.
Boston & Albany R.R. 8¾%	100	New York Central R.R.
Cleveland & Pittsburgh R.R. 7% Cap.	50	Pennsylvania R.R.
Delaware R.R. 8%	25	Pennsylvania R.R.
Erie & Pittsburgh R.R. 7%	50	Pennsylvania R.R.
Nashville & Decatur R.R. 7½% Orig.	25	Louisville & Nashville R.R.
Northern Central Ry. 8%	50	Pennsylvania R.R.
Pittsburgh, Ft. Wayne, & Chicago Ry. 7% Pfd.	100	Pennsylvania R.R.

PRIOR-LIEN STOCK. Prior-lien stock is placed ahead of other stock in respect to dividends, or assets, or both. It is thus a type of preferred stock. It should be distinguished from *senior* stock. If a company issued both common and preferred stock at the same time, the preferred would be considered senior stock, but it would not be a prior-lien stock. If a new issue of preferred stock were subsequently put in ahead of the old preferred stock this new issue would be a prior-lien stock, and it would also be a senior stock. An example of a prior-lien stock is the Alleghany Corporation $4 Cumulative Convertible Prior Preferred, which was issued in 1953. This stock has a prior lien over the other preferred and common stock both in respect to dividends and to assets upon dissolution.[7] In a few instances companies have outstanding a prior-lien stock issue even though there was no other stock except common outstanding. An example is the Wheeling & Lake Erie Railway Company 4 Per Cent Cumulative Prior-Lien Stock.[8]

In order to place an issue of stock ahead of another issue it would, if so provided in the contract, or in the statutes, necessitate the consent of a prescribed number of the shares. This is sometimes done when a corporation is in financial difficulty and can secure

[7] This stock has prior claim to dividends over the company's old $2.50 Preferred Stock (for which it was exchanged), the $5.50 Cumulative Preferred Series A, which was outstanding at the time, and of course, the common stock. It also has a prior claim over the other stocks in event of liquidation of $80 a share. This latter figure is also its call price. The stock voting as a class has the right to elect two of the directors. A two-thirds vote of the Prior Preferred is required to alter materially any provisions of the stock, or to issue any prior or parity stock. The stock is convertible into 16 shares of common stock of the company.

[8] This stock has a preference over common of $4 cumulative dividends per annum, and in the event of liquidation it gets $100 and accrued dividends before the common receives anything. It is noncallable. The "prior" lien and the common are the only classes of stock outstanding. The prior-lien stock was exchanged for the company's old 7 per cent prior-lien stock in 1936.

new capital only by getting the old stockholders to subordinate their issue to a new one.

BANKERS' SHARES. If a company's stock sells at too high a price, the market for it will be restricted, with the result that in relation to the earnings or assets of the company the stock might be selling for too low a price. If the company were to sell additional stock at this time, it would be relatively expensive financing in view of the dividends being paid.

Instead of selling the new shares directly to the public, the issuing company places them with a bank or trust company. The financial institution issues nonvoting certificates of beneficial interest against the deposit of the company's shares. These certificates are called *bankers' shares,* or *subshares.* A much larger number of these certificates are issued than the number of shares deposited. Dividends are paid by the issuing company to the trust company. The latter then prorates these dividends to the holders of the bankers' shares.

The bankers' shares, which greatly outnumber the corporate shares, can be sold at such a relative low price that a much wider market can be obtained than if the stock was directly sold to the public. Thus, in relation to the dividends being paid, the company obtains cheaper financing. Bankers' shares are rarely issued.

DEFERRED STOCK. This type is one on which dividends are deferred until the expiration of a stated period or until after the happening of a particular event. The dividends on this stock are usually not paid until after they are paid on one or all the other stock issues. Using the term in a broad sense we could say that when both common and preferred are outstanding the common is a deferred stock. But the term "deferred stock" ordinarily applies to a stock that does not receive dividends until after they have been paid not only on the preferred, but on the common as well. This type of stock is used much more in England than in the United States.

FOUNDERS', PROMOTERS', AND MANAGEMENT SHARES. In some instances a special class of stock called *founders' shares, promoters' shares,* or *management shares* is given to the promoters of a corporation or to some of the top management. This is really another name for deferred stock. Dividends are not paid on it until after a specified amount has been paid to all the other classes of stock. When this type is issued the number of shares is much less than in the other classes of stock. In some instances all the profits, after a specified rate is paid to the other types, may go to these shares. In some cases the profits are divided evenly between this type of stock as a class and the other classes. Since the number of founders' shares is relatively small, the *per share* dividends would be relatively large. As mentioned above in connection with deferred stock, these shares are used more commonly in England than in the United States.

DEBENTURE STOCK. This term is rarely used in the United States, but when such a stock has been issued it has been a type of preferred that came ahead of the other stock of the company.[9] The term is more commonly used in England where it applies to a *bond*, and not a stock. In some instances the bond is secured by a mortgage and in other cases it is not secured.[10] In the United States the word "debenture" is used to apply to a bond which is not secured by property. But we call these obligations *debenture bonds*, and not debenture stocks.

Questions

1. (a) Distinguish between stock and a stock certificate. (b) Of what practical value might it be to distinguish between the stock and the certificate?
2. Distinguish between the authorized, the issued, and the outstanding stock of a corporation.
3. Distinguish between the capital, and the capital stock of a corporation.
4. If a company has only one class of stock outstanding, what is it usually titled on the balance sheet?
5. (a) Why is it advisable not to indorse a stock certificate which is put up as collateral for a loan? (b) What would be done in lieu of an indorsement?
6. (a) When stock is transferred near a dividend date, what determines whether the transferor or the transferee is entitled to the dividend? (b) If the directors of Company X, whose stock is listed on the New York Stock Exchange, declare a dividend to stockholders of record January 15, when will the stock go ex-dividend?
7. When stock is transferred near the time of the annual meeting, what determines whether the transferor or the transferee is entitled to vote the stock?
8. (a) Indicate briefly the nature of the liability of corporate shareholders. (b) Who may be held liable when partly-paid stock is transferred?

[9] An example is the Dennison Manufacturing Company 8 Per Cent Cumulative Debenture Stock. This stock has a preference in respect to dividends over the A common and the voting common. In liquidation it is entitled to $160 and dividends ahead of the other stock. The stock is callable also at $160 and accrued dividends. It has no ordinary voting power unless dividends are $12 in arrears, when it has the right to elect approximately two thirds of the board of directors, and to exercise ordinary voting rights with the voting common, each debenture share to have ten votes, and each voting common share to have one vote. These voting rights continue until all accumulated dividends have been paid.

[10] The Canadian Pacific Railway Company has outstanding a secured perpetual bond issue which is called a "4 Per Cent Consolidated Debenture Stock" issue.

9. (a) What is meant by treasury stock? (b) Who votes treasury stock? Who receives dividends on it? (c) Indicate the reasons for the origin of treasury stock and the circumstances under which it might be acquired.

10. (a) List the reasons why a corporation might reacquire its own stock. (b) List the various ways that a corporation might reacquire its own stock. (c) Indicate briefly the nature of the legality of a company purchasing its own stock.

11. (a) What are the reasons, if any, for corporate stock to have a par value? (b) What are the shortcomings, if any, of par-value stock to the issuing corporation?

12. What are the advantages of no-par stock from the viewpoint of the issuing corporation?

13. What are the possible disadvantages of no-par stock from the viewpoint of the issuing corporation?

14. (a) Must no-par stock have a "stated" value? (b) If a stated value is required for no-par stock, is it necessary to specify it in the articles or certificate of incorporation?

15. At what value should no-par stock be carried in the balance sheet of the issuing corporation?

16. (a) Distinguish between the following stock values: par value, book value, net tangible asset value, and real value. (b) Give a hypothetical example of an abbreviated balance sheet of a corporation which has preferred stock outstanding, and compute the per-share book value of the preferred and the common stock. (c) Indicate several circumstances under which the determination of the book value of stock would be of considerable practical value.

17. (a) Give a hypothetical example of the computation of the price-earnings ratio. (b) Of what practical value is the price-earnings ratio? (c) Why should too much emphasis not be placed on this ratio?

18. What is meant by the "common-stock theory of investment"?

19. Indicate what is meant by each of the following: classified stock, guaranteed stock, prior-lien stock, bankers' shares, deferred stock, founders' shares, and debenture stock.

20. Is the British terminology concerning corporate stock any different from that used in the United States? Explain.

Problems

1. The following is a balance sheet of the New Corp. as of Dec. 31, 19-1:

Assets		*Liabilities and Net Worth*	
Cash	$ 50,000	Payables	$ 200,000
Receivables	100,000	Preferred Stock	1,000,000
Inventory	300,000	Common Stock	2,000,000
Plant	3,250,000	Surplus	1,500,000
Good will	1,000,000		
Total	$4,700,000	Total	$4,700,000

The preferred stock bears a 7 per cent cumulative dividend, and both it and the common have a par value of $100 per share.

(a) Assuming that the preferred and common share alike in assets upon dissolution, and that all accumulated dividends have been paid on the preferred to date, what is the book value per share of the common stock? (b) If the preferred stock is entitled to its par value only upon dissolution, what is the book value per share of the common? (c) If the preferred stock is preferred over the common in respect to assets upon dissolution to the extent of $110 per share and accrued dividends, and no dividends have been paid on it for the past two years, what is the book value per share of the common? (d) What is the book value per share of the preferred stock?

2. The articles of incorporation of the Amalgamated Corp., filed at the Secretary of State's office on Jan. 2, 19-1, provided for the issuance of 50,000 shares of common stock with a par value of $100 per share. The following day Mr. Hopkins, Mr. Chase, and Mr. Douglas turned over the property to the corporation, and each received $1,000,000 in stock in payment for the property.

The next day each donated to the corporation $200,000 of the stock, which was not canceled by the corporation. On Jan. 5, $400,000 of this stock was resold to Mr. Stone for $320,000 in cash. On the same day Mr. Reynolds contracted to purchase $100,000 of the donated stock from the corporation on Feb. 1 at the price of $75 per share, payment to be made on Feb. 1. On Jan. 6 Mr. Harlan and Mr. Holmes each subscribed for 1,000 shares at par, paying 20 per cent down and agreeing to pay the balance on call. The following day these subscriptions were accepted by the directors. On Jan. 10 the directors called for another 20 per cent to be paid on the stock. Mr. Harlan met the call but Mr. Holmes was unable to do so, and the corporation canceled his subscription by appropriate resolution adopted by the board of directors.

On Jan. 11 Mr. Hughes contracted to purchase 1,500 shares of this unissued stock at par. It was agreed that he was to deposit 20 per cent of the contract price with the company immediately and 20 per cent additional each month for 4 months, at the end of which time the stock certificate was to be delivered to him. In the meantime the company agreed to pay him 3 per cent interest on the money deposited.

Assume that you are called upon to submit a report to the treasurer of the company on Jan. 12 showing the status of the company's stock at that time. Indicate the amounts that you would show under the following heads:

(a) Authorized stock
(b) Issued stock
(c) Outstanding stock
(d) Unissued stock
(e) Full-paid stock
(f) Part-paid stock
(g) Treasury stock

3. A company has assets of $600,000; liabilities of $100,000; capital stock of $400,000; and surplus of $100,000. The stock, which has a par value of $100 per share, is given up by the shareholders for no-par stock with a stated value of $50 per share, the exchange being on a share-for-share basis.

(a) Indicate three different ways in which the no-par stock may be shown on the balance sheet. (b) As a stockholder in the company, which of these methods would you favor? Why? (c) If you were a creditor of the company, which method would you prefer? Why? (d) Which method would be considered the best accounting practice? Why?

4. The Standard Corp. was organized June 1, 19–1, with an authorized capital stock of 10,000 shares of no-par stock. On June 3, 5,000 of these

shares were sold to the public for $40 per share. On Sept. 1 of the same year an additional 2,000 shares were sold for $30 per share.

(a) Do you think that it was legal to sell the 2,000 shares at this relatively low price? (b) Do you think that it was fair to the shareholders who purchased the first shares sold? Why? (c) Would the last 2,000 shares sold have to be first offered to the original shareholders before they could be sold to the public? Explain.

Chapter 7

PREFERRED STOCK

General Nature of Preferred Stock. As its title indicates, *preferred stock* is a type of stock which is preferred over common stock in some way. In practically all, if not all, preferred issues outstanding, the stock is preferred over the common in respect to dividends. It usually is preferred over the common also in respect to assets upon dissolution. In recent years most of the preferred issues have been cumulative in respect to dividends. Commonly the voting right is restricted.

The specific rights, preferences, or limitations depend upon the statutes of the state in which the company is incorporated, and upon the provisions relating to it in the articles of incorporation, the by-laws, and the stock certificate. We, therefore, cannot make general statements regarding the rights of preferred stock and have them apply to all preferreds. The rights of any specific preferred stock depend upon the specific contract under which it is issued.

Preferred, like common, stock may be no-par or par value. When the latter, the par may be \$100, \$50, \$25, \$1, or any amount specified in the articles. Unlike the common, preferred stock must have a specified dividend rate since it is entitled to this amount before any dividends can be paid to the common. (Some companies by custom pay a fixed amount on the common each year, but this rate is not specified in the contract. For example, American Telephone and Telegraph pays a \$9 dividend each year.) When the preferred is no-par, the dividend rate must be expressed in dollars and cents, but when the stock is par value it may be stated in per cent. The latter might, however, be misleading unless the particular par value is known. For this reason the annual dividend rate on par preferreds is generally expressed in dollars per share and this rate is used in the title of the particular stock in order to identify that issue. (Some companies have a number of different preferred issues, each with a different dividend rate.) Following are the titles that would be used for the three selected issues: Atchison, Topeka and Santa Fe $2.50 Noncumulative Preferred, Pacific Gas and Electric $1.50 Cumulative Preferred, and Union Pacific $2 Noncumulative Preferred. The Atchison stock has a par value of $50, and a dividend rate of 5 per cent, Pacific Gas and Electric has a $25 par and a dividend rate of 6 per cent, and Union Pacific has a par value of $50 and a dividend rate of 4 per cent.

Why Preferred Stock Is Issued. Many people do not want to assume the risks that go with common stock, and they are desirous of a regular and fixed dividend. Bonds are a type of security which offer greater safety and a more regular return than common stocks, but because of these favorable features, the rate of interest paid on bonds is relatively low. Preferred stock is a sort of compromise security which offers less risk and greater certainty of return than common stock, but a higher return than can be obtained on a bond of the same company. Preferred stock appeals more to the investor or semi-investor than does common stock. The speculator, as distinguished from the investor, may be more desirous of buying common stock.

The reason a corporation sells any type of security is to get money. Quite often at the time a company is formed the common stock is handed out to the promoters and organizers for their services, and for the property, if any, which they turn over to the corporation. Preferred stock is then sold to the public to secure the additional capital needed.

In the past many preferred stock issues, particularly in the railroad field, have arisen at the time of reorganization. Some of the bondholders were usually asked to turn in their bonds and accept preferred stock in exchange. The preferred stock might appeal to them more than common stock, so the company offered this type of security to induce them to give up their bonds.

At times the market may be more favorable to stocks than to bonds, but for some reason the company does not want to sell common stock, or the public may want something better than common stock, so preferred stock is sold. Preferred stock is sometimes a suitable type of security to issue in connection with a consolidation or merger. It is often used at this time in exchange for securities of other companies, or sold for the additional capital needed.

From the standpoint of the common stockholders and the issuing corporation, preferred stock provides a means of getting additional cash without letting the new shareholder participate in the management or in future abnormal earnings. Since the dividend rate is usually limited, any earnings on the stock in excess of this rate will add to the common stockholders' equity. This is called *trading on the equity*, or *leverage*, and will be fully discussed in Chapter 8 in connection with bonds. In some instances it is given to shareholders for their accrued dividends. Some corporations have given preferred stock as a bonus in connection with the sale of bonds or common stock.

Legal Nature of Preferred Stock. In Chapter 5 the rights of stockholders were listed. Among these were the right to vote and the right to receive dividends when declared by the board of directors, and the right to assets upon dissolution. Owners of preferred shares are stockholders and therefore are entitled to all of their rights, unless the contract provides otherwise. As far as the law is concerned, all of the shareholders, regardless of what type of stock they hold, are treated equally, unless otherwise provided. It follows from this that the preferred shareholders have the same rights as those having common shares if such rights have not been altered in the contract under which the stock was issued.

The fact that we call the stock "preferred" implies that some preference over the common has been given to it in the contract. Where it is specified that the stock is voting, or that it is cumulative with respect to dividends, it is then clear what rights are possessed by it in respect to these features. Many preferred stock contracts, however, specifically state some of the rights of the preferred, but they are silent concerning other features. The question then arises how the preferred ranks as compared with the common with respect to these unmentioned features. The stated rights or preferences might be interpreted as either giving other preferences or as limiting the stock in other respects by implication. It is for this reason that something will be said about the common-law rights of the stock; in other words, what is the attitude of the courts on these particular points?

Preference as to Dividends. If a stock was labeled "preferred," but no specific dividend rate was stated and there were no other provisions relating to its rights included in the contract, it would be difficult to escape the conclusion that the stock was really only common stock. It would be possible in some of the states to issue a stock with a preference over the common with respect to assets upon dissolution, but state no dividend rate, and still call it "preferred stock." Undoubtedly a court would hold that this stock was not preferred over the common in respect to dividends since there is no rate stated to indicate to what extent it was preferred.

In practice, however, practically all, if not all, the preferred stocks which are outstanding have a stated dividend rate. If the stock is called "preferred" and has a stated dividend rate the courts will hold that it is preferred over the common with respect to dividends, even though the contract does not specifically state this. In the discussion of the legal rights of preferred stock it will be assumed that the stock being considered has a stated dividend rate.

To understand the rights of preferred stock it is necessary to distinguish between interest and dividends. Interest on a debt owed is a fixed charge of the company—a debt—and it must be paid regardless of whether or not the company earns any profits. Dividends, on the other hand, constitute a distribution of the profits. There must be profits either current, or accumulated from the past, or a surplus arising from some other source, before the board of directors can legally declare a dividend. After a legal dividend has been declared it constitutes a debt of the corporation.

Even if the company has a profit or surplus from which dividends can be paid, the board of directors is under no legal obligation to declare dividends to the preferred or other stockholders. In fact, if the profits are small or the corporation needs the money for future uses, the board of directors may pass the dividend. The only compulsion that exists is that the directors must pay the preferred its dividend in any one year *if* they wish to declare dividends to the common. The preferred shareholders cannot compel the directors to pay them anything as long as the board is acting in a fair manner. In exceptional cases, when the profits have been enormous and the money was not needed in the business, the courts have, upon action brought by the shareholders, compelled the directors to pay dividends. But if the board is acting honestly and believes the money is needed in the business, a court will ordinarily not substitute its own judgment for that of experienced businessmen.

The board of directors is usually elected by the common shareholders or their proxies, either because the preferred is not voting, or because the number of common shares greatly exceeds the number of preferred shares. In many instances also the directors are owners of large blocks of the company's common stock. It would seem natural to expect that directors would tend to favor the common shareholders, even in some instances at the expense of the preferred shareholders.

From a legal standpoint, then, it would appear that the preferred shareholders do not have a very secure position as regards dividends. Actually, however, a board of directors will usually declare the preferred dividends where there are profits sufficient to pay the dividend without seriously jeopardizing the future operation of the company. To pass the dividend under these circumstances would probably affect the market for the company's stock and produce an adverse effect on the company's credit.

The principal advantage of the preferred over the common is the preference as to dividends. As we have stated, however, if there is no surplus the directors cannot declare a dividend. If the profits are sufficient to pay the preferred, but not enough to pay the common, the directors may pass the preferred dividend because they believe the money might be needed by the company in the future. If the company has large earnings and can pay dividends on both the preferred and the common, then there is not much advantage in having the right to get the dividends first. This reasoning appears to put the preferred in a rather weak position, but it does indicate the possibilities. In fairness to preferred stock it should be stated that in many instances the preferred shareholders get regular dividends while the common shareholders receive them only spasmodically. Also the rate paid on the preferred is sometimes higher than is paid on the common.

Cumulation

Cumulative Dividends. If dividends on a particular preferred stock are *cumulative,* it means that if dividends at the stated rate are not paid in any year they accrue into subsequent years, and must be paid *before* any dividends can be paid to the common.

If a company issued a preferred stock which did not have a stated dividend rate, it undoubtedly would not be held to be cumulative by the courts since there is no way of knowing at what rate to cumulate the dividend. But as we have already stated, preferred stocks as a practical matter have a specified rate stated in the contract. If the contract further states that the stock is cumulative or noncumulative, or words to this effect, then it is clear as to the stock's rights. But assume that the stock has a stated dividend rate but nothing is said in the contract concerning cumulation. Will the courts hold it to be cumulative or noncumulative? The courts reason that if a definite per-annum rate is stated, such as 5 per cent, and there is no statement that it is noncumulative, the stock should be entitled to this amount *each* year, and that if it is not paid in any year, the dividend will *cumulate* into subsequent years.

Even if the stock is cumulative, the dividends on it do not have to be paid. What was said above relative to the legal right of preferred stockholders to dividends applies also to cumulative stock. If there is no surplus, the law will not permit the directors to pay the dividend. If there is a profit or surplus sufficient to pay the accrued dividend, the board of directors do not have to declare the dividend. The only compulsion is that the cumulated dividend must be paid *before* any dividends can be paid to the common shareholders.

Although the cumulative feature in a preferred stock is desirable from the viewpoint of the investor, its value should not be overestimated. If a company can pay regular dividends on its preferred stock, it will generally do so regardless of whether the stock is cumulative or noncumulative. If the company earns nothing the dividend cannot be paid. The value of the cumulative feature comes into play when the company after some lean years during which the dividends are passed, runs into prosperous years and has to pay the arrears on the preferred before it can pay any dividends to the common.

If the dividends on the preferred have accrued for a number of years the stockholder rarely receives the full amount in cash. To attempt to pay the arrears may mean that the common will have to go without dividends for many years even after the company's earnings increase. This affects the market for its stock, and may make it difficult for the company to borrow money, or if it can secure loans, it may be at a relatively high interest rate. Again, it should be remembered that the control of the corporation is usually in the hands of the common shareholders or their proxies.

Various methods or compromises are used to get rid of the accumulated dividends. In some instances the corporation offers the shareholders new preferred or common stock for the dividends. The new preferred may be an issue with different rights from the stock on which they are paying the dividend. Sometimes the shareholder is asked to take part of the dividend in cash and the balance in stock. In a few cases the directors have promised to resume current dividends on the preferred if the preferred shareholders would give up their right to the accrued dividends. The preferred stockholders cannot be compelled to accept the compromise settlement. In practice, however, the preferred shareholders are usually not organized and are therefore in a weak bargaining position, and they commonly accept the plan advanced by the management.

In the past, preferred stock was commonly forced upon bondholders in exchange for their bonds in railroad reorganizations, and it was usually noncumulative. It was rare to find a cumulative railroad preferred stock before 1900, but most of the railroad preferreds issued since then have been cumulative. Although many of the early industrial preferreds were noncumulative, since 1897 the bulk of them have been cumulative. Preferred stocks of public utilities and public utility holding companies issued since 1920 have practically always been cumulative.

NONCUMULATIVE PREFERRED STOCK. If a preferred stock is *noncumulative* it means that if the dividend is not paid in any year it is gone forever, and the shareholder will have no claim to it in subsequent years. Some court decisions in the past, which have met with the approval of some of the legal writers, however, held that even if a preferred stock was made noncumulative by contract, it would, nevertheless, be cumulative in those years in which profits sufficient to pay the dividend had been earned. The United States Supreme Court in 1930, in the famous Wabash Railway case, however, held that if a stock is noncumulative, it remains so even if the company earns profits sufficient to pay the dividend. The words of the court on this point were as follows:

> We believe that it has been the common understanding of lawyers and business men that in the case of non-cumulative stock entitled only to a dividend if declared out of annual profits, if those profits are justifiably applied by the directors to capital improvements and no dividend is declared within the year, the claim for that year is gone and cannot be asserted at a later date.[1]

Since noncumulative preferred stock does not appeal to the investing public, we find that it has been used mainly in the reorganization of insolvent companies, recapitalization of solvent concerns, and as a stock dividend.

Participation

RIGHT OF PREFERRED STOCK TO PARTICIPATE IN DIVIDENDS. A preferred stock is said to be *participating* when it has the right to share with the common in some way after the stated rate on the preferred has been paid. When we speak of a *nonparticipating* stock we are referring to one which has no further right to dividends in any one year after its stated rate (plus any accrued dividends in the case of cumulative stock) has been paid. The term "participating" is sometimes used also to apply to the right, if any, of the preferred stock to share in some way with the common in assets upon dissolution after the par or a specified amount has been paid to the preferred.

[1] *Wabash Ry. Co. v. Barclay*, 280 U.S. 197, at 203 (1930).

If a preferred stock is specifically made participating or nonparticipating in the contract, then its rights in this respect are clear. But in some instances the contract is silent on this point and then the question arises whether the stock is participating or nonparticipating. This is a matter for the courts to decide.

In considering this question it is well to keep in mind that preferred stock has all the rights of common except as they may be changed by the statutes of the state or the contract under which the stock is issued. If a corporation were to issue a stock which had a preference over the common in respect to assets upon dissolution, but there was no specified dividend rate stated, the courts would undoubtedly hold that the stock had equal rights with the common in respect to dividends. In other words, it would be participating. This follows because the stock has the same rights as the common unless otherwise indicated. Furthermore, since no dividend rate is stated, there is no indication of a limit on the amount of dividends which should go to the preferred stock.

Actually, however, when corporations issue preferred stock they specifically give it a stated dividend preference. The question that confronts the court is this—is the statement of the dividend rate to be construed not only as a statement of preference, but also as an implied statement of limitation? The courts are not in agreement on this point, so we cannot make a definite statement and say that it is one way or the other. But we can say this: the great weight of authority holds the stock to be *nonparticipating*.

In Pennsylvania, however, the courts have definitely held that when the stock was not made nonparticipating by contract, it would be *participating*. The reasoning behind this is the point previously stated, that preferred stock has all the rights of common unless otherwise changed. If the preferred received its stated rate and the common got all the rest, this would be putting a limitation on the preferred if the amount paid to the common exceeded that which went to the preferred. This would be depriving the preferred of its rights. So, unless the stock is specifically made nonparticipating, it should be held to be participating.

The high-court decisions in the other states which have decided on such points and in England, however, have held that the preferred is *nonparticipating* unless it is specifically made participating by contract. Does this violate our rule that the preferred is just like the common except as changed by law or contract? These courts take the attitude that when a preferred stock is given a stated preference as to dividends that this impliedly is a statement of limitation as well. In other words, they are still adhering to the principle that the preferred is just like the common except as otherwise provided, but they believe that the stated dividend rate is a statement of preference, and an implied statement of limitation.

Several other arguments are presented by the courts in holding the stock to be nonparticipating. One is that in their opinion most people when buying preferred stock think that it is entitled to only its stated rate in any one year. Furthermore, in some of the cases which came before the courts, the company had in some of the years paid the preferred its stated rate, and then paid the common a larger amount. The preferred stockholders had not objected to this practice in the past, so they evidently believed that their stock was nonparticipating. In a few of the cases some of the directors who voted for the larger common dividends were preferred stockholders.

Another point which is made by the courts is that the stated preference as to dividends is given to the stockholders in lieu of the right to participate in dividends equally with the common. Looking at it from the standpoint of the common stockholders, the common shareholders give the preferred stock first chance to any dividends, and frequently first claim as to assets upon dissolution, so they are taking more risk than the preferred. This being so, the common shareholders should be the ones to reap the returns if the company is unusually successful.

If the dividend in question is one payable in stock of the company, special consideration should be given to it. Let us assume in a particular case that the amounts of preferred and common stock outstanding are the same. We will assume also that the preferred is voting and that it has equal rights with the common in respect to assets upon dissolution. If, after the preferred and common had received the stated rate of dividends, the company paid an additional dividend in stock to the common only, the right of the preferred in regard to control and in regard to its share in the assets upon dissolution would be altered. It was pointed out in Chapter 5 that shareholders had the pre-emptive right to get new stock in the corporation in order to maintain their degree of control and their equity in the company. The courts in some of the states have therefore held the preferred to be participating under circumstances similar to these when the dividend was a stock dividend. In some of the cases holding this way, the preferred was specifically made nonparticipating by the particular contract. Our main interest here, however, is in respect to the common-law right of the stock to participate in a cash dividend.

By far the larger percentage of preferred stocks issued are nonparticipating. It would be difficult to estimate the exact number, but of the preferreds listed on the New York Stock Exchange, over a long period of years, slightly more than 87 per cent were nonparticipating.[2]

There are three different types of participating preferred stock which may be provided for in the contract. They are as follows:

Simple participation. When the preferred gets its stated rate and the common a like rate or a fixed amount per share, and then the balance of the dividend is split equally per share (or at the same percentage rate) between the preferred and the common, it is called *simple participation* (sometimes also referred to as *fully participating*). In Pennsylvania, where the stock is held to be participating unless made nonparticipating in the contract, simple participation is the type which the courts give to the preferred stock. An example of simple participating preferred stock is the Moody's Investors Service $3 Cumulative Participating Preferred. This stock has a preference of $3 cumulative dividends ahead of the common, and then after the common receives $2.25 in dividends in any year, the preferred participates with the common share for share in any further dividends declared.

Immediate participation. The contract under which the stock is issued sometimes states that the preferred is entitled first to its fixed rate, and then if any more dividends are paid, the preferred immediately participates on an equal basis per share or designated amount with the common. In other words, the common does not get a stated rate before the preferred participates. This is called *immediate participation.* An example is the Arden Farms Company $3 Cumulative Preferred Stock. This stock is entitled to a $3 cumulative dividend ahead of the common, and then whenever a dividend is declared on the common, each share of the preferred is entitled to an amount equal to one fourth of the dividend declared on the common share, but the additional dividends on the preferred are limited to $1 per share in any calendar year.

Special participation. Any type of participation other than the two mentioned above would be called *special participation.* The different types used in practice are too numerous to mention, but the following would indicate the extremes. The preferred is en-

[2] This is the approximate percentage for all preferred stocks listed on the New York Stock Exchange from 1885 to 1934. W. H. S. Stevens, "Stockholders' Participation in Profits," *The Journal of Business of the University of Chicago,* April. 1936, and July, 1936.

titled to a preferential dividend of 6 per cent, and then after the common has received a similar rate, the preferred is entitled to all the additional amount paid that year. Or, the preferred is entitled to its stated rate of 6 per cent, then the common is paid the same rate, if declared by the directors, and if any more dividends are declared that year, the preferred get an additional 2 per cent and the common get the balance. A type of special participation is illustrated by the Philadelphia Transportation Company $1 Participating Preferred. After this stock and the common have both received $1 in dividends in any year, the preferred is entitled to participate in any further dividends with the common, but the preferred share is entitled to 1½ times the amount per share paid to the common in such additional dividends.

VOTING RIGHTS. Unless the voting right is taken away from preferred stock, it has the same right to vote as common stock. According to the statutes in the various states this would mean one vote per share on each matter that came before the meeting. In Illinois the voting right cannot be taken away from the preferred, but in the other states there is no objection to providing for restrictions on the voting right. The common law gives shareholders the right to vote, so the preferred would have this right unless the contract otherwise provided.

It is common practice to restrict the voting right of the preferred, but it is usual to provide that the preferred will have the right to vote on certain questions, or under certain conditions. In some instances the contract provides for class voting which gives the preferred the right to elect a designated number of directors. The voting rights of the General Motors Corporation $3.75, and $5.00, preferred stocks, stated below, are typical of an industrial concern.

> The shares have no voting power except if dividends are in default for a period of six months, when holders of the preferred shares would have the right to elect one-fourth of the board of directors so long as the default continues. The preferred also have the right to vote on selling, conveying, transferring, or otherwise disposing of the property and assets of the corporation as an entirety, and the creation of mortgages.

A further voting right of the General Motors preferred shares will be mentioned later in connection with protective provisions.

Although it was common practice in the past to make railroad preferred stock voting, perhaps not more than 20 per cent of preferred stock of all types of industries outstanding today have full voting rights. A number of these voting preferreds were issued by corporations organized in Illinois, where the law requires that all classes of stock shall have the right to vote. Practically all of the "nonvoting" preferred stocks, however, have the right to vote for directors (either ordinary voting or class voting) if dividends are in default for a specified period of time, or the right to vote on mergers, consolidations, sale of assets, etc., or to vote on the issuance of additional preferred stock or bonds.[3]

One of the reasons that "nonvoting" preferred stock is practically always given some contingent voting right is to add to its marketability. Investment bankers may insist on the inclusion of such rights. Another is the fact that the New York Stock Exchange will no longer list a preferred stock unless it has at least the following voting rights: (1) right to elect not less than two directors if the dividends are in arrears for the equivalent of six quarterly periods, and (2) a two-thirds affirmative vote of the preferred as a class on any charter or bylaw amendments which materially affect the position of the preferred stock.

The restrictions which are placed on the general voting right of preferred stock are not too serious. Most stockholders, whether they be common or preferred, do not take an interest in the corporate management. Furthermore, the preferred stockholders are usually interested in their stock as an investment and not as an instrument for controlling the corporation. Even where the preferred stock has ordinary voting powers, the number of common shares outstanding generally exceeds the number of preferred shares, so that the vote of the preferred would mean little. In the case of class voting, however, this would not be the situation.

It is only fair that the preferred should be given the right to vote as a class on all matters that would affect their relative position in the corporation. Since the main advantage of the preferred is to

[3] A study of 1,094 preferred stocks listed on the New York Stock Exchange showed that only 5.7 per cent had no voting rights at all. W. H. S. Stevens, "Voting Rights of Capital Stock and Shareholders," *The Journal of Business of the University of Chicago,* October, 1938, pp. 311–40. A study of 250 *industrial* preferred stocks issued in 1944–1946 revealed that *none* of them was denied the voting right completely. A total of 25 per cent of them had full voting rights, but the remaining 75 per cent had the right to vote for directors if dividends were in arrears for a specified period, to vote on mergers, etc., and the issuance of senior securities. J. F. Bradley, "Voting Rights of Preferred Stockholders in Industrials," *The Journal of Finance,* October, 1948, pp. 78–88. A more recent study of 72 preferred stocks issued by various types of industries, including public utilities, during 1946–1950, showed that only 18 per cent had general voting rights. But 86 per cent of them had various types of voting rights in event dividends were in arrears for a specified period, 87½ per cent could vote on major changes such as mergers, sale of assets, etc., and approximately 89 per cent had the right to vote on the issuance of senior securities. Donald A. Fergusson, "Recent Developments In Preferred Stock Financing," *The Journal of Finance,* September, 1952, pp. 447–62.

receive a preferential dividend, it seems proper that they should, as a class, be given the right to receive representation on the board of directors when the dividends are in arrears for a specified period of time.

Right to Assets Upon Dissolution. In the event of dissolution of a corporation, the claims of the creditors always come first. If there is anything left, then it is distributed to the shareholders. If the statutes of the state and the contract are silent as to the right of the preferred, then the common law says that the assets shall be divided evenly per share between the preferred and the common stock. In other words, the preferred has no preference in respect to assets, and also it is not limited as compared with the common.

Preference as to assets upon dissolution is rare among railroad preferreds, but a majority of the preferreds issued by public utilities and practically all the industrial preferreds have this preference. The extent of the preference varies, but quite commonly it is preferred up to the par value, or stated value, of the stock. In some instances the preferred is entitled to par in the event of involuntary dissolution, but par and a slight premium in case of voluntary liquidation. A $100 preferred stock, which may be callable at $110, may be entitled to $110 in event of voluntary dissolution and $105 in case of involuntary liquidation.

Of the stocks which have a preference as to assets, close to 90 per cent call for a preference not only up to the par value, or a specified amount, but also in respect to any accrued dividends. This preference may also be given effect if the company is merged into another company, or when it is reorganized.

Several legal questions are involved in connection with the preference as to assets. If a particular preferred stock calls for par, or a stated amount in the case of no-par stock, and accrued dividends, but at the time of dissolution there are no profits or surplus, is the preferred stock entitled to the accrued dividend before anything is paid to the common? Some courts have held that the preferred is not entitled to the dividends,[4] while others have held that the stock is entitled to the preferrential dividend.[5]

[4] *Michael v. Cayey-Caguas Tobacco Co.*, 190 App. Div. 618 (N.Y.) (1920). In *Hull v. Pfister & Vogel Leather Co.*, 235 Wis. 653 (1940), it was held that the preferred was not entitled to be paid accrued dividends out of capital surplus created by reduction of capital stock.

[5] *Willson et al., Executors v. Laconia Car Co. et al.*, 275 Mass. 435 (1931); *Fawkes v. Farm Lands Investment Co.*, 112 Cal. App. 374 (1931); *Pennington v. Commonwealth Hotel Construction Corp.*, 155 Atl. 514 (Del.) (1931); *Drewry-Hughes Co. v. Throckmorton*, 120 Va. 859 (1917).

This question cannot be said to have been settled in the United States, but the weight of authority is that the preferred is entitled to the preferential dividend upon dissolution even if not earned. It should be kept in mind that we are here referring to a stock which has specifically been given a preference in respect to dividends upon dissolution. If no such preference is given, the preferred would not be entitled to it, unless such dividends were declared by the board of directors, and a surplus would have to be present before they could declare a dividend. But if the preferred contract calls for par and accrued dividends ahead of the common upon dissolution, most courts take the attitude that this relates to a return of capital, and not profits, and that a corporation can contract for the return of capital in any way that it desires.

It was stated above that unless otherwise provided the preferred and the common would share alike in assets upon dissolution. But as we have also mentioned above, the majority of preferred stocks of public utilities and industrials are specifically given a preference as to assets upon dissolution by their contracts. The same question arises here as in the case of the stated preference as to dividends. Does the stated preference as to assets impliedly limit the stock to the preferential amount? The courts in the United States are not in accord on this question, but most of the decisions have held that the stated preference as to assets impliedly limits the stock to this amount. In other words, the weight of authority is that the stock is *nonparticipating in assets* where it has been specifically given a stated preference as to assets.[6] Of course, if the stock specifically stated that it was participating in assets in addition to being preferred as to assets, this would control. An example is the Moody's Investors Service $3 Cumulative Participating Preferred. The contract provides that this stock is first entitled to $50 per share and accrued dividends in event of liquidation, and then after the common gets $50 a share, the preferred participates equally share for share with the common in any further distribution of assets.

The preference as to assets is given in order to increase the marketability of the stock. But the practical importance of this right is overestimated by the average buyer. A corporation does not fail because it has stock outstanding. Debts are what cause failure. Creditors always have the right to be paid in full before

[6] *Murphy v. Richardson Dry Goods Co.*, 326 Mo. 1 (1930); *Clark Williams et al., Appellants v. Alfred H. Renshaw et al., Respondents*, 220 App. Div. 39 (N.Y.) (1927); *Hatch et al. v. Newark Telephone Co. et al.*, 34 Ohio App. 361 (1930); *Niles v. Ludlow Valve Mfg. Co.*, 196 Fed. 994 (1912).

anything is distributed to the stockholders. In many instances after they are paid, nothing remains for the shareholders. In such a case the preference of the stock would mean nothing. As long as the company continues to operate, the preference never comes into play. So it would seem that in most instances the shareholder does not profit from the preference as to assets. The value of this preference in most instances is only the consolation of knowing that *if* the corporation dissolved, and *if* anything was left after the creditors were paid, the preferred would be paid first.

Perhaps we have been a little too critical of the value of the preference as to assets feature. We have been speaking only of failure and liquidation. The preference as to the assets feature has been respected in some instances when a corporation has been merged with another, reorganized, and in the case of a public utility, dissolved under the Public Utility Holding Company Act.

PROTECTIVE PROVISIONS IN PREFERRED STOCKS. Preferred stock is quite commonly sold as the senior security of the company. If additional preferred stock having the same or a prior claim to dividends is issued, the status of the original preferred would be materially altered. The status of the stock might also be changed materially by incurring more debt or by the depletion of cash or surplus by excessive dividends to the common, or the use of current assets for expansion purposes. Since the preferred is ordinarily nonvoting, or if it is voting, the common nevertheless usually controls by virtue of having more shares than the preferred, the holders of the latter are not in a position to protect themselves against the actions that might be taken by the common shareholders and the directors. For this reason investment bankers commonly insist that certain protective provisions be inserted in the preferred stock contract. The following are illustrative of the various types of such provisions.

Anti-dilution clauses. The contract may provide that no bonds or preferred having the same or prior claim may be issued. A more common provision is that no such securities may be issued without the consent of two thirds or three fourths of the preferred shares. This provision is often contained in the contract even though the preferred is nonvoting on ordinary matters. In the General Motors Corporation preferred stock contracts, referred to earlier in the chapter, it is provided that the company without the consent of 75 per cent of the preferred shares cannot create any bonds, mortgages, or specific liens on its properties except existing obligations on hereafter acquired property and renewal of such obligations, and the pledging of securities to secure cash advances maturing within three years.

In some instances the preferred might be helped by the issuance of a prior-lien stock. This might enable the corporation to secure needed funds which would prevent its failure.

Maintenance of certain ratios. Some of the ratios listed below are really in the nature of anti-dilution clauses but are given here under the heading of ratios.

Current ratio. In some instances it is provided that directors cannot pay dividends or otherwise voluntarily use cash for expansion when it would result in a reduction in the current ratio (ratio of current assets to current liabilities) below 2½ or 3. Or, such action cannot be taken if it would reduce the net current assets (current assets less current liabilities) below a certain percentage, such as 150 per cent, for example, of the preferred stock.

Ratio of assets to preferred stock and bonds. The contract may provide that dividends on the common cannot be paid if it would reduce the total assets to less than twice, for example, the amount of bonds and preferred stock outstanding.

Ratio of earnings to preferred dividends. Another type of provision is that no dividends may be paid on the common unless the company is earning its preferred dividend by a stated number of times, such as, for example, three times. Or, it may be provided that no new preferred stock can be issued unless the company is earning the dividend on its present preferred and the amount which it contemplates issuing at least, for example, 2½ or 3 times.

Ratio of preferred to common stock. In order to have a substantial buffer of common stock behind the preferred, it is sometimes provided that the amount of preferred outstanding cannot at any time exceed, for example, one half the amount of common stock.

Surplus and dividend reserves. Occasionally the contract under which the stock is issued states that no dividends may be paid to the common if it would reduce the surplus below a specified figure, or below a stated ratio of the preferred stock. In some instances a specified reserve for dividends on the preferred must be set up and maintained before any dividends may be paid to the common.

In the contract under which the General Motors Corporation preferred shares are issued the corporation covenants not to pay any cash dividends on the common stock unless aggregate of common and surplus shall exceed $335,700,600 by an amount not less than $100 for each share of preferred outstanding in excess of 1,875,366 shares, and net current assets are more than $75 for each share of outstanding preferred.

Callable Feature. Unless the contract under which the stock is issued provides otherwise, a corporation cannot force the stockholder, either common or preferred, to give up his stock. It is the usual practice, however, in the case of industrial preferreds to make the stock callable by the company at any time. When callable, it is usually at a premium of from 5 to 20 per cent over the par value, or stated value or issue price in the case of no-par stock.

At the time the stock is issued the company may have been able to sell only preferred stock. And it may have been necessary to give it a preference not only with respect to dividends and assets, but other protective features which might in the future result in some embarrassment to the corporation or hamper its future financing. Later on, the company may have a good market for its common stock, or its earnings may have produced an amount sufficient to retire the preferred stock. Anticipating such events, industrial companies commonly make their preferred callable.

From the standpoint of the shareholder, the call feature may prove to be a disadvantage. The interests of the preferred stockholder and the corporation are not the same. The corporate policies are determined by the directors, who are usually elected by the common shareholders. What benefits the preferred may be at the expense of the common, and vice versa. When the corporation's credit improves, or its earnings increase, it may decide to exercise the call feature. At this time the preferred would be a better investment than when it was originally sold.

The call price is usually at a premium in order not to detract too much from its marketability, and to soften the blow when the privilege is exercised. It will be found in practice that the market price of a preferred stock will rarely exceed its call price. It should be kept in mind that the call feature is at the option of the corporation, not the stockholder.[7]

[7] The $5 cumulative preferred stock of the General Motors Corporation, mentioned several times in the chapter, is entitled to $100 and accrued dividends in event of liquidation of the company, but it is callable at $120 and accrued dividends. The General Motors $3.75 cumulative preferred is also entitled to $100 and accrued dividends upon liquidation. (These two issues of preferred are no-par and they have a *pari passu* [equal] preference over the common both with respect to dividends and assets upon liquidation.) The $3.75 General Motors Preferred is callable through Nov. 1, 1956 at $104; through Nov. 1, 1961 at $103, through Nov. 1, 1966 at $102; through Nov. 1, 1971 at $101; and thereafter at $100. The three utility preferreds mentioned at the beginning of the chapter are not callable. These were the $2.50 Atchison, Topeka and Santa Fe, the $1.50 Pacific Gas and Electric, and the $2 Union Pacific preferred stocks.

COMPULSORY REDEMPTION OF PREFERRED STOCK. A number of preferred stock issues, particularly in the industrial field, contain provisions which compel the issuing corporation to buy back a certain amount of the preferred stock annually. The amount to be purchased usually varies according to the earnings of the company. There are several reasons for the inclusion of such a clause in the issue. Among industrial companies, as distinguished from railroads and public utilities, senior issues of securities, such as bonds and preferred stock, are commonly looked upon as a temporary method of raising funds. When the opportunity of paying them off arises they should be retired. Furthermore, if the corporation is buying back a certain amount of the preferred stock annually, this will create an additional market for the stock, and thus tend to keep the price up. Also, as the issue is being retired, the shares remaining outstanding will have a relatively more secure position. The retirement of the preferred also improves the position of the common stock.

An obligatory redemption clause in the preferred stock contract raises a serious legal question. Can a corporation be compelled to buy back its preferred stock even if it has agreed to do so in the contract? An answer to this question necessitates an examination of the statutes of the states, the court decisions, the ability of the corporation to pay its debts, and the surplus position.

We have already referred to the "trust-fund theory," which holds that the capital stock is a trust fund for the benefit of creditors. Although this is a misnomer, it is nevertheless true that a corporation cannot use its funds to retire its stock when it would impair the company's ability to pay its debts, or cause insolvency. If the firm used its "surplus" to retire the stock there would be no violation of the trust-fund theory. But even here, the stock should not be retired if it would seriously affect the ability to pay debts, or cause insolvency.

The statutes of the leading states permit a corporation to retire its stock. The fact that a redemption clause was in the contract at the time the stock was issued would strengthen the right. In some instances the statutes state that the stock can be retired only from surplus. In some states the corporation would have this right even in the absence of such statutes. In either case, however, the redemption would not be permitted if it would make it impossible for the firm to pay its debts. For these reasons the preferred stockholders may be unable to compel retirement of the preferred stock even though there was an obligatory redemption clause in the contract.

In order to redeem the stock a company may buy it in the market, or if it is callable, exercise the call feature. Since the stock will probably not be selling in the market for more than its call price, the company might buy it in the market. Furthermore, when stock is called in it is usually the entire issue which is so treated. In some instances the stock is retired by asking for tenders on the part of the shareholders.

Preferred Stock Sinking Funds. A considerable number of industrial preferred stock contracts call for the corporation to set up a *sinking fund* or *retirement fund* for the retirement of the stock. This is particularly true where the retirement is compulsory. A sinking fund constitutes a separate account to which funds are transferred for the express purpose of retiring the stock. It will be discussed more fully in Chapter 13 in connection with bonds.

In some instances the setting up of the sinking fund is compulsory, while in other cases it rests with the discretion of the board of directors. What was stated above relative to the unenforceability of compulsory redemption clauses under certain circumstances, applies with equal force to compulsory preferred stock sinking funds.

While the presence of a sinking fund tends to strengthen the position of the preferred and make a better market for the stock, if the money put into the fund is needed in the business, the fund might be of questionable value to the preferred stockholders.

Convertible Preferred Stock. Many preferred issues, particularly those sold by industrial companies, contain a clause which gives their holders the right to *convert* it into common according to the terms of the contract. In contrast to redemption, conversion is at the option of the stockholder.

The principal reason for the inclusion of such a clause is to add to the marketability of the preferred stock. At the time the stock is sold, the company may not have had a market for its common, but people would buy the preferred because of the advantage in dividends and cumulative features. But many of these same persons would like to have the common stock if the credit of the company improved and if the earnings increased. The common might then be more attractive than the preferred because it might increase in price on the market, and the dividends may be more than those paid on the preferred.

From the standpoint of the issuing company, the conversion feature may have been necessary in order to sell the stock, or to sell it with the designated dividend rate at the particular price. In other words, the cost of the financing would be less. But if the preferred holders exercise the conversion right, it would be at a time when the company would probably choose to have the preferred remain outstanding rather than have more of the common out. In the long run, however, the conversion of the preferred might benefit the company because it would eliminate the preferential cumulative dividend, and if they were present in the contract, eliminate any provisions which might restrict the future sale of senior securities.

Approximately 35 per cent of all publicly offered preferred stock issues sold from 1933 to 1952 had some sort of conversion privilege attached.[8] Industrials accounted for almost 89 per cent of the convertible preferred issues.[9] The contract may provide that conversion can be made at any time, or it may limit the time for conversion. Dewing[10] states that fixed time limits are unusual on convertible stocks, but a study of preferred shares sold in the period 1948–1952 showed that 64 per cent of the convertible issues had a time limit for conversion which averaged about 10 years.[11]

CONVERSION RATIO. When a convertible preferred stock is issued, the contract contains a stated price at which the common may be acquired upon conversion, or the number of shares of common which may be obtained for each share of preferred. This is called the *conversion ratio*. Thus a particular contract may state that the conversion price is $50, or it may state that two shares of common can be obtained upon the conversion of one share of preferred.

When a stated conversion price is given, this indicates the price that will have to be given for each share of common. In the case of par stock, the preferred is used in exchange value at its par value. Thus, if the preferred had a par value of $100, and the conversion price was $50 (this means that the common can be acquired at $50 a share), the shareholder could obtain 2 shares of common for each share of preferred converted.

The subject of conversion will be discussed in more detail in Chapter 12, when we consider convertible bonds. Most of the dis-

[8] C. James Pilcher, *Raising Capital With Convertible Securities*, Bureau of Business Research, University of Michigan, Ann Arbor, Michigan, 1955, p. 6. This study included public offerings in excess of $300,000 each.

[9] *Ibid.*, p. 19.

[10] Arthur S. Dewing, *The Financial Policy of Corporations* (5th ed.; New York: The Ronald Press Co., 1953), p. 264.

[11] C. James Pilcher, *op. cit.*, pp. 48–49. These preferred stocks included practically all of the convertible preferreds issued in 1948–1952, for which a prospectus accompanied the New York Stock Exchange Listing Application.

TABLE 6

SELECTED GROUP OF CONVERTIBLE PREFERRED STOCKS LISTED ON THE NEW YORK STOCK EXCHANGE

Issue and Dividend Rate	*No. of Common Shares Per Preferred Share*	*Current Call Price of Preferred*
Abbott Laboratories $4	1.70	106½
Alleghany $4 Pr.	16.00	80
Allis-Chalmers $3.25	2.00	103
American Airlines $3.50	4.83	102
American Brake Shoe $4	2.49	101
Ashland Oil $1.50 2nd	1.50	31
Chesapeake & Ohio $3.50	1.60	105
Dixie Cup $2.50 A	1.25	52
Lone Star Gas $4.75	3.80	103½
McCrory Stores $3.50	5.00	104
National Distillers $4.25	2.60	103
Republic Pictures $1	1.1025	15
Safeway Stores $4.30	2.174	102
Worthington Corp. $4.50	3.6832	100

cussion there will apply with equal force to convertible preferred stock.

SUMMARY OF PREFERRED STOCK RIGHTS. We have been discussing the common-law and statutory rights of preferred stock, and also provisions which may be included in the contract to alter these rights. Perhaps it would be advisable at this time to summarize the common-law rights of preferred stock, and to indicate the rights of the typical preferred stock found in the market. Since preferred is practically always, if not always, preferred as to dividends, the listing below will pertain to a preferred stock which has specifically been given this preference.[12]

[12] The voting rights of a sample of 72 preferred stocks issued in 1946–1950 were stated in the footnote on page 138. The percentage of these stocks possessing other features are as follows:

Contractual Rights	*Per Cent*
Cumulative	100
Participating	1
Convertible	29
Liquidation preference	100
Callable	100
Sinking fund provision	51
Limitation on common dividend	82

Donald A. Fergusson, "Recent Developments in Preferred Stock Financing," *The Journal of Finance*, September, 1952, p. 452.

Common-Law Rights	*Rights of Typical Preferred Stock*
Cumulative	Cumulative
Nonparticipating (most states)	Nonparticipating
Voting	Nonvoting (unless dividends are in arrears. Also right to vote on corporate changes and issuance of senior securities.)
Not preferred as to assets	Preferred as to assets
Participating in assets	Nonparticipating in assets
Noncallable	Callable
No sinking fund	Sinking fund (industrials)
Nonconvertible	Convertible (industrials)

INVESTMENT WORTH OF PREFERRED STOCK. It is difficult to generalize on the investment worth of any type of security. Some preferred stocks are excellent investments, others poor ones. But in concluding our discussion on preferred it might be of some value to compare it as a class with common stock and bonds. The latter will be discussed in the following chapters. Bonds represent debts of the issuing corporation. The company is obligated to pay the interest on the bonds and the principal amount upon maturity regardless of whether or not it has any earnings.

In comparing preferred stock with the other types of securities, we will assume that the preferred stock has the rights, preferences, and limitations usually given it. That is, we will have in mind a stock which is cumulative, but nonparticipating in dividends, nonvoting on ordinary matters, callable, and preferred, but limited in assets upon dissolution.

It is sometimes said that a preferred stock is midway between a common stock and a bond. That is, the dividends are apt to be more certain and regular than those on common stock, but they do not constitute a debt as is the case with bond interest. The dividends on the preferred are limited in amount as compared to the common, which makes it somewhat similar to a bond in this respect. The preferred dividend, however, would be expected to be larger in amount than the interest paid on bonds. The common is voting, but the preferred is similar to a bond in that it is nonvoting, at least on ordinary matters. The common is not redeemable or callable, whereas the preferred may be by the terms of the contract. This compares somewhat with the call feature and maturity of bonds.

Despite what has just been said, we cannot escape the fact that preferred stock is stock. The preferred shareholder is an owner in the business and not a creditor. Dividends can be paid only if there is a surplus, and even then whether or not they are paid rests with the discretion of the board of directors.

A somewhat exaggerated statement is that preferred stock has the disadvantages of both bonds and common stocks and the advantages of neither. That is, it is limited in return similar to the bond, and like the common, is not sure of getting dividends. Not being a credit instrument, there is no obligation to pay the dividend or the principal amount back to the shareholder, and unlike the common stock, it ordinarily is nonparticipating and therefore does not share in any abnormal success which the company may have.

Other things being equal, it would be better to own a preferred stock of a company that has no bonds outstanding, and where the consent of two thirds or three fourths of the preferred voting as a class would be necessary before any bonds could be issued. Naturally, it would be better to own the preferred stock of a good company, even if bonds were outstanding, than the preferred of a weak company. There are a number of preferreds that have bonds ahead of them which are excellent investments.

Questions

1. (a) Why might a corporation issue preferred stock rather than some other type of security? (b) Why might a person buy preferred stock rather than some other type of security?
2. In general, what rights are possessed by preferred stock as compared with common?
3. If a company issued a stock labeled "7 per cent preferred stock," and no other preferences or limitations are stated in the contract or the statutes of the state, indicate the rights of the preferred as compared to the common in relation to the following points: cumulation; participation rights, if any, with respect to dividends; right to assets upon dissolution; and voting rights, if any.
4. Is there any legal or moral obligation on the part of the board of directors to declare dividends on the preferred stock? Explain.
5. What preferences and limitations, as compared with common stock, are possessed by the typical preferred stock?
6. From the standpoint of the shareholder, what is the practical value of the cumulation as to dividends feature of preferred stock?
7. Indicate various types of participation in dividends features which may be provided for in preferred stock contracts.
8. Indicate the nature of contractual features that are sometimes placed in the preferred stock contract relating to voting rights.
9. If the preferred stock contract specifies that in event of dissolution the stock is entitled to its par value and accrued dividends ahead of the common, must a "surplus" be present on the books before the preferred is entitled to the accrued dividends? Explain.
10. Does the giving of a preference as to assets upon dissolution impliedly limit the preferred stock to that amount? Explain.

11. Ascertain whether the statutes of your state give any preferences or place any limitations on preferred stock. If so, indicate what they are.

12. Indicate the various types of "protective provisions" which are sometimes placed in the contract for the protection of preferred stock.

13. Indicate the right, if any, of a corporation to call in its preferred stock. Are sinking funds ever provided for the redemption of the preferred stock?

14. If a preferred stock which is selling in the market for $80 a share, and which has a par value of $100, is convertible into common stock at $60 a share, how high would the common have to go in order that a person would break even by converting? Assume the price of the preferred remains the same as stated above.

15. Indicate in general the investment worth of preferred stock as compared to bonds and common stock.

Problems

1. The Standard Corp. was organized on Jan. 2, 19-1, and within a few days sold $2,000,000 of 7 per cent preferred stock and $2,000,000 of common stock, both having a par value of $100 per share. The stock was sold at par, and there was no paid-in surplus. Net earnings after taxes for the first 5 years were as follows:

Year	*Earnings*
19-1	$ 25,000 (deficit)
19-2	5,000 (deficit)
19-3	0
19-4	310,000
19-5	840,000

All the available earnings were paid out in the form of dividends each year to the extent permitted by law. If you owned one share of the preferred and one share of the common stock, how much in dividends would you receive on each share for each of these years if the preferred stock was:

(a) Noncumulative and nonparticipating? (b) Noncumulative and participating? (c) Cumulative and nonparticipating? (d) Cumulative and participating? (e) If the statutes of the state and the contract were silent as to cumulation and participation features?

2. The preferred stock in the preceding question was issued under a contract that stated that it was entitled to par and accrued dividends ahead of the common in event of dissolution of the company. Assume that the company merely broke even on its operations for the year 19-6, but at the end of that year it sold out to a competitor for $5,140,000 in cash that was distributed to the shareholders. If you owned one share of preferred and one share of common stock how much would you get for each share? (Assume that the dividends stated in the preceding question have been paid.)

3. The New Corp. has outstanding $3,000,000 in common stock; $2,000,000 in 7 per cent noncumulative, nonparticipating preferred stock; and $1,000,000 in 6 per cent first mortgage bonds. Mr. Astor said that he would not purchase any of the preferred stock because it had the weakness of the common stock without its advantage and the weakness of the bonds without their advantage.

(a) What did Mr. Astor probably mean by that statement? (b) Do you think he was correct? Explain.

Chapter 8

CORPORATE BONDS

Bonds Compared With Stocks. Although all corporations secure at least part of their capital from the sale of stock, many of them, particularly railroads and public utilities, borrow part of it. When an individual borrows money from a bank, savings and loan association, or finance company, he executes a note in favor of the lending institution, promising to pay the amount borrowed at a specified time with interest at a stated rate. But when a corporation wants to borrow millions of dollars, no one individual or company has that amount to lend, or if they did, they would not want to lend it to one company.

When the corporation borrows a substantial amount of money, it is, therefore, necessary in most instances to borrow it from a number of different persons or companies. The instrument which embodies the promise to pay the debt, which is given to the lender, is called a *bond.* So, when a corporation sells bonds it is borrowing money. These bonds are similar to notes except that they are generally of longer maturity than notes and there is more formality surrounding their issue.

Stocks and bonds are both referred to as *securities,* but there is a considerable difference between these two types of securities. Following is a summary of their principal differences.

1. *Bonds represent debts.* The stockholders are the owners of the business, whereas the bondholders are its creditors. Although bonds are the obligation of the corporation and not of the stockholders directly, we might say that the latter collectively, through their corporation, owe the money. The bonds can be satisfied, however, only from the corporate property, as long as the stockholders have no liability on their stock. Upon dissolution of a corporation, the bondholders must be paid in full before anything can be given to the stockholders.

2. *Bonds must be paid off.* Since the bonds represent a debt, they must be paid upon maturity. As a practical matter the corporation may be financially unable to pay them when they fall due and some compromise settlement may be worked out. But as a legal matter they must be paid or the bondholders can take steps to foreclose the corporate property for the satisfaction of their claims. Stocks, in contrast, do not come due. Preferred stocks may be callable, but they do not have a due date.

3. *Interest on bonds a debt.* Not only must the corporation pay the principal amount of the bonds upon maturity, but it is also obligated to pay the interest semiannually or annually, according to the terms of the agreement. It is practically always provided that failure to pay the interest will also make the principal amount of the bonds due. Except for "income bonds" (Chapter 11), this obligation to pay interest is present regardless of whether or not the corporation has any earnings. In contrast, dividends on stocks cannot be paid unless there are earnings or an accumulated surplus, and they are paid only if declared by the board of directors.

4. *Interest is a fixed amount.* The amount of the interest on a bond is fixed at the time the bond is issued and remains the same throughout its life. As we have already seen, the dividends on stock may fluctuate from year to year.

5. *Bonds are nonvoting.* The bondholders, being creditors rather than owners, ordinarily have no voice in the management of the company; in other words, bonds are nonvoting. As we have already seen, stock carries the right to vote unless such right is restricted by the contract. In some instances the bond contract provides that certain proposals, such as the issuance of additional bonds, will have to be approved by a designated percentage of the bondholders. Upon failure or insolvency of the company they may dictate to the directors under threat of foreclosure.

PRACTICAL DIFFERENCE. The above represents the legal difference between bonds and stocks. In some instances the contract will give the bonds certain features that are possessed by stocks; these will be pointed out later in our discussion. Preferred stocks, as we have already seen, may have a stated cumulative dividend, may be made nonvoting, and upon dissolution may be preferred, though limited, in the distribution of assets. These features tend to make the preferred stock somewhat similar to bonds. But despite these features, there still remains the principal distinction that the stockholders are owners and the bondholders are creditors.

The actual legal rights accruing to the bonds are not always enjoyed by the bondholders. The latter are oftentimes unorganized and do not press for the strict observation of their rights. As a practical matter, it is often realized by the bondholders that if the corporation has to default in the payment of the interest, they may gain more in the long run by permitting it to operate rather than by exercising their legal right to foreclose. When corporations fail they are rarely liquidated. The usual procedure is for the corporation to go into the hands of a receiver or trustee in bankruptcy. This will prevent the bondholders from foreclosing on the corporate property. Following this the concern will commonly go through a reorganization rather than a liquidation. The treatment accorded the bondholders will depend upon the types and amounts of securities outstanding, the seriousness of the failure, and the bargaining power of the security holders. Despite this, however, the bondholders will receive better treatment in the reorganization than the stockholders. So, in actual practice the difference between bonds and stocks may be relative rather than absolute.

Bond features

DENOMINATION OF BONDS. The usual *denomination* of a bond is $1,000. This is commonly called the *face value,* or *par value.* This represents the amount that will be paid to the bondholder upon maturity of the bonds. Bonds may originally be issued for more or less than their face value, and the amount that must be paid for them after original issue depends upon the market price. In many instances bonds are callable by the issuing corporation at a slight premium from the face value.

Bonds may be issued with a face value of more or less than $1,000. Some corporations have issued them with a face value of $500 or $100. The Series E United States Savings bonds have a face value as low as $25. Bonds with a face value of $100 or less are sometimes referred to as *baby bonds.*

The relatively high face value prevents their purchase by the general public. Bonds are usually purchased by investors who have considerably more than $1,000 to invest. Corporations feel that the printing, selling, and transferring costs would be too high relative to what they would obtain to issue them in denominations of less than $1,000.

STATUS OF GOLD BONDS. Because of the unfortunate experience with a depreciated paper currency following the Civil War, it became common practice for both governments and corporations to issue *gold bonds.* These were bonds that were payable both in respect to interest and principal in "gold dollars of the present weight and fineness." In 1933, Congress enacted legislation which made null and void the gold clause in bonds. Later that year the gold content of the dollar was reduced by approximately 40 per cent, and the government called in all gold coins and gold certificates.

With gold no longer available to pay off the bonds, it was thought by some that the gold bonds should be discharged with the payment of a sufficient number of devalued dollars to equal the value of the dollars which were originally paid for the bonds. The Supreme Court of the United States, in a five-to-four decision in 1935,[1] however, held that the government or private companies could discharge their gold bonds with the payment of the contractual amount in any coin or currency which at the time is legal tender for public and private debts. Although the federal government has never defaulted in the payment of its debts, some have referred to this act on the part of the government as an abrogation of the contract.

Maturity of Bonds. When corporations borrow from commercial banks for a period of 30, 60 or 90 days they execute a *note* to the bank which contains their promise to pay the principal and interest. They also sometimes borrow on notes for periods up to five years. In some instances the maturity of the note will be ten years, or longer. These notes are similar to bonds but usually there is less formality surrounding their issue. When a corporation obtains a large loan from an insurance company it may execute notes with maturities greatly in excess of ten years.

When the maturity of the obligation is five years or more it is usually referred to as a bond. Those which have a maturity of from five to fifteen years are commonly called *short-term* bonds. When the maturity runs over fifteen years and up to forty years, they are referred to as *medium-term* bonds. *Long-term* bonds have a maturity in excess of forty years.

Long-term bonds are more commonly found in the railroad field than among public utilities and industrials. Many of these were issued in reorganizations, in exchange for shorter-term securities. Several examples of long-term railroad bonds are the Northern Pacific Railroad Company's 3 per cent general lien bonds, which mature in the year 2047, and the New York Central Railroad Company's 4½ per cent refunding and improvement mortgage gold

[1] *Norman v. Baltimore & Ohio R.R. Co.,* 294 U.S. 240 (1935).

series A, which come due in 2013. An unusual case is the Elmira and Williamsport Railroad Company's 5 per cent income bonds which mature October 1, 2862.[2]

We formerly considered that, due to the vital nature of their services and the relative stability of their earnings, a large bonded indebtedness was a more or less permanent feature of railroad finance. The competition of automobiles, trucks, buses, airplanes, and pipe lines has in recent years changed our ideas about the sheltered position of railroads. Also, the depression of the 1930's taught us that even the railroads should in good times reduce their bonded indebtedness. Many of them took advantage of their large earnings during and after World War II to materially reduce their indebtedness. Public utility bonds seldom run for over 50 years, and the average industrial company bond has a shorter maturity than in the case of public utilities.

There have been a few isolated cases where perpetual bonds have been issued. The Green Bay & Western Railroad Company's Non-Cumulative Income A and B Debenture Bonds have no maturity date, but the contract provides that they will become due only upon sale, liquidation or reorganization of the company. They are listed on the New York Stock Exchange.[3] The Canadian Pacific Railroad Company has outstanding a Perpetual 4 Per Cent Consolidated Debenture Stock which, despite its title, is a perpetual bond.[4] The British Consols are a well-known example of perpetual bonds. The latter are callable by the government, but they have no maturity date. In regard to the principal amount, a perpetual bond is more like a stock than a bond, but it is similar to other bonds in respect to interest. The idea of borrowing money without providing for its repayment is contrary to our accepted principles of debt. Perpetual bonds could benefit either the issuer or the holder depending upon their face rate of interest, and the future trend of interest rates in general.

INTEREST RATE. Bonds have a fixed rate of interest which must be paid the same as any other debt on the dates due. Interest on

[2] These bonds were issued in 1863; hence from the time of issue they have a life of 999 years. Furthermore, these bonds are noncallable. They are guaranteed as to interest by the Pennsylvania Railroad Company, and they are traded in the over-the-counter market.

[3] More will be said about these bonds in connection with participating bonds in Chapter 11.

[4] This bond issue is also listed on the New York Stock Exchange. It is noncallable. By legislation it has been given a first lien on all the company's assets and earnings. The fact that it is called a "Debenture Stock" issue is probably due more to British practice than to the fact that the issue does not have a maturity date.

bonds is usually due semiannually on the first or fifteenth of the month, such as January 15, and July 15, although in some instances the interest is paid annually. The rate of interest is expressed as a percentage of the face value of the bond. When the interest is paid semiannually the amount paid each six months is one half the stated rate. The face rate of interest is called the *nominal yield.*

The rate of interest a bond bears is set at such an amount that the bond can be sold by the issuing company at or near its face value. The rate of interest which a corporation must pay on its bonds depends upon the general interest rates prevailing in the market at the time the bond is issued, the supply and demand of money, the general credit of the company, the nature of the particular bond issue, the length of maturity of the bonds, and the price at which the corporation proposes to sell the bond in the market.

After giving due consideration to the above factors, investors will pay such a price for a bond that the rate of return on their money, which is called the *yield,* will be the amount demanded. The following factors would tend to make the face rate of interest relatively low: low prevailing interest rates in the market, large supply of loanable funds, high credit rating of issuing company, a well-secured senior bond, a short-term bond, and a relatively low offering price on the bonds. When interest rates are relatively low, the shorter the maturity of the bond, the lower will be the yield demanded by investors. When bonds are sold at a premium or discount the loss or gain in the principal amount at maturity (or at call date) is considered a deduction from or addition to the current interest being received by the holder.

TABLE 7

WEIGHTED AVERAGES OF YIELDS ON NEWLY ISSUED DOMESTIC BONDS
UNITED STATES, SELECTED YEARS

Year	*Railroads*	*Industrials*	*Utilities*	*All Corporates*
1955	4.12%	3.65%	3.33%	3.56%
1954	3.53	3.30	3.17	3.22
1949	3.85	3.20	3.07	3.13
1944	3.22	3.22	2.98	3.09
1939	3.52	3.09	3.46	3.36
1934	5.09	6.04	4.86	5.03
1929	5.02	5.76	5.21	5.34
1924	5.34	6.43	6.03	5.96

SOURCE: *Moody's Industrial Manual,* Moody's Investors Service, New York, 1956, p. a18, and letter from same service dated October 25, 1956.

Computing Bond Yields. If a person buys a bond at its face value and sells it at the same price, his *yield* will be the same as the face rate of interest. If, however, he pays more or less than the face value, or if he pays the face amount and sells it for something different, the yield will be more or less than the face rate of interest.

Let us assume that a person bought a 4 per cent 10-year bond at 108⅝. Since bonds are quoted in percentage of their face value this means that he paid $1,086.25 for a $1,000 face value bond. The fact that a premium was paid for the bond indicates that the corporation could borrow money at less than 4 per cent interest. The purchaser will get $40 a year interest on the bond. But if he holds the bond until maturity, he will get back only $1,000. Thus, he will lose $86.25 of his principal. The actual yield on the bond will obviously be less than 4 per cent for two reasons. First, the 4 per cent face rate is based on the face value of the bond and not the purchase price, and second, the premium is lost. We can determine the approximate *yield to maturity* with the following formula.

$$\frac{\text{Annual interest} - \text{Annual amortized premium (or, + Annual amortized discount)}}{(\text{Cost price} + \text{Maturity value}) \div 2} = \text{Approximate yield to maturity}$$

Substituting the above figures in the formula we get the following,

$$\frac{\$40 - \$8.625}{(\$1{,}086.25 + \$1{,}000) \div 2} = 3 \text{ per cent}$$

If the bond was bought at a discount from the face value, the annual amortized discount would be added to the annual interest, as indicated in the formula. The above formula does not give the exact yield but it is close enough for ordinary purposes. The actual yield can be found in standard bond tables which are available without charge in banks, trust companies, bond houses, brokerage offices, etc. They can also be found in libraries and samples of them are usually in investment and personal finance books.

If a premium bond is callable by the company before its maturity date, then the purchaser should consider his *yield to call date,* instead of maturity. The call price would then be used instead of the maturity value in the formula, although the two may be the same. There are two reasons why the yield on a premium bond should be computed to call date rather than maturity. First, the fact that the bond is selling at a premium indicates that the corporation's current borrowing rate is less than the face rate on the bonds. Therefore, it would be cheaper for a corporation to call in its bonds and put out an issue with a lower face rate. So the probability is that a corporation will exercise the call feature on a premium bond. The purchaser should, therefore, be realistic and compute his yield to call date. The second reason for doing this is that it is conservative practice since it gives a lower yield.

If a callable bond is selling at a discount it is indicative that the corporation's current borrowing rate is more than the face rate on the bond, and therefore it is probable that the bonds will not be called in. Therefore, the yield should be computed to the maturity date. Furthermore, computing the yield on a discount bond to maturity will give a lower yield, therefore it is the more conservative method to use.

If a person buys a bond some time before its call or maturity date, and expects to hold it only a short period of time, he should not compute his yield to either the call or maturity date. In other words, if he is not going to accumulate the amount of the discount or lose the premium, then he should ignore this in computing the yield. A person under these circumstances should use the *current yield* computation. This is done by dividing the face rate of interest by the purchase price of the bond. To use the figures in the above example, if a person bought a 4 per cent bond for $1,086.25, the current yield would be little more than 3.68 per cent. If a bond which has only a short time to run until maturity is selling at a substantial discount, it is probable that it will not be paid at maturity, so it would be advisable to use the current yield rather than the yield to maturity, even if it is contemplated that the bond will be held for some time.

If it is probable that the bonds will be paid off at maturity, the price of both discount and premium bonds will gradually work toward the face value as the maturity date approaches.

In purchasing a bond in the market the buyer must pay the seller the quoted price plus any accrued interest. In other words, the quoted price of bonds does not include any interest which has accrued since the last payment date. This is in contrast to stocks whose quoted price reflects any anticipation of dividends. Corporate bonds sold for "regular way delivery" on the New York Stock Exchange call for delivery the fourth business day following the sale. Regular way delivery on government bonds however is the next day following the sale. Accrued interest is computed from the last interest payment date up to, but not including, the day of delivery. Thus, if a corporate bond on which interest is paid semiannually on January 1st and July 1st, is sold on March 28th, it would be delivered regular way on April 1st (March has 31 days). Interest accrued from January 1st through March 31st, or one fourth of a year's interest, will be paid by the buyer in addition to the quoted price of the bond.

There are two instances when bonds are quoted flat, i.e., when the quoted price includes any accrued interest. These are income bonds (with a few exceptions), which will be described later, and bonds that are in default.

Relationship Between Bond Prices and Interest Rates. A particular 4 per cent bond may originally sell for its face value. If the credit of the issuing company remains about the same, but interest rates in general drift lower in the market, people may be willing to invest their money at a lower rate of interest than formerly, so they may bid up the price of the 4 per cent bond to a premium.

Conversely, if interest rates in general would advance, then people could get a higher rate of return. If they could buy a 4½ per cent bond at its face value, they would pay less than that for a bond similar in nature, but which bore a face rate of only 4 per cent. In other words, a rise in interest rates would cause a drop in the price of existing bonds. It is thus seen that bond prices result from people demanding a particular yield. During and for some time after World War II, however, the government kept interest rates low by putting a peg under the price of government bonds. The government wanted interest rates to remain relatively low in order that the refinancing of the huge national debt would not cost too much. By buying the bonds on the market through the Federal Reserve Banks at pegged prices, the price of the bonds was prevented from falling, and thus the yield was maintained at a low figure.

Regardless of how bond prices, and thus yields, may fluctuate in the market, however, the yield to a particular individual is always computed on the purchase price of the bond.

Although *yields* on short-term and long-term bonds tend to move together, the short-term yields follow the business cycle more closely and go to greater extremes in both directions than do the yields of long-term bonds. The *prices* of long-term bonds, on the other hand, fluctuate more than do the prices of short-term bonds. The following indicates the prices at which a 3 per cent bond would sell to yield 4 per cent, and the prices at which a 4 per cent bond would sell to yield 3 per cent. As is noted, when the bond is selling at a discount or a premium the longer the maturity, the greater is the discount or premium.

Maturity in Years	*Price of a 3% Bond in a 4% Market*	*Price of a 4% Bond in a 3% Market*
5	95.51	104.61
10	91.82	108.58
20	86.32	114.96
30	82.62	119.69

If market interest rates would decline from 4 to 3 per cent, investors would pay the face value for a 3 per cent bond. This would result in an increase in the price of the 30-year, 3 per cent bond, of 17.38, but a rise of only 4.49 in the price of the 5-year maturity. Referring now to the last column above, if the market rate of interest would rise, from 3 to 4 per cent, the price of the 4 per cent 30-year maturity would fall 19.69, while the price of the 5-year maturity would fall only 4.61.

It should be kept in mind that in the above example we were assuming that people would buy the various maturities on the same yield basis. This was done in order to show the comparative effects on the prices of long-term and short-term bonds of a change in market interest rates. As a practical matter, investors usually demand different yields on different maturities. When interest rates are comparatively low, long-term securities sell on a higher yield basis than do short-term securities. In order not to sacrifice too much in the way of yield by buying a short-term bond, and not run the risk of losing too much on the price of a long-term bond resulting from an increase in interest rates, the medium-term bonds are recommended for the average investor.

Registered Bonds. With respect to the payment of interest and principal, bonds are classified as (1) registered, (2) coupon, or (3) registered-coupon. A fully *registered bond* is one which contains the name of the owner on the bond, and which is registered in his name on the company's records (usually maintained by the registrar). This is similar to the registration of stocks.

Interest on a fully registered bond is paid by check directly to the registered holder. When the principal is due it is paid to such holder upon presentment of the indorsed bond. If a holder wants to transfer it, he must indorse it. For the purchaser to be recognized by the issuer as the owner, it will be necessary to surrender the indorsed bond to the transfer office of the company and have a new one issued in his name.

If a person buys an unindorsed registered bond, he does not necessarily get title. If the indorsement is forged, then no one can acquire title to it. The advantage of a registered bond thus lies in its safety. A thief or finder cannot pass good title to an unindorsed registered bond. It is also less trouble to receive the interest by mail than to clip the coupons and present them for payment, which must be done with a coupon bond.

The disadvantage of a registered bond is that it is more trouble to transfer than a coupon bond because of the necessity for indorsement, and the fact that the buyer has to get it registered in his own name. As a result, the registered bond will usually sell for slightly less than a coupon bond of the same issue.

If a registered bond is put up as collateral for a loan the banker will want the right to have the bond transferred to his name in event of default in the loan. If the bond is indorsed then it would still have the owner's indorsement on it after it is returned to him when the loan is paid. Rather than indorse the bond, it would be better for the owner to attach to it a signed *bond power of attorney.* This would give the bank the right to have it transferred to its name in event the loan is not paid.

The registered bond may be preferred by an institutional investor, such as an insurance company, which might contemplate holding it until maturity. The treasurer of a company or a trustee might prefer it because of the relative safety from loss or theft.

Coupon Bonds. This type contains a series of dated coupons which are clipped by the owner on the appropriate dates and sent to the issuing company or given to a bank for collection. The coupons are payable to bearer. Unless the bond is registered as to principal, the principal amount is also payable to bearer. Title to this bond passes by delivery. It is not necessary to indorse it, nor does the buyer have to get it transferred to his name. An innocent purchaser for value gets good title to the bond.

As mentioned above, the coupon bond usually sells for slightly more than the registered bond. The usual price differential is from one quarter of a point to one point ($2.50 to $10.00 on a $1,000 bond). Most buyers of corporate bonds (and U. S. Treasury bonds) prefer the coupon bond.

The principal disadvantage of the coupon bond may be inferred from the above. There is greater danger in holding the bond because of the possibility of loss or theft. For this reason coupon bonds should always be kept in a safe place, such as a safe deposit box. It is advisable for a person to keep a record of the serial number of all types of bonds he owns, particularly coupon bonds, in order to aid in identification of the bonds in the event that they are lost or stolen. The list of the numbers should be kept in a different place from where the bonds are kept.

If a person loses a bond he should immediately notify the company or its registrar, giving full particulars. In order to secure a new bond, however, the issuing company will usually require that he put up a surety bond to protect the company in event the bond shows up in the hands of an innocent purchaser for value.

Another possible disadvantage of the coupon bond is the trouble of clipping the coupons. This may not seem to be much of a job to the average reader, but in the case of large institutional investors, and also for some individuals, it is quite a task. Furthermore, since the coupons may come due at different times on different bonds, an extensive investor may find it quite troublesome to have to make frequent trips to the bank to get the coupons and send them in for collection. Furthermore, if the coupons are not sent in on time, the bondholder will lose the opportunity of getting interest on the interest due. In the case of registered bonds the interest is always sent on time, so the bondholder can invest the interest. Since the company does not have the names of the coupon bondholders, it will be necessary for them to watch the financial newspapers for any anouncement of a call. This is another disadvantage of coupon bonds.

When bonds are called by the company, all interest on either the registered bond or the coupon bond ceases on the date the bonds are called.

In the case of large bond isues, both registered and coupon bonds are usually issued. It is then generally provided that the registered and coupon bonds can be exchanged for each other at the option of the holder. Usually a charge of from $1 to $2 per bond is made for the exchange. If such an issue is listed on the New York Stock Exchange, all purchases and sales are assumed to be the coupon bonds.

Registered-Coupon Bonds. Corporations sometimes issue a bond which is registered as to principal but coupon as to interest. Or the bond may originally be sold as a purely coupon bond but with the owner being given the right to have it registered as to principal at his option. Such bonds are sometimes called *registered-coupon bonds.* The interest coupons are payable to bearer, but otherwise the bond is treated as registered. The owner's name appears on the back of this type of bond.

Redemption and Call Features. Unless so provided in the bond, it is not redeemable or callable before its maturity. The

United States Savings bonds, Series E, H, J, and K are redeemable at the option of the holder after a specified period of time at redemption prices stated in the bond. Other government bonds and all corporate bonds are not redeemable at the holder's option. Neither can the corporation call them in until their maturity date unless a call feature is included in the contract.

It is common, however, for corporate bonds to have a provision in the contract giving the corporation the right to *call* the bonds in at any time, or at specified times. Holders of registered bonds will be notified by mail of a call. When bonds are called in, the interest on them ceases. But even if they are not turned in on time the holder still has a right against the company for the principal amount, or the call price, and any interest due up to the call date. Companies usually set up funds to take care of outstanding bonds which are called. If the bonds are not turned in within a period of from seven to fifteen years after the call, depending upon the period of the statute of limitations in the particular state, the debt may be outlawed and the corporation would not have to pay them off.

The call feature works to the disadvantage of the bondholder, since the call would probably be exercised at the time when the holder would desire to hold on to the bonds. In order not to detract too much from their marketability, corporations commonly set the call price at a slight premium over the face value.

Trustee of a Bond Issue. When an individual borrows money there are only two parties involved—the borrower and the lender. But when a corporation borrows by selling bonds there are three parties to the agreement—the borrowing corporation, the bondholders, and a *trustee*. The trustee is supposed to represent the interests of the bondholders. The borrowing corporation deals with the trustee rather than with the individual holders. When the bond issue is secured by a mortgage on the corporate property, legal title to the property is transferred to the trustee (in some states the trustee holds a lien) who holds it in trust for the benefit of the bondholders. It would be impractical to give separate mortgages to thousands of individual bondholders. Trustees are used, however, even if the issue is not a mortgage one, to facilitate the dealings between the bondholders and the corporation.

The trustee is selected by the company or the investment banker who is selling the issue, or they may jointly make the decision. The trustee is usually a trust company which has experience in this work and which has a permanent staff to take care of the details. In some instances an individual is appointed as a cotrustee. The trust company, being a corporation, may not have the authority to transact business in other states in which some of the corporation's property may be located, but an individual trustee can represent the corporation in all states. The trust company, on the other hand, does not have the limited life of an individual.

In the past, trustees often neglected the interest of the bondholders and favored the corporation which selected them. As a result, the federal government in 1939, adopted the Trust Indenture Act. This Act applies to all security issues which must be registered with the SEC (Securities and Exchange Commission) except foreign government bond issues and corporate issues of $1,000,000 or less. The following are among the more important provisions of the Act relating to trustees.

1. One of the trustees must be a corporation with capital and surplus of not less than $150,000, organized in the United States and authorized to exercise corporate trust powers, and subject to supervision or examination by federal, state, or territorial authority. Banks and trust companies with at least the minimum stated capital and surplus would qualify as trustees. The Act also provides that individuals may be appointed cotrustees.
2. In a situation where a conflict in interests would arise such as where the trustee is acting under another indenture of the same issuer, or where the trustee or its officers are affiliated with the issuer or underwriter, the trustee must either resign, remove the conflicting interest, or notify the security holders and let them exercise their powers of removal.
3. The issuing corporation is required to furnish a list of bondholders to the trustee at stated intervals, which lists must be made available by the trustee to individual bondholders upon demand.
4. The trustee must submit an annual report to the bondholders indicating the nature of any advances made by the trustee to the corporation, the condition of the property held in trust, and other relevant matters.
5. The trustee must notify the bondholders of all defaults within ninety days.
6. In the event of default the trustee must exercise his defined powers and rights with the same degree of care and skill as a prudent man would exercise or use under the circumstances in the conduct of his own affairs.

Duties of the trustees. The duties of the trustees vary according to the indenture (the latter is described below) but the following are typical.

1. *Authentication* of the bonds. In order to give protection to the bondholders against overissue and forgery, the trustee authenticates the bonds by signing a statement such as the one below, which is called the *certification of the trustee.*

    This bond is one of the bonds described in the within mentioned deed of trust.

    ______________ Trust Company

    By ______________

    Trust Officer

2. *Collection and disbursement* of interest and principal. It is the duty of the trustee to collect the money from the corporation and disburse the interest and principal payments to the bondholders. This is a routine task which the trustee is usually better equipped to handle than the corporation.
3. *Sinking fund.* If the indenture provides for a sinking fund to retire the bonds, it is usually the duty of the trustee to secure the money from the corporation and acquire the bonds.
4. *Protection of security.* If the bonds are issued under a mortgage, it is the duty of the trustee to see to it that the mortgaged property is not dissipated. When other securities are pledged as collateral behind the bonds, the trustee is the custodian of the collateral. He must also attend to the substitution of the collateral in the event that some of the securities pledged are retired.
5. *Protection of bondholders.* It is the duty of the trustee to make the corporation observe all the provisions included in the indenture for the protection of the bondholders. In the event of default, the trustee must take the steps indicated in the indenture. If the issue is secured by a lien on real estate or other property, he must take the proper steps to foreclose the particular property.

THE BOND INDENTURE. The three-way agreement between the issuing corporation, the trustee, and the bondholders is contained in a rather elaborate contract called the bond *indenture.* Other titles used for this document include the following: *trust agreement, deed of trust,* and *mortgage and deed of trust.* In general the indenture contains all the details in connection with the bond issue and the relationships between the corporation, the trustee, and the bondholders.

Contents of the Indenture. Following are the provisions which are usually contained in the indenture.

1. The indenture starts out with the names of the parties to the agreement. These are the issuing corporation and the trustee. The bondholders are the beneficiaries under the trust.

2. Next is the preamble which states the purposes of the indenture, the legal authorization for the issuance of the bonds, the form of the bonds and of the interest coupons, if they are coupon bonds, and the certification of the trustee.
3. The granting clause which contains a detailed description of any property mortgaged, or any securities put up as collateral.
4. A statement of the maximum amount of bonds to be issued under the indenture. If all the bonds are not to be issued at once, a statement of the amount to be issued immediately will usually be stated, followed by a statement of the conditions under which the additional bonds may be issued.
5. Clauses, or *covenants,* for the protection of the bondholders. These include the following: agreement of the corporation to keep its mortgaged property in proper repair, to maintain insurance on the property, to set up depreciation reserves, to pay property taxes, and agreement not to place a prior lien on the property.
6. The procedure to be followed by the bondholders to levy on the mortgaged property in case of a mortgage issue, or to pursue their rights as general creditors.
7. An *acceleration clause* which states that if any default in interest payments occurs, the principal of the bonds will become due and payable.
8. Any provisions for a sinking fund to retire the bonds.
9. Any provision for calling the bonds before their maturity.
10. Rights, if any, to convert the bonds into other securities.
11. Any provision for the maintenance of minimum working capital requirements before dividends can be paid to the stockholders.
12. Definition of the powers, duties and liabilities of the trustee. These were dealt with above.

In connection with our discussion of trustees, some of the requirements of the Trust Indenture Act of 1939 were mentioned. Registration of a security issue is not complete until an indenture which complies with the provisions of the Act is filed with the SEC. The Commission's responsibility is to see to it that the indenture conforming to the Act is properly filed. But the Commission does not thereafter have any powers with respect to the enforcement of the provisions of the indenture. The indenture, however, like other contracts, is enforceable by the parties thereto. The requirements of the Act, however, make it mandatory to include in the indenture certain provisions for the protection of the bondholders in event of negligence or misfeasance on the part of the trustee, and forces the corporation to exercise greater responsibility. Failure on the part of the trustee or the corporation to comply with the provisions of the Act, however, means little unless the bondholders initiate action against them.

Reasons for selling bonds

TO SECURE CAPITAL. The obvious reason why any corporation sells bonds is to secure money. Some corporations are able to secure the capital needed from the reinvestment of earnings, but in many instances this source does not produce the amount of capital needed. Trade creditors are another source of working capital, but there is a limit on the amount of capital that may be secured in this manner.

Bank borrowings and the sale of short-term and long-term notes are another source of capital. And the sale of additional stock is always given consideration when planning for the acquisition of additional capital.

In former times borrowing was looked upon as a sign of financial weakness, and in some instances it still is, but today in many cases borrowing is indicative of financial strength. Our present interest is why corporations sell bonds instead of, or in addition to, the sale of notes and stocks, or instead of borrowing from the bank.

FINANCIAL CONDITION OF THE COMPANY. Since bonds represent a debt of the company both in respect to interest and principal, there are many instances where because of financial weakness of the company the market would not absorb a stock issue, but a bond issue could be sold. And it may be necessary in many cases to secure the bond issue with a mortgage on the company properties. The company under such circumstances has no alternative in securing new capital but to issue bonds.

CONDITION OF THE MARKET. The tendency is for people to buy stocks during the prosperous period of the business cycle, and bonds when business conditions are not so good. A corporation follows the preference of the public for bonds or for stock and would issue what is more economical under the circumstances.

CONTROL. The matter of participation in control is sometimes an important factor in determining whether a stock issue or a bond issue will be sold. Bonds do not possess the right to vote, but stocks, with the exception of some classified issues and some preferred issues, do. The voting shareholders who have the pre-emptive right may not have the amount of money needed to subscribe to the new stock, or may not want to invest any more in the same corporation.

In the case of the corporate giants with a large number of small stockholders, the sale of additional voting stock would probably not jeopardize their control, as the management is likely to continue to dominate the company through the use of the proxy system.

WIDER MARKET. Stocks and bonds are to some extent not purchased by the same class of buyers; in general, speculators tend to favor stocks, while investors prefer bonds.

In addition to individuals, many institutions are heavy investors. Many of these, such as banks, trust companies, trustees, and life insurance companies are either prohibited by the law from buying stocks, or if permitted, the percentage of their resources that can be invested in stocks is relatively small. Thus, a corporation may have more classes of bond buyers than stock buyers.

TABLE 8

COST OF NEW FINANCING IN TERMS OF PERCENTAGE YIELDS ON VARIOUS CLASSES OF SECURITIES, UNITED STATES, SELECTED YEARS

Year	*Moody's Composite Average of Yields on Corporate Bonds*	*Moody's Preferred Stock Yields**	*Moody's Common Stock Yields Covering 200 Common Stocks*
1955	3.25%	3.99%	4.06%
1954	3.16	4.00	4.78
1953	3.43	4.24	5.49
1952	3.19	4.06	5.50
1951	3.08	4.04	6.12
1950	2.86	3.83	6.27
1949	2.96	3.99	6.63
1944	3.05	4.40	4.81
1939	3.77	5.38	4.15
1934	4.96	6.34	4.11
1929	5.21	5.44	3.41

* Average of ten high-grade and ten medium-grade industrials and ten high-grade and ten medium-grade utilities for years 1949–1955. For earlier years, the utility stocks are not included.

SOURCE: *Moody's Industrial Manual,* Moody's Investors Service, New York, 1956, pp. a18, and a24.

COST OF FUNDS. As has been stated before, bonds ordinarily are sold in denominations of not less than $1,000, while stocks are usually sold at considerably less than $100 a share. Furthermore, bonds are ordinarily sold to investors in much larger dollar amounts than stocks, and are a much safer investment than stocks of the same company. Because of these facts, the selling costs connected

TABLE 9

GROSS PROCEEDS AND PERCENTAGE DISTRIBUTION OF NEW CORPORATE SECURITIES OFFERED FOR CASH SALE, UNITED STATES, SELECTED YEARS

Year	Total (millions of dollars)	Percentage Distribution			
		Bonds	Preferred Stock	Common Stock	Total
1955	$10,454	73.1%	6.1%	20.8%	100.0%
1954	9,516	78.6	8.6	12.7	100.0
1953	8,898	79.6	5.5	14.9	100.0
1952	9,534	79.7	5.9	14.4	100.0
1951	7,741	73.5	10.8	15.7	100.0
1950	6,361	77.3	9.9	12.8	100.0
1949	6,052	80.0	7.0	12.2	100.0
1948	7,078	84.3	7.0	8.7	100.0
1947	6,577	76.6	11.6	11.8	100.0
1946	6,900	70.8	16.3	12.9	100.0
1945	6,011	80.8	12.6	6.6	100.0
1939	2,164	91.5	4.5	4.0	100.0
1934	397	93.7	1.5	4.8	100.0

SOURCE: *Moody's Industrial Manual*, Moody's Investors Service, New York, 1956, p. a18.

with a bond issue of a given amount are lower than the costs of a stock issue of the same amount.

In addition to the above, the annual interest charges that a corporation must pay out on bonds are ordinarily less than would have to be paid in dividends on stock. Since bonds constitute a debt of the issuing corporation, while stock represents ownership, a person will ordinarily lend money to a corporation at a lower rate than he would demand from stock. In general, the bonds could perhaps be issued at one half the rate that the corporation is paying on its common stock. Of course, the bond interest must be paid regularly, while the payment of dividends rests with the discretion of the board of directors. But in order to maintain its credit and the market for its stock, a corporation will usually pay dividends when it can do so.

TRADING ON THE EQUITY. The term *equity* is used in different ways, but in corporation finance it means *ownership*. Thus, we speak of stocks as being *equities*, or *equity securities*. If a corporation has only common stock outstanding and it sells additional common stock at its book value, but the *rate of earnings on the stockholders' investment* remains the same, the *earnings per share* on the old stock would remain the same. But if instead of selling more stock, the corporation obtained the same amount of additional money by the sale of bonds, the rate of interest on which is less than the rate the company is earning on its capital, then the earnings per share on the stock would be increased. This process or procedure of using the stockholders' equity as a basis for borrowing money at a lower rate than the corporation hopes to earn on the bondholders' money is called *trading on the equity,* and referring to the stockholders' raised earnings position, the company is said to have *leverage.* A similar result may be obtained by the issuance of preferred stock with a fixed or limited dividend rate.

Let us assume that a company has $1,000,000 in stock outstanding, and an equivalent amount invested in assets. To simplify the example, we will assume that there are no liabilities, and also no surplus. For the time being we will ignore the federal corporate income tax. If the company earns, after all expenses, $100,000 a year, the earnings per share on the stock would be 10 per cent.

We will assume that the corporation wants to raise another $1,000,000 either through the sale of stock or bonds. If it sells the stock, and continues to earn 10 per cent on its capital, the total earnings would increase to $200,000, but the *earnings per share* would remain at 10 per cent. But if the company raised the $1,000,000 through the sale of a 3 per cent bond issue, the earnings (before taxes) on the common stock and after the bond interest was paid would amount to $170,000. This represents earnings per share of 17 per cent on the stock, instead of only 10 per cent.

We can carry the above example further to illustrate the effect of trading on the equity. If the company increased its *rate of earnings* on its capital from 10 to 15 per cent, the earnings per share on the common would be increased by only the same percentage, assuming the firm secured the additional $1,000,000 through the sale of stock. But if the bonds were sold instead, and the company could increase its rate of earning on its capital from 10 to 15 per cent, the earnings on the stock would increase to 27 per cent. This is computed as follows:

Earnings before interest	$300,000	(15% on capital)
Less: Bond Interest	30,000	(3% on $1,000,000)
Earnings on stock	$270,000	(equals 27% on stock of $1,000,000)

Trading on the equity, however, sometimes backfires on a corporation. If the earnings fall to the point where the company is earning a smaller rate on its capital than it is paying on the bonds, then the corporation would have been better off to have sold additional stock. To illustrate, let us assume that earnings fall to where they represent a return of only 1½ per cent on the capital. This means that the earnings would decline to $30,000. If the corporation had sold stock it would then be earning 1½ per cent on the stock. But if bonds had been sold, all of these earnings would be consumed in paying the bond interest, and the company would have earned nothing on its stock. If the company instead of earning something, suffers a loss, then the loss will be larger if it has to pay bond interest. From what has been said it is obvious that trading on the equity *magnifies both profits and losses.* In order to better visualize what has been said above, the comparative effects of selling stocks and bonds are summarized in Table 10.

Trading on the (common stockholders') equity can also be done by the issuance of a nonparticipating preferred stock. Since the dividend rate on the preferred would ordinarily be more than the interest on bonds, the use of preferred stock does not magnify the profits as much as when bonds are issued.

The term *leverage* is quite commonly used in practice to refer to what we have here described as "trading on the equity." Companies that have a large portion of their capitalization in the form of bonds are referred to as leverage companies. The term "leverage" is also sometimes used to apply to the situation where a corporation has a large surplus so that a slight increase in the rate of earnings on the invested capital will produce a relatively large increase in the earnings on the stock. The latter is referred to as *internal* leverage, whereas the former type is called *external* leverage.

FEDERAL INCOME TAX. In our discussion above of trading on the equity we ignored the federal corporate income tax in order to illustrate how leverage alone would effect profits and losses. As a practical matter, however, we cannot and do not want to ignore these taxes.

Bond interest is an expense which is deducted as such before arriving at the net profits on which the tax rate is based. Dividends on stock, on the other hand, are not expenses, but rather a distribution of the profits, and are not deducted before computing the income tax. This means that every dollar paid out in bond interest reduces by that amount the figure on which the tax is based. The federal corporate income tax rate has been changed several times in recent years and it will probably be changed in the future, but to illustrate the point, we will assume that the rate is 50 per cent. With this rate of taxation it means that if a corporation is enjoying a profit, the bond interest reduces the net taxable profit by the

TABLE 10

EFFECT OF LEVERAGE ON STOCKHOLDERS' EQUITY (TAXES IGNORED)

	Capitalization					
Item	*Stock* *$2,000,000*	*Stock* *$1,000,000* *Bonds* *$1,000,000*	*Stock* *$2,000,000*	*Stock* *$1,000,000* *Bonds* *$1,000,000*	*Stock* *$2,000,000*	*Stock* *$1,000,000* *Bonds* *$1,000,000*
Earnings before interest	$200,000	$200,000	$300,000	$300,000	$30,000	$30,000
Interest on bonds		30,000		30,000		30,000
Earned on stock (before taxes)	$200,000	$170,000	$300,000	$270,000	$30,000	0
Per cent earned on stock	10%	17%	15%	27%	1½%	0

TABLE 11

EFFECT OF LEVERAGE ON STOCKHOLDERS' EQUITY (AFTER TAXES)

	Capitalization					
Item	*Stock* *$2,000,000*	*Stock* *$1,000,000* *Bonds* *$1,000,000*	*Stock* *$2,000,000*	*Stock* *$1,000,000* *Bonds* *$1,000,000*	*Stock* *$2,000,000*	*Stock* *$1,000,000* *Bonds* *$1,000,000*
Earnings before interest	$200,000	$200,000	$300,000	$300,000	$30,000	$30,000
Interest on bonds		30,000		30,000		30,000
Earnings after interest	$200,000	$170,000	$300,000	$270,000	$30,000	0
Taxes (50%)	100,000	85,000	150,000	135,000	15,000	0
Earned on stock	$100,000	$ 85,000	$150,000	$135,000	$15,000	0
Per cent earned on stock	5%	8½%	7½%	13½%	¾%	0

amount of the interest, so that there is a tax saving equivalent to 50 per cent of the bond interest. In other words, if a corporation sells a 3 per cent bond issue, instead of a stock issue, and is operating at a profit, the tax saving reduces the effective cost of the bonds from 3 per cent to 1½ per cent. In Table 11 are the same data as stated above in connection with trading on the equity after correction for federal corporate income tax at the rate of 50 per cent.

If there is an excess profits tax on corporations, such as during and for a short time after World War II, if the earnings are high enough to be in the excess profits tax bracket, the amount saved in taxes by virtue of issuing bonds rather than stock would be proportionately greater than that shown above.

The reader should guard against an idea that savings can be effected by the unlimited issuance of bonds. It is not good financial management to pay out $1.00 in interest in order to save 50 cents in taxes. But as an alternative to stock financing, bonds will effect the tax savings illustrated above.

If trading on the equity is accomplished through the issuance of preferred stock, only the first example given above of the effect of leverage before income taxes would be applicable, since dividends, unlike interest, cannot be deducted before taxes. Taxes should be deducted before preferred dividends.

Classification of bonds

In the next several chapters we will be discussing various types of bonds. To get a better over-all picture of bonds let us first classify them. Several different methods of classification will be given before presenting the one which we will follow.

Character of Issuer. In referring to different kinds of bonds we sometimes have in mind a classification according to the character of the issuer. These are large groups which need breaking down for purposes of analysis. Following are the different types of issuers.

1. United States government
2. States and municipalities
3. Foreign governments and municipalities
4. Railroads
5. Public utilities
6. Industrials
7. Others

PURPOSE OF ISSUE. The purpose of selling any bond issue is to secure money. In some instances, however, such as a reorganization, or a refunding operation the issue may be exchanged for old bonds of the company. The money obtained from the sale of bonds may be used for many different purposes. Bonds may be classified according to the specific use to which the money is put. The names themselves may or may not be used in the bond title.

1. Adjustment
2. Bridge
3. Car trust
4. Consolidation
5. Construction
6. Dock and wharf
7. Equipment
8. Ferry
9. General
10. Improvement
11. Interim
12. Purchase money
13. Refunding
14. Reorganization
15. Revenue
16. Temporary
17. Terminal
18. Unified

METHOD OF RETIREMENT. Bonds can be classified according to the method used to retire them, as follows:

1. Callable
2. Noncallable
3. Convertible
4. Serial
5. Sinking fund

A bond issue does not necessarily have to have one of the above-listed features to the exclusion of the others. Several may be present in the same bonds. For example, a convertible bond may also be callable, or a serial bond may have a sinking fund behind it.

METHOD OF PAYING INTEREST. We have previously discussed registered and coupon bonds, so classifying bonds according to interest payment is done here for the sake of completeness.

1. Coupon bonds
2. Registered bonds
3. Coupon bonds registered as to principal
4. Interchangeable bonds

SECURITY. Perhaps the most commonly seen classification of bonds is that according to the security behind the bonds. In the following chapters dealing with bonds we will take them up according to the type of security, though not in the exact order in which they appear in the following classification.[5]

[5] This classification is in the main the one used by Arthur Stone Dewing, in *The Financial Policy of Corporations* (5th ed.; New York: The Ronald Press Co., 1953), pp. 194–95.

I. *Bonds secured by a lien on property.*
   1. Bonds secured by a first lien on real property or equipment:
      (a) General first mortgage bonds
      (b) Divisional mortgage bonds
      (c) Special direct lien mortgage bonds
      (d) Prior lien mortgage bonds
      (e) Equipment obligations
   2. Bonds secured by a junior lien on real property:
      (a) Second, third, etc., mortgage bonds
      (b) General mortgage bonds
      (c) Refunding mortgage bonds
   3. Bonds secured by a lien on securities:
      (a) Collateral trust bonds

II. *Bonds secured principally by only the general credit of the corporation.*
   1. Bonds which commonly have a lien on property:
      (a) Assumed bonds
      (b) Guaranteed bonds
      (c) Receivers' certificates
   2. Bonds which have no lien on specific property:
      (a) Debenture bonds
   3. Bonds the interest on which is partially or wholly conditional:
      (a) Income or adjustment bonds
      (b) Participating bonds

Questions

1. (a) Indicate the various differences between bonds and common stocks. (b) In what respects do preferred stocks resemble bonds more than they do common stocks?

2. Are good bonds a hedge against inflation or deflation? Explain.

3. Are bonds issued in low enough denominations to permit the small investor to purchase a diversified portfolio of them?

4. (a) Distinguish between bonds and notes. (b) What characterizes short-, medium-, and long-term bonds? (c) In what type of industry are long-term bonds more commonly found?

5. (a) Distinguish between the following kinds of yields: nominal yield, current yield, and yield to maturity. When should each be used? (b) Indicate when the investor should compute the long-term yield to the maturity date and when to the call date in the case of callable bonds. (c) What factors determine the price at which a particular bond will sell in the market?

6. (a) If interest rates in general would advance, what would happen to the price of high-grade bonds? Why? (b) Do changes in interest rates cause long-term or short-term bonds to fluctuate more? Explain. (c) When interest rates are relatively low, will long-term or short-term bonds sell on a higher yield basis? Explain.

7. Distinguish between registered and coupon bonds. Which would you rather purchase? Why?

8. (a) Are corporate bonds redeemable at the option of the holder? U. S. Savings bonds? (b) At whose option is the call feature exercised?

9. What are some of the principal features of the Trust Indenture Act of 1939?

10. List the principal duties of a trustee designated in a bond indenture?

11. Indicate the principal contents of a bond indenture.

12. Indicate the various reasons why a corporation might sell a bond issue rather than a stock issue.

13. If a corporation issues a 4 per cent bond, and the corporate income tax rates are 50 per cent, what is the real cost to the corporation of the interest?

14. Illustrate what is meant by "trading on the equity." What other term is applied to the same thing?

15. Indicate several different ways of classifying bonds.

Problems

1. The Federated Corp. was organized in the early part of 19-1 with a capitalization consisting of $1,000,000 in 6 per cent bonds; $2,000,000 in 7 per cent noncumulative, nonparticipating preferred stock; and $3,000,000 in common stock. All the stock had a par value of $100 per share. Earnings before interest charges on the bonds were paid and before taxes, were as follows (assume federal corporate income tax rate is 50 per cent):

Year	*Earnings*
19-1	$ 340,000
19-2	680,000
19-3	1,360,000

Because the company started out with a large paid-in surplus, all the available earnings were paid out each year in the form of dividends. Assume that you own ten shares of the common stock that you purchased at its par value.

(a) What percentage did you earn on your investment in each of these years? (b) If the company had been capitalized at the same amount as stated above but with common stock only, what percentage would you have earned on your stock in each of the years? (c) Expressed in terms of percentage, how much more did you earn in 19-3 under the circumstances stated in part (a) than in part (b)? (d) As a common stockholder would you prefer that there be bonds or preferred stock, or both, outstanding, or that only common stock be issued? Explain.

2. Assume that you purchased on original issue the Standard Corporation's 20 year, 4 per cent bonds for 110 ($1,100). Compute the following:

(a) Nominal yield, (b) Current yield, (c) Approximate yield to maturity.

3. Compute the three types of yield stated in Problem 2, above, assuming that you purchased the bond for 90 instead of 110.

4. If the bond in Problems 2 and 3 had been callable five years before its maturity should the long-term yield be computed to the call or the maturity date? Explain.

Chapter 9

MORTGAGE BONDS

NATURE OF A MORTGAGE. It was pointed out in the preceding chapter that when a corporation borrows money from a number of bondholders the agreement relating to the conditions of the loan is made with a trustee who represents the future bondholders. When the bond issue is secured by a mortgage, the latter runs in favor of the trustee. Our discussion of a real estate mortgage will be better understood if we simplify and describe it first from the standpoint of one individual giving a mortgage to another, rather than consider the corporation, the trustee, and the bondholders.

Let us assume that Adams borrows $100,000 from his *creditor* Brown, who will require that the *debtor* Adams give him a note or bond containing his written promise to pay the amount borrowed with interest at a specified rate and time. In order to add to the safety of the loan, Brown requires Adams to give him as security for the loan a mortgage on some real estate, which we will assume, consists of a lot and a building valued together at $200,000.

The correct meaning of the names which are applied to the parties involved is necessary for proper understanding. In the example given above, the debtor Adams, as giver of the mortgage, is called the *mortgagor*, and the creditor Brown, as receiver of the mortgage, is called the *mortgagee*.

So long as Adams makes the payments of interest and principal when due, Brown will not make use of the mortgage. But if a default occurs, then Brown may exercise his rights to the mortgaged property for the satisfaction of the loan.

The procedure of the enforcement and use of the mortgage varied considerably during its complicated legal history. The outcome was that the mortgagee could not immediately get possession of the property upon default of the mortgagor, but would have to foreclose by legal proceedings the property under mortgage and have a court sale of the property at public auction to satisfy his claim. And that is in final analysis the way a mortgage is treated today by the courts, although in different states there still are two different "theories" as to the exact legal nature of a mortgage.

The older concept still adhered to in many states says that the mortgage transfers *legal title* to the property to the mortgagee. The mortgagor, however, retains *equitable title* to the same property. This is sometimes called his *equity of redemption.* "Equitable title" has been defined as that title which the mortgagor possesses in order to get back legal title upon the discharge of his debt. The transfer of legal title to the mortgagee, however, is not complete. After transferring such title, a later clause in the mortgage, called the *defeasance clause,* states that as long as the mortgagor lives up to his agreement, the transfer of title to the mortgagee shall be null and void. This theory is called the *conveyance of title* theory.

The other theory, which is followed in some states, is that the mortgage is not a conveyance of title to property, but merely gives the mortgagee a *lien* on the property. This is the *lien theory.* The same result is obtained under both concepts. If a default occurs, the mortgagee forecloses to make his title good, or to get title to the property by virtue of his lien, depending upon which theory is followed in the particular state. The court then proceeds to sell the property in order to secure the money to satisfy the claim.

In the event that there are no other bidders for the property, or if they do not offer enough, the mortgagee buys it with his claim. If, however, the property sold brings more than the amount owed to the mortgagee and court costs, then the mortgagor gets the balance. But if the sale brings less than the amount owed, the debtor is still liable on his note or bond for the deficiency.

In actual practice the mortgage bondholders of a corporation commonly do not receive satisfaction in the precise way described, because the corporation may go into the hands of a receiver or a trustee in bankruptcy, who will prevent the bondholders from foreclosing. This commonly ends with a reorganization of the company rather than liquidation, and the bondholders receive whatever treatment had been agreed upon or was forced upon them in the reorganization plan. This will be described later in the book when we consider reorganization.[1]

NATURE OF JUNIOR MORTGAGES. In order to illustrate the nature of junior mortgages, we will again refer to the above example of where Adams gave Brown a mortgage on his property as security for the $100,000 loan. We assumed that Brown holds a *first* mort-

[1] See Chapters 34 and 35.

gage on the property. Adams may need additional money at the time he gets the loan from Brown, but the latter may not be willing to lend him any more. We will assume that Clark will lend him $30,000 with the security of a *second* mortgage against the property. Adams could transfer to Clark no better title than he himself possessed: an equity in the property, or an equity of redemption, after the first mortgage of Brown. So it is this which Adams now transfers (subject to the defeasance clause) to Clark as security for the $30,000 loan. When Adams gave Brown a first mortgage on the $200,000 property as security for a $100,000 loan, Adams' interest or equity in the property was reduced to $100,000. When he gave Clark a second mortgage as security for the $30,000 loan, then Adams' equity was further reduced to $70,000.

If Adams was then to borrow $5,000 from Douglas and give his equity after the first two mortgages as security for a *third* mortgage on the property, his equity would be reduced to $65,000. There is no necessity of obtaining the consent of Brown or Clark in order to give the junior mortgages that follow them.

Let us now assume that Adams defaulted in the payment of the loan to Brown who held the first mortgage. Brown will bring an action of foreclosure and sale. This action will be brought against Clark, Douglas and Adams, since they all have an equity in the mortgaged property. If the property was purchased at the court sale by Edwards, the proceeds (after court costs and taxes) would be applied on the first mortgage, and this would have to be paid off in full before anything would be paid to Clark who held the second mortgage. Then the money would be applied on the second, and Douglas would get something only after the second mortgage had been paid in full.

The purchaser of the property, Edwards, would get it free of all claims. If Edwards would not pay enough for the property to satisfy the claim of Brown, who holds the first mortgage, Brown would use his claim to bid in the property and the claims of Clark and Douglas would be wiped out so far as Brown is concerned. If Clark and Douglas feel that the property is worth any more than the $100,000 which is owed to Brown, they can bid more for the property. Any mortgagee that is not fully satisfied after the sale has claim against Adams for the deficiency.

If default occurred in the second mortgage and action for foreclosure and sale was brought by Clark (against Adams and Douglas), the purchaser of the property would take it *subject to* the first mortgage. In other words, the claim of the first mortgage continues. If the purchaser thought the property was worth $120,000, he would pay only $20,000 for it since he would be taking it subject to the first mortgage. Clark, the holder of the second mortgage, would receive the $20,000, and Douglas would, of course, receive nothing. The latter would still have a right against Adams for $5,000, but no longer a mortgage against the property, and Clark would have a right against Adams for $10,000, the amount of the deficiency. If Clark thought the property was worth more than $120,000, he could use his own claim and bid $30,000 for the property subject to the first mortgage.

The effects of foreclosure by the various mortgagees are shown in Table 12. It is assumed that Mr. Edwards buys the property at court sale, and that the proceeds from the sale are after all court costs and expenses have been paid.

Assuming a Mortgage. In the above example we indicated that when the second or third mortgagees foreclosed, the purchaser took the property *subject to* the first mortgage, or subject to the first and the second mortgage. The property remains as security for the debt, and in case of default the mortgagee could bring action for foreclosure and sale of the mortgaged property, but the buyer would not be liable for any deficiency. The original mortgagor would still be liable on his note for this deficiency.

If instead of buying property subject to a mortgage, the purchaser bought it *assuming* the mortgage, the mortgagee could come against the buyer for any deficiency. In the event that he merely indorses the note, instead of replacing it, then both the original mortgagor and the buyer would be liable on the note. Someone assuming the mortgage assumes the obligation which is embodied in the note or bond as well as in the mortgage.

Corporate Mortgage Bonds. In the above discussion we confined ourselves to individuals in order to simplify the material. When a corporation wants to borrow money in large amounts and/or for a long term it is usually necessary for it to sell bonds to thousands of buyers. It would be impractical, to say the least, for it to have to give a mortgage to each bondholder and to have to deal with each one separately. So the trustee is brought into the picture. Any mortgage behind the bonds is given to the trustee for the benefit of the bondholders. We can refer to the trustee as the *legal mortgagee,* and the bondholders as the *beneficial mortgagees.*

Closed-end Mortgage. When a corporation is authorized in the indenture to issue a fixed amount of bonds, such as $50,000,000 for

TABLE 12

RIGHTS UPON FORECLOSURE SALE OF MORTGAGED PROPERTY

Foreclosed by	*Action Brought Against*	*Proceeds of sale*	*1st Mortgagee (Brown) of $100,000 gets*	*2nd Mortgagee (Clark) of $30,000 gets*	*3rd Mortgagee (Douglas) of $5,000 gets*	*Mortgagor (Adams) gets*	*Purchaser (Edwards) gets*
1st mortgagee	Adams, 2nd mortgagee and 3rd mortgagee	$115,000	$100,000	$15,000 has claim against mortgagor for $15,000	Nothing. Has claim against mortgagor for $5,000	Nothing	Clear title
2nd mortgagee	Adams and 3rd mortgagee	$33,000	Still has 1st mortgage	$30,000	$3,000. Has claim against mortgagor for $2,000	Nothing	Title subject to 1st mortgage
3rd mortgagee	Adams	$7,000	Still has 1st mortgage	Still has 2nd mortgage	$5,000	$2,000	Title subject to 1st and 2nd mortgage
1st, 2nd, and 3rd mortgagees	Each as in above	$131,000	$100,000	$30,000	$1,000. Has claim against mortgagor for $4,000	Nothing	Clear title

example, and all of these bonds are issued at the same time, the issue is said to be a *closed,* or *closed-end* issue. The particular issue may be either secured by mortgaged property or it may be unsecured. The former is commonly referred to as a *closed-end mortgage.* In order to better bring out the relative advantages and disadvantages of open and closed issues, we will assume that they are secured by mortgaged property.

Generally speaking, the closed-end mortgage may benefit the particular bondholders, but it may be to the disadvantage of the issuing corporation. When a closed-end mortgage bond issue has been sold, no more bonds having the same lien against the particular property may be issued. Thus, the bondholders need not fear that their equity will be diluted by the issuance of additional bonds against the same property. If the firm wants to sell additional mortgage bonds against the *same* property, the mortgage will have to be *junior* to the issue which is outstanding. This is to the disadvantage of the corporation since the new issue, being a junior one, will have to bear a higher rate of interest than the senior issue. The company further suffers in that a number of relatively small bond issues will not have the market that would be enjoyed by one large issue.

Open-end Mortgage. If the indenture does not specify a maximum dollar amount of bonds that may be sold, the issue is said to be *open,* or *open-end.* The bonds may be secured by a mortgage, or they may be unsecured.

The open-end mortgage may work to the disadvantage of the bondholders in that if the corporation issued additional bonds under the same indenture, the equity of the bondholders would be diluted. From the standpoint of the issuing corporation, however, the open-end feature is desirable in that additional bonds having the *same lien* against the mortgaged property may be issued. Priority of issue under an open-end issue thus does not give priority of lien. The rate of interest that must be paid on the new bonds issued would be less than would have to be paid on a junior issue for two reasons. First, the bondholders would have an equal lien with the original bondholders, and second, the one large issue would attract a wider market than a number of different issues, particularly junior ones.

Open-end indentures provide for the bonds to be issued in *series.* Thus, designations such as Series A, Series B, etc., are indicative of an open-end issue (or limited open-end), except in the case of equipment trust obligations, which will be discussed later. The various series of bonds under an open-end issue may bear different face rates of interest, and their maturities too may differ.

LIMITED OPEN-END MORTGAGE. The indenture of a *limited open-end* issue permits the issuance of additional bonds up to a maximum specified amount. Under such an indenture a corporation might sell, for example, $10,000,000 of bonds today, but additional bonds under the same indenture and having the same claim could be sold at various times in the future, until a maximum of, for example, $50,000,000 in bonds had been issued. Thereupon the issue would become closed.

The limited open-end issue takes on some of the advantages and disadvantages of both the closed-end and the open-end issues. These should be obvious from what has been said above.

RESTRICTIONS ON OPEN-END ISSUES. The unrestricted issue of bonds under an open-end issue (and within the limit set in a limited open-end issue) tends to weaken the position of the bondholders. For this reason corporations find it difficult to sell an open issue of bonds (and in some instances a limited open-end issue) without writing into the indenture certain limitations, permitting additional bonds only when the equity or position of the existing bondholders would not be impaired.

The following types of restrictions on the issuance of additional bonds under an open-end issue are often found in indentures. The bonds may be issued:

1. Up to a specified percentage, such as 60 or 75 per cent of the cost of new property which is acquired by the corporation.
2. If the company is earning at least twice the interest charges on the bonds now outstanding and those proposed to be issued.
3. If the net current assets are at least a certain percentage of all the bonds or at least equal to the bonds outstanding and those proposed to be issued.
4. If the capital stock bears a specified relation to the bonds outstanding and those proposed to be issued.

AFTER-ACQUIRED PROPERTY CLAUSE. In order to market a particular issue of bonds it may be necessary for the corporation to secure them by not only the present property which is owned, but also by any property which the organization may acquire in the future. Such a clause in the indenture is called an *after-acquired property clause,* or simply an *after-acquired clause.* The present property and the type of property acquired in the future covered by the mortgage is carefully defined in the indenture. Usually, it is only the *real property* which is included.

From the standpoint of the bondholders, the presence of the after-acquired property clause in a bond issue tends to strengthen their position because the equity behind the bonds increases as the corporation acquires more holdings. From the corporation's viewpoint, however, such a provision may make future financing expensive, because it may be necessary for it to issue a mortgage bond to finance the new acquisitions, and the mortgage behind these bonds would have to be junior to the one outstanding which possesses the after-acquired property clause.

If the issue which contains such a clause is an open-end one (or a limited open-end issue which has not yet been closed), and considering any restrictions in the indenture, the clause will not be embarrassing to the company, since more bonds having the same lien may be issued to finance the new holdings. Looking at it from the viewpoint of the bondholders, however, the open feature in the issue would tend to weaken somewhat the value of the clause.

Thus, in short, the closed feature and after-acquired property clause tend to benefit the bondholders, while the open feature and the absence of such a clause tend to benefit the corporation. The open-end (or limited open-end) feature and the after-acquired property clause in the same issue offer a compromise between the bondholders and the corporation, and in practice these two features are commonly found in the same bond issue.

Avoiding the After-Acquired Property Clause. In the past, corporations which have had closed-end bond issues outstanding which contained such a clause have found it so much of a drawback that they have taken steps to avoid its effects. Such steps are:

Redemption of the bonds. If the bonds can be purchased in the market at a fair price, it may be advantageous for the corporation to buy back its bonds. In fact it may be desirable to even pay a substantial premium to get rid of the clause. If the bonds are callable, then they may be retired by the exercise of the call feature. If the corporation does not have the money on hand to retire the bonds and its financial standing is satisfactory, it may sell additional stock, or put out a refunding bond issue to secure the cash.

In some instances it may be possible to get the bondholders to exchange their bonds for a new issue which does not possess the after-acquired property clause. Some inducement such as a cash or stock bonus may have to be added. The corporation can also use the argument that the large new issue may have a much wider market than the old one.

Lease. Where the use of particular property is desired it may be leased rather than purchased. In this way the after-acquired property clause is not operative. This method is commonly used by railroads to finance the acquisition of rolling stock. Title to the property is taken by a trustee who leases the equipment to the railroad. Equipment trust obligations, in the form of car trust certificates, are issued to secure the amount of money needed in addition to the down payment made by the railroad. Acquisition of equipment in the way here mentioned will be described in some detail in the following chapter.

Purchase money mortgage. Another method is through the use of the *purchase money mortgage.* To acquire property, the corporation makes a down payment and executes notes or bonds promising to pay the balance. A mortgage is retained by the seller as security for the debt.

If the corporation had acquired legal title to the property, the old bonds with the after-acquired property clause would attach to the property, and any bonds that the company would issue to secure the money to pay the balance on the purchase price would have been junior to the old bonds. But the purchase money mortgage is placed on the property *before* the corporation acquires it, so this mortgage would have first claim against the particular property. Thus, the corporation acquired only equitable title to the property after the claim of the purchase money mortgage, and it is only this equitable title, or equity of redemption, which comes under the lien of the old bonds with the after-acquired property clause. In other words, these bonds would have a second mortgage on the property acquired.

If the seller wanted all cash for the property, legal title to the property could be transferred by the seller to a trustee, and purchase money mortgage bonds, guaranteed by the buyer of the property could be sold to the public through an investment banker the same as any other type of bond. Through the use of the purchase money mortgage the corporation is able to sell bonds that have a first claim on the new property and thus get the advantage of a lower interest rate than if they had acquired the property and then had to issue second mortgage bonds because of the after-acquired property clause in their old bonds.

Subsidiary corporation. In order to prevent the old bonds having the after-acquired property clause from obtaining a lien on new property, the company may form a subsidiary corporation and have that company take title to the new property. The stock of the subsidiary is acquired by the parent company. The subsidiary can then issue bonds having a first mortgage on the property as security.

The subsidiary may be a small, relatively unknown company and, therefore, may not be able to market its bonds economically. To secure the lowest possible interest rate, the parent could do one of two things. It could guarantee the principal and interest on the subsidiary's bonds, or it could acquire the bonds and put them up as collateral and issue its own collateral trust bonds. The stocks or bonds of the subsidiary would ordinarily not come under the claim of the after-acquired property clause bonds. The money obtained from the sale of the collateral trust bonds would be used to pay for the subsidiary's bonds. The subsidiary would of course use the money to pay for the new property.

Some courts, however, have held that where a corporation owns all the stock of a subsidiary and the two companies have the same officers and directors, and the subsidiary appears to have been organized in order to avoid the after-acquired property clause, the parent really acquires title to the subsidiary's property. In such an event the bonds having the clause would have first claim against the property of the subsidiary.

Merger. Another method is a *merger* of the company that has such a clause in its bonds into another company. We can best illustrate this with an example. Assume that Company A has bonds outstanding with this clause in the indenture. Company B buys the properties of Company A, and issues its stock to the stockholders of Company A in exchange for their stock. Company A is then dissolved. The bonds of Company A are assumed by Company B. Now if the company, which is all Company B now, acquires any additional properties, these properties will not come under the claim of the old A bonds, since Company A did not acquire any new property.

The above procedure may not be as easily accomplished as just described. The indenture under which the bonds having the after-acquired property clause are issued may contain a provision prohibiting the company from selling its mortgaged properties, or merging into another company. Or, the vote of a designated percentage of the bondholders may be necessary to accomplish it. It could also be provided in the indenture that to acquire the properties, the successor corporation would have to place future-acquired property under the claim of the bonds.

In passing we might inquire into the effect of the merger on bonds of Company B which contained the after-acquired property clause. Since this company is actually taking on additional holdings, its bonds containing this clause would have a lien on the properties of old Company A, but, of course, their claim would be junior to that of any mortgage bonds issued by Company A.

Types of mortgage bonds

FIRST MORTGAGE BONDS. A *first mortgage bond* has a first lien on property. When the term *mortgage* is used in connection with corporate bonds it is taken to mean a mortgage on *real* property, or *real estate,* as distinguished from *personal* property, such as stocks and bonds. This real property is owned by an industrial company, railroad, public utility, etc. When bonds are secured by a mortgage on real estate such as houses, apartments, office buildings, etc., they are commonly referred to as *real estate bonds,* or *real estate mortgage bonds.*

A first mortgage bond may have a first lien on all the corporate property, or the first lien may be on only a small part of the property. It may have a second or third claim on other property of the corporation.

In theory at least, if the interest or principal on a first mortgage bond is not paid, the bondholders through the trustee can take steps for foreclosure and sale of the mortgaged property. The first mortgage bonds are supposed to be paid off in full before anything can be applied to other bonds, or any money returned to the stockholders. In practice, corporations commonly go into the hands of a receiver when they are about to fail, or have failed, and the court then prohibits the bondholders from foreclosing on the property. A reorganization plan is then worked out with the consent of a specified number of the security holders, and the bondholders get whatever treatment was agreed upon in the plan. Thus, the first mortgage bondholders may get new securities in the reorganized company, or their interests may not be disturbed. In any case they are given better treatment than the junior bondholders. The difference between first, second, third, etc., mortgages may thus be a relative rather than an absolute one.

Despite the lien on physical property, the real or practical security for a first mortgage bond, the same as for any other type of bond, is based on the earning power of the company which issues the bond. An unsecured bond issued by a prosperous company with excellent management would be a safer investment than a first mortgage bond secured by an obsolete plant of a defunct company. Fixed assets, which are the security for mortgage bonds, bring only a small percentage of their cost or book value upon forced sale. They often possess little value unless they are used by a profitable business. The real value of any business asset, particularly a fixed asset, is usually expressed in the earning power of the company.

A company which does not earn a profit cannot pay the interest on its bonds for any long period of time. And it is probable that such a company could not pay off the principal of the bonds. The obligation to the bondholders is a debt, which legally has to be paid regardless of whether or not there are any profits. Companies will continue to pay on their bonds as long as they can because of the fact that the company would fail otherwise, and be forced out of business, or have to go through a reorganization. The threat of action on the part of the bondholders will force a company to meet the bond requirements. In the event that the company is unable to meet the interest on all its bonds, it will as far as possible continue to pay the interest on its first and senior obligations even if it has to default on its other debts. In practical analysis, then, the principal value of the first lien on the property which is possessed by a first mortgage bond comes from its first claim to the earnings.

In discussing mortgage bonds we should always keep this in mind. A mortgage bond is made up of two parts. First, the promise to pay the interest and principal which is embodied in the bond, and which is based on the general credit of the corporation, the same as any other type of bond, and second, the specific security for this promise to pay the debt which is contained in the mortgage. In the event of default on a mortgage bond, the bondholders through the trustee could proceed against the corporation on its promise to pay, and ignore the particular property which is mortgaged behind the bond issue.

After getting judgment against the corporation, the bondholders may then proceed to attach, or secure a lien on, the corporate property which is not already mortgaged. But by foreclosure of the lien which the mortgage bondholders already had against the specific mortgaged property, they would be a step ahead. Also, considering the fact that the corporation has failed, the promise to pay is not worth much since there is little or nothing behind it. So the mortgage bondholders usually find that their best course of action is to proceed against the particular property which is mortgaged.

Another point worth emphasizing is that the first claim of the first mortgage bondholders applies only to the specific property which is mortgaged. In other words, if Corporation A issued a first mortgage bond against Plant X, these bonds would not have first claim against Plant Y which is owned by the company. As regards Plant Y, the first mortgage bondholders would have no better right than any unsecured creditors of the company. From the standpoint of a going concern, however, the first claim to earnings which is possessed by the bonds really gives them a first chance at earnings which are derived from the use of both the mortgaged and the unmortgaged corporation property. But if the company failed and there was a strict foreclosure, the first mortgage bondholders would have a first claim only with respect to the particular property which is mortgaged as security for the bonds.

Divisional Bonds. *Divisional bonds* are those which are secured by a mortgage on only a section or division of the company's total property. They are found almost entirely in the railroad field. In most instances they are bonds which were originally secured by the entire property of a railroad which has since been acquired by a large railroad company or system. In some cases, however, they have been issued with the security of only a part of a company's property.

Although there may also be junior mortgage bonds secured by only a division of a company's total property, the term "divisional bond" is usually applied to only a first mortgage bond.

As is true of any mortgage bond, other things being equal, the more valuable the property that is mortgaged, the more valuable the bond. If the divisional bond is issued by the consolidated company itself, or is assumed by it, then the general credit of the large company or system is also behind the bond.

Since divisional bonds are ordinarily secured by first mortgages on branches or divisions which have been consolidated into one large company or system, they are sometimes called *underlying bonds.* This means that they have a claim superior to that of later issues of mortgage bonds issued by the consolidated company against its total property. The same idea is expressed when it is said that the safest bonds are those which "lie closest to the rails."

Special Direct Lien Bonds. When a bond is secured by some special-type property of a corporation such as a terminal, bridge, dock or warehouse, it can be classified as a *special direct lien bond.* It is noted that the security constitutes a smaller part of the company's property than in the case of a divisional bond. In some instances the type of security behind the bonds is indicated by the title of the bonds such as *terminal, bridge, dock,* or *warehouse bonds*. More will be said about these when we discuss joint bonds in a later chapter.

PRIOR LIEN BONDS. Such an issue is one which is put in ahead of one or more other issues in respect to security. A corporation cannot issue such bonds, of course, without the consent of the existing bondholders (unless their bonds are subordinated debentures). It may be to the best interests of the bondholders to agree to such a prior lien bond issue, as this may be the only way a corporation can secure money when it needs it. If a company has a first and a second mortgage bond issue outstanding, and the consent of the second is obtained to place a lien in just ahead of the second, the new issue would be considered prior to the second, but not prior to the first. Usually, however, a prior lien issue takes precedence over all the other bond issues. When this is the case, the first mortgage would become a second, and the second would become a third, etc.

We have used the words "senior" and "junior" several times in connection with bond issues. A *senior* bond issue is one which comes ahead of one or more other issues from the standpoint of mortgage security. A *junior* issue is one that comes after one or more others from the standpoint of security. Thus, a second mortgage would be senior to a third, but junior to a first mortgage. The placing of a prior lien ahead of the first mortgage would have the effect of making the first mortgage bond issue junior to the senior prior lien.

When a second mortgage is placed on the property after a first mortgage, it is incorrect to call the first a prior lien. Prior liens may be first mortgages, but first mortgages are not necessarily prior ones.

SECOND, THIRD, ETC., MORTGAGE BONDS. As was stated above in connection with mortgages, when a corporation has a first mortgage on its property, the most it can mortgage in favor of a second mortgage bond issue is its equity of redemption (equitable title) after the first mortgage. And when we were discussing first mortgage bonds we indicated that in event of strict foreclosure and sale the proceeds of the property would go to pay off the first mortgage bonds in full before anything could be paid to the second mortgage bondholders. Similar reasoning applies to a third and successive mortgages.

If the company is a going concern and has not defaulted on the first mortgage bonds, and if the second mortgage bonds become due before the first, they would, of course, be paid off first.

A second mortgage bond is secured by the general credit of the company the same as a first, but its claim to the mortgaged property is junior to the first. As long as the company is able to pay the interest and principal on all its bonds, it makes little difference whether you own a first or a second mortgage bond. Some of the latter have become firsts by virtue of the first being paid off. When any mortgage is paid off, those junior to it move up and take a position one step closer to the mortgaged property.

In appraising the investment worth of a second mortgage bond the size of the first mortgage must be taken into consideration. If the amount of the first mortgage bonds outstanding is insignificant, a second mortgage would be practically as good as a first one.

Other things being equal, a company must pay a higher rate of interest on a second mortgage bond than on a first, due to the greater risk. Due to the dislike of the investing public for second or third mortgage bonds, the words *second, third,* etc., are rarely used now in the title of a bond. Where these titles are still found the bonds are likely to be old railroad obligations which have withstood reorganizations, and are now probably first mortgage bonds by virtue of the underlying bonds having been paid off.

GENERAL, CONSOLIDATED, AND REFUNDING MORTGAGE BONDS. These titles are used for junior mortgage bonds instead of *first, second,* etc., for the reason mentioned above. A *general mortgage bond* is usually one that has a junior lien on all the property. It may have a second mortgage on some property, a third on other property, and a fourth on the rest of the property. It is commonly an open-end issue with the after-acquired property clause attached. As the senior liens become due, additional general mortgage bonds under the open-end indenture are issued to pay them off. Eventually the general mortgage bond may thus become a first mortgage on part or all of the corporate property. The term *blanket* issue is often applied to a general mortgage bond issue. In some instances the terms *improvement* or *extension* are used in the title.

A *consolidated mortgage bond* is usually the same as a general mortgage bond. The name is derived from the fact that it is often used to secure money to refund or "consolidate" the other bond issues outstanding, or to effect a consolidation of several companies. In some instances the term *unified* is used for this type of bond.

When a short-term debt, such as accounts payable or short-term notes, are converted into long-term debts, such as bonds, we speak of it as *funding* the debt. If an issue of bonds is used to retire another issue of bonds we say that the debt has been *re-*

funded. A *refunding mortgage bond* would therefore be a mortgage bond which is exchanged for other bonds of the company, or is sold in order to secure the cash to retire another issue of bonds. The proceeds of a general or consolidated mortgage might be used for the same purpose, so these titles are in practice almost interchangeable. Some corporations and investment bankers prefer the title *refunding* since it places emphasis on the fact that the underlying issues will be paid off with the proceeds, and thus the refunding issue will become better secured.

In some instances a combination of these names is used for the bond title; for example, *first and refunding mortgage, first refunding mortgage, first and consolidated, first consolidated and refunding mortgage,* etc. Care should be taken not to misconstrue a bond title. For example, a "first and refunding mortgage bond" has a first mortgage on at least part of the property, although the part may be relatively small. But when the title "first refunding mortgage bond" is used, it does not indicate that it has a *first* mortgage on any property. It is the "first" *refunding mortgage bond* which the company has issued, but it may have nothing better than a second or a third lien on the corporate property. In the past many corporations have intentionally used titles which would be deceiving to the public, but they would not be approved now by the Securities and Exchange Commission.

Some corporations, particularly railroads and public utilities, have a number of bond issues outstanding. These issues were sold at different times and they may have varying rates of interest. Also the issues may be relatively small and thus they may not enjoy a wide market. Generally speaking, the wider the market, the more economical it is for the corporation to sell the bonds. Furthermore, bondholders can secure more for their bonds of a large issue. So the fashion in corporation finance is to replace small issues with one large blanket issue of bonds which has the open-end provision and the after-acquired property clause.

Questions

1. What is the nature of the security behind a mortgage bond?
2. If mortgaged property sells for less than the face value of the bonds secured by the property, is the mortgagor liable for the balance? What instrument makes him liable?
3. Indicate the difference between buying property and assuming a mortgage, and buying the property subject to the mortgage.
4. (a) Distinguish between open- and closed-end mortgage bond issues. Which type would the investor ordinarily prefer? (b) What restrictions are commonly placed on the further issuance of bonds under an open issue?

5. (a) Indicate what is meant by the "after-acquired property" clause? (b) Indicate how corporations sometimes avoid the effects of the after-acquired property clause.

6. Explain clearly the difference between a first and second mortgage bond.

7. What type of property is ordinarily behind mortgage bonds?

8. Explain what is meant by each of the following types of bonds: purchase money mortgage bonds, divisional bonds, special direct lien bonds, prior lien bonds, first general mortgage bonds, and consolidated mortgage bonds.

9. Distinguish between funding and refunding a debt.

10. Would a corporation ordinarily prefer a number of small issues of bonds, or one large issue? Why?

Problems

1. Mr. Flint borrows $5,000 on a first mortgage and $2,000 on a second mortgage to buy a house and a lot. In addition to giving the mortgagees mortgages on the property, he, of course, gives them his personal notes for the amounts stated. When Mr. Flint is unable to continue interest payments on the money borrowed, the creditors foreclose against the property. The property is purchased by Mr. Drew at the court sale. Indicate the liability, if any, of Mr. Flint after the sale, the nature of the title received by Mr. Drew, the amount received by the first mortgagee, by the second mortgagee, and by Mr. Flint if the following amounts were realized at the sale following the foreclosure action instigated by the mortgagee indicated. (Disregard court costs, taxes, etc.)

Foreclosed by	*Amount obtained from sale*
(a) First Mortgagee	$4,000
(b) First Mortgagee	6,000
(c) Second Mortgagee	1,000
(d) Second Mortgagee	3,000

2. The following was the last balance sheet presented by the New Method Corp. prior to its liquidation:

Assets		*Liabilities and Net Worth*	
Accounts receivable	$ 100,000	Accounts payable	$ 100,000
Inventory	300,000	Notes payable	200,000
Plant	1,000,000	First mortgage bonds	400,000
Deficit	200,000	Second mortgage bonds	200,000
		Preferred stock	200,000
		Common stock	500,000
Total	$1,600,000	Total	$1,600,000

Newer methods introduced by competitors caused a sharp decline in the earnings of the New Method Corp. in recent years, and the creditors forced the company into receivership. After studying the business for some months the receiver reported to the court that liquidation of the business appeared to be the solution rather than reorganization, especially since that met with the approval of the creditors. It was thought desirable to sell the assets piecemeal rather than for a lump sum. The bonds possessed a mortgage against the plant. The preferred stock had a preference over the common in respect to assets upon dissolution to the extent of $110 per share. All the stock had a par value of $100 per share.

(a) How much and what percentage on the dollar would be received by each class of creditors if the particular assets were sold for the following amounts?

Accounts Receivable	$ 50,000
Inventory	150,000
Plant	500,000

(b) Do you think that the assets were carried on the last balance sheet at an inflated figure? Why or why not?

Chapter 10

OTHER SECURED OBLIGATIONS

Collateral trust bonds

General Nature. With one exception which will be noted below, *collateral trust bonds* are secured by stocks or bonds, or both, of other companies. Although the pledged securities, which are referred to as the *collateral,* may be turned over to the trustee by means of a *chattel mortgage,* it is preferred that the word *mortgage* not be used in the title of these bonds, since it is usually understood to apply to a bond which is secured by *real* property (real estate) rather than *personal* property (of which securities are a part).

The mechanics of issuing collateral trust bonds are similar to those for mortgage bonds.

In event of default, the holders of the bonds have the right, through the trustee, to foreclose on the pledged securities, subject to the conditions stated in the indenture under which the bonds are issued. If the collateral brings an amount insufficient to pay off the bondholders, the latter would have a right against the issuer of the collateral trust bonds for any deficiency. If, on the other hand, the collateral would bring more than the amount of the bondholders' claims, the balance would go to the issuing corporation.

Although foreclosure would enable the collateral trust bondholders to gain possession of the collateral, it would not necessarily give them a right against the physical property of the issuer of the pledged securities. If the latter were bonds, then these bonds would have to be in default before the collateral trust bondholders could go against that corporation's physical property. If the pledged collateral consisted of stock, then the bondholders would end up being stockholders, and not creditors, in the company.

Reasons for Issuance. As is the case with any bond issue, collateral trust bonds are sold in order to secure funds. But we are interested in why this particular kind of a bond issue is sold. The reasons can conveniently be explained under the headings of the types of securities which are pledged.

Securities of subsidiaries. In the case of a pure holding company, the only property which it owns are the securities of its subsidiaries. So, if this corporation wants to issue a secured bond issue the only kind open to it is the collateral trust type. The corporation could sell some of its subsidiaries' securities in order to get the money, but it may desire to hold them, particularly when the securities are stocks which are needed for control purposes.

The parent company may also use collateral trust bonds as a way of economically financing its subsidiaries. The latter may be small, new, and unknown to the investing public. Furthermore, their bond issues might be too small to attract a wide market. Under these circumstances they either could not sell bonds directly, or if they could, the cost of the financing would be relatively high. So the bonds are bought by the parent who puts them up as collateral behind their collateral trust bond issue. In this way they are able to sell a bond which is secured by a mortgage on the physical properties of the subsidiaries, and also by the general credit of the large parent company. Furthermore, the issue may be large enough to attract a wide market.

Some collateral trust bonds that are backed by securities of subsidiaries are not high-grade investment securities. If the ability to pay on the part of the issuer becomes imperiled and the bondholders start looking to the collateral for the satisfaction of their claims, they may find that the same factors which have adversely affected the parent company have produced a similar effect on the subsidiaries. Bonds of the subsidiaries are, of course, better security than stocks. In some instances both subsidiary bonds and stocks are pledged behind the bonds.

When we were discussing the after-acquired property clause, it was pointed out that corporations sometimes have subsidiaries take title to property to avoid having the property covered by the lien of bonds outstanding which contain this clause. The securities of the subsidiary may then be acquired by the parent company and pledged behind a collateral trust bond issue of the parent.

Control of properties worth millions of dollars has been effected in the railroad and public utility fields on the investment of little money, through the use of collateral trust bonds. Stocks of holding companies controlling many subsidiaries are bought by top holding companies with the money obtained from the sale of collateral trust bonds secured by the stocks acquired.

Securities of independent companies. In some instances collateral trust bonds are issued against securities of independent companies which are held as investments. The question may arise why a company needing money would not sell these investment securities instead of borrowing money on them. The securities held may be those of small companies and the market for them might not be sufficiently wide to attract a good price. They may be sound bonds that will yield a good return to maturity. Also, the amount of securities held may be so relatively large that if an attempt was made to sell them all at once, the market price would break. The current market quotation for securities is for only the relatively few that are being bought and sold. For these reasons a company might prefer to keep its investments and borrow money.

Some investment companies sell bonds in an attempt to increase the rate of earnings on their stock through the leverage principle which was previously discussed (Chapter 8). Since the only assets possessed by these companies are the securities of other companies, if they issue a secured bond it will have to be the collateral trust bond.

Company's own bonds. Occasionally some corporations will issue their collateral trust bonds or notes secured by a pledge of their own mortgage bonds. This procedure may appear peculiar to the reader, but there are reasons why this might be desirable.

The coupon or face rate of interest specified in the indenture of an open-end mortgage bond issue may be so low relative to the corporation's current borrowing rate, that additional bonds could be sold only at such discounts that would arouse suspicion on the part of some investors. (Open-end indentures, however, commonly permit varying rates of interest on different series.) Or, the maturity specified in the indenture may be longer than the period for which the company needs the money. So bonds of the open issue are not sold, but rather deposited as collateral for an issue of bonds with the rate of interest or maturity desired. Instances of these kinds are, however, rare.

A more common reason is to save in interest charges. The market conditions may be such that they can borrow on notes, which have relatively short maturities, at lower interest rates than on bonds. Or, interest rates may be relatively high at the time the company needs funds, so they issue notes hoping that by the time they come due, interest rates will be lower and they can refinance the notes with longer term obligations at a lower rate than would have originally been possible. These notes are secured by the company's open-end mortgage bonds. For all practical purposes the notes can be said to be secured by a mortgage on the company's property. In fact, in the past, in the titles of some of such obligations there may appear the term *first mortgage* in addition to *collateral.*

Securities and real property. Bonds are sometimes issued which are secured not only by the pledge of securities of other companies, but also by a mortgage on a part or all of the corporation's real property. Such bonds may be given a name which indicates the dual nature of the security, such as "first mortgage and collateral trust bond."

PAYMENT OF INTEREST, DIVIDENDS, AND PRINCIPAL ON PLEDGED SECURITIES. Any cash dividends or interest received by the trustee of the collateral trust bond issue are turned over to the corporation. Stock dividends or dividends that represent a return of capital rather than profit are retained by the trustee as security for the bonds. If the corporation which issued the collateral trust bonds defaults in the payment of interest or principal on the bonds, the trustee will retain any dividends and interest which are paid on the pledged securities.

When the principal of pledged bonds is paid, the trustee retains the cash until the corporation pledges additional securities of equivalent value.

VOTING PLEDGED STOCK. If the pledged stock is not transferred to the trustee's name on the books of the issuing company, although it usually is, the corporation issuing the collateral trust bonds can exercise the voting rights on the stock. When the stock is in the name of the trustee, he will ordinarily give proxies to vote the stock to the corporation issuing the collateral trust bonds. If the latter company defaults in the payment of principal or interest on its collateral trust bonds, the trustee will exercise the voting rights in the interest of the bondholders.

SUBSTITUTION OF PLEDGED SECURITIES. The indenture under which collateral trust bonds are issued contains provisions for the substitution of pledged securities in event that any of the pledged bonds are called or mature. A similar provision is made in relation to pledged stock in event the issuer is merged into another company, consolidated with other companies, or is reorganized.

Originally the pledged securities must bear some fixed ratio to the collateral trust bonds issued. In many cases the pledged securities must equal in value the bonds issued against them, while in others the pledged securities must exceed the value of the collateral trust bonds. In the event substitution of pledged securities is necessary the indenture will provide that the same ratio be maintained, or that the value of the securities substituted shall be the same as the old securities. The effect of these two provisions is the same.

Investment Status. Like any other type of secured bond, the investment worth of collateral trust bonds depends upon the credit of the issuer, and the value of the security behind the bonds. If the bonds are issued by a company which is strong financially, the question of the value of the pledged securities is not extremely important. As the general credit of the issuer becomes worse, the importance of the collateral increases. Although the collateral trust bond is the only kind of secured bond that can be issued by a holding company, it is usually found that those which have an excellent credit standing commonly issue bonds which are not secured by the pledge of any securities.

The credit of the issuing company is therefore the prime thing to consider in purchasing collateral trust bonds. If this is questionable, then the value of the collateral should be more closely scrutinized. But a person should hesitate to buy any bond which is issued by a company of questionable credit standing.

Other things being equal, diversified collateral of independent companies would appear to be safer than the securities of subsidiaries which are affected by the same factors as the parent company. Bonds are better security than stocks of the same companies. The indenture should be carefully analyzed to determine the value of the collateral in relation to the bonds issued against it, the provisions relating to the maintenance of this relationship, and the provisions concerning the substitution of securities. Where collateral trust bonds are issued solely as a means of obtaining control of other companies on a minimum investment, they should be purchased only after a thorough investigation has shown them to be of good investment standing.

Equipment obligations

General Nature. Generally speaking, *equipment obligations* are issued by railroads or car manufacturers to finance the acquisition of rolling stock, such as cars and locomotives, and are secured by this equipment. In years past, equipment obligations were generally issued by railroads that had all of their other property mortgaged, and which were in a weak financial condition. But in more recent years they have been issued by both strong and weak roads. Approximately 10 per cent of the entire railroad debt is in the form of these obligations, and this comprises a larger portion of the total debt than do collateral trust bonds.

When acquiring rolling stock, the railroad will make a down payment, varying from 10 to 25 per cent of the cost of the equipment. Equipment obligations are then issued for the balance of the purchase price. The obligations are retired serially each six months or year, over a period usually of ten or fifteen years. The latter maturity has been more common in recent years. The obligations are issued under one of three plans which will be briefly described.

Equipment Mortgage Plan. The *equipment mortgage plan* (sometimes referred to as the New York Plan) of issuing equipment obligations is similar to that of issuing ordinary mortgage bonds which we have already discussed. The railroad makes a down payment on the equipment and the car manufacturer transfers title of the equipment to the railroad. The railroad then turns over to a trustee legal title to the equipment as security for an issue of notes or bonds. These obligations, which are called *equipment mortgage bonds,* are sold ordinarily through an investment banker to secure the money necessary to pay the balance due on the purchase price.

The rolling stock which is pledged behind the equipment mortgage bonds is a type of personal property, and the deeding of title over to the trustee is accomplished under a chattel mortgage, the same kind of mortgage that is used in connection with collateral trust bonds. When we were discussing the latter it was indicated that the term *mortgage* was not used in connection with a bond issue when the security pledged was *personal* property, rather than *real* property, but it has been customary to refer to equipment obligations issued under this plan as "equipment mortgage bonds."

Several shortcomings are present in connection with the issuance of obligations under this plan. If the railroad has outstanding any old mortgage bond issues containing the after-acquired property clause, which many of them do, these old mortgages would attach to the property the minute the railroad acquired legal title to the property, provided, of course, that the indenture specified that rolling stock would come under the claim of the after-acquired clause. This would mean that the equipment obligations would be in the nature of *second* mortgage bonds as far as the equipment was concerned.

The other shortcoming is that in event of failure of the railroad and the appointment of a receiver or trustee in bankruptcy, since the railroad has equitable title to the rolling stock, it would come under the jurisdiction of the receiver or trustee. Thus, the trustee representing the holders of the equipment obligations could not foreclose on the equipment, a situation which is true of any mortgage bondholders in respect to the mortgaged property. Because of the weaknesses mentioned, the equipment mortgage plan is rarely used.

Conditional Sale Plan. In the *conditional sale plan* the railroad makes a down payment on the equipment the same as in the plan discussed above, and issues its serial notes or bonds for the balance of the purchase price. These bonds are sold through an investment banker to the public. The car manufacturer transfers title to a trustee. The latter retains this title until the railroad has paid off all the equipment obligations at which time title to the equipment passes to the railroad. This plan is the same as is used in the sale of consumer goods on the installment plan through the conditional sale arrangement.

In some states the conditional sale plan possessed practically the same weaknesses as the equipment mortgage plan. In Pennsylvania and a few other states the courts took the attitude that when a railroad made a down payment on the equipment and got possession of the property, that it acquired title to the equipment. This being the case, any bonds that possessed the after-acquired property clause that it might have outstanding would have a claim on the equipment, and thus the holders of the equipment obligations would have a junior claim to the equipment.

Even if the particular state in which the obligations were issued recognized the senior claim of the equipment obligations, the rolling stock might be located in states which took a different view in regard to the conditional sale arrangement, and the rolling stock might be attached by other creditors. Also, in those states which considered that the railroad received title to the equipment financed under this plan, in event of receivership of the company, the equipment would come under the jurisdiction of the receiver. These shortcomings led to the adoption of the Philadelphia Plan which will be discussed below.

In recent years statutes have been adopted in Pennsylvania, and perhaps all the other states which took a similar attitude toward the conditional sale as Pennsylvania, which specifically state that the holders of the equipment obligations issued under the conditional sale plan have first claim against the equipment. Despite this change, the conditional sale plan is rarely used when equipment obligations are sold to the public. The conditional sale plan has been used in a number of instances in recent years when the equipment obligations have been sold directly to large commercial banks, which hold them as investments.

Philadelphia Plan. The great bulk of the equipment obligations outstanding are issued under the *Philadelphia Plan.* This plan was devised to overcome the weaknesses inherent in the equipment mortgage and the conditional sale plans. From a legal standpoint, the documents used in connection with the acquisition of the equipment and the issuance of the obligations are carefully worded in order that no creditor or court can say that the railroad has any title to the equipment prior to the time the last equipment obligation is retired.

Title to the equipment passes directly from the car manufacturer to the trustee. (It will be recalled that in the equipment mortgage plan, the railroad got title, and then transferred it over to the trustee.) The railroad then *leases* the equipment from the trustee. That is why this plan is commonly called the *lease plan.* The railroad makes a down payment of from 10 to 25 per cent of the cost of the equipment. In effect this is really an advance rental payment. Equipment obligations are then sold through an investment banker to secure the necessary amount of money to pay the car manufacturer the balance of from 90 to 75 per cent, depending upon the amount of the down payment.

The equipment obligations sold under the Philadelphia Plan are in the nature of certificates of beneficial interest in the equipment and the lease. They are sometimes called *equipment trust certificates,* or *car trust certificates.* To the extent that they are certificates of beneficial interest in the equipment and the lease, they are more like stocks than bonds. But the railroad which leases the equipment indorses on the certificates a guarantee that it will carry out the lease agreement, and pay the proper rentals to enable the trustee to pay the dividends (really more like interest) on the certificates, and to meet the principal amount of the certificates as they mature. Because of the fixed maturity, the certificates resemble a bond. And because of the railroad's guarantee to pay the rentals necessary to meet the dividends and principal amount of the certificates, the latter are similar to bonds both in respect to the rate of return and obligation to pay back the principal amount.

The certificates, however, are not issued by the railroad—they are issued by the trustee who holds legal title to the equipment for the benefit of the certificate holders. It is only because of the agreement relating to the rental and the guarantee on the certificates that the railroad becomes obligated on the certificates.

Since the railroad has no title whatsoever to equipment while it is being financed, any bonds with the after-acquired property clause which it has outstanding would have no claim to this equipment. Furthermore, in the event of receivership of the road, the equipment will not come under the jurisdiction of the receiver or trustee in bankruptcy. This means that if the railroad does not keep up the rental payments even in receivership, the trustee can rent

---

NEW ISSUE

$2,250,000

New York, New Haven and Hartford Equipment Trust of 1956, No. 1

4⅝% Equipment Trust Certificates

To be dated July 1, 1956. To mature $150,000 each July 1 from 1957 to 1971.

Issued under the Philadelphia Plan with 20% cash equity

MATURITIES AND YIELDS

1957	4.25%	1962	4.75%	1967	4.75%
1958	4.35	1963	4.75	1968	4.75
1959	4.45	1964	4.75	1969	4.75
1960	4.55	1965	4.75	1970	4.75
1961	4.65	1966	4.75	1971	4.75

These Certificates are offered subject to prior sale, when, as and if issued and received by us, subject to approval of the Interstate Commerce Commission.

SALOMON BROS. & HUTZLER

DREXEL & CO. UNION SECURITIES CORPORATION

STROUD & COMPANY
Incorporated

August 1, 1956.

Figure 3. Equipment trust certificate. The above appeared in *The Wall Street Journal,* August 1, 1956.

the equipment to another railroad, or sell it. The threat of this action will cause the receiver to continue the rental payments even if he has to default in other obligations issued by the railroad.

Since the Philadelphia Plan is the one which is practically always used, the discussion which follows will apply particularly to this plan.

Terms of the Lease. The equipment obligations are retired serially, that is, a fixed amount of them come due each year. Usually the same amount is retired each year beginning at the end of the first year. The rental payments are arranged to retire the amount coming due each year and to pay the return on the outstanding certificates.

In the event that the railroad defaults in its rental payments, or fails to live up to other covenants in the agreement, all of the certificates become due immediately. The railroad agrees that, if this occurs, it will at its own expense deliver the equipment to the trustee at places which he designates. The trustee can thereupon rent the equipment to another road or sell it to secure the money to pay off the outstanding certificates. In addition to the rental payments, the railroad agrees to the following:

1. To keep the equipment properly repaired, and to replace any that is destroyed.
2. To keep the equipment insured.
3. To pay all taxes on the equipment.
4. To indemnify the trustee for any claims arising out of the ownership and use of the equipment.
5. To attach a metal plate to each piece of equipment stating the name of the trustee who owns the equipment.
6. To deliver the equipment to the trustee in event of default in the rental payments or failure to abide by other covenants in the agreement.
7. To file periodically with the trustee a statement showing the condition and location of the equipment.

Upon payment of the last rental installment, the trustee agrees to execute a bill of sale transferring title to the equipment to the railroad. If the road has any bonds outstanding with the after-acquired property clause, they would attach themselves to the equipment at the time that the railroad acquired title. But this is not a serious matter because the railroad has been able to finance the equipment with a senior obligation. In event of receivership after the road has acquired title, the equipment would come under the jurisdiction of the court. But here again this is of little importance because the equipment has been completely financed. It was when the railroad had to acquire money for the acquisition of the equipment that it was desirable that the equipment not come under the jurisdiction of the receiver or trustee in bankruptcy.

SECURITY BEHIND THE OBLIGATIONS. The rolling stock which is financed with equipment obligations wears out faster than other property, such as buildings. At first thought this might make it appear that the equipment obligations are poorly secured. But this is not the case. In the first place the obligations are issued only up to from 75 to 90 per cent of the cost of the equipment. So some margin of safety for the certificate holders exists from the start. The rolling stock will last at least twenty years, while the obligations are paid off over a period of ten to fifteen years. Furthermore, since the obligations are retired serially every year, they are being paid off at a faster rate than the equipment is depreciating. In other words, despite the relatively rapid depreciation of the equipment, the equity behind each $1,000 of obligations increases, rather than decreases, as the equipment wears out. This point can be illustrated with the diagram on the following page.

The margin of safety behind equipment trust obligations during their entire life is illustrated by the diagram in Figure 4. The original cost of the equipment, which is $3,000,000, is represented by the line A–X. It is assumed that the equipment is depreciated annually on a straight line basis over a 20-year period (no salvage value assumed). This is represented by the line A–Z. It is assumed that 20 per cent of the cost of the equipment, or $600,000, is paid at the time of purchase. This is represented by the line A–B. Equipment trust obligations in the amount of $2,400,000 are issued to complete payment for the equipment. It is assumed that the obligations are paid off in equal annual installments over a period of 15 years. The amount of obligations outstanding at any time is indicated by the line B–Y.

The amount of obligations outstanding and the depreciated value of the equipment at any time can be found quickly by drawing a line perpendicular to line X–Y and extending the line upward to intersect lines B–Y and A–Z. The margin of safety would be represented by the part of the perpendicular line which is between lines B–Y and A–Z. At the time of issue there is a margin of safety of $600,000. But there is only $1.25 in property behind each $1.00 of obligations. At the end of 10 years, there would be only $800,000 in obligations outstanding against equipment with a depreciated value of $1,500,000. Thus, the margin of safety would then be

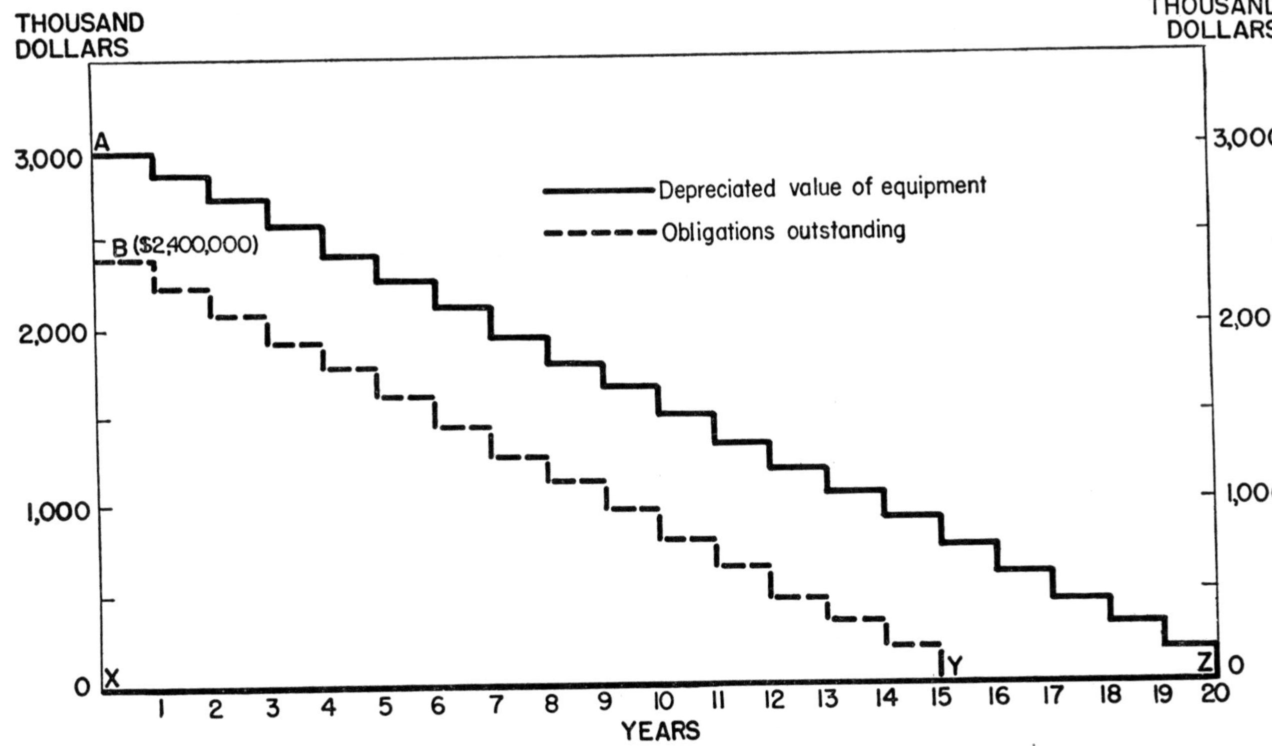

Figure 4. Relationship of equipment trust obligations to depreciated value of equipment

$700,000. At this time there would be $1.87½ behind every $1.00 of obligations. It is therefore evident that despite the depreciation in the property the obligations are better secured as time goes on.

INVESTMENT WORTH OF EQUIPMENT OBLIGATIONS. Equipment obligations are among the best, if not the best, railroad securities obtainable. Even roads that are financially weak have been able to secure money at a relatively low rate through the sale of these obligations. Following is a summary of the reasons why equipment obligations have such a high investment rating.

1. Rolling stock, which is the security for equipment obligations, is perhaps the most valuable property possessed by a railroad. Some branch lines, terminals, shops, etc., may be abandoned, and the road can get along, but it cannot operate without cars and locomotives. Generally speaking, the more valuable the security for a bond or certificate, the more valuable is the obligation. This is particularly true of equipment obligations.

In the case of most securities, the general credit of the issuing company is more important to the security holder than is the property which is pledged or mortgaged behind the obligations. Although the general credit of the railroad is important in the case of equipment obligations, the equipment which is behind the obligations is perhaps more important. This results from the fact that in the event that the company defaults in the payment of its rentals, the equipment can be rented to another road, or sold, and the obligations can be paid off.

2. The equipment is standardized and can be used by other roads. Hence in event of default it might be sold to another railroad.

3. The rolling stock is built on wheels and is on a standard-gauge track and can therefore be easily transported and rented or sold to another railroad in event of default.

4. A railroad is a type of public utility and its services are essential. Thus if it fails, the receiver or trustee and later the reorganized company will need the equipment.

5. The equipment obligations are paid off faster than the equipment depreciates, so that there is an increase in the equity of the outstanding obligations.

6. If the Philadelphia or conditional sale plan is used, in event of default the trustee or seller can seize the equipment, even if the company is in the receiver's hands. Section 77 of the Bankruptcy Act specifically provides that nothing in the Act will prevent the owner from taking possession of the equipment in compliance with the provisions of a lease or conditional sale contract.

Good Record. The superior nature of equipment obligations is evident from the experience of the past. Prior to the depression of the 1930's, there were only a few instances of where it was necessary to repossess the equipment or where other securities rather than cash were given to the holders of equipment obligations.

During the depression of the 1930's, companies having one third of the railroad mileage of the country were in the hands of receivers. Defaults in ordinary railroad bonds were common, but the record for equipment obligations was good. Only three railroads found it necessary to extend the maturity of the obligations. In only two railroads was it necessary to have the holders of such obligations exchange their securities for receivers' or trustees' certificates having the same par value as the obligations, but bearing a lower rate of return. Only in the case of one railroad did the holders of such obligations lose money. The Florida East Coast Railway defaulted and the equipment was sold by the trustee. The holders of its equipment obligations (Series D) received in 1937 only $440.58 for each $1,000 certificate. In 1944, an additional $152.96 was paid on each $1,000 certificate from the deficiency judgment. In 1951, the final payment of $108.27 was made on each $1,000 certificate. This made a total of $701.08 which was received for each $1,000 certificate.[1]

During the depression of the 1930's, when the other bonds of a number of roads which were in receivership were selling at only a small fraction of their face value, the equipment obligations were selling at a premium.

The high investment standing of equipment obligations is also reflected in the yield. In many instances these obligations sell on a lower yield basis than do the senior mortgage bonds. In fact the principal disadvantage of these obligations is the relatively low yield. Some investors do not favor them because of their relatively short maturities.

Due to the fact that equipment obligations mature serially, they are quoted in terms of yield, rather than price. The quoted bid-and-ask prices seen in the newspapers are the close for the preceding day and are an average for all the maturities. Quotations on particular maturities can be obtained from investment dealers.

Use in Other Fields. Although the primary use of equipment obligations has been by railroads, they have also been used in other fields. Oil, coal and steel companies have used these obligations to

[1] Harry G. Guthmann and Herbert E. Dougall, *Corporate Financial Policy* (3d ed.; Englewood Cliffs, N. J.: Prentice-Hall, Inc., 1955), p. 135 *n.*

finance their own cars. Marine companies have used them to buy ships. In a few instances they have been used by industrial companies to finance machinery. In recent years some of the commercial airlines have used equipment obligations to finance new planes. When used for this purpose their maturity has been shorter than in the case of railroads, five years being typical.

Equipment obligations issued by industrial companies do not have the same investment standing as those issued by railroads. Several things account for this difference. The equipment behind the industrial issue is less standardized and it usually becomes obsolete faster than railroad cars. Furthermore, an industrial is subject to more competition than a railroad, and in event of failure it may be liquidated rather than reorganized.

Land trust certificates

GENERAL NATURE. Real estate is often financed through the issuance of *land trust certificates*. Legal title to a particular piece of land is transferred to a bank or trust company which serves as trustee. A definite number of certificates of beneficial interest representing equitable ownership of an undivided part of the land are sold to the public to obtain the money necessary to acquire the land. These certificates, which are commonly called *land trust certificates*, are similar to equipment obligations issued under the Philadelphia Plan.

Although the legal nature of land trust certificates is similar to that of stocks, in actual practice they are more similar to bonds. The usual denomination is $1,000, although in some instances it is $500, and in a few cases as low as $100. They bear a fixed rate of return similar to bonds. The money to pay the return on the certificates comes from the rental payments made by the lessee of the property. Although the certificates do not have a maturity date, the contract may give the lessee an option to purchase the land at a specified price at a designated time. In such instances a call price, usually a premium over the face value, would be stated in the certificates.

INVESTMENT STATUS. In final analysis the investment worth of land trust certificates depends upon the value of the particular land. Since the income to pay the return on the certificates comes from the rental paid by the lessee, the credit of the lessee is an important consideration. If the site is an important one, probably the lessee can profitably use the property and will be able to make the rental payments. If a default in the rental payments is made, the claim of certificate holders, through the trustee, for ground rent would come ahead of any obligations that had been issued to finance a building on the land. If a particular lessee cannot meet the rental payments, the property might be leased to someone else. But as already stated, the value of the particular site may finally determine the financial ability of the lessee to meet the rental payments.

When land trust certificates are issued, a building is either already erected on the land, or it is soon to be constructed. Barren land would ordinarily bring little in the way of rent, and therefore any land trust certificates issued against the land may be of little value.

The agreement provides that the lessee shall pay the real estate taxes levied against the land. Since the certificates represent fractional ownership in the land, some courts have classified them as real estate and therefore have held that they are not subject to the personal property tax in the state. The income from the certificates is of course subject to the income tax.

Naturally, the value of land trust certificates is affected by the fluctuations in real estate values. Buyers of the certificates, the same as any other buyers of real estate, should see to it that they are not purchased when real estate values are highly inflated. Some shrinkage in land values could be stood by the certificate holders, however, since the value of the building would add to their margin of safety.

The relatively large denomination of land trust certificates tends to limit their market in the same manner as was discussed in connection with bonds. Since they are issued against a particular site, the value of which may be known only in the particular community, their market tends to be local in nature. Although the lessee may reserve the right to buy the land and retire the certificates, the certificates do not have a due date. Thus, the holder may have to sell them in the market in order to get back his money.

If the land is such that land trust certificates may be issued, an owner may obtain much more by the sale through the certificates than by the ordinary method of selling the land. This follows from the fact that through the use of the certificates the land is sold in small units to many buyers. When a company wishes to build a building or store on the land, the land trust certificate arrangement of getting the land through a lease will obviate the necessity of providing a large amount of cash to purchase the land. In some instances companies like department stores will sell the land on which their store is located through the use of land trust certificates and thus have the cash which would otherwise be tied up permanently in the land to use in their business.

Leasehold mortgage bonds

General Nature. *Leasehold mortgage bonds* are issued to finance buildings which are erected on leased land. Many companies do not want to tie up a considerable amount of money in fixed assets, such as land. So the company, which contemplates operating a department store, for example, leases the land for a long period of time. In many instances the lessee has the right to purchase the land at a designated price. In some cases the owner wants to sell the land rather than lease it. If this is the situation, the land may be sold through the land trust certificate arrangement described above, and then the company may lease the land from the trustee.

In order to help finance the building on the leased land, the company then issues bonds which are secured by the leasehold. If only one mortgage is issued, the bonds would have a first claim against the leasehold and would be referred to as "first leasehold mortgage bonds." Provision is made for the retirement of the bonds before the termination of the lease.

Investment Status. Despite the fact that leasehold mortgage bonds may have a first claim against the leasehold, they are in effect second mortgage bonds. This follows from the fact that the owner of the land (the land trust certificate holders in case they are issued) really has first claim against the building for the ground rent. Any shrinkage in real estate values would thus be felt by the holders of the leasehold mortgage bonds, and their equity would be wiped out before the holders of the land trust certificates would be affected. Because of this the leasehold bonds as a class are not rated highly as investment securities.

From what has been said it is obvious that bonds which are secured by the land as well as the improvements on the land are much better investments than those which are secured only by a leasehold.

Questions

1. (a) How do collateral trust bonds differ from mortgage bonds? (b) If it becomes necessary for the holders of collateral trust bonds to foreclose against the collateral, can they then foreclose against the real property of the issuer of the securities which are deposited as collateral? Explain.

2. What are the various reasons why a corporation might issue a collateral trust bond rather than another kind of bond issue?

3. Who is entitled to vote corporate stock which is pledged as security for a collateral trust bond issue?

4. Explain the difference between the three plans under which equipment trust obligations may be issued.

5. Why do equipment-trust obligations, particularly those issued under the Philadelphia Plan, rate so high as investment securities?

6. Would you recommend equipment obligations for the average investor?

7. How do you account for the way equipment trust obligations are quoted in the market?

8. Indicate the nature of land trust certificates and explain the circumstances under which they are issued.

9. Why might an investor prefer land trust certificates over the purchase of the land directly?

10. Indicate the nature of leasehold mortgage bonds and the circumstances under which they are leased. Do they have first claim against a building which is erected on the leased land? Explain.

Problems

1. The Northern R. R. Co. has among its bonds outstanding a mortgage issue containing the after-acquired property clause. The company is going to buy 2,000 additional freight cars for which it will have to pay $12,000,000. Considering its other needs for cash, the company cannot use more than $2,400,000 of its cash in acquiring the equipment.

(a) What type of obligations would you recommend that the company issue to provide the necessary money? Why? (b) Under what "plan" would you recommend that these securities be issued? Why? (c) Are these securities stocks or bonds? Explain.

2. Assume that equipment trust obligations to the amount of $9,600,000 are issued to finance the acquisition of the equipment mentioned in the above problem and that they are to be retired in 15 equal annual installments. Further assume that the average life of the freight cars is 20 years.

(a) How many dollars in property value are behind each dollar of obligations at the beginning of the first year? At the end of 5 years? At the end of 10 years? At the end of 14 years?

3. Look up the quotations of equipment obligations of several railroads.

(a) Explain the meaning of these quotations. (b) Compare the yield (return to the investor) on these obligations with some of the senior bonds of the same railroad. Assume investment at current prices. Judging from your results, which do you believe can be purchased with less risk? Why is this true?

4. The Drive-In Shopping Center Co. acquired eight lots from Mr. Neil on which to erect a building. The lots were acquired through the issuance to the public of $400,000 in land trust certificates. The building was financed by a $500,000 issue of first mortgage leasehold bonds. The certificates yielded the investor 5 per cent on the par value, and the bonds had a contract rate of 7 per cent. Both the certificates and the bonds had a face value of $1,000. The company leased the land from the First Trust Co., which acted as trustee for the certificate holders.

(a) Who owned the land? The building? (b) In the event the enterprise was a failure, who would have first claim against the land? Against the building? (c) Why didn't the company buy the land instead of leasing it? (d) Why was the rate of return higher on the bonds than on the certificates? How much higher was it, expressed in terms of percentage? (e) Do you think that Mr. Neil would prefer this means of sale rather than selling the land to one party for cash? Why?

Chapter 11

UNSECURED BONDS

MEANING OF UNSECURED. In the two preceding chapters we discussed secured bonds. These, as we have seen, are backed by a lien on real or personal property. When bonds are not so secured they are commonly referred to as *unsecured bonds*. All bonds, whether or not they are secured, are really backed by the general credit of the issuing corporation. Some authors, therefore, refer to unsecured bonds, as bonds secured by *general credit*. But it should be kept in mind that bonds which are secured by a lien on property are also secured by the general credit of the issuing company.

Included in this chapter are some bonds that are secured by a property lien. These are discussed here because their principal security is the general credit of the issuing, assuming or guaranteeing company.

As a class, secured bonds of course have a higher investment rating than unsecured bonds. The secured bonds of any particular company are safer than the unsecured bonds issued by it. But the unsecured bonds of one company may be a safer investment than the first mortgage bonds of another company. The bonds issued by the United States government, which are the safest in the world today, would be classed as unsecured bonds.

Both in England and the United States the first bonds issued by railroads were unsecured; mortgage bonds developed later.[1] Even today mortgage bonds are rarely issued in England. As pointed out earlier, too much weight should not be placed on the mortgage phase of a bond. From a going-concern standpoint, the ability of a company to meet the bond interest depends upon the earnings. Even in respect to the principal of the bond, the worth of mortgaged property depends upon what it will earn. So in final analysis the real worth of the mortgaged property behind a bond issue is expressed by the general credit of the issuing company. And

[1] Arthur Stone Dewing, *The Financial Policy of Corporations* (5th ed.; New York: The Ronald Press Co., 1953), p 215.

it is the general credit of the company which is behind the so-called unsecured bonds.

It should not be inferred from what has just been said that unsecured bonds of a company are just as good as its secured bonds. In fact, the reverse of this was stated above. The earnings will ordinarily be applied to the first mortgage bonds before the junior bonds receive any interest. In event of default, the first mortgage bonds are legally entitled to payment in full from the proceeds of the mortgaged property before the junior bonds receive anything.

Assumed bonds

Nature of Assumed Bonds. These are issued by a company which is later absorbed by another firm which takes on the obligation to pay the interest and principal on the bonds. About 80 per cent of the assumed bonds now in existence are those of railroads. The balance is found in the public utility and industrial fields. When the Kaiser-Fraser Corp. acquired the assets of Graham-Paige Motors Corp. in 1947, it assumed the Graham-Paige Motors Corp. Debenture 4's, which came due in 1956.

The assets of one company are acquired by another company either through a merger or a reorganization. Both mergers and reorganizations have been common in the railroad field, hence such assumed bonds are common. Our railroad systems have been built up by the mergers and consolidations of smaller companies. When a large system acquires the assets of a small railroad there are several things that might be done with the bonds of the latter company. They could be called in, if the call feature was in the contract. But that would take additional financing on the part of the system. In many instances, however, the bonds were not callable. They could be bought up in the market, but when it would become known that the large system was buying up the bonds, the holders would demand a considerable premium for the bonds. This might make their purchase too expensive. Hence the easiest and perhaps the cheapest thing to do would be to let the bonds of the merged company remain outstanding. When the large system acquires the assets of the small company it would thereupon assume the outstanding bonds.

Aside from mergers, practically all the rest of the assumed bonds have arisen through reorganizations. When a company fails and goes through a foreclosure sale, some of the bonds of the old company may be left "undisturbed," and thus they are assumed by the new reorganized company.

Nature of the Security behind the Bonds. In the following discussion we will suppose that the assumed bond has arisen through a merger. The assumption of the bonds may be by formal agreement, or it may be implied. In some instances the assumption obligation is printed or stamped on the face of the bonds. In other cases it does not appear on the bonds, but rather is contained in a supplemental agreement as one of the terms of the sale of the assets. In a few instances there is no formal agreement. But the courts have held that if one corporation acquires the assets of another company and the latter loses its identity and passes out of existence as a separate company, the bonds of the merged company are automatically assumed by the merging company.

What is the security behind an assumed bond? In the first place, the bonds have whatever security they had in the issuing company. Thus, if they were mortgage bonds, they still retain a lien on the specific property which is mortgaged. They may be senior or junior mortgage bonds or debenture (i.e., unsecured) bonds. The general credit of the issuing company is of course no longer behind the bonds since this company has ceased to exist. In addition to any mortgage, by virtue of the assumption, they become general credit obligations of the assuming company. Thus, they are on an equal footing with any other unsecured obligations, so far as the assuming company is concerned.

Investment Status. Because of the dual nature of the security, the investment rating of assumed bonds is sometimes a little difficult to determine. A company may assume a senior, a junior, and a debenture issue of another company. Although all of these rank equally so far as the assuming company is concerned, the senior mortgage, particularly if it is on a main line of a railroad, will have a much higher investment rating than the other issues. In event of failure of the assuming company, if its properties are worth no more than the amount of its senior bonds, then the assumed bonds would have to look to whatever security they had in the issuing property for satisfaction.

Although, as has already been stated, assumed bonds may be mortgage bonds (as regards the issuing company) it is noted that they are discussed in this chapter dealing with unsecured bonds. This was done partly as a matter of convenience, but partly also because the principal security of an assumed bond may be the general credit of the assuming company rather than the mortgage of the issuing company.

Guaranteed bonds

Nature of Bonds. A guaranteed bond is one on which the payment of interest or principal, or as usual both, is guaranteed by another company. In some instances it applies to the interest only, and in a few cases only the principal is guaranteed. The guarantee is usually stated on the face or reverse side of the bond, in which case the bond may be referred to as *stamped* or *endorsed*. This is commonly done when the guarantee is direct and is made at the time the bond is issued. In the case of a lease or consolidation, the guarantee may be stated in a supplemental agreement rather than on the bond itself. Guaranteed bonds arise in one of the following ways.

Lease. Guaranteed bonds, particularly in the railroad field, have commonly arisen through a lease. Company A may lease the property or road of Company B and, as one of the conditions of the lease, guarantee the interest and principal on B's bonds.

The purchase of property such as railroads requires a considerable amount of money, but the lease method offers a way of acquiring the use of the property without the immediate outlay of a large sum of money. The amount of the rental payments may be just sufficient to pay the interest on the bonds and the company's taxes. In some instances the rental payments also cover the dividends on the company's stock. In such instances, the dividends on the stock also would be guaranteed. Equipment trust obligations issued in connection with a lease, discussed in the preceding chapter, are a type of guaranteed security.

Financing a subsidiary. Parent companies sometimes guarantee the interest and principal on their subsidiary companies' bonds. The subsidiary may be small and relatively unknown, and thus it either could not sell its bonds or only at a higher interest rate. The parent company may possess good credit, and its guarantee of the bonds would enable them to be sold at a relatively low rate of interest. This would enable the subsidiary to pay more dividends to the parent. The guarantee would probably be contained in the bond. Many guaranteed bonds of this kind are found in the public utility field.

Consolidation. Guaranteed bonds arising through a lease were discussed above. They may also arise through other forms of combination. In some instances a company may acquire controlling interest in another company by agreeing among other things to guarantee the interest and principal on the bonds of the other company. It is to be noted that the company whose bonds are guaranteed remains in existence as a separate entity. If its assets are merged into the acquiring company, then the bonds are really "assumed," as explained above, regardless of whether they are referred to as guaranteed or assumed bonds.

Other instances. Guaranteed bonds sometimes arise through other methods than those listed above, but in some instances these are not strictly in the realm of corporation finance. In the case of small corporations some of the officers must personally endorse or guarantee their corporation's bonds before they can be sold, especially since the depression scare.

Prior to 1930, many real estate bonds were guaranteed by a building corporation or real estate holding company. Many of these bonds were issued against highly inflated values. With the depression which began in 1929, rental payments sufficient to meet the interest could not be obtained. The assets of the guaranteeing corporation were so small compared with the amount of its guarantee that they quickly failed and the guarantees meant little or nothing.

In the early history of this country many of the states guaranteed private loans that were made for the purpose of financing banks, canals, and railroads. Many of these ventures were unsuccessful and the states had to bear the loss. As a result of this experience, many state constitutions now prohibit the states from lending their credit to private business ventures.

INVESTMENT WORTH OF GUARANTEED BONDS. When guaranteed bonds which are guaranteed both as to interest and principal arise through a lease, the terms of the lease should extend beyond the maturity of the bond, as is usually the case, otherwise the guarantee of principal would mean little. Furthermore, the rental payments should be sufficient to pay not only the interest, but also to provide for the retirement of the principal.

The security behind guaranteed bonds is usually considered to be dual in nature: the obligation of the issuing company and the obligation of the guaranteeing company, and for purposes of analysis we should add a third—any mortgaged property of the issuer which may be behind the bonds. In a sense this is included in the obligation of the issuer, but we want to list it separately for proper emphasis.

In the case of railroad guaranteed bonds which arise through a lease of a railroad line, the general credit of the issuing company usually is not strong. The company probably was not very successful in operating as an independent line, and therefore felt that its security holders would be benefited by leasing itself to a large company or system. At the time of the guarantee probably the most important security behind the bonds is the general credit of the guaranteeing company. This is why this type of bond is commonly discussed in connection with unsecured bonds, although it may be backed by a mortgage on the property of the issuer. In practice guaranteed bonds frequently go by the name of the guaranteeing company.

The real test of a guaranteed bond, however, comes when the guaranteeing company gets into financial difficulties. Since the bonds are secured only by the general credit of this company, any mortgage bonds that the latter has outstanding will come ahead of the guaranteed bonds. The company may try to get the holders of the guaranteed bonds to accept some type of settlement which may amount to a repudiation of the guarantee. According to the Bankruptcy Act, if two thirds of the bondholders agree to a settlement the court can force the other bondholders to accept it.

In the event that the general credit of the guaranteeing company means nothing, the bondholders will have to fall back on the security of the issuing company. Probably the general credit of this company would be poor at this time, and the mortgaged property may not be of much value. If, however, the property consisted of a main line (or part of it) of a railroad, the company might lease itself to the reorganized company or to another railroad. Where the mortgaged property is indispensable to the operation of the system, then the bonds may not be asked to accept a compromise, or if the company is reorganized, they may be given good treatment.

In final analysis then, the investment worth of a guaranteed bond may depend upon the value of the property which is mortgaged behind it. This is borne out in practice. Different bonds of the same road, or bonds of different companies, all of which are guaranteed by a particular company, and thus are backed by the same general credit of the guaranteeing company, will sell on different yield bases as a result of variations in the issuing companies' security.

Guaranteed Bonds and Guaranteed Stocks Compared. In many instances when the interest and principal of a company's bonds are guaranteed, the dividends on its stock are also guaranteed by the same company. It should be noted that since stocks do not become due at any time, the principal amount represented by the stock is not guaranteed.

Since the guarantee puts the general credit of the guaranteeing company behind the securities, the obligation assumed on the stock for dividends is just as strong as the interest assumption on the bonds. In other words, the holders of the guaranteed stock would be in the position of general unsecured creditors of the guaranteeing company with respect to the dividend.

If the guaranteeing company fell into such financial condition that the guarantee would mean nothing, then the holders of the guaranteed bonds and stocks would revert to their original status as regards the issuing company. This means that the bondholders are the creditors and would, in event of default, have a right against the property of the issuer. The stockholders, being the owners, would have no right against the issuer's property.

Every company is obligated to pay its own bonds; but when we speak of a guaranteed bond we refer to one which is guaranteed by *another* company. Likewise, a guaranteed stock is one on which the dividends have been guaranteed by another company.

Joint bonds

NATURE OF JOINT BONDS. These are bonds on which the interest and principal are guaranteed by *two or more* companies. Like the assumed and guaranteed bonds, they commonly arise in the railroad field. When several railroads want to build and use in common some facility such as a terminal, dock, wharf, or bridge, they usually incorporate a separate company to build and operate it. This facilitates the procedure and also prevents any bond issues containing the after-acquired property clause, which any of the railroads may have outstanding, from attaching themselves to the new property.

The new corporation then issues its bonds to secure the money necessary to build the project. These are commonly secured by a first mortgage on the property. In order to make them marketable at a comparatively low rate of interest, the companies which are to use the property jointly and severally guarantee the payment of the interest and principal on the bonds. It should thus be noted that a joint bond is not jointly *issued* by two or more companies. It is issued by *one* company, but *jointly guaranteed* by the *two* or more companies. It should likewise be noted that although the joint bond is guaranteed, we reserve the term *guaranteed* to apply to a bond which is guaranteed by only *one* company. In the usual joint bond, it is *jointly and severally* guaranteed. This means that all the companies collectively guarantee the issue, and furthermore, that each one guarantees it. Thus, if any of the companies could not make good, the others could be held.

The stock of the corporation which is formed to take title to the property is divided up among the companies which will use the facility, and rental payments are made by these companies according to the use they will make of the property. The rents collected go to pay the interest on the guaranteed bonds and the company's taxes.

Security of the Bonds. The real security behind joint bonds is the general credit of the guaranteeing companies rather than that of the issuing company or the particular property which is mortgaged. This property is of a special nature that is usually of value only to the companies which use it. If it ceases to be of value to the guaranteeing firms, it would ordinarily not be of use to others. As long as the general credit of the guaranteeing companies is good, the guarantee will mean something, and the bonds will therefore be good.

If the guaranteeing companies fail, they will probably go through a reorganization. If the particular property which is mortgaged is no longer of any value to the companies, the guarantee may be repudiated when the court so decides. If the other property of the companies is fully covered by senior liens, the holders of the guaranteed bonds can do nothing about it. Needless to say, the general credit of the issuing company at this time would be nil. If, on the other hand, the property behind the guaranteed bonds is indispensable to the operation of the reorganized companies, the guarantee will be respected and the bonds will come out of the reorganization in good shape.

From what has been said it is obvious that joint bonds, perhaps even more so than assumed and guaranteed bonds, should be classed as unsecured (i.e., bonds secured only by general credit) rather than secured bonds. An example of a joint bond is the Cleveland Union Terminals Company First Mortgage 3¼ Per Cent Serial Bonds, which are secured by a first mortgage on the terminal (together with an after-acquired property clause) and the joint and several guarantee by The New York Central R.R. Co., The Cleveland, Cincinnati, Chicago and St. Louis Ry. Co., and the New York, Chicago & St. Louis R.R. Co., by endorsement.

Receivers' and trustees' certificates

Nature of Receivers' and Trustees' Certificates. When a corporation goes into the hands of a receiver in equity or trustee in bankruptcy because of failure or threatened failure, it is practically always in dire need of cash. While in the courts' hands, the corporate officials would not be permitted to sell new securities. Furthermore, considering the financial condition of the company at this time, no one would buy ordinary corporate securities. But additional cash may be a necessity in order to operate.

The solution of the problem is the issuance of receivers' or trustees' certificates. *Receivers' certificates* are issued when the company is in equity receivership, and *trustees' certificates* when the company is undergoing reorganization under the Bankruptcy Act; but since the nature of these two obligations is the same, we will use the term *receivers' certificates* in our discussion.

Such certificates are short-term notes issued by the receiver under authority of the court which is administering the receivership. The courts say that the certificates are not the obligation of the company, but rather of the receiver. Despite this fact there is no case on record in which the receiver or the judge ever paid anything out of his own pocket on a receivers' certificate. They are paid off from the assets of the company. The money necessary to pay them may come from the earnings of the company, or from the proceeds of a sale of new securities, or from an assessment of old security holders. In a practical sense, therefore, the certificates are similar to obligations of the company.

Priority Position. There is a common belief that receivers' certificates have a priority ahead of all the other obligations of the corporation. This is not necessarily the case. Their claim depends upon what specific priority the court gives them. It is customary for the court to give them a claim ahead of all securities which are in default and which will probably have to undergo some sacrifice in the reorganization. But they ordinarily would not be given priority over a senior issue of bonds which was not in default and which would be "undisturbed" in the reorganization. The priority is given by virtue of a court order rather than by the formal execution of a mortgage.

Since the certificates must be paid off from the earnings of the company or from money which it collects, they are really considered to be secured more by the general credit of the company than by the claim on property, and that is why they are discussed in this chapter dealing with general credit obligations.

In some instances a court will authorize subsequent issues of receivers' certificates. These may rank on equal footing with the ones previously issued or ahead or behind them according to the specific claim given them by the court.

The court will see to it that the certificates are paid off or that adequate provision has been made for their retirement, before receivership will be lifted. In some instances the failure is so serious that the holders of the receivers' certificates will be asked to accept inferior securities in exchange for their certificates, and in a few cases they have been asked to stand an assessment in order to come in on the reorganization.

Receivers' certificates are commonly made callable before their maturity date. In some instances the maturity date has been extended by authority of the court. Because of the priority given them, receivers' certificates ordinarily sell on a relatively low yield basis.

Debenture bonds

DEBENTURE BONDS DEFINED. Bonds which are secured only by the general credit of the issuing company, and thus have no claim on specific property, are called *debenture bonds.* As has already been sufficiently explained, the absence of specific mortgaged security is not necessarily a sign of weakness in the bonds; in final analysis the real security of all bonds is the general credit of the company. If a company which has only debenture bonds outstanding defaults in the payment of interest or principal, the bondholders through their trustee can take proper legal steps to secure a lien against the company's property. After this has been done the bonds may really become mortgage bonds. So, from the standpoint of security, debenture bonds are only a step behind mortgage bonds. If a company has both mortgage and debenture bonds outstanding, any lien on mortgaged property that would be obtained by the debenture bonds would be junior to that possessed by the mortgage bonds.

It should be kept in mind, however, that mortgage bonds have a senior claim only in respect to the particular property which is mortgaged. In respect to unmortgaged property the mortgage bondholders and debenture bondholders would stand on an equal footing.

Debenture bonds usually have a shorter life than mortgage bonds because of the difficulty of determining the ability of a corporation to pay off its general credit obligations in the distant future. They are issued more commonly by industrial corporations than by railroads and public utilities.

It is sometimes said, and with some truth, that debenture bonds are a sign of either weakness or strength. If a company has already outstanding a number of mortgages against its properties, a debenture issue would sell about as well as a third or fourth mortgage. If a company, on the other hand, has no mortgages against its properties and is in a strong financial condition, it may be able to market a debenture issue at a relatively low rate of interest without placing a mortgage against its properties. If a bond issue is sold by some types of corporations such as merchandising companies which do not own any real estate, it would have to be a debenture issue. Pure holding companies, whether railroad, public utility, or industrial, and investment companies have no real property, hence they cannot issue a mortgage bond. Aside from collateral trust bonds, debenture bonds are the only type they may issue.

When such bonds were first issued there was no trustee appointed to represent them, nor was there a separate agreement such as an *indenture*. (Care should be taken not to confuse the terms *debenture* and *indenture*.) The provisions relating to the issue were contained on the face of the bond. This procedure was similar to the issuance of unsecured notes. Without the trustee, a single bondholder could bring action against the corporation in event of default in the payment of interest or principal. After 1900, it became common to issue debenture bonds under an indenture giving an appointed trustee the power and duty to enforce the provisions in the agreement. This is the same procedure which had been used in connection with mortgage bonds. In addition to taking action which may be requested by a stated percentage of the bondholders, the trustee pays the interest and principal on the bonds after the issuing corporation has paid him the amount in a lump sum.

PROTECTIVE PROVISIONS IN DEBENTURE ISSUES. Due to the absence of specifically pledged property as security, it has become common practice to include in the agreement under which debenture bonds are issued certain provisions for the future protection of the bondholders. Following are the more commonly used restrictions or safeguards.

1. *Restrictions on mortgage indebtedness.* Investment bankers and investors commonly insist on a provision in the debenture agreement giving the bonds an equal claim on the property with any mortgage bonds subsequently issued.

2. *Restrictions against additional indebtedness.* In recent years it has become increasingly common to find in the agreements pro-

visions limiting or restricting the amount of additional indebtedness which may be incurred in the future. A common type of such provision provides that additional indebtedness can be incurred only if the company's average earnings for a designated number of years have been at least equal to 3 or 4 times the interest on the debt outstanding plus the additional debt which is contemplated. In some instances the contract provides that the net tangible assets must at least be equal to 2½ or 3 times the bonded indebtedness, including the proposed new issue. This type of limitation may be in addition to those stated above.

3. *Restrictions on dividends.* Another type of provision is that of preventing the payment of cash dividends on the stock unless certain ratios are maintained. For example, the current ratio may have to be at least 2 or 3 (this means that the current assets would have to be at least 2 or 3 times the current liabilities), or the net current assets (current assets less current liabilities) would have to be at least a stated amount, or the net tangible assets would have to be at least 2½ or 3 times the bonded indebtedness.

SUBORDINATED DEBENTURES. In recent years subordinated debentures have been used to an increasing extent by corporations to secure additional capital. A *subordinated debenture bond* issue is one which, according to the terms of the indenture, cannot be paid in event of liquidation, dissolution, bankruptcy, or reorganization, until payment has been made to the senior creditors. Senior creditors may be described in the indenture to include existing bank creditors, and holders of bonds and notes, or those who subsequently become such creditors. Debts such as accounts payable, dividends payable, and certain other types of current liabilities are usually described in the indenture as not constituting senior debt.

Although the principle of subordination is not new, the first issuance of bonds which possessed the subordination clause at the time of issue was the 5 per cent, ten-year subordinated debentures of the General Finance Corporation, which were issued in March, 1936. As a group, finance companies have been the principal users of subordinated debentures.[2] In recent years a number of other types of industrial corporations have made use of this type of bond. Among the largest was an issue of $101,751,000, by the Sinclair Oil Company in 1953, and one for $100,000,000 issued by Dow Chemical Company in 1952. There are only a few instances of the use of

[2] For an excellent article on this type of bonds, see "Subordinated Debentures: Debt that Serves as Equity," by Robert W. Johnson, *The Journal of Finance*, March, 1955, p. 1.

subordinated debentures by public utilities, and apparently none by railroads.

Subordinated debentures are issued in order to obtain additional capital, and at the same time broaden the base for future senior borrowing. A company may have outstanding the maximum amount of bank loans and other senior debt permitted in relation to the equity structure of the company. The money obtained from the sale of subordinated debentures will increase the base or security in a manner similar to the issuance of additional stock. Thus, in the future, the company may be able to obtain additional funds from bank loans or other senior debt at a relatively low rate of interest. The particular company may favor the subordinated debentures over the issuance of preferred or common stock for the following reasons. Since the bonds have a fixed rate of interest, the benefit of leverage may be obtained. Also, the interest rate on the bonds would probably be lower than the rate of dividends that would be paid on a preferred stock issue. Furthermore, the bond interest is deductable for income taxes, whereas dividends are not. And, of course, control is not affected by the issuance of bonds, whereas this is a possibility if additional stock is sold. From the market standpoint, insurance companies, pension funds, and other institutional buyers might, either because of law or practice, favor bonds over stocks. In order to add to their marketability, most subordinated debenture issues have been made convertible into stock of the issuing company.

SECURED DEBENTURES. After seeing debenture bonds defined, one may be surprised to see the term *secured debenture.* This title is sometimes used for a bond which is secured by some property, either real or personal, or both, but where the amount or value of the security is so small in relation to the face value of the bonds, it is thought advisable not to call the obligation a mortgage or collateral trust bond.

Income bonds

GENERAL NATURE. Income bonds are those on which the interest payments do not constitute a fixed charge unless earned, and which therefore do not have to be paid unless the company has earnings sufficient to pay them. The principal, however, comes due at a stated time and must be paid (or otherwise legal action may be taken to collect it), regardless of whether or not there are earnings. Although called *income bonds* in the past, in more recent years, due to the fact that the public has come to recognize their weak nature, they have been called *adjustment bonds,* and in a few instances *preference bonds.*

Income bonds first arose in railroad organizations and most of such bonds issued by railroads down to the present time have come into being in this way. In the depression of the 1930's, they were frequently issued in the reorganization of companies which had issued real estate mortgage bonds.

In the case of practically all railroad failures, the amount of the bond interest, called *fixed charges,* is excessive in relation to the earnings. About the only way the reorganized company can get back on its feet is to cut down the amount of these charges. So the reorganization plan usually calls for the issuance of income bonds in exchange for some of the junior bonds of the company. More will be said about this in later chapters dealing with reorganizations.[3] As we will then see, the bondholders usually can do nothing but accept these new bonds.

Most of the income bonds issued by railroads have been mortgage bonds, but their mortgage is usually a junior one. In an ordinary bond of this sort the value of the mortgage comes into play when the interest is defaulted, since this, according to the indenture, makes the principal amount due. But in the case of a mortgage income bond, if the interest is not earned it does not have to be paid, therefore the principal amount would not thereby become due. If the company earns the interest, it will ordinarily be paid on any kind of a bond. Thus, the mortgage phase of an income bond does not mean as much as in the case of an ordinary mortgage bond. In the event of default in the principal, however, the mortgage may benefit the bondholders, although it should be kept in mind that the mortgage is generally a junior one.

Interest Provisions in Income Bonds. The exact nature of the interest payments on an income bond depends upon the particular contract under which it is issued. The general statement made above that the interest is a fixed charge only if earned would apply in practically all cases. In some instances even if the interest is earned it must be declared by the board of directors, in a manner similar to the declaration of dividends on stock, before the bondholders can claim it.

Considering the inexactnesses that are present in the science of accounting, there may be some question from time to time whether or not there are earnings, and if so, their exact amount. In some instances the directors may juggle the figures around so that they

[3] See Chapters 34 and 35.

can make the earnings, or lack of them, appear as they desire. In some issues the indenture carefully defines what shall be considered expenses before arriving at the amount available for the income bondholders.

If the company has earnings, but an amount insufficient to pay the full rate, the indenture may provide that the amount earned shall be paid. In such instances it is commonly stated that the rate paid must be a multiple of even fractions, such as ½ per cent.

In the older railroad income bonds the interest was noncumulative, or noncumulative for the first few years and cumulative thereafter, but railroad income bonds issued after 1920 and those issued by other companies at the time of promotion have more frequently been cumulative from the time of issue. The 4½ per cent income bonds (due in 2022) which were issued in the reorganization of the New York, New Haven and Hartford Railroad in 1947, are cumulative only up to 13½ per cent. Any accumulated interest on income bonds must be paid before any dividends can be declared on the stock, or at the maturity of the bonds. If the bonds are noncumulative, interest not earned in a particular year will not be paid in a subsequent year even if the later earnings are more than sufficient to pay also the interest for the particular year. In a few instances bonds have been issued which were cumulative in years in which the interest is earned, but noncumulative in those years in which the interest is not earned.

Income Bonds Compared with Preferred Stocks. From what has been said above it is apparent that income bonds are somewhat like preferred stock. Neither is entitled to anything for a particular year in which there are no earnings and no declaration of dividends made by the board of directors. Both may be cumulative or noncumulative, depending upon the contract under which they are issued. Preferred stocks are also commonly limited in respect to the rate of return, similar to the bonds.

But there are several important differences between these two types of securities. Preferred dividends do not constitute a fixed charge, and do not have to be paid even if the company has earnings. Interest on income bonds, as we have seen, however, becomes a fixed charge if earnings sufficient to pay the interest is earned in any particular year. This interest would have to be paid before any dividends could be paid on the preferred stock. The principal of the bonds becomes due the same as any other debt of the corporation, whereas preferred stocks do not come due, although they may be callable by the issuing company.

From the standpoint of the issuing company, there are several reasons why it may prefer income bonds to preferred stock. These are as follows.

1. *Security holders prefer bonds.* From the standpoint of security, bonds are preferred over stocks. The fact that the security can be called a "bond" would have a psychological advantage and the old bondholders would be more ready to accept a reorganization plan if they were offered bonds instead of stock. Since the income bonds are ordinarily given to the old *bondholders* they are thus being issued to a type of investor who has preferred to own bonds. Furthermore, as we have already pointed out, the interest on the income bonds constitutes a fixed charge and must ordinarily be paid in those years in which the interest is earned.

2. *Restriction on stock ownership.* Life insurance companies have in the past been large holders of railroad bonds. These firms were in the past prohibited from owning stock. If in a reorganization they were given preferred stock in exchange for their bonds, they would have to divest themselves of such stock within a short period of time. Thus, they would oppose the stock. If the stock were forced upon them it would later be thrown on the market, which would depress the price and thus further impair the company's credit. Bonds, even though they are income bonds, could be held by the insurance companies. In recent years many state laws have been changed to permit the limited holdings of stocks, both common and preferred, by life insurance companies.

3. *Income tax savings.* Bond interest is an expense and can thus be deducted before arriving at the figure on which the income tax is based. Dividends, on the other hand, are not deductable since they constitute a distribution of the profits. Thus, even if the rate of return on the income bonds and the preferred stock would be the same, the bonds would result in a tax savings to the issuing company.

INCOME BONDS INFERIOR INVESTMENT. From what has been said, it is apparent that income bonds are ordinarily not sound investments. In the first place, the fact that they are issued is usually indicative of financial weakness. When they are secured by a mortgage, it is usually a junior mortgage. The uncertainty of earnings, and therefore the uncertainty of income, is an unfavorable factor.

In some instances income bonds have attained a good investment status by virtue of the subsequent success of the issuing company. A case in point is the 4 per cent adjustment bonds which were issued in the reorganization of the Atchison, Topeka and Santa Fe Railway Company in 1895. Regular interest has been paid on these bonds since their issuance with the exception of one instance in which there was a default in the payment of the semi-annual interest in 1938. Since the interest on these bonds is cumulative after 1900, this interest installment was later paid. These bonds, which are currently selling at a premium, come due in 1995.

Income bonds are ordinarily quoted *flat*. This means that any interest accrued or expected on the bond is included in the quoted price. When the bonds attain the investment status such as those of the Atchison mentioned above, the bonds are quoted "and accrued interest," the same as ordinary bonds.

In recent years an increasing number of solvent companies, particularly railroads, have issued income bonds to secure new money or to retire preferred stock issues. The main advantage to the issuing company of the income bond as compared with preferred stock is the tax savings. Furthermore, institutional investors may purchase the bonds. In a few instances, the income bonds have been subordinated debentures. For example, in 1953, the Federal Pacific Electric Company (formerly the Federal Electric Products Company) issued a $2,000,000, 6% Subordinated Income Debenture issue, due in 1968. Warrants were attached to these bonds for the purchase of common stock of the company. Some of the weaknesses discussed above of income bonds issued during reorganizations are not present in income bonds which are issued primarily because of the tax savings.

Participating bonds

PROFIT SHARING. As the term is ordinarily used in corporation finance, a *participating bond* is one which bears a fixed rate of interest, like an ordinary bond, and in addition is entitled to participate along with the stockholders in additional earnings to the extent provided in the contract. They are also called *profit-sharing bonds*. They have rarely been issued in the United States, but are more common in Europe. The participating feature is similar to that which appears in some preferred stock issues, but it should be remembered that the initial rate on the bonds is a fixed charge which must be paid regardless of whether or not there are earnings. Some participating bonds are secured by a mortgage, while others are debenture issues.

The fact that the participating feature is included is evidence that the bond could not be favorably marketed without it. In other words, participating bonds would be issued only by companies whose credit was not of the highest quality. The bond contains two features which ordinarily are not found in the same issue—the fixed rate of return which ordinarily is associated only with credit instruments, and the profit-sharing feature which goes with equity securities. Another type of security, the convertible bond, which will be discussed in the following chapter, offers the bondholder the security of a fixed rate of return and the chance, by conversion, to share in the earnings of the company. Conversion, however, terminates his position as a creditor of the company. In the case of the participating bond, the holder retains his position as a creditor entitled to a fixed rate of return, while he may also enjoy the right to participate along with the stockholders in additional earnings, although the participation right may be limited to a stipulated rate.

EXAMPLES. An example of a participating bond is the Baltimore & Ohio R.R. Co., First Mortgage, Series B Bond, which matures in 1975. These bonds have a fixed rate of interest of 4 per cent, and an additional 1 per cent contingent upon earnings in the preceding calendar year. This 1 per cent is cumulative and is payable to the extent earned (in multiples of ¼ per cent). Any accrued interest must be paid, however, at the maturity of the bonds. Bonds of this kind are sometimes called *split-coupon bonds.*

Some income bonds also have participating features. For example, the Green Bay and Western Railroad Company has outstanding Non-Cumulative Income Debentures, Series A and B. Payment of the interest is contingent upon earnings and is subject to the discretion of the board of directors. Distributed earnings accrue first to the Class A Debentures to the extent of 2½ per cent, then to the capital stock to the extent of 2½ per cent ($100 par), then both classes of securities share pro rata in further earnings until both have received 5 per cent each, then the Class B Debentures receive the balance of any earnings distributed. All of these securities were issued in a reorganization. The debentures and stock of the company are listed on the New York Stock Exchange.

Questions

1. Is there any security behind an "unsecured" bond? Explain.

2. (a) Are unsecured bonds more risky than secured bonds? Explain. (b) Considering the various types of bonds that are outstanding today, would you say that the safest ones are really unsecured bonds? Explain.

3. Explain the following relative to assumed bonds, guaranteed bonds, and joint bonds:

(a) Circumstances under which they arise. (b) Nature of the security behind them. (c) Their relative investment status.

4. Compare the relative status of guaranteed bonds and guaranteed stocks.

5. Indicate the nature of the security behind receivers' or trustees' certificates.

6. (a) Distinguish between the terms *debenture* and *indenture.* (b) What type of provisions are often inserted in the indenture of a debenture bond issue for the protection of the bondholders?

7. (a) Indicate the nature of income bonds. What other title is often used for them? (b) Are most income bonds debentures or mortgage bonds? (c) Of what importance would the mortgage feature of an income bond be?

8. Is there any reason why both the issuing corporation and the investor might prefer an income bond over a preferred stock? Explain.

9. Explain what is meant by a participating bond.

10. Without referring to the book, list the names of as many different kinds of bonds as you can.

Problems

1. The entire assets of the Metal Steel Co. and the All Products Co. were purchased by the United Steel Corp. The first-mentioned company had mortgage bonds outstanding against its plant amounting to $1,000,000, and the All Products Co.'s plant was mortgaged to the extent of $2,000,000. Both of these issues were assumed by United Steel. The bond issue of the Metal Steel Co. contained the after-acquired property clause.

The United Steel Corp. then issued $2,000,000 in mortgage bonds to get cash for further expansion purposes. This issue was secured by a first mortgage on United's old plant, and contained an after-acquired property clause. United then acquired the plant of the Strip Co. and used a purchase money mortgage of $1,000,000 as part payment for the plant.

Several years later the United Co. failed, and the following amounts were received for the properties at the court sale:

Metal Steel plant	$ 800,000
All Products plant	1,400,000
Old United plant	1,500,000
Strip plant	1,300,000
Other assets of United Corp. (unmortgaged)	500,000

(a) Indicate the exact nature of the liens of the various bond issues prior to the court sale. (b) Indicate the amounts that would go to the designated classes of bonds and what percentage on the dollar would be realized by each class of bondholders.

2. The Subsidiary Corp. was capitalized with $1,000,000 in first mortgage bonds, which were secured by a mortgage on its plant; $1,000,000 in 6 per cent preferred stock; and $2,000,000 in common stock. The Parent Corp., which had guaranteed both the interest and principal on the bonds and the dividends on the preferred stock of the Subsidiary Corp., was capitalized with $2,000,000 in first mortgage bonds, which were secured by a mortgage on the Parent new plant; $1,000,000 in 7 per cent debenture bonds; $1,000,000 in 6 per cent preferred stock; and $4,000,000 in common stock.

The dividends on both preferred stocks have not been paid for the past 5 years. Upon default in the principal on all the bond issues, the bondholders brought action that ultimately resulted in a court sale of the properties. The following amounts were realized from the particular assets indicated:

Subsidiary plant	$ 700,000
Parent new plant	1,200,000
Other assets of parent (unmortgaged)	1,800,000

(a) Indicate the nature of the lien or claim of each class of securities before the court sale. (b) Indicate the amount that will go to each class of security holders, and state the percentage on the dollar that each receives. (For purposes of solving this problem, assume that dividends on the preferred stock have accrued for 5 years, there is no accrued interest on the bonds, and disregard any court costs.)

Chapter 12

CONVERTIBLE BONDS, STOCK WARRANTS, AND OPTIONS

Convertible bonds

NATURE OF CONVERTIBLE SECURITIES. As the name indicates, a *convertible security* is one which can be converted into another type. In practically all instances the option to convert rests with the holder rather than with the issuing company. In most instances the convertible security is a relatively sound one with a more or less fixed or limited income return, and it is convertible into a more speculative security which lacks a fixed return but which has the right to reap the benefits of any future success the company may have. Thus convertible bonds are usually exchangeable for either preferred or common stock, and convertible preferred stock can usually be exchanged for common stock. The convertible security and the one into which it is convertible are issued by the same company. Convertible preferred stock was briefly discussed in Chapter 7. Much of what is stated in this chapter will apply also to convertible preferred stock.

In a few instances bonds have been convertible into securities of other companies which were held by the company issuing the convertible bonds. Isolated instances have occurred where preferred stock has been convertible into bonds issued by the same company. There have been a number of cases among railroads and public utilities where short-term notes have been convertible into long-term bonds which were put up as collateral behind the note issue.

EARLY USE. Convertible securities of one form or another have been used since the corporate form of organization was applied to business undertakings. Several spectacular uses of them have been made in the building up of the railroad systems in the United States.

In the latter part of the last century Commodore Vanderbilt was trying to wrest control of the Erie Railroad from Daniel Drew and his two associates, Jay Gould and Jim Fisk. Vanderbilt had acquired all the outstanding stock of Erie and an additional 50,000 shares from short sellers. Drew had been selling and was short of the stock. In order to save himself, Drew at a secret midnight meeting had the directors of the road issue ten million dollars in convertible bonds which were acquired by Drew. The latter then proceeded to convert these bonds into 100,000 shares of the common stock, and used them to cover his short sales. The balance of the stock he threw on the market and it was bought up by Vanderbilt. The latter had by this time overextended himself. In the meantime Drew and his associates fled to New Jersey to avoid arrest and took their money and the Erie's books with them. Finally a compromise was worked out whereby Vanderbilt was reimbursed from the treasury of the Erie Railroad, and Drew was required to turn over the management of the road to Gould.

Convertible bonds were used successfully by Edward H. Harriman in building up the Union Pacific system. In 1901 the Union Pacific sold to its stockholders $100,000,000 in 4 per cent convertible bonds. Part of the proceeds was used to acquire majority ownership of the Southern Pacific, and part to acquire a large stock interest in the Northern Pacific Railroad. Due to the successful operation of the road, the common stock of the Union Pacific rose to the point where practically all the bondholders changed over to the common stock by the time the conversion privilege expired in 1906. The conversion feature enabled the company to sell the bonds on a lower yield basis than if they had been straight bonds. The proceeds from the sale made it possible to acquire the stock of other companies, and conversion eliminated this bonded indebtedness. The Union Pacific successfully used convertible bonds in the same way in several later instances.

Extent of Use. In a study that was made of more than $60,000,000,000 corporate bonds and notes that were issued in the years 1909–1937,[1] it was found that 12.44 per cent of them were convertible securities. Most of these were debenture issues as can be seen from the following data which were taken from the study showing the percentage distribution of the 993 convertible issues classified according to industry and type of bond.

[1] Earl L. Knight, *Convertible Securities,* unpublished dissertation, Ohio State University, 1940, pp. 118, 149.

TABLE 13

PERCENTAGE OF CONVERTIBLE BONDS AND NOTES, CLASSIFIED BY TYPE AND INDUSTRY, FOR THE YEARS 1909–1937

Type of Industry	*First Mortgage*	*Junior Mortgage*	*Collateral Trust*	*Debenture*	*Total*
Industrial	37.0%	2.9%	5.3%	54.8%	100.0%
Public utility	14.5	7.0	15.5	63.0	100.0
Railroad	8.5	18.7	20.3	52.5	100.0
Financial	12.2	7.3	15.8	64.7	100.0
Total	26.8%	5.4%	10.0%	57.8%	100.0%

In a more recent study that covered all bonds issued from 1933 to 1952, it was found that slightly over 9 per cent of the total number of issues were convertible. Table 14 shows the total number of all publicly offered security issues during this period, including preferred and common issues, and what percentage of them were convertible issues.

TABLE 14

PUBLIC OFFERINGS; CONVERTIBLE ISSUES RELATIVE TO TOTAL, 1933–1952 (OFFERINGS IN EXCESS OF $300,000 EACH, AND EXCLUDING EQUIPMENT TRUSTS)

	Total Number of Offerings	*Number of Convertible Offerings*	*Per Cent Convertible*
Bonds	1,959	182	9.3
Preferred stocks	1,399	494	35.3
Total senior issues	3,358	676	20.1
Common stocks	1,764		
Total	5,122	676	13.2

SOURCE: C. James Pilcher, *Raising Capital With Convertible Securities,* Bureau of Business Research, University of Michigan, 1955, p. 7. Data for the table were from Sullivan & Cromwell, *Issuer Summaries, Security Issues in the United States—July 26, 1933 to December 31, 1949;* Ad Press Ltd., 1951, Vols. I and II; and *Investment Dealers' Digest,* Jan. 22, 1951; Jan. 21, 1952; and Jan. 26, 1953.

As might have been expected, the number of industrial convertible preferred stock and convertible bond issues greatly exceeded those issued by utilities, railroads, and financial institutions. The relative importance of convertible issues among these industries for the period 1933–1952 is shown in Table 15.

A good investment bond does not ordinarily need a conversion privilege attached in order to sell it. In many instances this privilege

TABLE 15

INDUSTRY USE OF CONVERTIBLE SECURITIES, 1933–1952
(PUBLIC OFFERINGS IN EXCESS OF $300,000 EACH, EXCLUDING EQUIPMENT TRUSTS)

	Preferred Stocks		*Bonds*	
	Number of Convertible Offerings	*Percentage of Total*	*Number of Convertible Offerings*	*Percentage of Total*
Industrials	438	88.7	134	73.7
Utilities	49	9.9	40	22.0
Railroads	1	0.2	7	3.8
Banks	2	0.4	1	0.5
Insurance companies	4	0.8	0	0.0
Total	494	100.0	182	100.0

SOURCE: C. James Pilcher, *Raising Capital With Convertible Securities*, Bureau of Business Research, University of Michigan, 1955, p. 19. Data for the table were from Sullivan & Cromwell, *Issuer Summaries, Security Issues in the United States—July 26, 1933 to December 31, 1949;* Ad Press Ltd., 1951, Vols. I and II; and *Investment Dealers' Digest,* Jan. 22, 1951; Jan. 21, 1952; and Jan. 26, 1953.

is attached to a junior grade bond in order to add to its marketability.[2]

WHY SOLD. In some instances, however, companies with exceptionally strong credit will issue convertible bonds in order to sell the bonds at a relatively low rate of interest, and also to prevent a depression in the price of the stock which might result if stock rather than the convertible bond was sold. For example, the American Telephone and Telegraph Company since the end of World War II has sold to its shareholders through privileged subscription in excess of $3 billion of convertible bonds. In September, 1955, A. T. & T. offered its 1,380,000 shareholders the right to buy $637,000,000 3⅞% Convertible Debentures due in 1967—the largest private financing ever undertaken. Shareholders received one "right"[3] for each share of stock held. With eight "rights" a shareholder could buy one $100 bond at its face value. A shareholder

[2] The 1956 *Moody's Industrial, Public Utilities, and Transportation Manuals* list the following number of publicly held domestic convertible security issues:

	Industrial	*Public Utility*	*Transportation*	*Total*
Convertible bonds	127	21	28	176
Convertible stocks	334	57	27	418
Total	461	78	55	594

[3] The issuance of "rights" under the privileged subscription method of selling securities is discussed in Chapter 17.

could then convert one $100 bond with $48 cash into one share of stock.

Unless otherwise provided, shareholders have a pre-emptive right to buy convertible bonds before they can be sold to the public. The purpose in selling any kind of security is to obtain money. But our interest at the present is why the conversion feature is added to the bonds, or why the company does not sell stock rather than bonds to obtain the money. The reasons follow.

1. *Cheaper financing.* The conversion feature adds to the attractiveness of the bond. As stated above, these bonds are usually of inferior security. People will give more money for a bond with a given rate of interest if the conversion privilege is attached. In other words, the company can sell such bonds on a lower yield basis than if they were not convertible. This speculative feature enhances the market for the bonds.

As would be expected, the conversion feature is added to bonds more commonly during the upswing of the business cycle when the stock market is bullish. People at that time hesitate to buy fixed dollar investments. The conversion feature permits them, if they should decide to convert, to share in the future earnings of the company, and to hedge against inflation by becoming owners in the business.

2. *Inability to market stock.* Although the convertible bonds may be sold during a period of rising stock prices, the particular company may not at the time have a market for additional stock. A market for the stock may exist, but considering the size of the new issue contemplated, the sale of additional stock instead of bonds might depress the market price of the stock too much.

3. *Elimination of bonded indebtedness.* If the bondholders convert, it will eliminate the bonds and substitute additional stock instead. Generally speaking, a company prefers to have stock rather than bonds outstanding. The fixed interest charge is eliminated and the company will not have to provide the money to pay off the bonds at maturity. The substitution of stocks for bonds broadens the stock base and reduces the indebtedness. This will facilitate borrowing in the future if it becomes necessary.

4. *Selling the stock for more than its worth.* Considering the price that is obtained for the bond which is later converted into stock, the net result is that the company obtains more cash per share of stock eventually outstanding than if the stock was sold originally. Perhaps we can best illustrate this with an example. Let

us assume that a company's stock is selling in the market for $75 a share. It sells for $1,000 a bond which is convertible into 10 shares of stock. If the stock subsequently rises to more than $100 a share the bondholder might convert. If he does convert, it results in the company's having obtained $100 for each share of stock which is exchanged for the bonds. Had the company sold the stock originally instead of the bonds it would have obtained only $75 a share. This means that the company by issuing the convertible bonds which are later converted, obtains 33⅓ per cent more money than if the stock had been sold instead of the bonds. If the company is paying a dividend of $6.00 a share, it means that the money obtained from the security sale is costing it 6 per cent instead of 8 per cent if stocks had been sold.

Disadvantage to Issuer. Although some or all of the above listed advantages of convertible bonds may be experienced by the issuing corporation, it may also encounter certain disadvantages. These are as follows:

1. *It may dilute earnings per share.* The shareholders who become such from the conversion of bonds would share in the earnings and dividends along with the old stockholders. Considering the fact that the interest rate on the bonds may have been relatively low, the result of conversion may be that the earnings per share and thus the dividends paid may be less than before the bonds were converted.

2. *Surplus may be diluted.* Since the bondholders upon conversion would share in the surplus of the company in the same manner as the old stock, the surplus attaching to each old share may be reduced.

3. *Price of stock may fall.* Because of the two points stated above, conversion may result in a drop in the market price of the stock.

4. *May be expensive.* Conversion would eliminate the *leverage* (trading on the equity) which had been experienced from the bonds. This is similar to the first point stated above. The rate of dividends being paid may be higher than the interest rate on the bonds. Furthermore, any increase in earnings would be shared by the old bondholders who now hold stock.

5. *Conversion occurs at wrong time.* The bondholders would convert only when they would profit from the exchange. Looking at it from the viewpoint of the issuing corporation, what would benefit the bondholder would probably harm the corporation.

At the time the convertible bonds were sold the public probably demanded bonds rather than stock, due to the fact that the company's credit position, earnings, or prospects for the future may not have been good. At this time the company would probably prefer a stock issue over a bond issue. Later when the earnings increase and the stock rises in the market, the bondholders convert. This is the time that the company could better stand the bond issue and it would prefer that the bondholders not convert their bonds. But the option rests with the bondholder and not the corporation.

6. *Control may be altered.* The bonds, of course, do not possess the voting right. When the bondholders convert into stock they would be entitled to vote in the same manner as any other stockholder (in some instances, however, the bonds are convertible into nonvoting preferred stock). This might result in the shifting of control from the existing management.

If the holders of the convertible bonds are the shareholders of the company, this and the preceding disadvantages would not be applicable. As a matter of law, shareholders entitled to the preemptive right, which was discussed in Chapter 6, would be entitled to buy the convertible bonds before they could be offered to the public. In some instances, however, the statutes or bylaws give the directors the right to sell convertible bonds to the public without first offering them to the shareholders.

7. *Taxes increased.* Since bond interest is an expense, it is deducted before arriving at the profit figure on which the federal and any state income taxes are based. The conversion of the bonds would eliminate this deduction and thus increase the taxes, since the dividends on the stock cannot be deducted for tax purposes. If an excess profits tax is in effect, this would be a still more serious consideration.

The corporation would also have to pay an additional state tax on the increase in stock similar to the organization tax. In many states the annual franchise tax is based on the amount of stock outstanding, so this would be higher after conversion takes place.

ADVANTAGES TO BUYER. From what has been stated above the advantages and disadvantages of convertible bonds from the viewpoint of the buyer might be apparent, but for the sake of completeness they will be briefly discussed.

1. *Security of a bond.* The holder of a convertible bond is a creditor of the company and thus occupies a more secure position than the stockholders. If the price of the stock does not advance to

the point where it would be profitable for him to convert, he can retain his creditor position.

2. *Chance for profits on bonds.* The higher the stock goes the greater will be the rise in the price of the convertible bond. In fact, the price of the bond will probably advance before the stock rises to the place where it would be profitable to convert since a further rise in the price of the stock will be anticipated.

While the bondholder is experiencing a rise in the price of his bond comparable to the rise in the price of the stock, he nevertheless has the relatively secure position of a creditor.

3. *Chance for profit on stock.* After the price of the stock advances beyond the break-even point, the bondholder can convert into the stock and make a profit by selling it. Or, he may hold on to the stock anticipating a further rise. Also, the dividends being paid on the stock will probably be larger than the bond interest he had been receiving.

A further advantage of converting, although more theoretical than practical, is that the former bondholder thereafter has the voting rights possessed by the stock.

Disadvantages to Buyer. As is true of all types of securities, there are certain disadvantages to the buyer. These are as follows.

1. *Pays higher price for the bonds.* The principal reason the issuing corporation adds the convertible feature to the bond is to enable it to secure more money for the bond. The bond buyer pays a higher price for the bond, or (saying the same thing) he gets a lower yield on the bond, than if the convertible privilege had not been present. If the price of the stock does not advance, the amount paid for the convertible feature is money lost.

2. *Pays higher price for stock.* The stock could have been acquired at a lower price at the time the bonds were purchased. Thus, whether he wants to be a stockholder in the company or a bondholder, he is paying a relatively high price in either instance.

3. *Instability of bond prices.* After the price of the stock has advanced beyond the point at which it would be profitable to convert, any further movement either up or down in the price of the stock will be followed by a proportionate change in the price of the bond. Whether he wanted to or not, the bondholder will find that he has become a speculator. Paper profits in either the bonds or the stock may be wiped out if the security is not sold at the right time. And the determination of when is the right time to sell is exceedingly difficult.

4. *Conversion eliminates security.* Once the bondholder converts he gives up his status as a creditor of the company and becomes a stockholder. The price of the stock may fall to relatively low levels, and the dividends on the stock may be cut or eliminated entirely.

CONVERSION RATIO. The *conversion ratio,* which is stated in the bond contract, expresses the amount of stock which may be obtained by the conversion of the bond. It may be expressed in terms of the number of shares of stock which can be obtained from the conversion of one bond. Technically speaking, this would be a *ratio,* or as it is sometimes called, *conversion rate.* In other instances the contract states the price at which the stock can be acquired. This is termed the *conversion price.* When a conversion price is stated, the exchange value of the bond is its face value. When the stock has a par value it may be provided that the bond can be converted into stock with a par value equal to that of the bonds. Thus a $1,000 (face or par value) bond might be convertible into 10 shares which have a par value of $100 each. This is merely another way of stating a conversion price. When no-par stock is used, a conversion price or ratio would have to be stated.

It should be kept in mind that the conversion ratio stated in the contract remains the same regardless of the fluctuation in the market price of the bonds or the stock. For example, if the conversion price of the stock is $125, a $1,000 (face value) bond can always be converted into 8 shares of stock, regardless of what may be the market price of the bond or the stock. The market prices are of importance, of course, when it comes to determining whether it would be profitable to convert.

In some instances the contract calls for an increased conversion price at the end of each successive period of years. Occasionally it is provided that the conversion price will increase after a stated fractional part of the bond issue has been converted. Sometimes the bondholders must pay some cash in addition to turning in their bonds, in order to get the stock; an example of this is the American Telephone and Telegraph bonds mentioned previously.

PRICE PATTERN OF CONVERTIBLE BONDS. In most instances, at the time convertible bonds are issued, the price of the common would have to rise before it would be profitable to convert. The market value of the bond is made up of two component parts which we may call the investment value and the conversion value. The *investment value* of the bond is a resultant of the worth of the bond as a credit obligation of the company. It bears a fixed rate of interest, and is secured by the general credit of the issuing company and any other security that may be pledged behind the bond. Although no profit could ordinarily be made by converting at the time the bond is sold, people will give a little more for the bond because it has the conversion privilege attached. This added value can be called the *conversion value.* After the stock has risen in price to the point where it would be profitable for the bondholder to convert, the bonds would also go up in price as a result of their conversion value. The market price at this time would reflect the conversion value rather than the investment value of the bond. Any drop in the price of the stock would be accompanied by a proportionate drop in the price of the bonds. But the bonds will follow the price of the stock down only to the point where the price of the bonds would represent their investment worth. Perhaps this can best be illustrated with the following example.

Assume that a company sells at their face value, 3-per-cent bonds which are convertible into stock at $100 a share. If the conversion feature had not been attached to the bond issue perhaps the company could have obtained only 95, instead of 100 for the bonds. The investment value of the bonds would thus be considered to be 95 ($950 for a $1,000 bond) and the additional 5 points would be the conversion value. We will assume that the stock into which the bonds are convertible was selling in the market at $75 at the time the bonds were issued.

If the stock would advance in price to $100 a share, the bondholder would break even by converting. So we may call this the *break-even point.* If the stock did make this advance in price the bonds would probably also rise in price because of the anticipated profit that could be made if the stock continued to advance in price. To illustrate better the price relationship between the stock and the bonds, however, we will be somewhat theoretical and assume that the price of the bonds remains at 100 while the stock is advancing to $100. If the price of the stock should advance from $100 to $110, it would be expected that the price of the bonds would also go up 10 points. This is true because one $1,000 bond could be converted into 10 shares of stock with a total worth of $1,100. So the bond would be expected to advance 10 points, or $100 in price. If the stock would advance to $150, for example, the price of the bonds would be expected to rise to $1,500. It is thus seen that after the price of the stock advances beyond the *break-even price,* the market price of the bonds will be determined solely from their *conversion value.*

If the price of the stock would fall, we would expect the price of the bonds to follow a similar course. For example, if the price of the stock fell from $150 to $120, we would expect the price of the bonds to drop from $1,500 to $1,200. But if the price of the stock should fall below $100, we would expect the price of the bonds to drop only to about $1,000, since this price represents the *investment value* of the bond, plus something additional for the speculative future value of the conversion feature. If the financial condition of the company would deteriorate to the point where it would appear improbable that the stock would ever get back to the place where it would be profitable to convert, the price of the bond would probably drop to about 95 ($950), which is what we assumed was the *investment value* alone of the bond. Of course if the condition of the company was such that the ability of the company to pay the bond interest and retire the bonds at maturity was questionable, the investment worth of the bonds might become considerably less than 95 ($950).

DETERMINING WHEN TO CONVERT. It would be profitable to convert whenever the market value of the total stock obtained exceeded the market value of the bonds to be converted. If the market price of the bonds is 100 ($1,000 for a bond with a face value of $1,000), and the conversion price is $100, in other words one bond is convertible into 10 shares of stock, it would be profitable to convert whenever the price of the stock went above $100. For every dollar the stock advanced, we would expect the bond to go up 1 point ($10 for each $1,000 bond). When the conversion price is not a round figure such as $100, and when the market price of the bond is not an even $1,000, it may be a little more difficult to determine the profitableness of conversion. For that reason it is desirable to set up a rule or formula to determine this.

The break-even price of the stock can be determined as follows:

$$\text{Break-even price of stock} = \frac{\text{Market price of bond}}{\text{No. of shares of stock obtained}}$$

It would be profitable to convert only when the market price of the stock exceeded the break-even point. To illustrate the use of the formula let us assume that a particular $1,000 bond purchased at $1,200 is convertible into stock at $125 a share. We will assume the stock is now selling for $130 a share. Would it be profitable to convert now? With the above conversion price it is obvious that one bond could be converted into 8 shares of stock ($1,000 divided by $125). Substituting in the formula we get the following:

$$\frac{\$1{,}200}{8} = \$150, \text{ Break-even price of stock}$$

This shows us that it would not be profitable to convert until the stock went above $150 a share (assuming the bond price remained at $1,200). We can easily test the accuracy of the formula. It obviously would not be profitable to convert until the market value of 8 shares exceeded $1,200, the price of the bond. To just equal the market price of the bonds, the shares would obviously have to sell at $150. If conversion was made when the stock was selling for $120, the bondholder would get only $960 in stock. He would thus lose $240 in conversion.

Perhaps a simpler way to get the break-even point is to multiply the conversion price of the stock by the market price of the bonds expressed in percentage of their face value.

$$\text{Break-even price of stock} = \text{Market price of bonds (expressed in per cent)} \times \text{Conversion price of stock}$$

Substituting the above figures in the formula we get the following:

$$120 \text{ per cent} \times \$125 = \$150, \text{ Break-even price of stock}$$

It might be of some value to determine what the *conversion* value of the bonds would be when the stock was selling at a particular price. This can be computed as follows:

$$\begin{matrix}\text{Conversion value of bond} \\ \text{(expressed in per cent)}\end{matrix} = \frac{\text{Market price of stock}}{\text{Conversion price of stock}}$$

Assuming the stock was selling for $175 a share, and that its conversion price was $125, by substituting in the formula we get:

$$\frac{\$175}{\$125} = 140 \text{ (per cent), conversion value of bond}$$

If the bond was selling for 140 per cent of its face value (it will be remembered that the market quotation for bonds is expressed in percentage of face value) that means that the market price for a $1,000 (face value) bond would be $1,400. We can get the same result by the obvious round-about method. Since 8 shares of stock can be obtained from the conversion of one bond, with a market price of $175 a share, the bondholder would get $1,400 in stock. So this would represent the conversion value of the bond.

Adjustment for Interest and Dividends. Price relationships between convertible bonds and the stock into which they are convertible do not work out exactly as indicated above. One of the reasons for this is that, as we have previously seen, bonds are quoted "and accrued interest," while stocks are quoted "flat." The market price of the bond thus does not reflect any interest which may be accrued on it, while the market price of the stock includes any accrued or anticipated dividend.

The particular contract under which the bonds are issued should be examined to determine what, if any, consideration has been given by the company to accrued interest and dividends. Generally the contract provides that the bondholder is entitled to any interest accrued to the time of conversion. But specific provision for accrued dividends is less common. Of course, if the former bondholder can get the stock registered in his name before the dividend date, he will receive the dividend, unless otherwise provided in the contract.

In some instances the contract provides that upon conversion the bondholder will be credited with any interest accrued on his bonds, and the company will receive credit for any accumulated or accrued dividends, and that any balance either way will be settled by cash payment.

UNEVEN NUMBER OF SHARES. In order to simplify the explanation above we assumed conversion prices which were evenly divisible into the face value of the bonds. But in actual practice things do not work out so precisely. For example, the conversion price may, instead of being $100, or $125, be some price such as $110. With the latter price one $1,000 bond could be converted into 9 shares of stock, but what becomes of the unused $10 part of the bond? The following alternate methods have been used in different instances.

1. Commonly the bondholder receives a warrant for $10. He could then buy up warrants worth $100 in the market and send them all in to the company in exchange for an additional share of stock, or, he could sell his warrant on the market.
2. The bondholder could send in his warrant plus $100 cash and get the additional share.
3. The company could refund him $10.
4. The contract may provide only for an even exchange. Thus the bondholder would lose the $10, unless he held bonds in multiples of $11,000 which amount could be converted into an even 100 shares of stock.

CONVERSION PERIOD. The period during which bonds are convertible is specifically stated in the contract under which the bonds are issued. The conversion period may be from the issue date of the bonds until their maturity date. In event the bonds are called in under a provision in the contract, (usually 30 or more days notice of redemption is given), it is usually provided that conversion can be made for a specified number of days, such as from 5 to 30, before the call date. When bonds are reflecting their conversion value in the market, many companies force conversion by exercising the call provision.

In the case of short-term bonds, which are more frequently issued by industrials and public utilities, the conversion period is commonly from issue date to maturity date, or a specified time approximating this period. In railroad bonds, which are more commonly long-term, the conversion period may begin some years after issue date, and terminate some years before the maturity date. In a survey of bond issues listed on the New York Stock Exchange during the period 1948–1952, it was found that 80 per cent were convertible at any time during the life of the bonds.[4]

Where the conversion privilege is of value to the bondholder and the conversion period expires before the maturity of the bond, the holder should either sell his bonds or convert into the stock before the termination of the period. Otherwise he may lose a sizable amount of money. We will illustrate this, using the same example that was used before. Assume that the investment value of a bond is about 95 and that it is convertible into stock at $100 a share. If the stock is selling in the market for $125 a share, the bond should be selling at about 125 ($1,250 for a $1,000 bond). The market price reflects the conversion value of the bond rather than the investment value. Now if the conversion privilege were to expire, the market price of the bonds would drop to about 95 ($950), the pure investment value of the bond. Conversion should also be made under these circumstances if the bond is called or if it matures.

If the company issuing the convertible bonds is merged into another company and thus loses its identity, the conversion privilege will thereby terminate. Where the privilege is of some value, conversion should be made before the merger. The contract under which the bonds are issued sometimes contains provisions which require a successor company to recognize the privilege.

PROTECTION AGAINST DILUTION. Unless provision to the contrary is made in the contract, the value of the conversion privilege may be weakened or destroyed by the company issuing stock dividends, or having stock split-ups. For example, let us assume a conversion

[4] C. James Pilcher, *op. cit.*, p. 48.

TABLE 16

SELECTED LIST OF BONDS CONVERTIBLE INTO COMMON STOCK

Bond	*Call Price**	*Convertible into Common Stock at (dollars per share)**
Bethlehem Steel, 3¼% Debentures, 1980	102.75	140.00
Canadian Pacific, 3⅛% Collateral Trust, 1970	101.10	25.00
Central Hudson G. & E., 3% Debentures, 1963	100.50	12.00†
Consolidated Edison, 3% Debentures, 1963	100.72	25.00
Detroit Edison 3¼% Debentures, 1969	102.75	25.00
Dow Chemical, 3% Subordinated Debentures, 1982	104.00	46.08
General Dynamics, 3½% Debentures, 1975	105.25	74.20
Inland Steel, 3¼% Debentures, 1972	102.62	55.50
Lockheed Aircraft, 3¾% Subordinated Debentures, 1980	102.75	50.00
Sinclair Oil, 3¼% Subordinated Debentures, 1983	102.75	44.00
Standard Coil Products, 5% Subordinated Debentures, 1967	105.00	18.50
Standard Oil (Indiana) 3⅛% Debentures, 1982	102.50	46.00

* In some instances the call price of the bonds and the conversion price of the stocks are different from those stated in the table for 1958, and subsequent years.

† $12.00 for the first $2,000,000 bonds converted, $12.50 for the next $2,000,000 bonds converted, $13.50 for the remaining $2,000,000 bonds converted.

price of $100 for the stock. The bond would have conversion value when the price of the stock went above $100. If, when the stock approached the price of $100, the company had paid a 100 per cent new stock dividend (instead of cash dividend), or issued two new shares for each old share (split-up), it would tend to reduce the market price of the stock to $50 a share. Now the stock would have to climb 100 per cent more in price before the conversion privilege would be of any value. This is comparable to a price of $200 for the old stock. And a price of that amount for the old stock would have meant a market price of 200 ($2,000) for the bond.

Most convertible issues sold in recent years contain antidilution clauses which protect the bondholders against the weakening of the value of the privilege. Such clauses state that the bonds would be entitled to the number of shares comparable to the old stock. Thus, in the example above, if the company had a 100 per cent stock dividend, or a two for one split, the bondholder could convert into 20, instead of 10 shares. Or, stating the same thing in another way, the conversion price of the stock would be reduced from $100 to $50 a share.

Similar clauses may be contained in the indenture to protect the bondholders from the dilution of the value of the privilege by issuing stock to the stockholders at a price below the existing market price. In some instances the contract will provide protection to the bondholders from such actions as the following: issuance of stock having a preference in respect to redemption or dissolution over the particular stock into which the bonds are convertible, issuance of another convertible security convertible into the stock at a lower price, and distribution of assets to senior security holders.

Other Types of Conversion. In our discussion above we have assumed that the convertible security was a bond and that it was convertible into common stock. This was done for simplicity reasons. It was pointed out at the beginning of the chapter that bonds are sometimes convertible into preferred stock, preferred stock is sometimes convertible into common stock, and notes are sometimes convertible into bonds. The part of the above discussion which is applicable in these instances should be apparent to the reader.

In a few instances two or more bond issues of a particular company have been convertible into the same class of stock. For example, the Atchison, Topeka and Santa Fe Railway had outstanding at one time three different issues of debenture bonds which were convertible into the common stock at par. There have also been cases where bonds were convertible at the option of the holder into several different classes of stock. A few companies have issued securities which were convertible into securities issued by their subsidiaries.

There have been a few instances involving close corporations where an issue of stock has been converted into bonds in an apparent attempt to get the income tax advantage of deducting the bond interest before computing the tax. The government will not permit the deduction of such interest where it appears that the conversion was done only in an attempt to obtain this tax advantage.

Hedge for Short Sellers of Stock. *Short selling* in stocks means selling stock which is not owned by the seller at the time of the sale. When a person sells the stock short he borrows the same number of shares and makes delivery to the purchaser. Later he will purchase the stock in the market and return it to the lender of the stock. Short selling is more fully discussed in Chapter 19.

We can best illustrate this with an example. Let us assume that a stock is selling for about $100. We will further assume that the company which issued this stock has bonds outstanding which are convertible into the stock at $100 a share and which are selling for about $1,000. If the stock should rise above $100, the bond would probably increase in price by about the same amount, assuming, of course, that the time is within the conversion period. If the stock should decline, however, the bond probably would not drop in price lower than approximately its investment value. Of course, the conversion privilege would probably be giving it some anticipated conversion value in excess of its investment value.

We will assume that a person sells short 10 shares at $100 a share. Later if the stock drops in price to $90 a share, he can buy it in the market and deliver the stock to the person who lent it to him at the time of the short sale. The profit would obviously be $10 a share, or a total of $100. The net profit would, of course, be less than this because of the taxes and commissions which would have to be paid. But the danger in a short sale is that the stock will go up instead of down. For example, if the stock went to $110, and he bought it to cover the short sale, a total loss of $100 plus taxes and commissions would be suffered.

Now let us assume that at the time of the short sale one of the convertible bonds was bought at a price of $1,000. If the stock declines to $90 probably the bond would not decline since its market price reflected practically only its investment value. A profit on the short sale of $100 (less taxes and commissions) would be realized, and the bond would be sold for about the same as its purchase price. All the speculator would be out on the purchase and sale of the bond would be the commissions.

But if the stock, instead of declining, had advanced to $110 a share the situation would be different. The short seller could convert his bond into 10 shares of stock and cover his short sale by delivering these shares to the lender of the stock. Or, since the bond would probably also rise in price to $1,100, he could sell the bonds at a $100 profit, and buy the stock in the market to cover his short sale. (The latter procedure would ordinarily result in a greater expense because of the additional commissions in selling the bonds and buying the stock). Either of these two methods would result in no net loss (other than taxes and commissions) to the short seller since the profit on the bonds would offset the loss on the short sale of stock. But had the bonds not been used as a hedge, the short seller would have suffered a loss of $100.

In using the convertible bonds as a hedge, care should be taken to see that the bonds are selling in the market for about their investment value. If the bond price reflected its conversion value, then a drop in the price of the stock would result in a fall in the price of the bond, and thus the loss on the latter would offset, at least in part, the gain on the short sale. For example, if the stock was sold short at $110 and the bond bought at about 110 (which would be the approximate price of the bond because of its conversion value), if the stock dropped to $100, probably the bond would fall in price by about the same amount.

If the price of a company's stock fell because of serious financial difficulties the bonds might also drop in price even if their market price had reflected only their investment value. Under these circumstances the bonds would not offer a good hedge in connection with the short sale of the stocks.

Conclusion on Convertibles. We have discussed convertibles at some length, perhaps out of proportion to their importance, due to the technical factors involved. Perhaps it would be advisable in conclusion to state something about their investment status.

In the first place the conversion privilege is apt to be attached to a junior-grade bond. The mere presence of the privilege may be an indication that the bonds are not of the highest security, or the credit of the issuing company may not be of the highest standing, otherwise the bond might perhaps have been sold without adding the conversion privilege. A prospective purchaser should be on guard and thoroughly investigate the company before buying any kind of bonds. In some instances, however, such as the American Telephone and Telegraph Company, the issuer is a strong company.

The buyer of a convertible bond is trying to get on both sides of the fence at the same time. The convertible bond attempts to carry with it the security of a bond, but the speculative opportunities of stock. As a bondholder he pays for the privilege which may never be worth anything, or he may not take advantage of it at the opportune time. If he does convert, he would have found it more profitable to have bought the stock originally instead of the bond. Furthermore, even if he converts when the stock is selling at a relatively high price, there is no assurance that the stock will be sold at a price which will return him a profit. The stock may later go down to the point where he would rather not have converted. But having once converted, he cannot later convert back to be a bondholder again.

To profit on stock a buyer should devote a considerable amount of time to studying the market. The average bond buyer may not be of this type. But having converted he becomes a stockholder who has probably not had much experience in this capacity. The net result may be a loss on the original money invested in the bonds. In fact if he gets the stock market fever, he may unwisely commit even more money to the stock market.

Despite the criticisms stated above, there is something to be said in favor of convertible bonds. Granted that it may be a junior grade bond, is it any worse off by having the conversion privilege attached? About the only disadvantage at the time is that the purchaser has to pay a slightly higher price for the bond. But this higher price may be justified. The holder is not compelled to convert. If the company is successful and the price of the stock rises to the point where it would be profitable to convert, the bondholder can make a profit on the stock. If he does not want to become a stockholder, he can sell his bond and make a profit. The money could then be invested in other bonds. If he retains the bonds or the stock after he converts, he may profit still further if the price of the stock continues to advance.

If the bondholder converts he may find that the annual dividends received on the stock will be greater than the interest he had been receiving on the bond. There also may be a tax advantage. Any profit made on the sale of the bond, or on the stock after conversion, would be considered a capital gain, and if the security has been held for at least six months this is considered a long-term gain, and the taxes on it would be less than on ordinary income. Furthermore, a stockholder is entitled to the dividend exclusion and dividend credit for income tax purposes.

Stock purchase warrants

Nature of Stock Purchase Warrants. The term "stock purchase warrant" is used by some to refer to different types of contracts, and in some instances several different words or phrases may be used to apply to any one of these various kinds of contracts. Using the term in its generally accepted meaning, a *stock purchase warrant* is a contract which is attached to a security at the time of its sale giving the holder of the warrant the right to purchase another type of security issued by the same company. We will use the term with this meaning, and then in the latter part of the chapter we will indicate the other terms which may be applied to it, and the other types of contracts to which the term is sometimes applied.

Type of Securities Carrying Warrants. In most instances the securities to which the warrants are attached are bonds or preferred stocks. The warrants usually call for the purchase of common stock, but in a few instances the warrants attached to bonds call for preferred stock. In a few cases the warrants have been attached to one class of common stock and gave the holder thereof the right to buy another class of common stock. The bonds carrying warrants are usually debentures. Generally speaking, warrants are more frequently attached to bonds and preferred stock of inferior quality.[5] They have been more frequently used by industrials, investment companies, and public utility holding companies than by other types of companies.

REASON FOR USE. The reason for the use of stock purchase warrants is probably apparent—they are "sweeteners" to facilitate the sale of the securities to which they are attached. In this respect they are similar to the conversion feature.

Extensive use of warrants began in the hectic stock market period, 1926–1929, and from a percentage standpoint perhaps they were more frequently used then than ever since. People were very much stock-minded at that time, and even if the company's credit was such that common stock could not be sold, buyers of bonds and preferred stock still demanded the right to share in any future earnings of the company through the right to purchase the common stock. Companies found it difficult to sell any kind of securities in the depression of the 1930's, but they found that bonds and preferred stocks were more readily salable if they had warrants attached, despite the fact that common stockholders suffered severe losses during and following the stock market crash of 1929.

PURCHASE PRICE OF STOCK WITH WARRANT. The price at which the warrant holder can acquire the common stock is higher than the price of the stock at the time the warrant is issued. Thus the price of the common stock would have to advance before it would be profitable for the holder to exercise the warrant. This is comparable to the situation with convertible securities.

DETACHABILITY OF WARRANTS. Some warrants are nondetachable from the security to which they are attached, or nondetachable for a specified period and detachable thereafter. In the case of the nondetachable warrant, only the holder of the security to which it is attached can exercise the warrant. To do so he must send the security with warrant attached and the money to buy the stock to the issuing company or a designated trust company representing the company. The company or its agent then sends him the stock and the old security after having detached the warrant.

[5] The 1956 *Moody's Industrial Manual* lists 93 different stock purchase warrants. Of these, 22 were issued in connection with sale of notes and bonds, 5 in connection with the sale of preferred stock, and the remaining 66 originated in other ways, including mergers.

TABLE 17

SELECTED LIST OF STOCK PURCHASE WARRANTS (DETACHED)

Company	*Purchase Price of One Share of Common Obtainable with One Warrant*	*Warrant Expires*	*Where Traded*	
			Stock	*Warrant*
Alleghany Corp.	$3.75	Perpetual	NYSE*	ASE*
Atlas Corp.	6.25	Perpetual	NYSE	ASE
Armour and Co.	15.00†	1964	NYSE	ASE
Great Northern Gas Utilities, Ltd.	5.00‡	1963	O-C*	O-C
Investment Co. of America	10.48§	Perpetual	O-C	O-C
Standard-Thomson Corp.	9.90	1961	ASE	O-C
Tri-Continental Corp.	17.76	Perpetual	NYSE	ASE

* NYSE—New York Stock Exchange; ASE—American Stock Exchange; O-C—over-the-counter.

† This price continues through December 31, 1959, then it increases to $20.00.

‡ The purchase price of the stock increases $1 each year on December 14, beginning in 1958.

§ One warrant entitles the holder to purchase about 10.97 shares of stock at $10.4832 per share.

In most instances the warrant is detachable from the security. The holder thereof can detach the warrant himself and either exercise it and buy the stock, or he can sell the warrant in the market, provided, of course, that it has a market value. Such warrants are payable to bearer.

Investment bankers and investors prefer detachable warrants, since they can sell the warrants without the security to which they are attached. The issuing company might prefer the nondetachable warrants since they would continue to improve the market for the security until the warrant was exercised.

DURATION OF WARRANTS. The duration of warrants depends, of course, upon the terms of the contract under which they are issued. In most instances the time within which they may be exercised is limited to a period stated in the contract. Ordinarily in the case of bonds, the life of the warrant is less than the life of the bond, in many instances approximately 5 years, which may be for about one-fourth of the life of the bond. Warrants attached to preferred stocks also frequently run for about 5 years. In some instances the price to be paid for the stock upon exercise of the warrant increases as time goes on.

If the security to which the warrant is attached is called by the company before the warrant has expired, the contract may provide that the warrant shall continue for the period stated. If the warrant becomes void upon redemption of the security, it is usually provided that the warrant can be exercised within a stated number of days before the redemption date. If the life of the warrant continues after redemption, a nondetachable warrant would become detachable.

Unless otherwise provided, if the company issuing the securities with warrants attached is merged into another company and thus loses its identity, the life of the warrants would terminate. The same would result from dissolution of the company.

In some instances no limitation is put on the life of warrants. In other words they are perpetual, unless, of course, their life is terminated by redemption of the security to which they are attached, or the company is merged into another one, or is dissolved.

ANTIDILUTION PROVISIONS. The warrant calls for the purchase of stock at a definite price per share, whatever that share may turn out to be at the time it is exercised. Such things as stock dividends and stock split-ups will dilute the value of the privilege in the same manner as was discussed in connection with convertible issues. In recent years the contract has usually provided that the purchase price of the stock with the warrant shall be reduced proportionately in event of a stock dividend or stock split-up.

Protection against other things, such as the issuance of stock with a claim senior to that which can be purchased by the holder of the warrant, the issuance of the stock to others at a price lower than the subscription price to the warrant holder, etc., may also be provided in the contract.

WARRANTS COMPARED WITH CONVERTIBLE PRIVILEGE. Warrants and the conversion privilege are attached to securities for the same reason—to increase the marketability of the particular issue. They both are usually attached to a security giving the holder the right to acquire another security junior to it. In most instances the security to be acquired will have to advance in price before it would be profitable for the holder to exercise the privilege. The exercise of both privileges tends to dilute the equity of the existing common stockholders. In other respects the privileges differ. We will assume the privilege is attached to a bond giving the holder the right to acquire common stock.

When the bondholder converts, the particular bonded indebtedness is extinguished and its place is taken by common stock. Thus, the fixed interest charge and the obligation to pay the principal of the bonds are eliminated. No new money is brought into the corporation. In contrast to this, when the bondholder exercises the warrant, he retains his bonds and buys common stock. Thus, the company's obligation to pay interest and principal remains, and its capitalization is increased by the common stock. The purchase of the stock brings new money into the corporation.

If the holder of the convertible bond wants to profit on the privilege he must either sell the bond and thus cease to hold any securities in the company, or he must convert it into stock and cease to be a bondholder. The warrant holder, as stated above, retains his bonds upon exercise of the warrant. Also, if the warrant is detachable, he may profit by selling the warrant alone and retaining his bonds.

The warrant holder will exercise the privilege only when the company is prospering and the price of its stock high. This may be the very time when the company is not in need of additional funds, but it has no control over the exercise of that privilege. Furthermore, when a company does need funds for expansion, etc., it needs a considerable amount of money at one time. Warrants may be exercised in small amounts over a relatively long period of time.

From what has been said above it is obvious that some would prefer the warrants over the conversion privilege. The only disadvantage of the warrant is that its exercise calls for the outlay of additional cash. But if the holder does not want to buy the stock, he can profit on the warrant by selling it in the market.

PRICE OF DETACHABLE WARRANTS. Since the warrant adds value to the security to which it is attached, even though the stock of the company is not selling sufficiently high to make the exercise of the warrant profitable, it is obvious that the market puts a value on the warrant even before it has any exercisable value. The fact that it is being sold detached may give it more value than if it were still attached to the security.

One warrant ordinarily gives a person the right to acquire one share of stock. This is the way it is usually quoted in the market. If a person owns a bond which entitles him to buy 10 shares of stock there would be attached to his bond one certificate evidencing 10 warrants. Antidilution clauses, however, may result in the warrant being good for an uneven number of shares.

A detached warrant which gives the holder the right to buy one share of stock at $20 a share would have no exercisable value if the stock was then selling at, for example, only $10 a share in the market. But actually the warrant may be selling in the market for $1 or $2. The stock may be advancing in price and speculators see the possibility that it may go above $20 in the near future, so they will bid up the price of the warrants in order to have a call on the stock if it should advance sufficiently in price. An example of this is the Tri-Continental Corporation warrants which carry the right to purchase 1.27 shares of the stock of the company at $17.76 a share.[6] In 1953 when the stock was selling on the New York Stock Exchange for only $16, the warrants were being sold on the American Stock Exchange for $4. (In 1956, when the stock was selling at $28, the warrants were quoted at $12.75.)

Part of the explanation of the above is that it takes less money to speculate indirectly in the stock through the use of the warrant than to buy the stock directly. This can be illustrated by the following hypothetical example. Let us assume that a company has detached warrants outstanding which enable the holder thereof to buy company's stock at $48 a share. We will assume that the stock is selling for $50 a share in the market. A warrant would obviously be worth at least $2. Actually the warrant would sell for more than this for reasons stated above. But we will assume for illustrative purposes that it is selling for only $2. Now if the stock price should increase to $52, a rise of only 4 per cent, the price of the warrant would increase by at least $2 (actually it would probably increase more than this amount). This would be an increase of 100 per cent. So with a given amount of money a person could make a much greater profit by buying the warrant than by purchasing the stock.

USE AS HEDGE IN SHORT SALE. Warrants can be used as a hedge in connection with a short sale of stock in a manner similar to convertible bonds. Using the above example, at the time of selling the stock short at $50, a person could buy a warrant for, we will assume, $2. If the stock goes down as contemplated, he will make a profit on the short sale. But the most that it is possible to lose on the purchase of the warrant is $2. If the stock had gone up, any loss suffered on the short sale would be at least made up by a profit on the warrant. Or, if the stock went up the warrant could be used to acquire the stock with which to cover the short sale, without any loss to the seller, other than taxes and commissions. If the warrant is selling for a relatively high price as a result of its exercisable value, it would not afford a hedge since, if the stock went down considerably, the warrant could also fall a large number of points.

HYBRID FORM. In some instances corporations have issued bonds which carried warrants for the purchase of stock and the contract

[6] The odd figures are a result of the operation of an antidilution clause.

provided that the face value of the bonds *can* be used in whole or in part instead of cash to purchase the stock. Where all of the bond is used to pay for the stock it is really a convertible bond regardless of what it may be called.

OTHER USES OF WARRANTS. The only kind of warrants mentioned above are those which are attached to a particular issue of securities at the time it is sold. This was the first use of warrants and still continues to be an important one. But in recent years there have developed a number of other uses of stock purchase warrants. These will be briefly discussed below. Aside from stating their use and the reasons therefor, we will not have to discuss the nature of the warrants since the explanation given above will apply with equal force to these other uses.

Reorganizations. The use of warrants in reorganizations did not begin until about 1920. In the past when a company failed in many instances the stock interest was "wiped out" and the stockholders were not made a part of the reorganized company, unless they paid an assessment, which is another way of saying they were asked to buy new stock in the company. The practice then developed of giving these shareholders, who had gone through the financial troubles of the company, but who had little or no equity left, warrants entitling them to buy stock of the reorganized company at a price higher than its value at the time the company emerged from the reorganization.

In some instances when a corporation goes through a drastic financial readjustment, in order to sell a new issue of stock, it will be necessary to attach warrants to these shares giving the stockholders the right to buy additional stock of the same class in the future at stepped-up prices. As an inducement to get investment bankers to handle the issue, they also may be given warrants in addition to their commissions. These are more commonly called "options," as will be pointed out later.

Refunding operations. When a bond issue becomes due it may be necessary for a corporation to put out another bond issue in order to retire the old one.

The success of a refunding issue depends upon a fairly large percentage of the bondholders accepting the new issue. As an inducement to get the bondholders to accept the new bonds, it may be necessary to attach stock purchase warrants to the bonds giving the bondholders the right to buy the stock of the company at prices usually higher than existing at the time the bonds are sold. This, of course, is similar to the use of warrants to aid in the sale of new securities, which was discussed at the beginning of the chapter.

Stock options

OPTIONS DISTINGUISHED FROM WARRANTS. It was pointed out above that there were some differences of opinion as to the meaning or use of the term "warrants." We have used the term "warrant" to apply to the contract which is attached (although it may be detachable) to a new issue of securities giving the holder thereof the right to buy another class of security. We will use the term *stock option* to apply to a contract for the purchase of stock which is *not attached* to any issue of securities, although it may be used in connection with the sale of an issue of securities.[7] These options are usually not transferable. Some writers refer to these contracts also as "warrants," but in practice they are usually called "options." Perhaps the exact terminology is not too important if we understand the nature of the contract being discussed.

The term "warrant" is sometimes used to apply to the piece of paper which evidences the right to acquire stock. Thus, it may be said that warrants are issued giving the holder the "option" to acquire the stock. When *stock rights* are issued under a privileged subscription, which will be discussed in Chapter 17, the contract evidencing the right may also be called a "warrant." When stock dividends are paid or stock of another class or another company is exchanged for a particular stock, a person may be entitled to a fractional share or a number of shares plus a fractional share. The company may issue "warrants" evidencing these fractional shares. We will now briefly discuss the various uses of stock options as defined above.

GIVEN TO INVESTMENT BANKERS. In the late 1920's it became common practice for investment bankers to insist upon receiving options as part of their compensation for selling a new issue of securities for a corporation. They were usually used in connection with the sale of common stock, but occasionally they were given with an issue of preferred stock or bonds. The options called for the purchase of common stock usually at a price higher than the selling price of the stock at the time they were given. They were usually not transferable. The options issued in the 1920's usually

[7] The term "stock option" is also used to apply to other types of contracts used in stock market operations. These are *puts, calls, spreads,* and *straddles,* which will not be taken up in this book, but which the reader can find discussed in books dealing with the stock market.

ran for a period of from one to five years, but those issued in the 1930's usually ran for less than three years.

Where the options permit the purchase of a substantial amount of stock, or more stock than the company has outstanding, control of the company could easily be acquired by the bankers, if they already did not have control. The probable dilution in the surplus and the earnings per share from the exercise of the options should be given serious consideration by any prospective purchaser of the stock under these circumstances. There has been a relative decline in the amount of options given to bankers.

Given to Corporate Promoters. In addition to being given stock in a new corporation, promoters are sometimes given options to purchase additional stock in the future at prices higher than the original offering price of the stock. As is true with options issued to other parties, they do not cost the company anything, and if the company proves to be successful they furnish a means for the promoter to receive additional compensation for his work.

Courts have upheld the giving of options to promoters, provided the conditions in connection with their use are fair and reasonable. In the past in many instances the number of options outstanding and their terms were not made public. Companies that must register their securities under the Securities Act of 1933 are now required to state in their registration statement and prospectus any options outstanding or to be created in connection with the particular security issue, and the specific terms of the options. The Act also requires that the names and addresses of all persons, who are to receive more than 10 per cent of the options, be filed.

Given to Corporate Officials. There has been a tremendous increase in recent years in the number of corporations which have given options to their leading officers. The reasons for giving them options usually falls under one of the following heads:

1. To induce a particular person to accept the position
2. To help retain an executive who is already employed by the company
3. To augment the other compensation received by an executive
4. To augment the pension plan for executives
5. To spur the executives on to make larger profits for the corporation

Although there are many able businessmen in the United States, those capable of successfully running our leading corporate giants are limited. This oftentimes results in considerable competition among companies for the services of these top-flight executives. Salaries, bonuses and commissions constitute ways of obtaining or retaining the services of an expert. But considering the attitude of stockholders, labor unions, customers, and the general public, there seems to be some limit on the amount that can be paid to executives in the form of salaries, bonuses and commissions. Furthermore, income taxes take the major part of such compensation. The exercise of stock options would also tend to increase the degree of control possessed by the particular officers.

Options to purchase the company's stock have become rather common as a means of giving greater compensation to executives, without necessarily impairing the company's public relations. Publicity is not given to the issuance of options in the same way as in the case of salaries. Furthermore, it does not cost the company anything, at the time, to issue options for the purchase of the company's stock at the same price or at a higher price than the stock is selling at the time the option is issued.

In some instances both the company and the executive look upon options as an addition to the regular pension plan operated by the company. The stock may not rise in price sufficiently high to make it profitable to exercise the options until the executive has retired or is about to retire. The stock so acquired may pay dividends of an appreciable amount during the remaining lifetime of the retired executive. Or, he could take a profit on the sale of the stock and invest the money in some other way.

It is questionable whether a corporate executive would work harder if he would receive more compensation. He is supposed to be putting forth his best efforts regardless of the amount of his salary. But having options to purchase the company's stock at what may prove to be relatively low prices in the future will certainly not cause him to work less.

In most instances perhaps the interest of the corporation and those of the stockholders are one and the same. But sometimes the corporate officials will take advantage of their position and take actions which might benefit them in the future even if they are not in the best interests of the stockholders. For example, the directors may retain profits in the business which really should be distributed to the shareholders in the form of dividends. This should result in an increase in the book value and market value of the stock. If the officials hold a substantial amount of stock in the company and have options to buy more stock in the future at prices higher than those existing at the time the options are given, they would tend to benefit from this action.

Tax Status of "Restricted" Stock Option. The income tax status of stock options varies according to the terms and conditions of their issuance. The most favorable (from the standpoint of the option holder) tax treatment is accorded the *restricted* stock option. To qualify as a restricted option, and get the best tax treatment, it must meet the following requirements:[8]

1. The option must be granted for reasons connected with the person's employment.
2. The option price of the stock must not be less than 95 per cent of the market price of the stock at the time the option is granted.
3. The stock must be held for at least six months after it is purchased.
4. The stock cannot be sold within two years from the date of the option.
5. The option can be exercised only while the optionee is still employed by the granting corporation, its parent or subsidiary, or within three months after leaving the company.
6. The option must be exercised within a period of 10 years from the time it is granted.
7. The option is nontransferable, except at death.[9]

With the restricted option no income tax is paid at the time the option is granted or at the time the stock is purchased. When the stock is sold, the difference between what is paid for it and the price obtained from its sale is reported as a capital gain. The maximum tax on a long-term capital gain is 25 per cent. This compares with a tax of 91 per cent that would be paid on ordinary income if the executive had an income in excess of $200,000. If a joint return is filed, the tax on the top part of ordinary income of a person who has a total income in excess of $200,000 would be 89, 90, or 91 per cent, depending upon the size of the income. It is thus apparent that a much greater part of the income derived from the sale of stock purchased by the exercise of a restricted stock option may be retained by the executive than if the same amount were paid in salary.

Problems in Connection With Warrants and Options. The statutes of some of the states specifically permit the issuance of warrants and options under the conditions set forth in the law. In

[8] Internal Revenue Code, Section 130A (d) (1).

[9] A further requirement is that the employee cannot own more than 10 per cent of the total combined voting power of all classes of stock. If he owns more than this, the option price of the stock must be at least 110 per cent of the market price of the stock at the time the option is granted. The 110 per cent options must be exercised within five years from their issue date.

some states corporations have sometimes issued them without any specific authorization in the laws.

Before issuing these privileges perhaps the corporation should have sufficient authorized, but unissued, stock on hand to enable it to meet the demands of the holders of the privileges. In the meantime, this ties up that amount of authorized stock. If the corporation has no authorized stock to meet the demands of the holders of the warrants or options, the shareholders cannot be forced to authorize it. In this event the holder of the privileges could not demand specific performance of the contract, but they would have a right in damages against the company for the difference between the option price of the stock and its market value.

In the case of par value stock, if the warrant or option gives the holder the right to buy the stock at a price below its par value, it would appear that he could be held liable in event of insolvency of the company for the difference between what he paid and the par value of the stock, unless it was treasury stock that was sold. Mergers, consolidations, reorganizations, recapitalizations, and the issuance of additional securities might complicate the legal rights of holders of the privileges.

Even though the requisite vote of the shareholders (or their proxies) has been obtained to grant stock options to executive officers, minority shareholders' suits have sometimes been troublesome to some companies. The management should not take any action which would result in harm to the corporation or to its shareholders. But where the stock options are granted as a type of compensation, and where the executive might remain with the company for a reasonable length of time before he can profit from the option, the company and its shareholders may actually benefit from their use. In such instances minority shareholders have no right of action against the corporation or the executives.

Unless the statutes provide otherwise, where the pre-emptive right is present, shareholders would have to waive their right to the stock before it could be sold to the officers under stock options. Protection should be provided the holders of warrants and options against dilution through stock splits, stock dividends, etc.

Questions

1. Why has the American Telephone and Telegraph Company sold convertible bonds, rather than another type of security, a number of times since World War II?
2. List the other reasons why convertible bonds are sold.

3. Explain what is meant by the statement that the buyer of convertible bonds pays more for the bond or stock into which it is convertible than the real worth of the bond or stock?

4. Explain the effects on the issuer and its shareholders of bonds being converted into stock.

5. What is meant by the conversion ratio?

6. Assume that a bond which is convertible into stock at $80 a share, is selling in the market for 90.

(a) How many shares of stock would you get by converting one $1,000 bond? (b) What is the "break-even" price of the stock? (c) If the stock advanced in price to $100, what would be the "break-even" price of the bond? (d) If the bond was selling in the market at $120, what would be the probable market price of the stock?

7. Indicate how accrued interest and dividends complicate the computation of "break-even" prices in the convertible bond and stock.

8. Can the holder of a convertible bond do anything about the company diluting the value of a share of stock through stock dividends and stock splits? Explain.

9. Explain how convertible bonds might be used as a hedge in connection with short selling.

10. Indicate in general whether you would recommend the purchase of convertible bonds and state your reasons.

11. Indicate the relative advantages both to the issuing company and to the investor of bonds convertible into stock, and bonds which have warrants attached for the purchase of the stock.

12. Indicate the relative advantages of nondetachable and detachable warrants from the viewpoint of both the issuing corporation and the investor.

13. Is the warrant holder given any protection against the dilution in the value of the shares of stock caused by stock dividends or splits? Explain.

14. Indicate the circumstances under which warrants might be used as a hedge in connection with short selling.

15. Indicate the various circumstances under which, or reasons why, warrants are issued.

16. Why might a warrant have a market value even though the stock can be purchased in the market at a lower price than through the exercise of the warrant?

17. Why might a speculator prefer trading in warrants rather than the stock which can be purchased through the exercise of the warrants?

18. Are warrants ordinarily attached to the better grade investment securities?

19. Indicate the distinction made in the book between warrants and options. Is this always observed in practice? Explain.

20. Indicate why corporate executives might prefer stock options over a salary increase. (Look up the present tax laws relating to profits made by corporate executives from the sale of stock which has been obtained through the exercise of warrants.)

Problems

1. Mr. Leland purchased twelve 6-per-cent debenture bonds of the New Era Co. on Mar. 16, 19-1, at 98. These bonds had a face value of $1,000 per

bond and were convertible into common stock of the company at any time between Jan. 1, 19-4, and Dec. 31, 19-9, at $125 per share. At the time the bonds were purchased the stock of the company was selling in the market for $108 per share. The fluctuations in the price of the stock follow:

Year	*High*	*Low*	*Year*	*High*	*Low*
19-1	110	53	19-6	100	70
19-2	61	32	19-7	137½	80
19-3	38	16	19-8	200	187½
19-4	49	30	19-9	150	125
19-5	60	50	19-0	150	137½

(a) How many shares of stock would Mr. Leland get if he converted his 12 bonds? (b) If the market price of the bonds remained at the sale price, would it have been profitable for Mr. Leland to convert his bonds in 19-4? Why or why not?

(c) If the price of the bonds remained at the sale price, how high would the stock have to get in order for him to break even on the conversion? Express this by the use of a formula in which:

a = price of the bonds (expressed in per cent of face value)
b = conversion price
x = break-even price

(d) What do you think should have been the theoretical high and low prices of the bonds in the following years: 19-7; 19-8; 19-9? (e) Relative to their 19-1 and 19-8 prices, what do you think should have been the market price of the bonds in 19-0?

2. Look up the following bonds: Inland Steel Co. Convertible Debentures, 3¼'s of 1972, and Colorado Fuel & Iron Corp. Convertible Debentures, 4¾'s of 1966, and ascertain the following for each bond:

(a) Terms of conversion. (b) Number of shares into which one bond is convertible, or conversion price of the common stock. (c) Market prices of the bonds and the stock into which the bond is convertible as of the same day this week. (d) Considering the conversion price of the stock and the market price of the bonds and stock, how much, if any, must the stock advance in price in order that a bondholder would break even by converting?

3. The Modern Aircraft Corp. was formed in 19-6 with an authorized capitalization of 2,000,000 shares of no-par common stock, and $20,000,000 of preferred stock with a par value of $100 per share. The preferred was 7 per cent nonparticipating and nonvoting. At the time of organization, 1,000,000 shares of the common stock were sold at $40 per share. In the Autumn of 19-8 the entire $20,000,000 in preferred stock was sold at par, and each share carried with it a warrant entitling the holder to purchase one share of common stock at $50. At the time the preferred was marketed the common was selling at $43 per share.

In the early part of April, 19-9, the market price of the common stock had gone up to $80. The company's surplus account had increased to $20,000,000. Orders sufficient to keep the plants operating three shifts a day for the next three years were on the books.

(a) Why do you think these warrants were issued by the company? (b) If the warrants were nondetachable, at what price do you think the preferred should be selling in April, 19-9? (c) If the warrants were detachable, how much would you pay for a warrant in April, 19-9? (d) Would the warrants sell for more or less than their "theoretical" value? Why? (e) Do you think that the market price of the warrant in April, 19-9 would depend upon the number of warrants outstanding? Explain. (f) From the standpoint of the issuing company, do you think the warrants should be detachable or non-detachable? Why? (g) As a director of the company, would you vote for the issuance of the warrants as stated above or for an alternative proposal to make the preferred stock convertible? Give your reasons. (h) Does the preferred stockholder who exercises his warrants and buys the common stock at $50 when it is selling in the market for $80 have any liability on the common stock? Explain. Would your answer be the same if the common had a par value of $100 per share? (i) Do you think the issuance of these warrants was fair to the old common stockholders? Why or why not?

4. The following relate to the warrants issued by the Tri-Continental Corp., which are traded on the American Stock Exchange:

(a) How many shares of stock may be purchased with one warrant? (b) At what price can the stock be obtained through the exercise of a warrant? (c) Look up the closing price of the warrants and the stock (the latter is listed on the New York Stock Exchange), of a particular day during the past week. How can you explain the reason for the market price of the warrants?

Chapter 13

BOND RETIREMENT, SINKING FUNDS, AND SERIAL BONDS

Bond retirement

Bonds Come Due. In some types of companies, such as public utilities, bonded indebtedness is looked upon as a more or less permanent part of the capitalization. This was true in the case of railroads for a long period of time after their development. Even if a bonded indebtedness is considered a permanent part of the capitalization, the particular bonds outstanding come due and must be paid off, even though their place may be taken by a new issue of bonds. When the business is subject to competition or is still young, and there is no assurance of what the future earnings may be, bonds are looked upon as a temporary means of obtaining funds, and the issuer has the intention to pay them off as rapidly as possible. New industrial companies as a class are of this type.

Methods of Retiring Bonds. There are three methods of retiring bonds, and any of these methods may be used to eliminate the bonds either at or before maturity. These methods are as follows:

Redemption. Bonds are said to be *redeemed* when they are paid off in cash. This may occur at the maturity of the bonds or before by the exercise of the call feature or by the purchase of the bonds in the market.

Refunding. If bonds are paid off by means of another issue of bonds, they are said to be *refunded.* The new bonds may be exchanged to the bondholders for their old bonds, or the new bonds may be sold in the market and the proceeds used to retire the old bonds. The latter procedure is really a method of redemption.

Conversion. Bonds may be paid off by the holders thereof *converting* them into stock. This was described in Chapter 12, and therefore nothing further will be said about it.

Redemption at Maturity. When the bonds are paid upon maturity it is a routine matter. The cash (actually a check) for the principal amount and the interest due for the last period is turned over to the trustee representing the bondholders and he distributes this to the bondholders in exchange for their bonds.

Redemption Before Maturity. The paying off of a debt as soon as possible appears to be a logical thing, but there are various reasons why it may be done. As will be obvious from the discussion, the circumstances present at a particular time may result in one or more of the reasons for extinguishing the bonded indebtedness, while other circumstances may dictate other reasons. Although the following are the reasons for redemption before maturity, they can also be considered as reasons why a corporation may be anxious to pay off its bonds upon maturity.

Elimination of fixed charges. The interest on the bonds must be paid regardless of the amount of earnings or cash possessed by the corporation. This fixed charge may in the future be a source of considerable embarrassment and may even cause the concern to fail. Realizing this, many corporations try to eliminate their bonded indebtedness, the principal as well as the fixed charge, as soon as the opportunity presents itself.

Fluctuation rather than regularity is the rule in business, particularly among industrial concerns. Earnings made in good times should be used to retire the bonds before another slack period. Many corporations, including railroads, took advantage of their large earnings during and after World War II to get rid of bonded indebtedness.

Reduction of fixed charges. In many instances corporations are forced to sell bonds at a time of high interest rates. Or, the company's credit at the time may be such that a relatively high rate was necessary in order to sell the bonds. Later interest rates may generally fall, or the company's credit may improve so that it could currently borrow at a lower rate than it is paying on its present bonds, and redeem the expensive old issues.

Elimination of stringent provisions. In order to add to the marketability of the bonds to be issued, the corporation may have been forced to include some protective provisions in the indenture, which it now would like to eliminate, e.g., the requirement to observe certain strict current-asset or cash ratios, before it may pay dividends; prohibitions against incurring of additional debt or bonded indebtedness; mortgage on after-acquired property, which might make future financing expensive. The redemption of such bonds will extinguish the stringent provisions.

Elimination of inflexible financial plan. In many instances corporations sell an issue of bonds secured by a first mortgage against all their property, when they are still comparatively small or young. The company may later develop and need to borrow more money, but the issue of first mortgage bonds it has outstanding may be closed and the company cannot issue any more first mortgage bonds against the same property. Under these circumstances it would be desirable for the company to retire the old bonds.

Investment of idle cash. If operations and financial management are successful, a corporation should from time to time have cash on hand. Only part of the earnings are ordinarily paid out to the stockholders in the form of dividends. The retained earnings may in part at least be represented by cash. This cash could be reinvested in additional plants, inventories, etc., or it could be invested in securities of other companies or in government bonds.

For rough periods in the future perhaps part of the retained earnings should not be reinvested in the company's operating assets, but in liquid securities. However, there are several drawbacks to this procedure. Commissions will ordinarily have to be paid to brokers both when buying and selling the securities. The rate of earnings on these conservative investments would probably be lower than the rate of interest the company is paying on its bonds; there would have to be constant supervision of the investments; then there is always the possibility that some of the money invested may be lost. In many instances the best investment a company can make is its own bonds.

The disadvantage of using the cash to retire the bonds is that the money would not be available in the event the company ran into a period of deficits or low earnings. But even here the retirement of the bonds would probably result in a better financial condition than if the money had been sunk into additional plant facilities. The elimination or reduction of the bonded indebtedness may open the way for the company, in a period of adversity, to secure new loans, which might have been impossible had the bonds not been retired.

Bolster market for bonds. The bonds of a particular corporation may fall in price more than the general market. This drop in price may result in some of the company's bondholders disposing of their bonds. Such a situation has an adverse effect on the credit of the company. A falling market for its bonds may cause also the company's stock to decline in price—which would tend to make a bad situation worse.

If the company has the necessary cash available, it might be advisable for it to buy up some of the bonds on the market, and thus to check the price drop or reverse its direction.

Economical method of retirement. If a corporation's bonds are selling in the market at a price considerably below their call or face value, material savings could be effected if the corporation would buy the bonds on the market and cancel them; it could be done in an orderly fashion so as not to cause too much of a price increase.

METHODS OF REDEEMING BONDS BEFORE MATURITY. The methods of redeeming bonds before they mature are as follows:

Exercise of call feature. It is the usual practice to insert in the bond indenture a provision giving the issuing company the right to call in the bonds before their maturity. The provision calls for a fixed time for redemption, which is commonly on an interest date. The indenture usually provides that notice, which in practice ranges from several weeks to several months, must be given to the bondholders in advance of calling in the bonds. Registered bondholders will be sent notice by mail; for coupon bonds the notice will be printed in designated financial publications.

It is commonly provided in the indenture that the issue is callable only as a whole, but in some instances it is provided that a specified amount less than this may be retired. In the latter case the numbers of the bonds to be called will usually be determined by lot. Purchase of bonds for sinking funds will be mentioned later in the chapter.

Purchase on market through dealers. The corporation may secure the services of an investment banker or broker to buy up its bonds on the market. Bondholders, at least at first, are not aware of the fact that the bonds are being purchased for retirement. Thus, they would not hold out for a high price. The broker or dealer can judge the market and buy in periods of weakness in such quantities that the price would not be run up. This method of retirement might be used when the bonds were not callable, or when they were selling below their call price.

Direct negotiation with bondholders. In some instances a corporation will negotiate directly with its larger bondholders, for the retirement of their bonds, or advertise for tenders of its bonds at a price not to exceed a specified amount. The disadvantage of dealing directly with the bondholders is that they will know that retirement is being attempted and thus hold out for a relatively high price.

DISADVANTAGES TO BONDHOLDER OF REDEMPTION. In this section we will be considering primarily bonds that are redeemed through the exercise of the call feature. Usually, when it is to the best interests of the corporation to retire its bonds before maturity, it would be to the advantage of the bondholders to continue to hold them.

Interest rates may decline, with the result that the company exercises the call feature and refunds the issue with one bearing a lower rate of interest. The bondholder would have preferred to retain the bonds bearing the relatively high rate.

Having secured his money back, the bondholder is now confronted with the problem of reinvesting at a time of low interest rates. Furthermore, there is commonly a brokerage charge or commission to be paid to buy new securities. For the bondholder it is somewhat of a nuisance to watch for call notices, particularly in the case of coupon bonds, unless he turns his bonds over to a trust company for administration at a specified fee.

To offset, at least in part, these shortcomings of the call feature, corporations usually make their bonds callable at a slight *premium* over their face value. The amount of the premium oftentimes approximates one year's interest on the bonds.

NATURE OF REFUNDING. The bonded indebtedness of a corporation is called its *funded debt.* If a company *funds* its debt, it means that it replaces short-term notes or open book accounts by long-term bonds. *Refunding* a debt means to exchange one bond issue for another bond issue.

In a refunding operation the bondholders are frequently asked, or given the opportunity, to exchange their bonds for the new ones. If not all the old bondholders will do this, bonds of the refunding issue will have to be sold for cash sufficient to retire the old bonds. Commonly the issue is underwritten by investment bankers to insure its successful sale.

A bondholder cannot force a corporation to pay off its bonds before they are due; nor can a corporation force its bondholders to give up their bonds before they are due, unless the issue contains a call clause. But if bonds are called, the bondholder can insist on cash.

REFUNDING AT MATURITY. In some instances, when a bond issue comes due, the issuing corporation may need its cash or liquid assets in the business, or it does not have available cash or liquid assets necessary for their payment. If a refunding issue is acceptable to the bondholders or can be sold to secure funds, the corporation may be glad of the opportunity to pay off its bonds in this manner.

Companies, such as public utilities, may prefer to have bonds outstanding. Since their rates are set so as to permit them to earn only a fair return on a fair investment, it may be to the interests of the stockholders to have a bonded indebtedness more or less permanently. In this way they benefit from the *leverage,* or *trading on the equity,* which was discussed earlier in the book. Thus when a bond issue becomes due, it is generally taken for granted that its place will be taken by a refunding issue. It would, of course, be more profitable to pay off a bond issue than keep redundant cash on hand permanently, but public utilities generally have a need for increasing amounts of cash as the demand for their services increases.

Refunding Before Maturity. Earlier in the chapter we considered the various reasons why a corporation might want to redeem its bonds before their maturity. The same reasons would apply with equal force to refunding before maturity.

Computing Savings on Fixed Charges Through Refunding. When interest rates in general decline, or when the credit of the company increases to the point where it can borrow at a lower rate than it is now paying, at first glance large savings in interest rates may be expected from a refunding operation. But we should carefully compute the actual savings before jumping to conclusions. Let us assume that a corporation has outstanding $10,000,000 in 4 per cent bonds, which come due in 20 years from now, and that it can secure the money at about 3 per cent today. If an issue of 3 per cent bonds is sold to refund the 4 per cent bonds it might appear that an annual saving of $100,000, or a total saving of $2,000,000 for the 20-year period, could be effected (compounding the interest would still increase the savings).

To compute the *actual* savings, however, we will have to consider the following factors:

1. Commissions to bankers
2. Printing costs
3. Expense to register with Securities and Exchange Commission
4. Legal fees
5. Maturity date of new issue
6. Call price of old issue
7. Income tax rates

To simplify our explanation we will also suppose that the corporation can sell the bonds to investment bankers at such a price that it will have left an amount equal to the face value of the bonds after paying bankers' commissions, printing costs, registration expenses, and legal fees. To simplify our illustration further we will assume that the refunding issue has a maturity of 20 years. The call price on the old issue, we will assume, is 105. In order to compute the savings correctly we will have to assume, in advance, a particular corporate income tax rate. It is realized that this rate will probably vary in the future, but for purposes of analysis we will assume a rate of 50 per cent.

To call in the old issue will require $10,500,000. Of this amount $500,000 represents the premium on the old bonds. At the time when this amount is spent, it can be deducted as an expense for federal corporate income tax purposes. By paying out this amount the company will save $250,000 in taxes, which it would have been paying had the old issue not been called. So assuming that the $250,000 saved is available to apply toward the retirement of the bonds, it will be necessary to issue only $10,250,000 in new bonds.

The interest on the new bonds would be $307,500 annually, or a total of $6,150,000 for the entire 20 years. But since the interest charge is deductible for income tax purposes, the actual net cost to the company would be only half this amount, or $3,075,000. Interest on the old bonds would have been $400,000 a year, or $8,000,000 for the 20-year period. Adjusting this for taxes, the net cost for 20 years would have been $4,000,000. Subtracting from this latter figure the net cost of the interest on the new bonds of $3,075,000, leaves a net interest savings on the new bonds of $925,000.

But if the refunding issue is sold, the company will have to pay off $250,000 more in the bonds than if they had let the old issue remain outstanding. Subtracting this amount from the net interest savings of $925,000, leaves us only $675,000 as the net savings that would be realized over the 20-year period by refunding the old issue.[1]

[1] A more accurate analysis would take into consideration the earnings that might be realized by the company each year on the amount that is saved in interest. A compounding effect would be produced since in each successive year the company will have the use of the money saved in interest plus the amount earned on it in preceding years. Offsetting this in part, however, would be the income taxes that would have to be paid on the earnings realized from the savings.

If the bonds are purchased each year for sinking fund retirement a different result might be obtained. Also some consideration might want to be given to the fact that annual provision might be made for the retirement of the additional $250,000 in bonds, which would reduce by that amount the funds available for ordinary business purposes (adjusted for any earnings that might be earned on sinking fund, and for income taxes).

Bondholders' Attitude Toward Refunding Bonds. Most of our discussion in connection with refunding has been from the viewpoint of the corporation. What is the attitude of the bondholders in respect to the refunding issue? The disadvantages to bondholders of redemption through the use of the call feature will apply with equal force here. If the corporation is asking the bondholders to accept the refunding bonds voluntarily before the maturity of their old bonds, the bondholders are in a relatively strong bargaining position. If the old bonds are being retired by exercise of the call feature, the bondholder does not have the option of retaining his bonds. But he does have the choice of taking the refunding bonds or demanding cash. The nature of the refunding bonds and the conditions of the investment market would determine which should be done. The fact that the refunding bonds will probably be purchased by a banker if they are not taken by the old bondholders would indicate that the terms of the issue are such that they could be sold on the market. In other words, the bondholder probably could not do much better by taking cash and reinvesting in other securities. Furthermore, if he did take the money, he would have the problem of selecting new investments and of costs in connection therewith.

Where an issue is being refunded at maturity the bondholders might be better off in the long run to accept the new bonds. One explanation would be the same as stated above when the old bonds are called. In some instances the financial condition of the company may be such that it could not pay off the old issue in cash. Forcing it might result in failure of the company. In the reorganization of the company the bondholders may often be forced to undergo some sacrifice. Realizing this possibility, the bondholders might feel that it was to their best interests to accept the refunding bonds.

Inducements to Refund. In order to entice the bondholders to exchange their bonds for those of the refunding issue, corporations oftentimes have to give them some inducements. One or more of these may be offered in the same issue. Some of these might be used when the company is trying to get the bondholders to refund voluntarily their bonds before maturity, or when it wants them to accept the bonds when they are being called, or upon maturity.

1. *Higher rate of interest.* In some instances the refunding bonds bear a higher face rate of interest than the old bonds. It is appreciated, however, that a corporation will not pay a higher rate on its bonds than is necessary. In fact the reason refunding issues

are oftentimes used is to reduce the fixed charges, as has been pointed out previously.

2. *Cash bonus.* Occasionally a corporation will offer the bondholders a cash bonus if they will exchange their bonds.

3. *Partial redemption.* In order to make the offer attractive to bondholders, corporations will sometimes offer to give the bondholders the chance to receive partial payments of the bond in cash, and the balance in new bonds.

4. *Sinking fund provision.* If the old issue had no sinking fund behind it, the company may provide for one in the refunding issue for the purpose of inducing the bondholders to refund. (Sinking funds are liquid assets to be reserved at regular intervals for the retirement of bonds.) This in itself would not appear to be much of an inducement because a sinking fund merely increases the probability that the refunding bonds will be paid off. The bondholder can demand cash immediately for the bonds he is holding if they have been called or if they have matured.

5. *Better security.* The refunding issue may be better secured than the bonds which are being refunded. For example the old bonds may be debentures while the refunding issue may be secured by a mortgage. Or, the bonds outstanding may be secured by a mortgage on only a small part of the corporation's property, while the refunding issue has a mortgage on all the property. Even if this were the case, the refunding issue, however, would not necessarily be in a better position. The mortgage behind the old issue may constitute a first claim on a very important part of the corporate property, and the amount of the old bonds outstanding may be much smaller than the refunding issue which is to be exchanged or sold.

6. *Wider market.* As indicated above, the refunding issue may be a much larger one than the particular issue or issues that are being refunded. The larger issue will attract a wider market, which will result in a higher market price. Also the refunding issue may be listed on one of the stock exchanges (the old issue may not have been listed); this might further increase its market.

7. *Guarantee by another company.* In some instances a parent company will guarantee the refunding bonds issued by one of its subsidiaries as an inducement to the bondholders to accept them. This guarantee may add materially to the investment worth of the bonds.

Extension of Maturity. At a time when a corporation's bonds become due, they may not only be unable to pay them off, but their credit or the market conditions may be so bad that they cannot even put out a refunding issue. The company may therefore ask the bondholders to agree to an extension of the maturity of the bonds for a designated period of years. The bondholders cannot legally be forced to agree to the extension, but they may be too unorganized to act with concerted force, or they may realize that in the long run they may profit more from an extension than from foreclosure action.

In some instances a minority of the bondholders will not agree to the extension, but if a sufficient amount of the bondholders do agree to make the plan successful, those not agreeing are paid off in cash.

Inducements to Extend. In some instances the corporation offers the bondholders some inducement to extend the maturity of their bonds. This may take the form of agreeing to an increase in the rate of interest on the bonds, or increasing the security behind the bonds.

In some cases, however, the bondholder is asked to make some additional sacrifice in addition to the extension of the maturity. The financial condition of the company may be such that it appears improbable that the company can pay the regular rate of interest on the bonds in the future. Where this is the case the bondholders may be asked to agree to a reduction in the rate of interest paid on the bonds. If the bonds possessed privileges such as conversion or stock purchase warrants, they are sometimes terminated when the extension in maturity is made.

Sinking funds

Meaning of Sinking Fund. A *sinking fund* consists of assets of designated amounts which a company sets aside at stated intervals for the purpose of redeeming all or a portion of the bonds of a particular issue at or before maturity. It gets its name from the fact that it is designed to "sink" the debt. The sinking fund may consist of cash, or part cash, securities of other companies, bonds of the same company but other than the issue for which the fund was set up, or bonds of the particular issue for which it was set up to retire.

Reasons for Sinking Fund. If it is expected that a debt is to be a permanent part of the capitalization of the corporation, and that upon maturity of a particular issue it will be replaced by a refunding issue, there is little necessity for a sinking fund. In most instances, however, it is contemplated that the debt is a temporary thing and that it will be paid off at maturity. This is particularly true in the case of industrial enterprises, and has been true to an increasing extent among public utilities in recent years. Where it is expected that the debt will be retired, a sinking fund is commonly recommended. The various reasons for setting up a sinking fund are as follows:

1. *Future difficult to predict.* A corporation may intend to pay off its bonds upon maturity by a refunding issue. But by the time the bonds come due the market conditions or the financial condition of the company may deteriorate so that the refunding issue could not be marketed or offered to the bondholders for their old bonds. At such a time a sinking fund might prevent failure of the company.

2. *Payment a financial strain.* Even if a company is successful and its bonds come due at a favorable time, providing for payment of a large issue such as, for example, $50,000,000, might cause a severe financial strain on a company. During the years of good earnings, large dividends may have been paid. Also large amounts may have been plowed back into fixed assets. A large "surplus" on the books is of little help unless some of the assets are in such form that they can be used to redeem the bonds. When a corporation has need for a large sum of money in the future to retire its bonds, it would be advisable for it to provide annually out of earnings a fixed amount so that when the time comes that they have to meet the bond maturity payment, they will have the money. In this way that money would not be paid out in dividends or invested in fixed assets.

The top managers of many companies are commonly rather old people, who probably would not worry too much about a company bond issue that comes due in 25 years. But if a sinking fund is set up to redeem the issue, it will be their concern to see to it that every year funds be provided sufficient to meet the sinking fund installment as well as other cash outlays.

3. *Increases marketability of bonds.* The presence of a sinking fund provision increases the attractiveness of bonds, and they are, therefore, more easily marketed. This may result in a slightly lower interest cost to the company. This added security gives price support to the bonds.

4. *Offsets property depreciation.* All property deteriorates from wear and tear and action of the elements. Thus, as time goes on,

the specific security behind the bonds may depreciate in value. If adequate depreciation reserves are set up, this may in part at least offset the depreciation, but there is no assurance that the reserve would be invested in comparable assets or assets which would come under the lien of the mortgage. If a sinking fund was set up this would give protection to the bondholders even if the property depreciated.

Railroad equipment depreciates relatively rapidly. Practically all equipment trust obligations which have been used to finance the acquisition of rolling stock and which have not been of the serial type, have had sinking funds behind them. Companies with wasting assets, such as mining corporations, also almost invariably have sinking funds behind their bonds which provide for the retirement of the bonds as the assets of the company are being depleted.

DETERMINING AMOUNT OF SINKING FUND INSTALLMENTS. The statutes of some of the states require sinking funds for railroad and public utility bonds. In other cases the contract under which the bonds were issued would have to be consulted in order to determine whether there was provision for a sinking fund, and if so, the method that would be followed in determining how much should be put into the fund from time to time. In some instances, even though there is no provision in the indenture relating to it, a corporation may voluntarily set up a sinking fund for the retirement of its bonds, but in such a case if the company subsequently decided to discontinue the fund, the bondholders could do nothing about it.

There are three different methods of determining the amounts of sinking fund installments. These are listed below and followed by a brief description.

1. Fixed regular installments
2. Installments varying according to the results of the business
3. Optional installments

FIXED REGULAR INSTALLMENTS. The most common method followed in the case of closed issues of bonds is the payment of a fixed amount of money, or money equivalent to a definite face amount of the bonds. Thus, if a corporation sold a $10,000,000 20-year bond issue, the sinking fund requirements could be set at $500,000 a year, or an amount necessary to buy $500,000 in face value of the bonds each year. Although the monetary amount is definite and the same each year, the sinking fund would not provide for the redemption of the entire issue if a premium had to be paid to get the bonds. If $500,000 face amount of the bonds had to be purchased each year for the sinking fund, adequate provision will have been made for the redemption of the entire issue.

If the issue is an open one, comparable provisions could be made. The annual sinking fund installment could be expressed in terms of money equivalent to 1/20 of the face value of the bonds, or an amount necessary to buy 1/20 of the bonds. This is the usual type of sinking fund for open issues.

In some cases the amount of money to be put into the sinking fund annually increases as time goes on. This is designed to conform to the ability of the corporation to make the payments. After the money obtained from the sale of the bonds has been invested in the company assets for a period of time it should be reflected in increased earnings. Another reason for increasing the sinking fund payments during the later years is—not to burden the corporation too much during the early years when the sum of interest charges is relatively high. As the amount of bonds outstanding is reduced by purchase with money from the sinking fund, the company will have less in interest to pay each year. If the bonds are kept alive in the sinking fund, the interest received on them will add to the fund. Or, if the funds are invested in other securities, the income from them will augment the fund. In some instances the fixed annual sinking fund installments will provide for the retirement at maturity of only part of the entire issue.

INSTALLMENTS VARYING ACCORDING TO RESULTS OF THE BUSINESS. Sinking fund installments sometimes vary according to the volume of business or profits of the company. This is done in order to make the payments correspond to the ability of the corporation to meet the installments. Often there is a minimum annual requirement regardless of the results of the business operations. Following are the variables on which the amount of the payments are based.

Gross volume of business or unit of output. In some instances the amount of the sinking fund payments depends upon the gross volume of business done by the corporation. This is more commonly found in railroad and public utility bonds than in those issued by industrial companies.

In the case of wasting asset companies, such as mining and timber companies, as the product is sold the assets behind the bonds are constantly being reduced. Depletion charges will offset this but the assets represented by depletion reserves may not be direct security for the bonds. If such bonds are not retired serially, sinking funds are practically always provided. Commonly the amount paid into the fund varies according to the number of tons of ore removed in the case of mines, or the amount of lumber cut. The latter is usually called a "stumpage" charge. Sinking funds for bonds issued by land companies commonly call for installment payments varying according to the amount of land sold.

Net income. In some instances the amount of the sinking fund payments varies according to the net profit earned by the company. This is desirable, for in the long run the money should come from profits. The latter, however, does not necessarily provide sufficient funds for the retirement of the bonds. Besides, the amount shown as earnings may vary somewhat according to the accounting practices followed. Some call for a fixed amount plus a designated percentage of the net earnings. When the payments are based on net earnings, the percentage of the earnings sometimes increases during the later years as was described above in connection with fixed amount sinking funds.

In the case of collateral trust bonds, sinking fund payments are sometimes based on the amount paid in dividends on the stock which is pledged behind the bonds.

Dividends. Some sinking funds call for a fixed amount or for a designated per cent of the earnings, plus an amount equivalent to dividends paid by the corporation in excess of a designated per cent, or plus an amount equivalent to a designated per cent of the dividends.

Optional Installments. In some instances the decision on whether or not sinking fund installments are to be paid, and on the amounts of such installments, are left to the discretion of the board of directors. Such provisions occur more commonly in bonds issued at the time of reorganization of a company. In some of these issues minimum amounts are specified. Usually the indenture specifies that a certain percentage of the bonds shall be retired before their maturity date. In some instances when the installment payments are contingent or optional, they are cumulative up to a designated amount so that whenever possible any arrears must be made up.

Optional sinking funds obviously do not add much strength to the issue. As long as the company is successful and can provide for a sinking fund, or can pay off the bonds, the fund does not add much. But it is at this time that the directors will probably make payments into the fund. At a time when earnings are low and liquid assets small in amount, the fund would add to the security of the bonds, but under these conditions the directors would probably pass over the payments into the fund.

Substitutes for Sinking Fund Payments. The indentures under which some bonds are issued provide that certain allocations of funds will be accepted as a substitute for sinking fund payments. For example, it is sometimes provided that if bonds having a senior lien or one equal to the bonds for which the sinking fund is set up, are paid off, it will be equivalent to the payment into the sinking fund of the same amount. In some instances, the contract provides that, if bonds for which a sinking fund is being established are paid off from funds other than the sinking fund, or if they are convertible into stock and have been converted, sinking fund payments equivalent to such amounts will not have to be made.

The logic of the above is probably apparent. The position of a particular issue is improved by the payment of a senior lien or one having an equal claim almost to the same extent as if the bonds had not been paid off and the money had been paid into the sinking fund for the particular issue. If the particular bonds are actually retired or redeemed by some method other than the use of the sinking fund, there is need for less money in the sinking fund.

Corporation's Obligation for Sinking Fund Payments. Where payment of sinking fund installments is optional with the directors, nothing can be done by the bondholders or their trustee if payments are not made. But it is different when the indenture calls for a definite amount to be paid into the fund each year, and the fund is administered by a trustee.

Default in the payment of a sinking fund installment may be treated the same as a default in the payment of the interest or principal on the bonds. In the past particularly, trustees had been inclined to do nothing about defaults in sinking fund payments. The trustees are selected and paid by the corporation issuing the bonds so that this might influence their actions.

In most instances a corporation will probably meet its sinking fund installments when it is possible for it to do so. If the company has no earnings or cash out of which the payments can be made, enforcement under such circumstances might result in the appointment of a receiver and the reorganization of the company. This would be a bad blow to the credit of the company and would adversely affect the bondholders who might have to undergo some sacrifice in the reorganization. If on the other hand, no action was taken and the company was allowed to get back on its feet, the sinking fund arrears might be made up and the bondholders would be paid off at maturity, as if there had been no default in the sinking fund payments.

The situation is somewhat different now in respect to trustees who are appointed for bond issues whose indentures come under the provisions of the Trust Indenture Act of 1939. This legislation requires the trustees to serve as fiduciaries of the bondholders rather than as servants of the corporation. Such indentures require the trustee to make complete reports to the bondholders informing them of any default. Furthermore, the trustees must act under the circumstances as a prudent man would in the conduct of his own affairs. If the company was able to pay into the fund but did not do so, it would be the duty of the trustee to bring action to compel the company to act. But if, on the other hand, the company was financially unable to meet the sinking fund payments, the trustee may correctly decide that to attempt to force payment might do the bondholders more harm than good.

SINKING FUND TRUSTEES. We have referred several times to the sinking fund trustee. In some instances the corporation which issues the bonds administers its own sinking fund. This is more commonly the case when the sinking fund payments are optional. When the company must pay a fixed amount or variable amount into the fund, it is the usual custom today to appoint an independent trustee to administer the fund. Sinking fund payments are then made to the trustee and he invests the money or purchases the bonds which are to be retired.

The indentures of securities that must be registered under the Securities Act of 1933, must meet the requirements of the Trust Indenture Act of 1939. This was discussed in Chapter 8. One of the provisions of this Act requires that corporations appoint an independent indenture trustee. It is the general custom to appoint the same trustee as the sinking fund trustee.

INVESTMENT OBJECTIVES OF THE SINKING FUND. An important consideration in connection with any sinking fund is how the fund is to be invested. There are three tests which should be applied to sinking fund investments. They are as follows:

1. *Safety.* The ultimate purpose to be served by the sinking fund is the retirement of the particular bonds for which the fund was established. It is therefore of importance to see to it that the fund is invested in relatively safe securities.

2. *Fair return.* Some consideration must be given to the rate of return which is earned on the sinking fund investments. The fund installments take money out of the business which otherwise might have been earning a good rate of return. Furthermore, the

corporation is paying interest on its bonds until they are retired. It would not be good financial management to pay 4½ per cent on your own bonds and earn only 2¾ per cent, for example, on bonds acquired through sinking fund investments. However, the rate of return on a bond varies in inverse proportion to the safety of the investment. Since the sinking fund is set up to insure the payment of these bonds, no chances should be taken on the investment of the fund. Therefore a trustee may demand higher grade investments for the fund than those bonds being retired by the fund.

3. *Liquidity.* Since the purpose of the sinking fund is to retire the particular bonds on or before maturity, it is important that the investments be sufficiently liquid so that they can be converted into cash whenever needed. When we speak of liquidity we have in mind not just the ability to sell, but the ability to sell without appreciable sacrifice. In other words, the investment should be such that it can be sold at about the same price as was paid for it. Such an investment would normally be high-grade bonds.

Types of Sinking Fund Investments. In cases where a sinking fund is set up at the time the bonds are issued, the indenture will usually state the kinds of property or securities in which the fund shall be invested. In general, there are four different types of sinking fund investments.

1. Improvements
2. Bonds of other companies
3. Other bonds issued by the same company
4. Bonds which the sinking fund was set up to retire

Improvements. In some instances the agreement provides that the sinking fund may be invested in new property or in improvements made to the original property. The reader may already be questioning whether such an investment meets the tests set forth above. The obvious answer is that it does not. It would lack the liquidity which should be possessed by a fund. Moreover, there may be some question as to the safety of the investment, and there is no assurance that it will bring in a fair return. If such an investment is called a "fund" it should perhaps be referred to as an *improvement* or *maintenance fund.* Actually this is not even a fund as we usually use the term "fund" to apply to assets which are set aside for easy conversion into cash for a definite purpose.

The idea behind a so-called sinking fund, such as an improvement or maintenance fund, is that the investment of the money in improvements or additions will increase the value of the property, which is the security for the bonds, and offset, in part at least, its normal depreciation. Also the additional property should increase the earnings of the company, which in turn would improve the investment position of the bonds.

Such sinking funds are now found almost only with the open-end bonds issued by public utilities. Many of these companies have constant need for funds for expansion purposes. Public utilities frequently refund their bonds rather than actually reduce their bonded indebtedness. Where this is the case, there is less need for the ordinary type of sinking fund.

Regardless of what might be said in favor of such investments, the fact remains that investment in ordinary corporate assets does not provide the funds with which to retire the bonds—and that is the real purpose of a sinking fund. Also, if the company management is charged with the administration of such a sinking fund, there is a temptation to charge to the "fund" money which should have entered the expense accounts by charges to repairs or depreciation.

Bonds of Other Companies. In many of the older issues of bonds the sinking fund was invested in securities of other companies, to be converted into cash upon the maturity of the bonds for which the fund was set up. Several objections can be made to this type of sinking fund. One is the problem of the selection of the securities and the administration of the fund. The bonds acquired should be only of good quality, otherwise the safety of the investment might be impaired. To get safety, the rate of return paid on the bonds would probably be lower than the company was paying on the bonds which the fund was set up to retire. Then there is always the question what price would be obtained for the bonds when it became necessary to sell them to obtain the cash to retire the bonds. In some instances, the funds have been invested in government bonds in order to get safety and liquidity. In the case of business corporations, this would invariably mean that the company would be paying out a higher rate than it was earning on the sinking fund. Sinking funds of this type are rarely found in modern issues.

Other Bonds Issued by the Same Company. A few bond issues that were sold in the past provided for the sinking fund to be invested in the company's own bonds which were senior to the particular issue for which the fund was established. The purchase of such bonds would strengthen the position of the particular issue for which the fund was established, but there are several shortcomings to this type of sinking fund. Anything which would have an adverse effect on the ability of the company to pay one issue of its bonds would produce a similar situation in regard to the other issues. If the bonds purchased are canceled, there would be no assurance of getting sufficient funds on hand to retire the issue for which the fund was established. If the bonds were kept alive in the fund they would have to be resold in order to get the cash to retire the other issue. The resale might cause the price to go down, and thus adversely affect the company's credit.

Bonds for Which the Sinking Fund Was Set Up. Investment of the sinking fund in the particular bonds for which the fund was established is the method most commonly followed today. Since the ultimate purpose of the fund is to retire these bonds, this procedure is sound and logical.

Buying the bonds for which the fund was set up meets the sinking fund investment tests better than any other form of investment. It is perhaps the safest of any form of investment. The purpose of the fund—to get the bonds out of the creditors' hands—is being achieved in a direct way. Thus, the liquidity test also is met better than if the sinking fund were invested in any other securities.

The test of income is also admirably met. If the bonds are purchased and canceled, the company will be saving that amount in interest. Should it keep them alive, the company would in effect be earning the same amount on the investment of the sinking fund as it is paying on the bonds, and all this is accomplished without any risk in the investment of the money.

In addition to the above stated points, buying these bonds on the market will help to maintain their prices relatively high. This, along with the gradual decline in the amount of bonded indebtedness, will improve the credit of the company and result in greater protection to the outstanding bonds.

There are several possible disadvantages to the purchase of these bonds. If the corporation had not reserved the right to call in the bonds, it may have to pay a relatively high price for them, and its buying will tend to push the price still higher. The purchase of the bonds narrows the market for the remainder of bonds outstanding. This, of course, is offset at least in part by the advantages already stated.

Methods of Acquiring Own Bonds. When the sinking fund is to be invested in bonds of the particular issue for which the fund was established, it is commonly provided that the company can make installment payments, in whole or in part, in the bonds that are to be retired. The acquisition of the bonds may thus be done by the issuing company, or the trustee may acquire them. Part of our discussion on redemption before maturity will apply also to the acquisition of the bonds for sinking fund purposes. The bond indenture will prescribe the way in which the bonds are to be obtained, which will be one of the following:

Call. In some instances the call price for sinking fund purposes is lower than the regular redemption price. (The latter is applicable to bonds which are called "for general corporate purposes," or words of similar meaning, as distinguished from bonds called for sinking fund purposes.) It is commonly provided in the contract that bonds for sinking fund investment will be drawn by lot. In some instances the sinking fund call price of the bonds decreases as time goes on.

Some indentures provide that registered bonds of the same issue will not be called until after all the coupon bonds of the same issue have been acquired. This is done because holders of registered bonds are usually investors who desire to hold their bonds as long-term investments.

Purchase in market. The indenture can provide that the trustee may purchase the bonds in the open market at prices not to exceed the call price.

Tenders. In some instances the corporation or the trustee asks the bondholders to sell their bonds at a price not to exceed a designated figure. The company will then accept the lowest offers for the amount of bonds to be acquired.

Disposition of the Bonds. When the bonds for which the sinking fund was established are acquired by the trustee, they may be kept alive in the fund, or they may be canceled, according to the provisions of the indenture. If the bonds are kept alive in the fund, the indenture may provide that they can be reissued under specified circumstances.

Since the ultimate purpose of the sinking fund is to retire the bonds, the simplest procedure would be to cancel the bonds as soon as they are acquired by the trustee.

Distinguished from Redemption Funds. Throughout our discussion of sinking funds we have referred to the retirement of *bonds* with the funds. In some instances so-called sinking funds are provided for the retirement of preferred or special kinds of *stock*. Since stock is not a debt, and therefore does not come due, even though it may be made callable, it is suggested that the term "sinking fund" be used only in connection with bonds. The term *redemption fund* would perhaps be a better one to apply to the fund which is set up for the redemption of stock.

DISTINGUISHED FROM SINKING FUND RESERVE. Thus far in the chapter we have been discussing sinking *funds.* These are, as we have seen, appropriations of *assets.* The sinking fund is built up by the transfer to it of cash or the particular bonds which are to be retired. If the bonds are canceled, they would not be carried in the fund, but they would then be deducted from the bond liability account.

Notice of Sinking Fund Redemption

THE SAINT PAUL UNION DEPOT COMPANY

First and Refunding Mortgage
Series "B" 3⅛% Bonds
Due October 1, 1971

NOTICE IS HEREBY GIVEN, pursuant to the provisions of the original and supplemental indentures securing the above-described bonds, that the following numbered bonds of this issue have been drawn by lot for redemption through the sinking fund on October 1, 1955, at the agency of the Trustee in the Borough of Manhattan, City and State of New York, at 100½% of face value, plus the interest then accrued thereon, viz.:

M 73	M 977	M1690	M2957	M3996	M4892	M5573	M6969
114	1001	1806	3002	4011	4908	5640	7001
144	1026	1828	3097	4031	4985	5672	7044
212	1038	1892	3136	4162	5047	5714	7236
238	1056	2001	3164	4185	5048	5777	7274
239	1096	2042	3201	4219	5094	5870	7346
282	1121	2067	3254	4238	5105	5873	7387
334	1179	2177	3356	4363	5266	5931	7467
357	1271	2280	3412	4443	5314	6071	7501
524	1307	2498	3422	4453	5318	6119	14600
643	1460	2501	3635	4490	5386	6172	14606
691	1540	2533	3660	4634	5427	6200	14625
729	1544	2537	3698	4703	5458	6352	14650
746	1592	2592	3739	4822	5494	6501	14732
753	1596	2949	3823	4867	5501	6523	
891	1687	2956	3846	4879	5548	6894	

Holders of certain fully registered bonds are also notified that all or portions thereof have been similarly called for redemption, as follows:

Bond No.	Amount Called
RM-23	$ 1,000
RU-30	80,000
RU-31	33,000

and that said bonds will be reduced as to principal accordingly. Such holders will be separately advised as to the serial numbers of coupon bonds called, which have been reserved for issuance in lieu of said fully registered bonds.

The agency of the Trustee is hereby designated to be the office of J. P. Morgan and Co., Inc., 23 Wall Street, New York, N. Y. Holders of the above-numbered bonds, and holders of fully registered bonds as to which all or portions have been called for redemption, are notified to present them promptly for payment at the specified time and place, with, in the case of coupon bonds, all coupons maturing after said redemption date attached. From and after October 1, 1955, interest on the bonds thus called for redemption will cease to accrue.

FIRST TRUST COMPANY OF SAINT PAUL,
Trustee
Saint Paul, Minnesota

Dated July 7, 1955.

Figure 5. Notice of sinking fund redemption. The above notice appeared in *The Wall Street Journal,* July 19, 1955.

The setting aside of a sinking fund does not reduce the profits or the surplus of the company. Since in the long run, cash used for sinking fund payments is normally generated from earnings, that part of the profits or surplus equivalent to the amount of cash set aside in the sinking fund is not available for dividends to the stockholders. But the stockholder who looks at the surplus account only, and sees it constantly increasing in amount, may wonder why the directors are not paying a larger amount out in the form of dividends. This can be illustrated with the following hypothetical example. Assume a corporation has the following abbreviated balance sheet.

Assets	$5,000,000	Bonds Payable	$1,000,000	Capital Stock	$4,000,000

It will be assumed that the bonds come due in 10 years, and that the company is going to set up a sinking fund for their retirement by paying into the fund $100,000 a year. The net profits after income taxes are assumed to be $400,000 annually, and it will be assumed further that dividends of 6 per cent will be paid on the capital stock (in the balance sheet the stock is carried at its par value). If the company does only a cash business, the balance sheet at the end of the first year, *after* the payment of dividends, will be as follows (to simplify the problem we will ignore depreciation):

Assets		*Liabilities*		*Net Worth*	
Cash	$ 60,000	Bonds payable	$1,000,000	Capital Stock	$4,000,000
Sinking Fund	100,000			Surplus	160,000
Other Assets	5,000,000				
Total	$5,160,000		$1,000,000		$4,160,000

Assuming ten years' operations with each year the same as the first year, the balance sheet at the end of the period (*before* the bonds are retired), would be as follows:

Assets		*Liabilities*		*Net Worth*	
Cash	$ 600,000	Bonds payable	$1,000,000	Capital Stock	$4,000,000
Sinking Fund	1,000,000				
Other Assets	5,000,000			Surplus	1,600,000
Total	$6,600,000		$1,000,000		$5,600,000

During this period the company has earned 10 per cent on its stock, but it has paid the stockholders only 6 per cent. Meantime, the "surplus" has been increasing at the rate of $160,000 a year, and at the end of the period stands at $1,600,000. Some shareholders would probably feel that the directors had not been paying a sufficient amount in dividends. But of the surplus of this amount,

$1,000,000 has really gone into the sinking fund and therefore is not available for dividend payments.

In order to give effect to the appropriation of money into the sinking fund, the accounting practice commonly followed is to set up a *surplus reserve,* equivalent in amount to the sinking fund. Thus each year when the $100,000 is put into the sinking fund, the surplus or profits account is charged with a similar amount, which is put into an account called the "Reserve for Sinking Fund." At the end of the ten-year period the "Surplus" account then would show only $600,000, and the Reserve for Sinking Fund would be $1,000,000.

The bonds would then be retired from the sinking fund. This would still leave the Reserve for Sinking Fund on the books. This account would then be charged with $1,000,000, and the Surplus account would be credited with the same amount. In other words, the amount in the Reserve account would be put back into the Surplus account.

We might then raise the question whether or not the shareholders might then expect more in dividends because of the relatively large Surplus account. Be that as it may, the bonds in the meantime have been retired, which is the ultimate objective of the sinking fund. Considering the cash position of the company, the $1,000,000 which is transferred back to the Surplus account is not all available for dividends.

In some instances a sinking fund reserve account is set up on the books without a sinking fund. This would perhaps be better than not setting up either account. The reserve account would appropriate part of the surplus, and therefore that amount could not legally be declared in dividend by the directors. To that extent then, cash or net assets equivalent to the amount of the reserve would necessarily be conserved in the business. Thus, the property behind the bonds would tend to increase. But these assets may not be in liquid form when needed to retire the bonds at their maturity. The sinking fund reserve, without the sinking fund, would appear to be more appropriate in the event that the bonds are to be refunded rather than retired.

Serial bonds

BONDS ARE SERIALLY RETIRED. When parts of a single issue of bonds have different maturity dates, the bonds are called *serial bonds.* It should be noted that all the bonds are issued at the same time. This, plus the fact that they mature in series, distinguishes the *serial* bonds from those which are *issued in series* under an open-end indenture. We have already discussed one type of serial obligation —the equipment trust obligations. Serial bonds are also quite common among municipalities.

In some cases all maturities of the serial bond issue bear the same face rate of interest, while in others the rate is different among the various maturities. When the face rate is the same, the different maturities can be purchased on different yield bases by paying different prices for the bonds.

Advantage to Issuing Corporation. There are certain advantages of the serial bond over the ordinary type bond with a sinking fund provision, and this accounts for the fact that an increasing number of public utilities and industrials are using them. These advantages will be briefly discussed.

1. *Broader market.* Within the one serial bond issue are short-, medium-, and long-term bonds. Thus the issue may appeal to the different classes of investors according to these various maturities. This would tend to decrease the interest cost to the corporation; short and medium maturities generally sell on a lower yield basis than long-term maturities.

2. *Economy of redemption.* If the corporation would redeem its ordinary bonds by exercising the call feature, it would be forced to pay the call price, which is usually at a premium over the face value of the bond. The serial bonds that come due each year, however, are retired by paying the face value.

3. *No sinking fund expenses.* When a sinking fund trustee administers the fund, the corporation must pay him a fee. There is no need for a sinking fund with a serial issue, so that the expenses of such fund are eliminated.

4. *Interest saved on bonds retired.* If a sinking fund is invested in bonds other than those for which the fund was established the probability is that they will bear a lower rate of interest than the company is paying on its own bonds. But in the case of bonds maturing serially the company no longer has to pay the interest on its own bonds.

5. *Safety.* When a sinking fund is invested in something other than the particular bonds which are to be retired, there is always the danger that some loss may be encountered when the investment has to be converted into cash. When the serial bonds are retired each year, however, they have already been paid.

Advantages to Investor. The advantages of serial bonds to the investor may be apparent from what has been said above, but for completeness sake we will summarize the points.

1. *Selection of maturities.* The investor can select whatever maturities he desires.

2. *No restraint on market price.* The market price of callable bonds will rarely rise above the call price. If the serial issue is not callable, there will not be this factor holding down its market price. Naturally, the price of serial bonds, like any other type of bonds, will approach the face value as the maturity date arrives.

3. *Greater certainty of payment.* If a corporation has to pay off part of its bonds every year, there is a greater probability that the issue will be paid off than if they did not have any maturities to meet for, say, twenty years. If the ordinary issue provided for annual sinking fund payments, there is less probability that these payments will be met than if the bonds actually became due each year, as is the case with the serial issue.

4. *Increased equity.* As bonds under the serial issue are retired, the equity behind the remaining bonds is increased. Even with rapidly depreciating property, such as railroad rolling stock, the equity behind the serial equipment trust obligations is increased as the property depreciates. Serial retirement is particularly desirable for wasting asset companies, such as mining and timber companies.

5. *Maturity date certain.* When a person buys a callable bond, and the usual type is callable, he never knows just how long he will be able to hold the bond. With a serial bond (assuming it is not callable) he is always certain when the bond comes due.

Callable Serial Bonds. Although there is more reason for making the ordinary type bond callable, serial bonds are in some instances also callable. Where this is the case some of the advantages of the serial bond listed above would not be applicable.

In the case of callable serial bonds, the indenture frequently provides that the bonds are callable in the reverse order of their maturity. In other words, the bonds with the longer maturity dates are callable first. Commonly the call premium is a stated percentage for each year of the unexpired term. Calling the longer maturities benefits the corporation in two ways. It provides for the swift elimination of the entire debt, since the early maturities are being redeemed currently. Furthermore, it results in interest savings as the face rate of interest on the bonds usually increases with the length of maturity.

From the standpoint of the bondholder, however, calling in the reverse order of maturity has an adverse effect. People who buy the short-term maturities want that maturity, but the long-term bonds are purchased by those who want a more permanent investment.

SINKING FUNDS FOR SERIAL BONDS. In our discussion above we have assumed that sinking funds were not provided for serial bonds. That is usually the case. In some instances, however, such funds have been established for serial bonds. The call feature stated above, which is in some of the serial issues, might be exercised and the bonds bought with the sinking fund.

There is, of course, not as much need for a sinking fund for serial bonds as for ordinary bonds, but if the company's assets are subject to extreme depreciation or depletion, there might be some necessity for such a fund.

MARKET ASPECTS OF SERIAL BONDS. We stated above as one of the advantages of serial bonds that the various maturities would attract a wider market. Even though that is true, since the amount of bonds of any one maturity is limited, the bonds would not be so well known, and therefore, each maturity would tend to have a limited market. If the various maturities have the same face rate of interest, and they sell on a different yield basis, which is usually the case, then the prices of the various maturities would be different. For this reason serial bonds are not listed on the exchanges, because it would be necessary to quote prices for each of the maturities. It is common practice to quote serial bonds, not in terms of prices, but in terms of yield. But here again, the yield quotation would be desired for the particular maturity under consideration.

Questions

1. (a) Can a corporation call in its bonds before they are due? Explain. (b) Can a holder force a corporation to redeem its bonds before they are due? Explain.
2. What are the reasons why a corporation might redeem its bonds before maturity?
3. What are the various methods that are used by corporations to redeem their bonds before maturity?
4. What are the possible disadvantages to the bondholder of a corporation redeeming its bonds before maturity?
5. Distinguish between funding and refunding a debt.
6. What inducements are sometimes offered to the bondholders to get them to accept new bonds instead of cash when their bonds mature?
7. Indicate how the premium paid to call in a bond issue is treated for federal income tax purposes.

8. Assume that the federal corporation income tax rate is 50 per cent. A company is considering the relative advantages and disadvantages of issuing a 4 per cent bond issue, or a 6 per cent preferred stock issue. Indicate the advantage of the bonds relative to the actual cost of the money.

9. If a company retires a $10,000,000 bond issue by paying out cash of this amount, has the company incurred any expense in paying off the issue? Explain.

10. What inducements are sometimes offered bondholders to get them to agree to an extension of the maturity of their bonds?

11. What are the various reasons for setting up a sinking fund for a bond issue?

12. Indicate the various ways of determining the amount of the sinking fund installments. Which of these do you think is best? Explain.

13. Is the failure to meet a sinking fund installment considered the same as failure to pay the bond interest? Explain.

14. Would you recommend that an independent trustee be designated to handle the sinking fund? Why?

15. Indicate the various ways in which the sinking fund could be invested. Which do you recommend? Why?

16. If a corporation is buying back its own bonds with the sinking fund, do you think the bonds should be immediately canceled?

17. Is there any difference between a sinking fund and a redemption fund? Explain.

18. Distinguish between the sinking fund and the sinking fund reserve. What purpose is accomplished by setting up each?

19. What are the advantages to the issuer of a serial bond issue?

20. Are serial bonds listed on the securities exchanges? Why or why not? How are they usually quoted in the market?

Problems

1. The Acme Manufacturing Co. has $500,000 in bonds outstanding which mature in 10 years. The bonds are callable at 105 and are selling in the market for 105. The face rate of the bonds is 7 per cent. The company's credit has improved to the extent that it can sell sufficient 5½ per cent bonds of a new issue at par to retire the remaining old bonds. Disregarding selling costs and interest on the interest saved (assume federal corporation income tax rate to be 50%):

(a) Would you recommend that the refinancing be undertaken? (b) How much in new bonds would have to be issued? (c) What would be the difference in annual interest paid out to the bondholders? This would favor which procedure? Considering the excess in principal amount of the new bonds over the old, what would the annual net savings be? (d) What is the total amount which would be gained over the 10-year period by following the procedure you recommend?

2. The Home Utility Co. on Dec. 31, 19-1, sold a $10,000,000 issue of 3½ per cent first mortgage bonds that matured in 20 years. These bonds were sold at 102 and accrued interest. The issue was a closed one and provided in the indenture for a sinking fund to retire the bonds. The bonds were callable at 105 on any interest date after the first 5 years.

During several of the ensuing years the treasurer of the company had considerable difficulty in raising enough cash to meet the sinking fund requirements because of the dividends that had been declared by the directors. Following this, in two other years several large stockholders complained of the passing of dividends in the face of a substantial increase in the amount of the surplus as shown on the annual balance sheet. (a) What method of sinking fund payments do you think should have been provided in the indenture? Why? Would your answer be the same if this had been an open issue? Explain. (b) What other kind of provision do you think should have been stated in the indenture that probably would have prevented the embarrassing situation in which the treasurer found himself and at the same time have done away with the possibility of dissatisfaction on the part of the stockholders? (c) What would you recommend that the sinking fund be invested in? Why?

3. Indicate the nature of the sinking fund provisions of the following bonds and state which type you as a bondholder would prefer: Cities Service Co. Sinking Fund Debenture 3's of 1977; The Hudson Coal Co. First Mortgage Sinking Fund 5's of 1962; and Walworth Co. Convertible Debenture 3¼'s of 1976.

Part III

PROMOTION AND FINANCING THROUGH SECURITIES

Chapter 14

PROMOTION OF A BUSINESS

Meaning of Promotion. As the term is ordinarily used "promotion" refers to the discovery or conception of a business opportunity and the marshaling together of men, money, and other property in an enterprise for the purpose of exploiting the idea. Promotions may take place in new or in old industries, as are indicated by the following types:

1. *Promotion of a company in a new field.* Whenever a new product or service is discovered or created, a company may be formed in this new field in order to exploit it and to gain the profits which might be forthcoming. Promotions of this type in recent years would include television, frozen-food lockers, and air conditioners.

As would be expected, promotions of this type are hazardous undertakings. The market for the product or service is pretty much unknown, and it is extremely difficult to predict costs. Moreover, the best price at which to sell the product is not known. In many instances expensive advertising or selling forces may have to be utilized in order to build up a market for the product or service.

When a new product is to be exploited it is sometimes advisable to turn over the manufacturing operations to other companies that have the equipment and personnel necessary to make the product; also the selling may be done by established agencies. Later, after the product has become established, the new company might consider taking over the manufacturing and selling operations.

2. *Promotion of a company in an established field.* This is perhaps the most frequent type of promotion. Examples of this kind of promotion would range from the establishment of a new corner grocery store, to the formation of a new automobile manufacturing company, such as Kaiser-Frazer Corporation. (This later became Kaiser Motors Corporation, and is now part of Kaiser Industries Corp.)

Despite the fact that the particular industry is established, there is considerable hazard in starting a new company in competition with those which have been established for some time. Pitfalls into which a new company may fall have probably already been encountered and avoided by the established concern, or the management has the necessary experience to avoid falling into similar ones in the future. The older companies will have the experience in management, manufacturing, selling and financing which may enable them to do better than the new company. A strong financial condition and a large research staff may be a further advantage of the established company.

With a system of private enterprise such as exists in the United States, the probability is that the various established industries have sufficient companies operating within their fields to supply the existing demand for their product or services. As the demand increases, more products can be sold, but most existing companies can expand their production to take care of the increased demand. The established companies can more easily expand than new companies can enter the field.

3. *Promotion of a combination of two or more existing companies.* According to Adam Smith, competition is the self-regulator of free enterprise. When competition gets too keen, however, businessmen often seek ways of lessening the pressure. Many of our trusts or combinations formed in the 1880's and 1890's, were effected in order to secure a monopoly or semimonoply in the field. Aside from the lessening of competition, there are other reasons why combinations are formed. Many of those formed in the 1920's, and the 1950's, as well as in other periods, were effected in the hope of securing economies in management, manufacturing, selling, or financing. In some instances, and this applies to many of those formed in the late 1920's, combinations are promoted by investment bankers in order for them to make a profit from the sale of securities.

Promotions of this kind have the advantage of a past record of earnings of the constituent companies. This enables the promoter to determine with some degree of accuracy the probable future earnings of the combination. Also excellent management can be provided for the combination from the best executives of the various companies entering the combination. Furthermore, the separate companies have established and trained labor forces. The goodwill that has been built up by the constituent companies can carry over to the new combination.

Effecting combinations of existing concerns is not an easy task. Many companies hate to give up their independence. The managements have to be sold on the idea, and they in turn must sell the stockholders on the combination. Many legal problems arise which must be solved. We will discuss combinations at some length in Chapters 29–31.

4. *Promotion of a new company, whose shares are sold to the public, to take over a privately owned business.* Some investment bankers seek out close corporations, and attempt to sell them on the idea to relinquish part or all of their stock holdings for a specified consideration. Thus, the banker is furnished with a stock issue which can be sold to the public with the resultant fee. Some owners take the initiative themselves and contact an investment banker to sell their interests.

There are various reasons why a proposition of this kind may be of interest to the owners of a business. Some owners want to diversify their investments. The company may have been managed by one or a few persons who have since died, leaving the family without experienced executives. In some instances the management is too old and has not had the foresight to train capable executives.

Tax considerations may be another reason. Dividends are taxed at the regular rate for the income of the particular individual, which may be an exceedingly high rate. But if the stockholders sell their stock, any gain will be reported as a long-term capital gain (assuming the stock has been held for more than six months), and the maximum tax on such a gain is 25 per cent. If the owners held the stock until their death, it might be difficult to establish a fair value on the stock for federal estate and inheritance-tax purposes. Furthermore, it may be necessary for the beneficiaries to sell an appreciable amount of the stock in order to get the cash to pay the estate and inheritance taxes.

Promoters

THE PROMOTER. The person who conceives the idea for the promotion and who brings together the men, money, and property necessary for the planned organization is called the *promoter.* When he directs his attention to the promotion of some needed product or service, or to the formation of a company that will essentially improve a service, he is performing a useful service to society, and may be successful.

We are sometimes inclined to use the term "promoter" for somebody who is prowling around trying to swindle the public out of money. There are such people, but in most cases the promoters of our business enterprises accomplish a considerable amount of good. We would be without the use of much of our wealth of goods and services today if it were not for the promoter. Somebody has to take the initiative. Many of our industries which supply us with what we today consider essentials were looked upon as rank speculations at the time they were started. The promoter must have the imagination to see the need for the product or service in the future, and have the courage to see the promotion through to completion when others are perhaps skeptical as to the success of the undertaking. He must have a practical turn of mind and foresee the profitableness of the venture.

Another requisite of a successful promoter is an impressive personality. He must be a successful salesman, radiating success, as it will be necessary for him to sell and resell his idea to other people. But he should not overdo his pressure to the point where people will turn against him. A promoter must cooperate and be able to give and take.

The promoter must also be an organizer. It is not common to find selling and organizing ability in the same person, but a promoter must possess both these qualities. The successful formation of a new company calls for proper organization of the men, money and materials into a workable unit. This is not an easy task. The successful promoter has to be a person of good health and good judgment.

Another factor of considerable aid in the promotion of a new company is money. Although the bulk of the funds for the formation of a company may finally come from other sources, it is often necessary for the promoter to have sufficient money of his own to finance all the preliminary investigations which are necessary before he can enlist the financial help of other people.

TYPES OF PROMOTERS. The kind of people with the necessary qualifications for successful promoters could come from any walk of life, but especially in recent years they generally belonged to certain categories. Following are the various types of promoters responsible for new business undertakings.

1. *Professional promoters.* Many of the businesses, particularly large combinations which were formed during the latter part of the last century, were promoted by what may be called *professional promoters.* Some of these combinations were of the trust form of organization, which were later declared illegal. Many of them were formed by use of the holding company device.

The lure of large profits caused many companies to enter the business field. As the number increased, competition became keener, and many businessmen welcomed an opportunity to combine and divide the markets, rather than compete for them. Tremendous profits from the combinations were visualized. There sprang up a type of promoter who did little else than investigate opportunities for effecting large combinations, and then took the steps necessary to bring about the organization. With several successful promotions behind him, he became a sought-for expert; inventors, manufacturers, or other people who had ideas for the launching of a new enterprise or the combination of existing companies would seek out the professional promoter. A good example of the professional promoter was Charles R. Flint, who promoted the American Chicle Co., the National Starch Co., the United States Rubber Co., and many others.

The professional promoter did not stay with the organization permanently. He effected the organization, took his stock and such other compensation that he could obtain, and left to seek new fields to conquer. In some instances he aided in securing finances for the organization. The professional promoter for business enterprises is almost a thing of the past. Perhaps one of the best examples existing today is the promoter of sporting events.

2. *Owners.* The great bulk of our businesses, particularly the smaller concerns, were started by the person who owns them or by his ancestors. One has only to look at the small retail stores, service establishments, and small manufacturing plants to realize this. Perhaps most people have the idea that they would like to become independent and "to go into business for themselves." And many of them attempt this one or more times before they die. But it is frequently discovered that starting and operating a business is not as easy as was visualized, and that independence is not commonly attained. Many of these businesses fall by the wayside shortly after they have been promoted.

In many instances the *owner promoter* is a person who has worked for a company for some time and has learned the business, and then seeks to capitalize on his knowledge. Some of the business combinations that are formed are promoted by the owners of one of the units.

3. *Business executives.* Somewhat similar to the owner promoter is the *business executive promoter.* A separate classification was needed here, however, because in some instances the executive

is a salaried employee and not an owner, or he may own only a small amount of the stock of the company for which he is working.

As was stated above, a person may conceive the idea of starting his own company after gaining experience from working for someone else for a number of years. Many of our large combinations were promoted by executives of business concerns in the same field in which the combinations were formed. Promotions of this kind are often very successful.

4. *Engineers, consultants, and lawyers. Engineers,* or *engineering firms,* often promote the formation of companies or combinations. Some of these got their start by being called in for consultation or investigation work by other promoters and investment bankers. In some instances they entered the field with experience gained from conducting a business management service. In recent years an increasing number of firms have entered the *industrial management consultant* field. These firms often promote or aid in the promotion of new companies or combinations of existing companies.

There is a considerable amount of legal work connected with the promotion of a new company or the combination of two or more companies. Usually a *lawyer* must be consulted at one or more stages of the promotion. In many instances, he is busy with all stages of the promotion. This does not necessarily qualify him for a promoter, but in many instances he is prominent enough in the work to so classify him. In some instances the lawyer gains enough experience, and realizes the profit possibilities from his work done for other promoters, that he starts out as a true promoter himself. Quite commonly the lawyer receives stock in the new company as part of his compensation, and in some instances he remains identified with the company as its legal counsel.

We owe a considerable amount of credit to the *inventor* who thought up or perfected the necessities and luxuries of life, which we enjoy today. Certainly, he is an important person in the promotion of a company to manufacture his product. But usually genius and good business judgment do not go hand in hand. It is also well known that most inventors, particularly at the time of their first inventions, do not have the necessary finances to produce and commercialize their product. In some cases the promoter appropriates the idea of the inventor for his own personal advantage. Thus the inventor is usually not a promoter.

5. *Investment bankers.* In the promotion of large companies or combinations it is customary to contact investment bankers to have them take over the sale of the securities necessary to provide the

needed money. When they merely handle the financing, they are not acting as promoters. But beginning in the late 1920's, it became common for investment bankers to initiate and carry through large combinations of existing companies; thus they became true promoters.

The investment banker makes his profit from the sale of securities. If he does not get enough business from it, he may look around for opportunities to combine a number of companies. If he is successful he can sell securities of the new company which is formed to take over the various companies. The money thus obtained is used to buy the old companies' assets, or the stock from the shareholders of the companies.

6. *Venture capital firms.* Investment bankers are usually more interested in selling securities of established companies than of new ones. Some are interested only in selling bonds. Practically all of them confine their attention to the very large companies and combinations. Thus, there has long been a need for some type of agency to finance the promotion of smaller new companies whose product or service appears to be worth while.

In very recent years there have been several such organizations formed. These include the Enterprise Development Corp., J. H. Whitney & Co., and Rockefeller Brothers, Inc. These organizations were formed by a few relatively wealthy people who realized the need for such services and who could see the profit possibilities.

These firms do not directly initiate the project. People with ideas and plans for a new company approach them to secure aid. If after a thorough investigation the project appears practical, the firm will advance the money and take stock in the new company. A well-known and successful company, the Minute Maid Corp., was financed by J. H. Whitney & Co. These firms are not really promoters, but they finance the new company. Since they play such an important part in the promotion and are relatively new, they have been briefly discussed.

Stages in promotion

THE STAGES. The subject of promotion is exceedingly difficult to write about since there are so many different types and sizes of promotions. Also there is so much detail in the formation of a new company or combination that we cannot hope to do here more than barely outline the essential material. What we say here will be brief and general. For convenience we have divided the subject of promotion into four stages.

1. Discovery of the idea
2. Investigation of the proposed project
3. Assembly of the various elements
4. Financing the company

Only the first three stages will be taken up in this chapter. The subject of financing the enterprise will follow.

DISCOVERY OF THE IDEA. There are various ways in which the idea for a promotion may originate. An inventor may suddenly hit upon a new idea or product, or a prospector may discover a deposit of ore, or a geologist may find a new pool of oil. Sometimes the research staff of a large organization may develop a new product or compound unexpectedly, or the invention may be the result of a well-planned and long worked-out process.

In most instances the conception of the idea is not so spectacular. A person or group of persons, while working for another company, may have given some thought over a long period to starting their own business. Or the gradual expansion of a flourishing business may give rise to the need for new organizations to carry on special phases of the production and selling of the product. The pressure of competition may often result in a combination which had been planned and worked out over a period of months or even years.

INVESTIGATION OF THE PROPOSED PROJECT. Investigation follows naturally after the conception of the idea. Few people will put money into a new enterprise, unless there is some assurance that it will be an economic success. This is particularly true when it comes to investment bankers. Ideas mean little from an economic standpoint, unless they are of a practical nature and can be profitably put into operation. The investigation might proceed along the following lines.

PRACTICAL VALUE OF IDEA. It seems to be human nature for people to be optimistic about the practical value of their own ideas. Their minds are so crowded with the favorable factors or possibilities that they often cannot see the inherent shortcomings.

If a person starts an enterprise in an established industry, he has little chance for success, unless he can make the same product or perform the same service at a lower cost or considerably better. In the case of combinations the investigation should attempt to determine whether any economies could be attained in management, manufacturing, selling, or financing.

The originator of the idea may first cautiously, without giving away his secrets, consult with competent people to get their ideas on the practical value of the project, before spending too much effort and money on it. These qualified people may be commercial and investment bankers, manufacturers, engineers, lawyers, and other successful businessmen. Probably in most instances they might be pessimistic about the proposed plan. This is always the conservative attitude to take, since the outcome of the venture is not known, and nobody would like to approve an undertaking which later might turn out to be a failure. But in most cases, the promoter should not consult these individuals before he has made a thorough investigation in order to discuss all problems intelligently and to estimate the value of the advice received.

It is realized, however, that in most instances our important industries of today would not have been promoted if their organizers had not been daring but had waited until they got the approval of many other people.

ESTIMATING GROSS REVENUES. It is of importance not only to determine whether the product or service is practical, but also to determine how many of the products can be sold and at what revenue. In many instances the volume of sales will depend upon the selling price. The selling price may depend upon operating costs or on the prices charged by competitors and again on the volume of sales. In general, there are three ways of estimating the gross revenues, and which one of them would be used depends on the type of product or service to be sold. These three methods are as follows:

Statistical method. In some instances it is possible to make an intelligent guess of the probable earnings of a new company by the use of certain figures which are obtainable.

The amount of income and the savings and spending habits of the people in a particular community may be estimated from such things as the volume of bank, and savings and loan deposits, bank debits, life insurance sales, sales and redemptions of United States Savings bonds, automobile registrations, etc. An analysis of such data will indicate the spending power of the particular community. This would be of value to the promoters of companies which would have a local market, such as, for example, a department store or a public utility. Figures are available showing the sales of department stores, per capita consumption of public utility services, such as gas and electricity, etc. In the case of department stores due allowance must be made for the current and probable future sales of existing companies. For retail stores in general, a check of the number of persons passing the particular location is of importance.

The retail trade is highly competitive and accurate forecasts are difficult to make. Proper management is always a very important factor.

In the case of public utilities which operate under monopoly conditions, a more accurate estimate of probable revenues is possible. If the particular community into which the utility is going to locate is similar in personal income, industry, standard of living, etc., to another community with a similar type of utility operating, the per capita consumption can be used as a fairly reliable indication of what the new company will be able to do.

When the market for the product is not local, it is more difficult to estimate probable sales. A study of the sales of existing companies in the field, however, might give some indication of what could be expected in the future. In the case of certain types of products market research organizations might be of value in estimating the probable demand.

Sample method. When some new type of consumers' goods, such as food, is to be put on the market, a particular representative community or area might be selected in order to test the demand for the product. From the results obtained a fairly good idea may be had of the probable sale of the product in a much wider market.

Contract method. In some instances it is possible to get contracts or commitments for a specified number of products before the company is started. For example, a person who is well-known to one or a few manufacturers might secure their agreement to take a certain number of the products annually. The product may be raw materials or machinery of some kind. Another example would be a company that gets a contract from a mail-order house to take all or a certain part of the total output. Orders of this kind, however, are usually given to established concerns rather than to new promotions. In some instances orders from the government for defense materials might be secured by businessmen who then form a new company to manufacture the materials.

Where orders for the product can be obtained in advance, it is not necessary to use guesswork in determining the probable sales. But after the particular contracts are completed, there is no assurance that they will be renewed. If they are not, then it will be necessary for the company to build up a system of distribution for its products. This might be difficult to do, and besides it would not be possible to determine the probable future sales. This is the usual shortcoming when the market depends upon one or a few customers.

Estimating Costs. The costs of doing business can, as a rule, be estimated more accurately than the volume of sales. Costs, however, depend in part upon the number of products sold, so that for their estimate it is necessary to assume a definite volume of production.

In the case of a manufacturing company, the costs would be broken down into materials, direct labor, factory overhead, administrative, and selling costs and taxes. The materials cost can be determined accurately, but, of course, changes in the price of raw materials would affect it. The direct labor costs can also be determined in advance with a fair degree of accuracy. In estimating the overhead costs attention will be given to the following: whether the factory building is owned or rented; the rate of depreciation on the building and equipment; cost of light, heat and power, supplies, amount of supervision needed, etc.

The administrative expenses are made up of the salaries of executives and office workers, supplies, postage, telephone and telegraph, depreciation on office equipment, rent, heat and light, and other office expenses. Assuming a certain scale of operations, these administrative expenses can be estimated fairly accurately.

Selling costs are difficult to estimate for a new company. When the products are to be sold on strictly a commission basis, the unit selling costs of course are known after the rate of commission is determined. If the marketing is to be done by salaried salesmen the costs are definite, assuming a predetermined number of salesmen and a set salary scale. But to sell a given number of products may require more salesmen than originally contemplated.

It cannot be determined in advance how much advertising will have to be done in order to sell a given volume of goods. But commonly a definite amount of money is allocated for advertising, and a program is worked out for the spending of this amount. Thus the advertising expense at first can be a definite predetermined amount.

In making estimates it is common to overestimate sales and underestimate expenses. Many expenses arise which cannot be forecast in advance. After a schedule of expenses has been worked out, it is therefore advisable to add to this an amount up to 10 per cent of the total for unpredicted items.

After the company gets started, adjustments will have to be made when it is apparent that the estimates have been wrong. In some instances this means the appropriation of additional funds for certain expenses, while in other cases an attempt may be made to cut down on certain expenses. Future budgets can be made in line with the operating results.

Although based on the "profit" of a company, income taxes are a real cost of doing business. After giving effect to all the expenses that come out of the income, it should be remembered that an appreciable part of the net income must be paid in federal income taxes.

Estimating the Funds Required. An important part of any promotion is the estimate of the amount of funds that will be needed to start the business. Sometimes the amount of money that is put into a business is actually just the amount that a particular person or group of persons have or are able to obtain.

Few businesses fail because of too much money. But a common cause of failure is insufficient capital. In many instances the lack of cash is merely a symptom of some other fault, but in some cases it is because too little capital was put into the business originally. As was stated above, it is common to overestimate income and underestimate expenses. Unless proper allowance is made for this, the funds raised to carry on operations may later prove to be insufficient.

It is easier to raise money before a company starts than after it has run into financial difficulties. If a company is raising several millions of dollars, it would probably be easy to secure several thousand additional at the same time. But if this was not obtained and later the company was hard pressed for cash, it might find it could not secure any additional funds. Thus, ample funds should be raised before the concern starts its operations. In determining the amount of funds that will be needed, consideration should be given to the following.

Promotion and organization expenses. In many instances the promoter pays the promotional expenses out of his own pocket before there is any sale of securities. But he will expect to be reimbursed for these expenses. In other cases the money for much of the promotional expenses must be advanced by others. The amount that goes to pay the promoter personally can be determined, but the amount that will be necessary for all the expenses incurred by him is difficult to estimate. Included in these is the compensation that may go to lawyers, accountants, engineers, marketing research firms, etc. In many instances the promoter will need a considerable amount of money in order to buy options on property which the company proposes to acquire.

The promoter often takes, or is forced to take, stock in the new company as part or all of his personal compensation. There is the feeling that if the promoter himself is sold on his proposition, he should be willing to accept stock. Furthermore, in many instances the promoter is anxious to take stock in order to reap the returns in event the company is successful. The amount of stock that goes to the promoter usually varies from 10 to 51 per cent of the total stock, or the total voting stock.

The organization expenses can be calculated fairly accurately. An understanding can be had with the lawyer in regard to his fees. The amount of the organization tax can be calculated when it is known what the capitalization of the company will be. If the company is going to have subsidiaries operating in other states, or will register in those states and pay the foreign corporation tax, this will have to be figured out. All expenses connected with the sale of securities will have to be given due consideration.

Fixed assets. The amount of money that will have to be raised to acquire the fixed assets varies greatly depending on the type of business, scale of operations, whether the plant or office space is to be owned or rented, etc. A company formed to build and operate a public utility or a large manufacturing plant will obviously need more money for fixed assets than would be needed by a selling organization.

There is a tendency on the part of many promoters to start a new business on too grandiose a style. At least that is their idea until they attempt to secure the necessary capital. Perhaps a great amount of money should not be sunk into a business until the probability of success is apparent. In many instances offices and plant facilities can be rented rather than purchased. If the product involves manufacturing operations, perhaps this or part of it can be done by other manufacturers. In the case of merchandising companies the renting rather than purchasing of real estate will materially lessen the amount that must be raised for fixed assets.

If the company has been having the various parts manufactured by others, it may gradually take over these operations after it has become established. The funds for such extension may come from a new security issue or in whole or in part from the reinvestment of profits.

In order to attract new businesses some communities will relieve a new concern of the real estate tax, or will not force it to pay the tax for a specified number of years. In some instances sites for the plant will be given to the company if it will locate in the community.

Current assets. Although most of the funds raised by a business are in the form of cash and, therefore, are current assets, when we speak of the current asset requirement we mean the amount that will be more or less permanently invested in current assets after the fixed assets have been acquired. A point oftentimes overlooked is that the initial working capital (current assets) needs will be greater than the regular working capital. After a concern has been in existence for some time the production, selling and collecting cycle will have been completed, and the company will need only a fixed minimum amount in working capital. But this fixed minimum is really a more or less permanent investment in the business. The problems connected with financing the current assets are discussed in Chapters 20–22, dealing with working capital. A point previously mentioned should be repeated. Unexpected sources of income are very rare, but unexpected expenses are very common.

ASSEMBLY OF THE VARIOUS ELEMENTS. The next step in the promotion of an enterprise is the bringing together of the men, money, and materials, and the formation and organization of the company. When more funds are needed than are possessed by the promoter, he must secure the help of others. Friends and relatives are a possible source of funds. A few wealthy individuals may be consulted in an effort to get the necessary capital. If the promoter has been successful in other promotions, he may be able to get capital from the people who financed his previous projects. In the case of very large companies, an investment banker might be consulted. Generally speaking, they are not interested in security issues of less than $10,000,000. Some investment bankers will not take over an issue of securities of a new or speculative company. But if an investment banker would take over the issue, this method of obtaining funds is recommended.

Perhaps the most important element in any company is the management. The selection of the executives that are to manage the company may thus be the most important part of promotion. In the case of small enterprises the people who are doing the promoting may themselves constitute the management. In other instances, particularly for the larger concerns, it is necessary to select salaried executives who are not connected with the promotion of the company. Key executives of established companies in the same line of business are always a possibility. Added compensation, of course, usually has to be offered to induce them to come with the new company. This may be a higher salary, or they may be offered stock in the new company, or options to purchase the stock at a price which might later prove to be a bargain.

If the securities are to be sold by an investment banker, he may insist that a member of his firm be on the board of directors. Commercial bankers and able directors of other companies, particularly if they have a stock interest in the new company, may be selected as directors. An able board of directors will usually select capable executive officers to run the company. If the president is to be the most important officer in the company, the success or failure of the concern will depend in large part upon who is selected for this office.

If the stock is closely held by a small group of people, these shareholders will have an important part in the selection of the directors. But if the company is a large one and a large number of shares are sold to many people, then the majority of the shareholders will actually have little weight in the selection of the board of directors.

Legal aspects of promotion

LEASES. In some instances the amount of money necessary to purchase real property which will be needed by the new company is enormous. When the use of the property may be acquired through the *lease*, this procedure might be advisable. Many merchandising concerns lease their real estate instead of purchasing it. In some instances existing companies sell their property to an institution and then lease it back. This releases money from fixed investment and makes it available for current use, and also it results in a savings in income tax since the rental payments are considered as an expense and are therefore deductible for income-tax purposes.

The company which gets the use of the property under a lease is called the *lessee*. The individual or company which owns the property is called the *lessor*. It is commonly provided that the lessee will pay all taxes and insurance on the property and keep it in proper repair.

The shortcoming of the lease is that the lessee may lose the use of the property at the termination of the lease. This is commonly overcome by the inclusion of the following provisions in the lease.

1. A long lease period so that for all practical purposes the company using the property is in about the same position as if it owned the property.
2. An option to renew the lease for a specified period of years at a stipulated rental.
3. An option on the part of the lessee to purchase the property at a specified price upon termination of the lease.

In some instances the amount of the rental payment is contingent upon the results of the operations. For example, land is commonly leased for oil drilling purposes for a rental payment equivalent to one-eighth of the crude oil produced.

OPTIONS. Frequently the promoter does not have the necessary amount of cash to purchase property, title to which is necessary for the proposed corporation. Or, if he does have the requisite amount of capital, he may not want to tie it up in the property until it is assured that the promotion and financing of the corporation will be completed.

A possible solution to this dilemma is for the promoter to secure *options* to purchase the property from the owners for a definite price. The owner of the property who sells the option is called the *optioner,* while the promoter, or purchaser of the option, is called the *optionee.* The option will give the optionee the exclusive right to buy the property for the period of time covered by the option. Where the option is taken by the promoter, rather than by the corporation, it will give him the right to assign the option. If the option is not exercised, the money paid for it will be lost. If, on the other hand, the property is purchased, the contract may provide that the amount paid for the option will be applied toward the purchase price of the property. It is to the interest of the promoter to see to it that the necessary amount of money be forthcoming to exercise the option. It is said that Henry Frick lost one million dollars when he failed to secure the amount of money necessary to exercise his option on the Carnegie plants just prior to the formation of the United States Steel Corporation.[1]

The question sometimes arises as to the rights of optionees in relation to innocent third parties. Let us assume that *A* sells to *B* an option to purchase a particular piece of property. Before the expiration of the option and before it is exercised, the property is sold by *A* to *C*. What are the rights of *B*? The answer depends upon the knowledge possessed by *C*, whether the particular state accepts options for recording, and whether the option has actually been recorded. If *C* had knowledge of the existence of the option, then *B* may still obtain the property. If *C* had no knowledge of the option, and it was not recorded, *C* would have good title to the property. *B* then would have a right in damages against *A*. Generally speaking, the amount of the damages would be the difference between the option price and the existing market value of the property. If the state accepted options for recording, which is the usual case, and the option was recorded, then *C* is assumed to have

[1] Charles W. Gerstenberg, *Financial Organization and Management of Business* (3d ed.; Englewood Cliffs, N. J.: Prentice-Hall, Inc., 1951), pp. 236–37.

had knowledge of the option, and *B* could obtain good title to the property.

When the optionee, or the person to whom he has assigned the option, has a legal right to the property, and the optioner refuses to sell the property, the optionee may sue in a court of equity for specific performance of the contract.

PATENTS. The promotion of some projects may be successful only if competitors are prevented from manufacturing and selling the particular product. Some inventions or products lend themselves to protection through the obtaining of a patent. A *patent* is a grant by the federal government of the exclusive right to the use of a certain process for a period of 17 years. Renewal of a patent is rare since it can be obtained only by special act of Congress.

It is impossible to secure a patent on an idea or a particular product. A patent can be obtained only on the device or process of carrying out the idea or making the product. Thus even though a patent is obtained on the process of making a new product, a competitor may make, and obtain a patent to make, the same product in another way. When securing a patent it is, therefore, important to patent not only the process which is desired, but all other novel processes which might be used to make the product.

Engineering talent is valuable in working out a particular process for manufacturing a product and in thinking up possible substitutes for this process which are also included in the patent. The services of skilled patent attorneys are commonly needed to determine whether the process is in conflict with other patents, and to describe the processes which are to be patented.

The obtaining of a patent on a particular process does not insure success of the promotion. The patented process must be one which lends itself to economical production of the product; the company must be properly organized, efficiently managed, and the product properly sold before its operations are successful. In many instances the promotion is of such a nature that no patents may be obtained.

COPYRIGHTS. Where the promotion depends upon the protection of a literary or artistic work such as a book, a song, a play, or a motion picture, a *copyright* may be obtained from the federal government for a small fee. Copyrights run for a period of 28 years and may be renewed for a like period. Somewhat similar to the obtaining of a patent or copyright is the registration of a trade name, trade mark, or slogan with the Patent Office.

Patents, copyrights, and registration of trade marks do not automatically give protection to the owner. If some other person or company infringes upon these rights, it is necessary for the owner to go to court in order to protect his property. This may involve a considerable amount of money even if it is proved that there was an infringement.

Legal Position of Promoter. Strictly speaking, a promoter is not looked upon as an *agent* for the proposed corporation since the latter is not yet in existence. But since the proposed corporation is in no position to protect itself, the law requires the promoter to exercise the degree of care and prudence exacted from a *trustee,* or *fiduciary.* He is thus required to exercise the utmost good faith toward the corporation which he is promoting. The fiduciary relationship exists from the time the promotion is begun, and lasts until it is completed. Thus it would apply from the time the promoter conceived the idea of the promotion until the corporation's management is in the hands of an independent board of directors.

Compensation of Promoters. In many instances the proposed corporation is not formed and the promoter may lose all the money that he has expended in connection with the promotion. When the organization is completed, the corporation is not bound by anything which is not contained in the statutes and the charter of the company. The corporation, therefore, from a legal standpoint, does not have to pay the promoter anything for his services. As a practical matter, however, it will usually agree to pay him because it recognizes the value of his services, or because this is necessary in order to get the promoter to turn over his contracts, etc., to the corporation, or because the promoter is in control of the board of directors.

Due to the fiduciary nature of the promoter's position, he is not legally entitled to a *secret* profit. In order for a promoter's profit to be legal therefore, he must disclose the amount of the profit to all the original subscribers to the stock, or if the organization of the corporation is complete, it must be disclosed to an independent board of directors. To get the profit then, it will of course be necessary for it to be approved.

If the promoter makes a secret profit and it is later found out, the corporation may maintain one of the following actions against him:

1. Rescind the contract, return the property to the promoter, and receive back whatever was paid for the property.
2. Retain the property and sue the promoter for the secret profit, or sue him for damages.

Liability of Promoter. The promoter remains liable on all pre-incorporation contracts until the corporation accepts or ratifies them. He may be liable even after the corporation has accepted the contract. If the promoter represented himself as a promoter at the time of making the contract, after the corporation is formed and accepts the contract, the promoter is relieved of any liability. But if on the other hand the second party to the contract thought that he was dealing with the promoter in his own personal capacity, then the promoter could still be held liable on the contract after the corporation had agreed with the promoter to accept the contract. Naturally if the second party wants to release the promoter and look solely to the corporation, he would no longer be liable. In Massachusetts, the courts hold that a corporation cannot accept or ratify a contract made before it was in existence. Technically what is done there is to have the corporation make a new contract with the second party on the same terms as those contained in the promoter's contract.

Promoters may also be held liable for violations of the securities laws (called "blue-sky" laws) which are found in most of the states. They may also be liable under the Securities Act of 1933 for misstatements of facts or omissions to state material facts in a registration statement signed by them. As stated above, promoters are liable for any secret profits made by them in connection with the promotion of a company.

Questions

1. Give a definition or description of what is meant by (a) promotion, (b) a promoter.
2. Indicate the various types of promoters we have had in the past. Which type do you think makes the best promoter?
3. Indicate how in a general way you would proceed to ascertain whether or not a grocery store would be successful in a particular locality.
4. Indicate how the amount of money needed for the promotion of a small machine shop might be kept at a minimum.
5. Assume that *A* sells *B* an option to purchase some real estate. Despite this *A* sells the property to *C*. Indicate the rights of both *B* and *C* with respect to the property, and what action might be taken against *A*. State any assumptions made.
6. Indicate the nature of patents and copyrights.
7. Can a promoter make a profit on his promotion? Explain fully.
8. If a promoter makes a secret profit, what action may be taken?
9. Explain the right, if any, of a promoter to compensation for his services.
10. Explain the nature of the liability of a promoter, both before and after acceptance by the corporation, on contracts which he made before the corporation was organized.

Problems

1. Mr. Landski, a mechanic employed by one of the larger automobile manufacturing companies, has perfected a device for registering the quantity of oil in the crankcase of the motor. The registering part of the device is to be installed on the dashboard of the car. Mr. Landski, who is now twenty-eight years old, immigrated to this country when he was eighteen and, after working at laboring jobs for several years in the East, finally went to Michigan, where he has been employed most of the time by several automobile manufacturers.

Work on perfecting this device has been done entirely by himself in his spare time outside the shop. His friends consist mainly of shopmen engaged in work similar to what he is doing. Although Mr. Landski has earned a relatively high wage for some years, he has saved little money and therefore does not have funds to promote this device. A new man, who, by his spending, appears to have some funds, heard of Mr. Landski's device from another shop man and offered to promote it if Mr. Landski would let him have complete charge of the promotion and give him half the profits.

(a) Do you think there is a need for a product of this kind? (b) How would you go about determining whether the device was salable? (c) Should the device be patented? (d) Do you think Mr. Landski should form his own company to manufacture and sell the product? (e) Should Mr. Landski accept the offer of the other shopman? (f) Do you think the company should start out on a small scale and branch out only by reinvesting profits, or do you favor large-scale operations immediately in order to secure the advantages of reduced unit costs? (g) Do you think that the company that is paying Mr. Landski's wages should be given the device without paying him anything for it? Why? (h) What would you advise Mr. Landski to do?

2. On January 2, 19-1, Mr. Adams turned over to the Standard Corporation, for which he was acting as a promoter, two lots and received $5,000 (par value) in stock in payment for each lot. Lot A was purchased by Mr. Adams for $2,000 about five years before he sold it to the corporation. Lot B was purchased by him for $3,000 about two years before the sale, and shortly after he started acting as the promoter for the corporation. At the time it was purchased by Mr. Adams it was intended that Lot B would be turned over to the corporation.

(a) Is Mr. Adams justified in accepting $5,000 for each lot? Explain. (b) What action might be taken against Mr. Adams? (c) Is there any way that Mr. Adams would be legally justified in accepting $5,000 for Lot B? Explain.

Chapter 15

CAPITALIZATION AND CAPITAL STRUCTURE

Capitalization

MEANING OF CAPITALIZATION. From the standpoint of a going concern, the *capitalization* of a corporation is the *amount of the issued stocks and bonds.* At the time of organization the amount of stock which the corporation is authorized in its charter to issue is referred to as the capitalization. After operations began, however, only the amount of the stock which is issued is commonly included in the capitalization. When treasury stock is present the question may arise whether the capitalization consists of the issued stock or the outstanding stock. It is recommended that the capitalization be taken to mean the issued stock. In other words, the treasury stock would be included in the capitalization. If corporations issued bonds, the amount of such bonds would be included in the capitalization. The amount of the capitalization would thereafter be altered as more stocks or bonds are issued or are retired.

It should be noted that some writers include only the stock in the capitalization. Occasionally a writer will treat the surplus of the company as part of the capitalization, but this practice is not generally recognized. If the surplus is "capitalized" through a stock dividend, then it would obviously be included in the capitalization.

DISTINGUISHED FROM CAPITAL AND CAPITAL STOCK. The capitalization is sometimes confused with the capital or capital stock of the corporation. The term *capital* has several meanings, but we will use it to refer to the assets of the company. *Capital stock* is the term used to apply to the total amount of stock of the company, as shown in the net worth section of the balance sheet. It may be necessary to distinguish between the authorized, the issued, and the outstanding capital stock.

Bases of Capitalization. A brief statement about the determination of the amount needed to start a new company was given in the preceding chapter. Our interest at this time is in the various bases of capitalization. Any one of the following three may be used:

1. Capitalization on the basis of assets
2. Capitalization on the basis of earnings
3. Capitalization on a nominal basis

Capitalization on the Basis of Assets. Capitalization on the basis of assets means the issuance of an amount of securities necessary to acquire the assets. Thus if the company needs $10,000,000 to pay for promotional expenses, cost of selling securities, the fixed assets and to provide it with the necessary amount of working capital, and to cover possible initial loss, it will capitalize at $10,000,000 and sell securities in this amount.

Where the company must issue stock to acquire its property, etc., it cannot be capitalized at less than the value of the assets. Capitalization on the basis of assets may enable a public utility to pay the security holders a fair rate of return since the company may set rates at such a point that it will earn a fair return on the valuation of its assets.

Since the earned surplus of a company represents an increase in the assets, to the extent that the company capitalizes this surplus through the payment of a stock dividend, it would be capitalizing on the basis of assets.

Capitalization on the basis of assets would ordinarily raise no legal problem whether or not the stock was fully paid. If, for example, $1,000,000 in par stock is given for $1,000,000 in assets, the stock would be considered fully paid. Also the accounting for this is simplified since it is not necessary to inflate the value of the assets in order to make the stock appear fully paid. Furthermore, no stock premium or discount accounts are needed.

If the corporation is a going concern and issues additional stock equivalent to the value of the assets acquired with the stock, the equity of the existing stockholders would not be diluted. For whatever the statement may be worth, it can also be said that capitalization on the basis of assets tends to make the book value of the stock more what it is supposed to represent than if some other basis of capitalization had been used.

Capitalization on the Basis of Earnings. Existing companies have a past record of earnings, and although there is no assurance that these earnings will continue the same in the future, the past does give some indication of what might be expected in the future. A new company never knows what it will earn, but the organizers always try to estimate the probable earnings as accurately as possible.

When a company capitalizes on the basis of earnings it issues such an amount of stock that the estimated earnings will represent a predetermined rate of earnings on the stock. For example, if it is estimated that the company will earn $1,000,000 a year, after taxes, and it is desired that the rate of earnings on the stock be 10 per cent, it will capitalize at $10,000,000. This is obviously 10 times the estimated annual earnings. This "multiplier" can be found by dividing the desired rate of return on the stock into 100. If this company hopes to earn 20 per cent on the stock, for example, it would capitalize at 5 times $1,000,000, or $5,000,000.

The question naturally arises as to how the rate of capitalization is determined. This is not an easy task. The answer depends upon a number of factors which would include the following: whether the company is already established or a new one being promoted, the nature of the industry, and the rate of return being earned by similar companies at the time.

If the company is already established and is increasing its stock, or a new company is being formed to take over a number of existing companies, the capitalization can be higher in relation to the earnings. Also the capitalization can be relatively high if there is a good assurance that the estimate of future earnings will prove to be correct. This would include the situation just stated, but it would also cover new companies. For example, the estimate of future earnings of a water company, or other public utility, such as an electric company or gas company will probably be more accurate than in the case of a new industrial enterprise, therefore the capitalization can be higher for the utility. A public utility might capitalize on an 8 per cent basis (12½ times estimated earnings), whereas an industrial might capitalize its earnings on a 25 per cent basis (4 times estimated earnings).

The rate of return currently being earned on existing prices of stocks also has some bearing on the rate of capitalization that will be used by a new company. For example, in 1929, 1946, and 1956 many companies' shares were selling at such a relative high price that the rate of return, based on current earnings and market prices of the stocks, was only 5 per cent. In 1950, however, many stocks were selling at such prices in the market that the earnings were 8 per cent. Other things being equal, a new company being promoted in 1929, 1946, or 1956 could be capitalized at a higher figure in relation to earnings than in 1950.

Perhaps by this time the reader is wondering just how a corporation can issue an amount of stock which has a fixed ratio to the earnings, without giving regard to the amount of money needed to acquire the assets and set the company up as a going concern, the question of whether the stock is fully paid, etc. In many instances the corporation is formed to take over the business of an individual proprietorship, or a partnership. It may be a small close corporation with only a few shareholders who are related or closely connected. In such instances the amount of stock issued is more or less immaterial. If it is decided that the desired rate of earnings on the capitalization would call for the issuance of capital stock of a given amount, it would not make any difference whether the book value of the assets was more or less than this amount.

If the book value of the assets was more than the amount of stock to be issued, the assets could be revalued downward to correspond to the par or stated value of the stock. If, on the other hand, the assets were valued at less than the amount of stock to be issued, they could be reappraised upward. This would raise the legal question as to whether the stock was fully paid. The rule usually followed by the courts is that in the absence of fraud the valuation placed upon the property by the board of directors is conclusive. And fraud is difficult to prove. Another procedure would be to leave the assets at their old value and write in a figure for goodwill to make up the difference.

In the case of a large company with thousands of stockholders, the problem may be a little more difficult. Certainly the company will have to issue stock in an amount necessary to acquire the assets, or necessary to get the money to buy the assets. To this extent it would be capitalizing on the basis of assets. But capitalizing on the basis of earnings may result in a capitalization higher than the value of the assets. Certainly the company will not give more stock than is necessary to acquire the assets; neither will they throw away the extra stock. But what happens to the stock? The amount of the stock issued in excess of the amount needed to acquire the assets will go to the promoters, organizers, and bankers who handled the issue. If the stock has a par value, it can be made to appear fully paid by valuing the assets at the same amount as the stock. If the stock is no-par, the question whether it is fully paid may not be raised.

Some people, particularly accountants, are inclined to object to capitalizing on the basis of earnings. This objection arises in part from the importance which they attach to the cost or balance sheet value of the corporate property. Legal objection may also be raised against this method of capitalization since the stock may not be considered fully paid if it is issued in excess of the cost value of the assets.

From a business standpoint, however, capitalizing on the basis of earnings appears to be practical. Business property is worth what it will earn—not what was paid for it or the value at which it is carried on the balance sheet. It is well known that when business properties are sold piecemeal under the hammer, the amount obtained from them is commonly much less than the original cost or the balance sheet valuation. Coupled with good management, these same assets in a going concern may be worth many times what they cost or the balance sheet value or what they could be sold for at a forced sale. Capitalizing on the basis of earnings may, therefore, result in the issuance of securities in amounts more nearly corresponding to the real value of the assets than if the capitalization had been based on the cost price of the assets.

In some instances capitalization on the basis of assets results in capitalizing on the basis of earnings. This is particularly true when one company issues stock to acquire the assets of another company, or when a combination is formed to acquire the assets or stock interests in a number of companies. In determining the value of the assets to be acquired, both the buyer and the seller will usually give considerably more weight to the past and present earnings than to the balance sheet values. In appraising the worth of business properties or stocks, earnings are the most important single factor.

Capitalization on a Nominal Basis. In some instances the amount at which a company will be capitalized does not have any relation to the cost of the assets or the earning power of the company. When this is the case we speak of the company as being capitalized on a nominal basis. A nominal capitalization might be used in any one of the following instances:

1. *Close corporations.* If a partnership is to be incorporated and no new money or new partners are coming into the enterprise, the amount of the capitalization is immaterial. Or the same may be true when only a few persons wish to start a new business. Quite often such corporations are capitalized at a figure much lower than the real value of the business. This may keep the organization tax and the annual franchise tax at a minimum. In many instances of this

kind the company will issue the maximum number of shares possible for the minimum organization tax in the particular state. In some cases a close corporation may be capitalized at a figure much higher than the real value of the assets. This may be done in order to make a favorable balance sheet showing.

If more stockholders are later admitted, or if the company has a public offering of stock, a recapitalization is commonly effected in order to make the amount of stock outstanding correspond more nearly to the real value of the company before the new stock is sold.

2. *Incorporation of estate.* A corporation formed to take title to an estate is really a type of close corporation, but due to its different nature it is listed separately. When adequate provision has not been made in advance, the death of a wealthy person may result in a more or less forced sale of the properties in order to make proper distribution to the beneficiaries, and to pay the inheritance and estate taxes. Thus a business which has been built up over a long period of time, and which a person intended should be continued after his death for the benefit of his family, may have to be terminated.

Where part of the estate consists of stock, several states might attempt to tax it under the inheritance tax laws. Complicated questions as to the right of a particular state to tax the property might arise when the corporation whose stock is owned is organized in another state, and transacting business in still other states, and where the owner of the stock kept the certificates in a different state from where he lived.

The incorporation of the estate prior to the death of the individual may facilitate the administration of the estate. The stocks and other property are turned over to the corporation and stock in this new corporation is taken by the individual. He may even transfer some of this stock to members of his family prior to his death. Upon his death all that would be subject to the inheritance and estate taxes would be the shares in the close corporation to which he still retained title. And these shares would probably be subject to the inheritance taxes in only one state. The shares and other property transferred to the close corporation would not be subject to the taxes since the owner of this property—the close corporation—still lives.

Provision should be made through life insurance or other liquid assets to provide an amount sufficient to pay the death taxes in order that none of the shares in the personal corporation would have to be liquidated.

3. *Temporary corporations.* During the early stages of promotion there may not be sufficient cash on hand to pay the organization taxes on the full amount of the capitalization. But there is need for a corporation of some kind in order to take title to options and property, make contracts, etc. So a temporary corporation with a small or nominal capitalization may be formed for this purpose. Later when arrangements are made for the sale of the securities, and the cash necessary to pay the taxes has been secured, the capitalization can be increased to the desired amount. For example, the United States Steel Corporation was first formed with a capitalization of only $3,000. In less than six weeks afterward the capitalization was increased to over $1,000,000,000.

LAWS AFFECTING CAPITALIZATION. The laws of some of the states place certain restrictions or qualifications on the capitalization of a corporation. A number of them, for example, set a minimum capitalization. This amount in most instances varies from $500 to $2,000 for ordinary business corporations. None of the states place a maximum on the capitalization.

In some of the states, although there may be no minimum capitalization provided, the laws require that a certain minimum of the capital be paid in before ordinary business transactions are begun —usually $500 or $1,000. In some instances it is expressed in terms of a percentage of the stock, and varies from 10 to 50 per cent. In some of the states the laws prescribe that a certain percentage or all of the authorized stock must be subscribed to either before the charter will be approved or before ordinary business may be transacted.

Some states limit the amount of preferred stock that may be issued to a stated percentage of the common. A few do not permit classified stock. A few of the states limit the amount of bonds that may be issued to a designated percentage of capital stock.

Overcapitalization and undercapitalization

OVERCAPITALIZATION. The term *overcapitalization* is used in two different ways, to apply to the situation, (1) when the amount of capital stock and bonds exceeds the value of the assets, or (2) when the amount of capital stock and bonds is excessive in relation to earnings. Either or both of these situations could be present at the same time.

The term is apt to be used in the first way stated above at the time of organization of the company, when properties are frequently acquired at inflated values. Sometimes properties are overvalued in order to make an excessive issue of stock appear fully paid. In many cases stock must be handed out rather freely in order to effect the formation of the new company. Organization expenses and other intangibles consume their share of the stock. It is probably safe to say that a large percentage of all new corporations that sell their stock to the public are overcapitalized at the time of their formation.

Even though the amount of stock may not be excessive in relation to the value of the assets at the start of the corporation, subsequent events, such as the following, may make it so: operating losses, undercharging of depreciation or obsolescence on the property, destruction of uninsured or underinsured property, declining prices, etc.

For a going concern it is perhaps better to apply the term "overcapitalization" to the situation where the stock outstanding is excessive in relation to the average earnings. The cost or book value of the assets is given no consideration.

If a particular company is being formed in an industry where the company should be capitalized on about an 8-per-cent basis, then it would be capitalized at 12½ times the estimated earnings. Thus if the average earnings after taxes are expected to be $100,000, the company might capitalize at $1,250,000. But if it turns out that the company's average earnings are only $50,000, this would represent earnings of only 4 per cent on the capitalization. With earnings of $50,000 on the 8-per-cent basis, the company should have been capitalized at only $625,000. Thus the company to the extent of half the capitalization is overcapitalized.

Overcapitalization on the basis of earnings might develop also from another situation. Even though a company might be earning the rate of return it originally contemplated, conditions may change so that prospective stockholders would expect a company of this kind to earn a higher rate of return. In such an event this particular company might be said to be overcapitalized.

The two different meanings of overcapitalization stated above may not be as different as it first appears. If a company issues more stock than the real value of its assets, it might be unable to earn a fair rate of return on the capitalization. Thus it might be overcapitalized both in respect to assets and to earnings. Or, even though a company issues stock equivalent to the cost value of the assets, if it is unable to earn a fair rate of return on these assets (and thus not a fair rate of return on the stock), then we could say that the company was overcapitalized in relation to the *real value* of the assets, as well as in relation to its earnings.

Unless otherwise indicated, when we use the term "overcapitalization" at the time of organization of a company, we will have in mind the assets relationship, but when speaking of a going concern, which will be the usual case, we will be referring to the earnings relationship. Overcapitalization results in what is referred to as *watered stock.*

DISADVANTAGES OF OVERCAPITALIZATION. Generally speaking overcapitalization is undesirable. It may adversely affect not only the corporation, but its stockholders, creditors, customers, and possibly, the public. Following are the disadvantages of overcapitalization.

1. *Corporation cannot pay a good dividend.* If a company is overcapitalized (in relation to earnings) it will earn only a low rate of return and therefore will be unable to pay a fair rate of dividends.

2. *Manipulation possible.* Because of the point stated above, the stock will sell for a relatively low price in the market. This may subject the stock to manipulation.

3. *Poor credit.* The conditions stated above will result in the company having difficulty in obtaining credit. It will be forced to pay a high rate of interest for whatever money it is possible to obtain.

4. *Future financing difficult.* If a company is overcapitalized it might not only be difficult to borrow money, but it might also be difficult or impossible to sell new issues of stock.

5. *May charge too much for product.* If the company is operating under monopoly or semimonopoly conditions the tendency would be for it to charge too high a price for its product or service in order to pay a fair rate of return on its stock.

6. *Possibility of stockholder liability.* If stock is issued in excess of value of the property obtained for it, there is a possibility that the stockholders may be held liable to creditors for the difference between the value of the property and the par value of their stock. This is a very remote possibility, and would usually apply only to the original purchaser of the stock.

7. *May cause financial embarrassment.* A company that is overcapitalized may strain itself, in paying unwarranted dividends, to the point of failure.

Remedies for Overcapitalization. Following are remedies for an overcapitalized state.

1. *Plow back earnings.* Perhaps most companies are originally overcapitalized in respect to assets and possibly immediate earnings as well. Many concerns will pay out in dividends only a part of the earnings and the balance will be reinvested in the business. These added assets broaden the earnings base of the company. After a period of years the water may thus be squeezed out of the stock, and a proper relationship may be achieved between the stock and the assets and earnings.

2. *Reduce the amount of stock outstanding.* A reduction in the amount of stock outstanding can correct an overcapitalized state, but this is sometimes difficult to effect. The stockholders will have to consent to a reduction in the number of their shares, and a charter amendment may be necessary. This may be accomplished with either par or no-par stock. The book value of the assets might be similarly reduced to offset the reduction in the capital stock account.

3. *Reduce the par value of the stock.* A reduction in the par value of the stock, or a reduction in the stated value of no-par stock, with a similar reduction in the book value of the assets could be done in order to correct overcapitalization. This action would necessitate the consent of the stockholders and a charter amendment.

Undercapitalization. Undercapitalization is just the opposite of overcapitalization. Thus, it may refer to either the situation where the value of the assets is in excess of the amount of stock outstanding, or where the company is earning a relatively high rate of return on its stock. If a company follows a conservative policy of retaining part of its earnings every year, the tendency will be for it to become undercapitalized.

The term "undercapitalization" is also sometimes used in a different sense. A company may have a capitalization or permanent capital sufficient to carry on its present volume of sales, but it may attempt to expand its sales rather rapidly without getting any more permanent capital into the business. The increased sales volume will call for an additional investment in inventories, accounts receivable, etc. All its working capital may be thus consumed, and the company may become short of cash. It may then be said to be undercapitalized. In some instances companies have failed because of an attempt to rapidly expand their sales without adding to their permanent capital.

The use of the term "undercapitalization" in the way just explained is not common, so when we use the term we will have reference to one of the two meanings first mentioned. Unless otherwise stated we will generally have in mind the earnings relationship, although as was pointed out in connection with our discussion of overcapitalization, the use of the term in relation to assets and to earnings may not be very different.

Disadvantages of Undercapitalization. As may be obvious, the shortcomings of undercapitalization are not so great as overcapitalization. In fact, undercapitalization may be a rather healthy state. But there are certain disadvantages which will be briefly discussed.

1. *Narrowing market for stock.* If a company is undercapitalized the earnings and dividends per share will probably be rather high. This will cause the stock to sell for a relatively high price, which will narrow the market for the stock for the same reason that more people can and do buy Fords than Cadillacs. The narrower market and the high price of the stock will cause too wide fluctuations in its market price, even though the percentage change may not be large. Generally speaking smaller fluctuations are more desirable.

2. *Future stock financing may be more difficult.* Because of the relative high price for the stock, if the company wants to sell additional shares in the future, it may find the market comparatively narrow.

3. *Future stock financing may be relatively expensive.* Although high earnings and dividends per share are favorable factors, they may result in higher financing costs. We will illustrate this with a hypothetical example.

Assume that a company is earning \$20 a share on its stock and paying \$12 a share dividends, and that this stock is selling in the market for \$200 a share. If the company could sell more of this stock at \$200 a share and continue to pay \$12 in dividends, the new money would be costing the company 6 per cent. If, however, the company had four times as many shares outstanding (without any increase in the assets), the earnings per share would have been \$5, and the dividends \$3 a share. Naturally the stock would be selling at a much lower price in the market. Because of the lower price the market would be much wider. Due to this fact the stock would probably sell on a lower yield basis than 6 per cent. Thus, instead of selling at \$50 a share, it might sell at \$55, or even \$60 a share. If we assume the latter figure, then for every four new shares the company sells it would collect $240. The dividends on these four shares would be $12. Thus the new money would be costing the company only 5 per cent, instead of 6 per cent.

4. *May invite competition.* If a high rate is being earned on the capital stock, due to an undercapitalized state, it might appear as if the particular type of business were highly successful. This might possibly invite competition.

5. *May arouse suspicion of consumers.* Too high a rate of earnings and dividends on the stock might cause consumers to think that they were being charged too high a price for the company's product or service.

6. *May cause demands for higher wages.* When the earnings and dividends per share are relatively high, the employees or union leaders of the company may think that they are not being paid enough in wages. This may result in union demands for higher wages.

Perhaps it should be mentioned in connection with the last three points that the total earnings of the company would be just the same if they had a larger amount of stock outstanding. But on the surface it appears to be different, since the per share earnings are less.

Remedies for Undercapitalization. As we have already stated, the disadvantages of undercapitalization are not so serious as overcapitalization. Nevertheless, for one or more of the reasons just mentioned, a company may want to correct it. One of the following methods may be used.

1. *Stock split-up.* A stock split results in an increase in the number of shares, although the figure for the total capital stock remains the same. Where the stock is par value, this necessitates a vote on the part of the shareholders to reduce the par value of the stock, and amend the charter. Thus, if the par value per share was $100, a two-for-one stock split could be accomplished by the issuance of two $50 par shares for each $100 par share. If it were a four to one split, four shares of $25 par would be issued for each $100 share. No-par stock would also be split, or a company might issue a larger number of no-par shares for its par stock, or a larger number of low par shares for its no-par stock. The effect of a stock split is to lower the market price of the stock, the earnings per share, and the dividends per share. The surplus account is not affected by a stock split-up. (Unless a special rule of the New York Stock Exchange is applicable, see pages 632-33.)

2. *Stock dividend.* Somewhat the same result as a stock split-up can be effected by the payment of a stock dividend. As long as the company has sufficient authorized stock, the stock dividend would not necessitate any action on the part of the shareholders since a charter amendment would not be necessary. When a stock dividend is paid, shares of the same type and par or stated value as those outstanding are given to the shareholders. This results in an increase in the capital stock account and a reduction in the surplus account by the amount of the dividend. Obviously a surplus would have to be present before the stock dividend could be used, whereas such surplus is not legally necessary to have a stock split-up. From a practical standpoint, however, if the company is undercapitalized, the great probability is that the surplus of the company would be relatively large. The effect of the stock dividend is to reduce the market price of the stock, the earnings per share, and the dividends per share in a manner similar to the stock split-up. Having consumed part of the surplus by paying a stock dividend, there would be less left, than when the stock-split is used, to pay dividends on the increased number of shares.

3. *Bond dividend.* Occasionally a corporation will pay a dividend which consists of its own bonds. The payment of interest on the bonds would reduce the net profit, and the per share earnings and dividends. The payment of the principal of the bonds would also take money out of the business and this would tend to correct the undercapitalized state.

4. *Large cash dividends.* The payment of large cash dividends is not ordinarily considered as a method of correcting undercapitalization. But this would decrease the surplus and would reduce the amount of the assets which could be used to produce earnings in the future.

5. *Reappraisal of assets upward.* The stock split-up and the stock dividend would not affect the assets side of the balance sheet. In other words, the rate of earnings on the assets would remain the same. If the company reappraised the assets upward it would appear to reduce the rate of earnings on the assets. Technically this would not be considered as correcting the undercapitalized state, since the capitalization is not affected.

When New Permanent Capital Needed. We mentioned above that the term "undercapitalization" is sometimes used to apply to the situation where a company has an insufficient amount of permanent capital to carry on its current volume of business. When this is the case, the remedy obviously is to sell additional stock or bonds.

Capital structure

MEANING OF CAPITAL STRUCTURE. The *capital structure* of a corporation consists of its issued bonds and stocks, and its surplus (surplus reserves included). As the term is used it refers not only to the total amount of these items, but also the nature and amounts of the various types of securities and surplus. The term "financial structure" is sometimes used instead of *capital structure*.

The inclusion of *surplus* in the capital structure is necessary because of several factors. Par value stock is frequently sold for an amount in excess of its par value. The excess over the par is carried to the surplus account, normally a capital surplus account. No-par stock also is often carried in the capital stock account at a lower amount than the consideration received for it. The difference is also credited to the surplus account. It is thus evident that there is as much reason for including this surplus in the capital structure as for including the capital stock. The part of the earnings that are not paid in dividends or absorbed by operating losses goes into the surplus account. This becomes part of the owners' equity the same as the capital stock. The surplus account is treated about the same as if it were part of the capital stock account when it comes to the determination whether a corporation can obtain a bank loan or float a bond issue.

Some writers would have titled this section The Financial Plan. This term may have two or possibly three meanings. Used in a general sense it refers to the (1) determination of the total amount of capital that will be needed, (2) determination of the kinds and amounts of securities that will be issued to provide this capital, and (3) determination of what is to be done with this capital. The term is used in a more narrow sense to refer to either the kinds and amounts of securities issued by a corporation, or these items plus the surplus. One of the reasons why the term is not used in this chapter is because of this inexactness in the meaning. The other reason is that there are many kinds of financial plans and financial planning which relate to the capital structure only in an indirect way.

Planning the capital structure is an integral part of the organization of a new corporation, but it also is a matter of constant importance to the going concern. What follows will apply to both new companies being formed and those which are already in existence.

IMPORTANCE OF CAPITAL STRUCTURE. One of the most important phases of promotion is the determination of the capital structure. Perhaps most business failures, particularly those during the early years, are caused by an improper financial structure. Few businesses fail because of too much cash, but too little cash is a frequent cause.

Most promoters are naturally optimistic and tend to overestimate the income and underestimate the expenses. Such a situation will result in failure within a short time. In working out the capital structure, therefore, it is imperative that it provide for sufficient money to enable the company to carry on operations. Although the estimate of the amount of money that will be needed may turn out to be substantially correct, an error may be made in the determination of how this money should be raised. Generally speaking a stock issue will not cause a company to fail, but a bond issue may do so. The company is not obligated to pay dividends on the stock or to repay the principal. But both the interest and principal of the bonds must be paid, regardless of the earnings, or the bondholders may take legal steps to foreclose on the corporate property. In some instances the company could stand a bond issue of a moderate amount, but an error is made in issuing too many bonds and not enough stock. What has just been said refers to old businesses as well as to those being started.

DETERMINATION OF AMOUNT OF MONEY NEEDED. We have already considered in a general way in the chapter on promotion how a company might go about determining the amount of money which it will need. This is an exceedingly important subject but one which is difficult to cover in an adequate fashion in a book of this kind.

The amount of securities issued may not correspond to the amount of money needed to set up the business, but we know that securities in amounts at least equal to the amount of capital needed must be sold. When a company is capitalizing on the basis of prospective earnings, the amount of the securities may be in excess of this. Summarizing, the company will need money for the following:

1. Promotion and organization expenses
2. Expenses of selling securities
3. Fixed assets
4. Current assets
5. Intangible assets
6. Money to cover possible early operating losses

FACTORS DETERMINING KINDS AND RELATIVE AMOUNTS OF SECURITIES. Our principal interest in this chapter is in the determination of the kinds of securities that may be issued to obtain the needed capital under various circumstances, and a general consideration of the relative amounts of these securities. These factors are many and varied, and in some instances are viewed from the standpoint of the corporate management and the stockholders, while in other cases from the standpoint of the investment bankers or the investing public. Any one or more of the following may influence the form of the capital structure.

1. Whether or not outside capital is needed
2. Size of the business
3. Age of the business
4. Stability of the earnings
5. Nature of the business
6. Nature of the assets
7. Level of interest rates
8. Taxes
9. Control
10. Government regulation
11. Preferences of investors and investment bankers

WHETHER OR NOT OUTSIDE CAPITAL IS NEEDED. If the business does not have to appeal to the public for funds, the probability is that it will issue only one class of securities—common stock. This would apply to the incorporation of a partnership, an estate, or other close corporation. Even when some securities have to be sold—perhaps to relatives or friends, or to local investors—when the issue is too small to appeal to investment brokers, common stock only will be issued. Risk to the company is much less in selling common stock, and buyers of securities might prefer a chance to share in future profits.

The company need not be small to confine its capitalization to common stock. Some of our large companies which are owned entirely by a family have only common stock outstanding. In some instances the small company has reached large scale production by expanding through the reinvestment of earnings. Thus, it may now be a large company with common stock as the only class of securities outstanding.

The question whether outside capital is needed is influenced by the rate of expansion of the company, the rate of earnings, and the dividend policy of the company. Concerns that expand very slowly may be able to rely on reinvestment of earnings for the needed capital. Companies that expand rapidly may be forced to go to the capital markets for funds, but the extent to which they must obtain outside capital would depend upon their rate of earnings. Even if a company is earning a good rate of return on its stock, if a substantial part of this is used for dividend payments the reinvestment of earnings may not provide all the capital needed.

It may appear at first thought that a company which is in constant need of capital for expansion purposes should follow a conservative dividend policy. The opposite, however, may occur. If a company's earnings will not furnish the capital needed, new security issues must be sold. In order to create a good market for its securities, a company may find it advisable to follow a very liberal dividend policy. A case in point is the American Telephone and Telegraph Company.

Size of the Business. Very small concerns are practically always capitalized with only common stock bought by the few owners or friends or relatives in order to share in any future success of the business. A nonparticipating preferred stock would probably not appeal to them. There would be no market for bonds of a small company.

Age of the Business. New companies, particularly in the industrial field, should be formed with a conservative capitalization; this means common stock and only common stock. A new enterprise should be prepared for rough going. Starting out with debt may prevent future financing and result in failure of the company. The broader the common stock base at the beginning, the greater is the chance of obtaining new capital in the future.

Older companies are established in the trade, have experienced management, and have a record of earnings and an earnings trend. This past experience is used as a means of predicting the possible future trend. With this background it can be ascertained with some degree of accuracy whether the company can stand a bond issue or whether it should attempt to sell additional stock.

Stability of the Earnings. The relative stability of the earnings may be an important factor in determining whether the corporation wants to issue preferred stock or bonds, and also whether the investment bankers or the public would want to buy them.

Generally speaking a company which is not sure of earnings in the future should issue only common stock. If the earnings are fairly sure, but fluctuating in amount, a small preferred stock issue might be sold. If the earnings are fairly sure and certain in amount the company might safely issue bonds.

If a company is already established, the past earnings records will be available and preferred stock or bonds might be safely issued. The earnings of companies selling a low-priced consumers' good that is used regularly will usually be more stable than one selling a high-priced luxury good that is purchased relatively infrequently. Industries such as public utilities supplying an essential service and operating under monopoly conditions will tend to have relatively stable earnings.

Nature of the Business. The nature of the business frequently has a bearing on the stability of earnings and therefore on the kinds of securities which should be issued. Public utilities are more stable in their earnings than are industrial companies. Companies selling low-priced goods or services tend to have greater stability of earnings than companies selling high-priced articles.

Nature of the Assets. If the company is in the retail merchandising business and does not own any real estate, it will probably not issue bonds, for it would have no assets that could be mortgaged as security. Steel producing companies, on the other hand, have large investments in fixed assets and commonly issue bonds.

Level of Interest Rates. If interest rates in general are high, a company may attempt to issue stock rather than bonds. Or if they are high, a short-term issue may be sold with the hope that at the maturity of the issue interest rates will be more favorable to long-term financing. On the other hand, when interest rates are relatively low, a corporation might favor a bond issue since the interest paid may be much lower than the dividends that might be paid on a similar amount of stock. Furthermore, the costs of selling bonds are usually lower than in the case of stock.

Taxes. In an earlier chapter we discussed the tax savings which are effected through the issuance of bonds. Bond interest is an expense which is deducted before arriving at the net taxable income, whereas dividends on stock are a distribution of the profits after the taxes have been computed on those profits. With a 50 per cent corporate tax, this means that a 4 per cent rate of interest on bonds would cost the issuing company only 2 per cent in view of the tax savings.

Control. The promoters or management commonly give consideration to the question of control when issuing securities. The amount of money needed may be so large that if common stock were sold, the organizers or present owners might not be able to retain control. Thus nonvoting preferred stock or bonds may be sold to the public instead of common stock. In some instances a nonvoting common stock may be issued. As previously indicated such stock, however, could not be listed on the New York Stock Exchange at the present time. Also, some states will not permit the issuance of nonvoting common stock.

In case a large amount of voting stock is to be sold, and the question of control arises, it is better to sell to many small investors throughout the country. In this way, control may be retained by the ownership of an exceedingly small amount of stock since the average stockholder sends his proxy to the proxy committee, which is controlled by the management.

Government Regulation. The public utilities commissions in some of the states, and the Securities and Exchange Commission in respect to companies that come under its jurisdiction, and the Interstate Commerce Commission in the case of railroads, insist upon a proper balance between the amounts of bonds, preferred stock and common stock issued by public utilities and railroads. New security issues of these regulated companies must be approved by the proper governmental body.

Preference of Investors and Investment Bankers. In many instances the kind of securities that will be issued by a new company is limited to what the investment bankers think the public will buy. During a period of business prosperity people prefer common stocks, but in a depression they may hesitate to buy any kind of security, or if they will invest their money, they will insist upon bonds only. Sometimes, people may be willing to take a chance on preferred stock when they would not buy common stock.

When the prices of stocks are rising, although the public may not want common stock at the time, they may insist that any bonds or preferred stocks they buy be convertible into the common stock, or that they carry warrants giving them the right to buy the common stock.

Additional Factors Relating to Financial Plan. Although the above factors usually determine the type of the capital structure, it is advisable to state a few additional points.

Issue weakest security first. A company never fails because it issues common stock. But many of them fail as a result of selling bonds. The conservative thing to do at the time of promotion is to issue only common stock. A company should save its best securities to the last.

At the time of promotion a company may be able to sell any kind of securities. But later on, it may run into financial difficulties and as a result the public may not be willing to buy any kind of its securities except a first mortgage bond. If such a bond had been issued at the start, the company would be unable to obtain any additional financing, and as a result it may fail. But if only common stock had been issued at the time of promotion, the company might be able to raise more money by selling a senior issue such as a first mortgage bond. Although a company does not anticipate financial difficulties at the time it is formed, experience has shown that most companies have financial trouble sometime during their life, and in many instances this comes soon after they are promoted. The issuance of stock, rather than bonds, broadens the base against which future financing may be effected.

Make financial plan simple. Many companies do their financing in a piecemeal fashion, with the result that they have a number of different stock and bond issues outstanding. The tendency, however, has been to simplify the capital structure. The presence of many different types of securities is confusing to the investor, and may cause him to wonder why the company had to issue so many. One stock issue, or one common and one preferred issue and one large open-end blanket issue of bonds is preferred over a large number of small issues. Furthermore, the financing costs may be lower per unit on the one large issue.

Give effect to financing costs. In selling an issue of securities two different costs must be kept in mind. One is the payment to the bankers for selling the securities, and the other is the annual cost of the capital to the company. Ordinarily, the safer the issue, the lower is the amount that must be paid to the bankers. It is also generally true that the safer the issue, the less is the amount that will have to be paid annually to the investor for the use of his money. A senior bond, for example, will sell on a lower yield basis than a junior bond of the same company. Preferred stock would carry a higher dividend rate than the interest rate on the same company's bonds. Common dividends of companies that pay regular dividends are usually larger than the preferred dividends.

In some instances, however, the prices of some common stocks are bid up so high in the market that they sell on a lower yield basis than the bonds or preferred stock issued by the same company. This, however, is usually only a temporary condition. It is of course understood that if the company does not pay any dividends on its common stock, the money obtained from selling bonds is more costly.

Leverage. Closely connected with the cost of financing is the leverage factor. We discussed this in Chapter 8. If conditions are favorable for the issuance of bonds, it may be found that the rate of earnings on the stock will be more than if additional stock instead of the bonds had been issued.

Capital structure—railroads

COMPLICATED CAPITAL STRUCTURE. The capital structure of railroads is more complicated than in other industries, due in large part to the failures, reorganizations, and combinations which have taken place in the field. At the time railroads were first formed their capitalization was relatively simple. Many of them were promoted as civic undertakings. Land was granted to them by the states and the federal government. Cities and states bought their bonds with the proceeds from the sale of their own bonds. Common stock was purchased by the businessmen and citizens of the particular community. In many instances bonds were issued to pay for the actual construction costs and the stock was given to the bondholders as a bonus, or it was given to the promoters and bankers who handled the financing of the company.

Failure was inevitable for most of the early promotions. The roads were built in advance of the need for their services. Railroads vied with each other in the extension of their lines into undeveloped territory. They were grossly overcapitalized, and bonds were issued in such amounts that the companies were unable to earn enough to pay even the interest on them. In the reorganizations that followed failure, much or all of the original stock interest was wiped out in many instances. Income bonds and preferred stock were forced upon the holders of junior securities in exchange for their old bonds.

The failure and competition of the railroads resulted in the combination of many lines into large systems. Since the various companies had their own bonds, common stock, and in some instances preferred stock, outstanding, the financial structure of the integrated system became very complicated. The large company which acquired the others would then either guarantee or assume, depending upon the method of combination, the securities of the combined roads. As the need for additional funds arose, new bonds of the combining company were sold. Since the properties of the small companies were mortgaged behind closed issues which had been sold at the time they were formed or reorganized, the new issue of the parent would have to be a junior blanket issue on the entire properties. In most instances the investing public expects railroad bonds to be secured by a mortgage on the physical property.

Many of the bonds issued by railroads contained the after-acquired property clause. In order to avoid its effects until after the newly acquired property had been paid for, it became the common practice for railroads to finance their rolling stock through the issuance of equipment trust obligations. The joint bond was also issued to finance common terminals, bridges, docks, etc., in part to avoid the after-acquired property clause, and in part because of the expediency of having joint use property owned and operated by a separate corporation. The typical financial structure of the large railroads is thus a complex one.

TREND TOWARD SIMPLIFICATION. Although early reorganizations in many instances resulted in the issuance of additional bonds, in later years the companies emerged with fewer bonds and a less complicated financial structure. Since 1920, the Interstate Commerce Commission has had authority over the issuance of railroad securities, both in reorganization under the Bankruptcy Act and otherwise. This has resulted, particularly in the case of reorganizations, in a reduction in the amount of bonded indebtedness and fixed charges, and also in the elimination of worthless stock.

TABLE 18

CAPITAL STRUCTURE OF ALL CLASS I RAILROADS COMBINED IN THE UNITED STATES (IN MILLIONS OF DOLLARS AND PERCENTAGES)

Capital Structure	*Millions of Dollars*	*Percentage Distribution*
Long-term debt*	$ 9,854	37.1%
Capital stock†	7,809	29.5
Surplus	8,849	33.4
Total	$26,512	100.0%

* Includes unmatured funded debt, equipment obligations, long-term debt in default, and non-negotiable debt to affiliated companies.

† Includes all classes of capital stock. Approximately 79 per cent of this is common stock.

SOURCE: *Moody's Transportation Manual,* Moody's Investors Service, New York: 1956, p. a38.

The large earnings of certain roads over a long period of time has in many instances overcome the original overcapitalization. During World War II, extraordinary earnings enabled many roads to retire an appreciable part of their bonded indebtedness.

Railroad expansion has been over for some time. In fact, total railroad mileage has shrunk in recent years. There is still need for funds, however, for maintenance and modernization of properties, and for the acquisition of new equipment. The latter is now being financed almost entirely through the issuance of equipment trust obligations. Because of the relatively poor credit of railroads and the uncertain future of the industry, there have been few new stock issues sold since the 1920's.

In order for the bonds and preferred stock of railroads to be investment grade, Graham[1] states that in the case of bonds the interest should be earned at least five times before taxes, and in the case of preferred stock the sum of the interest charges and twice the preferred dividends should be earned at least five times before taxes.

Capital structure—public utilities

Railroads are sometimes included under the heading of public utilities, but it is customary to treat them separately as we have done. "Public utilities" include water, telephone and telegraph, gas, and electric companies, and other types of transportation and communications companies. These companies, as is also true of railroads, operate under monopoly conditions. In many instances, however, such as the gas and electric companies, they compete with each other. Differences exist among the various classes of public utilities, but they are not so great as those found among industrials.

WATER COMPANIES. Water companies are the oldest and most stable type of public utility. In most instances, particularly in the case of large cities, they are publicly owned, hence there is a relatively small amount of water company securities on the market. Because of the stability of their operations, water companies can stand a higher percentage of their capitalization in bonds than can other types of utilities.

TELEPHONE AND TELEGRAPH. All the landline telegraph business in the United States, except for some teletype and certain wire services which are carried on by the American Telephone and Telegraph Company, is handled by the Western Union Telegraph Company.

The telephone industry is dominated by the American Telephone and Telegraph Company. Although this company owns directly

[1] Benjamin Graham, *The Intelligent Investor* (rev. ed.; New York: Harper & Bros., 1954), p. 141.

certain interconnecting toll lines, it is primarily a holding company. It owns all the common stock of most of the operating companies and either a majority or a substantial interest in the other subsidiaries. The subsidiaries have been financed through the sale of common and preferred stock and bonds, but the trend has been toward the reduction in the amount of preferred stock and bonds. These securities have been sold primarily to the holding company which in turn has sold securities to the public to pay for those securities purchased from its subsidiary.

The holding company, the American Telephone and Telegraph Company, has followed a conservative financial policy. Only about one-third of its capitalization is in the form of bonds. And an appreciable amount of these bonds are convertible into stock. It has no preferred stock outstanding. The company has followed a stable dividend policy having paid an annual dividend of $9 a share ($2.25 each quarter) on the stock since 1922. Due to the nature of the company's business, its excellent management, and stable dividend policy, the stock is considered one of the best stock investments obtainable (from the standpoint of safety and dividend return).

TABLE 19

Capital Structure of American Telephone & Telegraph System (Consolidated)
(in millions of dollars and percentages)

Capital Structure	*Millions of Dollars*	*Percentage Distribution*
Long-term debt	$ 4,376	34.1%
Preferred stock	18	.1
Common stock*	5,704	44.5
Surplus	2,726	21.3
Total	$12,824	100.0%

* Minority interest in surplus is included in the minority common stock interests of $179 million.

Source: *Moody's Public Utilities Manual,* Moody's Investors Service, New York: 1956, pp. 602–3.

The largest independent telephone company in the United States is the General Telephone Corporation. The system controlled by this company has about 2,500,000 telephones in operation in parts of 30 states. Most of the area served consists of small communities and rural sections. The company also has large stock interests in telephone companies outside the United States, and in equipment manufacturing companies in the United States, Canada, and Europe. In recent years this company has expanded quite rapidly.

GAS COMPANIES. Gas companies have had to face the competition of electricity for many years. First, electricity pushed out gas for illumination purposes, and now it is making inroads in the field of domestic cooking. Offsetting this, however, has been the increased use of gas for domestic heating and industrial fuel. The increased production of oil has brought large quantities of relatively cheap natural gas which has been piped into metropolitan areas. If some time in the future the supply of natural gas were to diminish, the industry would have to rely more on the relatively expensive manufactured gas, with the result that some of the gas business would undoubtedly be lost. This would argue for conservatism in the issuance of preferred stocks and bonds. In a number of instances the same or a subsidiary utility, supplies both gas and electricity to a particular community. The earnings of such a company would tend to be stabilized since any reduction in the sale of one service might be offset by an increase in the other.

TABLE 20

CAPITAL STRUCTURE OF ALL NATURAL GAS OPERATING UTILITIES COMBINED IN THE UNITED STATES

(IN MILLIONS OF DOLLARS AND PERCENTAGES)

Capital Structure	*Millions of Dollars*	*Percentage Distribution*
Long-term debt	$3,556	57.1%
Preferred stock	410	6.6
Common stock	1,574	25.3
Surplus	682	11.0
Total	$6,222	100.0%

SOURCE: *Moody's Public Utilities Manual,* Moody's Investors Service, New York: 1955, p. a69.

ELECTRIC LIGHT AND POWER. By far the most important type of public utility, both from the standpoint of total assets and the amount of securities on the market, is the electric light and power industry. These companies have shown a remarkable growth and are continuing to expand. The use of electricity for illumination is firmly established, and its use as industrial power increases as industry expands. It has been used to an increasing extent for household appliances, and as stated above, for domestic cooking purposes.

To make the bonds a safe investment an operating company should have in recent years earned its total interest charges at least four times before taxes. If preferred stock is issued, the company should earn the sum of the bond interest and twice the preferred dividend at least four times before taxes. This applies to all types of operating utilities (railroads excepted). The reason why the preferred dividends are doubled is because taxes must be paid on the earnings before the dividends are deducted.[2]

The financial structure of electric light and power companies has been complicated by the formation of large holding companies on top of the operating companies and then pyramiding additional holding companies on the existing holding companies. This magnifies the leverage factor to a high degree. The income to meet the bond interest of the holding company that owns the operating companies' common stock must come from the dividends of the operating companies after they have paid their bond interest and preferred dividends. And this holding company must first pay its bond interest and preferred dividends before it can pay dividends on its own common stock. The same process applies to each of the successive holding companies. The top company's common stock would have such a great leverage that a slight fluctuation in the earnings and dividends of the operating companies would produce a tremendous effect in the ability of the holding company to pay dividends on this stock. The securities of public utility holding companies are thus much more speculative than those of operating companies. Under the Public Utility Holding Company Act of 1935, a number of unnecessary holding companies have been forced to dissolve, and many have had to simplify their financial structure.

TABLE 21

CAPITAL STRUCTURE OF ALL CLASS A AND B ELECTRIC UTILITIES COMBINED, IN THE UNITED STATES

(IN MILLIONS OF DOLLARS AND PERCENTAGES)

Capital Structure	*Millions of Dollars*	*Percentage Distribution*
Long-term debt	$13,322	50.5%
Preferred stock	3,281	12.4
Common stock	7,354	27.8
Surplus	2,461	9.3
Total	$26,418	100.0%

SOURCE: *Moody's Public Utilities Manual,* Moody's Investors Service, New York: 1956, p. a16.

[2] To earn the preferred dividend once after taxes, the company must, with a 50 per cent income tax, earn it twice before taxes. So if the proper margin of safety is four times the combined interest and preferred dividends, the company should earn the interest and twice the preferred dividend at least four times. This is the margin of safety indicated by Benjamin Graham (*op. cit.,* p. 141) to make the bonds and preferred investment grade.

OTHER UTILITIES. Traction companies, both urban and interurban, prospered during the early part of the century, but they started declining about the time of World War I due to the competition of the private automobile, buses and trucks. At the present time they are relatively unimportant except in a few metropolitan areas. Other utilities include pipelines, transportation companies such as trucking concerns, and communications, such as radio and television. We will not discuss the nature of the capital structures of these utilities.

Capital structure—industrials

TYPES OF INDUSTRIALS. The term "industrials" is sometimes taken to mean only manufacturing industries, but it is generally used in financial circles to cover all types of industries and companies other than railroads, public utilities, financial organizations, and real estate ventures. The greater part of this group is made up of companies engaged in the extractive, manufacturing and merchandising business. Industrial companies are more numerous and have a greater total invested capital than railroads or public utilities.

As a group, industrials are more speculative than the other types of industries. They are not protected by monopoly conditions as are the railroads and public utilities, and thus competition is always a factor to be reckoned with. The success or failure of an industrial is closely correlated with management. The average company is small and thus is not able to secure funds from the sale of securities through investment bankers.

EQUITY FINANCING GENERALLY USED. Due to the factors mentioned above, the typical capital structure of an industrial concern consists of only common stock and surplus. Funds for expansion commonly come from the reinvestment of earnings and depreciation reserves. Even if bonds or preferred stock could be sold, the security buyer may prefer common stock. This is due to the fact that there is considerable risk in buying any type of the typical industrial security, and if the buyer is going to assume this risk, he wants at least the opportunity to reap the rewards in event the company prospers.

Preferred stock and bonds are found more commonly among the large corporations than among the small ones. More industrials have bonds and preferred stock outstanding than bonds alone. Manufacturing companies have the highest percentage of bonds among the industrials, while merchandising concerns show the largest percentage of preferred stock. A larger percentage of the extractive

TABLE 22

CAPITAL STRUCTURE OF ALL CORPORATIONS, BY MAJOR GROUPS, IN THE UNITED STATES
(PER CENT)

Industry Group	*Long-term Debt*	*Preferred Stock*	*Common Stock*	*Surplus*	*Total*
Agriculture, Forestry, and Fishing	17.7%	2.2%	43.2%	36.9%	100.0%
Mining and Quarrying	17.1	3.1	26.3	53.5	100.0
Construction	18.6	2.7	26.1	52.6	100.0
Manufacturing	13.1	5.7	25.6	55.6	100.0
Public Utilities	42.2	6.1	29.2	22.5	100.0
Trade	12.0	4.9	28.8	54.3	100.0
Finance, Insurance, and Real Estate	28.3	3.0	23.6	45.1	100.0
Service	29.4	3.6	25.1	41.9	100.0
Other	20.9	6.5	71.3	1.3	100.0
All corporations combined	23.4%	5.0%	26.6%	45.0%	100.0%

SOURCE: Based on figures obtained from U.S. Treasury Department, *Statistics of Income for 1951,* Part 2, Table 4, U.S. Government Printing Office, Washington: 1955, pp. 78–87.

industry have only common stock than manufacturing or merchandising companies.

USE OF BONDS. Although bonds are issued at the time of promotion of a railroad or public utility, they are more apt to be issued by the industrial after it has become established. An industrial which shows a good earnings record may issue them for expansion purposes. In some instances bonds are issued when one company buys out another one. Consolidation frequently gives rise to a bond issue.

Reorganizations are another reason for bonds in the capitalization of an industrial. Railroads usually come out of a reorganization with fewer bonds than they had at the time of failure, but industrial reorganization frequently results in bond issue though none existed before.

Due to the great differences among industrial companies, it is difficult to state when bonds can safely be issued or what is the maximum amount that should be issued. If the circumstances are such that bonds can be issued, they should be limited in amount so that the company would be able to earn the interest charges at least seven times before taxes (this applies to investment grade). It would also be advisable that the bonds of the typical industrial company (assuming it is the type that can issue bonds) should not exceed the excess of current assets over current liabilities. Another rule of thumb for industrial mortgage bonds is that the bonds should not exceed 50 per cent of the replacement value (less depreciation) of the particular mortgaged property.

TABLE 23

CAPITAL STRUCTURE OF CORPORATIONS IN SELECTED MANUFACTURING INDUSTRIES IN THE UNITED STATES

(PER CENT)

Industry	*Long-term Debt*	*Preferred Stock*	*Common Stock*	*Surplus*	*Total*
Apparel	10.2%	7.7%	34.6%	47.5%	100.0%
Beverages	18.9	6.5	16.1	58.5	100.0
Chemical Products	12.1	8.1	21.9	57.9	100.0
Electrical Machinery	12.8	3.8	25.5	57.9	100.0
Food and Kindred Products	15.2	7.8	27.0	50.0	100.0
Furniture and Fixtures	9.9	5.1	29.9	55.1	100.0
Leather Products	9.3	7.0	28.9	54.8	100.0
Motor Vehicles	5.8	5.4	14.0	74.8	100.0
Paper Products	14.4	7.0	21.6	57.0	100.0
Petroleum	14.3	1.5	34.6	49.6	100.0
Primary Metals	17.2	7.2	25.3	50.3	100.0
Rubber Goods	22.5	9.7	15.6	52.2	100.0
Stone, Clay, and Glass Products	10.1	4.1	29.9	55.9	100.0
Textile Mill Products	11.2	7.0	22.5	59.3	100.0
Tobacco	30.0	11.3	24.1	34.6	100.0

SOURCE: Based on figures obtained from U.S. Treasury Department, *Statistics of Income for 1951*, Part 2, Table 4, U.S. Government Printing Office, Washington: 1955, pp. 81–85.

It should be emphasized that the capital structures of various types of industries and companies shown in the tables in this chapter are for companies that are in existence. Many of these companies have been established for years and have been able to accumulate large surpluses. It will be noted that in the case of manufacturing industries in most instances the surplus comprises over 50 per cent of the capital structure. In many cases the bonds were issued only after the companies had become firmly established and were able to show steady earning power. The fact still remains that the typical industrial concern should be capitalized with only common stock.

Although bond debt is looked upon as a permanent part of the capitalization of a railroad or public utility, this is not the case in the typical industrial. At the time bonds are issued, provision should be made for their retirement. They are commonly callable and have sinking fund provisions attached. When earnings permit, industrial bonds are commonly retired.

Use of Preferred Stock. A corporation that could safely issue bonds could also safely issue preferred stock. Since the preferred dividends are not a fixed charge, some corporations would qualify for a preferred stock issue when they should not issue bonds. But a company should be fairly sure that the earnings would adequately cover the bond interest and preferred dividends. The earnings, before taxes, should be at least seven times the sum of the interest charges and twice the preferred dividends to qualify the preferred stock as investment grade. The conversion feature is used more frequently with industrial preferreds than with other types of preferred stock.

Capital structure—financial and real estate corporations

Financial Corporations. There are many types of financial corporations, but we will confine our attention here to banks, savings and loan asociations, insurance companies, and investment companies.

Generally speaking, financial corporations issue only one type of security—common stock. By nature these companies are engaged in what is considered to be a conservative line of business, and they, therefore, follow conservative practice in the obtaining of funds. Furthermore, institutions such as banks, savings and loans, and insurance companies in a sense owe money to the depositors, savers, or policyholders and it is felt that these people should have the first and only claim against the company.

Mutual savings banks, all federal savings and loan associations and savings and loan associations formed in all except a few states have no permanent stock. They are mutual undertakings and are thus owned by the holders of the savings accounts. Mutual insurance companies are likewise owned by the policyholders.

Investment companies will be discussed in detail in Chapter 32. The open-end trusts, which have become so popular with the investing public in recent years, issue only common stock. Some of the closed-end trusts issue preferred stock and bonds.

Real Estate Corporations. In most instances a railroad, public utility, or industrial corporation finances the acquisition of real estate by the issuance of its own bonds. In some cases, however, such as for a merchandising company, a separate real estate corporation will be formed to hold title to the property, and it will be financed separately from the merchandising company. Real estate projects such as apartment buildings are often financed by a separate corporation which is formed for that purpose, and which holds title to the property.

In some instances the site is financed by the sale of land trust certificates, which were discussed in Chapter 10. The land against which the certificates are issued is then leased to the company which may erect a building on the land financed through the issuance of leasehold mortgage bonds. Or, a company may issue first mortgage bonds secured by a claim against both the land and the building.

TABLE 24

CAPITAL STRUCTURE OF FINANCE, INSURANCE, AND REAL ESTATE CORPORATIONS, IN THE UNITED STATES

(PER CENT)

Industry	*Long-term Debt*	*Preferred Stock*	*Common Stock*	*Surplus*	*Total*
Finance	14.7%	4.2%	27.1%	54.0%	100.0%
Insurance	.8	.5	13.8	84.9	100.0
Real Estate	61.7	2.2	19.6	16.5	100.0

SOURCE: Based on figures obtained from U.S. Treasury Department, *Statistics of Income for 1951,* Part 2, Table 4, U.S. Government Printing Office, Washington: 1955, pp. 85–87.

Real estate corporations will often issue the maximum amount of bonds they can sell, which is frequently equivalent to the cost of the property. Or, bonds and preferred stock will be issued for the full cost of the property. The common stock is then retained by the promoters and commonly represents no tangible investment. Since real estate developments commonly occur during a period of prosperity, the building costs are usually inflated. The drop in prices in the subsequent deflationary period may result in the value of the property being less than the amount of bonds outstanding against it. Not only is the stock interest wiped out, but considerable sacrifices may be suffered by the bondholders.

Questions

1. Distinguish between the terms "capital," "capital stock," and "capitalization."
2. Indicate the different bases on which a corporation might capitalize. Which one would you recommend? Why?
3. When would a company be likely to capitalize on a nominal basis?
4. Indicate the different meanings of over- and undercapitalization.
5. What are the disadvantages of over- and undercapitalization (in relation to earnings)?

6. If a company does not have sufficient working capital to carry on its present volume of sales is it necessarily undercapitalized? Explain.

7. Does the size or type of capitalization affect the amount of corporate organization and franchise taxes that must be paid? Explain.

8. Is it necessary to secure the approval of shareholders for a corporation to alter the amount or type of its capitalization? Explain.

9. Indicate the difference, if any, between the capital structure and the capitalization of a corporation.

10. What factors determine the nature of the capital structure?

11. How does the nature of the company and business to be transacted influence the type of capital struture?

12. Under what circumstances should the tax factor influence the nature of the capital structure?

13. What are some "axioms" that might be formulated in regard to the capital structure?

14. Under what circumstances can the matter of control be given considerable weight in the formulation of the capital structure?

15. What factors have played a part in the capital structures that we find existing today for many railroads?

16. What types of companies must have their capitalizations approved by the Interstate Commerce Commission? The Securities and Exchange Commission?

17. Indicate how the capital structure of a new industrial company would probably differ from that of a new electric power and light company.

18. Indicate the nature of the capital structure of financial corporations and account for it.

Problems

1. The American Corp. presented the following balance sheet as of Dec. 31, 19-1:

Assets		*Liabilities and Net Worth*	
Cash	$ 50,000	Accounts Payable	$ 200,000
Accounts Receivable	150,000	Bonds Payable	1,000,000
Inventory	600,000	Capital Stock	2,000,000
Machinery	1,000,000	Surplus	1,600,000
Land and Buildings	3,000,000		
Total	$4,800,000	Total	$4,800,000

(a) Which items might be considered the "capital" of the corporation? Which interpretation do you prefer? Why? (b) Which items might be included in the "capitalization" of this company? Which interpretation do you prefer? Why?

2. The Smith Corp. issued $2,000,000 in stock for assets that had a resale value of $1,800,000, and the Jones Co. exchanged $1,000,000 in stock for assets that had been appraised at $1,200,000. Average annual net earnings for the first 3 years were $400,000 and $30,000, respectively. No securities other than those stated above were issued by the companies. (a) Is either company overcapitalized? Which one? (b) Is either company undercapitalized? Which one? (c) What disadvantages might result from being over-

capitalized? Undercapitalized? (d) How could overcapitalization be corrected? Undercapitalization?

3. The Consolidated Corp. has estimated that its average annual earnings before interest charges will amount to $2,000,000. It has been decided that the company will issue four times as much stock (in amount) as bonds and that the capitalization will be based on the estimated earnings (before interest). Indicate the amount of bonds and the amount of stock that will be issued if the earnings are capitalized at (a) 10 per cent. (b) 20 per cent.

4. The Illuminated Power and Light Company is contemplating the issuance of $10,000,000 in 4 per cent first mortgage bonds, and $5,000,000 in 6 per cent preferred stock. The combined common stock and surplus is expected to be about equal to the amount of preferred stock issued. What would the earnings have to be in order that the company could earn its combined interest and preferred dividends twice?

In working the problem please give effect to the following: Assume a federal corporate tax rate of 50 per cent. To earn the preferred dividend once after taxes it therefore would be necessary to earn it twice before taxes. (Taxes are, of course, computed after interest has been deducted.)

Chapter 16

SECURITY BUYERS

Classification of Security Buyers. As industry and trade have developed in the United States the amount of investable surpluses has constantly increased. Corporations must depend upon the savings of the people both for their initial capital and for part of the money needed for expansion purposes. Individuals do not always invest directly in corporate securities. In many instances the investment is indirect as the individual investor puts his money into a financial institution, and the latter then buys the securities.

Following is a classification of security buyers each of which will be briefly discussed.

1. Institutional investors
   (*a*) Commercial banks
   (*b*) Savings banks
   (*c*) Savings and loan associations
   (*d*) Trust companies and trustees
   (*e*) Life insurance companies
   (*f*) Fire and casualty insurance companies
   (*g*) Eleemosynary, religious and educational institutions
   (*h*) Investment companies
2. Ordinary business corporations
3. Employees
4. Customers
5. Individuals
   (*a*) Investors
   (*b*) Speculators
6. Corporation's own shareholders

Institutional Investors. The amount of institutional investing has been increasing rapidly in recent years. More and more the public is putting money into financial institutions rather than into securities. But since the institutions invest the people's savings in corporate securities, we can think of the public being indirect buyers of securities to this extent. Since the financial institutions buy for investment purposes, they are not apt to throw the securities on the market at the first sign of a decline in price. For this reason the institutional buying has had a stabilizing effect on the market.

Commercial banks. The kind of credit which commercial banks supply to industry is primarily short term. In recent years, however, term loans and loans granted jointly by several banks have been longer in duration.

Most commercial banks have savings accounts in addition to demand (checking accounts) deposits. The bank will invest its demand deposits in short-term loans which may be liquidated at any time to meet the claims of the demand depositors. The money represented by the savings accounts, or at least a part of it, may be invested in longer-term loans and investments.

The principal type of security purchased by banks are obligations of the United States government. Some state and municipal bonds are also bought. Corporate bonds are bought to only a limited extent. Those that are purchased are definitely of the highest grade. Corporate stock can be acquired only under certain circumstances, and then the amount is limited, so that for all practical purposes we can say that banks do not buy stocks.

The national and state banking laws limit the amount of securities, except United States government obligations, which may be purchased by banks.

Savings banks. Mutual savings banks are found in only 17 states. They are concentrated in the New England states, Delaware, Maryland, New Jersey, New York, and Pennsylvania. Like the commercial banks, their investments are regulated by statutes. Securities that may be purchased by savings banks are termed *legal investments,* or are said to be on the *legal list.*

The principal investments of savings banks are real estate loans, principally mortgage loans on residential property. Next in importance are United States government obligations. The rest of the investment portfolio is made up mainly of public utility and railroad securities and state and municipal bonds.

Savings and loan associations. The primary investment of savings and loan associations is real estate mortgages. Most of them, however, have part of their secondary reserves invested in United States government securities. In a number of the states they are also permitted to buy state and municipal bonds issued in the particular state, but to date relatively few of them have acquired any appreciable amount of state and municipal bonds. Since savings and loans will be subject to the federal corporate income tax after their reserves have reached a specified amount, state and municipal bonds, which are tax exempt, will in the future in some instances make good investments for them.

Trust companies and trustees. Some trust companies carry on a commercial banking business as well as a trust business. Where this is done the investment of funds represented by the banking end of the business is governed by the same laws applicable to commercial banks. The following relates to the funds held by the trust company under various trust agreements. What is said will apply with equal force to individual trustees.

The trust agreement may state what type of securities may be purchased. When this is not done the state statutes relating to trustee investments are applicable. These statutes vary among the states but are classified into two groups, (1) those which specify that only securities which are on the *legal list* may be purchased, and (2) those which state that the trustee may purchase any security which a *prudent man* might purchase for his own account (called the *prudent-man rule*).

In addition to United States government and state and municipal bonds, the legal list usually limits the investments to real estate mortgages, high-grade public utility, railroad and industrial bonds. Under the prudent-man rule high-grade stocks may also be purchased.

The prudent-man rule was first adopted by Massachusetts, and it is sometimes referred to as the "Massachusetts rule." Due to the decline in interest rates and higher taxes there has been a decided shift to the prudent-man rule. At the present time slightly more than half the states follow it either as a result of statutes or court decision. It is worthy of note that New York enacted a statute effective July 1, 1950, which provides that trustees may invest up to 35 per cent "in such securities as would be acquired by prudent men of discretion, using intelligence in such matters, who are seeking a reasonable income and the preservation of their capital."

Life insurance companies. Life insurance companies have become one of the principal sources of investment funds in the United States. Premiums paid by holders of life insurance policies go to pay for the life protection afforded by the policy, and in all types of policies except term, also to build up a savings account for the policyholder, which is represented by the loan value or cash surrender value of the policy. Since the average policy runs for a long period of time before the company is compelled to pay anything out to the policyholder or the beneficiary, the insurance companies have large sums of money to invest.

The investments of life insurance companies are regulated by the statutes of the state in which the companies are formed, and to a certain extent by the laws of the other states in which they may be operating. These laws, however, are not as strict as those governing trustee investments. They are permitted to buy United States government bonds, state and municipal bonds, and to a limited extent real estate and real estate mortgages, and railroad, public utility and industrial bonds that meet specified standards. Some of the states also permit a limited amount of preferred stock that meets specified tests, and a few now permit a limited amount of common stock. In 1957, New York amended its laws to permit life insurance companies to invest up to 5 per cent of their assets, or one-half of their surplus, whichever is lower, in common stocks. To date they have been hesitant to invest a considerable amount of money in this way.

In some instances life insurance companies have purchased bonds directly from the issuing company rather than from an investment banker. This will be discussed in Chapter 18.

Fire and casualty insurance companies. Unlike life insurance, the total amount of the premiums paid for fire or casualty insurance goes to pay for the insurance protection. Thus, there is no "savings" feature present. Furthermore, the policies run for a period of only 1 to 5 years. For these reasons these companies do not have the money available for investment as do the life insurance companies.

They do, however, have a considerable amount of money available for investment. Although they were at first free to invest in whatever they desired, the tendency in more recent years has been toward the regulation of their investment portfolio, particularly in regard to the investment of required reserves. They, however, have much greater freedom than do life insurance companies. They have gone in for stocks much more than the life companies could, with the result that some of them have upwards of 50 per cent of their assets invested in this form of security.

Eleemosynary, religious, and educational institutions. Another increasing source of corporate funds are the charitable organizations, church groups, and universities and colleges. The assets of these institutions, naturally, increase along with the increase in population and the greater complexity of modern life. Moreover, with the increase in prices and lower interest rates, a larger amount of money is needed by these institutions. Another factor accounting for the growth of these organizations is the increase in income and death taxes. Donations to charitable organizations may be deducted up to a certain amount before arriving at the net taxable income. The part of the estate which is left to philanthropic organizations is not subject to the federal estate taxes or the inheritance taxes (in some states).

In some instances these organizations have their own staff that selects their investments, while in other cases they employ independent investment counsel. A person leaving money to these organizations may specify the type of securities in which the funds may be invested, but usually no such restrictions are present. In some of the states there are laws regulating the investments of this type of institution, but in general they are allowed much more freedom in investing than are trust companies and life insurance companies.

In the past the typical investment portfolio of these organizations was composed largely of bonds. Due to the increase in prices and the decline in interest rates, however, they have been investing a larger percentage of their funds in common stock in more recent years.

In some instances organizations of this kind have purchased bonds directly from the issuing company rather than buying them from an investment broker, in a manner similar to that of life insurance companies. Also in some cases they have purchased business property and then leased it back to the business.

Investment companies. Investment companies, which are also called "investment trusts," are organizations which invest the proceeds from the sale of their own securities in the securities of other companies. The securities of the other companies are purchased for investment rather than for control purposes.

Investment companies are subject to regulation by the Investment Company Act of 1940, but in general they are free to buy whatever securities they desire. In some instances the company is set up to invest in the securities of only certain industries. Some go in for diversification among the various industries. Others are set up to buy mainly common stocks while some concentrate on bonds or diversify their investments among bonds, preferred stocks, and common stocks.

The sale of stocks of the open-end companies has increased tremendously since the beginning of World War II, and this has resulted in a great increase in the funds the companies have had available for the purchase of securities. Investment companies will be discussed in detail in Chapter 32.

Ordinary Business Corporations. The ordinary business corporation is sometimes a purchaser of securities of other companies. Companies whose business is seasonal in nature, must have sufficient liquid investments on hand to meet the peak cash demand. Such investment is commonly in bank accounts and short-term government obligations. Funds being held for longer periods of time for such things as plant improvements and extensions are also often invested in government bonds.

Sinking funds call for the investment of money in government bonds or the particular issue for which the fund was set up. In some instances bonds of subsidiaries are purchased. In the case of parent or holding companies, securities, particularly stocks, of subsidiaries are purchased. Occasionally, a company will invest in the securities of other companies which supply them with materials, or customer companies.

Pension funds are providing more money every year for the purchase of stocks and bonds. There are in excess of 16,000 different funds in existence today. The value of their assets on January 1, 1955, exceeded 20 billion dollars. Although listed under corporate investors, most pension funds are administered by life insurance companies, trust companies and banks. Following the conservative practice typical of the industry, and also as prescribed by the law, the bulk of the pension funds the life insurance companies administer is invested in bonds and mortgages. Many banks and trust companies, however, invest approximately 25 per cent of the pension funds they handle in common stocks.

Some company pension plans which are administered by trustees other than life insurance companies invest heavily in the company's own stock. The Sears, Roebuck & Co. pension fund, for example, holds over one fourth of the company's outstanding stock. Approximately 98 per cent of the eligible employees are participating in the pension plan. In recent years many Sears employees who have been drawing only modest salaries have retired with small fortunes as a result of the pension plan.

Employees

Employee Ownership of Securities. The space here devoted to employee ownership of stock is out of proportion to its importance. Many of the institutions mentioned above are much heavier security buyers than employees. But since employee ownership of stock has peculiar conditions and problems, it was thought desirable to discuss it separately.

Employee-stock-ownership plans started at the beginning of the present century when the United States Steel Corp. adopted the plan in 1901. Other companies to make early use of the plan include the American Telephone and Telegraph Co., the National Biscuit Co., E. I. du Pont de Nemours & Co., Dennison Manufacturing Co., Firestone Tire and Rubber Co., Proctor and Gamble Co., and the Commonwealth Edison Co.

The greatest development in employee-stock-ownership occurred in the late 1920's, at which time about one third of the large corporations are estimated to have had a plan of one kind or another. The stock market crash of 1929 brought the movement to a halt, and in the years immediately afterward, four out of five of the leading employee-stock-ownership plans were given up. During the 1940's when the World War II business prosperity resulted in an increase in stock prices, additional companies either adopted the plan or revived their former plan which had been discontinued. Not many companies have stock-ownership plans, and of those that do, a majority call for the purchase of stock only on the part of executives or junior executives. In a study published in 1953, it was found that only 68 formal employee-stock-ownership plans were in existence among the larger American corporations, and of these only 28 were currently active.[1]

Advantages and Disadvantages to Corporation. Although the sale of stock to employees brings in new money to the issuing corporation, the same as a sale to anyone else, the primary purpose in most instances is not to obtain new capital. In some instances the sale of stock to employees may adversely affect the issuing corporation.

Advantages. The reasons for selling stock to employees amount to the same thing as the advantages to the corporation, and these may be outlined as follows:

1. Encouragement of thrift among employees
2. Improvement of company-employee relations
3. Reduction in labor turnover
4. Increase in labor efficiency
5. Greater diffusion of stock ownership
6. Economical way of selling stock
7. Tax savings to employee on stock profit

[1] National Industrial Conference Board, Inc., Studies in Personnel Policy, No. 132, *Stock Ownership Plans for Workers,* New York, 1953.

In most instances the amount of stock bought by the employees is not appreciable, and it is probably true that most plans are provided for purposes other than merely obtaining additional capital.

Companies are always seeking methods of improving their relationship with labor. Employees who develop the habit of thrift usually make better workers and are less likely to shift to another job. Labor turnover is expensive and anything to reduce it is eagerly sought by management. Labor unions are constantly making new demands on management, and some type of profit sharing plan tends to keep the demands of labor within reason. This point should be given more weight when the amount of stock held by the employees is appreciable, and where increased efficiency on the part of the workmen is more likely to result in higher dividends. In some instances when the issuing corporation continues to expand and increase its profits, employees have enjoyed large dividends over a period of years. In addition the market price of their stock may now be much higher than what they originally paid for it.

The last point listed above—tax savings—would generally apply only to high-salaried executives. With the present high income tax rates, a high-salaried executive has relatively little left after paying income taxes. A raise in salary of an appreciable amount leaves him little of the increase after taxes because all of it is taxed at the higher rate. Any profit made on the sale of stock held for more than six months, however, is considered a long-term capital gain, and the maximum tax on such a gain is only 25 per cent. Thus, selling stock to the executives, particularly at a price below its existing market price, may be more attractive to an executive than offering him a raise in salary. In some instances the stock buying is accomplished through the exercise of stock options, which we discussed earlier in the book (Chapter 12).

Disadvantages. Despite the possible advantages of employee-stock-ownership plans, in many instances they have not worked out well both from the standpoint of the issuing corporation and the employee. The disadvantages from the viewpoint of the issuing company may be outlined as follows:

1. The market price of the stock may decline.
2. The average employee cannot afford to take a loss.
3. The average employee is not familiar with stock market operations.
4. Dividends may be reduced or omitted.
5. Ill will may be created.
6. Labor union may be opposed to the plan.

Most companies do not have an employee-stock-purchase plan. Also, many companies which have had one in the past have discontinued it. In many instances it is felt that more ill will than goodwill is created by such a plan.

It is natural to expect that the employee would get interested in purchasing stock after the price of it had advanced considerably in the market. After he purchases, it may fall in price. The employee is usually given the right to buy the stock on the installment plan. In 1929, many employees found themselves owing more on the unpaid balance than the worth of their stock in the market. This makes the employee become disgruntled to say the least. In most instances of this kind, however, the company canceled the indebtedness and returned the money that had been paid. Even if the stock is fully paid at the time it declines in price, the average employee blames the company.

A temporary decline in the market price of the stock may not harm the employee if he would hold on to the stock for a long period of time. But like the average person he is inclined to sell it when the price declines. The average employee is not familiar with stock market operations, and he may interpret a technical decline in the market as a sign of reversal in the major trend of the market. The employee is usually not in a financial position where he could afford to take a loss on his investments.

In many instances an employee will interpret any move on the part of management in his behalf as something to be suspicious about. Even if the plan works out well, the employee may look upon it as designed to weaken his independence. In some instances labor union leaders are opposed to employee-stock-ownership plans because they feel it may weaken their power over the employees.

ADVANTAGES AND DISADVANTAGES TO EMPLOYEE. The advantages and disadvantages of employee-stock-ownership plans to the employee may be apparent from what has been said above, so we will merely summarize them here.

Advantages. The advantages of the plan from the viewpoint of the employee are as follows:

1. It may encourage thrift.
2. In many instances the stock can be bought below its market value.
3. In some instances the company will buy back the stock at the offering price.
4. The return on the employee's money may be higher than he would otherwise obtain.

Disadvantages. The disadvantages from the standpoint of the employee are as follows:

1. He may have to sell the stock at a loss.
2. The dividends may be reduced or omitted.
3. Too great a concentration of risk.

Type of Securities Sold. In most instances the type of security sold under the employee-stock-ownership plan is common stock. Among public utilities, however, preferred stock has sometimes been offered. In some instances the employee is given the choice between preferred and common. In a few cases the stock offered the employees has been a special type of stock.

Employees Eligible to Purchase Stock. In most of the plans which have been adopted the offer was open only to the executives and junior executives. Such a plan is more apt to be successful than one which is open also to the rank and file of the company employees. The executives are better able to assume the risks of stock ownership than are the ordinary employees. They may be able to buy an appreciable amount of stock, and their loyalty to the company will probably be greater than that of the average worker.

Mechanics of Plan. The mechanics of selling the stock vary considerably. In some instances the stock offered has never been outstanding. In such a case the stock would have to be released from the stockholders' pre-emptive right either by statutes or waiver before it could be sold to the employees. In some instances the stock is bought by the corporation in the general market, or has been acquired as treasury stock in some other way.

The stock may be offered to the employees at the market price, or at a price below this. In the latter event, the tendency would be to dilute the equity of the existing shareholders, but usually the amount of stock purchased by the employees is so small relative to the total amount of stock outstanding, that this is not a serious factor.

Following are the terms of the employee-stock-purchase plan of the American Telephone and Telegraph Company, which is one of the leading companies using a stock purchase plan. Any employee who has had more than three months' service with the company may buy one share for each $500 of his annual wages, with a maximum of 50 shares. The price paid by the employee is $20 below the average market price either for the month in which payment is completed or for the next succeeding month, whichever is lower, but in no event will the price be more than $150 per share nor less than $100 per share. Payment for the shares is in installments of $5 per share each month. The employee has the option to cancel the agreement at any time, in which event he can get back all the money paid in, or he can use this money to pay in full for a smaller number of shares than originally subscribed. Interest at the rate of 2 per cent per annum (compounded semi-annually) is allowed on employee deposits until the stock is purchased.

Method of Payment. In some plans the stock is paid for outright, but in most instances it is purchased on the installment plan. The company may deduct a specified amount from the employee's pay or the employee may pay the amount in cash each pay day.

Cancellation. The conditions governing the cancellation of employee stock-subscriptions depend upon the terms of the particular contract. In most instances if the payments are not made by the employee on schedule, the subscription will be automatically canceled by the company. The subscription may also be terminated if the employee no longer continues to work for the company. The employee is also usually given the right to cancel the agreement voluntarily. In the event the contract is canceled, the entire amount on deposit is paid back to the employee, sometimes with interest, even though the amount of money paid in would have been enough to purchase one or more whole shares.

Restrictions on Resale. After the employee has acquired the stock of his company there are usually no restrictions on the resale by him. However, where stock has been sold to the employee below the market price at the time, and where the purpose of the plan has been to improve labor relations rather than to secure additional capital, there are in some instances restrictions, either requiring the consent of the company before the stock may be sold, or it may be sold to the issuing company only. These restrictions are more common when the stock is not listed on a stock exchange.

Customers

Origin. The sale of stock to customers began on a large scale after World War I, in the public utility field, particularly among electric light and power companies, and continued until the stock market crash in 1929. In most instances the stock was preferred and usually it was nonvoting. The companies' regular employees often sold the stock, although in some instances special salesmen were hired to do so. House-to-house canvassing was often done. Stock of both operating and holding companies was sold.

Reason for Origin. Many utilities, following World War I, had difficulty in raising sufficient capital for expansion purposes through the regular channels. At the same time individuals had become acquainted with securities through the war bond drives. Furthermore, they had accumulated savings from the war and postwar prosperity, and thus had funds available for investment. Another reason why the utilities were interested in selling to the customers is that there would probably be less objection on the part of the customers to rate increases if they were shareholders in the company. The commissions earned by the employees in selling the stock was extra money in their pockets, and they therefore became happier with their job. In many instances the cost to the company of this method of selling stock was less than when it was sold through the regular channels.

Plan Rarely Used Now. The stock market crash in 1929 and the ensuing depression put an end to selling stock to customers. Many of the buyers lost a large part of their investment, particularly in the case of public utility holding companies. The Securities Act of 1933, and the Public Utility Holding Company Act of 1935, prohibited further selling of stock in this manner.

Customer ownership plans have not been used much outside of the public utility field. It has been used in some instances in merchandising. For example, wholesale grocers sometimes sell stock to retail grocers in an effort to get them to buy their goods from that company. In some instances a manufacturer will sell stock to retailers for the same purpose. The original United Drug Co., for example, sold stock to retail druggists who would handle their "Rexall" line of products.

Advantages and Disadvantages Summarized. Without further comment, we will list the advantages and disadvantages of customer ownership of stock.

Advantages. The advantages are as follows:

1. Another source of equity capital
2. Economical way of selling stock
3. Improve the capital structure, since customers are sold stocks and not bonds
4. Development of goodwill with customers
5. In case of public utilities, probably less pressure for government ownership if the company had a large group of stockholders, including the customers
6. Increases the earnings of the employee-salesman

7. Some of the company employees also stockholders as a result of the customer sale
8. Possible widening of the market for the company's products

Disadvantages. Following are the possible disadvantages of a customer-stock-ownership plan. It will be noted that most of these were the same points as mentioned in connection with employee stock ownership plans:

1. Possibility that the price of the stock might decline
2. Possibility that the dividends may be reduced or eliminated
3. Inability of the average customer to assume the risks of stock ownership
4. Unfamiliarity of average customer with stock market operations
5. As a result of some or all the above points, the plan may incur the ill will rather than the goodwill of the customer
6. Possible lack of banker advice about present and future financial matters

Individuals

NUMBER INCREASING. Employees and customers are, of course, included in the class of individual security buyers, but due to their special category, it was thought desirable to discuss these types of stock sales separately. The existing stockholders of corporations are also individuals, but due to peculiar conditions surrounding sales of stock to stockholders, we will discuss this by itself in the following chapter.

It is impossible to state the exact number of stockholders in the United States, due in large part to the fact that in many instances the same person is a stockholder in more than one corporation. If we took a list of the number of stockholders in all our corporations and added them together, we would get many duplications. Also some stock which people really own is carried in the names of brokerage firms.

THE 1952 BROOKINGS INSTITUTION STUDY. In the immediate past the number of stockholders in the United States has been estimated at somewhere between 5½ and 15 million, but it was not until 1952, that a rather complete study was made on the subject. At the request of the New York Stock Exchange, the Brookings Institution made a complete study of the stockholders in the United States of publicly owned corporations which was published in 1952, under the title *Share Ownership in the United States.*[2] It is to be noted

[2] Written by Lewis H. Kimmel, The Brookings Institution, Washington, D. C., 1952.

that this study covered only the *publicly owned* corporations. These embraced the companies whose stocks were traded on the New York Stock Exchange, the New York Curb Exchange (now the American Stock Exchange), and the 18 other stock exchanges, 373 unlisted banks, 149 unlisted investment companies, and 2,147 other unlisted companies of all types. Co-operative associations and companies whose stock was closely held were excluded from the study.

The study revealed that, at the beginning of 1952, there were 6,490,000 individuals in the United States who were shareowners in publicly owned corporations. This represented 4.2 per cent of the *total* population. Of these it was estimated that 6,350,000 were *adults*. Thus, about one out of every sixteen adults in the United States was a shareholder.

Because women outnumbered men as stockholders in some of our large corporations, such as American Telephone and Telegraph Company, it was thought that there were more women shareholders in the United States than men. But the study showed that of the total adult shareholders, 50.6 per cent were men, and 49.4 per cent were women. But considering the total number of shares held, it was found that men owned nearly 35 per cent more stock than women. The average holding for men was estimated to be 160 shares and that of women 115 shares. In other words, for every four shares owned by men, a little less than three shares were owned by women. The average stockholder owned stock of 4.1 different issues.

THE 1956 NEW YORK STOCK EXCHANGE STUDY. In 1956 the New York Stock Exchange made a study of the shareownership of public corporations in the United States.[3] This recent study revealed that the number of stockholders in public corporations had increased from 6,490,000 in 1952, to 8,630,000 in 1956—an increase of 33 per cent.[4] It is interesting to note in Table 25 that the proportion of women stockholders jumped from 49.8 per cent in 1952, to 51.6 per cent in 1956. One in every 12 adults owns stock in public corporations.[5] This compares with one in every 16 adults in 1952.

[3] "Public corporations" was defined as those companies with at least one stock issue traded on one of the country's securities exchanges, or otherwise available to the general public and owned by at least 300 stockholders.

[4] *1956 Census of Shareholders*, Department of Public Relations and Market Development, New York Stock Exchange, New York, N. Y., 1956. All the figures relating to the 1956 shareownership in the United States contained in this section were taken from this study.

[5] *Ibid.*

TABLE 25

INDIVIDUAL SHAREOWNERS OF PUBLIC CORPORATIONS BY SEX
(1956 CENSUS AND 1952 BROOKINGS)

		Individual Shareowners			
		1956 Census		*1952 Brookings*	
	Population	*Number*	*Per Cent of Total*	*Number*	*Per Cent of Total*
Males—All Ages	83,416,000 49.0%	4,175,000	48.4	3,260,000	50.2
Females—All Ages	86,852,000 51.0%	4,455,000	51.6	3,230,000	49.8
Total	170,268,000 100.0%	8,630,000	100.0	6,490,000	100.0

SOURCE: *1956 Census of Shareowners,* Department of Public Relations and Market Development, New York Stock Exchange, New York, 1956, p. 10.

The 1956 study showed that over half the adult shareowners are in households with incomes between $3,000 and $7,500 a year, and almost two-thirds in households earning under $7,500. The breakdown of the total population and shareownership by income groups is shown in Table 26.[6]

TABLE 26

INDIVIDUAL SHAREOWNERS BY INCOME
(1956 CENSUS)

*Reported Household Income**	*Population*		*Individual Shareowners*		
	Per Cent	*Number*	*As Per Cent of Population*	*Number*	*Per Cent of Total*
Under $3,000	34.1	34,020,000	2.8	960,000	11.6
$3,000-$5,000	36.5	36,470,000	5.9	2,160,000	26.1
$5,000-$7,500	19.0	18,940,000	11.6	2,190,000	26.4
$7,500 & Over	10.4	10,370,000	28.6	2,970,000	35.9
Sub-total	100.0	99,800,000	8.3	8,280,000	100.0
Not Classified by Income†	—	70,468,000	0.5	350,000	—
Total	—	170,268,000	5.1	8,630,000	—

* Based on 1955 income before taxes as reported by a responsible household member.

† Includes minors, members of Armed Forces, U. S. citizens residing abroad, transients, and people in institutions.

SOURCE: *1956 Census of Shareowners,* Department of Public Relations and Market Development, New York Stock Exchange, New York, 1956, p. 15.

6 The 1956 study by the New York Stock Exchange did not attempt to measure the dollar value of the stock holdings by the various shareowner groups.

Education appears to pay off when it comes to buying stock, as can be seen in Table 27. Only one person out of 59 with eight years or less of schooling is a shareowner in a publicly owned corporation; one out of every 10 high school graduates owns stock; but three out of 10 college graduates are shareowners. Those holding college degrees comprised 20.5 per cent of the total number of shareowners in 1952, but by 1956, the percentage had jumped to 29.4.

TABLE 27

ADULT SHAREOWNERS BY EDUCATION
(1956 CENSUS AND 1952 BROOKINGS)

		Individual Shareowners				
		1956 Census			1952 Brookings	
Last Year of School Completed	*Population*	*As Per Cent of Population*	*Number*	*Per Cent of Total*	*Number*	*Per Cent of Total*
8th Grade or less	35,840,000 35.9%	1.7	620,000	7.5	1,230,000	19.4
1-3 yrs. high school	17,950,000 18.0%	5.3	950,000	11.5	630,000	10.0
4 yrs. high school	28,630,000 28.7%	9.6	2,750,000	33.2	1,840,000	29.1
1-3 yrs. college	9,160,000 9.2%	16.8	1,540,000	18.6	1,330,000	21.0
4 or more yrs. college	8,220,000 8.2%	29.4	2,420,000	29.2	1,300,000	20.5
Sub-total	99,800,000 100.0%	8.3	8,280,000	100.0	6,330,000	100.0
Not Classified by Education	70,468,000	0.5	350,000	–	160,000*	–
Total	170,268,000	5.1	8,630,000	–	6,490,000	–

* 140,000 minors and 20,000 current students.

SOURCE: *1956 Census of Shareowners,* Department of Public Relations and Market Development, New York Stock Exchange, New York, 1956, p. 18.

Table 28 shows the number of adult shareowners classified by occupation. It will be noted that housewives (including nonemployed adult women) lead the list. This is accounted for in part by the fact that some men hold at least some of their stock in their wives' names in order to protect that part of their estate from business creditors. Furthermore, wives usually outlive their husbands, because statistics show that a woman will live about five years longer than a man of the same age; and many men marry younger women. Stock is also sometimes purchased in the wife's name or thereafter transferred to her in order to lessen the federal estate tax and the state death taxes. A final factor is that a wife, as well as the husband, may take the $50 dividend exclusion for income tax purposes if dividends of this amount or over are paid on stock which is held in her name. The table indicates that one out of four proprietors and executives is a shareowner; one out of six professional people owns stock; and one out of nine clerical and sales people is a stockowner.

TABLE 28

ADULT SHAREOWNERS BY OCCUPATION

(1956 CENSUS)

		Individual Shareowners		
Occupation	*Population*	*As Per Cent of Population*	*Number*	*Per Cent of Total*
Proprietors, Managers and Officials	4,640,000	24.6	1,140,000	13.7
Professional and Semi-Professional	5,620,000	18.0	1,010,000	12.2
Clerical and Sales	12,870,000	11.6	1,490,000	18.0
Housewives and Non-employed Adult Females	34,160,000	8.3	2,830,000	34.2
Non-employed Adult Males (including retired and dependent persons)	7,250,000	6.8	490,000	5.9
Service Workers	6,650,000	6.5	430,000	5.2
Craftsmen and Foremen	8,870,000	5.9	520,000	6.3
Farmers and Farm Laborers	4,700,000	4.9	230,000	2.8
Operatives and Laborers	15,040,000	0.9	140,000	1.7
Sub-total	99,800,000	8.3	8,280,000	100.0
Not Classified by Occupation	70,468,000	0.5	350,000	—
Total	170,268,000	5.1	8,630,000	—

SOURCE: *1956 Census of Shareowners,* Department of Public Relations and Market Development, New York Stock Exchange, New York, 1956, p. 20.

In addition to the 8,630,000 different shareowners in publicly owned corporations in the United States in 1956, the NYSE study showed that there were an additional 1,400,000 different people who owned shares in privately held corporations. Thus the total number of shareowners in this country is slightly in excess of 10,000,000.

INVESTORS. A distinction is commonly made in finance between investment and speculation, but the authorities are not always in agreement as to the difference. In some instances it would be difficult to draw the line. The difference between the two may be considered according to the degree of risk involved in the purchase of the security, the intent of the purchaser or the degree of his information about the particular security being purchased. In the opinion of the author, the term *investment* should be applied to the purchase of a security in which the degree of risk is relatively small, and where there is some assurance of an income or profit regardless of whether this results from a steady income or from an appreciation in the value of the security.

Certainly, the fluctuation in the purchasing power of money should be taken into consideration by the security buyer in determining if a security is an investment. There should also be some diversification between securities which are adversely affected by inflation and deflation. But a particular security that is otherwise considered a good investment should not be thrown out of the category simply because the purchasing power of the principal amount of the security may be less at maturity than when the security was purchased.

Investors buy the high-grade bonds, and high-grade preferred and common stocks. In many instances wealthy persons buy these securities for the income return or capital gain they are able to get. In some cases the reason for purchasing is for control purposes as well as for income return.

The purchase of securities by or for widows and orphans, who are interested in security of principal and a fair and steady income, is usually of the investment type. Many persons, who are not classed as wealthy, regularly purchase securities as part of their investments.

Securities purchased by investors are commonly held for long periods of time. Corporations like to have their stocks and bonds held by this class; it exerts a stabilizing effect on the market price of the securities, and enables the corporation to secure better future financing. Investment securities are purchased both directly from the issuing company and on the general market.

SPECULATORS. The term *speculation* is variously defined as the purchase of securities which are relatively risky, or applied when the intent in buying is for rising appreciation in the value of the securities, or when the purchase is made without a thorough investigation of the particular company and its security. In the opinion of the author, the degree of risk more than anything else would characterize speculation.

Bonds are ordinarily thought of as more in the investment class than in the speculation category, but many of them are relatively risky, and are definitely to be classified as speculations. Preferred and common stocks fall into both classes. Generally speaking, however, common stocks as a group are classified more as speculations than the other types of securities. Speculation may take place both in the purchase of securities which have already been issued and in those which are being originally issued by the corporation. Of course, speculations differ in degree of risk.

Some feel that speculation is harmful. But the speculation which takes place both on the stock exchanges and in the over-the-counter market is also beneficial in making for greater liquidity, setting values on securities, and aiding the corporation in its future financing. Perhaps more important is the original buying of securities of new companies. Practically all of our necessary and important industries today were considered rank speculations at the time of their formation. It is only because of the courage and foresight of thousands of speculators that such companies were able to start business.

Is there any difference between "speculation" and "gambling"? From the standpoint of the individual participant, there probably is not much difference, if any. From the social standpoint, however, it is sometimes said that speculation is the assuming of an already existing risk, whereas *gambling* creates the risk assumed. In speculation there is an assumption of a risk which might be beneficial from the viewpoint of society, whereas gambling is sometimes considered a vice.

The sale of stock to stockholders will be taken up in the next chapter. Later we will discuss sale to investment bankers. In passing, attention should be called to the fact that ordinarily investment bankers are not thought of as a class of security buyers since they usually buy the securities for the purpose of reselling them to others.

Questions

1. List the different classes of security buyers.
2. Which classes of security buyers are restricted by laws with respect to their investments? Why?
3. If an ordinary business corporation has cash which is not needed in the business why might it invest this money in securities rather than pay it out to the shareholders in the form of dividends?
4. (a) What are the advantages and disadvantages to the issuing corporation of employee-stock-ownership plans? (b) What attitude do the labor unions take toward employee-stock-ownership plans?
5. Indicate what you know about customer-stock-ownership plans.

6. Why has it been difficult to determine the number of shareholders in the United States?

7. The following refers to the New York Stock Exchange study on stock ownership in the United States.

(a) How many shareholders of publicly owned corporations are there in the United States? (b) What percentage of the shareholders were women? (c) What is the total number of shareowners in the United States?

8. Do you believe that more people in the United States should be encouraged to buy corporate stock? Why or why not?

9. Distinguish between investment and speculation. Is speculation the same as gambling? Explain.

10. If your parents, immediate relatives, or friends own stock, attempt to secure the answers to the following questions:

(a) Did they thoroughly investigate the issuing company before buying the stock? (b) Are they investing or speculating? (c) What was their primary motive in buying the stock? (d) Do they watch the market price of the stock closely? (e) Are their stock holdings sufficiently diversified?

Problems

1. (a) Classify the security ratings found in Moody's *Manuals* according to whether you think they represent high-grade, medium-grade, or speculative securities. (b) Compare the Moody ratings of securities with those issued by Standard & Poor's. (c) Do higher ratings indicate that more money can be made through the purchase of the particular security? Explain. (d) Compare the yields (based on current prices) of four railroad bonds with different Moody ratings. Which yields the most? Compare the yields of four industrial bonds with different Moody ratings. Which yields the most? Which of these industrial bonds do you think is the safest investment? Why?

2. Institutional investors invest a large percentage of their money in bonds, but a very small amount, if any at all, in stocks. How do you account for this?

3. An investment counselor in New York City recently was advising his clients to switch part of their holdings from bonds to stocks. The reason he gave was that the large national debt and the always-present fear of a widespread world war would cause prices to rise and that therefore stocks would be better investments than bonds.

(a) Do you think that a large national debt and world war would raise or tend to raise prices? Explain. (b) Would stocks be a better investment than bonds in a period of rising prices? Explain. (c) Are there any reasons why a life insurance company might prefer investment in bonds rather than stocks even in a period of rising prices? Explain.

Chapter 17

PRIVILEGED SUBSCRIPTIONS

MEANING OF PRIVILEGED SUBSCRIPTIONS. As ordinarily used, the term *privileged subscriptions* applies to the additional stock which a corporation offers to the existing shareholders, in proportion to their present stock holdings in the company and usually at a price below the then existing market price per share. As a rule, the new issue is common stock, and in the great majority of the cases, the offer to buy is extended only to the existing common shareholders.

In many instances, however, the term "privileged subscriptions" is used whenever the company offers any kind of securities to any of its existing security holders. For example, it may be used when the shareholders are given the right to buy bonds, or when the bondholders are offered the right to purchase stock of the corporation.

REASONS FOR USE. When a corporation selects a particular method of selling its securities it is usually done only after due consideration of the relative merits of the various other methods. The advantages and disadvantages of most of these were stated in the previous chapter.

There are two reasons why the privileged subscription plan is used, (1) legally the corporation may be compelled to use this method, or (2) it may be considered to be the best method under the existing circumstances. Sometimes however, both reasons may coincide in the same case. The two reasons will now be briefly discussed.

LEGAL OBLIGATION. In Chapter 5, when we were discussing shareholders' rights it was pointed out that, subject to some qualifications, shareholders had at common law a *pre-emptive right* to be offered new stock before it could be sold to the public. The reason for this legal right was to permit the shareholders to maintain the same degree of control in the company and to preserve their equity in the surplus of the company.

To illustrate this, let us assume that a particular corporation has only common stock authorized in its charter, and that a particular person or faction owns 51 per cent of this stock. Whoever owns 51 per cent of the stock could control the election of all the directors, or if cumulative voting was followed, at least a majority of them. If the stock capitalization of this company was to be increased 100 per cent by the sale of the new stock to the public, the person or group which formerly owned 51 per cent of the stock would now find that its 51 per cent equity had been reduced to 25½ per cent. This amount of stock is not sufficient to insure control of the company.

As a practical matter, it is understood that the above stated procedure would probably not occur. The directors would either consist of the people who owned the 51 per cent, or they would be controlled by these shareholders, and thus they would probably not follow a procedure which would change the control of the company.

The other reason given for the pre-emptive right was to enable a shareholder to maintain his same equity in the surplus of the company. This can best be explained through the use of an example. Let us assume that a corporation has the following abbreviated balance sheet:

Assets	$1,600,000	Liabilities	$ 100,000
		Capital stock (par value $100)	1,000,000
		Surplus	500,000
Total	$1,600,000	Total	$1,600,000

We will assume that the market value of the stock and its book value are the same, that is, $150 a share. If this company were to sell another $1,000,000 in stock to the public at its par value, the surplus would then be spread over twice as many shares, and thus result in a reduction of the book value (and possibly the market value) per share from $150 to $125. In other words, the old shareholders would lose $25 a share, and the new shareholders would gain this amount.

If the old shareholders were given the right to buy the stock, then for every share they held they could purchase a new one at its par value, which added to their original investment worth $150, would give them two shares, each now valued at $125. In other words, the $25 lost on the old share is made up in the value of the new share.

It should be noted that the *privileged* subscription may be a misnomer on two counts, (1) being offered the right to buy the stock first is hardly a privilege if the law forces the corporation to follow this procedure, and (2) it is not necessarily a privilege for the shareholders to be allowed to invest more in order to maintain their degree of control and equity in the surplus of the company.

WHEN NOT SUBJECT TO PRE-EMPTIVE RIGHT. In Chapter 5 some of the exceptions to the pre-emptive right were listed. These will be stated again here with some additional explanation.

Continuing sale of original issue. Generally speaking the pre-emptive right does not apply to the original stock authorization, particularly if it is continually being sold. If the right were applicable it would mean that whoever first bought the stock would have to be offered all the rest of it before it could be offered to anyone else, and any purchasers of the stock not taken by this shareholder would have to be offered the rest of the stock before it could be sold to any other person, etc. This obviously would be a highly impractical situation. Furthermore, rights of the shareholders with respect to control and equity in the surplus have not yet been established. They are, therefore, not harmed by not getting the pre-emptive right.

If only part of the original authorized stock was sold at the time of promotion of the company, and some years later the rest of it is to be sold, the pre-emptive right would apply to the subsequent sale since the shareholders' rights with respect to control and equity in the surplus have been established already.

Treasury stock. Stockholders do not have any pre-emptive rights in respect to treasury stock. The law reasons that the existing shareholders are not worse off after the treasury stock has been resold to the public than they were before the stock had been reacquired by the company. It should be noted, however, that after the treasury stock has been resold by the company it is entitled to the pre-emptive right the same as any other shares of the same class.

Nonvoting, nonparticipating preferred stock. The law recognizes the pre-emptive right as a fundamental right of shareholders, and such right, therefore, applies to preferred stock, unless it is taken away by contract, statutes, or by implication. Since the reason for the pre-emptive right is to enable a shareholder to maintain his degree of control and equity in the surplus of the company, a preferred stock which is nonvoting and nonparticipating with respect to the surplus would not at common law have the pre-emptive right.

"Nonparticipating" can apply to two different situations, namely, (1) limited to stated dividend rate per annum, or (2) limited to a stated amount in event of dissolution of the company. In denying the pre-emptive right because the preferred had no equity in the surplus, the courts usually apply this to cases where the stock is limited to a stated amount in assets upon dissolution. In some instances where the preferred and common stock share alike in assets upon dissolution, the courts have allowed the preferred to "participate" in a *stock* dividend due to the pre-emptive right, although it is doubtful if they would have ruled that the preferred would have been entitled to participate (beyond their stated rate) in a cash dividend.

To definitely determine the pre-emptive rights of preferred shareholders it is necessary to carefully examine the particular contract under which the stock is issued, and the court decisions and statutes of the state under consideration.

Stock exchanged for property. It is generally held that stock which is issued for property other than cash is not subject to the pre-emptive right. Thus stock can be issued for assets or in connection with a merger or consolidation without first offering it to the existing shareholders, even though the stock is of the character that would be subject to the pre-emptive right if sold for cash.

There appear to be several reasons for this rule. In some instances the only way a merger or consolidation could be effected is through the exchange of stock. If the stock had first to be offered to the shareholders, and they took the stock, the merger or consolidation could never be effected, unless it could be accomplished through the use of the money obtained from the sale of the stock to the shareholders. The other reason is that presumably the stock is exchanged for property of equal value to the stock which is exchanged for it. Thus the equity of the existing shareholders in the surplus of the company would not be affected. The statutes of many of the states prescribe that stock issued to effect mergers, consolidations, etc., shall not be subject to the pre-emptive right.

When right denied by statutes or contract. The statutes of many of the states prescribe if or how the pre-emptive right may be allowed or denied. A few, such as California and Indiana, provide that shareholders do not have the pre-emptive right, unless it is reserved for them in the corporate charter. The Ohio statutes provide that—"Except as otherwise provided in the articles, the holders of the shares of any class of a corporation, except shares which are limited as to dividend rate and liquidation price, shall, upon the sale for cash of shares of the same class, have the right, during a reasonable time and on reasonable terms and conditions fixed by the board of directors, to purchase such shares in proportion to their respective holdings of shares of such class, at such price as may be fixed in the manner provided. . . ."[1]

The statutes of some of the states provide that the pre-emptive right does not apply to stock issued for consideration other than cash, to stock sold to employees, stock issued in connection with the conversion of another issue of securities, treasury stock, stock issued as a dividend, or stock on which the pre-emptive right has been waived by a designated percentage of the stock entitled to the right. It is obvious that in some instances the statutes have merely codified the common law rule on the point. Some states have specifically indicated whether or not the pre-emptive right applies to original issues. For example, the New York statutes provide that the pre-emptive right does not apply to the originally authorized stock unless it has remained unissued for two years.

Practical Reason for Privileged Subscription. For some years now the private placement of bonds with institutional investors has been a favorite method of selling bonds. But these investors either are not permitted to purchase stocks or, if permitted, only a limited amount may be acquired. Although bonds are sometimes offered for sale to the corporation's shareholders, it is rare for bonds to be offered to the old bondholders. One of the reasons for this is that many of the bonds outstanding are coupon bonds and the company, therefore, does not know who the owners are.

With stock the situation is different. The existing shareholders of a company have a greater interest in the company than perhaps any other group, except the employees. If the company has been enjoying large earnings and paying liberal dividends, the shareholders may be anxious to purchase additional stock in the company. Particularly is this true if the stock is offered to them at a price below the existing market price at the time.

From the standpoint of the issuing company, the existing shareholders may be the best market for the new stock. The existing stock is registered in the name of the particular stockholder and the latter's name appears on the company's records. The most important point from the standpoint of the company is that the stock can usually be sold to the existing shareholders much cheaper than by any other method. The alternative is usually sale through an investment banker, and that would mean paying the banker a certain percentage of the proceeds. In some instances, when a corpora-

[1] Revised Code of Ohio, Sec. 1701.40. The section also contains provisions relating to the exemptions from the pre-emptive right.

tion sells its stock directly to the shareholders, it arranges with investment bankers for a standby syndicate to take up any shares which are not sold by the company. But the cost of this is far less than if the bankers undertook the sale themselves.

Procedure

MECHANICS OF PRIVILEGED SUBSCRIPTION. The proposal to sell stock under the privileged subscription method is initiated usually by the finance committee of the board of directors, the board of directors itself, or one or more of the executive officers of the company, and sometimes upon the advice of an investment banker. The board of directors would adopt an appropriate resolution authorizing the issue. If the additional stock to be issued has not been authorized in the charter, then a stockholders' meeting would have to be called to vote upon an amendment to the charter to approve the new issue. The charter amendment would have to be approved by the state.

If the new issue is one that would have to be filed with the Securities and Exchange Commission, this must usually be done despite the fact that the sale is being made to only the shareholders, since sale to the shareholders is ordinarily not considered to be a private sale. Filing with the appropriate state securities commission would also have to be done. If the particular stock is listed on a stock exchange, the exchange must also be notified of the action which is to be taken.

The number of new shares issued under a privileged subscription is always much less than the number of old shares outstanding. The ratio may be, for example, one new share for each five or ten old shares held. The board of directors will state in their resolution that stockholders of record as of the close of business of a specified day, usually a week or two hence, will be entitled to subscribe to the new stock. This is called the *record date*. Shortly after the record date the company will mail out to the shareholders *subscription warrants*, which evidence the right of the shareholder to subscribe to a specified number of new shares. All the terms of the issue will be stated on the warrant, including the subscription price, the bank, trust company, or company office which will receive the subscription, the final date for the exercise of the subscription, and the date when the new stock will be issued. On the reverse side of the warrant is a subscription agreement which the shareholder can complete if he wishes to subscribe to the new stock, and an assignment form which will be completed in event the shareholder desires to sell the warrant to someone else. The shareholder is usually given a period of from two to eight weeks to subscribe to the new stock. If the warrant is not exercised or sold before the end of the subscription period, it becomes worthless.

The subscription warrants just described should not be confused with the stock purchase warrants which are sometimes issued as a sweetener in connection with the sale of bonds or preferred stocks, or which are issued to investment bankers as part compensation for the underwriting and sale of an issue of securities. These latter warrants run for a long period, and in some cases are perpetual. The subscription warrant should also be distinguished from stock option warrants which are sometimes issued to officers of a company enabling them to purchase stock at a price below the existing market price of the stock.

We stated above that the subscription warrant evidenced the right of the shareholder to subscribe to a specified number of new shares. This warrant also evidences another kind of "right," or "rights." The latter has a technical meaning. Under the privileged subscription the shareholder is given one *right* for each old share he possesses. It is these *rights* which enable the shareholder to subscribe to the new stock. The warrant is merely a piece of paper which evidences or shows the number of such rights which are possessed by the shareholder.

If the company offers the shareholders the right to subscribe to one new share for each ten old shares owned, then a person owning ten shares would receive *one* warrant evidencing his *ten* rights. If he owned fifty shares he would get one warrant representing 50 rights. It is thus to be noted that the value of a right is the value attaching to each old share and not the value attaching to each new share.[2]

If a person does not own enough shares to entitle him to one full share of the new stock, or if he owned an odd number of shares so that he would be entitled to subscribe to a number of new shares, but have a few rights left over, the procedure to be followed will be stated in the contract. Many companies will issue fractional

[2] The type of right just discussed is sometimes called the "New York right." (This is the method followed on the New York Stock Exchange.) Formerly on the Philadelphia Stock Exchange rights were quoted in terms of the value attaching to each new share; these were called "Philadelphia rights." Under this system a shareholder would receive only as many "rights" as the number of new shares to which he could subscribe. Some years ago the procedure was changed to conform to the New York practice, so at the present time on the Philadelphia-Baltimore Stock Exchange the value of a right is expressed as the value attaching to each old share, the same as is done on the New York Stock Exchange.

warrants for the odd rights. These can be sold, or the shareholder can purchase a sufficient number of additional fractional warrants to entitle him to an even share. To illustrate, let us assume that the new offering is one for ten. The person who held 56 shares would receive a warrant evidencing his right to subscribe to 5 new shares (50 rights), and a fractional warrant evidencing his right to subscribe to 6/10's (6 rights) of a new share. By purchasing a warrant for 4/10's (4 rights) of a share, he could subscribe to an additional share of the new stock. In some instances the company will give the shareholder the right to use cash to make up for the additional rights needed.

The privilege is quoted in the market as the price per *right* (not the price per *warrant*—the latter would be meaningless since warrants call for any number of *rights*). Rights may be bought and sold in the market just like shares of stock, and the warrants are comparable to stock certificates. If a warrant represented 50 rights, the holder could if he desired sell 20 of the rights and have a new warrant made out for the remaining 30 rights. The broker would handle the details and the old warrant would go to the company's stock transfer office where one warrant for 20 rights would be made up for the purchaser, and a new warrant for 30 rights would be delivered back to the seller.

Value of rights

DETERMINING THE VALUE OF RIGHTS. Let us assume that a corporation has the following abbreviated balance sheet (for simplicity we will asume that the company has no liabilities):

Assets	$13,000,000	Capital stock (par value $100)	$10,000,000
		Surplus	3,000,000
Total	$13,000,000	Total	$13,000,000

This company wants to raise an additional $2,000,000 through the privileged subscription sale of its stock. The directors decide to offer the new stock at par to the shareholders in the ratio of one new share for each five old shares held. We will assume that the book value and market value of the stock are the same. The value of a *right* can be calculated through the use of the following formula:

$$\frac{\text{Market price of old stock} - \text{Subscription price of new stock}}{\text{Number of old shares necessary to get one new share} + 1} = \text{Value of a right}$$

Substituting the figures in the hypothetical example given above, we get the following:

$$\frac{\$130 - \$100}{5 + 1} = \$5, \text{ value of a right}$$

In the above example we assumed that the market value and book value of the stock were the same. This was done so that the determination of the value of a right through the use of a balance sheet could be better understood. Rarely, if ever, would the two values be the same. As a practical matter, the market value of the stock rather than the book value should always be used in the formula. In the continuing analysis we will, nevertheless, assume the two values to be equal.

EXPLANATION OF VALUE OF RIGHTS. It was stated above that a *right* expressed the value attaching to each old share in connection with a privileged subscription. Perhaps a balance sheet analysis will explain what the formula gave us. After all the new stock has been sold to the shareholders in the example given above, the balance sheet will be as follows:

Assets	$15,000,000	Capital stock (par value $100)	$12,000,000
		Surplus	3,000,000
Total	$15,000,000	Total	$15,000,000

Before the new stock was sold the company had 100,000 shares of stock outstanding. Since the surplus amounted to $3,000,000, each share had an equity of $30 in the surplus. After the new stock was sold the company had outstanding 120,000 shares. Since the new stock was sold at its par value, no new surplus came into the company. Since all shares of the same class are equal in all respects, it follows that the surplus of $3,000,000 will be spread over 20,000 additional shares. Therefore, after the new stock is sold the equity of each share in the surplus is reduced from $30 to $25. If a person owned five of the old shares, the equity of each share would be diluted to the extent of $5, or a total dilution of $25. This $25 in effect attaches itself to the new share, which cost only $100, and gives it a value of $125. So what is lost on the old shares is made up in the value of the new share.

The value of a *right* can be expressed in several ways. It represents the value lost on each old share. Or, we can say that it represents the value in subscribing to the new stock. Since the value of each share is going to be reduced by $5, no matter whether or not the shareholder takes the new stock (assuming that a banker or the public will buy the stock if he does not do so), and since it would be worth $25 to subscribe to a share at $100 if it was going to be worth $125 immediately, then the five rights necessary to get the new share should be worth $5 each. Or, assume a person does not own any stock in the company but he can buy *rights* on the market to subscribe to the new stock at $100. Knowing that the new stock would be worth approximately $125, he would give $25 for the rights necessary to get the new share. And, since it takes five rights to get the share, he would pay $5 for each right.

Quotation of the Rights. If the stock is listed on, for example, the New York Stock Exchange, it is probable that the rights will also be listed. Before trading in the rights can begin the Exchange makes sure that all the requirements regarding authorization for the issuance of the rights by the board of directors and stockholders of the company and, if necessary, by the SEC and Interstate Commerce Commission have been met. The Exchange will then announce the day on which trading in the rights can begin. At this time the rights will be traded on a "when issued" basis, since they are not available at this early date.[3] The seller will give the buyer a contract promising to deliver the rights when they are issued. In the quotation of securities on the financial page of the newspaper "when issued" will be indicated by the use of the letters "wi" immediately after the name of the *right*. As soon as possible after the warrants evidencing the rights have been mailed out to the shareholders, the Exchange will announce the day on which rights will be traded "regular way." The absence of the letters "wi" will indicate that trading is "regular way."

Until about the time of the "record date" (day on which the stockholders of record will be entitled to the rights) the old stock will sell "rights-on," or as it is sometimes called "cum-rights." In other words people buying the old stock while it is selling "rights-on" will get the stock recorded in their names on the books of the company in time to receive the rights. When a person buys the stock too late to get it recorded in his name before the record date, the stock will be said to be selling "ex-rights." The first day that the stock sells "ex-rights" it will be indicated by the use of the letters "xrts" following the name of the stock.

The Exchange will set the "ex-rights" date, which at the present time is usually the third full business day before the record date.

[3] Years ago, when there was some preliminary announcement of declaring rights, such rights would have been traded on the New York Curb Exchange (now the American Stock Exchange) on a "when, as, and if issued" basis. The Securities Act of 1933 now prohibits such trading.

The reason for this date is as follows. Since March 3, 1952, all stock sold "regular way" on the New York Stock Exchange must be delivered on the fourth full business day following day of sale. In other words, stock sold on the 10th of the month must be delivered on the 14th. If a person buys stock at least four days before the "record date," then he will get delivery by the time of the record date. But if he buys it only three days before the record date he will not get delivery until the day after the record date. Therefore, the third day before the record date is usually designated as the "ex-rights" date.[4] If the record date is, for example, January 8th, the stock would sell "rights-on" through January 4th, but it would sell "ex-rights" on January 5th.[5]

We might further illustrate the quotation of stock and rights by referring to the hypothetical situation several pages back where the balance sheet was used. Assume that the privileged subscription was announced in May, and that the following dates were stated in the contract:

June 10. Record date.
June 17. Rights issued.
July 10. Rights expire.

We will further assume that the rights are listed on the New York Stock Exchange, that all requirements have been complied with, and that the Exchange designates June 2, as the date on which trading in the rights may begin on a "when issued" basis. Applying this to the previous example where the corporation offered its stockholders the right to subscribe to one new share at $100 for each five old shares owned, the rights should theoretically sell for $5 each. Since the rights were to be issued June 17, the Exchange might designate June 18, as the date on which trading "regular way" will begin. The value of the right will not change any simply because it is traded "regular way." The rights would then continue to be traded in until July 10.

Since the record date is June 10, the "ex-rights" date will probably be designated as June 7. In other words, the stock will sell

[4] If the stock is bought four or five days before the record date the purchaser will be paying for the *right* since the stock will be selling "rights-on." Although he will get delivery before the record date, it may still be too late to get the stock recorded in his name on the books of the company. The seller, being the stockholder of record, will actually get the *right*, but since the price he got for the stock included the value of the right, he is really not entitled to the *right*. Therefore, in a situation of this kind, the buyer's broker will get a "due bill" from the seller's broker calling for the right.

[5] Different dates were used here than before in order that the reader may not confuse the regular way delivery and ex-rights dates.

"rights-on" through June 6. In the example above, the stock should therefore sell at the theoretical price of $130 through June 6. On June 7, however, the stock theoretically should open at $125. Any further change in the price of the stock would be due to factors independent of the privileged subscription.

DETERMINING VALUE OF RIGHTS WITH STOCK EX-RIGHTS. In the formula given above for the determination of the value of a right we used the "rights-on" value of the stock since we were interested in immediately ascertaining the value of a right. After the stock sells "ex-rights," it is necessary to make a slight change in the formula. The change consists in dropping the "1" (one) which appears in the denominator. The formula would then appear as follows:

$$\frac{\text{Ex-rights price of stock} - \text{Subscription price}}{\text{Number of old shares necessary to get one new share}} = \text{Value of a right}$$

Substituting the figures given in the above example, we get the following:

$$\frac{\$125 - \$100}{5} = \$5, \text{ value of a right}$$

The reason for dropping the "1" in the above formula is as follows. The ex-rights price of $125 expresses the per share value of all the stock after the subscription has been completed. By subtracting the subscription price of $100 from the ex-rights market price of $125, we get the figure of $25, which represents the value of the *opportunity* to subscribe to one new share. Then we need divide by only "5" to reduce the value to a per share basis, or in other words, to get the value of one *right*.

ACTUAL PRICE OF STOCK AND RIGHTS. We have used the word "theoretical" several times in reference to the value of the stock and rights in the above example. This was necessary for several reasons. In the first place the general market may fluctuate to such an extent that the price of the stock and rights of the particular company under consideration may be affected. Also, we have explained the price of the right in terms of book values. It is realized that rarely would a stock sell in the market for its exact book value. Despite this fact it has been found that the formula is fairly accurate in determining the value of the right and the ex-rights value of the stock.

Being able to buy stock at a price below its existing market price is usually looked upon as a "privilege," and when the privileged subscription is rumored or announced there is sometimes a tendency for the stock to advance slightly in price. In attempting to ascertain any effect on the market price of the stock due consideration would, of course, have to be given to any change in the market in general and any factors independent of the privileged subscription which would affect the price of the stock of the particular company.

Some of the books state that the stock and rights will usually sell higher at the beginning of the subscription period than thereafter. (Independent of the drop in price when the stock goes ex-rights.) The explanation usually given is that many shareholders either do not understand the nature of the privileged subscription and therefore wait until they learn more before selling their rights, or if they do know what it is all about, they may not act until they are forced to do something because of the closeness of the expiration date of the rights. Since many of the shareholders will sell their rights rather than subscribe to the new stock, it is argued that more of this selling will take place near the end of the period.

There is a theory in the stock market that if enough people believe something is going to happen and act accordingly, then probably the thing will not happen. Applying this to the situation at hand, if enough shareholders believed that the rights would sell highest at the beginning of their life, then they would be anxious to do their selling at that time. The effect of the large volume of selling would tend to depress the price. And conversely, the absence of selling near the end of the period would tend to firm the price. As a matter of fact rights sell highest during the early part of the subscription period in only about half the cases. They are highest during the latter part of the period in a little over one-fourth the cases, and highest during the middle part of the subscription period in a little less than one-fourth the cases.[6]

We have already stated that the rights tend to sell at their theoretical value. In other words, the price of the rights and the stock tend to sell at parity with each other. Thus, the rights tend to advance when the stock price goes up, and to fall when the price of the stock declines. In some instances, however, the rights will sell at a price higher than their theoretical value while in other cases they will sell for less than the theoretical value. Arbitrage tends to keep the prices pretty much in line. If the rights are sell-

[6] For studies on actual cases, see Harry G. Guthmann and Herbert E. Dougall, *Corporate Financial Policy* (3d ed.; Englewood Cliffs, N. J.: Prentice-Hall, Inc., 1955), pp. 365–66; and Arthur Stone Dewing, *The Financial Policy of Corporations* (5th ed.; New York: The Ronald Press Co., 1953), pp. 1158–60.

ing for a relatively low price, speculators will sell the stock short (short selling is explained in Chapter 19) and buy sufficient rights to subscribe to the amount of shares necessary to cover the short sale. The short sale of the stock tends to depress its price, while the buying of the rights tends to increase their price; hence the prices of the rights and stock are brought back into line. If the rights are selling at a relatively high price people will hesitate to buy them, but they will buy the stock since it is relatively cheap.

Other factors affecting the relative prices of the rights and the stock are the comparative costs and convenience of buying the stock on the market and acquiring it through the exercise of rights. It costs more and ties up cash to buy the stock on the market since besides the price the broker's commissions must be paid. This tends to cause the rights to sell at more than their theoretical value. But it is more convenient to call up a broker and have him buy the stock on the market than to complete the blanks on the warrant and send it in to the proper office. This tends to cause the rights to sell at less than their theoretical value.

After reading about these various factors which produce opposite effects in the price of both the rights and the stock, the reader is probably bewildered as to whether the rights should or will sell at more or less than their theoretical value. If this is true, then perhaps the author has accomplished his purpose. The only conclusion that can be drawn is that it is uncertain whether the rights will sell at parity or above or below parity. However, it should be kept in mind that the prices of the rights and the stock generally move in the same direction, and that price of the rights tends to approximate the theoretical value.

Long-Run Effect on Stock Price. In the discussion above we were concerned with the price of the stock during the short period of the life of the right. A speculator or investor is also interested in what happens to the price of the stock over a period of time after the privileged subscription has ended. No definite conclusions on this point can be drawn from past experience.

At first glance it might appear that since the new stock is sold below its existing market price, that the surplus per share remains diluted more or less permanently compared with what it would have been had the privileged subscription not taken place. Or similarly, the issuing company gets less for the new shares and has, therefore, less in assets per share than formerly. Consequently, the earnings per share, and possibly the dividends per share, might be less than before the privileged subscription.

But we should distinguish between the book value and the market value of the stock. The fact that stock under a privileged subscription might be offered at 30 per cent below its existing market price, does not necessarily mean that it is being offered at 30 per cent below its book value. Or, to take an example, a stock may have a par value of $25 a share, a book value of $35, and a market value of $40. Now if new stock was offered under a privileged subscription at $35 a share, there would be no dilution at all in the surplus attaching to the old shares. If the earnings on the book value of the assets continued at the same rate as before the privileged subscription, and the same percentage of earnings were paid out in dividends, there is no reason why the new stock, and of course, the old stock, would not eventually sell at the same price per share as before the privileged subscription.

Even if there is a dilution in the surplus per share as a result of a privileged subscription, it does not follow that the price of the stock will remain depressed permanently. The privileged subscription generally can be used only by successful companies. If the earnings of the company continue to increase as a result of expansion or increased business, the earnings and dividends per share might be even larger in the future. This would ordinarily cause the stock to sell for a higher price than before the privileged subscription. Of course had the new stock been sold at the market value rather than less, the earnings per share would probably have been even larger since the company would have had the use of more dollars per share.

Since privileged subscriptions can be used successfully only during prosperous times, which is generally true of the sale of common stock under any other method, it is to be expected that the market price will tend to rise as time goes on.

Where the offering price under a privileged subscription is not too far below the market price, and where the proportion of new shares to old is not too great, the "ex-rights" price will not be much lower than the "rights-on" price. This slight drop can usually be made up rather quickly if the market in general continues steady or advances. In situations of this kind the issuing company usually continues the same rate of dividends per share on all the stock as was formerly paid on the old stock. Under these conditions there is no reason why the new and old stock should not sell at least as high as before the privileged subscription. The American Telephone and Telegraph Company has used the privileged subscription under these circumstances many times in the past and the stock has usually quickly made up for the drop in the price which occurred when it went ex-rights.

WHAT TO DO WITH THE RIGHTS. Every shareholder receiving rights under a privileged subscription has to decide what to do with them. In our discussion we will first assume that the market price of the stock drops ex-rights by the theoretical value of the right, and that it remains at this price. The shareholder may do one of the following:

1. Take no action.
2. Sell the rights.
3. Subscribe to the new stock.

Take no action. It can generally be stated that a shareholder should not sit idly by and do nothing. He should either sell the rights or subscribe to the new stock. To explain the effects of the shareholder's actions with respect to the disposition of his rights we will again refer to the hypothetical situation stated above where a company offers its shareholders the right to subscribe to one new share at $100 for each five old shares held, and where the market price of the old stock was $130. As we computed above, the *right* in this case would be worth $5, and the stock would sell at $125 ex-rights. Since $5 worth of the company surplus will be taken away from each share, the shareholder, owning five shares, will lose a total of $25 if he lets his rights expire.

Many shareholders do not understand what the privileged subscription is all about, and as a result they do nothing. Others think that it is merely a scheme to sell them more stock (which is sometimes the case), and therefore they throw away the rights.

Sell the rights. Since the shareholder should ordinarily not let his rights expire, his alternative is either to sell the rights or exercise them and purchase the new stock. Which of these he should have done, only future events can reveal. But this we know, it is always better to sell the rights than to let them expire. If the rights are sold it amounts to the same thing as selling part of the stock. If the shareholder who owned five old shares sold his five rights, he would get $25 in cash (less commissions). Since in our example his old stock would decline in price $5 a share after it went ex-rights, or a total of $25 for the five shares, he would merely break even by the sale of the rights.

Subscribe to the new stock. To exercise the rights by subscribing to the new shares, it would be necessary for the shareholder who owned five old shares to put up an additional $100. This cash together with the five rights would enable him to get one additional share. This additional share would be, according to our assumptions, worth $125. So he, in a sense, gains $25 on this share. But each old share drops $5 in price, and therefore his five old shares are worth in the aggregate $25 less. By subscribing to the new share, the shareholder merely breaks even—the same as if he had sold his rights.

This again raises the question—should the rights be sold, or the new stock purchased? The answer depends upon whether the stock in the long run will advance in price from the day it sold ex-rights.

Of course, the shareholder may feel that he already has enough money tied up in the particular company; or he does not have any money to invest in the new shares; so he may either sell his rights, or if he has enough he may sell part of his rights to enable him to subscribe to a few new shares without putting any new money into the company.

Action by Outsiders. An outsider could also profit from the purchase of the stock in somewhat the same manner as a shareholder. If it is thought that sometime after the subscription is over the stock will work back up to its old price, anyone could purchase the stock while it is selling "rights-on," or buy enough "rights" on the market to get the desired amount of new stock. The other alternative would be to purchase the stock in the market "ex-rights." Any of these methods would result in profit *if* the stock goes up in price after its initial drop caused by it selling "ex-rights."

Conditions for success

Requisites for Success of Subscription. As is true of the sale of securities by any method, a corporation should be fairly sure that the privileged sale will be successful before it is undertaken. One way to insure that all the stock will be sold is to have it underwritten by investment bankers. This will be discussed later. At the present time we are concerned with requisites for a successful sale regardless of whether or not it is underwritten. But from a practical standpoint, the following requirements would probably have to be met before a banker would undertake the risk of underwriting the sale.

1. A favorable outlook for business and stocks
2. The money used for profitable purposes
3. Wide distribution of old stock
4. New issue relatively small
5. Price of new shares relatively low in relation to price of old shares

A favorable outlook for business and stocks. It is obvious that a privileged subscription should be more successful during a prosperous period than during a depression. If the shareholders feel that business conditions will continue to improve and that the stock market will go bullish, they will be more inclined to buy additional stock than if the outlook for the future were gloomy. Moreover, they will have more money available for the purchase of stock during this phase of the business cycle.

Aside from the emergency need for funds, companies will also have a greater need for funds when they are expanding, and despite the higher construction costs, companies commonly do their expanding during prosperous times.

The money used for profitable purposes. The shareholders will have to be convinced that the new money will be used for profitable purposes. Perhaps one of the best assurances that the shareholders can have of this is a past record of good earnings and dividends.

Wide distribution of old stock. A wide distribution of stock is conducive to the stabilization of the price of the stock. But wide distribution is almost a necessity when it comes to the privileged subscription sale. If the stock is closely held in large blocks by a relatively small number of holders the probability is that many of them will not subscribe to the new stock. Since such shareholders already have a relatively large amount tied up in the company, they may not want to put any more eggs in that basket. Each shareholder would have to subscribe to a large number of new shares in order that the sale be successful, and many of them may not have the necessary money to do this, and will sell part or all of their rights on the market. Some will sell enough rights to subscribe to a few new shares without putting up any new capital. The bigger sale of the rights on the market will depress their price, and correspondingly the price of the stock. In extreme cases the rights will cease to have any value in the market, which means that the privileged subscription would be a failure.

If, on the other hand, the stock is widely scattered the individual shareholders will not be called upon to invest much more capital in the business. They, therefore, will be more inclined to exercise the rights by subscribing to the stock than to sell them in the market. Furthermore, although some of the rights evidenced by fractional warrants will be sold in the market, there might be a demand for rights on the part of many shareholders who need only a few more in order to subscribe to a whole share.

Perhaps another point should be mentioned here, but it is not known how much weight should be given to it. Small shareholders are usually more gullible than people who own a substantial amount of securities. When the stock is widely scattered it is generally held by persons of all walks of life. The average stockholder does not realize that as far as book values are concerned, he is no better off after the privileged subscription than before. He believes that he is getting a bargain when he is offered the opportunity of buying new stock at less than its existing market price, and he is, therefore, inclined to exercise the rights and buy the new shares.

New issue relatively small. In order that the privileged subscription be successful the proportion of new shares to the old shares should not be too great. The explanation in the preceding item applies with equal force here. If the proportion of new to old is too great it would necessitate the investment of a relatively large amount of new money on the part of the shareholders in order that the sale be successful. The unwillingness or inability of the shareholders to do this would result in their selling the rights on the market; thus the price of both the rights and the stock might be depressed to the point that the sale of the stock would be unsuccessful.

On the other hand, if the shareholders are asked to buy only a small fraction of a new share for each old share held, there is greater probability that they will utilize the rights by subscribing to the new stock. Thus, there is greater chance of success.

Perhaps the point will be better understood by the use of figures. Let us again refer to the example used above where the shareholder is given the right to subscribe to one share at $100 for each five shares he owns. Suppose that a person owned 50 of the old shares. At the price of $130 per share, the value of his equity in the company would be $6,500. He is now being asked to buy 10 new shares at a price of $100 each. In other words, he is being asked for only $1,000 more. But if the shareholder had been asked to subscribe to one new share for each *two* owned, it would require an outlay of $2,500 to take the 25 shares. Since the shareholder already has $6,500 invested in the company, (or his investment is worth that amount) there is a greater chance of getting an additional $1,000 out of him than there is of securing $2,500.

If a company needs a considerable amount of money, it would be better to have several privileged subscriptions over a period of time, each for a relatively small amount, rather than one large one.

The number of new shares issued in relation to the old shares varies in practice, but one new share for each four, each five, and each ten old shares were the most common relationship found in the past.

Price of new stock relatively low. One of the most important requisites, if not the most important, for a successful privileged subscription is that the price at which the new stock is offered to the shareholders be considerably below the existing market price of the old stock. The new stock should never be offered at less than a 10 per cent discount from the price of the old stock, and it would be better if the price was at least 25 per cent below the old stock.

If the price of the new stock is placed too near the market price of the old stock, it follows that the value of a *right* will be low. Therefore any factors adversely affecting the price of the rights and the stock might cause the prices to drop so much that the right would become worthless, or practically worthless, with the result that the sale would be a failure.

In the example we have been using above where the market price of the old stock was $130, and the offering price of the new was $100 (one new share for each five old), the theoretical value of a right was found to be $5. But if the offering price of the new stock was, for example, $118 instead of $100, the theoretical value of a right would be only $2. A drop in the price of stock of about 9¼ per cent would result in the right becoming worthless. (This would be a drop of approximately $12 a share, which would mean that the stock would be obtainable in the market for $118.)

Looking at the same problem from the viewpoint of the typical stockholder, the lower the offer price of the new stock as compared with the existing price of the old stock, the greater will be the bargain which he thinks he is getting.

Other things being equal, it would appear to be advisable to have a larger spread between the offer price of the new stock and the price of the old stock when the subscription is not underwritten by investment bankers.

UNDERWRITING PRIVILEGED SUBSCRIPTIONS. Since the issuing corporation is never sure that all the new issue will be taken up by the shareholders, it may have the privileged subscription underwritten by one or more investment bankers. As will be explained in the following chapter, the banker for a fee will agree to take up any stock which remains unsold at the end of the period. This would be the *standby* syndicate arrangement.

The nature of the arrangement between the issuing company and the banker varies according to individual cases, but usually the banker is paid a *standby* fee of 2 to 3 per cent of the subscription price of the entire issue to compensate him in event he has to take over part of the issue. In some instances he is paid this fee and then the contract calls for another fee of perhaps 2 or 3 per cent on all stock which he must take up. In some instances the agreement calls for additional fees ranging from 2 to 5 per cent depending upon the amount of stock which he has to take up.

If the market price of the stock drops below the subscription price of the new stock before all the stock has been subscribed, the banker will have to take up all the unsubscribed stock. He may immediately sell this new stock on the market at a loss, or he may hold it for a while waiting for the price to come back.

The advantage of having the issue underwritten is greater than would appear from what has already been said. Investment bankers can give advice to the issuing company about the best time to offer the new stock, and the other conditions of the issue. Also, the fact that the shareholders know that bankers have underwritten the issue will give them more confidence in the stock, and they, therefore, will be more inclined to subscribe to it.

The bankers may also buy up some of the stock or rights in the market during the subscription period when the market is weak, thus tending to stabilize the price and improve the chances of a successful sale. Such stabilizing action can be done only with the approval of SEC. In some instances bankers have, with proper approval, sold the stock short some time in advance of the privileged subscription so that their covering operations (buying in the market) during the subscription period would tend to steady the price.

Sale of Preferred Stock and Bonds. Since preferred stock is commonly made nonvoting and limited as to assets of the company, it would not be entitled to the pre-emptive right. Likewise, if a new issue of such stock was to be sold, the company would not be legally bound to offer it to the old shareholders first. The same is true of bonds. Ordinary bonds have no pre-emptive rights to new stock, and shareholders have no pre-emptive rights to a new issue of bonds.

As a practical matter, however, corporations sometimes offer new issues of preferred stock or bonds to their shareholders because they feel that this is the best or cheapest way of selling the new securities. In the case of preferred stock or bonds which are convertible into common stock the situation is a little different so far as legal rights are concerned. Since the control and equity in the surplus of the company are affected by the conversion of such preferred stock or bonds into the common stock, courts generally hold that the common shareholders have a pre-emptive right with respect to them. The statutes of some of the states, however, provide that the pre-emptive right does not apply to them.

When preferred stock or bonds are offered to stockholders under the so-called "privileged subscription" method, the problem of deciding the value of a *right* is somewhat more complicated than when common stock is being offered. In the latter case the existing stock has a market price and therefore the value of the offer, or in other words, the value of the right, can be easily computed. But no preferred stock or bonds, at least of the same character being offered, may be on the market so that the shareholder does not know their worth as a straight preferred stock or as a bond. By comparing them with similar securities of the company, or similar securities of similar companies, however, a fairly close approximate value can be attached to them.

When the security being offered is a convertible, such as a convertible bond, the shareholder has the same problem as just mentioned, but it is complicated by the fact that he may not know whether to value the privilege according to the worth of the bond as a straight credit obligation, or to appraise it from the standpoint of its conversion value. Then too, another problem adds complications. When common stock is being offered under the privileged subscription, the subscription period is only a few weeks. Therefore, the dilution effect on the surplus attaching to the old shares occurs almost immediately. But the bonds may be convertible over a ten-year period, for example, and the conversion may be made gradually over that period. That raises the question whether the shareholder should appraise the conversion worth of the bond in terms of the existing price of the old stock, or whether he should give effect to the "ex-rights" price of the stock.

The most practical procedure to follow in this case, and the one that is taken by the great majority of the shareholders, is to let the market place set the value on the right. Through competition the so-called "experts" will determine the value of the convertible bond, and thus the value of a right. If the bond is worth more as a result of its convertible feature, then the value of the right would be set accordingly. As a practical matter, the issuing company in order to sell the bonds would offer them under such conditions that there would be some advantage in subscribing to them. The shareholder, however, has the same problem here as in the case of the sale of new common stock. Should he sell the *rights* or subscribe to the bonds? The explanation given in connection with new stock applies with equal force here, with one exception. The bond offers a type of hedge and it can be held for a relatively long period before the shareholder has to decide whether to convert it or hold it. If he holds it, however, he will have paid a relatively high price for the bond since the purchase price reflected its conversion value. This same reasoning, of course, applies to the purchase of convertible bonds under any method of sale.

Perhaps we should not leave the determination of the value of the right under these conditions to the so-called "experts," since it is hoped that some of the readers will become the experts. The determination of the value of a right is easy after the bonds are being quoted in the market. If listed they will probably be quoted on a "when issued" basis after all the requirements relating to their issue have been completed. Bonds being sold under the privileged subscription method are commonly offered in denominations as low as $100, rather than the usual $1,000, in order to minimize the number of fractional warrants. In the following formula for determining the value of the right, a $100 denomination is assumed.

$$\frac{\text{Market price of bonds} - \text{Subscription price of bonds}}{\text{Number of shares necessary to get one bond}} = \text{Value of a right}$$

The above formula presupposes that we know the market price of the bonds. Before the bonds are being bought and sold on the market we can estimate their probable value in the way stated above. But as a practical matter it is probable that the conversion value of the bond would be greater than its worth as a straight obligation. So, in most instances we can start out by determining the bond's conversion value.

If a bond which can be converted into stock worth $115, can be subscribed to for $100, the market price of the bond should be approximately $115. In some instances some cash has to be given along with the bond to get the stock. If in the example just given, it takes one bond and $5 in cash to get one share of stock, then the bond should sell for approximately $110 in the market. This still leaves one question unanswered, does the $115 figure represent the worth of the stock before or after giving effect to the dilution of the surplus resulting from the conversion? As stated before, the conversion may take place gradually over a long period of years and therefore the dilution will not be immediate. This would argue for not taking into account the future dilution in determining the conversion value of the bonds. The American Telephone and Telegraph Company has sold convertible bonds through the privileged subscription method to its shareholders a number of times since the end of World War II.

Questions

1. Indicate the type of securities which are usually offered, and the type of security holders to whom they are offered, under a privileged subscription.
2. Why do corporations use the privileged subscription method rather than some other one in selling securities?
3. (a) Indicate the nature of the pre-emptive right of shareholders to subscribe to new stock offered by their corporation. (b) What are the exceptions to the pre-emptive right?
4. Does one "right" under a privileged subscription entitle the holder thereof to one new share? Explain.
5. Indicate when a stock will sell "cum-rights" and when "ex-rights".
6. In determining the value of a right, should the book value or the market price of the old stock be used? Why?
7. Is the privileged subscription a misnomer? Explain.
8. Has the American Telephone and Telegraph used the privileged subscription much in connection with the sale of new stock? With the sale of bonds? Explain.
9. What should a person do with the rights which he receives in a privileged subscription? Explain thoroughly.
10. What are the requisites for a successful privileged subscription?

Problems

1. The Midwestern Manufacturing Co., whose stock is listed on the New York Stock Exchange, presented the following balance sheet as of Dec. 31, 19-1:

Assets		*Liabilities and Net Worth*	
Cash	$ 10,000	Payables	$ 100,000
Receivables	200,000	Capital Stock	3,000,000
Inventory	690,000	Surplus	1,200,000
Plant, etc.	3,400,000		
Total	$4,300,000	Total	$4,300,000

The stock has a par value of $100 per share, and its present market price is the same as its book value. Assume that you own nine shares of the stock. On Jan. 3, 19-2, the company announced that its capital stock was to be increased 33⅓ per cent through the sale to present stockholders of additional shares at par. The rights are to be given to stockholders of record as of Jan. 20, 19-2, and the new shares may be subscribed to through Mar. 20, 19-2. It is assumed that by the latter date all the new stock has been subscribed. (a) What is the value of one "right" in this case? (b) Construct a new balance sheet giving effect to the new financing. (c) Using the data contained in the two balance sheets, prove why the right is worth the amount that is obtained from use of the formula. (d) Assuming that a correction has been made to rule out changes in the price of the stock caused by the ordinary fluctuations of the market, indicate, in general, the relative prices at which you would expect this stock to sell on the following dates: Jan. 2; Jan. 4; Jan. 17; Mar. 18; Apr. 15. (e) Indicate the relative prices at which you think the rights would be selling on the dates stated in part (d). (f) How many rights will you get? How many shares of new stock can you acquire with these rights? (g) Compare your investment and its worth (1) before the new stock is issued, (2) after all the new stock is sold, assuming that you acquired the number of shares to which you were entitled, and (3) after all the new stock is issued but assuming that you have thrown away your rights. Assume that the stock is selling at its book value on Mar. 30. Have you gained or lost anything by following procedure (2) or (3)? Explain.

2. Look up the most recent sale by the American Telephone and Telegraph Company of convertible bonds through the privileged subscription method, and indicate the terms of the privileged subscription.

Chapter 18

INVESTMENT BANKING AND REGULATION OF SECURITY ISSUES

Investment banking

NATURE OF INVESTMENT BANKERS. When the terms "banking" or "banks" are used the average person is apt to think of *commercial banking*. Commercial banks usually maintain both checking and savings accounts for individuals and businesses. The funds so acquired are invested in short-term obligations or loaned to business concerns, usually for a short term, for such purposes as financing inventories, paying accounts, meeting payrolls, and other working capital purposes. In some instances commercial banks will lend money to business firms for a relatively long period, but essentially they are interested in short-term loans only.

Investment banks, on the other hand, are interested in long-term financing—the kind that is secured by companies through sale of stocks and bonds. Furthermore, the investment banker does not *lend* the money to the company. Rather he *buys* the stocks or bonds, and then resells these securities to one or more of the classes of security buyers discussed in Chapter 16.

Investment bankers started out handling bonds only. Later some of them took over also the sale of stocks, but their primary function is still the sale of bonds rather than stocks. Because of this investment banks, whose appearance is more like a business office than a commercial bank, are often called *bond houses*. It is to be noted that the investment banker is a principal in buying securities rather than an agent for someone else.

In addition to buying securities from the issuing corporation, some investment bankers will also buy securities which have already been issued, and sell them to other buyers. In connection with the original distribution of securities, some investment bankers will buy the securities from other investment bankers and then sell them to institutions and individual investors.

The stock brokerage business is oftentimes confused with investment banking. There is, however, a fundamental difference between them. The *broker* merely acts as an agent for the buyer and seller. He does not take title to the securities. He merely acts as a go-between for the buyer and seller, and collects a commission from either the buyer or the seller according to whose order he is executing, the buyer's or the seller's. The order that goes through a broker is for securities which have already been issued by the corporation.

Confusion between brokers and investment bankers is more common when the same firm, through different departments, carries on both investment banking and brokerage business.

Services Performed by Investment Banker. Although the primary function of the investment banker was stated above, we want to discuss this in more detail and to add some other functions performed by him.

1. *Middleman.* There are always companies wanting capital and investors seeking investment opportunities. But without the services of the investment banker, it would be difficult for the two to get together. The corporation wanting capital is an expert in the manufacture, assembly, or sale of some particular product or service —not in securities. Individual investors are likewise engaged in their respective pursuits and have no opportunity to know the various companies that want funds. The investment banker acts like a wholesaler or retailer in that he secures the goods, in this case the securities, from the various issuers and sells them to the consumer or investor.

The cost to the issuer by selling through an investment banker is ordinarily less than if he attempted to market the securities directly to the investor. The banker has a security sales organization built up and this organization has contacts with other bankers and with the investing public.

2. *Assurance of successful sale.* If the issuing corporation attempts to sell its securities directly to the investor, it is never sure that the sale will be successful. Only part of the issue may be sold. This would have an adverse effect on the price of the securities, and furthermore, the company would not get all the money that was needed. In order to accomplish what was desired, it may be necessary to raise the total amount of money originally planned. When the sale is made to an investment banker the issuer has more assur-

ance of selling all the securities, and also all the money will be coming in at the same time. This latter is often essential.

3. *Advice on the issue.* The investment banker is an expert in securities and the securities market. He knows what type of securities are selling and can thus advise the issuing company on the best type to sell at the particular time. He is also well acquainted with the current yields on other securities and, therefore, is in a good position to advise the company on the face rate of interest or dividend rate which should be set on the securities.

Timing is an important factor in marketing securities. The investment banker is in a position to know when the securities should be placed on the market. If the issuing company attempted to sell the securities directly, the timing may be off, with the result that all the issue could not be disposed of, or the selling price might have to be lowered considerably to sell the entire issue.

4. *Securities usually well placed.* If the issuing company attempted to sell its own securities they might be sold to the existing stockholders, the employees, or to people in the particular locality. Anything that might adversely affect the corporation may result in the securities being thrown back on the market.

When securities are sold through an investment banker they are usually "well placed." The banker has a sales organization built up throughout the country, and contacts are usually made with the investment class rather than with speculators. These investors are usually interested in the securities for the long-run pull. They are not apt to sell them as soon as the first signs of weakness appear in the market prices.

5. *Market support.* The price quotations for securities are for the relatively few which are being sold on the market. When a substantial part of an entire issue is placed on the market, at or about the same time, the tendency is for the price to fall. This has a marked influence on the price of the securities already sold and on the value of the part of the issue which is yet to be sold.

When the securities are sold through investment bankers, the latter commonly support their price by buying some of the securities on the market whenever the price weakens. This point will be discussed further later in the chapter.

6. *Continued financial advice.* Not only may the advice of the investment banker be utilized at the time the securities are sold—he may continue to lend his aid for an indefinite time. Since the reputation of the banker is affected by the performance of the

securities which he has sold, he will be interested in the future success of the company. He serves often as a financial adviser to the company during the entire time the securities are outstanding. In some instances he is made a member of the board of directors, which in some cases he insists upon.

When future financing is needed by the company, particularly if it is important to the people to whom he sold the securities, he would be more inclined to buy new securities of the company than investment bankers who had had no past connection with the company.

7. *Aids the promotion of sound enterprises.* An investment banker is particular about the securities which he undertakes to sell. It is a business proposition with him. Naturally he will buy only those securities which he thinks he will be able to sell successfully. Thus companies which are not needed, or which will probably not prove to be successful, will be turned down by the banker. On the other hand, he will take over the securities of those companies which he thinks are selling a product or service that is wanted by the public. If the banker turns down an issue, the company may never be started. Those companies which he believes are needed will be promoted. Thus, from the social viewpoint, the investment banker is performing a useful service.

Advantages of Bankers to Investors. The discussed functions of the investment banker were at the same time the advantages to the issuing company. From what was said, the advantages of the banker to the investor is more or less obvious, but will be briefly stated as follows:

1. *Issuer has been investigated.* Before an investment banker will take over an issue of securities, he will conduct a very thorough investigation of the issuer. Lawyers check property titles, patents, and contracts; engineers determine the value and physical condition of the properties; and accountants make a detailed check of the company's books. The production and marketing methods and labor relations are gone over. And of course, considerable weight is given to the efficiency of the management. All of this means that when an investor buys securities of an issue which has been taken over by an investment banker he is assured that a very thorough examination of the issuer has been made, and that in the opinion of the expert banker, the security issue will prove to be successful. The average investor is in no position to ever make such an investigation himself.

It should not be inferred from the above that all issues which bankers handle will turn out well. Bankers vary as to the extent to which they investigate an issue, and their judgments are naturally not the same, and it is impossible for anyone, including bankers, to know what will take place in the indefinite future.

2. *Assurance of proper security contract.* The staff of the investment banker will check the charter and bylaws of the issuer to determine if the security issue is properly authorized and that all the legal requirements have been complied with. They will have the necessary protective provisions inserted in the agreement, and these will be worded in such a way that the courts will uphold them. Although the banker is interested in the profit he will make from selling the securities for the company, he knows that the terms of the issue must be attractive to investors in order to sell the securities successfully.

3. *Maintenance of market.* This point which was mentioned before, and which will receive more attention later in the chapter, is obviously to the advantage of the investor.

4. *Advice of banker.* The investment banker's continued advice to the issuing company on financial matters would turn out to the advantage also of the holder of the securities. If a person buys securities through an investment banker, he may come to this source for future investment information. The banker is an expert in this field and is capable of giving sound advice, but he might, of course, be somewhat biased in his opinions by what securities he still has on his shelves to sell.

5. *Representative of the investors.* Security holders are usually unorganized and therefore cannot act with concerted force. If the company gets into financial difficulties or undergoes a reorganization, the investment banker that sold its securities often takes the initiative and represents the interests of the security holders. The latter, therefore, may receive better treatment in the reorganization than if the banker had not been in the picture.

Types of Investment Bankers. From the standpoint of type of organization, investment banks have been formed as individual proprietorships, general and limited partnerships, and corporations. As would be expected, corporations now carry on the greater part of the business, although there are a few partnerships left.

In the 1920's, it was characteristic of many investment banks to specialize in one type of securities, such as bonds, or stocks, or railroad securities, or municipal bonds; but beginning in the 1930's, and continuing to the present, most investment banks handle various types of securities. A few, however, handle only one type of security, or specialize in that type. For example, Halsey, Stuart & Co., Inc., is the only large house of its kind in the country today that handles only bonds, while the C. F. Childs and Company specializes in United States government bonds.

Some investment banks act only as wholesalers, some only as retailers, while others combine the functions of wholesaler and retailer. Such companies as Dillon, Read & Co., Inc., do not maintain a regular retail sales organization. Their primary function is to buy the securities from the issuing company and sell them to other investment bankers, who in turn sell them to financial institutions and to the public. Although these houses are classed as wholesalers, they do some selling directly to institutional investors. But this is classed as *institutional,* rather than *retail,* selling. These wholesalers handle large issues which are sold on a national scale. Some of the investment banks, such as Halsey, Stuart, and Co., Inc., buy securities from issuing companies and sell them to other investment bankers, institutions, and to the public. They are thus performing both the wholesale and retail functions, as well as engaging in institutional selling.

A final type is the house that is engaged primarily in buying securities from members of the selling group or from individual investors, and selling them to someone else. They may on occasion buy a local issue directly from the issuer, and in some cases they will be members of an underwriting or selling group. The term *investment dealer,* or *bond house,* would probably be a better title for them than *investment bank.* In some instances these houses merely arrange for the purchase or sale of securities for an individual, thus acting as a broker. The main business of a dealer of this kind is in the over-the-counter market.

Many of the large investment banks have branch offices in the larger cities throughout the country. Salesmen work out of these offices calling on the retail trade, banks, and other institutional investors.

DEPARTMENTS OF A LARGE INVESTMENT BANK. A large investment bank that buys securities from the issuing company and sells them to other bankers, institutions, and to the public is departmentalized in a manner similar to other large concerns. These departments will be briefly described.

Buying department. The buying department, as the term would indicate, has to do with the purchase of the securities from the issuing company. The bank may learn of the issue from different sources. The issuer may have done business with the particular bank before or will seek out the banker even though they had not had previous connections. A traveling representative or branch office of the bank or an independent "finder" may bring the business to the banker. In recent years, to an increasing extent, the bank learns of the new issue through advertising of the issuer for bids.

Needless to say, the work of the buying department is highly important. It is oftentimes said, and with a great deal of truth, that an issue well bought is half sold. The buying department uses the services of other departments such as the statistical and legal departments in the investigation of the issuer. Independent lawyers, engineers, and accountants are often hired to make a study of the company.

Although a particular bank may be large, the decision to buy or to refuse an issue is made by a few persons. They may be the partners of the firm or its principal officers, or a committee composed of some of the leading officers of the company.

Syndicate department. In the case of large issues, syndicates or groups are formed both to purchase the issue and to sell it. We will describe these operations later. A syndicate department selects the other members of the buying group and the members of the selling group to which the buying group will sell the securities. In some banks, however, the buying department makes up the purchase group, while the syndicate department organizes the selling syndicate.

Sales department. When the house is not exclusively a wholesaler, it will have a selling department. This organization will have salesmen whose duty it is to call on institutional and individual buyers. In some houses a salesman may confine his activities to only one of these groups. Salesmen may also call on other investment houses or dealers.

Trading department. The trading department may engage in stabilizing operations after the new securities have been sold. It is often necessary for a banker or syndicate to buy back part of the securities sold when the market price tends to become depressed. This aids in the sale of any unsold part of the issue, and tends to keep those securities sold from being thrown back on the market.

In many instances a new issue handled by the investment banker is disposed of by taking in other securities in exchange for the new issue. It then becomes the duty of the trading department to sell these securities.

Statistical or research department. This department aids the buying department by making whatever studies are needed when considering a new issue of securities. It will also make studies of particular industries, companies, or securities. The statistical department will answer inquiries from investors and dealers in regard to particular securities. It will usually examine the holdings of investors free of charge, and make recommendations regarding the sale and purchase of specific securities. In some houses there is an investment advisory department which takes over some of the work of the statistical department stated above.

Accounting department. This department handles the bookkeeping work the same as in other types of businesses. It will also keep the records in connection with buying and selling groups and aid in the settlement of these accounts.

Syndicates

Relation of Banker to Issuing Company. In our discussion we have assumed that the investment banker or group of investment bankers purchase the securities outright from the issuing corporation and then sell them to other bankers or investors. This is the usual arrangement, but it is only one of the following three types of agreements between the banker and the issuer.

1. Firm commitment
2. Stand-by commitment
3. Best-effort commitment

Firm commitment. The *firm commitment* is the type we have been discussing where the banker or group of bankers buy the securities directly from the issuing company and then sell them to investors, other bankers, or institutions. The price that is paid for the securities is negotiated between the banker and the issuing company or is established by competitive bidding. The profit made by the banker is the *spread* between the purchase price and the selling price, less expenses connected with the purchase and sale.

When the banker agrees to buy the securities, all the responsibility for selling them is on his shoulders. The issuing company gets its money from the investment banker before the securities are sold to the public. This type of commitment carries the highest "spread," and is the one most commonly used. After we have described the stand-by and best-effort commitments, the rest of the chapter will deal primarily with the firm commitment.

Stand-by commitment. In case of the *stand-by commitment,* the issuing company will sell its own securities, and the investment banker or group of investment bankers will merely "stand-by" and "take-up" and sell any securities which the issuing company is unable to sell. It thus becomes a firm commitment to the extent of any unsold securities. This type of commitment is most commonly made when the company attempts to sell securities to its existing stockholders under the privileged subscription, which was discussed in the preceding chapter. It is also sometimes used when a company offers its security holders a new type of security in exchange for the securities which they hold.

The amount and basis for computing the banker's commissions under the stand-by commitment vary according to the particular agreement. In some instances the banker estimates the amount of securities which he may be compelled to take over, and charges the company a fixed fee or a fixed percentage of the entire issue. In most instances, however, the banker gets both (1) a *stand-by* fee of a designated percentage of the entire issue, and (2) a *take-down fee* of a designated percentage of all securities which he must take over and sell.

Best-effort commitment. In the *best-effort commitment* the investment banker does not agree to buy any of the securities. He merely agrees that he will use his best efforts to sell as many of the securities as possible. Thus, he is really only acting as an agent in selling the company's securities. This type of arrangement is usually made when the issue is a speculative common stock, whose sale is doubtful. This arrangement is also sometimes used when a company wants to sell a better quality issue, but where it is not necessary that the entire issue be sold. In the case of the best-effort commitment, the banker is paid a commission only on the securities which he sells.

PURCHASE AND SELLING SYNDICATES OR GROUPS. In many instances the purchase of an issue of securities may require many millions of dollars. The particular investment banker may not have the amount of capital available to buy the issue, or not want to risk an enormous amount in one company. For this reason the banker may call in other investment bankers to help him buy the issue. This group of bankers is called the *underwriting syndicate,* or *purchase group.*

In order to aid in the sale of the securities, the purchase group may or may not form a special organization called the *selling syndicate* or *selling group,* to whom the securities are sold. These groups will now be described.

Purchase Group. When the issue is large in size the investment banker who originated it may call in other investment bankers to buy a share of the issue along with him. Any of the following terms are applied to the group thus formed: *purchase syndicate, purchase group,* or *underwriting syndicate.* In order to avoid confusion with the *selling syndicate* or *group,* we will refer here to this buying organization as the *purchase group.* The investment banker who originated the issue will usually serve as manager of the group.

Purchase agreement. The *purchase agreement* is the contract that is made between the members of the purchase group and the issuer. Prior to 1933, it was common practice for the various members of the group to buy the securities for their joint and several account; thus if any member did not pay for his share of the issue, the other members could be made to stand it. After the adoption of the Securities Act of 1933, however, the practice has been for each of the members of the purchase group to severally contract for the purchase of his particular share of the issue directly with the issuer, although all of the participants are included in the same purchase agreement. This limits the liability of each participant both in respect to the penalties provided by the Securities Act, and in respect to the unsold securities.

The purchase agreement covers all essential matters, such as the time and place of delivery of the securities, stipulates how and when payment shall be made, conditions that must be performed by the company before the actual purchase of the securities, etc.

In the past, the agreement was effective as soon as it was signed by the parties, but the Securities Act of 1933 provides that the securities can be offered to the public only after at least 20 days have elapsed from the time the securities have been registered with the Securities and Exchange Commission. Changes made by the Commission (effective in 1952) in the regulations permit a speedier sale provided the proper information has previously been given to the prospective buyer.

It is now common practice to include "market-out" clauses in the agreement, giving the purchase group the right to terminate the agreement if certain events occur before there is a public offering of the securities. Such events are, for instance—declaration of war involving the United States, closing of the stock exchanges, declaration of bank moratoriums, the discovery of a false statement in the agreement, instigation of a law suit against the issuing company, and other events which might adversely affect the financial position of the company. Since such "market-out" clauses have been inserted in agreements, there have been few instances where such events have occurred, but even where they have, the bankers have usually not tried to take advantage of them.

A notable exception, however, occurred in 1948, when Otis & Co. and two other investment bankers backed out of their agreement to sell 900,000 shares of the common stock of the Kaiser-Frazer Corp., predecessor to the Kaiser Motors Corp. and Kaiser Industries. It was agreed, among other things, that if any important litigation was started against the motor company before a specified time, the investment bankers would not be bound to take over the issue. Less than an hour before the time the agreement was to have been effective, suit was brought by a lawyer (a stockholder of the Kaiser-Frazer Corp.), asking the court to prevent the sale of the stock, alleging that the financial position of the company had resulted in insecurity and uncertainty among the stockholders of the company and the prospective purchasers of the company's products. It was contended by Kaiser-Frazer that the suit was instigated by the bankers as a means of getting out of the agreement. Action was then brought by Kaiser-Frazer against Otis & Co., and countercharges were brought by the latter company. The Securities and Exchange Commission then got into the fight because of the refusal of the bankers to sell the securities and because of the alleged misleading earnings figures on the part of the motor company in the registration statement. After six years of litigation, representatives of Kaiser Motors Corp. and Otis & Co. announced in early 1954, that both companies were dropping all charges and countercharges and that an agreement had been reached. Subsequently the Securities and Exchange Commission announced that it was also dropping the actions it had brought.

Agreement among purchasers. The *agreement among the purchasers* is a contract made between each purchaser and every other purchaser in the group, and also between each purchaser and the manager of the group. Following are some of the more important contents of this agreement: the amount of securities to be purchased by each member, the amount of money to be deposited immediately by each member, provisions relating to the payment and delivery of the securities, liability of the members, expenses assumed by the members, authority and compensation of the manager of the group, provisions, if any, relating to price stabilization operations, and the effective date and termination date of the agreement.

In connection with the *purchase agreement* it was indicated that it was common practice for each member of the buying group to purchase his share of the securities directly from the issuer, and that he would, therefore, be liable only for that amount of securities. This is referred to as the *limited liability account,* or *divided account.* The agreement, however, may provide that in event not all the securities should be sold, each member would have a liability for them in proportion to his original subscription. This liability continues until the account is closed out. When the agreement provides for this type of liability it is called the *unlimited liability account,* or, *undivided account.*

The advantages of the divided account to the banker who has an effective sales organization are obvious. After taking down the amount of securities to which he subscribed, he has no further liability. But the divided account is not preferred by those bankers who are not sure of being able to dispose of their share of the issue. The divided account is the one usually used in the sale of corporate securities which have a common maturity date.

The undivided account, however, is widely used in the case of municipal bonds and corporate securities which have serial maturities, such as railroad equipment obligations. In the case of serial bonds, certain of the maturities can more readily be sold than other maturities. If the account was divided, some of the leading bankers would take down their allotment in the maturities which were easily marketed, leaving the less desirable ones for the other bankers. For this reason such accounts are commonly undivided, so that the banker who got the preferred maturities may still be forced to take some of the other maturities.

The above discussion of the purchase group has referred to the *firm commitment.* As pointed out earlier, this group could, instead of actually purchasing the securities, have made a *stand-by* or a *best-effort commitment.*

Selling Group. It was stated above that the purchase group may be the only syndicate present in the distribution of a security issue. In such a case it would be referred to in most instances as an *underwriting syndicate.* This syndicate would then sell the securities through its own sales organization to institutions, individual investors, and maybe also, to investment dealers.

The tendency in recent years has been to include a larger number of investment bankers in the originating group. Also a larger proportion of the securities are being sold by members of this originating group without the use of the selling syndicate than was formerly the case. This is particularly true in the case of municipal issues and corporate issues that are of the best quality, or which are small in amount.

In the case of corporate securities, however, there is often a group of bankers or dealers between the purchase group and the investor. Since the nature of this group differs in practice, and different terms are applied to the same type of group as well as the same terms to different types of groups, confusion abounds in the literature.

The object of the investment banking set-up is to get distribution of the securities to the final investor. Generally speaking, the greater the number in the purchase group, the greater will be the number of bankers who can be prevailed upon to enter the selling group. Likewise the greater the number in the selling group, the greater will be the number of investors who can be contacted. Consideration is given to the geographic distribution of the securities in the selection of members of the purchase and selling groups.

When a selling syndicate is set up, members of the purchase group commonly also participate in the selling syndicate. Thus, they in effect receive double commissions, one for underwriting the issue, and the other for aiding in the sale. In the trade it is said that they "take down" a part of the issue for sale by their own organization. The manager of the purchase group may also set aside part of the issue for sale to institutional investors. The balance of the issue is "given up" for sale to the other members of the selling group.

The provisions relating to the sale of the securities are contained in a *selling group agreement,* which is a contract between the purchase group and the selling group. The following provisions are included in the contract: terms of sale to the selling group, and prices to be charged by them for the securities, provisions relating to the payment for and delivery of the securities, invitation to dealers to subscribe to the issue, or to confirm allotments reserved for them, and provisions relating to termination of the agreement.

As may be inferred from the above, one type of arrangement is for the purchasing group to allot the dealer a designated amount of the securities, and ask the dealer to confirm this by a specified time. When the confirmation is received, the dealer becomes liable on a firm commitment for that amount of securities. The other type is an offer on the part of the purchase group to the dealer to subscribe to part of the issue. In this case the purchase group reserves the right to reject part or all the subscription.

There is a distinction sometimes made between the phrases "selling syndicate," and "selling group." The National Association of Securities Dealers, Inc.,[1] uses the term "syndicate" when the members of the organization are committed to take the securities, and the term "group" when there is no such commitment. Using the words with this meaning, selling groups are now more commonly used than selling syndicates. Despite the attempt to make a distinction between a "syndicate" and a "group," in practice the words are commonly used interchangeably.

COMPENSATION PAID TO INVESTMENT BANKERS. The compensation received by the investment bankers for underwriting and selling securities varies according to a number of different factors. Generally speaking, the better the quality of the issue, the lower is the compensation. Thus, lower yield bonds carry lower compensation than higher yielding bonds. The amount paid the bankers for handling bonds is less than that paid for handling a stock issue of the same company. The tendency is for the compensation to be a lower percentage for a large issue than a small one. In many instances, however, the larger issues are those of companies that are financially strong.

In the case of securities that can be sold in large blocks, e.g., to institutional investors, the amount paid to bankers is usually a lower percentage. During periods of prosperity when securities can be readily sold, the commissions for selling are of course lower than during a period of depression.

The difference between what the issuing company gets for the securities, and what the investor pays is called the "spread." This, of course, represents the bankers' compensation. This spread covers what is paid to the purchase group and its manager and to the selling group. In the case of large issues of high-grade bonds the spread would be between ½ to 1 point. In other words, the bankers compensation would be between ½ to 1 per cent, or between $5 and $10, per $1,000 bond. Normally the spread on bonds would be between 1 and 2 points, on preferred stocks between 2 and 4 points, and on common stock between 7 and 10 points, although in some instances the spread on common stock may run as high as 20 points. The amount of the spread that goes to the various middlemen varies widely, but normally the manager of the purchase group would get about 10 per cent, the purchase group itself about 30 per cent, and the selling group about 60 per cent.

[1] Rules of Fair Trade Practice, Article II, Sec. 1 (g), (h).

The spreads stated above represent the *gross* income from the underwriting and selling. Out of this income the bankers would have to pay all the expenses connected with the purchase and sale of the securities and their other expenses. In some instances the spread is so small that a slight change in the market may wipe out entirely the profit to the bankers. Occasionally they are forced to hold the securities for a while until the market improves. In some cases the bankers are forced to sell the securities for a lower price than they paid for them.

PRICE STABILIZATION. The price of securities that are already on the market is determined by the relatively few securities which at any one time are being bought and sold in the market. When a new issue of securities is being sold, the effect of a relatively large quantity on the market at the same time is to depress their price. If the market price of those securities which have already been sold, weakens, it may jeopardize the sale of the remaining part of the issue.

In order to maintain the price of the securities, the manager of the purchase group is commonly given the right to buy and sell the securities in the market. The agreement usually limits the amount of the account to from 5 to 10 per cent of the entire issue. The manager may sell these repurchased securities in the market, or he may force the members of the purchase group to take them up in the proportion to which they originally participated in the group.

Although the manager will attempt to maintain the price of the securities at or near the offering price during the life of the syndicate, if the market slips very much, he may have to keep lowering the price offered for the securities. In some instances the price falls so low that all attempts at stabilization are abandoned.

Since pegging the market is a form of manipulation, it can legally be done under the Securities Exchange Act of 1934 only with the consent of the Securities and Exchange Commission. Daily reports must be filed by the manager of the purchase group disclosing all stabilizing operations.

COMPETITIVE BIDDING. In the discussion of purchasing securities by investment bankers thus far we have been considering the method of direct negotiation between the banker and the issuing company. To an increasing extent in recent years securities have been sold by the issuer advertising for sealed bids on the part of investment bankers rather than by direct negotiation.

In most states public sealed bidding is required for state and municipal bond issues. United States Treasury bills are also sold in this way. Since 1941, the Securities and Exchange Commission has required, with a few exceptions, that issues of public utility holding companies subject to the Public Utility Holding Company Act of 1935, and the operating subsidiaries of such companies, be sold only by sealed bids. In 1950, the Federal Power Commission (this body has jurisdiction over public utilities which operate across state boundaries, but which are not subject to control by the Securities and Exchange Commission) issued an order requiring, with certain exceptions, public bidding for the security issues that come under its jurisdiction. In some instances the state laws also require competitive bidding for public utility issues. Since 1944, the Interstate Commerce Commission has, with some exceptions, compelled competitive bidding for public sale of all railroad issues over $1,000,000.

When investment bankers learn of an issue to be offered through bids, some of the leading bankers alone or in connection with a number of other bankers will take steps toward bidding on the issue. Copies of the registration statement will be obtained from the issuer, and the latter may hold meetings at which the nature and terms of the issue will be explained and discussed. The bankers will then submit sealed bids for the issue. The banker getting the issue may then proceed to sell it through syndicates in the same way that we have described in private negotiations. As is true of most things, there are advantages and disadvantages of competitive bidding.

Advantages of competitive bidding. Following are the advantages of competitive bidding. In most instances these are from the viewpoint of the issuing company.

1. Higher price obtained from the issue. In the case of private negotiations between the investment banker and the issuing company, the latter is more or less forced to take the price for the securities offered by the banker. In the case of competitive bidding, however, each banker knows that other bankers are bidding on the issue, and thus each one will tend to bid the highest price possible in order to get the issue. It is thus argued that competitive bidding results in the lowest financing cost to the issuer.

2. Will not lead to banker control. In some instances the system of private negotiation has led to banker control of some companies. The particular banker would advise the company on financial matters and handle its security issues from time to time. The banker would often insist that a member of his firm be on the board of directors as long as any of the securities were outstanding. It is

argued that under the more impersonal system of competitive bidding on each issue this banker control would not develop.

3. The underwriting business will not be concentrated in the hands of a few large bankers. It is argued by some that the private negotiation system of handling securities has resulted in a few large firms getting most of the business, and that competitive bidding would tend to break this up.

Disadvantages of competitive bidding. Following are the arguments against competitive bidding.

1. Intimate banker-issuer relationship destroyed. Under the private negotiation system the investment banker acts as a financial adviser to the issuing company. His services are often valuable in setting the terms and conditions of the issue, and he may continue to advise the company while the securities are outstanding and even after they have matured. When a new issue is being considered, the same banker would probably be called in. It is argued that competitive bidding would break up this desirable arrangement.

2. Issue may be overpriced. Due to the competition of bankers, the price paid the company for the particular issue may be relatively high. As a result the banker might price the issue to the public at a higher price than would have been the case under private negotiation. If the issue is overpriced, it will probably fall in price later, which may thus adversely affect the issuer, the investor and the banker. In reply to this argument it should be stated, however, that in general investors will not pay more for the securities than they are worth.

3. May result in the issues being handled by only a few large bankers. The proponents of both private negotiations and competitive bidding argue that the other method will result in a relatively few large bankers getting most of the underwriting business. The argument against competitive bidding is that since it tends to result in a relatively high price to the issuer, the banker will have to keep his compensation to a minimum. This may result in the spread becoming so small that only the relatively few large bankers will get the business.

4. Inflexibility. When the sale takes place through private negotiation, the terms can be changed to fit the market conditions at the time the issue is put on the market. But in the case of competitive bidding the terms are set and the bankers are asked to submit their bids. In the meantime the market may advance or decline before the issue is sold.

5. Ineffective under adverse circumstances. If the issue is a small one, or an issue of a company that is not well known, or a company that has a poor financial standing, there may be no bids submitted for it. Likewise when the market is unsettled, bankers may hesitate to bid.

Private Placement. An important trend in recent years has been the elimination of the investment banker in the sale of securities. Some institutional investors, particularly the life insurance companies, have been buying bonds directly from the issuing company. In some instances bonds have been privately placed with commercial banks and pension funds. One issue may be sold to one institution or a small number of such institutional buyers. Practically all of the securities which are privately placed are, of course, bonds. Prior to 1933, the amount of securities privately placed was negligible as compared with the total amount of securities issued, but since 1950, approximately 50 per cent of all bonds issued have been sold privately.

Reasons for development of private placement. They are as follows:

1. No registration cost. The Securities Act of 1933 requires that security issues which are to be publicly offered in interstate commerce must, with certain exceptions, be registered with the Securities and Exchange Commission. This entails a considerable expense to the issuing company. Securities that are privately placed do not have to be registered.

2. No waiting period. The Securities Act provides that no registered securities may be sold until the effective date of the registration statement. And the effective date is usually 20 days after the statement is filed with the SEC. During this period the market may break and jeopardize the successful sale of the securities. When the issue is privately placed, however, there is no waiting period that must be observed.

3. Avoiding liability for officers and directors. The Securities Act provides certain liability for officers and directors for any misstatements of material facts or omissions of material facts in the registration statement. Some corporate officials look upon private placement as a means of escaping this possible liability.

4. Save bankers' commissions. Although the bankers' spread is relatively small, on a large issue it amounts to a considerable sum. No such commissions need be paid with private placement.

5. Good investment for institutional investor. The assets of life insurance companies have been increasing rapidly over a period of

years. Interest rates were on the decline from 1932 to 1946, and insurance companies had difficulty investing their money in high-grade securities which bore a fair return. The insurance companies naturally have had to compete with each other in buying bonds offered through investment bankers. With the tremendous resources available, they started contacting the issuing company directly. In many instances the insurance company has been able to buy the securities at a cheaper price than through an investment banker.

Advantages of private placement. The advantages of private placement are practically the same as the reasons for its development, which have just been stated. It will be noticed that these advantages are from the viewpoint of the issuer and the investor, and not the eliminated investment banker. Probably both benefit in many instances: the issuer may get a little more, and the investor may pay a little less than if the issue had been sold through a banker.

TABLE 29

GROSS PROCEEDS OF NEW CORPORATE SECURITIES OFFERED FOR CASH SALE, BY TYPE OF OFFERING, UNITED STATES, SELECTED YEARS

(MILLIONS OF DOLLARS)

	Publicly Offered		*Privately Offered*		*Total*	
Year	*dollars*	*per cent*	*dollars*	*per cent*	*dollars*	*per cent*
1955	6,825	65.3	3,628	34.7	10,453	100
1954	5,844	61.1	3,719	38.9	9,563	100
1953	5,580	62.7	3,318	37.3	8,898	100
1952	5,533	58.1	4,002	41.9	9,534	100
1951	4,326	55.8	3,415	44.2	7,741	100
1950	3,681	57.8	2,680	42.2	6,361	100
1949	3,549	58.7	2,502	41.3	6,052	100
1948	3,991	57.2	3,087	42.8	7,078	100
1947	4,342	66.0	2,235	34.0	6,577	100
1946	4,983	72.2	1,917	27.8	6,900	100
1945	4,989	83.1	1,022	16.9	6,011	100
1939	1,458	67.4	706	32.6	2,164	100
1934	305	76.9	92	23.1	397	100

SOURCE: *Moody's Industrial Manual,* Moody's Investors Service, New York, 1955, p. a17. Data for 1955 obtained from *Statistical Bulletin,* United States Securities and Exchange Commission, February, 1956, p. 3.

Another possible advantage of private placement is that, if the issuing company should run into difficulty, it might be easier to effect an adjustment with the institutional owner than if the securities were scattered among many individual investors.

Disadvantages of private placement. Private placement results in a loss of the underwriting and selling commissions to the investment bankers, but the following disadvantages are from viewpoints other than the banker.

1. Inability of issuer to buy back securities at a discount. When securities are sold through the regular channels, opportunities often exist where a corporation can buy back its bonds on the market at substantial discounts. But when the securities are privately placed, the life insurance company will probably hold on to them until their maturity, at which time the issuer will have to pay back the full face value of the bonds.

2. Future financing may be more difficult. If the issue is privately placed, no general market is built up for the company's securities, and unless the same or some other institutions want to buy them, the issuer may have some difficulty in disposing of the securities.

3. Fewer high-grade securities available for others. It has been only the high-grade issues which have been privately placed with life insurance companies. That means that other investors, including the smaller institutional investors, do not have a chance to buy them. As the result, the tendency would be for these other investors to buy securities of lower quality, and the financial stability of the smaller institutions might be affected.

Brokerage fees to bankers. If large institutional investors, such as life insurance companies, approach the issuing company about a new bond issue, or vice versa, the investment banker, of course, is out of the picture.

The more recent trend has been for an investment banker to act as a "finder." He will make it his duty to know companies that need financing, and insurance companies that want to invest. In some instances the investment banker is approached by the insurance company, while in others the issuing company may call him in. In acting as a "go-between" the banker receives merely an agent's or broker's fee for making the arrangement between the buyer and the seller. The fee which he receives, usually ranging from 1/10 to 1 per cent of the issue, is smaller than the amount he would receive if he underwrote and sold the issue.

Regulation of security issues

NEED FOR PROTECTION. There has long been a need for laws to protect the buyers of securities. In ordinary sales of goods we have the rule or doctrine of *caveat emptor,* which means, "let the buyer beware." Under this rule of law the buyer is supposed to be able to see the goods and to judge their quality. If the seller makes any fraudulent misrepresentations in regard to the goods, the buyer has a legal right to bring suit, and if he can prove that fraud exists, he may recover the amount of his losses. But to do this he must take the initiative and prove fraud, which is usually difficult to do.

This law relating to ordinary goods proved very ineffective when it came to security selling. Securities are intangibles and it is impossible to judge their quality merely by inspection. The statements that accompany the security sale are highly important, but the average person is not capable of interpreting them. But even in cases where fraud is present and provable, relatively few buyers would take the time and spend the money that would be necessary to prosecute.

In many instances the sellers are well aware of just how far they can go without actually breaking the law. Although they will not make fraudulent statements, they will often fail to state all the facts. They will present only the favorable factors and remain silent on the others. In many instances they will merely give exaggerated statements of opinion.

State laws

Nature of State Laws. Beginning with Kansas, in 1911, all states now, except Nevada, have special laws relating to the sale of securities within their jurisdiction. These are called "blue-sky laws."[2]

In general there are three types of state securities laws. One type requires that the issuer register the security issue and receive the approval of the state securities commission before it may be sold. This type law is found in 43 of the states. In 32 of the states the laws authorize some state official, such as the attorney-general, to obtain court injunctions to prevent or stop the sale of fraudulent issues. Obviously, some of the states which have this fraud type statute, also require the approval of the issue before it may be sold. Only four states, Delaware, Maryland, New Jersey, and New York, have the fraud acts exclusively.

In 44 of the states security dealers and brokers must be approved and licensed by the state before they may transact business. Most of the states have all three of the types of laws stated above. Atten-

[2] The name is said to have originated from the fact that the laws were designed to stop the sale of securities of corporations that were formed to exploit the resources of the "blue sky."

tion should be called to the fact that, although most writers mention the licensing of security dealers and brokers, when they are discussing state security laws, they usually divide the classes of legislation into only two classes, the first two listed above.

EXEMPT SECURITIES. When the state law requires the approval of security issues before they may be sold, there are always a number of exempt securities. These include securities which must be approved by some other state commission, government, state and municipal bonds, and securities of other than ordinary business corporations. Following are the types of securities that usually do not have to be approved by the securities department:

1. Those issued by the United States, a state, or political subdivision
2. Stocks or shares issued by banks, savings and loan associations, trust companies, and insurance companies
3. Securities classed as "legal investments" in the state
4. Securities, such as those issued by railroads and public utilities, which must have the approval of the public utilities commisson in the state
5. Real estate securities
6. Securities that are listed on approved stock exchanges
7. Securities issued by nonprofit organizations

EXEMPT TRANSACTIONS. Although the security may be one that should ordinarily be listed, the nature of the particular sale may be such that approval of the state is not necessary. The following are included in these exemptions:

1. Sale of stock to existing stockholders
2. Sale or issuance of securities in a reorganization
3. Judicial sales
4. Sales to one or a few persons

WEAKNESSES OF STATE LAWS. Although the state securities laws have been effective in stopping the sale of most fraudulent issues which have been sold within the particular state, there are certain weaknesses in the state laws. Following is a summary of the most important shortcomings.

1. *Laws applicable only to intrastate sales.* The principal weaknesses of the securities laws of the various states is that they apply only to sales made within the state. The authority of the particular state is limited by its own boundaries, so that any laws enacted by the legislature of that state apply only to that particular state.

Many security issues are sold on a national scale. So long as the transaction crosses the state boundaries it is interstate in nature and subject to control by the federal government, and not the state. Sales that are completed outside the state by mail cannot be controlled by the particular state.

2. *Incompetent and dishonest officials.* In many instances the officials who are appointed to administer the securities laws are persons who have been appointed in reward for political favors granted. They are commonly not acquainted with the securities business. In some instances a particular security issue will be approved because of pressure brought on the official or in return for some personal favor.

3. *Fraud Acts not adequate.* The fraud statutes do not accomplish all the objectives that should be sought after in a securities law. Where this is the only kind of security law in the state, it is not necessary for a company to file information about itself and the securities it plans to issue. The approval of the state is not necessary for the sale of the securities. The state only has the power to stop the subsequent sale of the securities if it believes fraud has been committed. This is somewhat like locking the stable after the horse had been stolen.

4. *Too many exempt securities.* The laws vary among the states as to what securities or transactions are exempt from the law. Some of these were listed above. In many of the states there are too many exempt securities and exempt transactions. In some states all guaranteed securities are exempt. Some exempt any security which is listed in designated securities manuals, or which is listed on a stock exchange.

5. *Questionable intent of some laws.* In some of the states the securities commission is given the authority to determine whether in its judgment the company will be serving a useful purpose or will be successful. It is doubtful if any commission is capable of deciding these questions. Considering the caliber of some of the commissions, there could be little doubt about their inability to determine such matters.

Many of our important industries and companies today would probably never have been started if a state commission had had to pass judgment whether they thought the enterprise would be successful. Furthermore, it may be dangerous to our capitalistic economy to give anyone such power.

SECURITIES ISSUED BY PUBLIC UTILITIES AND FINANCIAL INSTITUTIONS. Our discussion of state regulation of securities applies in most instances to the securities of ordinary business corporations.

Most of the states have public utility commissions which have the power to set rates and pass on security issues of railroads and public utilities within the state. Also, a banking (or similarly named) commission, usually has the right to approve or disapprove the issuance of securities of banks and other financial institutions.

In the case of financial institutions, whose operations are more or less local in character, the commissions are probably adequate. Many of the public utilities and their holding companies, however, are large and their activities cross many state lines, so the state regulation of their security issues has not been very effective.

The Federal Securities Act of 1933

Reasons for the Law. We pointed out above the weaknesses inherent in the state securities laws. Despite these shortcomings the state laws are still applicable. But there has long been felt a need for more stringent regulation, and for federal control over those issues which involve interstate commerce.

Prior to 1933, the federal government, through the Interstate Commerce Commission, regulated the securities issued by railroads. In 1909, Congress passed the Mail Fraud Act, under which the postal department was given the right to stop the sending of misleading and fraudulent statements regarding securities, and other goods and services, through the mail. Penalties were provided for the violation of the law. The postal department, however, did not have an adequate staff to enforce the law. Even if some persons were forced to discontinue sending fraudulent statements through the mail, no relief was afforded by the law to those individuals who had been defrauded.

The need for federal regulation of security issues has been realized since the end of the last century. Following World War I, several bills were introduced into Congress for such a law, but no legislation was enacted. After the stock market crash of 1929, and the start of the depression of the 1930's, however, the President, Congress, and the investing public realized the urgent need for such a law.

The practices followed by many companies and investment bankers during the late 1920's were misleading, to say the least. Aside from meeting the securities laws in the particular states, they were free to sell the securities in any manner desired. In most instances, inadequate information was given about the particular issue being distributed. Where the information was given, in many instances it was in such a form that it could not be understood by the average investor. In many cases the issuer or banker would not make any incorrect statements, but they would intentionally fail to give all the facts. Only the favorable factors would be listed. If the most recent financial statement was not favorable, an older one which showed better results might be used. There was a close relationship in many instances between commercial banks, investment banks, and investment trusts. The shareholders and creditors of the banks and investment trusts might be adversely affected by the investment bank dumping the securities it could not sell to the public into the lap of the bank or investment trust.

Basic Purpose of the Law. The basic purpose of the Securities Act of 1933 is to compel the issuer to give all the pertinent facts relating to the particular security issue, in order that the investing public would have a means of determining the investment worth of the issue. The law requires that not only must the information given be correct, but also that the issuer give all the material facts about the company and the issue. Thus, the truth, and the whole truth must be given. At the time of its enactment, the legislation was often referred to as the "Truth in Securities Act."

The late President Franklin D. Roosevelt, in his 1932 campaign and afterward, urged the enactment of laws that would give protection to the small investor. He said that banks, and other institutions that collected and handled other people's money, occupied a trust position and that the law of fiduciaries should be applicable to them. The rule of *caveat emptor,* he said, should not apply to the sale of securities, but rather we should adopt the rule of "let the seller beware."

The Securities Act of 1933 merely requires full disclosure of all the facts. It was not intended that the federal government should pass upon the soundness of the security issue. As long as all the pertinent information is given in a truthful fashion, the government has no power to disapprove the issue. The Act requires that the front page of every prospectus must certify that "The Commission has not passed on the merits of any securities registered with it. It is a criminal offense to represent that the Commission has approved these securities. . . ."

Administration of the Act. The Securities Act of 1933 originally gave the Federal Trade Commission the power to administer the various provisions of the law. Legislation passed the following year, the Securities and Exchange Act of 1934, set up a commission, called the Securities and Exchange Commission (SEC), to administer both Acts. The Act of 1934, which regulates the stock exchanges and the sale of securities thereon, will be discussed in the following chapter.

The SEC is composed of five commissioners who are appointed by the president with the advice and consent of the Senate. They are appointed for a term of five years. For purposes of administration, the United States is divided into eight zones, with a regional office in each zone.

Principal Provisions of the Act. The Securities Act of 1933 requires that, with certain exceptions, before any new offering of securities can be made to the public through the use of the mails or interstate commerce, the company must file with the SEC a *registration statement,* containing certain specific information about the company and the issue.

To bring the information to the attention of prospective investors, the Act requires that a copy of the *prospectus,* which contains about the same information as the registration statement, but in abbreviated form, must be made available to every buyer at or before the completion of the sale. There, of course, is nothing in the law which can compel a buyer to read the terms of the prospectus.

The fee for registering the issue with the Securities and Exchange Commission is 1/100 of 1 per cent of the aggregate price of the proposed issue, but not less than $25.

Exempt Securities. When the act was first adopted it was provided that issues not exceeding $100,000 in amount could be exempt from registration. In 1945, this limit was raised to $300,000. It was thought that the costs incident to registration would be too high in proportion to the amount of money obtained by the company when the issue was small in amount. The exemption is not automatic. It is necessary for the company to file an abbreviated registration statement, and get the approval of the SEC before the issue of $300,000 or less will be exempt. Public sale may then take place after five days. The other exemptions include governmental issues, issues that must be approved by other commissions, and securities issued by nonprofit organizations. Following is an outline of the exempt securities.

1. Issues of $300,000 and less, if approved by SEC
2. Securities issued by the United States, a state, or a political subdivision of a state
3. Securities issued by any state or national bank
4. Securities of savings and loan associations
5. Securities issued by railroads
6. Receivers' and trustees' certificates

7. Short-term notes and bills with a maturity of not more than nine months
8. Securities of nonprofit organizations
9. Life insurance and annuity contracts

Exempt Transactions. The Securities Act of 1933 covers only transactions involving the primary distribution of securities to the public. In the case of private sales, such as the sale of an issue of bonds to a life insurance company, or the sale of the issue to only a few persons, it is not necessary to comply with the Act.

Since the Act covers only those sales involved with the primary distribution of the securities, subsequent sales of the securities by persons, brokers, or dealers are not governed by the legislation. This is referred to as "trading" in the securities. Following is a summary of the type of security transactions which may take place without the necessity of registering the securities.

1. Sale of securities not involving a public offering
2. Sale of securities to existing security holders under certain circumstances
3. Exchange of securities with existing security holders
4. Resale of securities after primary distribution has taken place
5. Securities sold only to residents within the state of issuer

Registration Statement. The *registration statement* is an elaborate document, three copies of which must be filed with the SEC. The listing of the requirements of this statement is contained in 32 paragraphs covering several closely printed pages. The preparation of the registration statement and the prospectus, including the printing, often involves many thousands of dollars and may take months to prepare.

In general the registration statement covers everything that the Commission needs in order to approve the issue. Following are some of the more important requirements of the statement:

1. Names and addresses of directors, officers, promoters, underwriters, and of stockholders who own more than 10 per cent of the company's stock, and the amount of securities held by each, and the amount of securities of the new issue to be held by each
2. Payment made or to be made to promoters, and all remuneration paid to each director and officer, and to anyone else receiving in excess of $25,000 a year
3. Filing of important documents and statements including the following:
   (*a*) Copy of articles of incorporation and bylaws
   (*b*) Detailed current balance sheet

(*c*) Detailed current income statement
(*d*) Statement of the amount of stock and bonds outstanding and the detailed provisions of all securities
(*e*) Statement of all securities covered by options outstanding, or to be created in connection with the security issue being registered, and the names and addresses of persons who are to receive more than 10 per cent of the options
(*f*) Terms of material contracts made, not in the ordinary course of business, including any management contract involving bonuses, and profit-sharing arrangements

4. Statement of net proceeds, offering price, and names of underwriters of any securities sold within two years preceding the filing of the registration statement
5. Elaborate detailed information relating to the particular issue being registered, including the following:
(*a*) Nature and amount of the security issue, and all underlying agreements relating to the issue
(*b*) Specific purposes of selling the issue
(*c*) Proposed price at which the securities will be offered to the public
(*d*) Estimated net proceeds which will be obtained from the sale of the securities
(*e*) Detailed list of itemized expenses incurred by the issuer in connection with the issue
(*f*) Commissions and any other type of compensation, directly or indirectly, received by the underwriters in connection with the sale of the securities
(*g*) Copy of opinion of counsel in respect to the legality of the issue

Effective Date of Registration Statement. The law provides that the effective date of the registration statement shall be 20 days after it has been filed. The Commission may, however, shorten this period if it believes such action is justified by the circumstances. The securities cannot be sold or offered for sale until the effective date of the registration statement. During the 20-day period, which is known as the "cooling period," the Commission examines the registration statement to determine if it meets the requirements of the Act. If the material is satisfactory, it will be approved and will become effective automatically 20 days after the filing date.

If some of the material is incomplete or inaccurate, the Commission will issue a "stop order," and notify the issuer what additional information is needed. The stop order prevents the statement from becoming effective, until it is properly amended. Even after the registration statement becomes effective, the Commission may, after

15 days notice, and opportunity for a hearing, issue a stop order suspending the effectiveness of the statement. The Commission will notify the issuer of any failure to conform with the provisions of the Act by means of a "letter of deficiency." Informal conferences between the Commission and the issuer, at which differences are ironed out, have largely eliminated the need for a stop order after the registration statement has been approved.

THE "RED-HERRING" PROSPECTUS. One of the purposes of the cooling period is to enable dealers and the public to learn as much as possible about the issue prior to the time it is offered for sale. But the formal prospectus cannot be given to the purchaser until after the registration statement has become effective.

To supply dealers and prospective buyers with information about the nature of the particular issue, there developed the practice of giving widespread distribution to dealers, institutional investors and some individual investors of the "red-herring" prospectus. This preliminary prospectus received its name from the fact that it contains a statement printed in red lettering on the side of the page, and in language prescribed by the Commission, that the prospectus is not an offer to sell or the solicitation of an offer to buy, and that no orders can be received until after the effective date of the registration statement.

The rules set up by the Commission prescribe what can be contained in the "red-herring" prospectus. It should have a fair summary of the more important parts of the registration statement, and it should not contain an opinion or recommendation as to the investment worth of the securities. The Commission requires that a copy of the real prospectus must be sent to anyone who received a "red-herring" prospectus.

The "red-herring" prospectus was originally sent only to security dealers. Realizing that the prospective buyer should legally secure more information about the securities to be sold, the Securities and Exchange Commission in 1952 used its "definitive powers" to make certain changes in the Securities Act of 1933. On security issues registered on and after October 27, 1952, the Commission permits investment bankers to send out during the waiting period as many "red-herring" prospectuses as they like to dealers along with copies of new "identifying statements." The latter includes a statement that it is not an offer to sell, the name and type of business of the issuer, the price, yield, redemption, convertible and warrant provisions of the security, the type of exchange on which the issue will be listed, an opinion of the issue's legality as an investment for savings banks, insurance companies, and fiduciaries, and a statement regarding tax exemptions, if any. The identifying statement may be published in newspapers, mailed, or handed out to prospective buyers. It may contain a "tear-off" blank which a prospective purchaser can use to request a "red-herring" prospectus from a dealer. If the Commission believes that a wide distribution of these identifying statements has been made to many prospective buyers, it may shorten the waiting period to less than 20 days.

THE PROSPECTUS. The registration statement is available to prospective investors both at the home and the regional offices of the Securities and Exchange Commission, and photostatic copies of it may be obtained for a small fee. The statement, however, is a long detailed volume and is read by few except investment bankers and large institutional investors. The fact that the buyer would have to take the initiative and secure a copy also detracts from its use.

Realizing the shortcomings of the registration statement, the Securities Act requires that a *prospectus* must be given to every buyer or person solicited either before or at the time of sale of the securities. This prospectus must contain a summary of the more important provisions of the registration statement. It is the desire of the Commission that the prospectus be in such an abbreviated form that people will read it, but considering the requirements, the fear of corporate officials and bankers that they may be held liable for failure to state the whole truth, causes them to be somewhat wordy. The result is that many prospective buyers do not read the document.

A copy of the prospectus must be filed with the Commission at the same time that the registration statement is filed. Since circulation is given to the prospectus, every effort is made to indicate that the Commission by approving the registration statement and prospectus has not put its stamp of approval on the security issue. To that end the law requires that the following statement be written in bold-face type on the front page of every prospectus.

> THESE SECURITIES HAVE NOT BEEN APPROVED OR DISAPPROVED BY THE SECURITIES AND EXCHANGE COMMISSION. .... (insert name of issuer) has registered the securities by filing certain information with the Commission. The Commission has not passed on the merits of any securities registered with it. IT IS A CRIMINAL OFFENSE TO REPRESENT THAT THE COMMISSION HAS APPROVED THESE SECURITIES OR HAS MADE ANY FINDINGS THAT THE STATEMENTS IN THIS PROSPECTUS OR IN THE REGISTRATION STATEMENT ARE CORRECT.

In the case of securities that must be registered, the issuer and bankers must be careful not to make any offers of sale or solicitation of orders without accompanying them with a prospectus drawn up in proper form. Some announcement or advertisement which was not intended by the issuer or banker to be a prospectus or offer to sell, might be construed by the Commission to be such an offer or prospectus. The Securities Act of 1933 defines a prospectus as follows:

> The term "prospectus" means any prospectus, notice, circular, advertisement, letter, or communication, written or by radio, which offers any security for sale; except that (a) a communication shall not be deemed a prospectus if it is proved that prior to or at the same time with such communication a written prospectus meeting the requirements of section 10 was sent or given to the person to whom the communication was made, by the person making such communication or his principal, and (a) a notice, circular, advertisement, letter, or communication in respect of a security shall not be deemed to be a prospectus if it states from whom a written prospectus meeting the requirements of section 10, may be obtained and, in addition, does no more than identify the security, state the price thereof, and state by whom orders will be executed.[3]

ADVERTISING REGULATED. Under the Securities Act of 1933 and its administration by the SEC, the prospectus must be given to anyone to whom an offer to sell a registered security is made. Because of this the issuing company or investment bankers could not make an offer to sell the securities through advertising. In the past only an announcement of the issue could be made in newspaper advertising. This was referred to as a "tombstone advertisement," or "tombstone prospectus." Such an advertisement could contain only the type of securities being sold, the amount, the price, and the names of the dealers. It was necessary to state in the advertisement that it was not an offer to sell or solicitation of an offer to buy, that an offering is made only by the prospectus, and the names of the dealers from whom copies of the prospectus could be obtained. This advertisement could be made only after the effective date of the security registration.

In 1955, however, the SEC liberalized the rules to permit a limited form of advertising for new issues both before and after the effective date of the registration. Now the advertisement may give a brief description of the offering company's business, information relating to the pricing and underwriting of the issue, and a statement whether the offering is being made by the issuing company itself or in behalf of stockholders who wish to sell.

[3] Sec. 2 (10).

Penalties Provided by the Act. In order to induce full compliance with the provisions of the law, the Securities Act of 1933 provides for a number of penalties in event of violation of any part of the statute.

We have already referred to the fact that the Commission may issue a *stop order* if it believes the issuer has not complied with the provision of the law. In addition, if the Commission believes that any person has or is about to violate the law it may apply to the federal courts for an *injunction* against the violation. The Commission may also give evidence of the violation to the Attorney General who is authorized to institute criminal proceedings against the violator.

The Act provides for both *criminal* and *civil penalties* in event of violation of the law. In regard to the first, the law provides that any person who willfully violates the Act or the rules of the Commission, or any person who willfully makes any untrue statement or omission in a registration statement is guilty of a crime and may, upon conviction, be fined not more than $5,000 or imprisoned for not more than 5 years, or both.

The *civil* liabilities are a little more complicated. If the seller fails to file a registration statement or if the contents of the prospectus are not correct, or if the prospectus or communication includes an untrue statement of a material fact, or omission of a material fact, he can be made to return the purchase price of the security, or if the purchaser has sold the security, the latter can recover damages from the seller. It is to be noted that the penalties for these particular violations of the law run in favor of only the immediate purchaser. The purchaser would be unable to collect if it could be proved that he had knowledge of the untruth or omission. The seller could escape the liability if he could prove that he did not know of the untruth or omission and "in the exercise of reasonable care" could not have known of it.

The second type of civil liability arises when the registration statement contains an untrue statement of a material fact, or an omission of a material fact. This is a liability for damages for the difference between the amount paid for the security and (1) the value at the time of suit, or (2) the price at which the security was disposed of in the market before suit, or (3) the price at which the security was disposed of after suit but before judgment, if the damages are less than under (1). The damages may, however, be reduced if the defendant can prove that the depreciation in the value of the security was caused by something other than the defect in the registration statement. The liability which we have just stated, in contrast to the one stated in the paragraph immediately preceding, runs in favor of not only the immediate purchaser, but all subsequent purchasers as well. Of course, if it can be proved that the purchaser knew of the defect in the registration statement, he would be unable to collect.

The original Securities Act permitted the purchaser to collect damages even if he did not rely on the misstatement or omission at the time of making the purchase. An amendment made in 1934, however, provides that if the purchaser acquired the securities after the issuer has published an earnings statement covering a period of at least twelve months beginning after the effective date of the registration statement, he would have to prove that he relied on the untruth or omission in the registration statement in purchasing the securities.

In order to enforce the civil liability the purchaser must bring action within one year after the discovery of the untruth or omission, but not more than three years after the securities were offered to the public or were sold.

Persons Liable Under the Act. In case of failure to file a registration statement, or failure to give a prospectus, or in the event the prospectus contains untruths or omissions of material facts, the law provides that the person who sells the security is liable. This would include the issuer and investment bankers.

When the suit is because of untrue statements or omissions of material facts in the registration statement, the following are liable:

1. The issuer
2. Every person who signs the registration statement
3. Every director who was serving as such at the time the statement was filed, or who with his consent was named in the registration statement as about to become a director
4. Every accountant, engineer, appraiser, or "any other person whose profession gives authority to a statement made by him, who has with his consent been named as having prepared or certified any part of the registration statement, or as having prepared or certified any report or valuation which is used in connection with the registration statement, report, or valuation, which purports to have been prepared or certified by him"
5. Every underwriter

In connection with the liability of the underwriter, he is liable for only that part of the issue which he underwrote.

Avoidance of Liability. We have mentioned above that liability can be avoided if it can be proved that the decline in the value of the securities was due to some cause other than the untruth or omission in the registration statement.

Every person except the issuer may avoid liability by proving any one of the following:

1. That he resigned from the office or relationship stated in the registration statement prior to the effective date of the statement, and that he notified the Commission of such resignation
2. That he had no knowledge of the particular part of the registration statement under consideration becoming effective, and that after becoming aware of the true facts he resigned, notified the Commission, and gave reasonable public notice that the registration statement became effective without his knowledge
3. That after reasonable investigation he had reasonable grounds to believe, and did believe at the time the registration statement became effective that the statements made were true and that there were no omissions of material facts

In regard to "reasonable investigation" and "reasonable grounds to believe" stated under (3) above, the original Act defined the standard of reasonableness as that "required of a person occupying a fiduciary relationship." Criticism of holding those responsible to such a high degree of care resulted in the Act being amended in 1934, to provide that "the standard of reasonableness shall be that required of a prudent man in the management of his own property."

Value of Civil Liability Provisions. There have been some criticisms of the civil liability provisions of the Securities Act. There have been relatively few instances of security buyers bringing action, and in those that have arisen, only a small percentage have resulted in convictions. This, however, may be an indication of the value of the liability provisions. Because of the possibility of their imposition, issuing corporations, their directors and officers, and investment bankers have been especially careful to meet the requirements of the law.

One weakness of liability penalties of this kind is that the purchaser must first take the initiative before these civil liabilities will be invoked. Most investors do not read the registration statement or the prospectus, and therefore they have no knowledge of any violation in the law. Furthermore, even if they suspect a violation, they are not apt to instigate action. The average person avoids law suits because of the time, trouble, and possible expense that may be connected with it. Security holders are usually unorganized and individual holders rarely start any action.

Evaluation of the Securities Act of 1933. At the time of the enactment of the Securities Act there was a great need for more available information in connection with security issues which were sold in interstate commerce. In fact, undoubtedly there would have been much less money lost in the 1920's and immediately after the stock market crash in 1929, if we had had such a law on the books then.

There was considerable criticism of the law immediately before and after its adoption, particularly on the part of corporate officials and investment bankers. They were afraid of the liability provisions of the law. They were particularly frightened of the liability for the omission of any material fact. It was feared that the Commission might determine whether something was a material fact in the light of events at the time of a suit rather than at the time the registration statement was filed, or the prospectus issued. In view of subsequent events, it seems that their fears were unfounded.

Another criticism was the relatively high cost of registering an issue. The routine has been simplified somewhat since the adoption of the Act, and the limit of issues that can be exempt by the Commission has been raised from $100,000 to $300,000. Nevertheless, the cost involved in meeting the requirements of the Act are considerable, particularly in the case of relatively small issues.

The Act was never intended as a means of preventing the sale of speculative securities. So long as the registration statement and prospectus show all the facts and omit no material facts, the issue will be approved, no matter how speculative it may be. Investors will continue to lose money by the purchase of speculative securities. Moreover, losses arise from many things other than untruths and omissions in the registration statement and prospectus.

The issuing company learns many valuable things about itself because of the necessity of preparing the registration statement. This may also indirectly benefit the investor. Investment dealers who buy the securities from the underwriters and sell them to the public have a means of ascertaining much more about the securities than was possible before the adoption of the Act. Institutional investors, particularly those who buy large quantities of the securities, can determine the quality of the issue by an examination of the registration statement.

The average investor also has the information available to study the particular issue if he so desires. But as mentioned before, most people pay little attention to the registration statement and prospectus. Nevertheless, the issuing company and the underwriters are careful to conform to the requirements of the law because of the chance of liability. The requirements of the prospectus, coupled with the desire on the part of the issuer and bankers to avoid liability, results in the prospectus being too lengthy to be read by very many investors. Perhaps a shortening of the prospectus would be a step in the right direction.

There can be no doubt that the Securities Act of 1933 has resulted in the elimination of many fraudulent issues that would otherwise have been put on the market. Most of these do not come to light now since promoters would realize their inability to get the issue registered. In other instances, when they attempt to get them qualified, the Commission issues stop orders.

Questions

1. Distinguish between investment bankers and commercial bankers.
2. What services are performed for industry by investment bankers?
3. What are the possible advantages to the investor of having an investment banker take over the sale of securities?
4. Distinguish between the following kinds of agreements made between investment bankers and the issuer of securities: (a) firm commitment, (b) stand-by commitment, (c) best-effort commitment.
5. Describe the procedure followed in the organization and operation of a syndicate to handle the sale of an issue of securities.
6. Distinguish between the divided and undivided account syndicates.
7. Do you think the investor is helped or harmed by the price pegging activities of a syndicate? Explain.
8. Indicate the advantages and disadvantages of competitive bidding for securities both to the issuer and the investment banker. What type of securities are commonly sold in this way?
9. Indicate the advantages and disadvantages of private placement of securities to the various parties concerned and to investors in general.
10. Distinguish between investment bankers and securities brokers. May the same firm carry on the functions of both? Do investment bankers handle listed or unlisted securities? Explain.
11. What types of security transactions may take place in your state that are exempt from the securities laws?
12. Indicate the circumstances which led up to the adoption of the Securities Act of 1933. (Hereafter referred to as the Act.)
13. What are the principal provisions of the Act?
14. (a) What securities are exempt from registration under the Act? (b) What types of securities transactions are exempt from the Act?
15. Can the Securities and Exchange Commission (SEC) refuse registration of a particular security issue simply because it believes the issue to be too speculative? Explain.
16. Does the fact that the SEC has approved the registration of a particular security issue indicate in any way that it believes the securities are of good investment grade?
17. (a) Who may be held liable for the violation of the provisions of the Act? (b) What is the nature of the liability?

18. Do you believe that because of the Act the average investor has more information relating to the particular security being sold than if the legislation had not been enacted?

19. Do you know of any way to get the investor to read the prospectus?

20. What changes have been recommended in the Act?

Problems

1. The following is a balance sheet of the All-Metal Manufacturing Co. as of June 30, 19-1:

Assets		*Liabilities and Net Worth*	
Plant	$4,000,000	Capital stock	$6,000,000
Machinery	2,000,000	Less: Treasury stock	1,000,000
Inventory	1,300,000	Outstanding	5,000,000
Receivables	800,000	Surplus	3,000,000
Cash	200,000	Payables	300,000
Total	$8,300,000	Total	$8,300,000

The stock has a par value of $100 per share and is selling in the market for $160 per share. Mr. Gary owns 1,000 shares of this stock. The directors voted to sell 10,000 shares of the authorized but unissued stock to a syndicate composed of Coon, Kobe & Co., Pillin Deed, and the City National Co., at $140 a share. The syndicate was to buy the stock outright and attend to all details in connection with its sale. Mr. Gary objected to this sale to the syndicate, but the company nevertheless closed the deal. (a) Was Mr. Gary justified in objecting? Can he do anything about it? Explain fully. (b) If it had been 10,000 shares of treasury stock that were sold to the bankers instead of the unissued stock, would your answer to (a) above be different? Explain. (c) If the 10,000 shares of unissued stock had been exchanged for the Western plant of the Eastern Steel Co., would Mr. Gary have any recourse? Explain. (d) If the stock had been purchased by the bankers at a price that enabled them to pay all expenses in connection with the sale and make only a reasonable profit, would Mr. Gary be justified in objecting? Explain.

2. Mr. Flatbush of Kalamazoo stated in a recent article that he preferred to buy his securities in the market sometime after the original sale rather than from the investment bankers at the time the syndicate was selling the securities.. Why do you think Mr. Flatbush might prefer this means of purchase?

3. The following apply to the laws in your state pertaining to the sale of securities: (a) Must security issues to be sold in your state be registered with a state commission? (b) What types of security issues are exempt from registration? (c) What must be done to register an issue? (d) Does the commission have the authority to decide whether the particular issue can be sold? Explain. (e) Are security dealers and brokers required to have a license?

Chapter 19

BUYING AND SELLING LISTED SECURITIES

SECURITY MARKETS. In preceding chapters we have been concerned with the original distribution of securities, that is, the sale by the issuing corporation directly to the public or through the medium of investment bankers. It is through this primary distribution of securities that corporations secure their new capital.

Corporations, however, would find it difficult to sell their securities if there did not exist a market where investors could sell their securities at any time for a fair value. The resale by investors of securities which have already been outstanding is referred to as the *secondary distribution.* The places in which the securities are sold, or the channels through which they are sold, are called security *markets.* These are of two kinds, (1) the over-the-counter market, and (2) the organized security exchanges.

OVER-THE-COUNTER MARKET. Although our primary interest in this chapter is in listed securities, it is only proper that we state first briefly the nature of the over-the-counter market. In order to enclose everything that should be included, we can say that the sale of securities by any method other than on the organized security exchanges is considered to be in the over-the-counter market. Since so much of the business of this type is now done over the telephone, it has been said that a more fitting name for this market would be the "over-the-telephone" market.

The over-the-counter market in this country is made up of some 2,500 securities houses and over 1,500 branch offices that buy and sell almost any recognized security whether it is listed on some security exchange or not. Quotations on more than 25,000 over-the-counter securities are published annually. This compares with about 3,000 securities which are listed on the exchanges. In some instances the houses merely act as brokers and collect a fee for the execution of a security transaction. In other cases they will take title to the securities purchased and resell them to other dealers or to the public. When the dealers take title to the securities the sale will be said to take place by negotiation. The dealer may be willing either to buy or sell a particular security, and he will therefore quote a bid-and-ask price. These constitute the price at which he will buy and the price at which he will sell respectively. A prospective customer, however, may be successful in getting the spread between the two narrowed by "negotiation" with the dealer.

More security issues are to be found, and a greater dollar value of sales occurs in the over-the-counter market than on the organized security exchanges. All state and municipal bonds are sold only in the over-the-counter market. Although some U. S. government obligations are listed on the New York Stock Exchange, the bulk of the business in them is done in the over-the-counter market. Other securities which are either sold entirely in this market, or at least the greater part of the business is done in this market, include the following: open-end investment companies, bank- and insurance-company stocks, railroad-equipment obligations, serial bonds, real estate securities, and in general the securities of small or medium-sized corporations.

Although our primary interest here is in the secondary distribution of securities, it should be stated that many of the dealers in the over-the-counter market are the same firms that handle the original or primary distribution of securities that are sold through investment bankers.[1]

The stock exchanges

ORGANIZED SECURITY EXCHANGES. An organized security exchange is a private organization formed and operated to facilitate the purchase and sale of securities by its members. A security exchange itself does not buy or sell any securities. The bulk of the business done on a security exchange is performed by brokers executing orders for their customers.

The membership on an exchange is more or less fixed, and if a person wants to become a member, it will be necessary to purchase a membership from a member who wants to sell. Bid-and-ask prices are kept on file at the exchanges for those who are interested, and may also be found in the financial press. Approval of the particular

[1] For additional material on the over-the-counter market see *Understanding the Over-The-Counter Securities Market,* Securities Publishing Division of Commodity Research Bureau, Inc., New York, N. Y., and "National Association of Securities Dealers," by Homer V. Cherrington, *Harvard Business Review,* November, 1949, pp. 741–59.

exchange, however, is necessary before any person will be admitted as a member. Only members are permitted to trade on the floor of the exchanges. Any orders to buy or sell listed securities that are received by a member of an exchange must be executed on the floor of the exchange.

There are 14 exchanges in this country that are registered with the Securities and Exchange Commission as a "national securities exchange," and four others that are exempt from registration.[2] The largest of the registered exchanges is the New York Stock Exchange, and the second largest is the American Stock Exchange (formerly the New York Curb Exchange). Expressing it in round numbers, approximately 85 per cent of the market value of all stocks sold on national securities exchanges is sold on the New York Stock Exchange, and about 8 per cent is handled on the American Stock Exchange. Thus the balance of about 7 per cent is the amount that is handled by all the other exchanges located outside New York City.

Although the exchanges are referred to as "stock exchanges," even in their formal titles, most of them also have bonds listed.[3] But the bulk of the trading done on the exchanges is in stocks.

THE NEW YORK STOCK EXCHANGE. Due to the relative importance of the New York Stock Exchange, we will describe the nature of its organization and operation. The American Stock Exchange will be mentioned only with respect to its differences from the New York Stock Exchange (which is often referred to as the "Big Board").

The New York Stock Exchange was founded in 1792. It is organized as a voluntary association, and its constitution provides for 1375 members. (The Exchange has bought back and retired nine of the memberships.) Up until 1953, only individuals were eligible for membership, but in that year the constitution was amended to

[2] The following are the 14 registered exchanges: American Stock Exchange, Boston Stock Exchange, Chicago Board of Trade, Cincinnati Stock Exchange, Detroit Stock Exchange, Midwest Stock Exchange, New Orleans Stock Exchange, New York Stock Exchange, Pacific Coast Stock Exchange, Philadelphia-Baltimore Stock Exchange, Pittsburgh Stock Exchange, Salt Lake Stock Exchange, San Francisco Mining Exchange, and Spokane Stock Exchange.

The four exempt stock exchanges are as follows: Colorado Springs Stock Exchange, Honolulu Stock Exchange, Richmond Stock Exchange, and Wheeling Stock Exchange.

The Philadelphia and Baltimore exchanges were consolidated in 1949, with the principal office now in Philadelphia. The Midwest Stock Exchange (located in Chicago) was also formed in 1949, by the consolidation of exchanges located in Chicago, Cleveland, St. Louis, and Minneapolis-St. Paul. The Los Angeles and San Francisco exchanges were combined in 1957, to form the Pacific Coast exchange.

[3] About 97 per cent of the bond trading done on the various exchanges is handled by the New York Stock Exchange. The greatest volume of bond trading, however, takes place in the over-the-counter market.

permit corporations to own memberships.[4] Memberships on the Exchange are sometimes referred to as "seats."

The number of security issues listed on the New York Stock Exchange varies from month to month. There are approximately 1,500 stock issues and about 1,000 bond issues listed. Strict standards must be met by a security in order to be listed. Only large, strong companies that have established earning power are eligible. The total market value of the stock or the net tangible assets must be at least $8 million, and the annual earnings must amount to approximately $1 million. The company must have a minimum of from 1,500 to 1,800 shareholders, and the Exchange prefers that there be a good distribution of the shareholders by states. Shareholders of less than 100 shares are heavily discounted. The total number of shares outstanding must be at least 400,000 shares, exclusive of concentrated holdings. The company is required to maintain a transfer agent and registrar in the Borough of Manhattan.

The company whose stock is listed must pay an initial fee varying according to the number of shares, but the minimum fee is $2,000. An annual fee must also be paid for a period of 15 years after listing. The amount of this fee also varies according to the number of shares, with a minimum of $500 a year.

Once a security is listed, the issuing company cannot voluntarily remove the security without the approval of 66⅔ per cent in amount of the securities. But even if this approval is obtained, the security will not be delisted if 10 per cent or more of the individual security holders disapprove of its delisting. The New York Stock Exchange, however, may take the initiative in having a security delisted because of its being called in by the company, or exchanged for another security, or because the issuing company is hopelessly insolvent and its securities have little value. The Exchange may delist the common stock if it is held by less than 250 stockholders, after substantially discounting odd-lots; if the common shares outstanding, exclusive of concentrated or family holdings, total less than 30,000; if the total market value of the common shares, exclusive of concentrated or family holdings, is less than $500,000; and if the market value of the total common stock or net tangible assets applicable to that stock is $2,000,000 or less and the average net earnings after taxes for the last three years is $200,000 or less.

ADVANTAGES OF LISTING TO THE ISSUING CORPORATION. The advantages of listing apply to listing on any of the national securities exchanges, but they apply with particular emphasis to the New York

[4] As of January 1, 1956, there were 25 corporate members.

Stock Exchange. As has been said before, the issuing corporation cannot initially sell an issue of securities on or through the New York Stock Exchange. The issue must first be sold to the public either directly by the issuer, or through investment bankers, and adequate distribution of the security obtained before it is eligible for listing. The sales of the company's shares that take place on the exchange thereafter represent sales made by the company's shareholders to other persons or companies.

From what has just been said the reader may conclude that listing benefits the shareholders and prospective shareholders of the company rather than the issuing company itself. Actually both benefit. The advantages of listing to the issuing company are as follows:

1. *Wider market.* If a security issue is listed on the NYSE it will enjoy a much wider market than otherwise. The wider market may give stability to the security and usually result in a higher price.

2. *Sale of new securities facilitated.* If at the time a new issue is being sold, publicity is given to the fact that application to list the securities will be made, this will improve the market and enable the company to float the new issue at a lower interest or dividend rate than would otherwise be the case.

3. *Advertising value.* Publicity connected with the listing probably improves also the market for the company's products.

4. *Indication of strength.* The fact that a company's stock is listed on the NYSE is an indication that, at the time of listing, the company was a large and successful one with bright hopes for the future. It should be realized, however, that some time after listing it may decline in importance.

Advantages of Listing to the Investor. Listing a stock on the New York Stock Exchange has certain advantages to the shareholders or prospective shareholders of the company. The principal advantages are as follows:

1. *Assurance that NYSE standards have been met.* The company must be large, must have established earning power and the future must appear favorable. Furthermore, it is an indication of a good distribution of the stock. The investor is assured that the securities have been legally issued, that the stock certificates are probably not counterfeited, and that there will probably not be an overissue of stock certificates.

2. *Stock will sell at a higher price.* Due to the wider market for the stock and the publicity given the company, it is probable that a shareholder can get a better price when selling his securities than if they had not been listed. It should be realized, however, that for the same reason, a higher price will probably have to be paid for the securities.

3. *Ready and continuous market.* People owning securities which are not listed may be unable to sell them at a particular time or only at a relatively low price. If, on the other hand the stock is listed, the investor knows that he may dispose of his securities at any time, and that he is getting the best price obtainable at the particular time.

4. *Higher collateral value.* Bankers are more willing to lend money on the collateral of listed securities, and a higher percentage of the market value of the security can be borrowed. This follows from the fact that the bankers know that if the loan is not repaid, they can at any time sell the collateral at the best obtainable price.

5. *Assurance of adequate information.* The investor in listed securities has the assurance that, due to the requirements of the NYSE, adequate information about the issuing company and its securities will be available at all times.

6. *Reasonable commissions.* The NYSE sets the minimum commissions that may be charged by its members to buy and sell listed securities. In practice these have become the maximum rates that are charged by members. If listed securities are purchased or sold through a nonmember, however, higher rates may be charged since the nonmember will have to pay the regular commission rates to a member to execute the order. Many nonmembers, however, charge only the NYSE rates. They handle the orders as a service to their customers, hoping thereby to obtain also profitable business.

Composition of NYSE Membership. The "seats" on the New York Stock Exchange are owned by several different classes of members, described below.

1. *Commission brokers.* Approximately 635 members of the Exchange are classed as *commission brokers.* These are members of brokerage firms who execute orders on the floor of the Exchange for their customers and charge for it the regular commission rates.

Partners of commission-broker members must agree to abide by the rules of the Exchange and are referred to as *allied* members. They, however, possess none of the rights of the regular members.

2. *Specialists.* About 348 members of the Exchange are *specialists.*[5] As the title would indicate, these members specialize in the execution of orders of one or more different stocks. They act as brokers for other brokers, such as commission brokers. The latter commonly give the specialists orders which they have that are to be executed only at prices that are somewhat far away from the market prices existing at the time. Specialists may also buy and sell stocks on their own account. They are subject to strict rules of the Securities and Exchange Commission which were designed to prevent the specialists from taking advantage of their customers for their own personal profit.

3. *"Two-dollar brokers."* The so-called *"two-dollar brokers"* also execute orders for other brokers, particularly when the latter are too busy to handle the orders, and they may trade on their own account. They are also called *floor brokers.* There are 196 members of this kind. They formerly received a commission from the broker for whom they were executing the order of $2 per 100 shares of stock, and this accounted for the title, but rates have since been changed and now average about $3 per 100 shares.

4. *Odd-lot dealers and brokers.* In the case of most stocks listed on the NYSE the smallest unit that can be bought or sold on the floor is 100 shares. Since many people want to invest in less than this amount, several *odd-lot* firms have developed which will deal in units of less than 100 shares. Representatives of these firms hold 17 memberships on the NYSE. In order to help them carry on their business, these odd-lot houses have 83 stock exchange members who act as "associate brokers" and execute their orders on a commission basis. Thus, the odd-lot dealers and brokers account for a total of 100 memberships. More will be said about odd-lots later in the chapter.

5. *Floor traders.* Floor traders buy and sell stocks on their own account on the floor of the Exchange, and do not execute orders for other persons. In recent years their number has diminished, and today there are only 22 memberships of the Exchange who are in this group.

6. *Bond brokers and dealers.* Bond trading is separated from stock trading on the floor of the Exchange. Those specializing in bonds may act as dealers and buy and sell bonds on their own account, or they may act as brokers in executing orders for other per-

[5] The number of each type of Exchange member stated in this chapter is as of the beginning of 1956.

sons. There are 30 such members on the NYSE. (These are included in the various types of members stated above.)[6]

AMERICAN STOCK EXCHANGE. It was pointed out before that the American Stock Exchange is the second largest exchange in the United States. Until January of 1953, it was called the New York Curb Exchange, and many today still refer to it as the "Curb." Much of the discussion above relating to the advantages of listing, the different types of members, etc., apply with equal force to the American Stock Exchange. The organization and operation of the latter are patterned very closely after the New York Stock Exchange, so we will merely indicate the differences between the two exchanges.

The American Stock Exchange is newer and smaller than the New York Stock Exchange. The NYSE really has only one class of members (although partners of members are called "allied" members). The American Exchange has 499 *regular members* who carry on their business in a manner similar to that of the members of the NYSE. A great majority of these members are members of firms that have one or more memberships on the NYSE. In addition to the regular members, the American Exchange permits an unlimited number of *associate members.* At the present time there are 335 associate members. These members are not permitted to trade on the floor of the Exchange, but they may have their business transacted by regular members at a greatly reduced schedule of commission rates. Most of the associate memberships are held by persons who are members of the NYSE.

Trading on the American Exchange takes place in both *listed* and *unlisted* stocks. Listed stocks must meet the standards set up by the Exchange before they are accepted. Unlisted stocks, on the other hand, are those which have been admitted for trading upon application of a member of the Exchange. The issuing corporation has nothing to say about it, neither does it pay any listing fee. No new stocks have been admitted for unlisted trading privileges since March 1, 1934, because the Securities and Exchange Act of 1934 virtually prohibited any addition to the list. Of a total of 815 stock issues traded in on the American Exchange, 527 are fully listed and 288 have unlisted trading privileges.

The listing requirements of the American Exchange are not as stringent as those of the NYSE. The American will list stocks of

[6] The above stated types account for 1,301 memberships. Nine memberships were bought back by the Exchange in 1953 and canceled. As of January 1, 1956, 11 memberships were in the names of deceased members, and 54 members were inactive.

relatively new companies even if they have no established earning power if it appears that they are soundly financed and have good prospects for the future. The American Exchange prefers that the company have assets of at least $1 million, and that there be at least 100,000 shares of stock publicly distributed in the hands of at least 500 shareholders. The American Exchange thus will list stocks of newer, smaller, and more speculative companies than will the NYSE. Many of the companies whose stocks have been listed on the American Exchange, however, have developed into large and seasoned companies, and many of them have in the past been accepted for listing by the New York Stock Exchange. The American Stock Exchange has more foreign issues, particularly Canadian stocks, listed than does the NYSE. The initial listing fees are also lower on the American Exchange, and there is no annual fee.

Bonds are also traded in on the American in a manner similar to the New York Stock Exchange. Of the 78 different bond issues on the American Exchange, however, only 21 are fully listed and 57 have unlisted trading privileges.

Regulation of the securities markets

SECURITIES EXCHANGE ACT OF 1934. Many of the practices carried on in the securities business in the past, particularly in the 1920's, were contrary to the best interest of investors, but it took the stock market crash of 1929 and the depression of the early 1930's to force action designed to improve the situation. One thing that was needed was the regulation of the issuance of new securities. This was accomplished by the Securities Act of 1933, which was discussed in the preceding chapter. The other need was for the regulation of the resale of securities after they had been issued, and the regulation of the stock exchanges and other markets through which these sales and purchases took place. This was accomplished by the enactment by Congress of the Securities Exchange Act of 1934.

The Act also provided for the creation of the Securities and Exchange Commission whose job it is to administer the Securities Acts. Later it was given the authority to also administer the following: the Public Utility Holding Company Act of 1935, the Trust Indenture Act of 1939, the Investment Company Act of 1940, and the Investment Advisers Act of 1940.

REGISTRATION OF EXCHANGES. The Securities Exchange Act of 1934 requires all national securities exchanges to register with the Securities and Exchanges Commission. Several local exchanges have been exempt from this requirement. Registration involves the filing of a considerable amount of detail relating to the exchange and its rules and regulations, and makes the exchange subject to the provisions of the Act and the rules and regulations of the Commission.

The exchange must pay to the Commission an annual fee equal to 1/500 of one per cent of the aggregate dollar amount of the sales of registered securities. The exchanges pass this fee along to the seller of securities.

Registration of Securities. Members of the exchanges are not permitted to buy or sell any security listed on the exchange unless the security has been registered with the Commission. The company whose security is listed on a registered exchange must therefore file the information required with the Commission. At the present time the data required by the Commission for registration are about the same as the NYSE requires for listing the security.

The following types of securities, however, are exempt from the requirement of registration: (1) direct obligations of the United States government, (2) obligations issued or guaranteed by corporations in which the government has an interest, (3) direct or guaranteed obligations of a state or political subdivision thereof, and (4) securities exempted by the Commission.

Margin Requirements. The Act orginally set the margin requirement for the purchase of securities, but the power to decide margins later was transferred to the Federal Reserve Board. The enforcement of the minimum margin requirements, however, is left with the Commission. More will be said on margin buying later in the chapter.

Manipulation Prohibited. Before the Act was passed, the New York Stock Exchange prohibited certain types of manipulation, but the legislation added to these and provided severe penalties for their violation. In general the Act prohibits any practice or device which interferes with a free and orderly market. False or misleading statements relating to the securities are prohibited. The same is true of any artificial means of causing the price of a security to rise or fall. The Commission is given the power to decide the conditions and the circumstances under which price stabilization in connection with the issuance of new securities may take place. The Commission also has the authority to prohibit or regulate short selling.

Segregation. Many of the members of a stock exchange act as broker in executing orders for other brokers and the public and also as dealer in buying and selling on their own account for their own personal profit. It has been felt by many that some of these members have taken advantage of the buying and selling public for their own personal advantage. Without proper regulation it has been realized that this is possible and that it had been done in the past.

The exchanges have for many years prohibited a member from making a profit as a dealer and getting a brokerage commission on the same transaction. But the Act gives the Commission the authority to compel a member to act at all times only as a dealer, or only as a broker. This is referred to as *segregation.* For example, the Commission could prohibit all floor trading and permit the members of an exchange to act only as a broker and execute orders for others. To date, however, the Commission has not forced segregation, but it has adopted rules and regulations which closely define the trading functions of the floor trader, the specialist, and to some extent the odd-lot dealer.

INFORMATION ON STOCK HOLDINGS. In some instances in the past, directors, and officers of corporations have used their office of trust to profit personally at the expense of the shareholders whom they were supposed to represent. If they expected to pay an extra dividend which was not anticipated by the public, they might quietly buy up the stock prior to the meeting date. Or if they expected to cut the dividend, or pass it entirely, they might sell the company's stock, and even go short.

The Act requires that at the time of registration of the security with the Commission all officers, directors, and persons owning 10 per cent or more of any class of stock file with the Commission the amount of their holdings. Or if anyone comes into this category thereafter, he must file his holdings. Furthermore, the Act requires that all such persons stated above report to the Commission monthly any purchases or sales of their company's stock, within ten days after the close of the calendar month. The Commission releases this information to the press.

SHORT-TERM PROFITS OF INSIDERS. The framers of the Act felt that corporate officers and large stockholders should not be able to profit from short-term speculation in their company's stock. To that end the Act provides that if any director, officer, or person owning 10 per cent or more of any class of stock makes a profit on the sale of his company's stock which he held for a period of only six months or less, a suit may be instigated by the corporation, or a shareholder acting on behalf of the company, to recover the profits for the corporation. It is to be noted that the Act does not prohibit such a profit. It only states that if a short-term profit is made by an insider, it may be recovered *if* suit is brought against the person.

Officers, directors, and shareholders owning 10 per cent or more of any class of stock are also not permitted to sell the company's stock short.

PROXY REGULATIONS. A large percentage of the voting in large corporations is done through proxies. In past years it was not uncommon for the proxy form to contain merely the announcement of the time, place and purpose of the meeting, and the name or names of the person who would act as proxies for the shareholder. By signing the proxy and sending it in to the company, the shareholder gave his proxy the power to vote more or less as he chose.

The Commission, acting under the Securities Exchange Act, has adopted a long list of requirements for the proxy statement. A copy of the proxy must be filed with the Commission ten days before it can be sent out. The following are among the more important provisions that must be included in a proxy sent out for a listed stock.

1. Statement of who is soliciting the proxies and who is paying the cost of the solicitation.
2. If auditors are to be selected at the meeting, or a committee to select the auditors, the names of the auditors or committee nominees must be stated.
3. The names and amounts paid to the directors and the three highest paid officers whose direct remuneration exceeded $30,000 during the previous fiscal year.
4. A list of the nominees for the board of directors showing the total amount of stock owned by each.
5. The direct remuneration paid by the company during the last fiscal year to all directors and officers, without naming them.
6. Space must be provided for the shareholder to vote For or Against the various proposals that will come before the meeting. The proxy may provide, however, that if he does not express himself the vote will be cast in the way indicated.

PERIODIC REPORTS. The Act gives the Commission power to require corporations to file with the Commission and the exchanges such information as may be necessary to keep the registration statement up to date. Annual financial statements are required, and the Commission has power to compel the filing of quarterly statements. These reports are available in the offices of the exchanges and the Commission. The average investor, however, rarely ever would request statements from these offices. The various financial services and the financial press, however, get information from these sources and give publicity to the data.

TERMINATION OF REGISTRATION. The Commission has the power to deny registration of a security issue, or to suspend registration, or to withdraw the security from registration if in its judgment the issuing company has failed to comply with the terms of the Act or the rules and regulations adopted by the Commission. When such action is taken the security can no longer be traded in on the national exchanges. It is, however, preferred by the Commission that the exchanges themselves take the initiative in requesting such action.

OVER-THE-COUNTER MARKETS. Thus far our discussion of the Securities Exchange Act of 1934 has dealt with only the national securities exchanges and the securities that are listed on such exchanges. The Act did not contain specific provisions relating to the over-the-counter market, but it did give the Securities and Exchange Commission the power to make such rules and regulations as it saw fit for the regulation of this segment of the securities market. The Act was amended in 1936 to provide for the registration of all securities brokers and dealers. The Act was further amended in 1938 by the Maloney Act which provided for the formation and registration of associations in the over-the-counter market for the purpose of adopting rules and regulations for the self-government of the business. To date, only one such association has been formed, the National Association of Security Dealers.

The National Association of Security Dealers has drawn up an elaborate body of rules dealing with fair and uniform practices to be followed by its members. Members' markups or commissions must be fair and nondiscriminatory. Price concessions may be made to other members of the organization, but securities dealers who are not members must be charged the same price as is charged the public.

Buying and selling

EASE OF BUYING AND SELLING. It is a very simple matter to buy and sell listed stocks and bonds. Our emphasis will be on stocks, but most of what is said would apply with equal force to bonds. We will assume that the stock is listed on the New York Stock Exchange, but the procedure would be practically the same on any other exchange.

In order to buy stock all that is necessary is to give the order to a stock broker and put up the necessary amount of money. The local broker will wire the order in to his correspondent or home office in New York. This office will immediately telephone the order to the company's telephone clerk on the floor of the exchange. The clerk will call the company's floor man (odd-lot orders will be explained later) and give him the order. The latter will go to the "post" at which the particular stock is sold, and, if it is a market order, buy the stock at the lowest price obtainable. A confirmation of the purchase will be sent back to the buyer. All of what has just been described (with the possible exception of the confirmation) takes place in a matter of only a few minutes.

TYPES OF ORDERS. There are several different types of orders that a person may give in buying and selling stocks and each have their advantages and disadvantages. We will discuss only the more common type of orders.

Market orders. A *market order* to buy is executed immediately at the lowest price obtainable. A market-sell order will also be executed immediately, at the highest price obtainable. When a brokerage firm's representative on the floor of the exchange receives a market order to buy a particular stock, he will go to the post at which that stock is traded and ask the specialist what the market is in that stock. The specialist may say "30 to ¼." That means he will buy the stock at 30, or sell it at 30¼. The purchaser's broker will then probably bid 30⅛ for the stock. If no one will sell it at that price, he will then buy it from the specialist, or whoever made the quotation, at 30¼. If this had been a sell order, the broker would have tried to sell the stock at 30⅛, and if he could not do so, he would then let it go for 30.

The advantage of a market order is that you are sure of getting it executed immediately. Since there are always bid (buying) and ask (selling) quotations on all stocks, you can always buy or sell immediately if you are willing to buy or sell at the "market." This is of importance if you are buying in a rapidly advancing market, or selling in a fast falling market. (Markets fall faster than they advance, so the sell market is used more commonly than the buy market order). The disadvantage of the market order is that you may pay more for the stock, and you may get less for it, than if you had specified a price at which you wanted the order executed.

Limited orders. A *limited order* is one that specifies a price at which the order is to be executed. But it is the broker's duty to get a better price than that specified if it is possible to do so. Comparing this with the example of the market order stated above, a person may give the broker an order to buy the stock at 29¾. The floor representative of the firm would ask the specialist the market in the particular stock and if he replied, as in the above example,

"30 to ¼," the broker would know that he could not buy the stock then at 29¾, since the specialist had been bidding 30. So, the broker would probably turn the order over to the specialist who would record it in his book. If the market later declined to the point where the stock could be bought for 29¾ or less, the order would be executed.

Before putting in a limited order the purchaser or seller may ask for the market on the stock, and his broker would wire through to the exchange and get the bid and ask prices (there is no charge for this service). The limited-buy order would then be put in below the market (below the ask price, or even below the bid price, as in the example just given). The limited-sell order would be put in at a price higher than the bid price (or perhaps even higher than the ask price). For example, a limited-sell order might be put in at 30⅛, or higher. The ordinary fluctuations of the market during the day or week may lower or raise the price of the stock to the point where the limited order can be executed.

The advantage of the limited order is that you may pay somewhat less, and get somewhat more, than if a market order had been put in. The disadvantage of the limited order is that you may never (or at least within a given period of time) be able to buy or sell the stock. If your order is to buy, the market may keep on advancing indefinitely, and never get down to the price where your order can be executed. After the market has advanced you may put in a new order to buy the stock at a price considerably higher than if you had bought it at the "market" originally. The same reasoning in reverse applies to the limited-sell order.

Unless otherwise specified, a limited order is good only for the day it is given to the broker. If not executed that day, it will automatically be canceled. If you so desire, however, you may make the order "open," in which case it will, if not executed, remain alive after that day. You may specify the period you want the order to remain open, such as "this week," etc.

Stop-loss orders. At the time an order to buy at 29¾ (or at the market) is given, an order to sell the stock at, for example, 27¾ "stop," may also be placed with the broker. Such an order is called a *stop-loss order.* It is given for the purpose of limiting a possible loss. In the above example, if the market on the particular stock should decline to 27¾, the stop-loss order would automatically become a market order to sell at the best obtainable price. If a sale was made at 27¾, probably the stop-loss could be executed at the same price. If so, the most that the purchaser would lose would be two points. If the stop-loss order had not been in, the price might have declined for a considerable length of time, and the purchaser may have eventually sold out at a much greater loss. That is the advantage of the stop-loss order.

The disadvantage of this kind of an order is that the market may get down to 27¾, or slightly below and you would be sold out. The market may then reverse itself and go up many points over a period of months or even years, but you do not profit from this since you have been sold out. Had the stop-loss order not been in, perhaps you would have held on to the stock and profited from the rise. It is obvious that the stop-loss order should not be placed too close to the existing market price, otherwise the ordinary fluctuations in the market might sell you out.

Another precaution should be observed. If the stop-loss order to sell had been put in at 27¾, as in the above example, as the market declined a person might become afraid that he would be sold out, so he might cancel the order, and place a new stop-loss order at 25, for example. A further decline might give rise to a similar fear, with the result that this order might be canceled and a new one placed at, for example, 23½. The same procedure might be continued with further declines. If a person follows this practice, the stop-loss order will be of little benefit. The stop-loss order to *buy* will be discussed in connection with short selling.

BUYING ON MARGIN. When a person purchases stock and pays for it in full he is said to have bought the stock *outright*. Stocks, however, may be bought partly on credit, like many other commodities. The amount which is paid down at the time of purchase is called the *margin*. The Federal Reserve Board fixes the margin required, and at the present time the margin must be at least 50 per cent of the cost of the stock.* Thus if a share of stock is bought at $100 a share, a margin of at least $50 must be deposited with the broker. The broker's correspondent office in New York uses the stock as collateral and borrows from New York banks the other $50 which is needed to buy the stock. The purchaser pays interest to the broker on the amount borrowed, which is called his *debit balance*.

It is obvious that with a given amount of money more shares can be purchased on margin than can be bought outright. For that reason marginal buying results in a larger percentage profit on the money invested, or if the stock goes down, a larger percentage loss

* The margin for buying and selling short was raised to 70 per cent in August, 1958, and to 90 per cent in October, 1958.

is suffered than if the purchase had been outright. Of course, the profit or loss is realized only when the stock is sold.

Some people will overextend themselves in marginal buying. Should the stock decline in price, the margin will be decreased. According to the rules of the New York Stock Exchange, the broker must compel the purchaser to maintain a margin of at least 25 per cent of the existing market price of the stock. In the example given above, if the stock declined 33⅓ per cent, or from $100 to $66⅔, the margin would be decreased by the amount of the decline, or $33⅓. Thus, the margin now would be only $16⅔. The latter amount is just 25 per cent of the existing market price of $66⅔. Therefore, more margin would have to be put up if the market drops further. If the purchaser is unable to do this, the broker will be compelled to sell him out. Considerable sacrifices may have to be made by the purchaser to get additional funds to maintain the margin. If he is unable to secure additional money, he will be sold out at an appreciable loss. Had the purchase been outright, the stock could still be retained even though it had declined in price.

Marginal buying also enables a person to *pyramid* if the stock goes up sufficiently high. The purchaser may use part of the book profits which he makes as additional margin. Against this he may borrow more money and purchase additional shares. This process will result in increased profits *if* the stock continues upward since more shares are held. But if it drops in price, the loss will be greater for the same reason.

Buying and Selling Odd-Lots. Most of the stocks listed on the New York Stock Exchange can be bought or sold on the floor of the Exchange only in units of 100 shares or multiples of 100 shares. To buy some stock like American Telephone and Telegraph at $180 a share, for example, would require an outlay of $18,000 if the purchase is outright, and at least $12,600 if bought on a 70 per cent margin. Most people do not have this amount of money available for the purchase of stocks. Or if they do have that amount, they may not want to invest the entire amount in only one stock.

In order to take care of those who want to buy and sell in quantities of less than 100 shares, several *odd-lot* houses in New York have developed a tremendous business of buying shares in units of 100 shares on the floor of the exchange, and then selling them to the public in any amounts from 1 to 99 shares. They likewise will buy these "odd-lots" from the public, or from the brokers representing the public, and assemble them in units of 100 shares and sell them on the floor. These odd-lot house members or their associate brokers operate on the floor of the exchange. When a broker's telephone clerk gets an odd-lot order he will immediately send it directly to a representative of an odd-lot house for execution.

In addition to paying the regular commissions to his broker, the purchaser or seller of an odd-lot of stocks must pay the odd-lot house *a differential.* This differential is ¼ of a point ($.25) per share for stocks selling at $40 and above, and ⅛ of a point ($.12½) for stocks selling below $40 a share. Following is an illustration of the execution of the three types of orders described above in odd-lots.

In the case of a *market* odd-lot order, the odd-lot house representative will wait until the next sale of a round lot (100 shares or multiple of 100 shares) and then add ¼ or ⅛ to this (depending upon the price of the stock) for a purchase order, and subtract ¼ or ⅛ in the case of a sell order. Thus, if a person put in an order to *buy* 10 shares of A T & T at the market, the odd-lot house would charge the buyer ¼ point (since the stock sells for more than $40 a share) more than the price at which the next sale of a round lot takes place. If the next sale made on the floor after the odd-lot broker received the order was at $180, the odd-lot buyer would be charged $180¼. In addition, the buyer would have to pay the regular commission rates to his own broker. If the order had been to *sell* at the market, the odd-lot house would pay the seller $179¾.

In the case of a *limited* odd-lot order, the odd-lot broker will execute it only when he can make the ¼ or ⅛ differential. Thus, if a person put in an order to *buy* 10 shares of A T & T at $180, the odd-lot house will sell it to him at $180 only when the market (a sale of 100 shares or multiple thereof) goes down to $179¾. If the order had been to *sell* at $180, the odd-lot house will give him that for the stock only when the market goes to $180¼.[7]

The odd-lot stop-loss order will be executed whenever the market (sale of 100 shares or multiples) reaches or goes through the price specified in the order. If the order is to sell, the seller will get ¼ or ⅛ of a point (depending upon the market price of the stock) less than the price of the sale which made the order effective. Thus, if a person put in an order to sell 10 shares of A T & T at 177 "stop," the order would be executed when there was a round lot sale at 177. The odd-lot seller would then receive 176¾.[8]

[7] Slightly different rules are applicable if the effective round-lot sale is more than ¼ of a point (for stocks selling at $40 and above), or ⅛ of a point (for stocks selling below $40) from the price specified in the limited order.

[8] If the price of the stock fell from 178 to 176, for example, without hitting 177, the sale at 176 would make the odd-lot order effective. and the odd-lot seller would receive $175¾.

Stop-loss orders to *buy* will be explained below in connection with short selling. If a person put in an order to buy 10 shares of A T & T at $183 "stop," the order would be executed whenever the stock sold in round lots at $183 or higher. If the stock sold at exactly $183, the odd-lot buyer would pay $183¼.

There are 317 stocks listed on the New York Stock Exchange in which a round-lot is only 10 shares. These are the less active stocks. About 85 per cent of them are preferred stocks. Trading in 233 of the 10 share unit stocks takes place on "Post 30," which is located in one corner of the new trading floor and the other 84 stocks are traded in at the other 18 posts.[9] Odd-lots in these stocks would be any number of shares from 1 to 9. The odd-lot business at Post 30 is handled by two firms of specialists. A higher odd-lot differential is charged for these stocks than for the 100 share round-lot stocks.

If an order is for an amount of stock that represents both a round-lot and an odd-lot, the round-lot will be treated as such, and the remaining shares will be handled as an odd-lot. Thus, in case of the 10 share unit stocks, if an order for 15 shares was received, 10 shares would be handled as a round-lot, and 5 shares would be treated as an odd-lot. In the case of 100 share unit stocks, if the order was for 250 shares, the 200 shares would be handled as a round-lot, and the remaining 50 shares would be considered an odd-lot order.

SHORT SELLING. One of the most confusing phases of stock market activity to the beginning student is the practice of short selling. When a person sells stock which he does not own, he is said to be *short selling* or *selling short*. The most natural question that follows is, how can a person sell something which he does not possess? The answer is simple. He borrows the stock and makes delivery.

The short seller is a "bear." He expects prices or the price of a particular stock to go down. (A "bull" expects them to go up.) Like anyone else, he would like to buy low and sell high. And since he thinks prices are relatively high at the particular time, and that they will be lower later, he would like to sell at the particular time and then do his buying some time later when prices have fallen. The "bull" does or hopes to do the same, but he buys first and sells later. The short seller sells first, and buys later. The following illustrates the steps involved in short selling.

Assume that Mr. *A* believes that A T & T is relatively high at $180. So, he places an order with his broker to sell 100 shares of A T & T short, at $180 or at the market. The broker will require him

[9] These figures are as of September 21, 1955.

(rules adopted by the Federal Reserve Board) to put up a margin of at least 50 per cent, or $9,000. This is to protect the broker if the price goes up. Mr. *A*'s broker sends the order through and the stock is sold to Mr. *B* on the floor, we will assume at $180. Mr. *B*'s broker will pay Mr. *A's* broker the $18,000.

In order to make delivery of the stock to Mr. *B*, Mr. *A*'s broker will borrow 100 shares of A T & T from Mr. *C*. Why will the latter lend his stock? Because Mr. *A*'s broker lends Mr. *C* the $18,000 which was obtained from Mr. *B*. Formerly Mr. *C* would have paid interest on the money borrowed, but in recent years the loan of the money is made without interest for the privilege of getting the stock. Occasionally, people like Mr. *C* will borrow the money without paying interest and in addition will demand a "premium" of $1.00 a day per 100 shares on the loaned stock. When no interest is paid for the money nor premium for the stock, the stock is said to be lending "flat." Mr. *C* can demand his stock back at any time, or Mr. *A* can demand the money back at any time upon proper notice. If Mr. *C* wants the stock back Mr. *A* can buy it in the market, or if he does not believe that it is the right time to buy the stock, he might borrow it from someone else on the same terms that he borrowed it from Mr. *C*, and return it to the latter.

We will assume that A T & T goes down to $175, and that Mr. *A* wants to close out his short sale. Mr. *A* will therefore buy 100 shares of A T & T from Mr. *D* at $175. Mr. *A* will then return the 100 shares to Mr. *C*, and the latter will return the loan of $18,000. Mr. *A* will use $17,500 of this to pay Mr. *D* for the stock. The net result is that Mr. *A* sold the stock for $18,000 and bought it for $17,500, thus making a profit of $500, less commissions and taxes.

Of course the market does not always move in the direction anticipated by the short seller. If the market had started up and had gone to $185, for example, Mr. *A* may have become afraid that it was going to continue to advance, and decided to close out the short sale at that time. If so, he would have to pay a total of $18,500 for the stock, and thus would lose $500, in addition to commissions and taxes.

It should be realized by the short seller that he does not know what his losses may be. When a person buys stock outright, the most that he can lose is the total investment, since the lowest the stock can go is zero. But the short seller stands to lose from the stock advancing in price, and theoretically there is no upper limit to the price which a stock may reach.

The short seller, however, may use the stop-loss order to limit his losses in a manner similar to the buyer. At the time Mr. *A* sold the stock short, he might have put in an order to *buy* the stock at $183 "stop." If the market advanced to this point, the stop-loss order would become a market order to buy at the lowest price obtainable. Perhaps this would be $183. In that event, the maximum loss that would be sustained by Mr. *A* would be $300, plus commissions and taxes. Or, if the stock fell to $175, and Mr. *A* felt that it might go lower, but he was afraid it might start back up, he might put in an order to buy at $177 stop, and thus protect a profit of $300. The stop-loss (to sell) order can, of course, also be used by the ordinary buyer of stocks to protect a profit as well as to limit a loss.

There has been considerable criticism of the practice of short-selling. The Securities and Exchange Commission has the power to regulate it, or to prohibit it. To date they have seen fit only to regulate it. In an attempt to prevent short selling from accelerating a falling market, the SEC adopted a rule that short selling can take place only at a price higher than the last regular sale of the stock, or at the same price as the last sale, provided this price was higher than the last preceding different price. Perhaps this can be illustrated better than explained. Assume that regular sales of the stock occurred in the following order: $180, $179¾, $179¼. A short sale could be made only at a price of $179⅜ or higher. With the stock headed down in this manner the probability is that no one would buy the stock at $179⅜. And someone would have to buy it or otherwise a short sale could not take place. To illustrate the other part of the rule, we will assume the market moved as follows: $180, $179¾, $179⅞, $179⅞. A short sale could be made at $179⅞ (if someone would buy it) or higher, since, although this is the same price as the last regular sale, it is nevertheless higher than the last preceding different price.

BROKERS' COMMISSIONS. Both the buyer and the seller of stocks must pay a commission to the broker for handling the order. The New York Stock Exchange, and the American Stock Exchange set the minimum commission rates that may be charged by members for the execution of orders in listed stocks. If a person buys stocks and holds on to them, he will have only the buying commission to pay. But if he sells, then the commission for selling must be paid.

For purposes of computing the capital gain or loss on the sale of stocks, for income tax purposes, the commissions paid may be added to the cost of the stock, and subtracted from the amount received from the sale of the stock.

Table 30 shows the minimum rates charged by members of the NYSE. These rates became effective May 1, 1958.

TABLE 30

NEW YORK STOCK EXCHANGE COMMISSION RATES ON STOCK

Money Value of 100-Share Unit	*Commission Charge for 100-Share Unit*
If less than $100.00	As mutually agreed (usually 6%)
$100.00 to $399.99	2% of Money Value + $4.00
$400.00 to $2,199.99	1% of Money Value + $8.00
$2,200.00 to $4,999.99	½% of Money Value + $19.00
$5,000.00 and above	1/10% of Money Value + $39.00

The above rates apply to round-lot shares selling at $1.00 per share and above. As noted in the table, the commissions are figured on the money value per 100 shares of stock bought and sold. To illustrate the application of the rates we will assume that a person bought or sold 300 shares of stock at $25 a share. The money value of 100 shares would be $2,500. That is in the $2,200.00 to $4,999.99 bracket, so we take ½% of $2,500, which gives $12.50. To this we would add $19.00. Thus the commission for 100 shares would be $31.50. Since the order was for 300 shares, the total commission would be three times $31.50, or $94.50. The commission on odd-lots is computed the same as for round-lots, and then $2 is deducted. Assume, for example, that a person bought or sold 40 shares (round-lot assumed to be 100 shares) of stock at $25 per share. The money value involved is $1,000. Applying the 1 per cent rate to this we get $10, and adding the $8 gives us $18. From this we subtract $2, which gives us a commission of $16.

The New York Stock Exchange rules provide, however, that notwithstanding the rates stated above, when the amount involved is $100 or more, the maximum commission charges for each transaction of 100 shares (or the odd-lot transaction) shall not be more than $1.50 per share, or $75 per single transaction, but in no case less than $6 per single transaction.

The commission charges are less than indicated above if a person sells his stock within 14 calendar days from the time he purchased it (or, in the case of a short sale, if he buys the stock within 14 days from the time he sold it short). If the "round turn" is made within 14 days, the above indicated commissions are reduced by 50 per cent, and then $5.00 is added for each round-lot of 100 shares, or $3.00 for each odd-lot.[10] This is subject to the minimum commission of $6 per single transaction. To illustrate, it was indicated above

[10] If a round lot is less than 100 shares, the regular commissions are reduced by 50 per cent, and then $5.00 is added for each 100 shares or fraction thereof. This, however, is subject to the minimum commission charge of $6 per transaction.

that the commission to buy 300 shares of a $25 stock would be $94.50. If this stock was sold within 14 days, we would compute the selling commission by taking 50 per cent of $94.50, which is $47.25, and then add to this $15.00 (3 times $5.00), which gives us a commission charge of $62.25. If 40 shares of the stock were sold within 14 days from their purchase, the ordinary commission of $16, as computed above, would be reduced by 50 per cent, and $3.00 added. Thus, the selling commission would be $11.00.

TRANSFER TAXES. Both the federal government and New York State levy taxes on the transfer of stocks. Since all stocks sold on the New York Stock Exchange must be transferred in New York City, the New York tax applies to all stocks sold on that exchange. Since these taxes are on the transfer, they do not have to be paid by both the buyer and the seller. The law states that they are to be paid by the *seller.*

Federal stock transfer tax. The federal stock transfer tax is as follows:

> Four cents on each $100 (or fraction thereof in excess of $50) of the actual value of the total shares sold, but in no case will the tax be more than 8 cents on each share. The minimum tax on any transaction is 4 cents.

The above rates became effective January 1, 1959. To illustrate the application of the federal tax, we will assume that a person sold 100 shares of stock for $30 a share. Thus the sale involved $3,000 of actual value. Each $100 of value is taxed 4 cents, so the total tax would be $1.20. If 100 shares were sold for $300 a share, the actual value would be $30,000. But the tax would not be $12.00 since this exceeds 8 cents per share. The tax in this case would be $8.00. If only one share was sold at $30 the minimum tax per transaction of 4 cents would be applicable. It is noted that the new transfer taxes are the same regardless of whether the stock is par or no par.

Prior to 1959, when an odd-lot house sold an odd-lot of stocks, it passed on the federal transfer tax to the buyer. The new law provides that the tax will not be applicable to sales of odd lots by an odd-lot house. Thus the odd-lot buying public no longer must stand the federal transfer tax. But the seller of odd lots to the odd-lot house will, of course, continue to pay the tax.

New York State stock transfer tax. The present New York State stock transfer tax is based on the selling price of the share, and does not distinguish between par and no-par stock. The tax rates are as follows:

Selling Price of Stock	Tax per Share
Less than $5	$.01 per share
$5 but less than $10	.02 per share
$10 but less than $20	.03 per share
$20 or more	.04 per share

Thus, if a person sold 100 shares of stock at $30 a share, the tax would be $4.00, regardless of whether the stock was no-par or par, and regardless of its par value.

In order to prevent the odd-lot investor from having to pay the transfer tax on both purchases and sales, the New York law at the present time does not tax the sale made by an odd-lot house to the buyer of odd-lots. Therefore, the odd-lot house does not charge the buyer with the tax. Thus, the New York tax is paid only by the seller, whether he sells in round-lots or odd-lots.

Aside from New York, the only other states having stock transfer taxes are Massachusetts, Pennsylvania, Florida, South Carolina, and Texas, but only the first two mentioned have stock exchanges.

Securities and Exchange Commission fee. The Securities and Exchange Commission charges the exchanges an annual fee of 1/500 of one per cent of the aggregate money value (one cent for each $500, or fraction thereof, of money involved in the sale) of all sales of registered securities. The exchange levies this tax on each sale, and it is paid by the seller. Obviously, the tax rate is so small that we can, for purposes of discussion, ignore it.

MONTHLY INVESTMENT PLAN. In 1954, the New York Stock Exchange inaugurated the *Monthly Investment Plan,* which is available through many members of the exchange. Under this plan a person may invest a fixed amount of money at regular intervals over a long period of time. The amount invested may be as small as $40 every three months, or as large as $999 a month. This amount is used each period to purchase a particular stock. A separate plan is arranged for each different stock which is purchased. The investor is credited with the exact number of shares or fractional shares that his money will buy (after giving effect to commission charges). Credit is received for dividends on fractional shares as well as on whole shares. On commitments of less than $100, the commissions are 6 per cent, but they are not subject to the ordinary minimum fee of $6 per transaction.

DOLLAR AVERAGING. The investment of a fixed amount of money at regular intervals is called *dollar averaging.* The Monthly Investment Plan arrangement described above illustrates a type of dollar averaging. Since the fixed amount of money will buy few shares when they are high in price, and relatively many shares when they are low in price, it will be found that the average *cost* (per share) to an investor of his stock over a long period of time will be less than the average *price* of the stock during the same period. Dollar averaging takes the "emotion" out of stock buying and thus usually prevents an investor from making the common error of "buying high and selling low."

SECONDARY DISTRIBUTIONS. Single transactions on the New York Stock Exchange or on any of the other exchanges, or in the over-the-counter market (after original offering), ordinarily involve only a relatively small number of shares of a particular issue. The total number of shares traded by the auction method on the exchanges for any day in fact comprise only a small percentage of the total number of shares listed of the particular stock. In some instances a relatively large number of shares might be offered for sale at one time. This might result from the sale of shares held in an estate, which in some cases is necessary in order to get money to pay the inheritance and estate taxes. Or it may represent important holdings of shares by company officials, by investment companies, trust companies, or other institutional investors.

Whenever a relatively large block of stock is sold or is offered for sale at one time, the price will be driven down with the result that the seller by his own efforts receives less for the stock than its intrinsic worth. Before 1934, the only alternative to this was to sell the stock in small amounts over a period of time. But this would ordinarily not meet the objective of the seller, and in some instances the sale had to be made immediately. So, manipulative devices were used to bolster the stock so that the market could absorb the large block at one time without unduly depressing the price.

After the enactment of the Securities Exchange Act of 1934, manipulative practices were prohibited, and severe penalties were provided for any violation of the law. This, plus the fact that the market was "thin" in the late 1930's, led to the practice of selling large blocks of securities in the over-the-counter market after the close of the New York Stock Exchange. This is called a *secondary distribution.*[11] The permission of the Exchange is necessary for such sale. Generally speaking, the block of securities to be sold must be at least as large as a month's balance of regular trading on the NYSE. A group of investment bankers or brokers will form a tempo-

[11] In 1956, the Alfred P. Sloan Foundation, Inc., sold 1,278,833 shares of General Motors Corp. common through a secondary distribution.

rary syndicate or group for the purpose of selling the block of securities, and some selling pressure will be exerted. The offering price of the stock will be at or slightly below the closing price for that particular day. The sale may be underwritten by investment bankers in the same manner as a primary offering. Both members and nonmembers of the Exchange can buy the stock. An attempt will be made to sell the entire block of stock before the opening of the Exchange the following morning. If this cannot be done, the offering will usually be withdrawn in order not to conflict with the ordinary trading in the particular stock on the Exchange.

The original seller under the secondary distribution, which may be an investment company, receives a fixed amount for the stock, which is slightly less than the closing price for the particular day, but undoubtedly more than if the stock had been sold in the ordinary fashion. The bankers or syndicate selling the stock receive a fee which may be from two to five times the amount of the ordinary New York Stock Exchange commission. (The Exchange requires that it be at least twice the Exchange commission rates.)[12] The buyer of the stock does not have to pay a commission. Price stabilization (for which permission must be obtained from the SEC) is usually used by the syndicate in connection with secondary distributions. Secondary distributions are sometimes called "secondary offerings," "off-the-board offerings," "dusk to dawn sales," and "block sales."[13] Secondary distributions of the type described here are also sometimes used for unlisted securities.

As the "off-the-board offerings" of listed stocks became more numerous, particularly the American stocks being sold by foreign governments at the start of World War II, the New York Stock Exchange became concerned about the volume of listed stocks being sold in the over-the-counter market. This resulted in the Securities and Exchange Commission amending its rules in 1942 to permit *Special Offerings* to take place on the floor of the national securities exchanges during regular trading hours. Such sales can be arranged when it is apparent that the market cannot absorb the block of stock within a reasonable time in the regular way without

[12] In a secondary offering of 280,000 shares of Atlantic Refining Co. stock in 1954, the total fee amounted to \$1.65 per share. Of this amount, 15¢ went to the syndicate manager, 35¢ to the underwriting syndicate, and \$1.15 to the sellers. *Business Week*, October 2, 1954, p. 118.

[13] It should be noted that we are using the term "secondary distribution" here in a technical sense to refer to the off-the-board offering of a block of securities. We have previously used the term in a general sense to refer to the resale of stocks on the market after the original issue, such as the sales on the organized stock exchanges.

unduly depressing the price, and where the number of shares is not large enough to justify a secondary distribution.[14]

In 1953, two additional procedures to handle block sales of stocks were authorized by the NYSE. These were called *Exchange Distributions,* and *Specialist Block Purchases.*[15]

In recent years it has become apparent that special procedures were also needed to handle the *purchase* of large blocks of stocks by institutional investors, pension funds, etc. Effective October 22, 1956, the NYSE authorized what are termed *Special Bids, Exchange Acquisitions,* and *Specialist Block Sales* to facilitate such purchases.[16] These correspond to Special Offerings, Exchange Distributions, and Specialist Block Purchases, mentioned above.

Questions

1. Indicate the nature of the over-the-counter market. What type of securities are sold in this market?
2. Do the registered securities exchanges themselves buy or sell any securities?
3. Indicate the advantages to the issuing corporation of having its stock listed on the New York Stock Exchange (NYSE).
4. Indicate the advantages to the investor of listing on the NYSE.
5. What are the requirements for listing a stock on the NYSE?
6. What different functions are performed by members of the NYSE?
7. How does the American Stock Exchange differ from the NYSE?
8. What are the principal provisions of the Securities Exchange Act of 1934?
9. (a) Can officers and directors buy and sell their own stock? What restrictions and limitations are put on them? (b) Can an officer or director make a short-term profit in his company's stock? Explain.
10. Indicate what must be contained in the proxy statement of a registered stock.
11. What are the relative advantages and disadvantages of the market and the limited order?
12. When is a stop-loss order for a round-lot executed, and what price is paid or received for the stock?
13. How many shares of a stock selling at $20 a share can be purchased under existing margin requirements with cash of $10,000? How low could this stock go in the market before the broker would be compelled to call for more margin under the present New York Stock Exchange rules?

[14] Special Offerings are described in *Rules of Board,* New York Stock Exchange, May 1, 1953, Rules 490–497. Rules renumbered October 22, 1956, to 490-A through 497-A.

[15] These are described in *Rules of Board,* New York Stock Exchange, May 2, 1955, Rule 498, and *Rules of Board,* June 1, 1953, Rule 353. Rules renumbered October 22, 1956, to 498-A, and 353-A.

[16] *Rules of Board,* New York Stock Exchange, October 22, 1956, Rules 353-B, 490-B through 497-B, and 498-B.

14. Indicate what would constitute the effective sale, and how much per share a person would pay for an odd-lot transaction if the order was: (*a*) A market order. (*b*) A limited order. (*c*) A stop-loss order.

15. Indicate the advantages and disadvantages to the investor of stop-loss orders.

16. (*a*) Indicate the mechanics involved in a short sale of stock. (*b*) Is it more expensive to buy on margin than to sell short? Explain. (*c*) Explain the Securities and Exchange Commission rule relating to short selling.

17. Indicate who must pay the federal and the New York stock transfer taxes on both round-lots and odd-lots.

18. Are odd-lot sales included in the published figures for the total sales on the New York Stock Exchange?

19. Explain fully how an odd-lot trader is at a disadvantage as compared to a person trading in round-lots. What constitutes an odd-lot at "Post 30"?

20. Explain the nature of the Secondary Distribution plan for secondary offerings of stock.

Problems

1. The following refers to the business or financial section of your local newspaper: (a) Are the current market prices of some stocks listed on the New York Stock Exchange given? The American Stock Exchange? (b) Is the daily volume of sales on the New York Stock Exchange given? (c) Are any over-the-counter securities quoted? Which ones? (d) Are any stock averages or indexes quoted? If so, which ones?

2. What newspapers or magazines relating to the stock market are in your school library?

3. Mr. Smith puts in an order to buy 10 shares (round-lot 100 shares) of a particular stock. After the order reaches the odd-lot dealer, sales of 100 share units took place at the following prices in the order indicated; 20⅛, 20, 19⅞, 19¾. Indicate which sale of a round-lot made his odd-lot order "effective," and how much per share he would pay for the stock if the order was: (a) A market order? (b) To buy at 20⅛ stop? (c) To buy at 20?

4. Compute the New York Stock Exchange commissions, federal transfer tax, and New York transfer tax on the following transactions: (a) 200 shares of stock sold at $20 a share (par value $10 a share). (b) 50 shares (odd-lot) of stock sold at $80 a share (no-par). (c) 50 shares (odd-lot) of stock sold at $3 a share (no-par).

Part IV
WORKING CAPITAL

Chapter 20

WORKING CAPITAL

Types of Assets and Their Financing. Corporate finance involves the raising of funds to finance both the fixed and the current assets. The *fixed assets* are those which will remain more or less permanently in the business, such as land, building, and machinery. They are sometimes referred to as the *permanent assets.*

The *current assets,* on the other hand, are those assets which in the ordinary course of business can or will be turned into cash within a year or less. Included in the current assets are cash, accounts and notes receivable, and inventory. (In some instances marketable securities are also included.) This class of assets is also sometimes referred to as the *circulating capital, liquid assets, quick assets* (erroneously so), and *working capital.*

The liabilities of a business are also classified as fixed and current. The *fixed liabilities* are the long-term debts, such as bonds issued by the concern. The *current liabilities* are those debts which at the time of their inception are intended to be paid off within a period of one year or less. Included in such liabilities are the accounts and notes payable, and taxes and wages owed by the company.

The fixed assets are practically always financed with permanent capital, which is obtained from the sale of bonds or stock, and from depreciation allowances and the reinvestment of earnings. The current assets are also financed, in part, from the proceeds of bond and stock sales, depreciation allowances, and the reinvestment of earnings, and in part from the current liabilities.

Definition of Working Capital. The term "working capital" is frequently used in corporation finance, but not always with the same meaning. Despite this confusion, we will use the term since it is commonly found in accounting and business practice. When the term *working capital* is used it refers either to (1) the total current assets, or (2) the excess of current assets over current liabilities. We cannot say that one definition is correct and the other wrong. Many accounting and financial writers use the term in the second way, meaning the excess of current assets over current liabilities, but the author prefers the first definition. Something can be said both for and against each interpretation.

When listing the various items or accounts that comprise the working capital, writers always list the current asset accounts. This would argue for the total current assets definition of the working capital. Besides it is always stated that short-term bank loans, for example, are a source of working capital. This would also indicate that they had in mind the total current assets concept of working capital, because if we considered the working capital to be the difference between the current assets and the current liabilities, then a short-term bank loan would not increase the working capital since for every dollar increase in the current assets as a result of the loan, the current liabilities would be increased by the same amount. The third argument in support of the total current assets concept of working capital is that the particular assets may be "working" in the business even though they are offset in part by current liabilities. It is for these reasons that the author prefers the total current assets concept of working capital.

The arguments in support of the current assets concept of working capital stated above, are, of course, the arguments against the other definition. What can be said in favor of treating the working capital to be the difference between the current assets and the current liabilities? Probably the only one is this: all the current assets shown on the balance sheet are in a sense not available for new commitments in the business, since they are offset in part at least by the current liabilities. If we state the amount of working capital to be the difference between the current assets and current liabilities, we will know the amount of the current assets that are more or less "free" for use in the business. In reply to this argument, however, it can be said that the paying off of a current liability is using a current asset, and therefore we are interested in knowing what the total current assets are. Perhaps this discussion can be best understood through the use of the following illustration of the current assets and current liabilities of companies A and B.

Item	*Company A*	*Company B*
Current assets	$1,000,000	$1,000,000
Current liabilities	800,000	200,000
Difference between current assets and current liabilities	$ 200,000	$ 800,000

We would say that *A* and *B* each had working capital of $1,000,000, or that it was $200,000 in the case of *A*, and $800,000 in the case of *B*, depending upon which definition we assumed. If we use the first definition, we would get the impression that company *A* was in just as good a current financial position as company *B*. But relatively speaking, company *B* is in a much better current position than *A*. As used in this text, however, current financial position and working capital are not the same thing. Both company *A* and company *B* have $1,000,000 worth of current assets which must be financed. The fact that company *A* has financed these current assets with current liabilities to a greater extent than company *B* does not alter the fact that the working capital is the same for both companies.

An exact definition of "working capital" is not so important as stating something in a way that can be easily understood by the reader. The term "current assets" is understood by all to mean the total current assets. Likewise, "net current assets" means the difference between the current assets and the current liabilities. The same reasoning may be applied to the working capital. We can assume that the term "working capital" refers to the total current assets, and if we want to refer to the difference between the current assets and the current liabilities, we can use the term "net working capital." This is exactly what is done in many instances. Standard and Poor's, for example, use the term "net working capital" in this way, although Moody's use the term "net current assets." In some instances a writer will use "gross working capital" when he wants to be sure the reader will understand that he is referring to the total current assets rather than to the difference between the current assets and current liabilities.

In order that there will be no misunderstanding about the use of the terms in this book, it will be repeated that "working capital" will be used to refer to the total current assets, and when we want to speak of the difference between the current assets and the current liabilities, we will use the term "net working capital," or "net current assets."

Kinds of working capital

CLASSES OF WORKING CAPITAL. In our discussion it will be of convenience to divide working capital into the following classes:

1. Fixed working capital
   (*a*) Initial working capital
   (*b*) Regular working capital

2. Variable working capital
   (*a*) Seasonal working capital
   (*b*) Special working capital

FIXED WORKING CAPITAL. The *fixed working capital* is the minimum amount that is needed in the business. This amount varies among different businesses and within the same business depending upon managerial policies and the results of business operations. This kind of capital is divided into initial, and regular working capital.

Initial working capital. As the term indicates, the *initial working capital* is the amount needed when a business begins operations. A large amount of cash is required at this time in order to purchase all the items that are necessary. Inventories must be purchased and processed, but collections from the sale of such inventories may not take place for several months. Sufficient money will have to be on hand to meet the payrolls and pay the many other expenses for a relatively long period of time. It usually takes some time before a new business reaches a profitable stage. It is therefore necessary to provide working capital sufficient to absorb losses during this initial period.

Regular working capital. After the business has gone through the formative stage and collections start rolling in, it will be found that a certain amount of working capital must be tied up in the business at all times to carry on a given volume of sales. This minimum amount necessary is called the *regular working capital.* It is true that cash will be collected from the sales and accounts receivable, but new inventories will have to be purchased and new credit granted. Thus, a certain fixed amount will have to be maintained in working capital all the time. If sales increase, a larger investment in working capital is called for. And if the sales volume continues at this higher level indefinitely, the increased amount of working capital will be needed permanently in the business.

The amount of regular working capital required varies greatly among different types of businesses. An electric light and power company, for example, which has no "inventory" to sell, and which does a cash business, would require much less regular working capital than a retail furniture store or jewelry store doing practically all its business on credit. Some of the more detailed factors which affect the amount of working capital needed will be explained when we take up the various working capital items.

VARIABLE WORKING CAPITAL. The *variable working capital* is an amount that is needed in addition to the regular working capital. It can be classified into seasonal and special working capital.

Seasonal working capital. Some businesses are seasonal in nature, that is, their manufacturing or selling period is concentrated over only part of the year. A vegetable or fruit cannery and a manufacturer of Christmas toys are examples of such types of business.

The working-capital needs of seasonal businesses fluctuate greatly during the year. As they are buying and processing or manufacturing to take care of the seasonal peak sales, the cash is constantly drained, accounts payable increase, and possibly it may be necessary to borrow at the bank to take care of the purchases and expenses. Most businesses have some seasonal fluctuation in working capital needs.

As orders start coming in, the inventory will be lessened and the cash and receivable accounts will increase. At the same time the need for cash for purchases and expenses lessens. As sales increase, this process continues, and the cash account will now show a large balance from the liquidation of the inventory and collection of the accounts.

Special working capital. Any type of working capital other than initial, regular, and seasonal, is classed as special. Since cash is one of the items included in working capital, any need for additional cash would call for an increase in working capital. The following are among the more common needs for additional cash or other forms of working capital.

1. Entering a period of prosperity. Prosperity usually results in an increase in prices and in sales for the more successful concerns. As prices increase, more cash is required to buy the same quantities of raw materials. Furthermore, sales are probably increasing at the same time, and this will require additional money for raw materials. At the same time, wages and other expenses are mounting, and thus still more cash is required. Although this appears to be a special situation at the time, as long as prices and sales are maintained, such additional working capital becomes part of the regular working capital.

Even if general prosperity is not present, in some instances the price of the raw materials of the particular company may increase in price, and the company may want additional cash to stock up before prices advance still further.

2. Entering a period of depression. From what has been said above, it may appear peculiar that special working capital may be

needed when a depression or recession hits. But such may be the case. Normally a company should cut down on its purchases when the country is headed for the recession or a depression. But unfortunately, you cannot be sure that such a period is at hand. Many companies will believe that what later proves to be a depression was only a slight setback in a period of prosperity. As a result they continue to expand inventories. As the recession gets under way, sales will begin slipping off, and collections will become slow. Unless purchases are cut and production schedules curtailed, the company will feel the need for additional working capital to carry the receivables and added inventory.

3. Contingencies and emergencies. Certain contingencies frequently arise which call for additional cash, such as—shutting down of the plant for a long period due to strikes, floods, fires, etc., uninsured property losses resulting from floods and fires which necessitate the investment of additional money in the business, litigation and unfavorable court decisions, and rise in wages.

4. Miscellaneous. Other reasons that would call for additional working capital would be the following: research projects, introduction of new manufacturing processes, or new products, advertising campaigns, inauguration of pension plans, etc.

Working capital items

In the discussion above we were concerned with fixed and variable working capital as a total figure. Businesses, however, must give attention to the amounts of each of the individual items that go to make up the total working capital. We will, therefore, now consider separately the working capital items of cash, inventory, and receivables.

CASH. As individuals we all know the importance of cash. This item is of no less importance to the business concern. In fact, of all the balance sheet items, cash is probably the most important.

A business starts out with cash obtained from the sale of stocks or bonds, or from the investment of the proprietor or the partners. This cash is used to buy fixed assets and inventory, and to pay the operating expenses. As the inventory is sold, accounts or notes receivable and cash including the profit margin, take its place on the books of the company. Collection of the notes and accounts puts money into the cash account. This cash is again used to buy inventory, and the rotation starts all over again. It is thus seen that the current assets, or working capital, circulate in the business. This is why working capital is sometimes called "circulating capital."

The success of the business depends upon the expenditure or investment of the cash in such a way that it returns more cash or other assets to the business than was expended. Although it may merely be a symptom of some underlying major trouble, the immediate cause of failure of practically any business is insufficient cash.

The amount of cash needed varies greatly among different companies, and under different circumstances within the same company. In some instances a company may, after some years of experience, set the desired cash account figure at a definite amount, or at a certain percentage of current assets, total sales, or current liabilities. In many cases the amount of the cash is merely a result of the business operations. Successful concerns may have relatively large cash accounts, while their less successful competitors may have relatively small cash balances, although their cash needs may be greater. Following are factors which affect the amount of cash needed.

1. *Initial requirements.* When a company first starts operations it needs a relatively large cash account. The various fixed assets, other than those for which stock was exchanged, as well as inventory must be purchased. Furthermore, it may be some time before the raw materials and work in process are completed into the finished product. Then the goods must be sold, and perhaps some time will elapse before the accounts are collected. The cash requirements during this initial period, before the production-sales-collection cycle gets into operation, are usually heavy.

In addition to the direct costs of materials and labor, there must be sufficient cash to pay for the overhead and administrative and selling expenses. In some instances large outlays will have to be made for advertising. Sufficient cash should be provided to cover possible losses usual during the first few months of operations. After carefully estimating the expenditures and receipts, it is conservative and good business practice to figure that the expenditures have been understated, and the receipts overstated. Unexpected sources of income are not so common as unexpected expenses. Due allowance should be made for this in setting up the cash budget.

2. *Terms of purchase.* A company that buys on a cash basis will need more funds at the start than one that buys on credit. But where discounts are given, it may be more economical to provide for the additional cash needed to take advantage of the discounts.

3. *Terms of sale.* If a company sells for cash it will need less cash at first than if the sales are on credit. The longer the credit period granted, the greater will be the cash needs.

4. *Volume of sales.* As sales increase more cash will be needed to purchase additional inventory and to finance additional accounts and notes receivable. This heavy cash requirement for the increased sales volume is similar to that required when the company initially started business. As sales increase many companies try to carry on the greater volume without an increase in the permanent working capital. The increased cash requirements for materials, labor and other expenses drain the cash before collections start coming in from the increased sales. Many expanding companies fail as a result of not having sufficient cash to meet payrolls, bank loans, and the claims of other creditors.

5. *Contingencies and emergencies.* This was discussed above when we considered the special working capital.

6. *Profit margin.* Since the sale of products at a profit will eventually result in an increase in cash flow, this should be given conservative consideration in determining working capital needs.

7. *Use of profit.* In considering the effect of profits on cash needs, consideration will have to be given to what shall be done with the profit. The profit might be sunk into fixed assets or it might be used to increase inventory purchases to take care of increased sales. If the profit, or part of it, is paid out to the stockholders in the form of dividends, then it would, of course, not be available for use in the business.

8. *Nature and amount of current liabilities.* Other things being equal, a company with small current liabilities would need less cash than one with a large amount of current liabilities. The maturity date of the various current liabilities is an additional factor to consider.

INVENTORY. In the case of merchandising and manufacturing companies the inventory is a very important part of the working capital. In many instances the success or failure of the business depends upon the handling of the inventory. This is particularly true in the event of rising and falling prices. The three major types of inventory and the factors which determine the amount of each type that should be kept on hand are discussed below.

1. *Raw-materials inventory.* The proper size of the raw materials inventory varies greatly among businesses. Under ordinary circumstances no larger inventory should be maintained than is necessary. This is the amount that is needed to keep up with the production schedule. In some instances, however, when the source of raw materials is uncertain, or when the time involved in getting

the materials to the factory is not definitely known, or when prices are increasing, a larger amount may be invested in raw materials.

Where the raw material used is a seasonal agricultural product, it will probably be necessary to stock up on the products at the end of the growing season. It may be advisable to purchase large quantities in case the suppliers' plant would be on strike or threatened by a strike. In some instances it is advisable to purchase larger quantities than would otherwise be the case in order to secure quantity discounts.

2. *Work-in-process inventory.* Generally speaking, the longer the production period, the greater will be the amount that will have to be tied up in work-in-process inventory. A ship building company, for example, will have a relatively larger work-in-process inventory than a cannery. The inventory will also have to be relatively large when the particular company manufactures a number of sizes, shapes, and colors of the product.

3. *Finished-goods inventory.* A number of factors affect the amount of finished-goods inventory that should be kept on hand. Since the company is in business to make a profit from the sale of its product, it is obvious that the finished-goods inventory should at all times be sufficient to fill the orders as they come. In case of seasonal business, the inventory may have to be unusually large at certain periods in the year. In some instances a seasonal business will try to keep up the manufacturing process throughout the year in order to lessen overhead costs and to give steady employment to at least some of the workers. Thus, finished-goods inventories will accumulate throughout the year to be liquidated during the selling season.

A company that sells from various distributing points throughout the country will have to maintain a much larger inventory than one which sells from only one place. As in the case of the work-in-process inventory, the more sizes, shapes, and colors carried, the greater will be the need for a large finished-goods inventory.

Available storage space is another factor that may influence the size of the inventory. The production schedules, however, should be such that the economies of large-scale production are realized. But too large an inventory may be uneconomical because of the excessive investment. Under normal circumstances the finished-goods inventory should not be much larger than the amount that can be turned out in the length of time that it will take to sell the inventory. In other words, if the company can turn out $100,000 in new products in a period of three months, and this is an economical run, and assuming the finished goods inventory on hand can be sold within three months, the size of this inventory should not be much in excess of $100,000. Since some allowance should be made for a breakdown or slow-up in production, and also for sales in excess of the estimate, the inventory under these circumstances should be somewhat in excess of the $100,000.

Inventory turnover. Some of the inventory factors discussed above are reflected in the "inventory turnover" figure. The *inventory turnover* is calculated by dividing the average inventory into the cost of goods sold. If the inventory is "taken" only once a year, the average is found by adding the beginning and ending inventory, and dividing the sum by two. When monthly inventories are taken or calculated, an average of the monthly figures should be used.

It is to be noted that the sales are taken at their *cost* figure rather than at the "sales" figure, in order to eliminate the profit element from the sales figure. If the actual "cost of sales" figure is not obtainable, then the estimated "mark-up" is added to the average inventory figure, and this is divided into the total "sales." Following are examples of both methods.

Let us assume that a company's beginning and ending inventories were $90,000 and $110,000 respectively, and that the sales expressed in cost were $400,000. Dividing $400,000 by $100,000 ($90,000 + $110,000 divided by 2) equals 4. Thus the company turned its inventory 4 times. If the cost of sales was not known, but it could be seen from the financial statements that the total sales were $480,000, and if it was known or estimated that the company marked up its merchandise by 20 per cent (note that we are assuming that the selling price was set at 20 per cent in excess of *cost*), we could calculate the turnover by the other method. (In some instances the "mark-up" is expressed as a percentage of the *selling price*). Adding 20 per cent, or $20,000, to the inventory figure, we get $120,000. Dividing this figure into the sales of $480,000, we again arrive at the figure of 4 as the inventory turnover.

More significance is attached to the inventory figure in the case of merchandising concerns, such as retailers, jobbers, and wholesalers, than in the case of manufacturing companies. The latter have three kinds of inventory: raw materials, work in process, and finished goods. The work-in-process and finished-goods inventory valuations have labor and overhead costs included in addition to the raw materials. If inventory turnover is calculated for a manufacturing concern, it would have to be confined to the particular inventory under consideration. Each of the types of inventory turnover would be computed as follows:

$$\text{Raw material turnover} = \frac{\text{Raw materials going into work in process during period}}{\text{Average raw material inventory during period}}$$

$$\text{Work-in-process turnover} = \frac{\text{Work in process transferred to finished goods during period}}{\text{Average work-in-process inventory during period}}$$

$$\text{Finished goods turnover} = \frac{\text{Cost of goods sold during period}}{\text{Average finished goods inventory during period}}$$

The rate of inventory turnover varies greatly among different types of businesses. For example, a chain grocery store will turn its inventory many more times a year than will a furniture or jewelry store. In considering turnovers, only concerns in the same line of business should be compared. The rate of turnover is highly significant. If we assume two companies with the same annual sales, the one with the faster turnover will require less capital tied up in inventory, and because of the smaller inventory less space and, therefore, a smaller overhead. Or if two companies have the same inventory, the one with the quicker turnover will have larger sales and, assuming they have the same mark-up, larger profits.

If two companies have the same amount invested in inventory, the one with the quicker turnover will require just as much initial working capital as the other company. A company with a rapid turnover will ordinarily suffer fewer losses from obsolescence and shopworn merchandise than one with a relatively slow turnover.

Inventory valuation. An important management decision in most businesses is the choice of an inventory valuation method. A number of different techniques are followed in practice. Each of these has a different effect on the valuation of working capital in the balance sheet, as well as on the amount of profits. After the physical inventory is taken at the end of an accounting period, the problem arises what dollar value to place on that inventory in the balance sheet. If a high dollar value is used (in other words if inventory is overvalued), profits will be overstated. If the ending inventory is overvalued, the actual cost of goods manufactured or sold will be less by the amount of the overvaluation, and the gross profit will be higher than if the proper valuation had been used. A higher gross profit means a higher net profit and results in higher income taxes.

Undervaluation of inventory on the balance sheet has the opposite results on the profit. Undervaluation of balance sheet inventory means that cost of goods sold will actually be higher and profits will seem less with correspondingly reduced taxes. During periods of high taxes, many businesses are interested in undervaluation of balance sheet inventory so that taxes will be less. It is important that anyone studying the working capital position of a corporation or its profit picture have an understanding of the inventory valuation technique used and its effect on the amount of working capital and on profits and taxes.

Following are the major methods used in inventory valuation:

1. First-in, first-out
2. Average cost
3. Last-in, first-out
4. Cost or market, whichever is lower
5. Inventory valuation reserves

1. First-in, first-out. Many businesses find it difficult to determine the actual cost of the inventory on hand. Where purchases of the same item are made several times during the inventory period at varying prices, it is difficult to tell which cost items are still on hand at the end of the period. One common practice used is to assume that the first purchased were the first ones used in production or sold. This is the *first-in, first-out* inventory valuation method, which in practice is called FIFO. Actual cost figures are used for all items purchased during the period. It is then assumed that all items on hand in inventory were the last ones purchased and are priced accordingly. The result is that the book value of the inventory at any time is close to the existing market price. In periods of rising prices, this would mean that the inventory would be stated at higher prices than under other methods and that profits would also be higher with correspondingly higher taxes.

2. Average cost. Under the *average cost* method, a weighted average of the cost prices of an item is determined and this is used as the basis of the inventory valuation on the books. In periods of rising prices, this method results in a lower valuation on balance sheet inventory and lower profits and income taxes than the FIFO method.

3. Last-in, first-out. The *last-in, first-out* method of valuation is particularly popular in periods of rising prices because it results in a lower value on balance sheet inventory and lower profits and income taxes. Under this system, which is called LIFO, cost prices are used and it is assumed that the last items purchased were the first items used or sold. Thus, the balance sheet inventory reflects earlier prices rather than the latest market prices. Under this

method, the latest market prices enter the cost of goods sold, and, therefore, make cost and profits reflect current market prices of inventory. Valuation of inventory on the books under this method, becomes out of line with existing inventory prices. Many firms changed to the LIFO method of inventory valuation for tax purposes during and after World War II when prices were rising sharply. In this way, profits reflected current costs and were therefore less than they would have been under average cost or FIFO. This technique resulted in lower taxes for the companies which used it during this period.

4. Cost or market, whichever is lower. When the cost prices of each individual item in inventory is available, companies do not have to worry about LIFO or FIFO or average cost as they know the actual costs involved. Some companies actually value their inventories at cost but others are more conservative and use the lower of cost or market. Under this method, profits from rising inventory values are not taken until the inventory is sold, but losses from declining inventory values are taken as the decline takes place. This is probably the most commonly used method of inventory valuation. In periods of rising prices, the inventory is still carried on the books at cost although replacement value would be much higher. This method results in a conservative statement of profits during periods of both rising and falling prices.

5. Inventory valuation reserves. Because of the possible loss or reduction in profits that may come from a reduction in prices, many companies will carry on their books a reserve for decline in inventory values. This reserve is shown as a deduction from the inventory account on the books. This is conservative practice and is followed by many concerns. It is similar, of course, to the "cost or market, whichever is lower" method, stated above.

Receivables. The *receivables* of a company consist of both *accounts receivable* and *notes receivable.* Since notes are given to take care of an account, or are given to the seller at the time of the sale, instead of having the obligation remain on open account, we will not treat accounts and notes separately. When reference is made here to accounts receivable, the same reasoning would apply in most instances to notes receivable.

A company that sells on account will usually have more bad debts than one that sells for cash. But selling on account may increase the sales to the point where the profits are higher even after the bad debts have been charged off. The function of the credit department is not to follow an ultraconservative policy which will result in the least amount of bad debts, but rather a policy which will result in the greatest profits.

The larger the amount of receivables the greater will be the amount of cash tied up. But if the larger receivables are a result of an increase in sales, this may be an advantage to the company. The situation is different, however, when the large volume of receivables is a result of inefficient collection procedure. It should be remembered that the longer an account is outstanding, the less is the chance of collecting it.

The sales department, in its efforts for greater sales, is ordinarily optimistic and is inclined to recommend credit policies that are too liberal. The credit department or the company treasurer, on the other hand, may tend to be too stringent. In order to earn the maximum in profits, perhaps a policy halfway between the liberal and conservative attitudes should be recommended.

The following factors are important in determining the amount of working capital that will be tied up in accounts receivable:

1. *Credit sales.* Almost all manufacturing and wholesaling and many retailing concerns sell at least a portion of their goods on credit. If all of a company's sales are for cash, there is no need to have any capital tied up in receivables. On the other hand, if all sales are credit sales, a sizable amount of capital will be required to carry the receivables. The greater the percentage of sales on credit, the greater the need for capital to carry accounts and notes receivable.

2. *Length of credit period.* The longer the period of time granted buyers to pay accounts receivable, the greater the need for capital to carry the accounts. For example, a firm granting thirty-day terms and having the same amount of credit sales will have more receivables than a firm which grants only seven-day terms. Receivables turnover is an important factor in determining working capital needs.

The *receivables turnover* is calculated by dividing the annual net credit sales by the average monthly receivables. It is to be noted that the sales are taken at their sales price, since the profit margin is also reflected in the receivables. The receivables turnover can be used to check the efficiency of the credit and collections department, and also to determine the quality of the receivables.

Let us assume that a company has annual net sales of $1,500,000, of which $1,200,000 are credit sales made on the 2/10, net 30, basis, and that the average monthly receivables is $100,000. Dividing

$1,200,000 by $100,000 gives us a receivables turnover of only 12 times a year. This means that the average account is outstanding 30 days. We could conclude from this that either no one took advantage of the discount, or that some did take the discount, and the accounts of some of the other customers have been outstanding for more than 30 days, and have thus been overdue. The latter would probably be the correct assumption. This would indicate that some of the accounts are probably of doubtful quality. The credit department should immediately (in fact this should have been done before) check the individual ledger accounts for the overdue accounts and take the proper action.

3. *Discounts offered.* The terms of credit extended to customers vary according to the line of business and among different companies within the same industry. Included in terms of credit are discounts which may be given to the customers if the bill is paid within a stated period. These cash discounts are offered as an inducement for the buyer to pay his bills promptly. The more attractive the discount terms offered, the more likely the buyer is to pay within the discount period. Thus there would be less capital needed to carry accounts receivable if very attractive cash discounts are offered by the seller. The price of the goods sold after deducting the cash discount should cover all costs and profit to the seller. The extra income obtained when the discounts are not taken should be sufficient to repay the seller for the cost of carrying the account for a longer period of time and all possible bad-debt losses. The seller has to take into account his own costs of capital in setting his credit terms.

4. *Collection effectiveness.* Special efforts devoted to collecting accounts when due will normally result in less overdue accounts. Many overdue accounts can be collected with the expenditure of collection effort. A certain amount of collection effort can be helpful in reducing capital needs for receivables. Collection procedure must be tempered to maintain as much good will as possible.

5. *Other factors.* Obviously, the total volume of sales, as well as the percentage of sales on credit, is a factor in determining financing needs for receivables. The amount of care exerted in granting or rejecting credit applications will influence inversely the amount tied up in bad debts and overdue accounts. Seasonal factors will influence the variable portion of the receivables accounts. The types of business involved has a great deal of influence on credit terms which in turn affect the volume of receivables.

Questions

1. What are the different interpretations of the term "working capital"? Which do you think should be used? Why?
2. Indicate the different kinds of working capital and state how each should be financed.
3. Under what circumstances do you think a corporation would be justified in putting money obtained from a short-term loan into fixed assets?
4. What factors determine the amount of inventory which a manufacturing company must carry?
5. Indicate how a company computes its finished goods inventory turnover.
6. Indicate the various methods of inventory valuation. Which do you recommend? Why?
7. How is the receivables turnover calculated? Of what significance is it?
8. What determines whether an item is to be classified as a current liability or a fixed liability?
9. What factors determine the amount of working capital which will be tied up in accounts receivable?
10. Should the credit and collection policy of a company be such that no bad debts will be experienced? Explain.

Problems

1. The inventory (at cost) of the Quality Department Store on January 1, 19-1, was $70,000. As of December 31, of the same year it was $80,000. Net sales for the year as shown in the income statement amounted to $600,000. The average "mark-up" for the store was 25 per cent of the selling price. What was the inventory turnover for the year?

2. The Acme Manufacturing Company follows the first-in, first-out method of inventory valuation. The inventory on hand on January 1, consisted of 600 units at an average cost of $1.00 per unit. It is the policy of the company to purchase additional inventory each four weeks (beginning in the fifth week of the year) sufficient in amount to last for a four-week period. The first purchase was at $1.10 per unit, and the second purchase was at $1.20 per unit. The production schedule for the first quarter of the year calls for 100 units of inventory to go into production each week. Show in columnar form the purchases, issues, and balance on hand in terms of units, unit cost, and total cost, for the first nine weeks of operations.

3. James White is considering building and operating a hot dog stand near where a large atomic plant is being built. The contractor has agreed to build the stand for $4,600 complete with equipment. It is estimated that the construction of the plant will take four years, after which time it is thought that the stand would be practically worthless so far as business is concerned. White's father has agreed to lend him the $4,600 needed to build the stand. White estimated that he will gross $9,000 a year, and that his annual operating expenses will be $2,200 a year. He figures he will therefore net $6,800 a year. (a) Why would more than $4,600 probably be needed for this project? (b) What expenses were probably not given any consideration by White?

Chapter 21

WORKING CAPITAL MANAGEMENT

IMPORTANCE OF WORKING CAPITAL CONTROL. The major contributors to cash flow are sale of inventory and collection of receivables. Lack of control over these working capital items has left businesses with insufficient cash flow to maintain solvency. The financial embarrassment caused by inability of generating cash to pay obligations may seriously affect credit rating and future possibilities of a business. Good working capital management should prevent even temporary embarrassing situations.

MAINTENANCE OF WORKING CAPITAL. After attaining the proper levels in the various working capital items, as discussed in the previous chapter, a business is faced with the problem of maintaining working capital at its proper balanced position. Constant management is required to maintain proper levels in the various working capital accounts. Cash and financial budgets, if used correctly, aid in establishing proper proportions. Sales expansion, dividend declarations, plant expansion, new product lines, increased salaries and wages, rising price levels, etc., put added strain on working capital maintenance. The financial officer of the corporation should be constantly aware of any changes of this type and plan for proper adjustments. Working capital must not be allowed to accumulate in excessive inventories or in large receivables due to a poor collection program. On the other hand, the needs of the business are not met and profit possibilities are lessened if inventories are inadequate or if funds are insufficient to grant proper credit terms. Working capital maintenance is dependent upon the constant and smooth circulation of cash into inventories, into receivables, into cash.

IMPORTANCE OF ADEQUATE WORKING CAPITAL. From the advantages of adequate working capital which are briefly discussed below, it will be apparent what disadvantages would result from inadequate working capital.

1. *It permits efficient operation.* A concern that has ample working capital will be able to operate efficiently. Raw materials in sufficient quantities will be obtainable. Purchasing in larger lots may mean lower prices. Payrolls can be met on time without worry or the necessity of borrowing at high rates of interest. All of this will improve the morale of the management and tend to make it more efficient.

2. *Credit is maintained.* One of the most important factors in the success of many businesses is the maintaining of good credit with banks and suppliers of raw materials. Credit rating agencies classify business concerns on their capacity, willingness, and promptness in paying debts. Companies that have a good credit rating need not in normal times worry about securing raw materials on credit or borrowing at the bank for some needed purpose.

3. *Discounts may be taken.* The savings by taking advantage of cash discounts in purchase of goods may be substantial. Adequate working capital will enable a company to take these discounts and thus obtain materials at a lower price than that paid by other companies that are unable to pay in time at discounts. This will enable the particular company to either undersell some of its competitors, or, if the same price is charged for the goods as is being charged by other concerns, to realize a higher profit.

4. *Depressions may be weathered.* The chances of a company weathering a depression are much better if it enters the period with ample working capital. When a depression hits, sales fall off and collections become slow. But the company's liabilities must be paid, and banks may call in loans sooner than would otherwise be the case. Although less cash may be needed for raw materials and labor, many of the fixed expenses remain the same during a depression. During critical periods there is no substitute for cash.

5. *Emergencies and contingencies.* Emergencies of one kind or another may require additional cash, such as law suits, adverse court decisions, increased taxes, and many other unexpected things. Companies also need some surplus cash to maintain minimum bank balances, and cash or liquid securities to meet their income tax payments. Ample cash or the equivalent enables a company to expand or to buy out other companies, effect mergers, branch out into more diversified lines, carry on adequate research, and it may prevent failure of the company when adverse contingencies or depressions hit. The cash should not be kept idle but should be invested in

relatively safe securities which return an adequate yield compatible with the safety of the investment.

Redundant Working Capital. It is, of course, better to have too much working capital than too little. Many companies make it a policy to carry more working capital than is currently needed in the business. Before World War I, it was customary for corporations to rely on banks for much of their working capital needs. This resulted in financial difficulties and failure of many concerns in the depression of the early 1920's. Later in the same decade when earnings were large, many companies retained a considerable amount of their profits to add to working capital more than was immediately necessary. The market for securities was also good at this time and many companies raised money which was not immediately needed from the sale of securities.

During and after World War II, the practice of corporations financing all their own working capital needs continued with increased momentum. It is now considered good financial judgment to carry more cash and liquid assets than are currently needed in the business. This enables the management to free itself of financial worries and to concentrate on the fundamental processes of manufacturing and selling products or supplying services. If it is found that there is no need for the surplus cash for any of the purposes outlined above, then the company should pay it out in dividends to the shareholders.

There may be certain disadvantages resulting from the retention of too much in current assets, although it should be restated that too much is better than too little.

1. *The management may become inefficient.* When managements have to work hard to meet payrolls, to take discounts and earn enough to carry on research and expand, they tend to be more efficient in many instances than when there is always cash at hand for all these purposes. Waste may creep in which otherwise would not be present.

2. *Relation with credit sources not maintained.* If a company always has plenty of cash on hand, it will not have to maintain close relations with banks and other possible sources of short-term capital. This may possibly result in the inability to get capital at some time in the future when adversity strikes.

3. *Return on investment may be low.* If a company has more cash on hand than can be profitably employed, the return on the total assets of the company will be lower than would otherwise be

the case. The earnings on the capital which is put to use may be adequate, but when this is spread over the total assets, the rate of earnings may be low. If all assets in regular use are earning 8 per cent, and the company has 25 per cent of its assets in surplus funds invested in 2 per cent government bonds, earnings on total assets would be only 6.5 per cent. Another company in the same field with no surplus funds may be earning 8 per cent on total assets. Lower relative earnings is the price the first company must pay for its too conservative approach.

Budgets

Importance and Function of Budgets. Without unlimited sources of capital, many companies would find themselves hard pressed for money on frequent occasions unless they anticipated their needs some time in advance. Practically all large businesses, which have thousands of employees and which turn out a variety of products from a large number of different departments, find that keeping budgets is essential to their successful operation. Most successful small corporations with few employees also maintain budgets although they are less complicated. Successful and profitable operation of a business can be obtained only when the various elements of the business are maintained in proper balance with each other.

The budget is one of the tools of control utilized by good business management. The preparation of a budget coordinates the various departments of a business, and anticipates the capital requirements for various purposes. It is used as a standard for comparison of efficiency of actual operations to budgeted operations. Each department has to study its relation to the entire organization and to the ultimate profit of the enterprise. This advance planning and objective look at the department's place in the organization leads to better coordination between departments and to more profitable operations.

The budget, if properly prepared and operated, gives the financial officer of the company warning of new capital requirements so that he may provide for these requirements well in advance of their actual need. Without the budget, the financial officer would have difficulty in estimating and providing for future capital needs.

The budget establishes a standard of performance for the period against which actual results can be compared. The comparison of actual results with the budget may point out any weak spots in the organization.

The fact that a business maintains budgets and plans scientifically for future operations may aid in obtaining additional credit. If a concern can point out to a bank why it needs additional funds and where the money will come from to repay loans, that concern will receive more favorable treatment from the bank than a firm operating without advance planning. Proper use of budgeting is a sign of good management. In today's complicated business world, budgets are essential to efficient business management.

Different Types of Budgets. The use of budgets varies within different industries and among different corporations. Some concerns budget for one year in advance, others for six months or quarterly. Some concerns budget certain needs on a weekly basis. Most of the large American corporations prepare both quarterly and annual budgets and some even go so far as to budget for five or ten years in the future. It is obvious that the longer the period of the budget, the less accurate the budget can be.[1] But even though it will be less accurate in forecasting corporate needs, long-term budgeting may be very useful as a guide for future planning. Budgeting projected far into the future will necessarily require revision as conditions change and more information about the future becomes available.

Some firms may project their complete income statements as far as a year in advance and draw up a *pro forma* balance sheet showing the anticipated financial condition at the end of this period. Where the income statement is projected into the future, it is necessary to budget all items that enter into this statement. The same applies where a *pro forma* balance sheet is desired. Since every income and expense item and all the assets and liabilities appear on these statements, it is obvious that it is necessary to prepare budgets which affect every phase of the company's operations. Manufacturing budgets are utilized by industrial concerns in which attempts are made to control the production cycle and manufacturing expenses. Expense budgets are often prepared for all departments to keep costs in line with expected income. The working capital and/or cash budget is essential for good financial planning. The sales budget or forecast is the basis for all other budgeting and on its accuracy will determine the success of the entire budgeting program. Since it is beyond the scope of this book to undertake the task of explaining how the entire budgeting operation works, only the sales and the cash budgets will be discussed further.

[1] In some instances, however, a six months' budget, for example, may prove to be more accurate than a budget for one month since mistakes tend to average out over the longer period.

The Sales Budget or Forecast. Before a budget of cash flow or expenses can be prepared, the total size of the operation involved must be forecast. The volume of sales determines production needs which in turn determines the amount of many expense items. Cash income and outgo vary with the volume of business transacted. The construction of any business budget, therefore, has to start with the sales estimate. Forecasting of sales for the coming period is of such importance that the final figure is often set by the board of directors after the sales department and budget committee have presented their estimates. The controller and the various departments involved then proceed to prepare their budgets on the basis of the projected sales volume figure.

Several methods are used in attempting to forecast sales for a future period. A common technique is to project past results into the future, with some modifications for changed conditions, such as the introduction of new products, different competition, and the oscillations of the general business cycle. Another technique which is less commonly used is to sample the market for expressions of future buying intent. In certain lines, such as industrial goods, this method may be satisfactory, but it would be extremely difficult to follow in many consumer industries. Under this technique, the forecast is established on the basis of what selected customers state they intend to purchase during the coming period. If the sample is properly chosen, it should be indicative of the buying anticipations of other customers. Of course, anticipations and actual purchases do not necessarily coincide. A third, and more common, technique is based on anticipated future conditions. Generally, this involves an estimate of the total market potential and then the individual company's share of that total market is estimated. In many instances, a combination of techniques is used along with a great deal of judgment on the part of the forecaster to set a figure for future sales or income.

The Cash Budget. Since our primary interest in this chapter is working capital, we should be concerned more with the working capital budget than other possible budgets. The working capital budget involves the anticipation of the amount of capital that will be needed to purchase and carry the various working capital items such as inventory, accounts receivable, and cash. Although the cash budget does not cover all the items that comprise the total working capital, it covers what is perhaps the most important one. The cash budget will, therefore, be discussed in some detail.

Anticipated cash receipts from all sources and cash disbursements of whatever nature will appear in the cash budget. Some of the sources or application of the cash may not come under the head of working capital, but nevertheless as long as they are cash items they will be included in the cash budget. For example, the raising of cash by means of a stock issue and investing the money in fixed assets does not come under the head of working capital, but the cash position of the company, which is vitally important in considering its working capital position, is affected by the raising and investing of cash.

The elementary accounting student who has become somewhat familiar with the income statement and balance sheet, but no other accounting reports, may find the cash budget a little confusing. The income statement shows the income and expense items as they are incurred regardless of whether or not the cash is actually received or paid out. Depreciation is treated as an expense the same as cash paid out for payrolls, but since no cash is paid out for it, such charge has no place in the cash budget. An investment in another form of asset takes cash out of the business in the same manner as the payment of expenses but does not affect the income statement. When it comes to the cash budget we are interested in only the actual receipt and disbursement of cash.

ITEMS IN THE CASH BUDGET. We stated above that the cash budget includes all anticipated receipts and disbursements of cash regardless of whether or not they were strictly working capital items. Thus the anticipated receipt of cash from the sale of securities and the disbursement of cash for buildings or income taxes, etc., are contained in the cash budget. We will assume that this has already been done, so that the discussion following will refer to the working capital items that appear in the budget.

Although some companies' cash budget may be made out for a year, others may include a period of only six months or, if the company gets out financial statements each quarter, the budget may be for only three months. In some instances a general budget will be made out for a year, but the detailed cash budget may be for only three or six months.

As a company gets into the early part of the budget period, the actual experience may be different from that anticipated, with the result that the budget for the remaining part of the period may have to be adjusted accordingly. In some instances the actual results experienced may call for looking about for ways to cut expenses. It should be remembered, however, that the budget is merely a means to the end, and not the end itself. If a change in the budget is necessitated as a result of the subsequent operations, then perhaps the budget should be changed rather than attempting to make the business operations conform to the budget. For example, if sales are larger than anticipated, it will necessitate the changing of a large number of cash disbursement items. It would be foolhardy for a business to cut down on sales in order to make the expenses incurred conform to the budget. Following are some of the details that are to be considered in connection with the working capital part of the cash budget.

CASH RECEIPTS. Monthly estimates will be made of the cash receipts from the following sources.

Sales. In drawing up a budget the logical place to start is with the sales department. The receipt and disbursement of cash depend upon the volume of sales. The sales for the budget period should be made out in terms of both the dollar volume and the unit volume. Then it will be necessary for someone to estimate what percentage of sales will be for cash and the percentage on credit. Credit sales are not an immediate source of cash. Only cash sales immediately enter into cash receipts.

Accounts receivable. From the credit sales information an estimate of the accounts receivable (and notes receivable) will be made for each month. In order to determine when the cash from the accounts will be collected, it is necessary to consider the terms of sale. If payment of the accounts are to be made within 30 days from the date of sale, then sales on credit for one month will be collected the following month. Due consideration will have to be given, however, to estimated slow collections and bad debts.

Other cash receipts. Although the cash sales and collection of accounts and notes will make up practically all the total cash receipts, any other anticipated source will of course also be listed. These might include interest and dividends received as well as cash received from sale of assets or securities.

CASH DISBURSEMENTS. To determine the total disbursements of cash, monthly estimates will be made of the following disbursements.

Purchase of materials. Based on the sales budget, the production department will be asked to submit a production schedule for the goods which are supposed to be sold. This will show the amount of materials or inventory which will go into the product and amount of direct labor cost. After giving effect to the inventory of raw materials, work in process, and finished goods on hand, the minimum inventory which is to be maintained, and the length of the production period—an estimate will be prepared of the amount of purchases which will have to be made each month. The terms of purchases will be taken into account and an estimate will be made of the amount of cash that will be needed each month to purchase the materials or to pay for the accounts payable arising from the purchase.

Labor. From the production schedule an estimate will be computed of the amount of direct labor that will go into the product each month. Care should be taken, however, not to confuse the labor cost as shown on the production department's cost-accounting records, and the actual outlay of payroll cash. We are here interested in the latter. Due consideration will have to be given whether a week or two of wages are "held back" on the factory workers. It will also be found that, although there may be the same number of work days in two different months, one month may contain four "pay days," while the next month may have five.

Other factory expenses. In addition to the materials and direct labor costs, the manufacturing process will necessitate other expenses such as indirect labor, materials, and supplies. These go into the cost of the product as "indirect expenses" or "overhead." In making up the cash budget, however, we are concerned not with the overhead expenses as they appear on the cost records, but rather with the actual outlay of cash for these items.

Administrative and selling expenses. Administrative and selling expenses, which include salaries, supplies, rent, light, heat, insurance, advertising, etc., must, of course, also be taken into account. But here again, we do not use the same figures that appear in the income statement, but rather the estimate of monthly cash disbursements to cover these various items.

Other cash disbursements. The cash budget covers not only working capital items but also anything for which cash disbursements will have to be made.

CASH BALANCE. At the bottom of the cash budget the difference between the total receipts and disbursements for each month will be shown. The cash on hand at the beginning of the period will be noted, and after giving effect to this and the difference between the monthly receipts and disbursements, a cumulative total of the cash balance should be written in. Business firms usually like to maintain a minimum cash balance of a certain amount. After considering this, we can calculate from the figures in the budget the amount of excess cash or deficiency which will be present at the end of each month. If a deficiency exists, then the company will know in advance when it must secure the cash through a bank loan or some other source.

When budgets are made out on a monthly basis, the treasurer or disbursing officer is more interested in the day by day availability of funds than in the monthly totals. In other words, the budget may show that the excess of cash receipts over disbursements for a particular month may amount to, for example, $50,000, but this is no consolation to him if he has to meet a bill of $30,000 by the 10th of the month for purchases made the preceding month. Likewise, the total net cash receipts for the month of March, for example, will not be available to meet an income tax installment due March 15.

Practical Budget Considerations. Perhaps it should be re-emphasized that a budget is only an estimate. Changes will constantly have to be made in the figures when it is found that actual experiences do not turn out as anticipated. Workable budgets must be flexible. Budgets are only as good as the use made of them. It is useless to prepare a budget if some effort is not made to live up to it. Rather than ignore a budget once it was found to be out of line, good management will revise the budget and continue to use it as an expense control. The importance of the cash budget to working capital management cannot be overemphasized.

Application of Funds Statement. Unlike budgeting, the application of funds statement is used to analyze past rather than future operations. This statement explains the origin of increases or decreases in working capital or cash over a period of time. This information can be used as a guide for working capital management in the future. Knowledge of the total change in investment in working capital over a period of time (obtained from comparative balance sheets) is no more important than knowledge of why and how these changes took place. The *application of funds* statement provides this information.

The major sources of working capital or "funds" include net income, depreciation, increase in current liabilities, sale of fixed assets, sale of securities, and amortization of prepaid expenses, or other non-cash expenses. The major uses of working capital are retirement of long-term debt, repurchase of corporate securities, reduction in current liabilities, dividend payments, purchase of fixed assets, and operating losses. A study of these sources and uses of funds may reveal why the total working capital may have moved in an opposite direction from accounting profits or deficits. Other uses of this information are to indicate the draining of funds to meet dividends or extra-heavy liability repayments. The effect of operating losses is indicated as well as diversion of funds to finance fixed-asset expansion. The influence of depreciation accounting on working capital is clearly indicated. An example of an application of funds statement follows:

Application of Funds
for the Year Ending December 31, 1956

Source of funds:		
Net income		$ 480,540
Depreciation charges		234,680
Sale of preferred stock		1,200,000
Increase in current liabilities		68,290
		$1,983,510
Use of funds:		
Repayment of mortgages	$500,000	
Purchase of fixed assets	986,440	
Preferred dividends paid	30,000	
Common dividends paid	266,800	1,783,240
Change in working capital (increase)		$ 200,270

Represented by:	1956	1955	Change
Cash	$ 436,200	$ 483,890	−$ 47,690
Accounts and notes receivable	1,132,230	781,060	+ 351,170
Inventories	802,340	905,550	− 103,210
Working capital	$2,370,770	$2,170,500	+$200,270

Credit rating maintenance

Importance of Credit Rating. The principal factor determining the amount and terms of credit and loans obtainable by a concern is its credit standing or credit rating. Credit rating is an intangible concept which becomes established in the minds of creditors or potential creditors and which refers to the future ability and willingness of a debtor to pay his debts. The credit rating of a debtor may vary substantially over periods of time. Various credit-granting institutions may assign different ratings to the same debtor. The credit rating indicates the ability to obtain credit on satisfactory terms. A firm with a good credit rating finds little difficulty in borrowing to meet short-term capital needs, but one with a poor credit rating may be unable to borrow when the need arises or may have to pay extremely high interest rates or agree to unreasonable terms, to obtain a loan. A firm's reputation in paying bills and meeting maturities when due and its available capital and financial standing determine its credit rating in the minds of creditors. A well-run concern will jealously protect its credit rating. A good credit rating can be a firm's most important asset in times of financial stress. Poor credit may result in a deficiency of working capital and perhaps financial embarrassment. The well-managed business will make every effort to maintain a good credit rating or to improve its credit rating. Important to an understanding of how to maintain a good credit rating is an understanding of what creditors consider in establishing a credit rating for an individual firm.

CREDIT RATING FROM THE CREDITOR'S VIEWPOINT. Creditors consider the four *C*'s of credit in establishing credit ratings. These are *character, capacity, capital,* and *collateral. Character* includes the willingness of the debtor to pay his debts. If a debtor has been prompt in paying his bills in the past, it is assumed that he will continue to be so, unless conditions change. A debtor that has consistently been slow in payment of accounts will generally have a very poor credit rating regardless of his financial condition or capital. Creditors look to experiences of others in granting credit. This information is readily obtainable through credit interchange bureaus and such organizations as Dun & Bradstreet, Inc. Slow payment of an account does not affect a firm's credit rating with just that one creditor. Generally, all other creditors, or potential creditors, will know all about the slow-pay account. Failure to pay a bill may cause cancellation of credit by other creditors as well as by the one involved.

Capacity implies the earning ability of the company. Capacity will be judged by an analysis of the firm's financial statements. Earnings records will be studied and probable trends in earnings determined to judge the ability of the business to repay debt. The ability of the management, amount of competition in the industry, general industry conditions, and the stage of the business cycle will all be taken into account in attempting to judge future earning power. The purpose for which the capital obtained on credit will be used is considered in its effect on the probable future earning-power of the business.

Capital has to do with the worth of the business and, therefore, is another indication of its ability to pay. Not only total capital is taken into account, but also, owners' equity, other liabilities outstanding, liquidity of capital items, and use being made of capital. The amount of other debt outstanding is important as it limits the claim of a new creditor on the assets in the event of financial difficulty. In addition to the amount of other debt, the lien involved and the maturity dates are important to a new creditor in determining his position in event of liquidation as well as his chances of repayment under normal circumstances. The working capital position is of particular importance, as it tends to indicate liquidity and ability to meet short-term loans. If the net working capital is relatively small, firms will be reluctant to grant credit or make loans as they will question the ability of the company to pay. The nature of the working capital items, and their turnover rates, are important in this regard.

Collateral is of importance to certain creditors. Collateral involves a pledge of specific property and gives the creditor obtaining the pledge an advantage in collection over other creditors with no specific claim against property. If collateral is involved, the value and liquidity of the property pledged is of importance. The value of the pledged property to the operation of the concern is also considered. Even if collateral is pledged, the ability of the corporation to pay based on its earning power or current position is generally a more important credit-rating consideration due to the expenses and difficulty of foreclosure on pledged property.

Another factor which creditors will consider in determining credit-rating of debtors might be called "conditions." This would include the present status of the business cycle and general credit and business conditions throughout the country. In addition, credit is always limited by the ability of the creditor to lend and how well the proposed loan fits into the creditor's maturity and diversification plan. Creditors require substantial financial information from the debtor and the ease with which this information is obtained may influence the granting of credit.

Working Capital Ratios. In analyzing the credit rating of debtor firms, creditors place considerable emphasis on certain ratios. The individual businesses, themselves, may find it advantageous to use these ratios in studying their own financial position. Potential investors as well as creditors make substantial use of ratio analysis. Of particular importance in this discussion of working capital are a group of working capital ratios which aid in studying the current financial position of corporations. Two very useful working capital ratios, receivables turnover and inventory turnover, were discussed in the previous chapter, so nothing further will be said about them. We will now consider some of the more important remaining working capital ratios.

Current ratio. This is perhaps the most important ratio used in analyzing the working capital. The *current ratio* is the ratio of current assets to current liabilities. Thus, if the current assets amount to $2,000,000, and the current liabilities are $1,000,000, this would be a ratio of 2 to 1. Although we are speaking of the current *ratio,* it is usually not expressed in ratio form, but rather as a simple number. In the above example we would divide the current liabilities into the current assets, and the resultant figure of "2" would be the current ratio.

The current ratio expresses the ability of the company to pay its current liabilities. In the daily operation of a business it is the current liabilities that the management must be concerned about rather than a bond issue which may not come due for 20 years. The current liabilities are ordinarily repaid, not from the proceeds of a bonds or stock issue, but rather from the cash on hand, or what will be collected from the accounts receivable or the inventory. In other words, the current liabilities are repaid from the current assets. The current ratio shows the margin of safety of the company with regard to the payment of its short-term debts. Or another way of saying the same thing, it shows how much the current assets may shrink without imperiling the ability of the company to meet these debts.

There is a rule of thumb that the current ratio should be at least two. That is, the current assets should be at least twice the current liabilities. With such a ratio, the current assets could shrink in value 50 per cent, and the company could still pay its current liabilities. This 2 to 1 ratio should not be taken too seriously. It does not apply to any particular business. What constitutes an adequate current ratio would vary according to the particular industry, company, season of the year, and period of the business cycle. A company with a rapid current assets turnover will usually require a lower current ratio than one with a slow turnover. Furthermore, the amounts of the particular items that go to make up the ratio are of great importance. For example, a current ratio of 2 to 1 would undoubtedly be adequate if practically all the current assets were cash and equivalent, but it might be wholly inadequate if the bulk of the current assets are slow-moving merchandise or overdue receivables.

"Acid test" ratio. The *acid test* ratio is the relation of current assets after inventory has been deducted (sometimes called the *quick assets*) to the current liabilities. The amount of the cash and receivables (and marketable securities) indicate the ability of the

company to meet its current liabilities better than when the inventory is added to the other current assets. The rule of thumb is that the cash (and equivalent) plus the receivables should be at least equal to the current liabilities. From what has already been said, it is evident that the ratio used in the acid test is sometimes referred to as the *quick ratio.*

Working capital turnover. The working capital turnover is found by dividing the average working capital (current assets) into the net sales for the year. The average working capital can be determined by taking one half the sum of the working capital at the beginning of the year and at the end of the year.

The working capital turnover indicates the number of dollars of sales that are produced by each dollar of working capital. In other words, it shows the efficiency of the working capital. Generally speaking the more rapid the turnover, the more efficient is the financial management of the concern. Too high a turnover, however, may result from insufficient cash or inventory and might prove to be embarrassing if raw material prices increased appreciably, or some other need for additional cash arose. The turnover figure may be compared with past turnover figures for the same company, and with those of similar companies in the same line of business.

Since the working capital position can be altered appreciably by a change in current liabilities, independent of the sales of the company, it might be advisable to calculate the turnover of the *net* working capital (current assets less current liabilities) instead of the *gross* working capital (current assets) turnover.

Working capital financing

PERMANENT FINANCING. From the preceding discussion it should be obvious that there is a need for permanent investment in working capital. The regular working capital of a corporation is a permanent capital requirement and should be more or less permanently financed. Part of the regular working capital is sometimes financed through short-term loans, with the hope of paying off the indebtedness with the profits earned. The wisdom of such a procedure can be questioned. In the first place, the profits may not be realized for a long time, and in some instances, never realized. The embarrassment that would be caused by the short-term loan under these circumstances is readily apparent. Or even if profits are realized soon, they may not be available for retiring a debt. A successful new business would be expanding its sales volume. This would call for an increase in the amount of regular working capital. Or even if the sales remain the same, at least part of the profit may be paid out in the form of dividends.

A business that attempts to finance its regular working capital by means of bank loans, or other forms of short-term credit, will soon run into difficulties. Although the turnover of inventory and accounts receivable will result in the receipt of cash, this cash must be expended again for materials, labor, and other expenses. So the minimum amount of working capital needed at all times is just as fixed in the business as is the investment in land, buildings, and other fixed assets. This being the case, the regular working capital should be financed by permanent capital obtained through the sale of stock or bonds, or acquired through reinvestment of earnings, rather than from short-term sources.

Short-term Financing. Seasonal and special working capital may be financed through short-term sources, for these needs are only temporary. As the peak season passes or as the special purpose is consummated, enough additional cash should be generated to repay the sources of the temporary working capital. This is not true of fixed working capital, since the cash generated (less the profit) is needed to replace the inventory and receivables producing the cash. Many corporations have found themselves financially embarrassed because they have attempted to finance some of the permanent working capital needs from temporary sources. Only variable working capital needs should be temporarily financed. At least part of each major working capital item is needed permanently in the business. Only a portion of the cash, receivables, and inventory in any business would be temporary or variable working capital.

If a company having a seasonal business keeps enough cash on hand at all times to meet the seasonal load, it will have redundant cash during part of the year. It would be losing the opportunity to earn a return on this money. Furthermore, too much cash on hand might tend to encourage extravagance on the part of the corporate officials. Since the extra-seasonal working capital is needed for only a few months, it is common for companies to depend upon the commercial bank or their trade creditors to finance at least part of it.

Advantages of Short-term Financing. Borrowing for short periods of time has certain advantages over long-term borrowing or other forms of more permanent financing. Short-term financing may be lower in cost than permanent financing. Since it is easier to determine a debtor's ability to pay in the near future than in the distant future, risk in granting long-term credit is greater than short-term. Since risk is greater, higher interest rates may have to be paid for long-term financing than for short-term. There may be less time involved in granting short-term credit and less credit-checking expense so that the lender may charge less because of lower costs of making short-term loans.

In some instances, short-term credit may be the only source of additional capital to a business. This is true particularly for small companies. It may be expedient to use short-term financing while arranging more permanent financing from other sources. Certain kinds of short-term financing are almost automatic for certain businesses. The purchase of goods is normally made on credit so that a firm usually obtains short-term financing when it purchases merchandise. Short-term credit arises almost automatically from the practice of paying labor some time after the work has been performed, and of paying taxes in periods after they have accrued.

Short-term financing may be more flexible than long-term financing. If temporary needs are financed short-term, as the need for funds is reduced, the accumulated cash can be used to repay the short-term borrowing. When short-term sources are used, it is easy to expand and contract working capital as needs dictate. Funds raised from long-term sources are in the business more or less permanently, and repayment, and new long-term financing are more difficult.

Disadvantages of Short-term Financing. Short-term financing has a major disadvantage in the early repayment provisions. This factor can be the cause of much financial embarrassment and grief to the business concerned. Liquid funds may not be available to meet short-term loans as they mature. Short-term financing for permanent needs requires constant refinancing—both in good times and bad. The problem of arranging for repayment of short-term loans when due may occupy the major portion of management's time and ability. Inability to meet a short-term maturity may ruin a firm's future credit-rating and thereby its ability to obtain capital in the future. Short-term financing can be very risky to the business, unless it can foresee sources of cash to repay the short-term loans when due.

An added disadvantage of short-term financing may be high cost. While the same type of financing from the same creditors may be at a lower rate on a short-term basis than long-term, some sources of short-term financing may be very expensive. When short-term financing is the only credit available to a firm, it may be available only at very high rates. Use of short-term financing may reduce the ability to obtain additional short-term financing in the future. In recent years a number of companies have issued subordinated debentures in order that future financing, both long- and short-term, may be made easier.

Questions

1. Indicate the advantages experienced by a company which has adequate working capital.
2. What are the possible disadvantages of redundant working capital?
3. Indicate the different kinds of budgets which may be kept by a large manufacturing company.
4. Indicate the importance of the cash budget and explain the procedure involved in making it out.
5. What is meant by an "application of funds" statement?
6. Indicate what is meant by the four *C*'s of credit. Which do you think is the most important? Why?
7. What is meant by the current ratio? What is an adequate current ratio?
8. What is meant by the "acid test" ratio? Do you think this is a more important ratio than the current ratio? Explain.
9. Indicate how the working capital turnover is computed? Is it always desirable to have as rapid a working capital turnover as possible? Explain.
10. Indicate the possible advantages and disadvantages of financing working capital through short-term as compared with long-term borrowing.

Problems

1. The Bord and Baylor Department Store is to open its doors for the first time on Jan. 2, 19-1. Sales for the first 6 months are estimated as follows:

Month	*Sales*
January	$20,000
February	25,000
March	30,000
April	35,000
May	35,000
June	30,000

It is anticipated that 20 per cent of the sales will be cash and 80 per cent net 30 days. The gross profit on sales (profit before any expenses, except inventory) is expected to be 20 per cent. All purchases and expenses are to be paid immediately in cash. Fixed expenses will amount to $1,000 a month, and variable expenses will amount to 10 per cent of the sales. (Bad debts are included in variable expenses.) The company will start out with cash of $1,000 and inventory of $16,000, and it does not want these accounts reduced below these figures during any month. Make calculations below on a monthly rather than a daily basis. Assume that all estimates are correct. (Ignore federal income taxes, and assume that inventory sold in a particular month is purchased that month.) (a) Prepare a three-column report showing the cash income and cash outgo and the excess of one over the other, with proper notations as to source or purpose for each month. (b) If the company does not borrow any money, how much cash will it need at the start, exclusive of the original $1,000 in cash and the initial inventory of $16,000? How would this cash be obtained? (c) Assuming that no money is borrowed, list the individual current asset accounts as of the end of each month. (d) If the company could borrow at 7 per cent straight interest, would you recommend that money be borrowed for working capital? Why? If so, when should this be borrowed? (e) If the company has only the $1,000 in cash and the $16,000 inventory to begin business and has to borrow all the rest needed, indicate how much it would have to borrow and the duration of the loans if the total interest charges are kept at an absolute minimum. Assume the following for purposes of answering the question: straight 7 per cent interest paid at the beginning of each month on the loan of the previous month; the amount needed for a particular month is borrowed for that entire month; the excess of cash income over outgo for any particular month is available at the beginning of the month to pay off the loans; expenses stated above do not include interest charges. (f) If no money is borrowed, how much profit would the company make for the six-month period? (g) As a practical matter, would you make any allowances for the possibility that the estimates given would not prove to be correct? Explain fully.

2. Racy's Department Store presented the following balance sheet as of December 31, 19-1:

Assets		*Liabilities and Net Worth*	
Cash	$ 75,000	Accounts Payable	$ 250,000
Accounts Receivable	250,000	Capital Stock	1,500,000
Inventory	825,000	Surplus	300,000
Building	900,000		
Total	$2,050,000	Total	$2,050,000

(a) Compute the current ratio. (b) Compute the "acid test" ratio.

Chapter 22

SOURCES OF WORKING CAPITAL

Sources. There are quite a variety of sources of working capital, but not all of these are available to every company. Some sources are commonly used in particular industries while other sources are used in almost all types of industries. Individual companies within an industry vary considerably in their use of various sources of working capital.

In an earlier chapter we classified working capital into fixed and variable. Generally speaking, the initial or fixed working capital is that which is needed permanently in the business, and should therefore be obtained from long-term sources. Variable working capital can be raised from short-term sources. In our discussion of the subject we will classify sources of working capital according to long-term and short-term types. Long-term sources of working capital include both (1) the owners of the business and (2) the creditors.

Long-term financing of working capital

Stocks. The safest way to provide the initial working capital is through the sale of preferred or common stock. This should be done at the time of the promotion of the company. This part of the working capital is going to remain in the business permanently and, therefore, it should be financed with permanent capital.

Since they represent equity and there is no repayment required, stocks are the safest permanent source of working capital. If the volume of sales increases and continues at the high level for the indefinite future, an increased amount of permanent working capital will be needed. Stocks are a good permanent source of these additional fixed working capital needs.

Retained Earnings. The retained earnings constitute another way of having the owners finance the working capital requirements.

This is a safe method to use since there is no repayment required. Naturally, the initial working capital cannot be obtained from this source, but additional fixed working capital needs are often supplied in part from retained earnings.

In some cases, the earnings of the company may be too slow in accumulating to furnish the additional working capital needed for expansion purposes. A large part of the earnings may have to be paid out in taxes, and at least a part of what is left may be given to the shareholders in the form of dividends. Thus what the company has left may be insufficient to finance the expansion called for at the particular time. In most instances, however, depending upon the rate of earnings and the amount needed for expansion, the retained earnings may furnish at least a part of the working capital needed.

The reader should guard against the error of assuming that whatever is left of the profits, after taxes and dividends have been paid, is available for expansion purposes in the form of cash or other kinds of working capital. The difference between the profit shown on the income statement and the change in the cash account for the period should be obvious to one who has studied elementary accounting. When a sale has been made the income statement shows the profit made even though no cash as yet has been collected from the buyer. Also, a company may show a large profit, but the cash account may be much less than at the beginning of the period. The money may have been used during the period for the purchase of additional inventory, or even to acquire some fixed assets.

Depreciation. In at least one respect, the amount of cash available for expansion purposes may even exceed the amount of the profits that are left after taxes and dividends. This results from the depreciation charge which will be more fully discussed in Chapter 24. Depreciation is a legitimate cost of doing business. The federal government permits its charge-off as an expense before arriving at the net taxable income. The handling of this item in accounting is to charge it as an expense in the income statement, and to set up a bookkeeping reserve of an equivalent amount which is subtracted from the appropriate asset account. No cash, however, is set aside at the time in a fund to replace the particular asset.

Thus if a company does business on a cash basis only and none of the asset accounts (other than cash) are increased or none of the liability accounts decreased during the period under consideration, the cash account should show an increase greater than the amount of profits left after taxes. This additional cash equivalent to the

TABLE 31

USE OF NET PROCEEDS FROM CASH SALE OF NEW CORPORATE SECURITIES
UNITED STATES, SELECTED YEARS
(IN MILLIONS OF DOLLARS AND PER CENT)

Year	*Total*	*Plant and Equipment*	*Working Capital*	*Retirements**	*Other Purposes*	*Total*
1955	$10,263	53.0%	26.0%	12.2%	8.8%	100%
1954	9,418	56.2	18.0	19.7	6.1	100%
1953	8,755	64.5	26.4	3.0	6.1	100%
1952	9,380	67.3	19.9	7.0	5.7	100%
1951	7,607	67.2	18.7	11.1	3.0	100%
1950	6,261	47.5	16.6	30.2	5.7	100%
1949	5,959	62.5	14.8	17.4	5.3	100%
1948	6,959	60.7	24.5	11.4	3.4	100%
1947	6,466	52.7	18.3	26.4	2.6	100%
1946	6,757	31.4	17.2	48.0	3.4	100%
1945	5,902	10.8	7.5	79.4	2.3	100%
1939	2,115	8.0	7.3	83.5	1.2	100%
1934	384	8.3	6.8	82.0	2.9	100%

* Includes all retirements of funded debt, other debt, and preferred stock for the years 1934–1954. For 1955, it includes only retirement of securities. Data for 1955 obtained from *Statistical Bulletin*, February, 1956, p. 5, United States Securities and Exchange Commission.

SOURCE: *Moody's Industrial Manual*, Moody's Investors Service, New York, 1955, p. a17.

amount of the depreciation reserve could very well be used to finance additional working capital. Of course, the particular fixed asset which is being depreciated will have to be replaced at the end of a relatively long period of years. But, perhaps the profits earned from the additional investment in working capital may over this period return enough to replace the asset. In some instances part of the additional cash resulting from the depreciation charge is being constantly invested in fixed assets. The depreciation charge is normally an important source of additional working capital to a company.

SALE OF ASSETS. Occasionally corporations will sell fixed assets that are no longer needed in the business. Whether the company makes a profit or not, the cash obtained can be conveniently used for permanent working capital. Many companies have sizable amounts invested in government bonds or other securities. When the securities owned are not held for control purposes, they could be sold to provide additional working capital.

BONDS AND NOTES. More or less permanent working capital is sometimes obtained through the sale of bonds or long-term notes.

Generally speaking, this would not be as safe a method as the sale of stock, since the interest charges on the bonds and notes must be paid just the same as any other kind of debt, and furthermore, cash will have to be taken out of the business to retire the obligations at their maturity, or the firm must have a credit-standing which will enable it to refund the obligations.

Loans from Officers and Directors. In the case of many companies, particularly small concerns, the principal officers or directors often lend the company money both for short- and long-term working capital. In some instances this may be the only source of capital open to them at the time.

Sale-and-Lease-Back Arrangements. Many companies have large amounts of money tied up in buildings and land. Only the depreciation on the buildings, and not on the land, may be charged off against income for tax purposes, and the rate of such depreciation is subject to approval by the government. Some companies have sold all or part of their buildings and at the same time entered into an agreement to lease back the properties from the purchaser. The rental payment, of course, covers both buildings and the land, and can be deducted in its entirety for income tax purposes. These payments are sufficiently large in amount to constitute in effect a fast write-off of the properties over a relatively short period of years. The agreement will provide for an option to renew the lease upon its termination at a greatly reduced figure. This type of arrangement gives the company the use of a sum of money without the issuance of any additional securities. Furthermore, during the period of the lease, income taxes will be reduced by virtue of the rental payments. It is usually provided in the agreement that the lessee will pay all taxes on the property and keep it properly insured and maintained.

The purchaser of the property is usually either a life insurance company or a nonprofit organization, such as an educational institution or a charitable foundation. The rentals represent a higher return on the investment than could be obtained through the purchase of bonds. Furthermore, life insurance companies pay income taxes under a special formula which results in lower taxes than ordinary business corporations, and nonprofit organizations pay no income taxes when they do not own the business outright.

In some of the older sales and leases, a clause was inserted giving the lessee the option to buy the property upon termination of the lease. The courts, however, have held that where such a clause is present, the original sale by the lessee was not a bona fide one, and that only the amount of the rental payments that would be equivalent to depreciation on the buildings could be charged for income tax purposes. In recent years there have been several instances where life insurance companies have entered into agreements with industrial concerns to build the plants themselves and lease them to the companies. For example, the New York Life Insurance Company built and leased properties costing $10,000,000 to the Continental Can Company.

The sale of the property provides funds which may be used for working capital. It reduces the amount of capital tied up in fixed assets and thus releases capital for current uses. Although the capital applied to purchase the fixed assets in the first place was a source of long-term financing to the corporation, the sale-and-lease-back arrangement can be considered a source of working capital because the arrangement releases funds for working capital uses. Since the lease arrangements are generally of a long-term nature, this type arrangement may be considered a long-term source of working capital.

Intermediate financing of working capital

Intermediate Financing. Intermediate financing is a term used to define borrowing for a period longer than one year but for a shorter period than would strictly be considered long-term. Intermediate financing may run five or even ten years. Many such loans are repaid in installments and are, therefore, generally considered amortized loans. Intermediate financing is used in many cases as an interim kind of financing, which will eventually be replaced by a more permanent source of capital. The intermediate financing is used until the long-term sources can be developed. The major long-term source generally relied upon to replace intermediate financing is reinvested earnings. If it is expected that sufficient earnings will accumulate to provide the needed funds in a period up to ten years, intermediate financing may be used rather than long-term sources because it is more flexible and the obligation can be retired as the earnings accumulate. Another use of intermediate financing is for capital requirements which will last for longer than one year, but less than the time normally considered permanent. A company may be expanding its working capital for the next four or five years to handle increased business during that period, but it may not expect to maintain the higher level of operations after the next four or five years. Short-term sources would not satisfactorily supply this need and long-term sources would leave the business with excess capital after the four- or five-year period.

Term loans are the major source of intermediate financing but installment financing of equipment purchases is another source. Both of these types of intermediate financing will be discussed further below.

TERM LOANS. Term loans are granted by commercial banks and life insurance companies. In some instances, several lenders will join together in making a single large loan to a company. Term loans are made for periods slightly in excess of one year up to ten years. Many are made for a five-year period, but the majority of them are made for periods of less than three years. The loan is paid off in installments during the life of the loan, with a relatively larger payment being made at the maturity of the loan. Manufacturing concerns are the principal users of this type of loan. The total amount of the usual loan is from $100,000 to $250,000, although in the case of large companies the loan may be greatly in excess of these amounts. Loans to small businesses are usually secured by a mortgage on real estate or equipment, but those granted to large companies are commonly unsecured.

The term loan contract often contains certain covenants designed to protect the lender, similar to those that are commonly inserted in a bond indenture. Dividends may be restricted if they would reduce the working capital position below a specified amount. Limitations may be imposed on the incurring of additional debts or the placing of liens on the property.

INSTALLMENT FINANCING OF EQUIPMENT PURCHASES. Although not a technique for financing working capital, installment financing of equipment purchases will be discussed here as a type of intermediate financing. The ability of a corporation to finance equipment in this manner means that the company can use funds which would otherwise apply toward the purchase of equipment for working capital purposes. This type of financing is considered an intermediate source since it is generally repaid in installments over a period of several years. This type of financing is generally utilized by commercial and industrial enterprises.

Equipment installment financing takes three general forms. The manufacturer of the equipment may sell it on installment terms to the purchaser. In this case, the manufacturer or distributor is directly financing the purchaser of the equipment. This is possible only if the manufacturers or distributors are well financed with available capital to carry accounts or notes receivable for a long period of time. As this is not always the case, equipment financing could take the form of bank borrowing with the equipment pledged as collateral for the loan used to pay off the manufacturer. In this case, the bank would be providing the purchaser of the equipment with capital to pay off the manufacturer. The third possibility is the sale or assignment of the account or note to a financial institution by the manufacturer. Under these circumstances, the financial institution is supplying the manufacturer with capital to carry his accounts or is actually carrying the accounts for him by purchasing them.

In all three of these arrangements, the loan is for the express purpose of financing the purchase of industrial or commercial equipment. The loan will require a down payment of a sizable amount so that the purchaser has sufficient equity in the equipment to make it financially desirable to continue payments. These down payments range from one-fifth to one-third generally, but may be as high as 50 per cent. The length of the payment period varies with the needs of the purchaser, but is limited by the years of use in the equipment and by the possible obsolescence rate. The equipment should be fully paid off far in advance of its loss of full value.

These loans are of the installment type. The principal is amortized over the life of the loan. Interest charges are generally figured on the original unpaid balance and are paid as part of the regular monthly payments. A quoted rate of 5 per cent on the original unpaid balance would be considerably higher in actual cost since the original balance is outstanding only until the first payment is made and the interest continues at the same amount for the life of the loan. The loans are either secured by a lien against the equipment or the title to the equipment rests with the creditor. Loans of this type generally run from twelve months to five years depending on the useful life of the equipment.

Financing of railroad cars and other similar equipment (see Chapter 10) is generally long-term rather than intermediate financing.

Government Agencies. Several government agencies, in recent years, have become a source of financing to many American corporations. These loans have been for various purposes, but are often used as a source of additional working capital. These are discussed under intermediate financing as the term of the loans generally runs more than one year, but less than a period which would be considered long-term.

In an effort to aid business and pull the country out of the depression that was well under way, the federal government, in 1932, formed the Reconstruction Finance Corporation, commonly referred to as the RFC. The objectives of this corporation were "to provide emergency financing facilities for financial institutions, to aid in financing agriculture, commerce, and industry, and for other purposes." To provide funds for the organization, the government purchased stock and advances were made by the Treasury Department.

As the title suggests, the Reconstruction Finance Corporation was formed to give financial assistance to business which was in the midst of a severe depression. But the organization was not terminated after the recovery from the depression had been made. Of course, even after business conditions had improved, the RFC still had to stay in existence to collect the money that was outstanding. But this was not the only reason for its continuation. Loans continued to be made. We had not been out of the depression many years until the defense program was launched. The RFC was generous in making loans to concerns that were engaged in or that turned to defense work. After our entry into World War II, the need for additional financing became even greater for both old and new companies. The objective of the RFC had changed completely from that of aiding sick businesses to that of helping industry turn out war materials. In addition, many loans appeared to have been made as a matter of political expediency.

The RFC continued to operate after the close of hostilities, lending to all types of businesses under its expanded powers. Shortly after the election of President Eisenhower, steps were taken to liquidate the RFC. No new loans could be made by it after September 28, 1953, and it was dissolved in June of 1954. The Small Business Administration (SBA) was set up in place of the RFC, but it has neither the power nor the funds that were possessed by the RFC. As the title indicates, its loans are confined to small businesses and are designed to give aid where banks are unwilling or unable to provide needed intermediate financing. The SBA first attempts to get banks to grant the loans, or to have them grant a specific percentage of particular loans. Loans up to $250,000 may now be granted for a period of 10 years (in certain instances, 20 years) to businesses with less than 500 employees. The Small Business Administration statutes were amended in 1958 to permit the formation of Small Business Investment Companies to provide capital for small businesses. The investment companies are financed jointly by private investors and the SBA.

Legislation enacted in 1934 permits the Federal Reserve banks to make loans directly to private businesses. Prior to that time they dealt only with banks. The loans can be granted through banks, or as stated, they can be made directly to business concerns. According to the statutes, the loans can be made only when the particular business cannot get financial assistance from the usual sources. The maximum maturity of the loans is five years and is to be repaid in installments. Before they may be granted they must be approved by an industrial advisory committee of the particular Federal Reserve district. These loans reached a peak in 1935 but have fallen off to the point where they are of negligible importance today.

Although we have mentioned Federal Reserve loans under the head of those granted by governmental agencies, it is understood that the Federal Reserve banks are not, strictly speaking, federal agencies. All the stock of these banks is now owned by the member banks in the particular district. But the tie-up between them and the government is so close that listing them in this category is not inappropriate.

Short-term financing of working capital

BANK LOANS. Bank loans have long been an important source of short-term working capital, but their relative importance has declined in recent years. Several different factors have accounted for this. Many businesses, particularly the larger ones, act as their own bankers. That is, they sell securities to furnish the needed capital. In addition, many companies retain an appreciable part of their earnings. Also many additional sources of working capital are available to businesses which were not present years ago. Some concerns have cut down on the amount needed for working capital due to the practice of carrying smaller inventories. Despite what has just been said, commercial bankers still remain an important source of working capital to many businesses.

Although a company will usually confine its borrowing to one bank in the community, where the company has plants or places of business in several cities, it may borrow from banks in some of the other localities.

It is highly desirable for a business to have good relations with its bank. Since practically all companies have checking accounts, this establishes one type of connection, and because of this relationship, which might have extended over a relatively long period of time, the particular company may be able to obtain a loan when needed. But naturally banks are more particular in selecting debtors than in picking their creditors. Banks are sometimes criticized for their willingness to lend money to a company which does not need it, and their reluctance to lend it when really needed. Some experienced businessmen advise young businesses particularly to negotiate a loan at a bank when they actually do not need the funds so that a favorable relationship will have been established with the bank. Then, when they actually have need for a loan, the bank might be more favorably inclined to grant it. Following are a number of different ways in which money may be obtained from commercial banks.

Ordinary (unsecured) loans. The usual commercial bank loan is made on an unsecured note with a maturity ranging from 30 days to one year, 90 to 180 days being common. Before obtaining a loan it is the usual custom for the bankers to go over the financial statements of the company and credit reports on the company, and after giving due consideration to the management, present status, and future prospects, to establish a "line of credit" for the company. This establishes a maximum amount which the company can borrow during a period of time without a credit recheck by the bank. The terms of the loan including the interest rate to be paid are included in this agreement. Since such loans are intended by the bank to be of a temporary nature, the bank likes to see all the loans paid off within a period of one year. Furthermore, it is preferred by the bank that the company remain out of debt for at least a 30-day period even though a new loan may be secured within a short period of time.

A line of credit has the advantage to the company of a known amount of obtainable credit. Even though it is not all needed at the time of the application, it can be taken up at any time during the year if the company needs the funds. Also, it saves credit checking each time a new amount is desired and gives the company a better basis for financial planning since it has an established known line of credit.

When the bank has some doubts about the ability of the company to repay the loan in the future, it may require the maintenance of certain ratios and put a limit on the salaries paid to officers, and the amount of dividends which may be paid to the shareholders. The line of credit agreement usually extends for a one-year period and may be renewed at the end of that time, or a new one with different provisions may be drawn up for the next year. Although the line of credit agreement does not force the bank to make the loan if conditions should materially change after it has been drawn up, the bank will usually abide by its terms, unless radical changes occur.

When the bank has some doubts about the ability of the company to repay the loan, which may be the case particularly with small or young companies, they may have some of the officers of the company personally indorse the company notes. When this is done such officers could be held personally liable for the loan in event of the inability of the company to pay. Such a loan would be classified about halfway between an unsecured and a secured loan.

It is customary for a bank to "discount" the borrower's note. In other words, the bank will deduct the interest in advance from the principal amount of the loan, and credit the account of the borrower with the balance. Thus the effective rate paid by the borrower on the money that he actually gets to use will be higher than the rate of interest agreed upon. On a 180-day (6 months) loan, 6 per cent (annual rate) discounted is the equivalent to approximately 6.19 per cent since the borrower is paying $3.00 for the use of $97 for six months instead of $100. In the past, banks commonly required that the borrower maintain a minimum balance in his checking account of from 10 to 20 per cent of the principal amount of the loan. In such instances the effective rate of interest paid on the money that was actually available to the borrower was considerably in excess of the contract rate. If a 20 per cent balance were maintained on a six months, 6 per cent $100 loan, the borrower would be paying $3.00 interest but would receive the use of only $77. (This would be an effective rate of 7.79 per cent.) In recent years the practice has changed and many banks no longer require such minimum balances. But since banks usually require or expect that the borrower will maintain his checking account at that particular bank, certain balances will be maintained in order to meet the checks which are written in the ordinary course of business.

Loans secured by securities. Loans are often made by banks to individuals with stock or bonds as collateral security. Banks also commonly lend to investment bankers and security dealers on such security. But such loans are not ordinarily made to other types of businesses. If a company has marketable securities on hand it would normally liquidate them instead of securing a bank loan. In some instances, however, the company might have only a temporary need for the cash and want to hold on to the securities for a more or less permanent investment. Or, the securities may represent investments made in subsidiary companies which are being held for control purposes. In some instances a loan secured by the securities may be preferred over their sale because the market value of the particular collateral may be relatively low at that time. In these cases, businesses may use bank loans secured by such collateral.

Securities which are listed on one of the leading exchanges, such as the New York Stock Exchange or the American Stock Exchange, are preferred by the banks since their market values are known constantly, and they can be liquidated in a matter of minutes if the loan is not repaid. Listing is particularly important when the security is a stock. Bankers, of course, will ordinarily accept only negotiable securities as collateral for a loan and will lend only a portion of the market value of the securities. The securities will have to be indorsed or they will have to be assigned to the bank by the completion of a separate assignment form. The latter is preferred by the borrower over the indorsement. If the securities are indorsed, after they are reacquired by the borrower when payment of the loan is made, they will still contain the indorsement, which means that title to them can be passed by delivery of the particular security. Thus, a thief or finder could pass good title to an innocent purchaser for value. When a separate assignment form is attached to the security rather than indorsing it, the form may be destroyed when the collateral is returned to the borrower. Such a security can be more safely kept by the borrower, since his indorsement or completion of another assignment form would be necessary before anyone would get title to the property.

Loans secured by mortgages. Some businesses, particularly small concerns, sometimes find it necessary to mortgage their real estate or equipment as security for a bank loan. Real estate, however, is rarely used as security by large companies for the purpose of securing short-term working capital. Small companies, or concerns with poor credit ratings, may find it necessary to pledge real property even for short-term needs as they are unable to obtain an unsecured loan and have no securities to pledge. This real property, will, of course, have to be free of other encumbrances.

Loans secured by inventory. Chattel mortgages on inventory are rarely used as security for bank loans since the particular company will be constantly selling the inventory and the legal difficulties involved in obtaining clear title under a chattel mortgage would be too great each time an item of inventory is sold. When inventory serves as security for a loan, the documents commonly used as collateral are a special type rather than a chattel mortgage. Companies that are engaged in the business of shipping, storing, and processing standardized staple commodities—such as butter, coffee, corn, cotton, eggs, rubber, silk, and tobacco—frequently use claims to these commodities as security for bank loans. These claims take the form of bills of lading, trust receipts, and warehouse receipts.

A *bill of lading* is a document issued by a railroad or other common carrier when goods are delivered for shipment. This document serves as a receipt for the goods, documentary evidence of title, and a contract to deliver the goods. A *straight* bill of lading passes title only to the consignee (buyer), is not negotiable, and therefore cannot be used as collateral for a loan. The *order* bill of lading, on the other hand, gives title to the consignee or to anyone else to whom he may indorse the bill of lading. This kind of a bill of lading is thus negotiable, and can be indorsed to a bank as security for a loan. It is necessary to surrender the bill of lading to the railroad in order for the buyer to get the goods. The procedure followed for this type of transaction will be briefly described.

The seller draws a *draft* or, as it is sometimes called, a *bill of exchange* on the buyer for the amount due for the goods. This draft orders the buyer to pay the money to the seller or to some other payee designated by the seller. The seller turns the draft and bill of lading over to his bank. The latter sends these instruments to the buyer's bank. If the draft is payable on sight, the buyer's bank collects the amount of the draft from the buyer, gives him the bill of lading, and remits the money to the seller's bank. Thus the buyer must pay the draft before he receives the bill of lading from the bank. Without the bill of lading, he cannot obtain the merchandise from the carrier. If it is a *time* draft, the "acceptance" of the buyer on the draft is obtained before he can get the bill of lading to claim the merchandise. The draft then comes back to the seller's bank. In event that the seller wants his money out of the draft before its maturity, the bank will discount it. That is, the bank will advance the seller the money after it has deducted the appropriate amount of interest. When the draft is payable to the seller, the latter will, of course, have to indorse it before the bank will give him the money.

Trust receipts for staple commodities and durable consumers' goods, such as automobiles, radios, televisions, refrigerators, and stoves, which are commonly sold to consumers on the installment plan, are often used as security for bank loans. This device is used in the following manner.

The buyer arranges with the bank for a loan sufficient in amount to pay for the particular merchandise. The buyer then orders the merchandise from the manufacturer and instructs him to draw a draft on the particular bank for the amount of the invoice, and to send this together with the bill of lading to the bank. Before releasing the bill of lading to the buyer, the bank will make him execute trust receipts in favor of the bank for the goods. The trust receipt specifies that the bank is the legal owner of the property and that the borrower will hold such property, or the proceeds from the sale of such property, in trust for the benefit of the bank. When the articles are sold the proceeds are used to repay the bank loan, and the particular trust receipts are canceled.

Warehouse receipts are used as security for bank loans in about the same manner as trust receipts just described above. In fact the latter may also be used along with the warehouse receipts. When the buyer gets the goods he stores them in a public warehouse and gets warehouse receipts. The latter are then turned over to the bank and the trust receipts are canceled. Reduced to its simplest form a warehouse receipt is a receipt for goods which are stored in a public warehouse. Such warehouses must be licensed, and to be licensed they must be bonded. The receipts are made out in the form prescribed by the Uniform Warehouse Receipts Act, which Act also prescribes uniform procedures to be followed and rights of the parties to the instrument.

A warehouse receipt may be either negotiable or nonnegotiable in form. In the case of the *negotiable* receipt the goods may be delivered to the designated person or to whomever he may order delivery to be made by means of indorsing the receipt. If made out in favor of the purchaser of the goods the receipt by proper indorsement can be passed on to the bank to serve as security for a loan. When the *nonnegotiable* warehouse receipt is used the stored goods can be delivered only to the person designated in the receipt. If the buyer is designated, then a bank would not accept the receipt as security for a loan. But if the receipt is made out directly to the bank it can be used as collateral for a loan. In fact the nonnegotiable form is more frequently used (made out to the bank or finance company) since the warehouse will release goods if the bank requests it by mail without the necessity of sending in the receipts every time that some of the goods are to be released. When the negotiable form is used, the warehouse will require that the receipt be sent in each time any of the goods are to be released. Since the receipt through an indorsement may call for delivery of the goods to the bearer, there is danger of theft or loss when the bank parts with possession of the instrument.

Since independent public warehouses are not always near the place of business of the borrower, considerable time, expense, and trouble may be entailed in storing the goods. In recent years the practice of *field warehousing* has evolved as a practical means of financing with inventory as security. Under this arrangement a designated part of the borrower's property is set aside and leased for a nominal rent to a field warehousing company. This may consist of a particular building, room, or even part of a room. Appropriate signs must be posted indicating that the goods and space are under the control of the warehousing company. The latter puts a designated custodian, properly bonded, in charge. In most instances the custodian is an employee of the borrower who is familiar with the handling of the goods. Only the custodian may issue the receiving records from which the regional office of the warehousing company makes out the warehouse receipts, and no one else may release the goods on orders signed by the holders of the warehouse receipts. In short, the arrangement is designed to create an independent warehouse on the premises of the borrower.

In some lines of business the public warehouse may be more satisfactory than the field warehouse arrangement, but if the particular business is a manufacturer or distributor who must repackage the products, or a retailer who must have his merchandise close at hand, the field warehouse may be better. Particularly is this true where the business has a continuous need to borrow for inventory purposes.

In general, warehouse receipts are commonly used in connection with the storage of nonperishable commodities such as cotton, grain, lumber, tobacco, and wool, or such standardized goods as canned foods, and consumers' durable goods.

Loans secured by accounts receivable. In the past, banks hesitated to lend on the security of accounts receivable, because they felt the risk was too great and the cost too high in relation to other types of loans which they were able to make. Furthermore, the laws of some of the states, many of which have since been changed, would not permit the assignment of the accounts unless the persons owing the account were notified of its assignment. Due to the falling-off in ordinary bank loans in the 1930's, banks began giving more attention to lending on the security of accounts receivable. Furthermore, the business became more profitable when they were able to add some additional charges for this type of arrangement.

Although the bulk of the accounts receivable financing is done by finance companies, factors, and commercial credit companies, an increasing portion is being handled by commercial banks. Most of these bank loans are made on the *nonnotification* plan. That is, the person or firm that owes the account is not notified that it has been pledged as security for a loan. In the past particularly, and this still applies in many lines of business, persons or firms owing accounts interpret it as a sign of drastic financial weakness if the holder of the account pledges it as security for a loan. Furthermore, these persons owing the accounts would usually prefer to deal with the original party to the account.

The borrower will make a formal agreement with the bank covering all the terms and conditions of the loan that is to be secured by the accounts receivable. Included in this will be the maximum percentage which will be lent on the accounts. This amount ordinarily varies between 65 and 90 per cent, with 75 to 80 being common. When the borrower needs money from time to time he will prepare a list of the accounts to be assigned and will then execute a note to the bank for the amount of the loan. The bank will usually mark on the borrowing company's ledger that the particular accounts have been assigned to the bank. Some states require that this be done in order that the assignment be valid. Before drawing up the agreement, the bank will have taken into consideration the credit standing of both the company borrowing the money and the ones whose accounts are pledged, the size and age of the accounts, etc.

Since with the ordinary bank loan of this kind, the firm owing the account is not notified that it is pledged, it will make payments on the account directly to the immediate party to the account and the latter will turn his money over to the bank. If checks are given, they may be indorsed directly to the bank.

Since the borrower must sign a note in favor of the bank for the amount of the loan, if the accounts are not paid the borrower will be liable to the bank. If the borrower is unable to pay, and no other arrangement is worked out with the bank, the latter can as assignee of the accounts take whatever action the borrower could have taken against the parties owing the accounts.

Discounting notes and drafts. In some lines of business, such as the fur and jewelry trade, notes given by the buyer are often discounted by the seller with a bank. In this way the seller gets his money out of the goods immediately by paying the bank a discount or interest charge to hold the note until its maturity. The note will be indorsed by the seller, and thus both the buyer and seller can be held liable on the instrument. This is sometimes called "two-name" paper for this reason. Banks hesitate to do much business of this kind because in many instances a note is given by the buyer only after the account is past due.

"Bills of exchange," "drafts," and "trade acceptances" may also be discounted at the bank. The seller draws a *bill of exchange,* or as it is more commonly called, a *draft* on the buyer for payment of goods on a debt due. The seller may draw this draft payable to himself. After signed acceptance by the buyer, the seller, not wishing to hold the draft until its maturity, indorses the draft and sells it to the bank at a certain discount.

Drafts that arise in connection with the purchase of goods and are accepted at the time of the sale and have a maturity in conformity with the original terms of sale are called *trade acceptances.* Such a draft has a higher standing in banking circles than those given for overdue accounts or purposes other than the purchase of goods. Despite efforts of bankers and credit men to encourage the use of trade acceptances, they are not commonly used. Competition and custom result in businessmen continuing to use the open book account.

Bankers' acceptances. Bankers' acceptances are used almost exclusively in foreign rather than in domestic trade. The procedure involved in connection with these acceptances is as follows. The buyer of goods makes arrangements with his bank to "accept" by signature drafts drawn on the bank by the seller of the goods. The bank furnishes the buyer with a "letter of credit" indicating its agreement to accept the drafts up to a stated amount for specified merchandise, and this letter of credit is sent to the seller. Upon sale of the goods the seller draws the draft and sends it through an agent or other bank to the buyer's bank for acceptance. The bill of lading will commonly be attached to the draft. After the "accepted" draft has been returned to the seller, the latter may discount it at his bank or sell it in the open market. In the meantime the buyer will have made an arrangement with his bank to furnish it the money needed to meet the draft at its maturity.

The buyer pays his bank a fee for accepting the draft, but it should be noted that this fee is a commission only for the bank putting its credit behind the draft. The buyer presumably will have the money at the bank when the draft becomes due. Whoever buys the draft from the seller is the one who immediately furnishes the cash. The seller, of course, will have to pay a discount when he sells the draft, but since it has been accepted by a bank, rather than an ordinary business, the discount rate will be relatively low.

Relative Importance of Bank Loans to Small Business. In the past adequate statistics have not been available on the extent to which small- and medium-size business depends upon external sources for funds and the sources of these funds. Because of this the U.S. Department of Commerce (Office of Business Economics) made a study of the financing of small- and medium-size business for the year ending June 30, 1954.[1] The industries covered were manufacturing, contract construction, wholesaling, and retailing.[2] The survey covered firms that were in existence in the early part of 1951 and those which were newly formed in the 1951–1953 period. It will be noted in Table 32, which was taken from that study, that only 44 per cent of the firms wanted outside funds. The remaining 56 per cent either did not need outside capital or they depended upon their earnings and depreciation "reserves" for the capital.

Of those firms which wanted outside capital, 93 per cent of the total amount desired was represented by loan capital. This is shown in Table 33. It will also be observed from the same table that 97 per cent of the outside funds actually obtained was from loans. Equity capital represented only 3 per cent of the total funds obtained.

Banks constituted the major source of borrowed capital for small- and medium-size business. It will be noted from Table 34 that slightly over 78 per cent of the total number of loans were granted by banks. Approximately half of the loans obtained were for a period of 90 days or less. Over two-thirds of them were for less than one year.

TRADE CREDITORS. The most important source of short-term working capital to many, if not most, businesses is trade creditors. When a firm sells goods on credit, it is supplying the buyer with working capital in the form of inventory. This is represented by an account payable on the books of the buyer. In some instances, notes are given when the account cannot be paid within a certain period of time. Some businesses have so little working capital that it is necessary for the seller to finance the entire inventory. In these cases, the buyer does not pay for the goods before he has sold them. This is not an ideal way of doing business.

Occasionally sellers will actually lend cash to concerns which buy their products. This is usually done for short periods of time and commonly in connection with the starting of a new enterprise,

[1] Loughlin McHugh and Jack N. Ciaccio, "External Financing of Small- and Medium-Size Business," *Survey of Current Business*, U.S. Department of Commerce, Office of Business Economics, October, 1955, pp. 15–22.

[2] Only single-unit firms with one or more employees were included, and none of the largest firms in any of the industries was included. Ninety per cent of the firms employed fewer than 20 workers, and 95 per cent of the firms had fewer than 50 employees.

TABLE 32

DEMAND FOR OUTSIDE FUNDS BY SMALL- AND MEDIUM-SIZE BUSINESS IN THE UNITED STATES FOR THE YEAR ENDING, JUNE 30, 1954

(per cent)

Financing Status	*All Firms*	*Established Firms**	*Newer Firms*†	*Industry*			
				Construction	*Manufacturing*	*Wholesale Trade*	*Retail Trade*
All firms	100.0	100.0	100.0	100.0	100.0	100.0	100.0
No outside funds wanted	56.0	57.1	46.8	51.9	50.8	50.9	59.7
Outside funds wanted	44.0	42.9	53.2	48.1	49.2	49.1	40.3
Obtained all funds wanted	23.9	23.7	25.3	25.4	25.8	29.4	21.8
Did not obtain all funds wanted	20.1	19.2	27.9	22.7	23.3	19.8	18.5
Obtained some funds	13.3	12.6	19.2	14.3	16.3	14.3	11.9
Obtained no funds	6.8	6.6	8.7	8.4	7.0	5.5	6.6

* Firms in business prior to March 1951.
† Firms which started business after March 1951.

SOURCE: "External Financing of Small- and Medium-Size Business," *Survey of Current Business*, U.S. Department of Commerce, Office of Business Economics, October, 1955, p. 18.

TABLE 33

PROPORTION OF AGGREGATE DEMAND FOR OUTSIDE FUNDS OBTAINED BY SMALL- AND MEDIUM-SIZE BUSINESS IN THE UNITED STATES FOR THE YEAR ENDING JUNE 30, 1954
(per cent)

	All Firms	*Established Firms*	*Newer Firms*
Loan demand			
Total	100	100	100
Obtained	76	76	75
Not obtained	24	24	25
Equity demand			
Total	100	100	100
Obtained	33	30	45
Not obtained	67	70	55
Aggregate demand			
Total	100	100	100
Obtained	73	74	71
Not obtained	27	26	29
Funds obtained			
Total	100	100	100
Loans	97	98	92
Equity	3	2	8
Funds wanted but not obtained			
Total	100	100	100
Loans	83	84	74
Equity	17	16	26
Aggregate demand			
Total	100	100	100
Loans	93	94	87
Equity	7	6	13

SOURCE: "External Financing of Small- and Medium-Size Business," *Survey of Current Business,* U.S. Department of Commerce, Office of Business Economics, October, 1955, p. 19.

or helping an old customer through a period of financial difficulty. It may be to the seller's long-run welfare to keep this client in business even though it means a loan of funds to keep him going. Normal trade credit, however, is granted in connection with the purchase of merchandise.

Trade credit is used so extensively because it is readily available and easy to use and because custom has dictated its use over the years. Some sellers offer trade credit because their competitors do so, and to stay in business they must compete on equal terms. Granting of credit has enabled some sellers to spread their sales more evenly over the year as they induce buyers to buy in slack seasons

TABLE 34

DISTRIBUTION OF NUMBER OF LOANS OBTAINED BY SMALL- AND MEDIUM-SIZE BUSINESS IN THE UNITED STATES FOR YEAR ENDING JUNE 30, 1954, BY SOURCE OF LOANS

(per cent)

	All Sources	*Bank*	*Individual**	*Other†*
All loans	100.0	78.3	9.1	12.6
To established firms	100.0	79.3	8.4	12.3
To newer firms	100.0	68.8	15.7	15.5
Established firms				
Construction	100.0	83.1	3.5	13.4
Manufacturing	100.0	80.3	8.5	11.2
Wholesale trade	100.0	79.3	10.1	10.6
Retail trade	100.0	76.8	9.2	14.0
Newer firms				
Construction	100.0	70.5	13.4	16.1
Manufacturing	100.0	67.9	12.2	19.9
Wholesale trade	100.0	70.6	16.4	13.0
Retail trade	100.0	67.7	18.7	13.6

* Partner, corporate official, acquaintance, or relative.

† Insurance companies and other financial institutions, supplier, equipment dealer, factor, government and other.

SOURCE: "External Financing of Small- and Medium-Size Business," *Survey of Current Business*, U.S. Department of Commerce, Office of Business Economics, October, 1955, p. 24.

and pay later. The buyer may find trade credit less costly than other available forms and the grantor may be more sympathetic to his borrowing needs than other possible lenders.

Cost of trade credit. Although it may be hidden in many cases, there is a cost involved in obtaining trade credit. If the seller does not charge the buyer for the use of credit with an interest charge or similar fee, he must obtain his costs of granting credit through the selling price of the merchandise. It costs money to sell on credit. There are bad-debt expenses to recover as well as substantial bookkeeping costs; there is the cost of providing the capital tied up in receivables all the time. Selling for cash avoids these expenses.

It is only under unusual circumstances that a seller charges interest for trade credit. Where no rate is charged and no cash discount included, the price of the merchandise includes the extra cost of the seller's granting of credit. If no discount is offered, the cost of using this credit will be determined by comparing prices with the cash prices of a similar seller. The cost of financing when cash discounts are offered is the amount of the discount.

An example of a term of sale which is widely used is "two ten, net thirty." This is usually written as follows: 2/10, net 30. This means that if the bill is paid within 10 days, a discount of 2 per cent will be allowed. If the bill is not paid within the 10 days, the full amount will be due at the end of 30 days. The time is computed from the date of the invoice; some cases from the first day of the following month.

A company will grant a discount for several reasons. Among these are the following: (1) it must be done because competitors do it, (2) it will increase sales, (3) if the discount is taken, the account cannot go bad, and (4) the buyer should pay interest on the amount owed if he does not pay within the discount period.

The discount rate figures out to be a high one when we express it on an annual basis. For example, let us take the standard term of sale of, 2/10, net 30. Assume that the goods are billed out at $100. If the buyer pays at the end of 10 days he will receive a discount of 2 per cent of $100, or $2. Thus he would pay only $98 for the goods. But if he waits 20 more days, he would have to pay the full $100. A charge of $2 for the use of $98 for 20 more days is equivalent to a charge of $36 (18 times $2) for the use of $98 for a year. Obviously this then would amount to a rate of 36.73 per cent. Terms of this type represent very expensive financing. It would generally pay a buyer to obtain funds elsewhere to pay for the merchandise in ten days than to take advantage of the extra twenty days offered at this extremely high interest rate. There is no cost to the buyer involved in taking advantage of the first ten days of credit offered. Well-run businesses will, however, be certain that all bills are paid before the end of the discount period where terms of this type are offered. Where the buyer cannot pay in time to take advantage of the discount, the net cost of the merchandise may be so high that the profits are small or that the buyer may not be able to compete successfully with other businesses that do take the discount.

Credit terms. The credit terms granted by sellers are important in determining the use and the cost of trade credit. Terms vary substantially between various industries and even between companies in the same industry. Terms may also vary between individual buyers based on their credit rating and the seller's willingness to lend to various types of risk. Most industries have what are considered standard credit terms. These terms are based on the length of the customers' production or marketing period, by the seasonal nature of the business, by the nature of the article involved, by the location of customers, and by competitive conditions. Credit terms vary from Cash in Advance, or Cash on Delivery, in the case of buyers with very poor credit ratings, to thirty, sixty, ninety, or even one hundred eighty day terms in certain lines of business for better customers.

Commercial Paper Houses. As compared with the amount of credit obtained from banks and trade creditors, the commercial paper houses are relatively unimportant. Commercial paper houses are really middlemen who buy notes from relatively large corporations and sell them primarily to banks. Although these houses formerly acted as brokers in the sale of notes and thus did not take title, at the present time they actually buy the notes and resell them to investors. The commercial paper house does not indorse the notes, hence it is not liable in event the note is not paid by the maker. From a practical standpoint, however, the houses in order to stay in business, handle only notes of high quality issued by well-known corporations.

Companies that use this means of obtaining capital are usually medium or large size. Perhaps the textile industry has made the greatest use of the commercial paper house. Others in the list include the foodstuffs, drug and chemical, farm implements, furniture, hardware and lumber industries.

The notes are made in even denominations such as $2,500, $5,000, $10,000, etc. In some instances the denominations may go as high as $100,000, or even higher. The total amount of the issue is usually greater than $100,000, and in some instances runs into the millions. The notes usually have a maturity of three, four, or six months. They are made payable to the order of the borrower, since it is not known at the time of issue who the creditor will be, and of course are signed and then indorsed by the borrower. They are secured only by the credit of the borrower. In other words, they are not secured by a pledge of any property, and since they are not indorsed by the commercial paper house, only the general credit of the issuing corporation is behind them.

These notes, which are referred to as "prime commercial paper," do not bear interest. They are sold at a discount to the commercial paper house. In addition, the commercial paper house receives a flat fee (commonly called "commission") of from ⅛ to ¼ of 1 per cent of the face value of the notes. Expressed on an annual basis a fee of the latter amount would be equivalent to 1 per cent on a 3 months' note, and ½ of 1 per cent on a 6 months' note. The principal compensation of the commercial paper house consists of this fee rather than the discount.

The commercial paper house sells the notes to investors, principally banks, at a slightly lower rate of discount, in other words at a higher price, than they paid for them. The notes are of course retired at maturity at their face value, so that as time goes on, assuming interest rates to remain about the same, the value of the notes increases. If the commercial paper house holds the notes for a time before selling them, part of the discount would accrue to its benefit. If interest rates should change materially while the house is holding the paper, the rate of discount would tend to go up or down, with a proportionate change in the rate of earnings of the commercial paper house. The return to the ultimate holder of the note consists of the difference between his purchase price and the maturity value of the note.

In the case of some companies the commercial paper house consists of only one department of the company. The other departments of the same companies carry on a brokerage and investment banking business.

The volume of business of the commercial paper houses declined from 1920 to 1931. Many of the companies that formerly used commercial paper houses, used them as a source of fixed as well as temporary working capital. The disadvantages of this approach were discovered by many of these companies in the crash of 1921. As a result, these companies now obtain their fixed working capital funds for long periods of time through the sale of stocks or bonds, and reinvested earnings. After 1931, the volume remained relatively stable until 1950. Since 1950, volume has doubled but has still not attained 1920 proportions. Most other financing institutions have volumes today far exceeding previous peaks. Although commercial paper formerly sold at a much lower rate of interest than ordinary bank loans, in more recent years banks have lowered the rate on ordinary loans so that while commercial-paper-house financing is still less costly than bank financing, the former cost differential is no longer present.

Advantages. The advantages of using the commercial paper houses as compared with ordinary bank loans as a source of short-term capital follow:

1. Lower cost. It was pointed out above that the cost of borrowing through the commercial paper house is usually lower than

for ordinary bank loans, although the difference is narrower than in the past.

2. Can obtain more capital. In borrowing from a bank on an ordinary loan the amount of the loan is necessarily limited since the particular bank's resources are limited, and furthermore, the amount that it can lend to any one firm is further limited. Through the sale of commercial paper the company can borrow from a number of banks. With the increase in mergers of large banks and the development of branch banking, however, larger loans from a particular bank are now possible. Furthermore, the practice has developed of having several banks join in a particular loan to a large company.

3. Borrower gets the use of all the money. Some commercial banks still require or expect the borrower to keep a minimum bank account of from 10 to 20 per cent of the amount of the loan. With commercial paper the borrower gets the use of the full amount of the money borrowed. As a practical matter, however, it is realized that the company will probably have part of this or at least other funds in its bank account at all times.

4. Ease of borrowing. If the alternative to commercial paper borrowing is getting individual loans from several banks, then each bank will have to make its investigation of the borrower. In the case of commercial paper the one commercial paper house makes the examination. These houses are experts in the line of business to which they cater and they are in an excellent position to judge the quality of the paper.

5. Prestige increased. The sale of commercial paper to a number of banks in different sections of the country adds to the prestige of the borrower. His credit becomes known and established in localities other than where his factories or places of business are located. This prestige will be of advantage if the borrower finds it necessary to borrow additional funds at a future time. This wider market enables the borrower to take advantage of lower interest rates in certain sections of the country, and to obtain loans from banks in areas where the slack season is on.

Disadvantages. Some possible disadvantages of using commercial paper houses rather than ordinary bank loans for short-term working capital are as follows:

1. Ordinary banking connections may be neglected. If a business relies too much on commercial paper for its short-term working capital needs, it may find sometime in the future that the paper is not marketable, and that an ordinary bank loan is difficult or impossible to secure because of the failure in the past to establish

relations with the bank. For this reason it may be advisable to get part of the working capital from ordinary bank loans even if some commercial paper is being sold. On the other hand, most businesses are able to establish relationships with banks by means of checking accounts and use of other bank services.

2. Paper must be paid off at maturity. When commercial paper is sold, the relationship between the borrower and the lender (banks usually) is an impersonal one. When the notes become due, the holders will demand payment. The inability to pay them might be very embarrassing to the borrower to say the least. In some instances, however, the commercial paper house will buy a new issue of notes to enable a company to retire the ones outstanding. If a company on the other hand is unable to pay off an ordinary bank loan the bank and borrower can talk it over with the result that a new loan may be made, or the maturity of the old one, or part of it, may be extended.

3. Can be used only by relatively large and successful companies. Commercial paper houses will buy the notes only of companies that are medium or large size and that are well established and successful. And these are the type of companies that can secure their working capital needs from other sources. The commercial paper houses and their customers are not interested in the notes of new, small, or unsuccessful companies. Perhaps this point is not really a criticism of commercial paper itself; certainly it is not a disadvantage from the viewpoint of the large successful company.

FINANCE COMPANIES. The nature of finance companies is commonly not understood by many since there are a number of different types of these companies, and they perform various functions. The situation is further aggravated by the fact that the same type of finance companies are referred to by different titles. The type of companies which we will briefly discuss here engages in one or both of the following types of business, (1) making loans on the security of accounts receivable, and (2) buying or lending on the security of installment paper. These companies may finance one or more of the following: manufacturers, wholesalers, retailers, and consumers.

In addition to being called *finance companies,* the following names are applied to these companies: *accounts receivable companies, automobile finance companies, commercial credit companies, discount companies,* and *installment finance companies.* Some include the *factor* under the heading of finance companies, but this is really a somewhat different institution and we will consider it separately. One type of "finance company" which is not included under this title is the *personal finance company,* or as it is sometimes called, the *small loan company,* or *consumer finance company,* which makes installment loans to consumers for purposes not directly connected with the purchase of goods.

Loans on accounts receivable. Borrowing money with the security of accounts receivable was discussed under bank loans so the material there stated, which has equal application to loans obtained from finance companies, will not be repeated. Both the *nonnotification* and the *notification* plans are used by finance companies, although the nonnotification one is more common. When the notification plan is used, payments on the accounts are made directly to the finance company which obtains power of attorney to indorse any checks, drafts, or notes made payable to the assignor of the accounts.

Borrowing on the security of accounts receivable enables a company to secure money which could not be obtained from other sources. The money obtained can be used to take discounts or can be reinvested in the working capital of the business. Even though the rate of interest charged on such loans is relatively high, this use of the funds will probably result in a large saving for the company. Furthermore, comparing it with an ordinary bank loan, no minimum balance need be maintained. Also the loans do not have to be made in advance of the need for funds or in larger amounts than immediately needed. Loans on accounts can be made from day to day as the money is needed, and the interest is computed daily and varies from 10 to 20 per cent, expressed on an annual basis. Where bank loans can be secured on the accounts, the rate of interest is usually lower than that charged by the finance company.

Discounting installment paper. The principal business of the finance company is discounting wholesale and retail installment paper, particularly in the automobile industry. With the expansion of automobile sales after 1920, there grew a need for some type of specialized finance company to finance the sale of this high-priced product. Banks were not equipped to handle installment sales paper, and furthermore, they felt the risk was too great. Some of the companies that were formed to finance automobile sales later started buying installment paper arising from the sale of other relatively high-priced products such as furniture, pianos, radios, television sets, refrigerators, washing machines, etc. Since the automobile paper makes up the principal part of the finance company's business, we will briefly describe the procedure followed.

The finance companies finance both the dealer and the consumer. The dealer puts up cash equivalent to from 10 to 20 per cent of the wholesale price of the cars and borrows the balance on his promissory note from the finance company. The manufacturer is instructed to draw a sight draft on the finance company for the balance due and to attach the bill of lading. In some instances the bill of sale is made out to the finance company. The finance company then releases the cars to the dealer under trust receipts. As the dealer sells the cars he remits to the finance company the amount due and the trust receipt is canceled.

When a purchaser buys a car he may make a down-payment of some amount, such as 33⅓ per cent of the purchase price, and borrow the balance from the finance company. This is done by the purchaser entering into a contract with the dealer or finance company and signing a promissory note for the balance due. In some instances the purchaser will sign as many notes as the number of monthly payments. The payments may run over a period of from 6 to 36 months. The car is either sold under a conditional sales contract, or under a chattel mortgage, depending upon which is favored in the particular state (laws relating to these two types of installment sales vary among the states). The contract and notes are sold by the dealer to the finance company, and payment on the notes is made by the purchaser directly to the finance company.

The dealer usually indorses the note "without recourse," which means that he will not be personally liable on the note if the maker is unable to pay it. Usually, however, the dealer makes an agreement that he will take over the car for resale after the finance company has repossessed it and pay the balance due the finance company. The dealer is in some instances required by the finance company to indorse the notes "with recourse" in the case of second-hand cars that are sold to poor-credit risks. By the use of this unqualified indorsement the dealer can be held personally liable on the note by the finance company if the purchaser of the car does not pay it.

The interest charged is on a discount basis, and furthermore the principal amount is paid off by installment. This makes the effective rate higher than appears at first glance. The effective rate of interest, expressed on an annual basis, may run from 10 to 18 per cent, depending upon the locality, risk involved, etc. The rate charged must necessarily be relatively high since it covers not only the interest proper, but also the investigation, financing, and collection costs. In addition to this charge, the purchaser is required to take out fire, theft, and collision insurance on the car payable to the finance company. In some instances the finance company owns or has affiliated with it an insurance company, so that it may also make a commission on the insurance sold. The amount of the interest, insurance and repayment of principal are figured out and divided by the number of months over which the payments are to be made, so that the purchaser pays the same amount per month to the finance company.

Since so many people have to buy automobiles on time payments, the amount of money tied up at all times is enormous. If there were no finance companies the manufacturers would have to finance the dealers, or the dealers would carry only a small inventory and then only by a relatively large investment in the business. By selling the installment paper to the finance companies, all the sales on credit have the same effect on the dealer as cash sales. This enables him to carry a large inventory on a relatively small investment in the business. Manufacturers realize that this will increase the sale of cars and some of them have formed their own finance companies to handle the business. In addition, of course, they can make a profit on the financing and maybe the insurance.

Finance companies receive part of their funds from the same source as any other types of corporations, that is, through the sale of common and preferred stock and debenture bonds. But half or more of their funds are usually obtained from ordinary bank loans and through the sale of commercial paper. In the past commercial banks have hesitated to lend directly on installment paper, but they have been willing to lend indirectly on it by lending to the finance companies which hold the paper. In recent years, however, banks have become interested in automobile paper particularly, and are now actively promoting this kind of business.

As stated above, the principal business of the finance company is the buying of installment paper and to a lesser extent, lending on the security of accounts receivable. In addition to these activities, many of them now also lend on inventories secured by trust and warehouse receipts, and on the security of equipment owned or purchased by a company.

FACTORS. We have already discussed the financing of accounts receivable by means of pledging them as security for a loan from a bank or a finance company. Another method of getting money from the accounts is to sell them to a factor. A *factor* is an individual or company that buys accounts outright. The process of buying accounts is called *factoring*.

Factoring started in the textile trade and is still used primarily in that field, although it has now spread to other industries, and is used both by manufacturers and wholesalers in New York and Chicago and other large financial centers. When factoring first started it was carried on by a manufacturer's selling agent who was located in the large trading centers and who acted as the exclusive selling agent for the particular mill. The entire output of the mill was taken by the agent who undertook the actual selling, granting of credit, and collection of the accounts. The agent was in a better position to judge the credit risks and obtain financing aid than was the manufacturer.

At the present time the factor usually confines his activities to the financial rather than selling end of the business. The manufacturer does the selling of the goods and then sells his accounts outright to the factor. Thus, the factor does the collecting, and any loss for uncollected accounts falls upon him. In other words, after the accounts are sold to the factor the manufacturer is no longer responsible. Customers of the manufacturer are notified to make payments on the accounts directly to the factor. In many instances the invoice is mailed to the customer by the factor.

Since the factor stands to lose on poor accounts, when the manufacturer first makes an arrangement for the factoring of his accounts, the factor will go over the accounts carefully and purchase only those that appear to him to be good. Thereafter the factor will have to pass on the credit standing of all prospective purchasers before the sales can be made, and all accounts arising from sales will be purchased by him. The agreement between the manufacturer and the factor is usually for a one-year period, but in practice the arrangement continues until one of the parties wishes to withdraw.

For buying the accounts receivable the factor receives two different types of compensation, (1) a commission or fee, and (2) interest. The commission or fee is dependent upon the degree of risk involved and collection costs, and is usually 1 or 2 per cent (the range is from ¼ to 4 per cent) of the face value of the accounts purchased the previous month. This is paid either in cash or deducted from the amount due from the factor for the particular month. This charge is intended to cover the risk which is assumed by the factor. The factor also receives interest, usually discounted at the annual rate of 6 per cent, on the amount of the accounts for the period equivalent to the credit period. (In some instances, this period plus 10 days—to take care of slight delays in the collection of the funds.) If the seller of the accounts leaves part of the proceeds with the factor, the latter may pay him interest at the annual rate of from 2 to 6 per cent. This, of course, would offset at least part of the interest charged the seller.

Perhaps an example would make the above more understandable to the reader. Suppose that accounts with a face value of $10,000 are sold to the factor on June 1, for a commission of 2 per cent, and interest at an annual rate of 6 per cent, with the terms of sale being 60 days. The factor would deduct interest of $100 (6 per cent interest on $10,000 for 60 days) and remit the seller the balance of $9,900 (less any fees due from the amounts purchased the previous month). The following month the fee of $200 (2 per cent of $10,000—note that the 2 per cent is not figured on an annual basis) will be paid to the factor. This is assuming that the seller leaves no funds with the factor.

Advantages. Following are the advantages of selling accounts to factors as compared to obtaining no credit, or utilizing one of the other sources of short-term credit.

1. May be the only source of funds available. In some instances a firm can sell its accounts when it would be unable to borrow against them from a bank or finance company. The funds so obtained can be used to expand the business, or less permanent capital will need to be tied up in the business.

2. No credits and collections department needed. When accounts are sold to a factor it eliminates the need for and expense of a credits and collections department.

3. Cost of credit definite and known. When a firm sells on credit it never knows exactly what credit losses will be encountered as sales are being made. The costs of selling the accounts to the factor are known, and bad-debt losses will fall on the factor.

4. Larger sales possible. Selling the accounts permits larger inventories and possibly larger sales. When a company carries its own accounts, it may hesitate to sell a large amount to any particular customer because of the risk of losses. A factor may not hesitate to buy the accounts because they will probably constitute only a small percentage of the total accounts which he holds. Hence, larger individual sales may be made when it is known that the accounts are to be sold.

5. Get use of entire amount. In comparison with a bank loan on the accounts, assuming a minimum balance to be maintained, sale of the accounts will give the company the use of the entire amount.

6. Current working capital ratio may be improved. A company may be able to improve its current working capital ratio by selling the accounts and using the proceeds to pay off bank loans or accounts payable. The following example will illustrate the point. Let us assume that the following is an abbreviated section of the company's balance sheet current items before sale of the accounts:

Before Sale

Accounts receivable	$100,000	Accounts payable	$100,000
Other current assets	300,000	Other current liabilities	100,000
Total	$400,000	Total	$200,000

If the accounts receivable are sold to the factor and the proceeds used to pay off the accounts payable (factor's charges ignored), the same section of the balance sheet will be as follows:

After Sale

Current assets	$300,000	Current liabilities	$100,000

Before the sale of the accounts the company had a current ratio of only 2 to 1 ($400,000 compared to $200,000), but after the sale and payment of the accounts the current ratio was improved to 3 to 1 ($300,000 compared with $100,000). The improved current ratio may enable the company to obtain more goods on credit, or to obtain more in bank loans than before the sale, or a bank loan may be possible now when it was impossible before.

Disadvantages. The various ways of securing capital always have disadvantages as well as advantages when compared with other sources. The following are the principal disadvantages of selling accounts to factors:

1. Relatively high cost. The cost of obtaining short-term capital through the sale of accounts to factors is a relatively expensive way of obtaining working capital. We can illustrate this using the figures in the hypothetical situation stated above where the fee was 2 per cent, and the interest 6 per cent a year, with a credit period of 60 days. The fee of $200 added to the interest of $100 gives us a total charge of $300. A charge of this amount is equivalent to a total charge of 18 per cent a year. ($300 for 2 months is equivalent to $1,800 for a year. A charge of the latter amount for the use of $10,000 would be at the annual rate of 18 per cent. The actual charge would be a little higher than this since the interest is discounted).

It is recognized however, that the total charge for factoring should not be compared with the interest charged on loans. The factoring charge includes an equivalent for the risk of bad debts and the billing and collection costs.

2. Possibility of smaller sales. Since the factor has to pass upon the credit standing of all prospective buyers, he may not permit sales to be made to certain firms, or he may limit the amount that may be sold to a particular firm. This, however, may be overcome at least in part by the points stated under advantages above, that larger sales may be possible.

3. Unfavorable customer reaction. Generally speaking, customers prefer to deal with the seller rather than with a factor. Furthermore, selling accounts is sometimes taken to mean that the seller is in desperate financial condition. Where factoring is common as in the textile trade, however, most of the customers will probably understand and look upon it as standard practice.

MISCELLANEOUS SOURCES. In the realm of larger concerns, parent or holding companies often have surplus cash that can be lent to the subsidiary companies. In some instances the parent or holding company will raise the money itself for the purpose of lending it to the subsidiaries. For companies that come under the jurisdiction of the Public Utility Holding Company Act of 1935, however, such loans are supervised by the Securities and Exchange Commission.

Although *industrial banks*, or as they are sometimes called, *Morris Plan banks* are engaged primarily in granting consumers' loans, some use is being made of them by businesses both for short-term and intermediate capital. Some big finance companies bypass commercial paper houses and banks for part of their funds by selling their commercial paper directly to individual and institutional investors. In fact, outstanding commercial paper placed directly by finance companies is about twice the amount of all paper outstanding handled by commercial paper houses. Customers of the business may provide working capital by advances on contracts before shipment.

Questions

1. Explain the procedure involved in the sale-and-lease-back arrangement, and indicate the principal reasons why it is used.
2. How do term loans differ from other types of bank loans?
3. What governmental agencies are at the present time engaged in financing private business?
4. What rate of interest do banks charge in your community for the typical 30-day business loan?
5. Distinguish between a straight and an order bill of lading. Can both be used as collateral for a loan? Explain.

6. Explain the procedure involved in securing a loan on the collateral of warehouse receipts.

7. Indicate what is meant by field warehousing and the reason for its origin and use.

8. When a loan is made at a commercial bank on the collateral of accounts receivable, does the person owing the account know that it is pledged? Explain.

9. Explain what bankers' acceptances are and how they are used.

10. List separately the sources of long-term and short-term working capital, discussed in this chapter.

11. Indicate specifically why cash discounts are usually large when figured on an annual percentage basis.

12. Should a buying company show cash discounts taken as an income item, or cash discounts not taken as an expense item? Explain.

13. What is meant by "trade credit"? Is it an important source of working capital to companies in the United States?

14. If a company does not charge interest on credit sales, should it sell to cash customers at a lower price? Explain.

15. What rate of interest is charged by the large department stores in your community on installment sales? Is all of this really interest?

16. Under what circumstances might a person be justified in paying a small loan company a rate of 36 per cent for a loan of $50 to pay cash for an article?

17. Indicate the advantages and disadvantages to the borrower of selling notes through commercial paper houses.

18. (a) What different types of companies are known as finance companies? (b) What different names are sometimes used for companies which handle automobile installment paper?

19. Indicate how the factor aids in working capital financing.

20. List the sources of working capital discussed in this chapter, and indicate in each case whether it is short-term or long-term working capital.

Problems

1. The Peerless Manufacturing Company is about to launch an expansion program which will call for approximately $5,000,000 in funds for additional property and working capital needs. The board of directors has been considering an issue of common stock to obtain the money. The company has been paying a 6 per cent dividend on its $100 par value stock. The stock has been selling slightly in excess of its par value in the market for some time. Corporate income tax rates can be assumed to be 50 per cent.

Mr. Williams, who is the president of the Standard Life Insurance Company, is a friend of Mr. Henry, the chairman of the board of the Peerless company, and suggested to Mr. Henry that he and his company consider the possibility of selling several of the plants to the insurance company in order to obtain the necessary amount of money. The plants could then be leased back for a long period of years.

Mr. Williams explained that all the rental payments could be deducted as an expense by the Peerless company before taxes, whereas none of the dividends on the stock could be deducted. He also called attention to the fact that as long as the Peerless company owned the plants, depreciation on only the building, and not the land, could be deducted for tax purposes. Mr. Williams explained that the insurance company would be content with 3½ per cent net return on its money if it could recover its investment within a 20-year period. The following proposal was worked out by the two executives and placed before the board of directors of both companies:

1. Two plants to be sold to the insurance company for $5,000,000.
2. The Peerless company to pay all taxes, insurance and maintenance on the plants.
3. The plants be leased to the Peerless company for a 20-year period for $337,500 a year.
4. An option be granted to the Peerless company to renew the lease for three additional 20-year periods at the nominal rent of $50,000 a year.

(a) Explain how the amount of the rental payments for the first 20 years would meet the objectives of the insurance company. (b) As a director of the Peerless company would you vote for the proposal to sell the plants and lease them back instead of issuing the additional common stock? Explain reasons for your answer and present figures to support it.

2. The Adams Manufacturing Co. paid for all of its expenses, except depreciation, in cash, and received cash for all income items for the past six months. Raw material equal to that sold was purchased each month. Profits for the period after charging depreciation of $10,000, but before taxes, amounted to $200,000. Assume the federal income tax rate is 50 per cent. All items on the balance sheet except cash, reserve for depreciation, and surplus were the same at the end of the period as at the beginning. How much did the cash account (after taxes) increase during the period?

3. The New Development Co. purchased some office furniture from the Easy Terms Furniture Co. The sale price was $120, but the furniture company agreed that this amount could be paid in six equal monthly installments, beginning one month after the date of sale. The company said that the New Development Co. would have to pay a carrying charge of 6 per cent, or $7.20, which amount was to be paid along with the final installment. What was the real rate charged by the furniture company? Would all of this carrying charge represent interest? Explain.

4. The New Development Company had $40,000 in current assets and $20,000 in current liabilities. The company then paid off $10,000 of the current liabilities, thus increasing the current ratio from 2 to 1, to 3 to 1. Does the higher current ratio indicate that the company is in a better current position? Explain.

Part V

ADMINISTRATION OF INCOME

Chapter 23

DETERMINATION OF NET INCOME

INTRODUCTION. Thus far in the book we have been concerned with the various forms of business organizations, giving particular emphasis to the corporation, the various types of securities that are issued to obtain funds, and the problems in connection with their sale, the promotion of a business, and the various sources of working capital. These are problems and relationships that concern the corporation and its owners and outside parties. We are now turning to the financial administration of a going business concern.

The primary purpose and *raison d'être* of every business organization is to make money for its owners. We realize the obligation owed to creditors, and to an increasing extent in recent years, the responsibility to the employees, and particularly in some types of industry, the responsibility to the users of the services furnished by the business. But the fact remains that a business is formed and operated to make profits for the owners.

In this chapter we are concerned with the financial steps in the process of earning this profit. Accounting records show to the owners how the profit is determined, and the accounting statement to display this is the *income statement*. This is also called the *earnings statement* or *profit and loss statement*. Subsequent chapters will discuss the nature of the earnings retained in the business, often called the *surplus*, which is what is left of the accumulated earnings after reserves have been set up and dividends paid. We will then discuss the various types of reserves and dividends, and dividend policies.

DEBITS AND CREDITS. Although we are here concerned with the subject of accounting to the extent only that is necessary in the determination of profits, it must be kept in mind that both the terminology and processes used by accountants are extremely important in attaining this objective. In these chapters we will make use of accounting to explain the various factors that refer to the administration of income. Although most readers of this book will have had one or more courses in accounting, we are going to say a few elementary things about "debits and credits," since a thorough grasp of their nature is essential for an understanding of what will be discussed.

For many decades accountants have used the "double entry" system of bookkeeping. By this is meant that for every debit against one account there must be a credit to another account. Such a system, among other things, aids in the location of bookkeeping mistakes, to the end that an accurate set of books may be maintained. Certain sheets of paper used in accounting records are divided into two sides by a line running down the center of the sheet. *Debits* are always recorded on the *left* side of the sheet or account, *credits* are entered on the *right* side. The term *charge* is commonly used synonymously with *debit.* In considering the items that go to make up an income statement, all the "income" items are *credits,* while all the "expense" items are charges or *debits.* Income items include such things as sales, interest income, etc., while cost of materials sold, labor, interest paid on debts, etc., are debit items. If a balance remains after all the expenses are deducted from the total income, it is called the *net profit* or *net income.* From what has been said it is obvious that this account, being the excess of total credits over the total debits, would be a credit.

Beginning accounting students are oftentimes confused when comparing the use of debits and credits in the income statement accounts with their application to the items or accounts that make up the balance sheet. The *balance sheet* shows the assets, liabilities, and net worth of the company. The *assets* are "debits," while the *liabilities,* and *net worth* are "credits." In a vague sort of way a person may think it confusing that something that you own which is called an "asset," should be a debit, while an income item is considered a credit. Likewise, it may seem peculiar at first that a liability or debt of the company is a credit, while an expense item that appears in the income statement is a debit.

We have said above that all debits must equal all credits. This applies also to the balance sheet. The value of all the assets is due either the creditors or the owners of the business. The liabilities show what is owed to the creditors, while the net worth shows the equity of the owners. The assets equal the sum of the liabilities and the net worth. Thus, the debits equal the credits.

Any profit made by the business would show in the balance sheet as an increase in the net assets (assets less liabilities), and be reflected in the net worth section by the same increase in the undivided profits or surplus. Thus, if the net assets increased $50,000 during the year, the net worth should increase also by $50,000. Speaking of this in terms of debits and credits, the net asset increase would add to the debits and the same amount added to the undivided profits would increase the credits.

The same reasoning can be applied to the liabilities and expense accounts. If a company has more expenses during the year than income, then it has suffered a deficit. In other words, debits in the income statement would exceed the credits. This would show up in the balance sheet as a decrease in the net assets. In other words, the credits would exceed the debits made to the asset accounts by the amount of the deficit. Another way of stating this is that if the gross assets remain the same, the liabilities (credits) will have increased by the amount of the deficit (which is a debit). What we have said can be summarized as follows:

Balance Sheet

Assets (debits) — Liabilities (credits) = Net Worth (credits)[1]

Income Statement

Income (credits) — Expenses (debits) = Net Profit (credit)[1]

THE INCOME STATEMENT. The *income statement,* whether it is called this or one of the other titles previously mentioned, shows the gross income received for the period, the expenses incurred, and the net income. Large corporations, particularly those whose stock is listed on one of the larger exchanges, publish income statements quarterly, but smaller companies usually issue them only once a year. This statement shows the net sales as income whether or not the goods have been paid for, and the expenses listed are those that are incurred regardless of whether or not there has been an actual cash outlay for the particular item. The excess of income over expenses is considered the net income for the particular period, regardless of the fact that it is not necessarily the excess of cash receipts over cash disbursements.

Even if the company does only a cash business and pays for all the expenses (except depreciation, which will be discussed later), although the excess of income over expense would show the excess of cash receipts over cash expenditures (depreciation ignored), it should not be concluded that this cash will show up in the cash account at the end of the period. Some of it may have been used to purchase additional inventory, or machinery, or some other item.

[1] If the result is a negative quantity, it would be called a "Deficit" (debit).

The Interstate Commerce Commission prescribes a standard form for the income statement for railroads. But in the case of ordinary business corporations, such as a manufacturing or merchandising company, quite a variety of different forms are found in practice. It is not our intention to discuss or even present these ramifications. We will be content with an abbreviated statement of a hypothetical manufacturing company.

Income Statement

The Standard Manufacturing Company

Year Ended December 31, 19–1

Gross Sales			$1,010,000
Less: Sales returns and allowances			10,000
Net Sales			$1,000,000
Cost of goods sold:			
Materials		$500,000	
Direct labor		175,000	
Indirect manufacturing costs		25,000	700,000
Gross margin (profit)			$ 300,000
Other operating expenses:			
Selling		$100,000	
Administrative		50,000	
Other		9,000	$ 159,000
Net operating income			$ 141,000
Nonoperating income:			
Interest received	$ 500		
Rent income	1,500	$ 2,000	
Nonoperating expenses:			
Interest paid		1,000	1,000
Net income (profit) before federal income tax			$ 142,000
Federal income tax[2]			68,340
Net income (profit) after federal income tax			$ 73,660

SALES. It was stated above that the sales figure shows the total sales regardless of whether or not collection has been made for them. Some companies show the gross sales and the deduction for returns and allowances, as we have done above, while others merely show the net sales after such deductions. Practice varies as to where "sales discounts" is to be shown on the income statement. Some show this item along with the returns and allowances as a deduction from sales, while others include it in the nonoperating expenses near the end of the statement. If some asset which is no longer needed in the business is sold at a profit, such profit is not ordinarily shown under sales. This is a nonrecurring item and it is

[2] The income tax is computed according to the 1956 rate, which is 30 per cent of the first $25,000, and 52 per cent on the balance.

usually included in the nonoperating income. The sales include the income only from the "stock in trade" of the company. In the case of railroads and public utilities the term "operating revenue" is used instead of the term "sales."

COST OF GOODS SOLD. In the case of merchandising companies, the "cost of goods sold" is arrived at in the following manner:

Inventory at beginning of period	x
Plus: Purchases during period	x
	x
Less: Inventory at end of period	x
Cost of goods sold	x

Where this method is used by processing or manufacturing companies, the inventories will include raw materials, work in process, and finished goods. Some companies follow the practice of showing purchases after purchase discounts have been taken, while others show the gross amount of the invoice under purchases, and show purchase discounts as a separate item under nonoperating income. The latter practice has the advantage of specifically showing to what extent the management is taking advantage of discounts.

In the case of manufacturing companies, particularly the larger ones that have cost accounting systems, cost of goods sold includes not only the cost of the materials which went into the goods sold, but the direct labor cost and indirect manufacturing costs. The cost of the materials can be obtained in the same fashion as the cost of goods sold for a merchandising company, that is, the purchases are added to the beginning inventory, and from this is subtracted the ending inventory. The cost accounting records, however, will directly show total cost of materials.

The direct labor covers the cost of the productive labor that was applied to the product. Generally speaking, this means the cost of factory labor on production work. The indirect manufacturing costs that go to make up the balance of the cost of goods sold is sometimes called "overhead," or "burden." Generally speaking, it includes such things as depreciation on the machinery and equipment used, operating supplies, rent, heat and light allocated to the production department, salaries of foremen and other supervisory factory employees, etc. Railroads and public utilities, of course, would not have a "cost of goods sold" in their statements. The various expenses are shown under the heading of "operating expenses."

Various titles are applied to the figure that is obtained by subtracting the cost of goods sold from the net sales. It is often called the "gross profit" or "gross profit on sales," but because of objections that can be raised to the use of either of these, some accountants merely label it "gross margin." Of course, we can then raise the question, "gross margin" on what? What the figure really represents is the gross profit on sales.

OTHER OPERATING EXPENSES. The statement above shows the principal expenses that come under the head of other operating expenses. Selling expense includes the salaries and commissions paid to salesmen, salesmen's traveling expenses, advertising, sales promotion, and other expenses which are allocated to the sales department. Administrative expenses include the salaries of the company officers and other administrative employees, insurance, stationery, postage, rent, light, and heat expense allocated to administration, etc.

Under "other" expenses would come any other operating expenses not listed under selling or administrative. Depreciation on the office furniture and fixtures might be one of these. In some instances, however, depreciation is included in the selling and administrative expenses.

The total other operating expenses are then subtracted from the gross margin to show the net operating income. Sometimes the caption "net operating profit" is used instead for this figure.

NONOPERATING INCOME. Nonoperating income is that income of the company which is not directly related to operations. In some cases the term "financial management income" is used instead of "nonoperating income," or that term may be applied to certain of the items that come under nonoperating income.

Dividends received on stock and interest received on bonds held by the company are included in this item. It is desirable to separate the nonoperating from the operating items in order that the income from the ordinary operations of the business can be clearly seen. Another item included in this section is any profit made from the sale of an asset, other than "stock in trade," which is no longer needed in the business. Such an item is sometimes referred to as nonrecurring income. A company, for example, may have been holding some real estate for a period of years thinking that use might be made of it sometime in the future. If this was sold at a large profit and the profit were included along with that from ordinary operations, the reader of the income statement would get a distorted picture of the relative efficiency of the company for that period. For these and other reasons, profit from an extraordinary transaction or nonrecurring item should always be shown in the nonoperating section. Another example of such an item would be that arising from the sale of securities of other companies which the company has been holding.

NONOPERATING EXPENSES. Expenses not related to operations are placed under the head of nonoperating expenses. Interest paid on bank loans or on bonds outstanding are included in this section. The points stated under nonoperating income above apply with equal force here. Any extraordinary or nonrecurring loss, such as on sale of some asset, other than stock in trade, would also be shown as nonoperating expense.

The difference between the nonoperating income and nonoperating expenses is then either added to or subtracted from the net operating income, depending upon whether the income exceeds the expense, or vice versa, and the resulting figure is the net income, or as it is sometimes called, the "net profit."

FEDERAL INCOME TAXES. The federal income tax is truly an expense and shows as such on the income statement. But since it is based on the "net income," the latter figure is computed, as shown on the income statement, before the taxes are deducted. The "net income" figure then is commonly shown "before" and "after" federal income taxes.

In passing we might recall a point that has been previously mentioned in the book. Since bond interest is an expense to be considered before arriving at net taxable income, the taxes are computed on what is left after the interest has been paid. Dividends, on the other hand, are not an expense. Hence the tax is figured on the net income before dividends have been paid. It therefore follows that the company which has bonds in its capitalization has the advantage so far as the deductibility of interest is concerned. With a tax rate of 52 per cent, this means that every dollar paid in interest costs the company really only 48 cents. But every dollar paid in dividends "costs" the company one dollar.

EFFECT OF NET INCOME ON BALANCE SHEET. The balance sheet shows the assets, liabilities, and net worth of a company as of a particular time. Corporations prepare and publish balance sheets at least once each year. The usual balance sheet shows the financial position of the company as of December 31, of the particular year. To illustrate the possible effect of a year's operation on the items that appear in the balance sheet, let us assume that the following was the balance sheet at the beginning of the year of the Standard

Manufacturing Company, whose income statement was shown above on page 538.

Balance Sheet
The Standard Manufacturing Company
As of Beginning of Year 19–1

Assets			*Liabilities and Net Worth*	
Current assets			Current liabilities	
Cash		$ 20,000	Bank loan	$ 25,000
Accounts receivable		40,000	Accounts payable	$ 20,000
Inventory		208,000	Total current liabilities	$ 45,000
Total current assets		$268,000		
U. S. bonds		20,000	*Net Worth*	
Fixed assets			Capital stock	$300,000
Machinery	$ 80,000		Retained income	133,000
Less: Reserve for Depreciation	20,000	60,000	Total net worth	$433,000
Land and Buildings	$150,000			
Less: Reserve for Depreciation	20,000	130,000		
Total fixed assets		$190,000		
Total assets		$478,000	Total liabilities and net worth	$478,000

After giving effect to the income and expenses for the year, as shown before in the income statement, the balance sheet for the end of the same year might appear as follows:

Balance Sheet
The Standard Manufacturing Company
Year Ended December 31, 19–1

Assets			*Liabilities and Net Worth*	
Current assets			Current liabilities	
Cash		$ 46,000	Accounts payable	$ 25,000
Accounts receivable		42,000	Federal income tax payable	68,340
Inventory		316,000	Total current liabilities	$ 93,340
Total current assets		$404,000		
U. S. Bonds		20,000	*Net Worth*	
Fixed assets			Capital stock	$300,000
Machinery	$ 80,000		Retained income	206,660
Less: Reserve for Depreciation	30,000	50,000	Total net worth	$506,660
Land and Buildings	$150,000			
Less: Reserve for Depreciation	24,000	126,000		
Total fixed assets		$176,000		
Total assets		$600,000	Total liabilities and net worth	$600,000

It will be noticed that the retained income (surplus) shown on the balance sheet at the beginning of the year amounted to $133,000, but at the end of the year it stood at $206,660. This was an increase of $73,660. This is exactly what the income statement shows the company made for the year after taxes. This is to be expected for several reasons. If there are no appropriations of the net income to reserve accounts, and if no dividends are paid, the accountant transfers the net income for the year to the undivided profits account. The other explanation is that the net assets (assets less liabilities) during the year should increase by the same amount as the net income for the year.

It will be noted that the cash account increased by $26,000, the accounts receivable account by $2,000, and the inventory by $108,000. This was a total increase in these assets of $136,000. But the machinery and buildings were depreciated (as noted from the increase in the reserve accounts) by $14,000. So the *net* increase in all the assets was $122,000. We find that, although the bank loan of $25,000 was paid off, the accounts payable increased by $5,000, and at the end of the year the company owed income taxes of $68,340. So the increase in the liabilities for the year amounted to $48,340. Subtracting this figure from the net increase in the assets gives us $73,660, which is the net income for the year after taxes as shown by the income statement. It appears from the statement that most of the profit for the year went into the purchase of additional inventory.

It is a little more difficult to attempt to follow through the transactions for the year from the cash standpoint. Undoubtedly all the accounts receivable on the books at the beginning of the year were collected by the end of the period. Also, probably all the accounts payable at the start of the year were paid off. Certainly we know that the bank loan of $25,000 was paid. But it is noted that the accounts receivable at the end were only $2,000 more than at the beginning of the year, and the accounts payable increased by only $5,000. Income tax appears to be the only expense for the year for which payment has not been made. Of course, the depreciation charge of $14,000 did not call for a cash outlay. Since the interest income and rent income do not appear as assets, they have apparently been collected in cash. With these facts in mind we can follow through and account for the cash.

The excess of the increase in the accounts payable ($5,000) over the increase in accounts receivable ($2,000) means that $3,000 in cash must be accounted for. The profits would add $73,660. The profits would have been greater to the extent of $68,340 if income taxes (which are still owed) had not been charged as an expense. And if the depreciation charge of $14,000, which took no cash out of the business, had not been made the profits would have been that much more. Adding these figures together shows us the net amount of cash to be accounted for.

Adjustment of accounts receivable and payable	$ 3,000
Net income for the year	73,660
Income taxes owed	68,340
Depreciation charges	14,000
Cash to be accounted for	$159,000

Referring to the two balance sheets, we find that the $25,000 bank loan was paid off, and that the inventory was increased by $108,000. This accounts for $133,000 of the cash. So we have to account for only $26,000 more. It will be noted that the cash account increased by exactly that amount. So, we have now accounted for all the increase in the cash. Following is a summary of what has just been said:

Payment of bank loan	$ 25,000
Increase in inventory	108,000
Increase in cash	26,000
Cash accounted for	$159,000

The reader should perhaps again be cautioned against confusing the net income and the cash. As we have just seen in the above example, the company earned a net income after taxes of $73,660, but the cash account increased by only $26,000. It is not recommended that the method we used above to account for the cash be used by the reader. To get a true picture of the flow of cash it would be necessary to give effect to every cash receipt and cash outlay. We can do this for the above company.

We will assume that the accounts receivable and accounts payable on the books at the beginning of the year are liquidated during the year. After comparing the inventories at the beginning and end of the year, and the cost of the materials which were sold, it is seen that the purchases must have been $608,000 for the year. But since $25,000 in accounts payable still remain on the books, only $583,000 in cash has been paid for the purchases. Since accounts receivable of $42,000 are on the books at the end of the year, only $958,000 of the net sales has been collected. To simplify matters, we will assume that the furniture was not carried at any value on the books, and that therefore the selling and administrative expenses did not include any depreciation. The depreciation totaling $14,000 was on the machinery and buildings, and is included in the indirect manufacturing costs. Following is a summary of the cash receipts and cash disbursements for the year:

Cash Receipts		*Cash Disbursements*	
Old accounts	$ 40,000	Old accounts	$ 20,000
Sales and new accounts	958,000	Bank loan	25,000
Nonoperating income	2,000	Purchases and new accounts	583,000
		Direct labor	175,000
		Indirect manufacturing costs (other than depreciation)	11,000
		Selling and administrative expenses	159,000
		Nonoperating expense	1,000
		Total disbursements	$ 974,000
		Excess of receipts over disbursements	26,000
Total	$1,000,000	Total	$1,000,000

As is seen from the above, the excess of cash receipts over disbursements for the year was $26,000, and this, as noted on the ending balance sheet, is the amount the cash account did increase. In attempting to determine the cash items as we have done above, proper attention must be given to any income items in the income statement which have not been collected, and any expense items which have not been paid. In our example we considered that all the income items were actually received in cash, and that all the expense accounts were paid for, except depreciation and income taxes.

The reader should always be careful not to confuse cash receipts with income, and cash disbursements with expenses. As noted in the above example, cash was received from the collection of the old accounts, but this did not show as *income* on the income statement. Likewise, an item may be earned during the year and show on the income statement as income, but the cash for it may not have been received during that year. In like manner, we saw that cash was disbursed to pay off the old accounts and the bank loan, but the paying off of a debt is not an *expense*, and thus does not show in the income statement. Also, the income statement may show some expense such as taxes, but if it is not paid during the particular year there will be no cash outlay for it during that year.

Ratios

RATIOS IN ANALYSIS OF STATEMENTS. Certain ratios are sometimes used in an analysis of the income statements of the same company for consecutive years in order to determine to what extent the company has gone forward or backward. They are also applied to the statements of two or more different companies covering the same period of time, for comparison purposes, but care should be taken that the figures are comparable. Equally successful companies in different industries or lines of business may show different ratios, owing to the fact that the nature of the industries is different; or the different ratios in the same industry may be due to the difference in size of the companies.

Another point that should be observed is the method of reporting used by the companies. The form of the income statement is not standardized, but in recent years there has been considerable progress made in that direction. In comparing two or more companies whatever adjustment may be needed to make the data comparable should be done before proceeding with a comparison of the ratios. Following are some of the more commonly used ratios that refer to data found in the income statement.

OPERATING RATIO. The *operating ratio* is the ratio of operating expenses to operating revenue. Although called a "ratio," it like many other ratios is expressed in *percentage*. It is computed as follows:

$$\frac{\text{Operating expenses}}{\text{Operating revenue}} = \text{Operating ratio}$$

The phraseology used above would have particular application to a railroad or public utility. If we want to apply it to a manufacturing or merchandising company it would appear in the following form:

$$\frac{\text{Operating expenses}}{\text{Net Sales}} = \text{Operating ratio}$$

Referring to the income statement of the Standard Manufacturing Company which appears on page 538, we see that the total operating expenses amount to \$859,000 (cost of goods sold + other operating expenses), and the net sales, \$1,000,000. The operating ratio for that company would be calculated as follows:

$$\text{Operating ratio} = \frac{\$859{,}000}{\$1{,}000{,}000} = .859 \text{ or } 85.9 \text{ per cent}$$

The operating ratio shows the percentage of each dollar of sales or revenue that is spent in operating expenses. It thus measures the efficiency of operations. Generally speaking, the lower the ratio, the greater is the efficiency of the company. Due consideration, however, must be given to the particular industry or industries studied, since the ratio varies widely among industries.

If we included the nonoperating expenses we could not measure the operating efficiency of the company. For example, the inclusion of the sale of some real estate no longer needed in the income would give us an exaggerated impression of the efficiency of the company. If bond interest (nonoperating expense) were included in the operating expenses, the company with the bonds outstanding would show a high operating ratio as compared to a company with only stock in its capitalization.

From a practical standpoint, however, we are interested in knowing the amount of bond interest that a company must pay, because this obligation must be met just as any other expense. But this has nothing to do with the operating efficiency of the company. Both the bond interest and the dividends on the stock constitute payments for the use of capital, and should not be given effect in computing the operating ratio.

Among other things, an efficient management is interested in cutting costs. With the high price of labor the introduction of labor-saving devices is one method of doing this. Anything that reduces expenses in relation to income will result in a decrease in the operating ratio, which, of course, is favorable. In some instances, however, a relatively low operating ratio may result from practices that are not in line with good management. For example, if a company does not spend enough to keep its machinery and equipment in proper running conditions for a long period of time, the immediate effect of this is a lower operating ratio. So here the operating ratio would be misleading, unless proper attention was also given to the amount being spent for maintenance. Likewise, inadequate depreciation charges would result in a more favorable operating ratio. But such a practice would result in an overstatement of earnings, and the company might not be in a financial position to replace the machinery when it is worn out. Thus the amount of the depreciation charges should also be taken into account when examining the operating ratio.

Companies are interested in making the maximum net earnings. As sales increase, expenses will also increase, but usually the expenses should not increase in proportion to the sales. Every concern has certain *fixed* costs that are incurred regardless of whether the company operates or not, or regardless of the volume of sales. Depreciation on at least some of the fixed assets would be an example. The administrative expenses might not increase much, if at all, with a relatively large increase in sales. In some cases companies will actually operate at a loss if they can sell their products at such a price that at least some of the income can be applied toward the fixed expenses, even though they cannot get enough to cover all the fixed expenses. Not to operate at all might mean an even greater loss.

In addition to the fixed expenses, the company will have costs or expenses that vary with the volume of sales. For example, the cost of the raw materials and direct labor might be a more or less constant amount per unit of output, and thus vary directly with the volume produced and sold. These are called *variable* costs.

As production and sales increase, the total expenses will, of course, also increase. But due to the more or less fixed costs, the expenses will not increase in proportion to sales. In other words, a company may show an operating ratio of 85 per cent for example, but an increase in the volume of production and sales may result in the ratio falling to, for example, 80 per cent.

There may be a limit, however, to which sales can be increased without increasing the fixed costs. After that point a slight increase in sales may call for additional facilities that would result in the fixed costs increasing out of proportion to the increase in sales. But businesses are interested in earning the maximum profits, and not in having the lowest operating ratio possible. For example, a company may have the following operating ratio:

$$\text{Operating ratio} = \frac{\$850{,}000\ (\text{expense})}{\$1{,}000{,}000\ (\text{sales})} = 85 \text{ per cent}$$

If the sales were doubled the fixed expenses might increase so much that the total expenses might go to \$1,800,000. The operating ratio would then be as follows:

$$\text{Operating ratio} = \frac{\$1{,}800{,}000}{\$2{,}000{,}000} = 90 \text{ per cent}$$

Thus this 100 per cent increase in sales might be possible only by increasing the costs more than 100 per cent, with the result that the operating ratio is increased from 85 to 90 per cent. But despite this, the company would prefer sales at the \$2,000,000 level since this would bring in operating profits of \$200,000 instead of only \$150,000 which was earned on a \$1,000,000 volume of sales.

If the company had increased sales only 50 per cent instead of 100 per cent, possibly the operating expenses would have increased to only \$1,200,000, for example, which is an increase of only slightly more than 41 per cent. The operating ratio would then be as follows:

$$\text{Operating ratio} = \frac{\$1{,}200{,}000}{\$1{,}500{,}000} = 80 \text{ per cent}$$

At this scale of operations the company would have operating profits of $300,000. This would obviously be better than pushing production up to the $2,000,000 sales volume as considered above. However, after adding the new facilities which caused the total expenses to increase faster than the sales, a further increase in sales might be possible with a lowering of the operating ratio. In other words, a business might make less in profits for a while as a result of addition to the fixed costs, but still this may be done because it may enable the concern to secure even higher production in the future and larger profits.

In connection with the subject we are discussing, businessmen sometimes refer to the "break-even point." This is the point which must be reached before a profit is made. The *break-even* point represents the number of units that would be produced and sold if the company made neither a profit nor a loss. Because of the more or less fixed costs, a profit will be earned after the break-even point has been passed. The break-even point for a particular company would vary from time to time as the selling price of its product is changed, or when the cost of raw materials and labor is changed.

In our discussion above we assumed that the unit sale price of the product remained constant. In many instances the unit cost of the product declines as more products are sold, with the result that the unit selling price for the product may be lowered.

RATIO OF NET OPERATING INCOME TO SALES. Another income-statement ratio is that of the *net operating income to sales.* This is sometimes called the *margin of profit.* Referring again to the income statement of the Standard Manufacturing Company on page 538, the ratio would be computed as follows:

$$\frac{\text{Ratio of net operating}}{\text{income to sales}} = \frac{\text{Net operating income}}{\text{Net sales}} = \frac{\$141{,}000}{\$1{,}000{,}000} = .141, \text{ or } 14.1\%$$

This ratio tells us that the operating income of the company is 14.1 per cent of the net sales. In other words, the company made an operating profit of 14.1 cents for every dollar of sales. It is obvious that the operating ratio discussed above and the margin of profit ratio express the same thing in two different ways. It will be remembered that the operating ratio shows what percentage of the net sales were consumed by operating expenses. Thus, a relatively low ratio is desirable. But the operating profit margin ratio shows how much of the sales dollar is carried through to operating profit. Therefore, a relatively high ratio is favorable.

At this point we have to say something about the use of the terms "profit" and "income." The former term has been in common use among corporations and other businesses for some time, but the tendency is now to use the word "income" instead. To some persons the term "profits" means the earnings of the company in excess of all expenses including the cost of the capital used. But as we know, dividends which are payments for the use of the stockholders' capital, are not considered an expense of the business before arriving at the net earnings, but rather as a distribution of such earnings. Although bond interest is treated as an expense, nevertheless, it is deducted after the "net operating income" has been determined. In some instances the use of the term "income" may be somewhat ambiguous, since the reader may not know whether reference is being made to the gross or to the net revenue (gross or net sales), the earnings from operations, or the net earnings of the company. Ordinarily, the term should not be taken to mean the income from sales or from the sale of services in the case of a railroad or public utility. Where reference is made to the "operating," or "net" income, these qualifying terms should be used. Unless otherwise indicated, "profits" should be taken to mean the same as "net income." Also if we use the term "earnings" it should be interpreted to mean the same as "net income," unless a contrary meaning is evident, or unless the term is qualified by the use of such words as "gross," "operating," etc.

NET INCOME TO CAPITAL INVESTMENT. The over-all efficiency of a company is reflected in the rate of return it is able to earn on the total capital invested in the business. First, we must consider what "income" figure we are to use, and then determine just what is meant by "invested capital." We will take these up in reverse order.

The "invested capital" could be taken to mean what the stockholder has paid in for his stock, or it could mean that figure plus the retained earnings and "surplus" reserves, or it could refer to the sum of the capital stock and retained earnings, plus the bonded indebtedness. If one company has capital stock of $6,000,000 and no retained earnings, and another company has capital stock of only $3,000,000, but has retained earnings of $3,000,000, the management of each company has the use of exactly the same amount of capital, namely, $6,000,000. So if we want to determine what rate of return they have made on the funds with which they had to work, we would have to add the retained earnings figure to the capital stock to get the total amount of capital. In other words, "invested capital" would include the surplus.

Now, what about bonds? The corporation owes the bondholders the amount represented by the bonds. Does this prevent us from saying that the bondholders' money is "invested" in the business? Certainly from the standpoint of the security buyer, we generally classify the bonds of a particular company as being a better, or at least a safer, investment than the stock of the same company. The bondholders' money is tied up in the business for a relatively long period of time. And when the bonds come due they may be refunded instead of paid off. Oftentimes stock, particularly preferred stock, is called in by the company. But in the meantime, we always consider all the funds obtained from stock as invested capital. There would appear to be sufficient reasons to justify the inclusion of bonds in the "invested capital" of a company. Furthermore, all dollars are alike, regardless of whether they come from the stockholders or the bondholders. In other words, the efficiency of the company's operating executives is revealed by what rate of income they make on the bondholders' dollar, just as much as that made on the stockholders' dollar. To summarize, the "invested capital" of a company consists of the capital stock, retained earnings (surplus), "surplus" reserves, and bonded indebtedness.

The next question is, what income figure is used to determine the rate of return on the invested capital? Perhaps after concluding what is included in the invested capital, the answer becomes obvious. But still there may be some question whether we use the net operating income, the net income before interest on bonds, the net income after bond interest, or the net income after federal income taxes.

Since we have included bonds in the invested capital, it is only fair that we use the income figure before deduction has been made for bond interest to determine what rate is being earned on that capital. If we used the net income after bond interest, differences would exist among companies in the rate of earnings due simply to the fact that one company may have bonds outstanding and another one has only stock. Or they may both have bonds outstanding, but different amounts, or the amounts may be the same, but the rate of interest paid on them is not the same for the companies. We are interested in what is left after bond interest, but when we want to measure the operating efficiency of companies as shown by the rate of return earned on the capital invested in the business, we must take the net income figure *before* bond interest has been deducted.

To get the true picture of the *operating* efficiency of the management as measured by the rate of return on the capital, perhaps we should take the net operating income figure. In other words, not only should interest on bonds be excluded, but any other nonoperating expense should likewise be omitted, and the nonoperating income should not be added. If this is done, however, attention should be called to the fact that the operating net income figure is being used. In practice when the rate of earnings on the invested capital is computed, the nonoperating income and nonoperating expenses, except bond interest, are included. In other words, the ratio is understood to express the relation of the net income from all sources, less the bond interest, to the invested capital.

Is the income figure that is used the income before or after federal income taxes? In some instances the net income before taxes is used in order to determine the operating efficiency of the management. Since taxes, however, are an expense of the business, the net income after taxes (but bond interest is not deducted), is frequently used.[3] To summarize, the ratio of net income to capital investment can be expressed as follows:

$$\frac{\text{Percentage earned on}}{\text{capital investment}} = \frac{\text{Net income before bond interest} - \text{Income taxes}}{\text{Capital stock} + \text{Retained earnings} + \text{“Surplus” reserves} + \text{Bonds}}$$

Referring to the income statement and the balance sheet of the Standard Manufacturing Company (the interest expense shown is for short-term loans) on pages 538 and 542, we would compute the net income to capital investment ratio as follows:

$$\frac{\$73{,}660 \text{ (net income after taxes)}}{\$300{,}000 \text{ (capital stock)} + \$133{,}000 \text{ (retained income)}} = .17, \text{ or } 17 \text{ per cent}$$

Net Income to Net Worth Ratio. Of practical consideration to the shareholders is the rate of earnings on their equity. When we speak of the shareholders' equity we mean the interest or ownership of the shareholders in the business. This is represented by the

[3] The shortcomings of deducting taxes are that the rate of earnings before taxes for two companies may be the same, but the earnings after taxes would be different and probably not comparable where one company had a different amount in bonds than the other company (or only one of the companies had bonds outstanding), owing to the fact that—(1) the deduction of bond interest lessens the the amount of taxes, (2) only corporations pay the corporate income tax, and (3) the over-all rate of taxation is lower for a company that has a relatively small income.

net-worth section of the balance sheet. In other words, the capital stock, retained earnings, and "surplus" reserves constitute the shareholders' equity.

When we speak of "earnings" in this connection, we mean the earnings actually available to the shareholders, regardless of whether or not they are paid out in the form of dividends. In other words, this is the net income left *after* the payment of bond interest and *after* the payment of federal income taxes. The shareholders are the owners of the company and both they and the management are interested in making as high a rate of return on the shareholders' equity as possible. Owners of the stock want to know how much is left after all expenses including interest and taxes have been paid. To summarize, the ratio of net income to net worth would be computed as follows:

$$\frac{\text{Percentage earned on}}{\text{shareholders' equity}} = \frac{\text{Net income left after deducting bond interest and income taxes}}{\text{Stock} + \text{Retained income} + \text{"Surplus" reserves}}$$

Referring again to the Standard Manufacturing Company's statements, the earnings on the shareholders' equity would be computed as follows:

$$\frac{\$73{,}660 \text{ (net income after taxes)}}{\$300{,}000 \text{ (capital stock)} + \$133{,}000 \text{ (retained income)}} = .17, \text{ or } 17 \text{ per cent}$$

In the case of the Standard Manufacturing Company the percentage earned on the shareholders' equity is the same as the percentage earned on the capital investment, since the company had no bonds outstanding.

The advantages or disadvantages of "trading on the equity" or, as it is more commonly called in practice, "leverage," shows up when we analyze this ratio. We will assume that Companies *A* and *B* each have invested capital of $6,000,000 in the forms shown below. The rate of return (before bond interest) for each company is assumed to be 12 per cent. The rate of interest paid on the bonds is 4 per cent. Federal income taxes are computed at the 1956 rates. The invested capital and the rate of return on the shareholders' equity is shown below:

Invested capital

	Company A	*Company B*
Bonds	0	$2,000,000
Capital stock	$6,000,000	2,000,000
Retained income (including "surplus" reserves)	0	2,000,000
Total	$6,000,000	$6,000,000

Earnings on shareholders' equity

	Company A	*Company B*
Net income before interest	$720,000	$720,000
Bond interest		80,000
	720,000	$640,000
Income taxes	368,900	327,300
Earned on shareholders' equity	$351,100	$312,700

To determine the rate of earnings on the shareholders' equity we would divide the above earnings by the total net worth, as follows:

Approximate rate of earnings on shareholders' equity

Company A

$$\frac{\$351{,}100}{\$6{,}000{,}000} = 5.85 \text{ per cent}$$

Company B

$$\frac{\$312{,}700}{\$4{,}000{,}000} = 7.82 \text{ per cent}$$

Even though both companies earned the same rate of return (before interest and taxes) on the capital invested, Company *B* earned a higher rate on shareholders' equity. This was due to two things. First, the company earned 12 per cent on the bondholders' money, but paid them only 4 per cent. The other factor was the fact that since bond interest is an expense deductible before computing federal income taxes, the taxes were lower for Company *B*, which therefore left in the company a larger amount in relation to the shareholders' equity.

EARNINGS PER SHARE. We have referred to the earnings per share elsewhere in the book (Chapter 6). But having just discussed the earnings on the shareholders' equity, it is advisable to follow through with the computation of the *earnings per share*, even at the expense of repetition. It will be recalled that the earnings per share are computed in the following manner:

$$\text{Earnings per share} = \frac{\text{Net income after taxes (earnings on shareholders' equity)}}{\text{Number of shares of stock outstanding}}$$

If we assume that the par value per share of the stock in the hypothetical example given above is $100, then we would compute the earnings per share as follows:

Company A

$$\frac{\$351{,}100}{60{,}000} = \$5.85$$

Company B

$$\frac{\$312{,}700}{20{,}000} = \$15.63\tfrac{1}{2}$$

As noted, the earnings per share means what the *company earns per share of stock,* and *not* what the shareholder gets in dividends.

But commonly the amount paid in dividends depends upon the amount earned by the company. Furthermore, whether or not the company pays the earnings out in dividends, it belongs to the shareholders.

Other Ratios. It will be recalled that in Chapters 20 and 21 we discussed working capital ratios. Those included were the following:

Inventory turnover
Receivables turnover
Current ratio
Acid test
Working capital turnover

We will say nothing further about these ratios here. In addition to these ratios and those discussed in the present chapter, there are a number of other ratios used for various purposes in connection with the analysis of a company or a number of companies. We will not discuss these other ratios for they are not as commonly used as those which we have taken up. Besides, if too many different ratios are listed, the reader might end up more confused than enlightened.

Questions

1. Indicate how the "cost of goods sold" might include different items depending upon the particular company being considered.
2. Should "sales discounts" be subtracted from the "sales" in the income statement, or shown as a nonoperating expense? Why?
3. Do you think "purchase discounts" should be subtracted from the cost of the purchases and the net shown under purchases, or that it should be shown as a nonoperating income item? Why?
4. When the net income of a corporation is reported for the year, is that before or after federal income taxes? Are reported "earnings per share" before or after taxes?
5. Ascertain whether the financial manuals use the same terminology as used in the book for the various captions in the income statement.
6. Is bond interest an expense of the business? Explain fully.
7. How is the operating ratio computed and of what value is it?
8. Explain how to compute the "net income to capital investment" ratio.
9. How does the "net income to net worth" ratio differ from the ratio stated in Question 8. Is the "net income" computed in a different way for the two ratios? Explain.
10. As a shareholder would you be more interested in the earnings per share or the dividends per share? Explain.

Problems

1. The Rapid System Manufacturing Co. published the following financial statements:

Balance Sheet
As of December 31, 19–1

Assets		*Liabilities and Net Worth*	
Cash	$ 40,000	Accounts payable	$ 310,000
Accounts receivable	300,000	Bonds	800,000
Inventory	800,000	Capital stock	1,500,000
Machinery	970,000	Surplus	500,000
Land and buildings	1,000,000		
Total	$3,110,000	Total	$3,110,000

Income Statement
For the year ended December 31, 19–1

Sales		$10,000,000
Cost of goods sold		8,000,000*
Gross margin		$ 2,000,000
Expenses		
Administration	$ 700,000	
Selling	1,100,000	
Interest on bonds	40,000	1,840,000
Net income before taxes		$ 160,000

* Includes materials, labor, and overhead applicable to production department.

(a) What is the "current ratio" for this company? Is it too high or too low? Explain. (b) What is the "capitalization" of this company? How much "capital" does it have? (c) What is the "operating ratio"? (d) What is the margin of profit? (e) The average inventory is the same as that shown in the balance sheet. The cost of sales shown in the income statement represented 60 per cent materials costs. What was the inventory turnover for the year? (f) What is the ratio of net income (before bond interest) to capital investment?

2. Assume that the company in the above problem paid a federal income tax of 50 per cent, and a dividend of 4 per cent on its stock (par value $100). If you purchased some of the company's stock at the beginning of the year for $150 a share what would be the (a) "Earnings per share" on the stock? (b) Yield you received?

Chapter 24

DEPRECIATION, OBSOLESCENCE, AND DEPLETION

Depreciation

NEED FOR CLARIFICATION. One of the least understood phases of business accounting is that of depreciation. The proper handling of this item is tremendously important in connection with charging the correct amount of expense for the accounting period, determining how much must be paid in income taxes, the amount of dividends which may be declared, and the replacement of the depreciated asset.

Depreciation is oftentimes confused with obsolescence and depletion. We will discuss the latter two after we have first explained the nature of depreciation. Depreciation charges are also often confused with maintenance and repair charges, betterments, replacements, and improvements. We shall, therefore, take up these items before discussing depreciation.

MAINTENANCE AND REPAIRS. Maintenance work must constantly be done on machinery, equipment, plant facilities, and other fixed assets used in a business. Things are constantly going wrong with property which is in daily use and proper maintenance work must be done to keep it in proper operating condition. Even though machines are in running condition they have to be oiled, inspected, etc., to remain in good shape. When breakdowns occur, the machines must be repaired and put in proper running condition. *Maintenance* and *repairs* are expenses of the business, properly charged as such against the period in which they occur.

REPLACEMENTS. Closely associated with maintenance and repairs are replacements of machine and equipment parts. In fact, maintenance and repairs frequently result in the replacement of certain parts of the equipment. Theoretically, if the replacement costs more than the depreciated value of the original part which is replaced, the excess should be charged to the appropriate asset account. In other words, the item should be "capitalized." The balance of the expenditure would be charged as an expense for the particular period. The annual depreciation charge for the particular asset in the future should be increased accordingly. In view of the fact that large companies are constantly replacing worn out parts, the time and expense involved in this accounting handling of the items is not justified by the results. It is therefore common for businesses to charge off replacements of parts to the repair or maintenance expense account for the period. In some instances companies charge off to expense all replacements which involve less than an arbitrary figure set by the particular company; costs exceeding that amount are charged to the asset account.

Despite proper maintenance and repairs, practically all fixed assets, except land, will eventually wear out, therefore proper depreciation charges should be made. It is sometimes argued that where the property consists of a large number of uniform small parts the replacement or repair of any one of which does not affect the life of the entire property, no depreciation charge is necessary since the property will never wear out. The roadbed of a railroad is an example. Ties and rails are being replaced constantly, and maintenance of the roadbed is continuous. The Interstate Commerce Commission, and generally the courts, however, do not agree with this viewpoint. Since 1943, railroads have had to charge depreciation, on the straight-line basis (see pp. 569 ff.), on their "way and structures."

Additions and Betterments. Some outlays of cash belong more appropriately under the head of *additions* or *betterments* rather than replacements. These items add to the value of the property and therefore, from a theoretical standpoint, should be written up as assets or as an increase in the asset values rather than charged to expenses. From a practical standpoint, however, some companies adopt a policy similar to that followed in replacements, that is, if the item involves less than a fixed amount, it is charged off to expense for the particular period, otherwise it is added to the assets.

Our reason for discussing maintenance, repairs, replacements, additions, and betterments at this point is that if the particular item is treated as an expense, it is written off as such in the particular period it is incurred. But if the outlay is "capitalized," i.e., added to the assets, it must be depreciated in future years.

Meaning of Depreciation. Practically all the property used by a business, except land, wears out over a period of time. From the standpoint of the farmer, even land "wears out" if it is not properly maintained. The wearing-out process results from two causes—(1) wear and tear from use and (2) action of the elements. Almost any type of asset, particularly one with movable parts, will wear out from use. Often the more the asset is used, the greater will be the deterioration. In addition to the wear arising from use, the action of the elements such as rain, ice, hail, freezing, thawing, heat, cold, etc., will cause most kinds of property to deteriorate. This goes on regardless of whether or not the property is used. Some property may deteriorate faster when it is not used since also maintenance might have been neglected.

The wear and tear and action of the elements result in a *physical* deterioration or *loss in substance* of the property. *Depreciation* is the *loss in value* of the property due to this physical deterioration. These terms should not be confused. Later in the chapter we will also distinguish depreciation from "obsolescence," and "depletion."

REASONS FOR CHARGING DEPRECIATION. There are four reasons:

1. To allocate the expense to the accounting period
2. To lessen income taxes
3. To value the particular asset at its current depreciated value
4. To replace the depreciated asset

ALLOCATING EXPENSE TO ACCOUNTING PERIOD. In proper accounting, all expenses incurred during a particular period should be charged against that period. This should be done regardless of whether or not the item is paid for during that period. If the life of a particular asset was no longer than the accounting period, then it could be charged entirely to an expense account immediately after it is acquired. But it would not be right to charge one year with the entire cost of an asset, such as a machine, when the future years are also going to benefit from it. When the machine is purchased it is written up as an asset, and is charged each year with its pro rata share of the depreciation.

The value of the loss in substance of an asset is just as much an expense or cost of doing business as the amount spent for labor and materials. The finished product should, therefore, bear the depreciation expense just as any other expense. The only difference is that after the particular asset has been purchased there is no further outlay of cash demanded until the asset must be replaced.

In accounting the depreciation is to be charged to the depreciation account, which appears as an expense in the income statement, with the amount of the depreciation for the accounting period. The contra credit is to the "reserve for depreciation" account, which is a valuation reserve and is deducted from the asset account on the balance sheet. The trend in accounting practice is to get away from the use of the term "reserve" when applied to "valuation reserves," like depreciation, since such "reserves" may be confused by the reader with "surplus reserves." The term "provision (or "allowance") for depreciation" is now being used by many companies instead of reserve, and it is recommended that this term be used in the financial statements. For purposes of discussion, however, we will use the term "reserve," rather than "provision," because it affords greater ease of expression. Later in the chapter we will give further consideration to the accounting for depreciation.

LESSENING INCOME TAXES. Before the federal income tax went into effect in 1913, few businesses paid attention to depreciation charges. But after that date, particularly in recent years, when tax rates have been so high, a considerable amount of attention has been given to this item.

From what has been said above, it is evident that depreciation is a legitimate expense of a business and should be charged on the company's books. But when it comes to income taxes, the businessman is happy to charge depreciation. If a corporation is paying an income tax of 52 per cent, for example, it means that every dollar charged off for depreciation lessens the net taxable income by that amount and saves the business 52 cents per dollar charged.

Generally speaking, only the cost price of an asset can be charged off as depreciation and this ordinarily must be done over a period of years corresponding to the life of the asset. The government has set up standard depreciation rates for various types of assets, and any pronounced departure from these might result in serious trouble for a company.

Even if a company charged off more depreciation than it should, it does not necessarily benefit. Overcharging depreciation would result in the asset being entirely depreciated before its useful life has expired. During the remaining years of its life, no further depreciation charges can be made. This would result in higher income taxes for these later years than if the correct rate of depreciation had been followed.

We have referred to the lessening of income taxes on the part of a corporation. This form of organization was used in the example, because the federal government has imposed a relatively high income tax on corporations. But it is also to the advantage of owners of unincorporated businesses to charge off depreciation on the business assets. Although the individual proprietorship and general partnership do not as a business organization pay the tax, the owners of these organizations must each year report their share of the business income on their personal income tax form. They too charge off depreciation on the business property in order to lessen the amount of net business income which they must report on their personal tax returns.

Some companies will prepare one income statement for the government and a different one for their shareholders. The one made out for the government may show the maximum depreciation charges possible. The published statement which goes to the shareholders may reflect a smaller depreciation charge, and therefore a larger net income. This is usually done for the purpose of making a better showing to the shareholders.

Under certain circumstances a company will write down the value of its fixed assets for the purpose of lessening depreciation charges. The fixed assets, or at least part of them, may have been acquired during a period of high prices. This becomes an important matter when a depression hits and the earnings decline drastically. In order to make a better showing to the shareholders, and possibly the creditors or future creditors, a company may reduce the book value of the fixed assets and charge this off against the retained income or a type of surplus account. The annual depreciation charges in the future will accordingly be lessened with the result that the deficit is decreased or the profit increased.

During World War II, a tremendous demand for war materials necessitated the building of new structures on the part of many companies that had war contracts. As an inducement to extend the plant facilities, the government granted permission to the companies to write off the cost, or a substantial portion of the cost, of the new plants over a five-year period. In other words, annual depreciation charges equivalent to about 20 per cent of the cost of the properties were permitted. This was done on the theory that the new plant facilities might be worthless after the war. The accelerated depreciation greatly reduced the amount that had to be paid in income taxes. The statutes provided that if the war ended before the five-year period had expired, a company would be permitted to readjust the depreciation charges upward for the past years. When the war ended in 1945, many companies refigured their depreciation charges for the past several years and received tax refunds in substantial amounts. Many of the new buildings are just as good today as when built, and are in constant use in the production of ordinary products. After having written off the entire cost of the new buildings during a few years, some companies have later put the buildings back in the balance sheet at some figure which represented only normal depreciation rates. But since the entire cost of the new facilities had been written off for tax purposes, none of the new depreciation charges are tax deductible.

Proper Valuation of Assets. Since the fixed assets are constantly depreciating, it would not be accurate to keep carrying them on the books at their cost figure. As the particular asset depreciates the accountant charges the depreciation expense account. The contra credit entry could be to the particular asset account, so that it would show the current depreciation value. But accounting practice is to credit a "reserve for depreciation" account. This procedure results in the asset always being shown at its cost price. The reserve account is deducted from the asset account on the balance sheet and the resultant figure is the current depreciated value of the asset.

The actual current *market* value of the asset may be more or less than the depreciated value, but the accountant is not concerned with this. The fixed assets, such as machinery and buildings, are going to be used in the business as long as they last or until the company terminates, and the proper balance sheet value is considered to be cost less depreciation, rather than the current market value, or the replacement value. From the standpoint of charging off depreciation as an expense, it is the actual cost (or cost less salvage value), not the current market or replacement cost that should be charged over the life of the asset. The same amount as is charged off is added to the reserve account.

Replacement of Depreciated Assets. As stated before, one of the reasons for the proper accounting of depreciation is to enable the company to replace the particular asset after it has been completely depreciated and is no longer usable by the business. It should be stated at the outset, however, that charging off depreciation as an expense, and setting up a "reserve" of similar amount, *does not directly* enable a company to replace the depreciated asset. The reserve account is merely an account, and all it consists of is some ink figures on the company's books. The reserve account may, for example, be for $10,000,000, but there is not one cent of cash or equivalent in the account.

The most that can be said in regard to the replacement of the particular asset is that the charging off of depreciation may result in less being paid out in the form of dividends, and as a result the *assets* (of one type or another) may be larger than would have been the case if no depreciation charges had been made. This can best be explained through the use of figures.

Let us assume that Companies *A* and *B* both start out business operations on January 1, with property and net worth accounts as represented by the following abbreviated balance sheet:

Assets		*Net Worth*	
Machinery	$1,000,000	Capital stock	$5,000,000
Other assets	4,000,000		
Total	$5,000,000	Total	$5,000,000

We will make the following additional assumptions: the machinery will last ten years, and have no scrap value; the other assets do not depreciate; each company will pay dividends equivalent to 80 per cent of the net income after federal income taxes; Company *A* will not charge off any depreciation on the machinery; Company *B* will annually charge off $100,000 depreciation on the machinery; and each company makes 10 per cent, before depreciation and taxes, on the original investment. The amount shown as taxes is according to the 1956 rates. The income statement would show the following for each year:

	Company A	*Company B*
Income before depreciation	$500,000	$500,000
Depreciation		100,000
Income after depreciation	$500,000	$400,000
Federal income taxes	254,500	202,500
Net income after taxes	$245,500	$197,500
Dividends	196,400	158,000
Retained income	$ 49,100	$ 39,500

After the end of the first year's operations the balance sheets for the two companies would appear as follows: (If any liabilities were present, it is assumed that they were deducted from the gross assets.)

Company A		*Company B*	
Assets		*Assets*	
Machinery	$1,000,000	Machinery	$1,000,000
		Less: Reserve for depreciation	100,000
	$1,000,000		$ 900,000
Other assets	4,049,100	Other assets	4,139,500
Total assets	$5,049,100	Total assets	$5,039,500
Net worth		*Net worth*	
Capital stock	$5,000,000	Capital stock	$5,000,000
Retained income	49,100	Retained income	39,500
Total net worth	$5,049,100	Total net worth	$5,039,500

From a comparison of the two abbreviated income statements several things are apparent. By not charging off depreciation, Company *A* has paid $52,000 more in taxes than was necessary. Considering that $100,000 of the machinery was consumed in the year's operations, the *real* net income after taxes would be only $145,500. But dividends amounting to $196,400 were actually paid. It is thus apparent that $50,900 of the dividends actually were paid from the "capital" of the company, rather than from the earnings. Also, after giving effect to the actual depreciation in the machinery, there is really a deficit of $50,900 present, rather than retained income of $49,100.

From the standpoint of the balance sheet, Company *A*'s machinery account is overstated to the extent of $100,000 since there is no reserve for depreciation for that amount. The so-called retained income is reflected in the "other assets" account.

The financial statements of Company *B* reflect the correct accounting of the depreciation. The income tax base is lowered by the amount charged off as depreciation. Not only are taxes lower, but the 80 per cent dividends amount to less than in the case of Company *A*, because the charging of depreciation results in a lower income before taxes. This also accounts for lower retained earnings on the part of Company *B*.

In examining Company *B*'s balance sheet it is seen that a "reserve for depreciation" account of $100,000 has been set up and this is deducted from the machinery account to give a true current depreciated value of the machinery. It will be noted that the "Other assets" of Company *B* increased by $100,000 more than retained earnings of $39,500. Ignoring the depreciation charge and the reserve for depreciation for the moment, Company *B*'s net income was $297,500. The dividends would reduce this to $139,500. In other words the net assets (assets less liabilities) actually increased by $139,500 (aside from the reduced value of the machinery). That is why the "Other assets" of Company *B* show an increase of that amount. The charging of $100,000 in depreciation does not take one cent out of the business; therefore, when we take the depreciation into account and lower the reported retained income by $100,000, the actual increase in the "Other assets" account remains at $139,500.

To illustrate the situation at the end of ten years, we will assume that the operating results and dividend policies of the two companies for each of the remaining nine years is identical to that of the first year. Following is how the balance sheets (the assets shown are after any liabilities have been deducted) for the two companies would appear:

Company A		*Company B*	
Assets		*Assets*	
Machinery	$1,000,000	Machinery	$1,000,000
		Less: Reserve for depreciation	1,000,000
	$1,000,000		$ 0
Other assets	4,491,000	Other assets	5,395,000
Total assets	$5,491,000	Total assets	$5,395,000
Net worth		*Net worth*	
Capital stock	$5,000,000	Capital stock	$5,000,000
Retained income	491,000	Retained income	395,000
Total net worth	$5,491,000	Total net worth	$5,395,000

Since Company *A* did not charge off any depreciation for the entire ten-year period, the shortcomings expressed above for the first year's operations apply with equal force to each of the ten years. The machinery is now worthless, according to our assumptions, and it must therefore be taken off the books. The elimination of this $1,000,000 from the assets will result in the obliteration of the entire retained earnings account of $491,000, and the creation of a *deficit* account in the amount of $509,000. Thus, the failure to charge off the depreciation has resulted in the payment of excessive taxes, and the payment of dividends from capital, with the result that a deficit now must appear on the company's books.

The next question is, how can Company *A* replace its worn-out machinery? At the beginning of the ten-year period there were $4,000,000 in "Other assets." Presumably this amount was needed in the business for inventory and other working capital and fixed capital assets, and is probably still needed. During the period the "Other assets" have increased by only $491,000. So possibly this represents the maximum assets that may be withdrawn from the business in order to purchase a new machine. Assuming that the new machinery will cost the same as the old, it may be difficult to acquire the new machinery. Either the company will have to use part of its needed working capital, or at least part of the money to pay for the new machinery may have to be borrowed. And there is always the practical consideration whether the company would be able to borrow the amount needed. Such are the shortcomings of failure correctly to handle depreciation of fixed assets.

The advantages to Company *B* of charging off depreciation for the first year, which were stated above, apply also to each of the other nine years. And furthermore, Company *B* will be in a much better position to replace the worn-out machinery. It will be noted that the "Other assets" of Company *B* increased by $1,395,000. The charging of depreciation not only reduced the amount of income taxes, but made also less available (retained income) for dividend payments to the shareholders. Thus the increase in "Other assets" was due in part to the accumulation of retained income, but $1,000,000 of it in effect resulted from charging off this amount as depreciation expense.

If only $4,000,000 in "Other assets" are needed to run the business on its present scale of operation, then $1,395,000 in *assets of one form or another,* would be available for the acquisition of new machinery. However, one point should be made clear: the charging of depreciation and the setting up of a reserve account of a similar amount does not in itself put the company in a *cash* position to replace the old machinery. As we have stated above, the reserve account is merely a bookeeeping entry—no cash or other assets are put into the reserve. It exists only as a bookkeeping account, and it should not be confused with a *fund* into which may be put cash or other assets. But, as we have also seen, the accounting for depreciation will result in the accumulation of additional assets in the business (unless deficits are suffered), and these additional assets will make it easier for the company to replace the machinery.

As a practical matter, if additional assets are acquired in the business as a result of operations, the business may expand constantly. Additional inventories or fixed assets may be acquired. Possibly, new machinery may be purchased gradually so that at the end of the ten-year period the old machinery, or part of it, will have been replaced.

It will be recalled, we assumed that 80 per cent of the income after taxes was paid in dividends. This resulted in smaller dividends for Company *B* than for Company *A*. It might be thought by the reader that this in itself would enable Company *B* to replace its machinery easier than Company *A*. But let us assume that Company *B* pays the same amount of dollars in dividends as Company *A*. This would reduce the annual retained income after dividends to $1,100, and reduce the annual increase in "other assets" to $101,100. The total increase in "Other assets" for the ten-year period would be $1,011,000. Thus, the company would still have additional assets in excess of the amount needed for the replacement of the machinery.

It is interesting to note that the annual savings in income taxes of Company *B* as compared with Company *A* amounts to $52,000.

In ten years (assuming the same rates) the savings would be $520,000. (The effect of compounding would result in an even larger saving.) Thus, the tax savings resulting from charging of depreciation would result in the accumulation of additional assets over the period to pay for more than half the cost of the new machinery.

The actual accounting of the replacement of the depreciated machinery could be done in one of two ways. The cash account or accounts payable would be credited depending upon whether the machinery was paid for or charged, regardless of which method is followed. Then the accountant could close out the reserve account against the asset account by debiting the reserve account and crediting the *old* asset account. The new asset account would then be debited with the cost of the new machinery. Or the same effect would be produced if the old asset account was allowed to remain on the books, and simply a debit made to the reserve account.

EXPERIENCE OF U. S. MANUFACTURING CORPORATIONS. Statistics relating to depreciation charges by U. S. manufacturing corporations for the years 1939–54 are shown in Table 35. It will be noted that the property accounts include land, on which depreciation charges are not made. The percentage depreciation charge figures would therefore be higher if based on the depreciable assets only.

As shown in the table the depreciation charges have increased considerably since pre-World War II, but that is to be expected in view of the appreciable increase in the property account. The latter has resulted both from the expansion in physical property in industry, and the higher prices at which the property has been acquired. But it will be noted that the 1939–40 depreciation was at the rate of about 4 per cent of the gross property valuation whereas in 1951–54 it had increased to approximately 5½ per cent. This percentage increase was due in large part to the stepped-up rate of depreciation permitted on certain types of properties during and since World War II. In the middle and latter part of the 1950's there was a tendency toward a lower rate of depreciation since much property had already been completely written off the books from the fast depreciation charges, and also because of the change in policy on the part of the government not to permit fast write-offs on many types of property. Many corporations, however, were able to step-up the depreciation charges on ordinary property due to the fast write-off provisions of the Revenue Code of 1954.

It was mentioned earlier in the chapter that the amount represented by the depreciation reserve is available for expansion in the

TABLE 35

PROPERTY ACCOUNTS AND DEPRECIATION CHARGES OF ALL MANUFACTURING CORPORATIONS, UNITED STATES, 1939–1954

(in billions of dollars)

Years Ended Dec. 31	*Gross Prop. Acc't.**	*Accrued Deprec. Res.†*	*Net Prop. Acc't.**	*Annual Deprec. Charges†*	*Deprec. to Prop. Gross*	*Deprec. to Prop. Net*
1939	$ 41.6	$18.5	$23.1	$1.6	3.9%	7.1%
1940	42.7	19.1	23.6	1.7	4.1	7.3
1941	44.9	20.2	24.7	1.9	4.3	7.9
1942	49.1	22.5	26.6	2.3	4.8	8.8
1943	51.6	24.6	27.0	2.7	5.3	10.1
1944	52.0	26.1	25.9	3.0	5.7	11.5
1945	53.9	28.7	25.1	3.5	6.6	14.1
1946	59.2	29.7	29.4	2.4	4.1	8.3
1947	66.8	31.4	35.4	3.1	4.7	8.8
1948	74.0	32.8	41.2	3.9	5.2	9.4
1949	79.1	35.0	44.1	4.1	5.2	9.2
1950	83.3	36.9	46.4	4.4	5.3	9.6
1951	92.1	39.5	52.6	5.3	5.7	10.0
1952	100.6	42.8	57.7	6.0	6.0	10.4
1953	112.6	50.2	62.4	6.3	5.6	10.0
1954‡	121.0	55.0	66.0	6.8	5.6	10.3

* Includes land.

† Includes amortization charges on defense facilities, and depletion charges on natural resources of minerals, petroleum, etc.

‡ Fourth quarter 1954 estimated.

SOURCE: National City Bank of New York, *National City Monthly Letter,* New York, March, 1955, p. 28. Data taken from U.S. Treasury annual "Statistics of Income" for 1939–52, and S.E.C.–F.T.C. "Quarterly Financial Report" for 1953–54.

fixed asset accounts or for additional working capital. It will be noted from the table that U. S. manufacturing corporations are able to obtain in excess of six billion dollars annually from this source.

USE OF ASSETS RESULTING FROM DEPRECIATION CHARGES. Although charging depreciation and setting up a reserve do not provide any cash with which to replace the assets, a company, such as our hypothetical Company *B* above, might attempt to set aside $100,000 annually for the eventual replacement of the machinery. But it would seem uneconomical to take this amount out of the earning assets each year for a ten-year period. Of course, it might be invested in U. S. Government bonds, but the rate of return on these would be relatively low. Commonly the amount equivalent to the reserve account just accumulates in the business and shows up as an increase in the inventory or other asset accounts. Naturally, it is the duty of the financial officer of the company to see to it that sufficient cash is available to replace the old machinery gradually or to replace it in its entirety at the end of the ten-year period.

If a company, like our Company *B* referred to above, does all its business on a cash basis and does not expand or contract, its cash account should increase each year by not only the amount of the retained income after dividends, but also by the amount of the depreciation charges of $100,000. Therefore, in examining the company's statements to determine the ability of the company to stand interest charges or some other outlay of cash, it should be realized that the company will increase its cash by $139,500 a year, and not by $39,500.

METHODS OF CHARGING DEPRECIATION. Under depreciation accounting, the value of the particular asset is written off over the period of its usefulness. The usual method is to deduct the salvage or scrap value from the cost of the asset and the balance is the amount written off. For reasons of simplicity, we will assume in our discussion that the particular asset has no scrap value and that therefore the entire cost is to be written off.

The estimated life of the various types of assets will have to be determined before setting up the depreciation schedule. The past experience of the particular company or that of other companies is useful in estimating the probable life. Due considerations will also have to be given to the Internal Revenue Service regulations for maximum percentage that may be written off annually so far as income taxes are concerned.

Some types of assets depreciate much faster than others. A company, for example, may depreciate its buildings over a period of from 50 to 60 years, and its machinery over a 10- or 15-year period. Dies, patterns, and jigs, on the other hand, might be written off over a period of from 1 to 5 years.

After having decided upon the period of time over which the asset is to be written off, the company must then decide upon what method will be used to determine the amount that will be written off each year, or accounting period. Following are the various methods that might be used.

1. *Straight-line method.* Under the *straight-line* method, each accounting year is charged with exactly the same amount of depreciation. This was the method used in our hypothetical example above. It is the simplest and by far the most commonly used method. The ease of setting up and following the schedule under this method is enough to recommend it. Furthermore, it is approved

TABLE 36

SUGGESTED YEARS OF USEFUL LIFE AND STRAIGHT LINE ANNUAL DEPRECIATION RATES FOR BUILDINGS, BY TYPES, UNITED STATES, 1956

Type of Building	*Useful Life (years)*	*Annual Depreciation Rate (per cent)*
Apartments	50	2.0%
Banks	67	1.5
Factories	50	2.0
Garages	60	1.7
Hotels	50	2.0
Loft Buildings	67	1.5
Office Buildings	67	1.5
Stores	67	1.5
Theaters	50	2.0
Warehouses	75	1.3

SOURCE: Based on Bulletin F of the Internal Revenue Service as reported in: Prentice-Hall Tax Service, *Federal Taxes, 1956,* Vol. 2, Prentice-Hall, Inc., Englewood Cliffs, N. J., pp. 14, 148.

by the Internal Revenue Service, the Interstate Commerce Commission, most of the state regulatory commissions, and generally by the courts.

It is obvious that under the straight-line method it is more or less assumed that the value of the property depreciates by the same amount each year. The current market value, however, may not actually decrease exactly the same amount each year. But the purpose of charging depreciation is to charge each period with its share of the expense and to provide for the replacement of the worn-out asset. This is done under the straight-line method. The property may actually decrease in market value less the second year than the first, but nevertheless the company got the same use of the property the second year as the first, and therefore, that year should bear as much of the cost as the first year.

If a company wants to have the total of the depreciation and maintenance or repair charges uniform during the entire period, the straight-line method would not be advisable since the maintenance charge on a machine, for example, is usually light when the machine is new, but heavy during the later years when the machine is old and constantly breaking down or necessitating greater maintenance.

2. *Production method.* Some companies charge depreciation according to the *production method.* The total number of operating

hours possible out of the machine is estimated and the depreciation is charged accordingly. Or, an estimate is made of the total number of units of product that can be turned out during the life of the machine, and the depreciation charged as so much per unit of output.

This method recognizes the realistic fact that the greater the operation of the machine, the greater will be the wear and tear, and therefore, more depreciation will take place. This method, however, gives no consideration to the fact that some depreciation will take place even if the machinery is not in use. From a practical standpoint, this method has the advantage of having heavy depreciation charges when production is high, and probably profits large, and low charges during slack periods when profits fall off. This would tend to equalize the net income. At the outset it would be necessary to determine how many hours the machine can operate, or how many units it can turn out. This would be difficult to estimate. But under the straight-line method it might be equally difficult to estimate the number of years the machine will last. The production method of charging depreciation can conveniently be used when a company has a cost accounting system in operation.

TABLE 37

SUGGESTED YEARS OF USEFUL LIFE AND STRAIGHT LINE ANNUAL DEPRECIATION RATES FOR SELECTED TYPES OF EQUIPMENT IN SELECTED INDUSTRIES, UNITED STATES, 1956

Industry	*Type of Equipment*	*Useful Life (years)*	*Annual Depreciation Rate (per cent)*
Bakery	Peeling Machines	15	6.7
Brewery	Kegs	10	10.0
Canning	Mixers	20	5.0
Cement	Kilns	30	3.3
Construction	Under ⅔ cu. yd. Trucks	3	33.3
Construction	Over 2 cu. yd. Trucks	8	12.5
Glass	Emery Mill	15	6.7
Iron and Steel	Blowers	25	4.0
Mining	Steel Mine Cars	10	10.0
Paper	Newsprint Machines	18	5.6
Rubber	Dryers	15	6.7
Textile	Banding Machines	30	3.3
Tobacco	Stemming Machines	15	6.7

NOTE: Salvage or scrap value is to be deducted before determining the dollar value of the equipment subject to depreciation.

SOURCE: Based on Bulletin F of the Internal Revenue Service as reported in: Prentice-Hall Tax Service, *Federal Taxes, 1956,* Vol. 2, Prentice-Hall, Inc., Englewood Cliffs, N. J., pp. 14, 143–44, 196.

3. *Fixed-percentage-of-declining-balance method.* The fixed-percentage-of-declining-balance method is similar to the straight-line method in that an estimate is made of the number of years the machine or other asset will last, but instead of charging off the same *amount* per year, the same *percentage* of the depreciated value is charged off each year. For example, if it is decided that the machine will last 10 years, it may be decided to apply the rate of 20 per cent ("double"-declining balance) a year on the depreciated value. Thus, if the machine cost $100,000, the depreciation for the first year would be $20,000. The depreciated value at the beginning of the second year would be $80,000, so during the second year it would be depreciated 20 per cent of $80,000, or $16,000. Continuing this process during the third, fourth and fifth years it would be depreciated $12,800, $10,240, and $8,192, respectively. This "double"-declining-balance method was first approved for federal income tax purposes in 1954.

Applying the 20 per cent to a diminishing value will never result in the machine being entirely written off since absolute zero is constantly being approached, but never reached. Therefore, it will be necessary to write off whatever balance remains during the last year the machine is used, or to switch to the straight-line method during the later years.

There are several arguments that might be used in favor of the fixed-percentage-of-declining-balance method. It results in heavy depreciation charges during the early years when the resale value would drop off relatively sharply. Also the maintenance charges should be relatively light during the early years, but heavy during the later years. Thus the total cost or expense of the machine as represented by the sum of the depreciation charges and the maintenance expense would tend more toward equality during the life of the machine. Also, the larger income tax savings would result in the retention of more assets in the business at the beginning of the period.

The arguments opposing the method are that it is more difficult to figure the depreciation charges, and that since the company does not contemplate selling the machine, there is no reason for carrying it on the books at a figure more in line with the market value. Furthermore, if income tax rates advanced during the later part of the life of the asset, the company would be harmed.

4. *"Sum-of-the-digits" method.* The "sum-of-the-digits" method of charging depreciation was first approved by the Internal Revenue Service for income tax purposes also in 1954. Under this method the

annual depreciation rate is represented by a fraction, the numerator of which is the number of years of useful life of the asset at the beginning of the particular year, and the denominator of which is the sum of years of useful life at the time the asset was acquired. This can also be best explained by the use of an illustration. Let us assume the same situation as above where a machine which cost $100,000 has an expected life of 10 years. The denominator of the depreciation rate fraction would be 55 ($10 + 9 + 8 + 7 + 6 + 5 + 4 + 3 + 2 + 1$). For the first year the numerator of the fraction would be 10. Thus, for the first year, $^{10}/_{55}$ths of $100,000, or $18,181.82 in depreciation would be charged off. For the second year $^{9}/_{55}$ths of $100,000 or $16,363.64 would be charged. This process would be continued until the tenth year when the charges would amount to only $1,818.18. It is to be noted that the depreciation rate each year, represented by the fraction, is applied to the original cost, and not to the declining balance, as in the method previously discussed.

This is an accelerated method of charging depreciation, somewhat similar to the fixed-percentage-of-declining-balance method described above, and therefore the same points there mentioned would apply to the "sum-of-the-digits" method. Under the latter method, however, the entire cost of the asset will be charged off over the ten-year period without the necessity of switching over to the straight-line method.

5. *Current market method.* Another possible method is to annually revalue the asset at its *current market* value and charge off the difference between this and the figure at which it is carried on the books. This is rarely ever done in business. It would be time consuming and difficult to determine the existing market value every year. Furthermore, since the fixed assets are not to be resold, there is no reason for carrying them at market values.

When a company is being bought out, or combining with another company, it may be necessary to determine the existing market values of the fixed assets. Many people figure depreciation on their automobiles to be the same as the decline in the market value for the particular period.

6. *Sinking fund method.* We have at several places pointed out that a fund represents the setting aside of cash or equivalent, while a *reserve* is merely a bookkeeping entry. The *sinking fund* method of charging depreciation is a misnomer because usually no *fund* is set aside. Other titles sometimes used, the *compound interest,* and *annuity* methods describe perhaps better the nature of this plan.

With the use of mathematical tables, it is ascertained what sum of money would have to be invested annually at interest of a predetermined rate compounded annually to equal the cost of the particular asset at the time it must be replaced. The amount of interest would increase each successive year due to the accumulation of annual installments and the compounding of interest on this increasing amount. As may be inferred from what has already been said, the annual installments are assumed to be equal in amount. But the sum of this given amount and the interest earned would increase each year due to the greater interest. A company using this method would charge depreciation, and credit the reserve for depreciation account, each year with the sum of the installment and the interest. Thus, it is apparent that the amount of the depreciation charged (and the amount credited to the reserve) would increase each successive year.

Aside from being complicated to figure, this method throws a burden on later years because the higher depreciation charges come at a time when the maintenance charges on the particular asset will also be heavy. Also, despite the fact that the particular property being depreciated will probably not be sold, the actual decline in the resale value of the property would be relatively high, rather than low, during the early period of its life.

But there is something to be said in favor of this method of charging depreciation. As we have pointed out earlier in the chapter, the charging of depreciation results in the accumulation of assets equivalent to the amount of the depreciation, despite the fact that *no fund* is actually set aside. This amount is usually not set aside in a special account, but is to be found scattered among the various assets. Therefore, it constitutes part of the earning assets of the company. The amounts added to the assets as a result of the charges for depreciation during the early years of the life of the particular asset are used in the business for a longer period than those which accumulate from the depreciation charges during the later years. Therefore, there is some justification for making the depreciation charges heavier during the later part of the asset's life.

The sinking fund method of handling depreciation is rarely used by ordinary business corporations, but some public utilities have adopted it.

7. *Arbitrary method.* Some companies, particularly in the past, have had no set depreciation policy. When earnings are large they charge off a large amount of depreciation and then when earnings fall off they cut down the depreciation charges. Although there may

be some connection between the rate of depreciation and the extent of the use of the particular asset, there is little correlation between depreciation and net income before the depreciation charges. This method, however, has the advantage of charging depreciation according to the ability of the company to stand the charges, and thus it tends to stabilize the net income. But it is realized that the assets will have to be replaced sometime regardless of whether or not the company has any earnings. This *arbitrary* method is not recommended, and of course, it would not meet with the approval of the Internal Revenue Service.

8. *"20 Per Cent" Deduction.* Since 1958 a business can take a 20 per cent tax depreciation deduction the first year (plus the first year's regular deduction of the remaining 80 per cent) on up to $10,000 a year investment in new or used "equipment" (not buildings or inventories) with a life of six years or more.

IMPORTANCE OF DEPRECIATION TO RAILROADS AND PUBLIC UTILITIES. For many years railroads and public utilities have been operated as monopolies and have been regulated in the interests of the public. In general the rates set for their services enable them to earn a fair return on a fair investment. Although there are some exceptions, in general the original cost of the property is taken as the investment.

The amount of the net income of railroads and public utilities would vary according to the amounts charged off in depreciation. And the amount of the net income is important when it comes to determining rates allowed by the commissions. In most instances these companies, as well as ordinary business corporations, use the straight-line method of charging depreciation.

DEPRECIATION RESERVES BASED ON REPLACEMENT COSTS. In a period of rising prices companies often find that to replace a particular asset may require twice as much as was originally invested in it. Under the current method of charging depreciation, other assets equivalent to only the original cost of the depreciated property will have been accumulated in the business by the time the property has to be replaced. As a result a company may find it difficult to finance the acquisition of the new assets. Because of this, some have advocated that during a period of rising prices, the assets should be depreciated on the basis of their replacement cost rather than the original cost. This would accomplish the double effect of charging depreciation currently on the basis of the replacement cost, and the accounting of this would result in assets equivalent to the replacement cost being accumulated in the business for the eventual replacement.

The traditional accounting for depreciation, however, is to write off the cost figure, since the particular period over which the asset is used should bear this cost, and only this cost. If more than the original cost were to be written off, then the particular asset would first have to be reappraised upward. That would not be considered conservative accounting particularly since the asset is not going to be sold in the market.

If additional depreciation charges were to be made as replacement costs increased, should, for consistency, the book value of the assets be reduced and the depreciation charges lessened when replacement costs decline? The accountant would oppose the lessening of depreciation charges since this would not be charging the period with the proper costs, and thus the net income would be overstated.

Despite the arguments that may be advanced for charging heavier depreciation as replacement costs increase, it is probable that businesses will go on charging it on a cost basis. The replacement of assets at higher figures is an important financial problem, but the proper company officers should anticipate this and take appropriate action to replace the assets when the time comes.

Obsolescence

NATURE OF OBSOLESCENCE. Some confusion exists in the writings and in business practices between depreciation and obsolescence. In some instances the two are distinguished but from an accounting standpoint they may be lumped together for purposes of charging the expense account and setting up a reserve account. The Internal Revenue Service still combines the charges for depreciation and obsolescence. Due to the difference between the two, however, it is suggested by the leading authorities that they both be recognized but handled separately from an accounting standpoint.

We have said that depreciation is the loss in value due to the physical deterioration of an asset. *Obsolescence,* on the other hand, is used to refer both to the becoming *out of date* and to the *loss in value* due to the asset's becoming out of date. In addition to becoming out of date as we ordinarily use the term, obsolescence includes also such things as unsuitability, or inadequacy due to modern developments, an increase in the scale of operation, a change in the production process, or changes resulting from some governmental action.

There is some difference of opinion among the writers whether depreciation and obsolescence can both take place at the same time, or whether the one that first causes the asset to be scrapped should bear the total charge. For example, even if a particular asset is becoming obsolete and eventually would have to be replaced, if it becomes worn out and fully depreciated before total obsolescence overtook it, should there have been any charges made for obsolescence? Or, suppose that the asset has to be replaced by a more efficient new model when it is only half depreciated. Should the entire cost of the asset be charged to obsolescence, or since it has been half depreciated, should only half of the cost be charged to obsolescence? We are interested in indicating the problem here and not in offering a proper solution.

It is undoubtedly more difficult to predict obsolescence than depreciation. Bringing a new model machine on the market may make the old ones obsolete overnight. And often nothing is known about the new model until it is out. It would be conservative accounting practice to expect the worst and therefore be liberal in respect to obsolescence charges. In this respect it would be advisable to be conservative in estimating the life of assets so that if obsolescence overtook the property, a relatively large part of it would have been charged off already.

Obsolescence has been an important factor for companies that generate electrical power and those that operate airlines. For some years now electric generating equipment and transport airplanes have become obsolete long before they were worn out.

ACCOUNTING PROCEDURES. Most companies make no charge for obsolescence. In some instances they are liberal in charging off depreciation due to the fact that they include something in it for obsolescence. Some companies specifically recognize obsolescence, but lump together "depreciation and obsolescence" in the financial statements. Courts and governmental and regulatory bodies generally take the position that the "depreciation" charge covers not only depreciation, but obsolescence as well.

Since depreciation and obsolescence are caused by entirely different factors, it would seem only logical to separate them for purposes of charging the income account. When this is done someone must decide just how much obsolescence is to be charged off. At best this must be guess work, and perhaps that is why most companies either ignore obsolescence charges, or include it in the depreciation charge.

The accounting entries for obsolescence would be the same as for depreciation, that is, it is charged as an expense and a "reserve for obsolescence" is credited. When depreciation and obsolescence are put into the same account, then the reserve would be deducted from the appropriate asset account. When the reserve for obsolescence is set up separately, it still may be combined with the depreciation reserve. The purposes accomplished by charging obsolescence are similar to those for charging depreciation, that is, the current period is charged with the cost, the net value of the particular asset is correspondingly reduced, and other assets equivalent in amount to the charges will accumulate in the businesses since dividends are restricted to the extent of the charges.

Obsolescence and Rising Prices. As explained, depreciation is charged off on the basis of the cost of the particular asset, and accordingly replacement of the asset is often difficult in a period of rising prices. Although not primarily designed to take care of that situation, the obsolescence reserve might facilitate the replacement of the particular asset. Whatever had been charged off as obsolescence would result in the accumulation of other assets of similar amount, just as in the case of depreciation. Therefore, from the asset position, replacement should be made easier. In some instances the cost of the replacement asset is more not only because of rising prices in general, but also because of improvements made in the asset. In other words, some obsolescence did take place, and therefore the charging of obsolescence was justified.

Amortization of Patents, Copyrights, Franchise, and Other Intangibles. Many companies carry intangible fixed assets such as patents, copyrights, franchises, trade-marks, and goodwill on the books at a stated value. These are usually amortized, in other words, charged off over a period of years. Patents last for only 17 years, and copyrights expire at the end of 28 years with an extension of another 28 years, so these should be completely written off by the time of their expiration. Quite often, however, their value ceases long before the exclusive legal right has terminated. Thus it would be conservative to write them off over a shorter period of time. Franchises also may be for only a limited time and should be written off during that period. Trade-marks and goodwill do not legally terminate, but conservative accounting practice would call for writing these items off over a reasonable number of years.

It is generally considered good accounting practice to carry goodwill on the books only if it was bought, and then it should not be valued at more than the cost price. Even though it may be purchased, some companies carry goodwill on the books at a nominal value of $1.

When intangible assets of the kind mentioned above are written off the books, the charge is ordinarily not called depreciation or obsolescence. The term "amortization" is usually used. Instead of setting up a reserve account, a credit is made directly to the asset account so that the book figure shows the net amortized value.[1]

Depletion

NATURE OF DEPLETION. *Depletion* takes place in connection with the exhaustion of *wasting assets* on the part of companies that own timberlands, oil and gas wells, mines, and quarries. When the mineral in a mine, for example, is exhausted, the property no longer has any value. When the minerals are sold, the difference between the income and expenses is not all profit. Part of the income represents the cost of the shrinking original property, that is, the gradual depletion of substance. Not to include this in the cost of the sales would be the same as not to include the cost of the inventory on the part of an ordinary manufacturing or merchandising company. If a mining company did not make a charge for the minerals sold, and the total net income after taxes was paid to the shareholders in the form of dividends, part of the dividends would represent a return of capital, and eventually the mineral lands would have no value.

ACCOUNTING PROCEDURE. Wasting asset companies prepare an estimate of the quantity of minerals, or whatever other material is involved, in the ground. Presumably this would be carried on the books at the cost figure. As the minerals are removed and sold a *depletion* charge is made against the income for the cost per ton, or whatever other measure is used. The corresponding credit is made to either the particular asset account or to a "reserve for depletion" account, which is deducted from the asset accounts on the balance sheet. Accountants prefer that the credit be made to the

[1] The term "*intangible* asset" is almost universally used to apply to such fixed assets as goodwill, patents, copyrights, franchises, etc. It is also used in connection with property taxes with a different meaning. The state may apply the tax to tangible personal property such as clothing, jewelry, automobiles, boats, etc., and/or to so-called *intangible* personal property such as stocks and bonds, bank accounts, etc. Where the tax is applied only to such things as stocks, bonds, bank accounts, money, etc., it is often called an *intangible* tax. From the standpoint of a company's balance sheet, we would certainly consider stocks and bonds (owned), money, etc., to be *tangible* assets and not intangible ones. Unless otherwise indicated, we will use the term "intangible assets" to mean goodwill, etc. Securities, etc., will be treated as personal property, unless otherwise indicated.

reserve account, particularly when "liquidating" dividends (these will be discussed in Chapter 26) will later be paid to the shareholders.

The depletion charge accomplishes the same as the depreciation charge. The income for the particular period is charged with the proper amount, and since the dividends are restricted to this extent, other assets equivalent to the charge accumulate in the business. This might be constantly invested in new mineral lands to take the place of those which have been depleted.

DEPRECIATION OF OTHER ASSETS. Wasting asset companies may have to give special depreciation treatment to other assets. For example, a tipple at a particular mine will be worthless after the exhaustion of the ore, so it, therefore, should be completely depreciated by the time the ore is exhausted. Ordinary depreciation policies, however, would be applied to property such as a refinery if the company had numerous other sources to draw from in event one ore deposit was exhausted.

DEPLETION AND INCOME TAXES. If a wasting asset company did not make depletion charges then it would in part be paying income taxes on money that represented a return of its own capital. At the present time the federal tax laws permit oil and gas producing companies, coal and metal and certain other types of mines to charge depletion of 50 per cent of the *net income,* or 27½ per cent of the gross income from oil (15 per cent of the gross income for metal mines), whichever is lower.

WHEN ASSETS ARE NOT TO BE REPLACED. If a company which operates only one mine is to be liquidated when the ore is exhausted, there is no reason for withholding from the shareholders the income that is represented by the depletion. In other words, part of the dividend would represent a return of capital. When such dividends are paid, the shareholders are informed as to what part of the dividend represents a return of capital. This should be done because the shareholder does not have to pay income taxes on that part of the dividends. According to the laws of most of the states, it is legal for a company with wasting assets to pay a dividend without first charging depletion.

Questions

1. What objectives are accomplished by the proper accounting handling of depreciation on the part of a business corporation?

2. Distinguish between maintenance or repairs, replacements, and additions or betterments. Why are they discussed in this chapter?

3. Does the overcharging of depreciation lessen the federal income tax? Explain.

4. Explain definitely how the proper accounting treatment of depreciation may result in the company being better able to replace the depreciated asset than if no depreciation charges had been made.

5. Indicate the various methods of charging off depreciation. Which do you favor? Why?

6. *(a)* What situation may be encountered during a period of rising prices by a company which charges depreciation on the basis of cost? *(b)* What drawbacks might there be to a policy of charging depreciation on replacement costs during a period of rising prices? If this policy is followed should it be continued during a period of falling prices? Why so or why not?

7. Distinguish between obsolescence and depreciation. Should the two be combined in the same account? Explain.

8. Assume that a half-depreciated asset is discarded because it becomes obsolete. What is the proper accounting procedure of writing off the asset and replacing it?

9. What accounting procedure should be followed in writing off intangible assets?

10. (a) Indicate the proper accounting handling of depletion charges. (b) What special income tax treatment is accorded companies which have wasting assets? (c) Indicate the shortcomings which may be encountered by a wasting asset company not making the proper depletion charges.

Problems

1. The asset side of the balance sheet of both the Old Co. and the New Co. is as follows:

Cash	$ 5,000
Inventory	95,000
Machinery	1,000,000
Plant	4,000,000

Both companies' average earnings before depreciation charges (and taxes) amount to $1,000,000 a year, and each of them follows a policy of paying out 90 per cent of their *net* income, after taxes, in the form of dividends, and investing half of the remaining income in United States government bonds. Assume federal income taxes to be 50 per cent.

Both companies state that the appreciation in the value of the plant will offset any depreciation, so no charge for the latter will be made. Both companies also agree that the machinery will be worthless in 10 years, but the Old Co. is not going to make any provision for depreciation or replacement "until the time comes when they have to replace it," whereas the New Co. will charge off machinery depreciation on a straight-line basis—treating this as an expense in the income statement and deducting a reserve of corresponding amount from the Machinery account on the balance sheet.

It is assumed that all the business is on a cash basis; that the liabilities remain the same; and that the Plant, Machinery (except for "Reserve" account in case of the New Co.), and Inventory accounts remain the same as stated above.

(a) List the asset accounts for each company at the end of the 10 years. (b) Can the Old Co. replace its machinery? (c) Can the New Co. replace its machinery? If so, what account will furnish the money to buy it? (d) What becomes of the Reserve for Depreciation account? (e) Assuming that the plant would appreciate in value an amount equal to the depreciation, would that be a reason for not charging off depreciation on the plant? Explain.

2. Select a company whose stock is listed on the New York Stock Exchange and ascertain what policy it follows with relation to the depreciation of its various types of fixed assets.

Chapter 25

RETAINED INCOME, SURPLUS, AND RESERVES

Retained income and surplus

TERMINOLOGY. After paying federal income taxes and dividends (if any) the balance of the net income shown on the income statement is carried to the net worth section of the balance sheet, and put into the account that represents the accumulated retained income from past years. The current retained income account in the income statement may be called something else than "retained income," as *net profit after dividends,* and *net earnings after dividends.* The account in the net worth section of the balance sheet into which the retained earnings are put is also known by different names, e.g., *retained income, retained earnings, accumulated income* or *earnings, earned surplus,* and *surplus.*

There is a definite trend to eliminate the word "profit" in connection with the income statement, since to some it may indicate excessive earnings, or earnings which are over and above what the company is entitled to. Some other term might also sound better to those who are socialistically inclined. As indicated above, the terms "income" or "earnings" are now used by many companies.

Accountants are also getting many companies to eliminate the term "surplus" in the net worth section of the balance sheet, and to substitute some title, such as "retained earnings," when it represents the accumulation of earnings from operations. When the "surplus" represents something else than the regular earnings, it is recommended that the source of the surplus be indicated along with the use of the word "surplus."

In our discussion we will use the term "surplus," as we have done in other connections in the preceding chapters, because it covers not only the retained income, but also the "surplus" arising from any other source. It is thus a simple word and can be conveniently used in writing or in discussion. Even though the tendency is to get away from using the term, it is still used when referring in general to reserves that are set up from the "surplus." That is, all such reserves are called "surplus reserves." The formal title applied to the account or reserve should indicate the purpose of the reserve, such as, for example, "reserve for betterments and improvements."

MEANING OF SURPLUS. The *surplus* of a company represents the excess of the assets over the sum of the liabilities and the par value or stated value (in the case of no-par stock) of the capital stock. Assuming that the capital stock account remains constant, any increase in the assets without as great an increase in the liabilities will result in an increase in the surplus. Also a decrease in the liabilities not accompanied by as great a decrease in the assets will increase the surplus. In other words, any increase in the *net* assets (capital stock account remaining the same) results in an increase in the surplus.

It should be noted that the surplus is a net worth account, and it should be stressed that it is merely an "account" on the books of the company. It is never anything real or tangible. It appears only as an ink figure on the company's books and on the balance sheet. This point is so fundamental that we are going to give a few examples even at the expense of boring the accounting student. Let us assume that a company starts out by selling $1,000,000 in stock at its par value. No other assets are owned and we will assume, to simplify the discussion, that no liabilities are incurred. A simple balance sheet of the company would appear as follows:

Assets		*Net Worth*	
Cash	$1,000,000	Capital stock	$1,000,000

As noted, the company has $1,000,000 in cash and not one cent in surplus. If all the cash was then spent for inventory, the company would have no cash and also no surplus. During the course of the year the company may sell this inventory and make a "net profit" after taxes of $100,000. We will assume that as the cash is received it is reinvested in additional inventory. The balance sheet would then appear as follows:

Assets		*Net Worth*	
Inventory	$1,100,000	Capital stock	$1,000,000
		Surplus (retained income)	100,000

The company now has $100,000 in "surplus," but not a cent in cash. Many people think that the "surplus" represents the *cash* which is not needed in the business. That is one of the reasons companies are getting away from using the term. From the simple example given above, it should be obvious that there is not necessarily any connection between the surplus account and the cash account. The surplus in a sense is a balancing account. It reflects any increase in the *net* assets for the period under consideration. If we are looking for the cash or other tangible property we must look to the assets section of the balance sheet and not to the net worth.

DEFICIT. A *deficit* is the opposite of a surplus. A deficit exists when the assets are less than the sum of the liabilities and capital stock. For example, let us assume prices decline with the result that the company in the above example would have to sell its inventory at such a low price that the company lost $200,000 during the second year of its operations. The balance sheet would then appear as follows:

Assets		*Net Worth*	
Cash (or inventory)	$900,000	Capital stock	$1,000,000
		Deficit	100,000
Total	$900,000	Total	$ 900,000

The effect of the operating loss is to wipe out the surplus entirely and to create in its place a deficit of $100,000. In some instances a company will list the deficit on the "assets" side, instead of subtracting it from the capital stock. Certainly a deficit is anything but an asset.

"EARNED SURPLUS" AND REALIZED SURPLUS. In most instances the term "earned surplus" is taken to mean the surplus that arises from the net income which is retained in the business. It will be recalled from the discussion of the income statement that the excess of income over expenses is considered the net income regardless of whether or not collections from the sales have been made. In some instances the "earned surplus" is narrowly construed to mean only the earnings from ordinary operations, or at least not including nonrecurring profit such as that arising from the sale of a building no longer needed in the business. As commonly used, and doubtless correctly so, "earned surplus" means all the retained net income regardless of the source.

The term "realized surplus" or "realized profits" is used synonymously with "earned surplus." Here again the question arises whether nonoperating and nonrecurring items are included. As in the case of "earned surplus," their inclusion is generally assumed.

Capital Surplus. Surplus that arises from some source other than the retained net income is called *capital surplus.* In some instances the term "unearned surplus" or "unrealized surplus" is used to describe this type of surplus, but perhaps these phrases are misleading, because in some instances the capital surplus has been "realized" if not "earned." For example, if stock with a par value of $100 is sold for $120 a share by the issuing company, a capital surplus of $20 is thereby created. To say that this was unearned or unrealized might not convey the correct impression.

There are many sources of capital surplus, and the appearance of the balance sheet can be changed materially through the handling of capital surplus. It is only fair to the shareholders and others who may be interested in the balance sheet that the surplus which arises from retained net income be distinctly shown, and that it not be merged with the capital surplus. The management should also split the capital surplus up according to source, and use a title for the various accounts which reveals the source of each kind of surplus.

Following are the sources of capital surplus:

1. Sale of stock for more than par or stated value
2. Forfeited subscriptions
3. Gifts made to company
4. Purchase of its own securities at less than par, stated, or face value
5. Reduction of "capital"
6. Reappraisal of assets upward
7. Sale of assets above book value
8. Mergers and consolidations
9. Recapitalizations and reorganizations
10. Elimination of certain reserves

Sale of Stock for More Than Par or Stated Value. If a company receives for its shares more than the par value in the case of par stock, or the stated value in the case of no-par stock, the amount in excess of the par or stated value is carried to the surplus account. The account would ordinarily be labeled "capital surplus," "paid-in surplus," or "premium on capital stock."

Financial institutions commonly sell their stock at a premium when they begin a business so that their balance sheet will make a good showing even before any income has been earned. Also, in some jurisdictions, banks must have a surplus equivalent to 20 per cent of their capital stock before they can pay dividends. Some have therefore sold par value $100-stock for $120, at the time of promotion so that they will be in a position to pay dividends without having to build up the 20 per cent reserve from earnings. After some years of successful operations the stock of many companies sells at a premium in the market. If such companies subsequently offer stock for sale it would probably be at a premium unless the privileged subscription was used.

There are some differences of opinion as to what should be done with the surplus account that arises from the sale of stock at a premium. It represents money paid in by the shareholders just the same as that portion which is carried in the capital stock account. But, so far as the law is concerned, it is not part of the "legal capital" of the company. Hence, unless there is some statute or court decision prohibiting it, such a surplus could be used for dividend payments to the shareholders. It is not recommended, however, that this be done. If dividends are paid from it, the shareholders should be notified as to the source. The statutes of some of the states, such as Ohio for example, provide that if dividends are paid from some source other than earned surplus or the surplus from the ordinary operations of the company, the shareholders must be notified of the fact. Surplus arising from sale of stock at a premium is sometimes called "paid-in surplus."

Forfeited Subscriptions. Although not common, forfeited subscriptions can give rise to one form of capital surplus. If persons have subscribed to stock and paid part of the par or stated value, but are unable to meet the subsequent calls for additional payments, their subscriptions may be canceled by the board of directors and the money already paid in may be retained by the company. Since the company would have the money, but no stock had been issued, the account collected would be credited to the capital surplus account. As in the case of all capital surplus items, the source of the surplus should be indicated in the account title. The statutes of a number of the states provide, however, that forfeited stock shall be sold at public auction. If it is sold for more than the unpaid amount due on the stock, the excess must be returned to the original buyer. In this case no "surplus" would result.

Gifts Made to Company. It is generally recommended that when gifts are made to a company the credit should be made to capital surplus. In some instances the account will be labeled "donated surplus." Cities will sometimes give land to a company as an inducement to get it to locate in the community. Large shareholders of close corporations sometimes give the company cash or other assets to enable it to recover from some financial difficulties. In some instances large shareholders will donate back part of the corporation's own stock to enable it to secure more funds. The stock so donated would be subtracted, ordinarily at its par value, from the outstanding stock and a credit of corresponding amount would be made to the donated surplus account. If the stock is subsequently sold for less than the par or stated value, the surplus account will have to be charged with the difference between the par or stated value and the selling price. The stock will be transferred back to the outstanding stock at its par or stated value.

Purchase of Securities at Less Than Par, Stated, or Face Value. When a depression hits and earnings fall off, the stock of many companies sells at substantial discounts from their par or stated value. As a result of collections from past sales and contraction in inventories, some companies find that their cash accumulates at a time like this. In some instances companies have taken advantake of this situation by buying back part of their stock on the market and canceling it. The reduction in the capital stock account being greater than the amount of cash expended for the stock, the surplus account is credited with the difference.

If the company's bonds are purchased in the market at less than their face value, a capital surplus account would be credited with the difference between these two values.

Reduction of Capital Stock. A reduction in capital stock is accomplished either by a reduction in the par or stated value of the shares or by a reduction in the number of shares outstanding. For example, a company with a $50 par stock outstanding may have the par of the stock reduced from $50 to $25 a share. If the number of shares outstanding remains the same, then the capital stock account will thereby be reduced 50 per cent, and the capital surplus account will be credited with this amount. To accomplish a capital stock reduction it is necessary to get the consent of the shareholders and the state to authorize a *charter amendment*. Such reductions will not be permitted when the effect of it is to impair the rights of existing creditors.

The other way of effecting a capital stock reduction would be to have a "reverse split-up." Shareholders, for example, may be asked to give up half of their shares. This may actually be accomplished by the company giving them one new share for each two shares held. If both the old and the new stock had a par value of $100 per share, a one for two exchange would reduce the "capital" by 50 per cent. As long as the par of the new share would be less than twice the par value (per share) of the old, a reduction would take place. Assuming that there is no reduction in the book value of the assets, any reduction in the capital stock figure would be credited to the capital surplus account. A number of companies effected a reduction in their capital stock during the depression of the 1930's. The surplus thereby created was in some instances used to absorb operating deficits.

The question as to the legality of a dividend paid out of the surplus arising from a reduction in capital stock has not been settled in most jurisdictions. In effect it amounts to the same as giving the shareholder back part of the original principal. In a technical sense, however, it would not come out of the "capital" of the company which has now been reduced from the original figure. It would seem good practice not to pay dividends from such a surplus. If they are ever paid from this source certainly the shareholders should be notified to this effect.

Although some jurisdictions by statutes or court decisions would prohibit dividends from surplus arising from a reduction in capital stock, particularly when it would or might impair the rights of creditors, there apparently is no objection to using such a surplus to absorb operating deficits and then paying dividends out of subsequent earnings. Had the reduction not taken place, the subsequent earnings would have gone to absorb the deficit, and could not have been used for dividend purposes.

In some instances when a company effects a reduction in its capital stock, the assets are reduced by the same amount as the capital stock account. This is done usually in a period of depression when prices and earnings are on the decline. The reduction in the book value of the assets will result in lower depreciation charges and thus improve the financial showing of the company. When the asset values are so reduced, no surplus is created by the reduction in the capital stock.

Reappraisal of Assets. In some instances a company will have independent appraisers revalue the company's fixed assets in line with existing values less depreciation. When the assets are revalued upward on the books, a credit will be made to a capital surplus account for the increase. In some instances a company will write up the goodwill account on the books and create a surplus of corresponding amount.

Most accountants would frown upon the practice of an upward reappraisal of the fixed assets. In fact, it is conservative accounting practice not to write up the value even of the inventories which are to be sold in the ordinary course of business. Since the fixed assets are not to be sold it is questionable whether they should ever be reappraised higher. Cost less depreciation continues to be the preferred way of carrying these assets. In some states, such as Ohio, for example, any surplus arising from the reappraisal of assets can be used for the payment of a stock dividend, but it cannot be used for a cash dividend.

Sale of Assets Above Book Value. Companies at times may find that they no longer need a particular building, warehouse, or vacant real estate which had been held for possible future uses. With the increase in real estate values which has taken place for some years in the past, such properties commonly may be sold for more than the value placed upon them on the company's books. The excess obtained from the sale over the book value would add to the earnings or surplus of the company. Sometimes this profit will be included in the "nonoperating" income section of the income statement. It should be realized, however, that not only is this income "nonoperating," but it is "nonrecurring" as well. Many recommend that income of this kind be credited directly to a capital surplus account.

From the standpoint of availability for dividends, surplus arising from the sale of assets above book values is in a different category from that arising from a reappraisal upward of the asset values. When the assets are sold, the earnings are actually "realized." In fact it may be in the form of cash in the bank, while some of the proceeds from the sales of the company's inventory may still be in the form of accounts receivable on the books. If the property sold must be replaced, then presumably all the cash obtained will be needed to buy the new property. If the property sold is not to be replaced, the surplus would be available for dividend purposes. But due to the special source of the surplus, and the fact that it is nonrecurring, the shareholders should be notified as to the source of the dividends.

Mergers, Consolidations, and Holding Companies. Mergers, consolidations and the formation of holding companies often give rise to a type of capital surplus.

Mergers. A *merger* is effected when one company absorbs another company. It is more fully discussed in Chapter 30. The merger is accomplished by Company *A*, for example, exchanging its stock with the shareholders of Company *B* for their stock at some ratio which is agreed upon in advance. Company *B*'s charter is surrendered and its stock canceled. The ratio of exchange of stock depends upon the size of each company, the number and classes of shares they have outstanding, the financial standing and earnings of each company, their management, and the bargaining power of the parties.

Whether or not a surplus arises through the merger, and if it does, the amount of such surplus, depends upon the par or stated value of Company *A*'s stock which is exchanged for the stock of Company *B*, and the valuation at which the net assets of Company *B* are carried on the books of Company *A*, and the amount of surplus which Company *B* had at the time of the merger. If we assume that Company *A* exchanges stock with a par value equivalent to the par value of Company *B*'s stock, and that the net assets of the latter company are carried on Company *A*'s books at the same valuation that Company *B* carried them, then any surplus of Company *B* would show up on Company *A*'s balance sheet as a type of surplus. Since *B*'s surplus helps to "pay" for the stock of Company *A*, it is in the nature of "paid-in surplus," and therefore should be carried on *A*'s books under this, or some other capital surplus title. The surplus may show up on Company *A*'s books at more or less than the figure at which *B* carried it, depending upon the amount of *A* stock exchanged for *B* stock, and the valuation at which *B* Company's net assets are carried on Company *A*'s books.

Consolidations. A *consolidation* results from the combination of two or more companies to form a new company. A new Company *X*, for example, is formed and it exchanges its stock with the shareholders of Company *A* and Company *B* for their stock. (Consolidations will be further discussed in Chapter 30.) The charters of Companies *A* and *B* are then surrendered and their stock canceled.

The amount of the surpluses of Companies *A* and *B* which will be carried to Company *X*'s books depends upon the same factors stated above in connection with the exchange of stock to effect a merger. If the rate of exchange is par for par, and the net assets are carried on Company *X*'s books at the same valuation as on the books of Companies *A* and *B*, then Company *X* should show under a "paid-in surplus," or some other form of capital surplus, the amount of the combined surpluses of Companies *A* and *B*.

In referring to the surpluses of Companies *A* and *B* in connection with mergers and consolidations, we have in mind the surplus arising from the retained earnings. Accountants prefer to show retained or earned surplus on the books of the merging or consolidated company as a form of capital surplus. In practice, however, many merging or consolidated companies carry the earned surplus of the other companies to their regular earned surplus account. Any capital surpluses of Companies *A* or *B* which are taken over by the merging or consolidated company may appear as a form of capital surplus on the books of the merging or consolidated company.

Holding companies. A holding company type of combination is effected by holding Company *X*, for example, exchanging its stock with the shareholders of Companies *A* and *B* for their stock. But in this case, Companies *A* and *B* retain their separate corporate entities. (Holding companies will be discussed further in Chapter 31.)

When the holding company and its subsidiaries prepare separate balance sheets no special problem relating to capital surplus arises. But when the holding company prepares a "consolidated" balance sheet for the entire system, then we have to reckon with the problem. In the consolidated balance sheet the assets and liabilities of the subsidiary Companies *A* and *B* are combined and shown as the assets and liabilities of holding Company *X*. All intercompany items are eliminated in the statement. The minority interests in Companies *A* and *B* are included in the liabilities.

If holding Company *X* carried its stock investments in Companies *A* and *B* at the value shown on the books of the latter companies, then no special capital surplus would arise from the consolidated balance sheet. But if the holding company carried the stock of the subsidiaries at less than the book value as shown on the subsidiaries' books, a capital surplus for the difference would appear on the consolidated balance sheet.

Recapitalizations and Reorganizations. The term "recapitalization" is usually applied to the recasting of the financial plan of a solvent company, although it is sometimes done to prevent threatened failure or insolvency. The amount of the par or stated value of the stock is often reduced in a recapitalization. The reduction in capital stock, discussed above, would be a form of recapitalization. If, after the recapitalization, the net worth is carried on the books at more than the par or stated value of the stock, a surplus would exist. If this surplus is greater than the combined earned and capital surplus before the recapitalization, the excess would be a type of capital surplus.

Reorganization usually is taken to mean the formation of a new company to take over another company that has failed or is about to fail. It is also applied, however, to the reconstruction of a company under the federal bankruptcy laws even though a new company is not necessarily formed. (Reorganization will be discussed in some detail in Chapters 34 and 35.)

In a reorganization usually the amount of the liabilities is reduced. This in itself would result in an addition to the surplus unless it was all absorbed in eliminating a deficit. The amount of the old stock may be reduced, or in some instances, increased. A reduction in the amount of the par or stated value would, of course, tend to increase the surplus account. It is usually recommended that surpluses of this type be treated as capital surplus.

In some instances in a reorganization the book value of the assets is reduced. Such reductions are an offset to the surplus or an offset to the additions in the surplus.

Elimination of Certain Reserves. In some instances in a reorganization certain surplus reserves of the old company are eliminated without a similar decrease in the valuation of the net assets. This would give rise to a capital surplus on the books of the reorganized company. Also aside from reorganizations, if any reserve has been set up from the capital surplus, the elimination of the reserve without a similar reduction in the net assets would result in an increase in the capital surplus. But if reserves have been set up from the *earned* surplus rather than the capital surplus, the elimination of the reserve without a corresponding reduction in the valuation of the net assets would result in an increase in the *earned* surplus.

Uses of Capital Surplus. Writers have probably had more to say about what should *not* be done with a capital surplus than what *should* be done with it. In several places above we indicated something about the legality or desirability of paying dividends from capital surplus. We will say nothing further about this at the present time since the next chapter will be devoted to dividend considerations. If dividends are not to be paid from capital surplus, or at least not from capital surplus arising from certain sources, what should be done with it?

In some instances nothing should be done with capital surplus. Take for example the surplus arising from the sale of stock at prices in excess of the par or stated values. This is in effect a type of paid-in capital and perhaps it should remain on the books as such in the same way that the capital stock remains on the books. The same reasoning may apply at times to surplus arising from the reduction in stated capital and that arising from a merger, consolidation, or reorganization.

A capital surplus created from writing up the value of assets or from their sale could be used to charge off losses resulting from the revaluation downward or sale of the assets. The charging off of intangible assets is usually considered conservative accounting practice, and in most instances no objection would be made to writing them off against the capital surplus.

Certain reserves that are commonly set up from the earned surplus, such as a reserve for betterments and improvements, could be set up from the capital surplus account. Or, if the reserve has been set up from the earned surplus, after the improvements have been completed perhaps it would be better to retain it in capital surplus or a capital surplus reserve rather than put it back in the earned surplus account.

The payment of a dividend in stock from the capital surplus would be desirable in many instances, provided the shareholders were informed as to its source, since this would permanently capitalize the surplus and thus prevent its use for cash dividends.

Reserves

Importance of Reserves. Corporate managements have the problem of not only deciding whether capital surplus can or should be used for dividend payments, but also that of deciding what reserves should be set up out of earnings or the earned surplus before arriving at the balance which is available for dividend payments. Other practical problems relating to dividend policies will be discussed in the following chapter.

In some instances the problem of setting up reserves merely involves a matter of business expediency. In some the tax situation is paramount, in other instances the matter of conservative accounting practice is the issue, while in some cases, if proper reserves are not set up, dividends may be paid from "capital"—a serious matter.

What Reserves Are. Before discussing the different types of reserves and their purposes, it is advisable that a clear understanding be had as to just what is meant by a "reserve." A person not acquainted with accounting terminology is inclined to think of a "reserve" as cash or equivalent which is "reserved" or set aside for a particular purpose. This is not the way the term is used by accountants or businessmen in connection with balance sheets. The term *fund* is usually used in financial statements to apply to the account which represents an appropriation of cash or equivalent for some specific purpose. The *sinking fund* for the retirement of bonds is an example, although in some instances a separate "fund" is not set aside by the company even when the term is used in the balance sheet.

A *reserve* is a bookkeeping account. From an accounting standpoint, it is always a "credit." Assets, such as "funds," are always "debit" balance accounts. As we will discuss in more detail below, a reserve account may merely represent a deduction from an asset account, a liability of the company, or the earmarking of surplus.

Because of the misunderstanding in regard to the meaning of the word ""reserve," mentioned above, many companies are eliminating its use and substituting such phrases as "provision for," "allowance for," or "appropriation for." This is recommended for purposes of published reports. For our purposes, however, it is much more convenient to use the term "reserve," and we will continue to do so.

Reserves are usually divided into three general types, as follows:

1. Valuation reserves
2. Liability reserves
3. Surplus reserves

VALUATION RESERVES. In the preceding chapter we have already discussed valuation reserves when we considered the reserves for depreciation, obsolescence and depletion. Another valuation reserve is the reserve for bad debts.

It will be recalled that the reserves are set up at the same time that the company makes a charge to the appropriate expense in the income statement. These reserves are deducted from the proper asset account to show the true depreciated or adjusted value of the particular asset. It is thus apparent that they are merely bookkeeping accounts.

In some instances where a company shows an abbreviated two-column balance sheet, the valuation reserves are listed under the liabilities, since they are "credit" accounts, rather than being deducted directly from the asset account. Occasionally a reserve such as for depreciation, depletion, or the writing off of intangible assets is called an "amortization" reserve.

LIABILITY RESERVES. Those who are not acquainted with accounting terminology would probably object more strenuously to calling a liability reserve a "reserve" than applying the term to a valuation reserve. A liability reserve is actually a current *liability,* or debt owed by the company. When used, it is applied to an expense which has actually been incurred, and for which a charge has been made in the income statement, but the cash has not yet been expended for it. A "reserve for interest" or "reserve for taxes," are examples. In some instances when the term "reserve" is applied to a liability, it is for an expense which has been incurred and is owed, but the exact amount owed is not definite at the time. This is sometimes the case with federal income taxes.

There is a trend away from the use of "reserve" as applied to a liability. Even when the amount of the federal taxes owed is not definitely known, many companies are now using a title such as "provision for federal income taxes" to show the tax liability. In some instances the liability for taxes or other expenses is shown under the caption of "accrued," followed by the name of the liability.

An increasing number of companies are establishing pension plans for their employees. In some instances annual amounts are paid to an insurance company or a trustee to cover the future payments. When this is done the plan is said to be *funded.* Many companies assume a liability for pensions but do not set up any separate fund at the time to cover the future payments. In some instances the balance sheet does not show any liability for the payments. In others a footnote is added to the balance sheet indicating the amount of the liability. Still other companies show the obligation under their liabilities. When the latter procedure is followed the liability may appear on the statements as a "reserve for pensions." In this case it is probable that the pension obligation was charged as an expense against the current income. Some companies set up a *surplus* reserve covering the pension. In some instances a company will set up a reserve for pensions covering the amount of the anticipated liability which is in excess of that which is funded with an insurance company or trustee.

SURPLUS RESERVE. Surplus reserves represent the appropriation of surplus. In practically all instances it is an appropriation of *earned* surplus, that is, the *retained* income. These reserves, as explained when we discussed reserves in general, represent nothing tangible. They merely earmark surplus. They are set up by debiting the surplus and crediting the reserve. Since the surplus itself is merely a balancing account and does not represent anything tangible, the reserve set up out of it likewise cannot be anything tangible.

The setting up of a surplus reserve accomplishes two purposes, (1) it specifically calls attention to the fact that the amount represented by the reserve is needed or may be needed for the purpose indicated in the reserve account title, and (2) it prevents the payment of dividends from that part of the surplus which is put into the reserve. If no surplus reserves were set up the "free" surplus would appear larger and the shareholders may think that the company should pay out more in the form of dividends. But the assets represented by the surplus may be needed for some specific purpose, and are therefore unavailable for dividends. Establishing the reserve and giving it a title that indicates the purpose for the retention of the surplus will result in better stockholder relations.

In some instances the surplus reserve is set up to show that assets of equivalent amount have been set aside in a separate fund for a specific purpose. The reserve for a sinking fund is an example. In other instances such as the reserve for improvements, no cash or fund is set aside, but the reserve indicates that cash or other assets are not available for dividends and should be retained in the business to facilitate the expansion program. The more important surplus reserves will now be briefly discussed.

Sinking fund reserve. The accounting procedure for sinking funds was discussed in a previous chapter but for completeness' sake part of it will be repeated here. A bond indenture may call for the setting up of a sinking fund, or a sinking fund reserve, or both. The fund itself provides the cash necessary to retire the bonds. But if the fund alone is set up, the size of the "free" surplus may cause stockholders to wonder why they do not receive larger dividends. The setting aside of cash in the fund makes the cash unavailable for dividends. From a legal standpoint, however, the establishment of the fund does not reduce the amount that may be paid in dividends. If the directors pay relatively large dividends, the equity behind the bonds would be reduced to that extent, and possibly the ability to meet future sinking fund payments may be affected.

If the sinking fund reserve and not the fund is set up on the books, the amount of dividends that may legally be paid is reduced accordingly, and the shareholders can see the purpose for which the surplus is being retained. But, although the limiting of the amount that may be paid in dividends tends to increase the assets, there is no assurance that *cash* or its equivalent will be available to retire the bonds at their maturity. Furthermore, since the fund is sometimes used to buy back the bonds regularly before their maturity, the absence of such a fund would result in the loss of this type of market support for the bonds. If both a sinking fund and a reserve are set up, the advantages of each are obtained without the disadvantages stated above of either one by itself.

A further point that should be mentioned here is, what happens to the sinking fund reserve when the bonds are retired? The answer is that nothing happens to it. The use of cash or a sinking fund to retire the bonds reduces the assets, but the bond liability is reduced by the same amount. Therefore, the net worth of the company is not affected. The reserve has accomplished its purpose of indicating that assets of the same amount were being retained to retire the bonds, and preventing the payment of dividends to the extent of the amount appropriated. It is therefore put back into the surplus account by debiting the reserve and crediting the surplus. Dividends could then be legally paid from such surplus, but from a practical standpoint the use of cash to retire the bonds may make such dividends impossible.

Reserve for expansion. The reserve for expansion may be so labeled, or it may be called a "reserve for additions, betterments, and improvements," or any one or more of these words may be used in the title. The purpose of this reserve is obviously to show the purpose for retaining part of the surplus, and preventing dividends to the extent of the reserve, with the result that the company is in a better asset position to carry on an expansion program.

The expansion, however, merely means the substitution of one asset for another, and therefore the net worth of the company is not affected. In other words, the reserve is not consumed by the expansion. It may therefore be put back into the surplus account after the program has been completed. Although cash dividends could legally be paid from this surplus, the expansion may have depleted the cash. Since the amount formerly shown in the reserve account is now permanently invested in fixed assets, it might be capitalized through a dividend payable in stock.

Reserve for working capital. The reserve for working capital is similar to the reserve for expansion, but attention is being called to the fact that the appropriation is for current rather than fixed assets. The restriction of dividends to the extent of the reserve does not of course automatically insure that the assets retained will find their way into additional working capital. The amount retained may gradually be invested in an additional fixed asset, or it might be used for debt retirement.

Reserve for dividend equalization. Certain advantages accrue from the payment of regular dividends, as will be pointed out in the following chapter. But earnings of most corporations fluctuate from year to year, particularly those which are more subject to the business cycle. Some companies will pay out a smaller proportion of their earnings when the net income is large, than when it is relatively low. In this way they may be able to stabilize the rate of dividends on the stock from year to year. In order to facilitate this procedure the company may set up a reserve for dividend equalization when earnings are large, and then draw on this reserve for the payment of dividends when earnings fall off. It is obvious that when this reserve is used for dividend payments, it is consumed. This is in contrast to the surplus reserves discussed above which are put back into the surplus account after their purpose has been accomplished.

Reserve for replacement of assets. In our discussion of depreciation it was pointed out that depreciation was charged and reserves set up on the basis of the cost value, and that replacement was sometimes difficult during a period of rising prices. In addition to the usual method of handling depreciation, a surplus reserve equivalent in amount to the difference between the original cost and the replacement cost may be set up. Through the retention of earnings that otherwise may have been paid out in dividends, the company may be in a better asset position to replace the depreciated property. If the replacement does cost more than the original asset, the reserve account is not thereby consumed. The new asset will be carried on the books at the total cost price, and thus the net worth is not affected. The reserve account could then be put back into the surplus account, or it could be retained to aid in the replacement of other assets. It should be kept in mind that the setting up of any kind of surplus reserve does not necessarily put the company in a better cash position for the disbursement of funds, but to the extent that dividends are prohibited, the company should be in a better asset position, if not a better cash position, than if the reserve had not been set up on the books.

Reserve against decline in asset values. Many companies carry their raw materials inventory at cost or market, whichever is lower. If the market price declines after the goods are purchased, the inventories are marked down and the charge is made against current income for the loss. In some instances a company will want in addition to make some provision for the possible further decline of an indefinite amount in the inventory. This may be done by setting up a surplus reserve. If the decline actually takes place the loss is written off against the reserve. Otherwise, the reserve can be continued for the possible decline in future purchases, or it can be put back into the surplus account.

Some companies, particularly those which own relatively large amounts of securities, especially stocks, set up a surplus reserve for the possible future decline in the market value of the securities. This is handled in the same way as the reserve for decline in inventory values.

Reserve for contingencies. Many companies carry a general surplus reserve called "reserve for contingencies." This is intended to take care of any losses for which provision has not otherwise been made. It may cover losses for which insurance is unobtainable, or possible losses in excess of the amount of insurance carried. In some instances a separate insurance reserve is set up.

Companies sometimes get involved in lawsuits relating to damages caused by the company's operations or possible patent infringements, and set up surplus reserves to cover adverse court decisions. In some instances it would be more conservative accounting to show some of these as current liabilities, particularly if it appears that the company will come out on the losing end of the case.

In some instances a contingency reserve is set up to help the company during a period when its profits decline because of the invention of new methods or processes or new models on the part of a competitor.

Secret Reserves. Occasionally the term *secret reserves* is used. This does not appear as a reserve at all on the books of the company. When the surplus of a company, after giving effect to the reserves that are set up on the books, is really larger than appears on the books and financial statements, the company is said to have a "secret reserve." This may be brought about in several different ways. The writing down or carrying of assets on the books at less than their real value is one way of creating a secret reserve. Excessive depreciation charges is one method of doing this. The conservative practice of writing down intangible assets may also result in such reserves. Charging such things as replacements, betterments and improvements to expense rather than writing them up as assets on the books will result in secret reserves. Also, charging to expense for the particular period items that should be partly deferred to subsequent periods has the same effect.

Overstatement of liabilities also has the effect of creating secret reserves. This could result from carrying what is really a surplus reserve as a liability reserve. The larger the amount of such a reserve, the greater the amount of the secret reserve.

Overstated Surplus. Although we are here discussing reserves, the material would be incomplete if we did not say a word about the opposite of secret reserves—overstating surplus. This in effect results from practices that are just the opposite from those that cause secret reserves. Such overstatements of surplus would include the following: writing up repairs, maintenance, and other expenses, as assets instead of charging them off as expenses; overstating the valuation of assets; charging off too little in depreciation; and an understatement of liabilities or failure to state all liabilities.

Deficits

How Deficits Are Created. The term "deficit" does not appear in the chapter title, but since it is the opposite of a "surplus," which is discussed in this chapter, we are justified in discussing it too. Earlier in the chapter it was stated that when the liabilities plus the capital stock as shown on the books were greater than the assets, a deficit existed. A deficit can be created in one or more of the following ways.

1. *Operating losses.* If a company operates at a loss and has no surplus, or has consumed more than its surplus by losses, then a deficit must appear on the books.

2. *Writing down asset values.* If the value of the assets has been overstated on the books and the assets are revalued in line with current values it may produce a deficit. The scrapping of equipment which has not been properly depreciated may also produce a deficit.

3. *Property becoming obsolete.* Occasionally the scrapping of machinery or equipment due to new inventions and processes will cause a deficit where obsolescence reserves have not been adequate to handle the write-off.

4. *Destruction of property.* The destruction of a large part of the total assets through some catastrophe such as a flood, earthquake, or fire, where insurance does not cover the total loss, may be the cause of a deficit.

5. *Writing up liabilities.* The writing up of liabilities which have been understated may produce a deficit. In some instances this results from not having proper contingency reserves.

6. *Unwise managerial practices.* Unwise managerial practices may result in operating losses and produce a deficit as pointed out above. But several specific practices should perhaps be mentioned separately. Unwise expansion may saddle the company with such additional expense that a deficit results. In some instances managements have declared dividends to the extent that the surplus was so depleted that subsequent operating losses resulted in a deficit.

How Deficits Can Be Eliminated. Following are the ways in which deficits are or can be eliminated from the books.

1. *Earnings.* The normal way of reducing or eliminating a deficit is to absorb it through future earnings. This may necessitate a new management, but we are not here concerned with the method.

2. *Reduction of "capital."* The deficit may be eliminated by reducing the par or stated value of the stock, or by reducing the number of shares without reducing the par or stated value, or both procedures may be accomplished at the same time. The proper statutory steps will have to be followed to accomplish this.

3. *Reduction in asset values.* If the assets are written down at the same time the capital is reduced, and in the same amount, this would offset the reduction in capital, and the deficit would remain. Or, the assets may be written down less than the capital reduced, with the result that part of the deficit would be eliminated. The depreciation charges in the future on the written-down assets, however, would be less, with the result that future deficits would be less, or a profit would result instead of a deficit, or a larger profit would be shown on the company's statements. This could be used to write off at least part of the deficit.

4. *Gifts of stock.* Some of the large shareholders may donate part of their stock back to the company. Either the cancellation or subsequent sale of this stock would reduce the deficit.

5. *Asset values written up.* If the assets are reappraised upward it would reduce the size of the deficit. With a deficit existing, however, it is probable that the assets are already being carried on the books at inflated values. Even if a deficit did not exist, it is not good accounting practice to write up the value of the assets.

6. *Reduction of liabilities.* The only time the liabilities should be reduced is when they are overstated, or when creditors forgive the company part or all the debts. If a deficit exists probably the liabilities are not overstated. In some instances creditors will cancel part of the debt in order to permit the company to remain in busines and continue to buy from them. This is sometimes accomplished through a composition settlement.

7. *Reorganization of the company.* If the company reorganizes either when solvent or insolvent, and the par, stated, or face value of the securities of the reorganized company are less than before, this would reduce the deficit accordingly.

In general, deficits may be reduced in the same ways as a capital surplus may be created, which we discussed earlier in the chapter.

The other methods were not listed here because of their impracticability.

Recording Deficit on the Balance Sheet. In some instances the deficit is carried on the asset side of the balance sheet and added to the assets to make them balance with the sum of the liabilities and capital stock. It may be labeled "Deficit," or "Surplus." This is poor practice since the deficit is not an asset, and it should not be handled in this way.

The proper way to show the deficit is as a deduction from the capital stock. And it should then be called a "Deficit." In some instances it is labeled "Surplus" even though deducted from the capital stock. Occasionally the deficit has been deducted from the capital stock and the balance has been shown under a caption, such as "Capital stock and surplus."

Questions

1. (a) Indicate definitely what is meant by the "surplus" of a corporation? (b) How should a deficit be shown on the balance sheet?
2. (a) Indicate the sources of capital surplus. (b) What can or should be done by a corporation with a capital surplus?
3. Indicate what disposition can legally be made or should be made with a surplus arising from the sale of a fixed asset at a price in excess of its book value.
4. Distinguish between valuation reserves, liability reserves, and surplus reserves. Give two examples of each.
5. What disposition is finally made of each of the following reserves: reserve for improvements, reserve for bad debts, sinking fund reserve, reserve for federal income taxes?
6. Indicate what is meant by a secret reserve and how it could arise.
7. What criticism is sometimes made of the use of the term "reserve"? What term might be substituted for it?
8. Look up the balance sheet of the General Motors Corporation and ascertain what reserves it has on the books.
9. Should reserves for contingencies and reserves for taxes be shown as a liability or in the net worth section of the balance sheet? Explain.
10. Indicate the various ways in which a deficit may be eliminated from the books. Which of these do you believe is the best? Explain.

Problems

1. On Jan. 1, 19-1, the net worth section of the balance sheet of the Peerless Metal Co. was as follows:

Capital stock	$3,000,000 (par $100)
Deficit	100,000

During the year the following transactions took place: $100,000 of the stock was donated back to the company, and half of this was sold for $80 a share;

one of the plants was reappraised from $1,000,000 to $1,500,000, and later in the year sold for $1,100,000; another plant was reappraised from $500,000 to $650,000; $1,000,000 (in par) of the unissued stock was sold for $120 a share; a new building was constructed at a cost of $200,000; $1,000,000 worth of the company's bonds were converted into unissued stock at $125 per share; earnings from ordinary operations were $400,000. (a) Indicate how the net worth section would appear at the end of the year. (The company's ledger has two surplus accounts: Surplus and Capital Surplus.) (b) What can the company do with its Capital Surplus?

2. (a) Is Surplus a tangible item? (b) Are cash dividends really paid from surplus? (c) The sales manager of a large industrial corporation, when asked how his company was going to finance the construction of a new office building, replied: "We are going to build it out of our surplus." When asked what he meant by "surplus," he pointed to the Surplus account on the balance sheet. Was the sales manager's statement technically accurate? Explain.

3. Indicate with respect to each of the following the general term that could be applied to that type of reserve account, the section of the balance sheet in which it should be placed, and contra "debit" entry that is made when the reserve is set up: (a) Reserve for Depreciation. (b) Sinking Fund Reserve. (c) Reserve for Betterments and Improvements. (d) Reserve for Dividend Equalization. (e) Reserve for Bad Debts. (f) Reserve for Obsolescence. (g) Reserve for Decline in Inventory Value. (h) Reserve for Federal Income Tax.

Chapter 26

DIVIDEND POLICIES

FACTORS AFFECTING DIVIDEND POLICIES. *Dividends* are the distribution of cash or other property to the shareholders. In most instances the dividend consists of cash and the source of the dividend is the current or retained earnings. This chapter will be concerned mainly with cash dividends. Dividends are declared by the board of directors and are paid to the shareholders of record as of the date set by the board. The question whether dividends can or should be declared by the directors is determined by a number of factors, chief among which are the following:

1. Law
2. Contractual arrangements
3. Nature of company business
4. Need for funds
5. Dividend policy

COMMON LAW. It is a common law rule that dividends cannot be paid from "capital." The "capital" of a corporation, as used in this sense, is usually defined to mean the capital stock. More specifically, it means the par or stated value of the stock, or the amount shown under capital stock in the net worth section of the balance sheet. Some courts have said that the capital is a "trust fund" or it is like a trust fund for the benefit of creditors. This, of course, is an inaccurate statement since there is no property set aside in trust. Furthermore, operating losses may reduce the capital of a company and nothing can be done about it by the creditors. Although the law looks upon the capital stock to be the legal "capital" of a corporation, from a practical standpoint the capital of a company consists of its assets. Dividends actually cannot be paid from the capital stock account. Dividends paid in cash or other assets are actually paid from "capital" (as we defined the term earlier in the book), but there must be profits or surplus on the books at least equivalent to the amount of the dividends before they may be paid.

What the law means therefore when it says that dividends cannot be paid from capital, is that no dividends can be paid if the net assets (assets less liabilities) are less than the amount of the capital stock as shown in the balance sheet, or if the payment of such dividends would reduce the net assets below the capital stock figure. The law reasons that creditors or prospective creditors grant credit on the strength of the amount shown as the "capital" of the corporation, and that it would be unfair or injurious to them if the directors paid dividends which would impair this capital.

The cases sometimes say that dividends can be paid only from the profits or accumulated profits of the company. This is not strictly true since usually at common law dividends can be paid to the extent of the company's surplus, regardless of the source of the surplus.

Statutory Law. The statutes of the various states contain provisions concerning dividends. Since these differ among the states, it is difficult to make general statements that would have application to all the states. The statutes of the particular state under consideration should be consulted to determine the law that is applicable. In many instances the statutes merely codify the common law rules. Others elaborate on this rule. Some define what is meant by "surplus." The statutes of some of the states permit dividends from current earnings even if a deficit exists. In some instances a stock dividend, but not a cash dividend (or other dividend payable in property), can be paid from "unrealized appreciation" in the value of the assets. The statutory provisions can be conveniently discussed under the following heads.

Dividends from surplus. The typical statutory provision states that dividends can be paid only from "surplus," or as some phrase it, dividends can be paid only from the excess of assets over the liabilities plus the legal or stated capital. In defining surplus or net assets the statutes of a number of the states provide that proper deductions must be made for depreciation, and bad debts. Some provide that deduction will also have to be made for depletion in the case of wasting asset businesses, although in Ohio, and some other states, no deduction need be made if so provided in the articles of incorporation.

The statutes of many of the states are silent about the availability for dividends of surplus arising from the upward reappraisal of assets. In Ohio the statutes specifically prohibit cash dividends from this source, but permit stock dividends.

Unless specifically prohibited by statutes, a dividend can legally be paid out of capital surplus. The statutes of some states, however, including California, Pennsylvania, Illinois, and Michigan, limit such dividends to stock dividends and those paid on preferred stock. In Ohio and some of the other states, if a dividend is paid from a source other than "earned" surplus, the shareholders must be notified as to its source.

The statutes of Delaware permit a dividend to be paid from the current earnings or those of the previous year even if a deficit exists on the books.[1] Such dividends, however, cannot be paid if the net assets are less than the preferred stock's preference as to assets, or if the dividend would reduce the net assets below that amount. Such a rule is liberal to say the least. A company, having only common stock outstanding, could theoretically by having alternating periods of earnings and deficits pay out practically all its assets in dividends. When creditors are present, however, either the statutes or the courts would prohibit the payment of dividends if the company was insolvent or the payment of such dividends caused it to be insolvent.

No dividends when insolvent. The statutes of about one-third of the states, including California, Illinois, Massachusetts, and Ohio, specifically state that a dividend cannot be paid when the company is insolvent or when the dividend would cause it to become insolvent. This raises the question as to what is meant by insolvency. Ordinarily, "insolvency" refers to a situation where the assets are less than the liabilities plus stated capital. This is sometimes referred to as the "bankruptcy" definition. As used in this way the rule is merely stating that a surplus must be present before a dividend may be declared. But in Massachusetts and Ohio, "insolvency," as used in the particular statute, means the inability to meet debts as they become due. This is using the term in the "equity" sense. Thus, in these states, even if a surplus is present, the statutes say that dividends cannot be paid if the company is insolvent or if the dividend would cause the company to become insolvent. But even in the absence of such statutes, equity courts in most of the states would prohibit a dividend under these circumstances if they were called upon to do so.

[1] Similar statutes are found also in California, Minnesota, and New Jersey. Dividends paid from current earnings with a deficit present are sometimes called "nimble dividends." Such dividends are permitted also in England.

Restrictions Imposed by Commissions and Regulation. The Public Utility Holding Company Act of 1935 provides that before dividends may be paid from capital or unearned surplus by a registered holding company or its subsidiary, approval must be obtained from the Securities and Exchange Commission. Any provisions in the state statutes or commission regulation relating to public utilities or financial institutions must be observed. Various accounting provisions concerning dividends are contained in the following legislation and must be followed by corporations subject to these particular statutes: Federal Communications Act, Federal Water Power Act, Interstate Commerce Act, and the Motor Carrier Act.

Contractual Arrangements. Restrictions on the payment of dividends are frequently found in the company's charter, bylaws, and bond indentures. Where preferred stock is present and has cumulative rights to dividends, all dividends in arrears and those for the current year must be paid before any dividends may be paid on the common stock. In event of liquidation the contractual right of the preferred with respect to any preference as to accrued dividends must be observed.

In some instances dividends may be paid only from earnings that arise after the particular securities have been issued. Both preferred stock and bond contracts sometimes contain provisions which prohibit dividends if the effect of their payment would be to reduce the net current assets below a specified figure, or if it would lower the current ratio below the specified one.

Nature of Company Business. The nature of the business conducted by the particular company commonly influences the dividend policy. Generally speaking, a company whose earnings are subject to wide fluctuations, such as many industrial companies, should follow a more conservative dividend policy than one whose earnings are more certain and regular. A public utility would illustrate the latter.

A company that comes under the head of a growth industry will constantly have need of funds for expansion purposes. This does not mean, however, that such a company will retain a relatively large part of the earnings. In many instances the earnings would not provide sufficient funds for expansion, so new securities must be sold from time to time. In order to maintain a good market for its securities the company may find it beneficial to follow a more liberal dividend policy.

Need for Funds. Although from a legal standpoint a corporation may have an adequate surplus for the payment of a dividend, from a practical standpoint the company's cash position and the expected need for funds in the future must be given serious attention before dividends should be declared. The need for funds will be discussed under several different heads. In discussing dividends in this connection we have in mind primarily cash dividends.

Working capital position. The proceeds from the sale of a company's product may temporarily be tied up in accounts receivable. After the accounts are collected the cash may be needed for the purchase of or the payment for additional inventory. If the company is expanding its sales, or if prices are rising, or both, the net proceeds from sales, including the profit, may be tied up in inventory. Thus, despite the presence of a "profit" on the books, the company may not be in a cash position to pay dividends. Or, the company may have adequate cash at the time but some bank loans are due and the cash must be conserved to pay them. In some instances all the funds will be needed to pay the accounts payable.

If the company is increasing its sales, larger amounts of working capital will have to be invested in raw materials, work in process, and finished goods inventories. The expenditures for labor will be higher, and some of the other expenses will also increase with sales. The cash derived from earnings may, therefore, be needed in the business.

Fixed capital needs. In many instances the company must rely on its earnings for funds needed for fixed capital purposes. When this is the case the company may be unable to pay any dividends for some years even though a sizable profit has been earned. Some of the reasons why cash must be retained for both working capital and fixed capital purposes are stated under the headings which follow.

Young companies. A young company cannot ordinarily obtain funds from the sale of securities in the market. With some exceptions, it is usually only the older and better established concerns that can do their financing from the sale of their stocks or bonds. A new company must usually depend upon the investment of its owners for the original capital needed. Thereafter, for some time, the reinvested earnings will be the only source of additional funds open to the company. In some instances bank loans may be obtained, but in many cases even these are unobtainable by new companies. Young companies must, therefore, follow a very conservative dividend policy if they expect to have the necessary funds for expansion purposes.

Small companies. Small companies, both young and old, cannot, in many cases, obtain funds from the sale of stocks or bonds in the general market. Bank loans may be available to small companies that are established, but ordinarily they cannot be obtained for long-term fixed capital purposes. Most small companies must, therefore, conserve a relatively large part of their earnings for expansion purposes, and thus it is necessary for them to be conservative in regard to dividends.

Stage of general business cycle. During periods of depression many companies cut their dividends. This results not only from the fact that their earnings fall off, but also from the desire to conserve funds for the uncertain period that lies ahead. Many would like to reduce their dividends as they start running into a recession, but often the recession is well under way or the depression is upon them before they realize what has happened.

Dividend Policy. The factors stated above, the law, contractual arrangements, nature of the company business, and need for funds, all have a bearing on the dividend policy of a company, but it was thought desirable to discuss them under separate heads. Following are additional considerations that determine a dividend policy.

Stable dividends. Many corporations strive to pay dividends of a fixed amount at regular intervals, such as each quarterly period. Naturally this can best be done by a large, well-established company whose earnings are relatively stable, and who can depend upon the sale of additional securities for expansion purposes. Public utilities as a class meet these requirements better than other industries. Even if earnings fluctuate somewhat, a stable dividend policy may be followed by the company paying out a relatively small percentage of its earnings during good years, and setting up reserves for the payment of dividends during lean years.

Advantages of Stable Dividends. Following are the advantages of a stable dividend policy.

1. *Stock is less speculative.* The stock of a company that follows the policy of paying out a fixed amount in dividends at regular intervals tends to become known more as an *investment* stock rather than a *speculative* stock. The so-called investor class, including some institutions, will buy it. This gives stability to the stock and widens its market.

2. *Aids future financing.* As a result of the stability in price and wider market for the stock, future stock financing is made easier. The stock will usually sell at a high price in relation to the dividends

being paid, so the cost of the money obtained from the sale of additional stock will be relatively low.

3. *Bonds may be classified as legal investments.* The laws of the various states prescribe requirements which must be met by a company, in order that its bonds may be purchased by savings banks, trustees, and other fiduciaries and financial institutions in the state. One of the requirements frequently found is that the company must have had an unbroken dividend record for a specified number of years, such as five years. The failure to pay dividends in one year would thus take the bonds off the legal list for at least five years. Bonds that qualify as *legals* attract a relatively wide market and sell on a relatively low yield basis. Thus, future financing through the sale of additional bonds is relatively easy and cheap.

4. *Future planning made easier.* When a stable dividend policy is followed a company knows at all times just how much will be required in the future to meet dividend payments. With this in mind the officials can better plan future financial requirements.

5. *Improves stockholder relations.* To an increasing extent corporations are realizing the importance of establishing and maintaining good relations with their stockholders. Nothing accomplishes this better than a policy of liberal and stable dividends.

Perhaps the best example of a stable dividend policy is that followed by the American Telephone and Telegraph Company. This company has paid dividends of some amount in each year since 1881. Beginning in 1922, and continuing through the present, a regular dividend of $9 a year ($2.25 quarterly) has been paid. This was done despite the fact that during the depression of the 1930's, earnings on several occasions dipped below the amount of the dividend. A selected list of companies that have paid dividends every year since the year indicated, although the amount of the dividend varied during the period, is shown in Table 38.

Distribution of stock. When a company's stock is held by a large number of persons, an attempt is usually made to follow a rather liberal dividend policy for reasons which have been stated above. But when the stock is closely held by a relatively small number of persons, the interests of the stockholders, officers, and directors may all be the same. If all or a substantial part of the earnings are needed or wanted for some particular purpose, there is no feeling of obligation on the part of the directors to pay dividends. The shareholders may prefer under these circumstances to forego the dividends.

TABLE 38

Common Stocks With Long-Term Dividend Records

Company	*Dividends Paid Each Year Since*
Pennsylvania Railroad Co.	1848
Washington Gas Light Co.	1852
Cincinnati Gas & Electric Co.	1853
Continental Insurance Company	1854
Corn Exchange Bank & Trust Co.	1854
Scovil Manufacturing Co.	1856
American News Co.	1864
New York & Harlem Railroad Co.	1866
Pullman Incorporated	1867
Westinghouse Air Brake Co.	1875
Parke, Davis & Co.	1878
American Telephone and Telegraph Co.	1881
Corning Glass Works	1881
Diamond Match Co.	1882
Standard Oil Co. (N.J.)	1882
Consolidated Edison Co. of New York	1885
United Gas Improvement Co.	1885
The Ruberoid Co.	1889
Boston Edison Co.	1890
Cannon Mills Co.	1890
Coca-Cola Co.	1893
Standard Oil Co. (Ind.)	1894
Burroughs Corp.	1895
Colgate-Palmolive Co.	1895
U. S. Playing Card Co.	1896
General Mills, Inc.	1898
Borden Co.	1899
General Electric Co.	1899
National Biscuit Co.	1899
Pittsburgh Plate Glass Co.	1899
Standard Brands, Inc.	1899
United Fruit Co.	1899
West Virginia Pulp & Paper Co.	1899
Yale & Towne Mfg. Co.	1899

Source: *The Exchange,* The New York Stock Exchange, New York, February, 1954, pp. 10–11.

Tax considerations. In the case of close corporations the tax angle may be the determining factor in deciding dividend policy for a particular year or years. In addition to the corporation paying the federal corporate income tax, the shareholders also have to pay the federal personal income tax on the dividends they receive. During prosperous times when the earnings of the corporation are large, probably the income of its shareholders is also large. Although the top part of their personal income may be subject to taxation at a high rate, the receipt of dividends may push the income into an even higher tax bracket. When the board of directors is composed of the shareholders, or when it is under the control of the shareholders, it may be agreed not to pay any dividends, or at least, not much in dividends that year. In subsequent years when the personal income of the shareholders is lower, and therefore subject to lower tax rates on the upper part of the income, the corporate earnings may be paid out in the form of dividends.

In a situation of this kind, or any other situation, care should be taken, however, not to violate the Internal Revenue Code.[2] The Code imposes an additional tax on any earnings (after an accumulated $100,000 exemption) which are retained beyond the "reasonable anticipated needs" of the business. Any such improper retained earnings can be taxed at the rate of 27½ per cent on the first $100,000, and 38½ per cent on the amount in excess of $100,000. In determining if earnings beyond the reasonable needs of the business have been retained, the government gives consideration to the following: whether the stock is closely held by a family or other small group, whether loans have been made to company officers or the shareholders out of money that could have been used for dividend purposes, and whether money has been invested in securities which have no relation to the normal business activities of the company.

It should be made clear that the retention of a relatively large portion of the earnings does not automatically subject the company to the additional taxes. The government must initiate the action, and the company is given the right to explain the reasons for the retention. The company policy may be justified by the fact that the money was needed for the purchase of additional inventory, for expansion purposes, for replacement of equipment, for contingency reserves, etc.

The special situation in regard to the tax status of stock dividends will be taken up when discussing stock dividends in the following chapter.

Other factors. The factors stated above are the principal ones which determine dividend policy. In some instances special circumstances may control. For example, a company may conserve cash for the retirement of a bond issue. Liberal dividends may be forthcoming because of the desire to create a good impression so that the management will get the shareholders' proxies or to insure the re-election of the management or to get better terms for a proposed merger or consolidation. In some instances liberal dividends have

[2] Sections 531–537, Internal Revenue Code of 1954 (formerly sec. 102).

been paid in order to induce the holders of convertible bonds to convert them into stock.

From the standpoint of society in general, it would tend to smooth out the business cycle if corporations would follow a regular dividend policy. When dividends are cut at a time of depression, which is the typical situation, it only makes a bad situation worse so far as the country in general is concerned. If the dividends could be maintained, so much more purchasing power would get into the hands of the shareholders. It might be a foolhardy policy on the part of the company, however, to pay liberal dividends in the face of uncertainty. It should also be realized that the directors are supposed to do what is in the best interests of the shareholders of the particular company.

DIVIDENDS DECLARED BY BOARD OF DIRECTORS. One of the powers of the board of directors of a corporation is the declaration of dividends. Naturally the cash position of the company, its need for funds, the earnings, amount of surplus shown on the books, the dividend policy followed by the company, etc., all have an important bearing on how much, if any at all, will be declared in dividends. In some instances the president of the company, or the finance committee of the board of directors, will suggest or recommend how much should be declared. But the final authority for the declaration of dividends is the board of directors.

Even if the earnings are relatively large, the board is under no obligation to pay dividends. The judgment of the board of directors is usually final in regard to dividends. If they believe the earnings are needed in the business for possible future contingency or for expansion purposes, the shareholders ordinarily can do nothing about it. In exceptional cases the shareholders may appeal to a court of equity to compel the declaration of dividends.

A classical example of the courts compelling the payment of dividends is the *Dodge v. Ford Motor Company* case,[3] which was decided by the Supreme Court of Michigan in 1919. In 1916, the time the suit was filed, the Ford Motor Company had capital stock outstanding in the amount of only $2,000,000. The surplus of the company, however, amounted to $112,000,000. The earnings for that one year were nearly $60,000,000. The cash on hand was over $52,000,000. The company had for some years been paying a regular dividend equivalent to 60 per cent a year on the stock, but this amounted to only $1,200,000 and in addition several extra dividends had been declared. Some of the minority shareholders brought suit

[3] 204 Michigan 459 (1919).

against the company contending that in view of the amount of the surplus, earnings, cash, the amount they were getting in dividends, and the use to which the earnings were being put, the directors should pay more in dividends. In a newspaper article Mr. Henry Ford was quoted as saying that it was his ambition "to employ still more men; to spread the benefits of this industrial system to the greatest possible number, to help them build up their lives and homes. To do this, we are putting the greatest share of our profits back into the business."[4] The court, however, said—"A business corporation is organized and carried on primarily for the profit of the stockholders. The powers of the directors are to be employed for that end. The discretion of the directors is to be exercised in the choice of means to attain that end and does not extend to a change in the end itself, to the reduction of profits or to the nondistribution of profits among stockholders in order to devote them to other purposes."[5] The court thereupon ordered the company to pay an additional dividend of $19,000,000. Later the Ford family bought up the shares which were held by minority shareholders.

In the case of preferred stock, if the contract calls for the payment of dividends each year in which profits are earned, which is a rare type of contract, the courts might compel the payment of the dividend if profits are earned. If dividends are declared on the common before the arrears on the preferred or the current preferential dividend is paid, recourse could be had to the courts to have the dividend rescinded, or to compel the declaration of the preferred dividend.

Declared Dividends Are Debts. After the board of directors has declared a dividend it constitutes a debt of the corporation. After declaration, but before payment, the dividend should show as a current liability of the company. If the company should fail, and assuming the dividend was properly and legally declared, the shareholders would be treated as general creditors with respect to the declared dividend. If, however, money was set aside in a special fund or bank account for the payment of the dividend, the shareholders would be treated as preferred creditors with respect to that fund. If a stock dividend is declared and has not yet been paid, the amount of the stock dividend should be shown along with the outstanding stock in the net worth section of the balance sheet.

Remedies for Improper Dividends. The statutes of the particular state under consideration must be consulted to determine the

[4] *Ibid.*, p. 468.
[5] *Ibid.*, p. 507.

remedies that may be had in event the directors improperly or illegally declare and pay a dividend. If such a dividend has been only declared and not paid, shareholders cannot get the court to force its payment. The directors could rescind the dividend and the shareholders would have no right against the corporation or the directors with respect to the dividend.

In many states directors are personally liable for the payment of illegal dividends. Usually receivers or trustees or a new management of the corporation can sue the directors to recover for the company any amounts paid in illegal dividends. As a rule, the statutes specify penalties for the payment of dividends from "capital." In some states, including New York, it is a misdemeanor, while in others it is a criminal offense. Usually the directors are not liable for improper dividends if they acted in good faith, and used reasonable care in the selection of the officers and others responsible for the preparation of the financial statements. If a director believes that a dividend is being illegally declared he should go on record in the minutes of the meeting as opposing the dividend, otherwise he may be held liable.

The ability to recover an illegal dividend from the shareholders is another matter. If the improper or illegal dividend causes insolvency, or causes the company to fail, it can be recovered in a number of states. If this does not result and if the shareholders were innocent and received the dividend in good faith, in a number of states recovery may not be had.

Dividend Terminology. In the following chapter we shall classify and discuss dividends according to the medium in which they are paid. At the present time, however, we are interested in classifications of dividends other than those relating to the medium of payment.

Regular dividends. Preferred stock carries a preferential dividend, expressed either in per cent or dollars per share, and this may be considered the regular dividend even though the stock may receive additional amounts if it is participating in some form. The term "regular dividend," however, is commonly used with reference to the common stock.

Classified common stock ordinarily carries a stated dividend rate in a manner similar to preferred stock, but again, the term "regular dividend" is usually applied to the ordinary common stock. Ordinary common stock does not carry a stated dividend rate, nor is any expressed in the charter or bylaws. But in practice the board of directors by their action in declaring a fixed amount of dividends

TABLE 39

COMMON STOCKS WITH QUARTERLY DIVIDEND RECORDS OF A HALF CENTURY OR LONGER

Company	*Quarterly Payments Began*
American News Co.	1864
Pullman Incorporated	1867
Erie & Pittsburgh R.R. Co.	1870
Pittsburgh, Ft. Wayne & Chicago	1872
Gold & Stock Telegraph Co.	1877
American Telephone and Telegraph Co.	1882
Washington Gas Light Co.	1885
Commonwealth Edison Co.	1890
Beech Creek R.R. Co.	1891
Consolidated Edison Co. of New York	1891
Boston Edison Co.	1891
Westinghouse Air Brake Co.	1894
West Virginia Pulp and Paper Co.	1895
The U. S. Playing Card Co.	1896
Parke, Davis & Co.	1897
Procter & Gamble Co.	1898
Raybestos-Manhattan	1898
Pittsburgh Plate Glass Co.	1899
General Electric Co.	1899
National Biscuit Co.	1899
United Fruit Co.	1899
Electric Storage Battery	1901
Acme Steel Co.	1902
Eastman Kodak Co.	1902
United Eng. & Fdry. Co.	1902
American Snuff Co.	1903
Beech-Nut Packing Co.	1903
Allied Chemical & Dye Corp.	1903
Central Hudson G. & E.	1903
The Texas Co.	1903
Yale & Towne Mfg. Co.	1904
American Brake Shoe Co.	1904
American Natural Gas Co.	1904
E. I. duPont de Nemours	1905

SOURCE: *The Exchange,* The New York Stock Exchange, New York, September, 1955, pp. 10–11.

at regular intervals establish what is thought of as the "regular dividend." This is commonly a quarterly dividend, although in some instances it may be semiannual or annual. In some instances the term "regular dividend" is printed on the dividend check. In many cases the directors and officers of the company refer to the dividend by this term, and a conscious effort is made to have a regular dividend rate established. The policy of the American Telephone and Telegraph, referred to above, is a good example. Most of the stocks of the leading companies listed on the New York Stock Exchange have what is looked upon as regular dividend rates on their common stock.

In practically all instances the regular dividend is paid in cash, although in a few cases a more or less "regular" dividend has been paid in stock or the regular stock dividend is paid in addition to the regular cash dividend.

Extra dividends. When companies which have established a regular dividend rate on their stock pay more than this amount in dividends, they usually label the additional dividend an "extra" dividend. The dividend is specifically called extra, because the company does not want the shareholders to expect that this amount will be paid regularly in the future. In many instances a separate check, different in color, and in some cases marked "extra dividend," will be made out for the extra dividend.

Some corporations pay their regular dividend during the first three quarters of the year, and then after viewing the results for the entire year, pay an extra in addition to the regular dividend at the end of the last quarter. In some instances this may be done to escape the possibility of the additional retained earnings tax, referred to above, being applied.

Although in most instances the extra dividend is paid in cash, in some cases it consists of a stock dividend or occasionally a dividend in property other than cash.

Declaring and paying dividends is sometimes referred to as "cutting a melon," and the dividends may be called "melons." In some instances this terminology is applied only to an extra or special dividend, and in others it is applied only to a dividend of appreciable amount.

Interim and final dividends. When corporations follow the practice referred to above of paying a regular dividend or a relatively small one during the first three quarters and then paying the regular dividend plus an extra, or a relatively large dividend, at the end of the year, the first three quarterly dividends are sometimes referred to as *interim* dividends, and the last one is called the *final* dividend.

Special dividends. An extra dividend is sometimes referred to as a "special" dividend. In some instances the term is applied not to the extra dividend as described above, but rather to an isolated or occasional dividend which is paid from the profits from some special or nonrecurring item such as the sale of some real estate which is not needed in the business.

Liquidating dividends. The distribution of cash or other property made to shareholders upon liquidation of the company is referred to as a "liquidating" or "liquidation" dividend. Usually it represents merely a return of part of the original capital contributed by the shareholders. Occasionally, however, the business may be sold for more than the amount of the capital stock, in which case part of the dividend would represent the surplus or profits of the company. In most instances, however, all such dividends consist of "capital." In the case of holding companies that are broken up as a result of a court order, or those being dissolved under the provisions of the Public Utility Holding Company Act of 1935, the dividend may, in part at least, consist of the securities of other companies.

In some instances the part of the dividend paid by a going concern which represents the depletion of a wasting asset company is referred to as a liquidating dividend.

Liquidating dividends, being a return of capital, are treated differently from ordinary dividends for income tax purposes. The part of a dividend which represents a liquidation dividend is not reported as ordinary income, but rather it is deducted from the cost of the stock. Thus, when the stock is sold, any profit made (as measured by the difference between the selling price and the adjusted cost price) is taxed as a capital gain.

Liquidating dividends may also be treated differently from ordinary dividends when preferred stock is outstanding. The provisions of the preferred stock contract concerning its right to assets upon dissolution will govern the right of the stock to liquidating dividends, rather than the clauses that relate to its right to ordinary dividends. Liquidation dividends are sometimes called "capital" dividends.

Questions

1. Indicate the various factors which determine whether a company can or will pay a dividend in any given year.
2. Explain what is meant when it is said that dividends cannot be paid from "capital."
3. (a) Can a corporation pay a dividend from capital surplus? Explain. (b) Can a corporation pay a dividend from income other than "earned"? Explain.
4. Should a large successful company that constantly needs funds for expansion follow a conservative or liberal dividend policy? Explain.
5. Indicate the advantages of a stable dividend policy to the company.
6. Indicate how the income tax laws might influence the dividend policy of a corporation.
7. Are directors under any obligation to declare dividends? Explain.

8. Are dividends ever a debt of the corporation? Explain.

9. Indicate what action might result from the declaration of unwarranted dividends.

10. (a) What is meant when it is said that a corporation "cut a melon?" (b) How often do large corporations, which follow a regular dividend policy and whose stock is listed, pay the dividends?

Problems

1. The following questions refer to the Peerless Metal Co. as of Jan. 1, 19-2. (See Problem 1, Chap. 25): (a) How much could the company pay out legally in the form of cash dividends? (b) Which particular source of surplus could better be used as a basis for a stock rather than a cash dividend? Why? (c) Which particular sources of surplus do you think inadvisable as a basis for cash dividends? Why? (d) List the additional information that you would desire before deciding upon any dividend action for the company. (e) Do the stockholders have any right against the corporation in respect to dividends? Explain.

2. The question of dividend action was before the directors of the Wear-Forever Corp. at their January meeting in 19-1. The company had recently tied up a considerable amount of money in inventories and was not in a cash position to meet the regular dividend. The president recommended that $90,000 be borrowed at the bank to enable the company to pay the regular 6 per cent dividend—a rate that had been paid for the past 13 years. (a) Is it legal to declare dividends when there is insufficient cash on hand to pay the dividend? (b) Do you think the president's recommendation might have been sound? Why? (c) Would the 13-year dividend experience of the company have any influence on you as a director in voting on the president's recommendation? Explain. (d) What additional information would you, as a director, want before acting on the president's recommendation?

Chapter 27

KINDS OF DIVIDENDS

Kinds of Dividends. Dividends paid by corporations take one of the three forms, namely, (1) those that are paid in cash or other property, (2) those that are paid in notes or bonds, and (3) those that are paid in stock of that company. It will be noted that each of these three different kinds of dividends affect different sections of the balance sheet. We will discuss each of the kinds of dividends that fall into the three groups. Following are the various kinds of dividends:

1. Cash dividends
2. Property dividends
3. Scrip dividends
4. Bond dividends
5. Stock dividends

Cash Dividends. To what has been said above relating to cash dividends we have to add only that "cash" dividends are not paid in cash but rather by checks. The larger companies have a bank or trust company act as their dividend paying agent. The addressograph plates bearing the names and addresses of the shareholders are kept by the institution, and the latter has a record of the number and kind of shares held by each shareholder. All the detailed work in connection with the making out of the checks and sending them to the shareholders is handled by the institution.

Property Dividends. Dividends payable in assets or property other than cash are called "property" dividends. Usually this property takes the form of securities of other companies. In some instances such a dividend is referred to as a "security" dividend. In some cases the property or security dividend is a liquidation dividend, but in others such a dividend may be paid by a going concern. The General Electric Company was forced by court decree to divest itself of the stock of Radio Corporation of America, and it did this in 1933 by paying a special dividend on its shares of 1/6 of a share of Radio Corporation stock. Some public utility holding companies have paid security dividends to their shareholders as a means of disposing of stock under the requirements of the Public Utility Holding Company Act. In some instances companies have paid dividends in government bonds which the company had been holding as an investment.

As an alternative to a security dividend, the company could sell the securities and pay a cash dividend. But the securities may be selling for more than the company paid for them, and the income tax would have to be paid on the profit. By paying the securities themselves out as dividends the corporation escapes the tax. The shareholders receiving such a dividend, however, would have to report them as ordinary earned income at the value existing on the day they are received.

Occasionally dividends will be paid in property other than cash or securities. Building lots, liquor and warehouse receipts for liquor have been distributed as dividends. As may have been inferred from what has already been said, a property dividend is ordinarily a *special* dividend.

From an accounting standpoint the payment of a cash or property dividend results in a debit to the surplus, or retained income account, and a credit to the appropriate asset account.

SCRIP DIVIDENDS. Dividends that are paid in notes of the particular corporation are called *scrip* dividends. The notes usually bear interest and, when a definite due date is stated, are also negotiable. They are usually classified as current liabilities of the company, particularly when they mature within a period of one year. In event of failure of the company, the holders of the notes would be treated just as any other general creditor of the company, provided the dividend had been legally declared. Scrip dividends are rarely used.

The reason for the use of scrip dividends is that the company does not have the necessary cash available to pay a cash dividend; or it has the cash, but wants to use it for another purpose and still does not want to "pass" the dividend. Thus it declares and pays a scrip dividend. If a company has actual earnings, and the cash has not been collected yet, but will be collected by the time the notes come due—then the scrip dividend may be justified. Or even if the cash is not now available but will be forthcoming from some other source, the dividend may be warranted. But in most instances when the scrip dividend has been used, the company should perhaps have passed the dividend at least until such time as it could pay a cash dividend. In some instances the earnings reported may be not real, due to the undercharging of depreciation or some other questionable accounting practice.

In a sense, the payment of a scrip dividend is an admission of the inability to pay a cash dividend. This situation should not be made worse by the assumption of an obligation in the form of the notes to pay cash out at some future time.

Any obligation of the company to pay preferred dividends before the common dividends cannot be satisfied by the payment of a scrip dividend to the preferred shareholders, unless it is so specified in the stock contract or the preferred shareholders agree to such action.

BOND DIVIDENDS. Bond dividends are similar to scrip dividends except that the obligation assumes a longer maturity date. Both scrip and bond dividends result in the lessening of surplus and an addition to the appropriate liability account. Bond dividends, like scrip dividends, are rare.

It is questionable whether a corporation should pay a bond dividend. They usually bear interest and the company, therefore, undertakes to pay an annual fixed charge and also the principal of the bonds when they become due. And this obligation is undertaken without getting anything in return except credit for declaring the dividend. The ability of the company to meet this obligation in the future is not known at the time. Moreover, if the company has several different classes of stock outstanding and the bond dividend is paid to only one of them, the other class of stock may be harmed thereby.

In one way at least the bond dividend may be preferred over the scrip dividend. If the company cannot pay a cash dividend at the time, it may be unable to meet the notes when they become due. A bond obligation of the same amount may be met, however, since the company has a longer period of time to secure the cash. In the meantime, however, interest will be continuing on the obligations.

It is not uncommon to see corporations paying cash dividends to their shareholders and at the same time selling bonds in the market. This would not seem much different in its effect on the corporation from retaining the cash instead of getting it through the sale of bonds, and declaring a bond dividend. A company might also consider a bond dividend as an alternative to a stock dividend. In each case the company retains the use of the money represented by the dividend. But before the earnings can be used to pay a dividend on the stock, income taxes must be paid on these earnings. But if a bond dividend is paid, the interest on the bonds is deductible before arriving at future net taxable income. Thus, in this respect, the corporation and its shareholders would benefit taxwise from the bond dividend. Any use of bond dividends on the part of close corporations for tax savings purposes, however, would undoubtedly be looked into by the Internal Revenue Service, and possibly the interest deduction would not be allowed.

Stock dividends

NATURE OF STOCK DIVIDENDS. So far as their relative importance is concerned, stock dividends rank next to cash dividends. A more lengthy discussion of stock dividends is advisable, and also a comparison of this type of dividend with stock split-ups, which are not dividends, will be made. For these reasons stock dividends are being considered last.

When a stock dividend is declared and paid, the surplus or retained earnings account is debited, as in the case of any other kind of a dividend, and the capital stock account is credited. In order to pay the stock dividend the company would, of course, have to have sufficient authorized capital stock, otherwise, it would be necessary to go through the procedure, and pay the taxes and fees, for a charter amendment to get the necessary amount of authorized stock. When a stock dividend is paid, it should be noted that the par value or stated value of the outstanding stock is not changed, and the stock represented by the dividend possesses the same par or stated value as the stock on which the dividend is paid.

It should be apparent that so far as book values are concerned, the stock dividend does not give the shareholder anything he did not possess before. Let us assume that the net worth section of the balance sheet of a company appears as follows.

Capital stock (par value $100)	$1,000,000
Surplus	2,000,000
Total net worth	$3,000,000

The book value of the stock in the above example is $300 a share. If the company now pays a stock dividend of 100 per cent, the net worth would be changed as follows:

Capital stock (par value $100)	$2,000,000
Surplus	1,000,000
Total net worth	$3,000,000

After the dividend each shareholder now has two shares of stock for each one share that he possessed before the dividend was paid.

The book value per share, however, has been reduced from $300, to $150. So the shareholder now has two shares with a book value of $150 each, instead of one share with a book value of $300. In other words, the shareholder's equity is not changed at all by the stock dividend. It is similar to having two five dollar bills instead of one ten dollar bill (although the par value is not reduced).

Reasons for Paying Stock Dividends. There are several good reasons for paying stock dividends. In some instances one reason may account for the dividend, while in other cases one or several other reasons may apply.

1. *Money is retained in the business.* The stock dividend is the only kind of a dividend that may be paid without taking any money or other property out of the business at any time. The payment of a scrip or bond dividend does not necessitate the payment of any money at the time, but their payment is only postponed. As has been pointed out several times before, the earnings of a company are rarely represented by cash; often they show up as more inventory and other assets. The earnings are said to be "plowed back" into the business. Perhaps a more accurate statement is to say they are absorbed by the business in the form of additions to the net assets. A company that uses its earnings for expansion purposes cannot, from a practical standpoint, pay cash dividends. The retained earnings or surplus is as permanent a part of the business as the assets represented by the capital stock. That being the case, there is no reason why the surplus should not be permanently capitalized by the payment of a stock dividend.

Even if the earnings were in the form of cash, but the company had a need for the funds in the near future, it would appear desirable not to pay the money out in the form of a cash dividend. The stock dividend may be recommended in such a situation.

2. *Pacify the shareholders.* Shareholders expect to receive dividends when there are earnings. In the event the company has used or needs the money in the business, it can retain the money and still pay a stock dividend. In this way the shareholder is pacified.

In most instances, however, a stock dividend represents a special or extra dividend. At the time it is paid the company will usually also pay the regular dividend in cash. As a rule, the stock dividend is not used as a substitute for the regular cash dividend. But even though the regular cash dividends are paid, if the retained earnings are still relatively large, the shareholders may expect additional dividends. It is in a situation of this kind that the stock dividend is frequently used.

If the shareholder wants his additional dividend in the form of cash, he can sell the stock obtained as a dividend in the market. Of course, this would lessen the shareholder's proportionate interest in the business and his degree of control. Also, his right to future dividends, as well as his right to assets upon dissolution of the company, would be diluted.

3. *Reduce the per share earnings and dividends.* If a company has a 100 per cent stock dividend, as in the example given above, since the number of shares are doubled without any new capital coming into the business, the earnings per share would tend to be reduced 50 per cent. Although a company likes to have large earnings per share, it does not want the figure to get too high. Extremely large earnings per share may cause labor, and particularly the labor unions, to think that the company is not paying high enough wages. Also customers may wonder whether or not the company is charging too much for its products. High per-share earnings may also result in an investigation to determine if the company is in violation of the antitrust laws. Naturally, the earnings will tend to be just as large after the stock dividend, but the fact that the per-share earnings seem moderate, due only to the stock dividend, will soon be forgotten.

If a company continues to pay out the same percentage of its earnings in the form of dividends, the 100 per cent stock dividend would tend to reduce the per-share dividends by 50 per cent. What was stated above in regard to the advantages of reducing the per-share earnings applies with equal force to the per-share dividends.

4. *Reduce the market price of the stock.* In many instances the principal reason for declaring a stock dividend is to reduce the market price per share of the stock. That could also be accomplished with a stock split-up, but this will be discussed later in the chapter. Although companies like to see their stock selling for a relatively high price, there is a limit. Too high a price narrows the market. Fewer people can buy the stock, and its price is subject to greater fluctuations, at least from the standpoint of dollars and cents changes. Listed stocks selling for over $100 a share are good candidates for stock dividends or stock splits. Even $60, or $80, might be considered too high a price for a good market.

The market price of stock becomes of considerable importance when a new issue of stock is being considered. If the stock is selling for a high price in the market, any new shares of the same class should be sold at approximately the same price, otherwise the new money would cost too much, and the equity of the old shareholders would be diluted. But the relatively high price may narrow the market so much that the company could not sell the stock for its real worth. Prior to the offering of the new stock, the company may therefore have a sizable stock dividend to reduce the market price of the stock, and thus enable the company to attract a wide market. Furthermore, part of the surplus of the company is distributed to the old shareholders by means of the dividend, and thus there is less chance of its dilution by the sale of new shares.

The reduction in the market price of the stock resulting from a stock dividend comes about from several factors although they are closely related. The reduction in the book value is one reason. More important, however, are the factors which were stated in the above section—the reduction in the per-share earnings and dividends.

PRACTICAL ADVANTAGES TO SHAREHOLDERS. Perhaps in most instances shareholders actually benefit from the payment of stock dividends. The possible advantages are as follows.

1. *Favorable future outlook.* Corporate managements usually think through the consequences of a stock dividend before paying it. They realize that the per share earnings and dividends will presently be reduced in proportion to the amount of new stock issued, and usually they would not authorize such dividend unless they thought that the future earnings were going to be as large or larger than those of the past. In some instances, particularly when the dividend is relatively small, the management indicates that they hope to maintain the same *rate* of dividends on all the shares as they were paying on the old shares. This would obviously necessitate more dollars to pay the future dividends. It is therefore probable that they expect earnings actually to increase in the future. The shareholders, and the investing public, realize this and interpret the declaration of a stock dividend as an indication that the management is optimistic in regard to the future.

2. *Larger dividends.* As stated above, in many instances the company continues to pay the same amount of dividends per share after a stock dividend has been paid. Since the shareholder holds more shares of stock after receipt of the stock dividend, his future cash dividends may be larger as a result of the stock dividend.

3. *Greater market value.* In many instances a stock dividend does not reduce the market price of the stock as much as its book value. This results from the fact that the stock will have a wider market, and the dividends may be maintained at the same rate. The

shareholder, therefore, commonly finds that the market value of the aggregate of his holdings after the stock dividend is greater than it was before. Even if the immediate effect of the stock dividend is to reduce the market value of the stock, later the market price tends to work up toward the old price, for the reasons stated above.

4. *Tax savings.* Cash dividends are taxable as ordinary income in the hands of the recipient stockholder. Stock dividends, on the other hand, are usually tax exempt. We will now discuss this subject.

Taxability of Stock Dividends. It was stated above that a stock dividend does not give the shareholder anything that he did not possess before. It was for this reason that the United States Supreme Court in 1920,[1] ruled that ordinary stock dividends are not income and therefore are not subject to the income tax. Starting in 1921, the revenue laws have specifically excluded ordinary stock dividends from taxation. According to the provisions of the law and later court decisions,[2] a stock dividend is not taxable if it does not give the shareholder an interest different from that which he had before the dividend, but taxable if it gives him a different interest. Thus, a dividend paid in *common stock* to the *common stockholders* would not be taxable. Likewise, if the company had *only* common stock outstanding and it paid a dividend in *preferred* stock to the shareholders, the dividend would *not* be taxable. But if the company had preferred stock outstanding and it paid a dividend in *preferred stock* to the common shareholders it would be taxable.

As a general rule, under the 1954 Internal Revenue Code, a stock dividend is tax exempt regardless of whether or not the shareholder's interest in the corporation is changed in any way as a result of the dividend, unless: (1) it is paid to the preferred stockholders in lieu of their cash dividend for the current or preceding year, or (2) the stockholder has a choice whether to take his dividend in stock or in cash or other property. (This is sometimes called an *optional* dividend.) Although preferred stock given as a dividend is tax exempt, it is taxable as ordinary income if the shareholder sells the preferred stock or redeems it.

When the stock dividend (other than one paid in preferred stock) is not taxable as ordinary income, the dividend reduces the *cost* price of the stock for purposes of computing the capital gains

[1] *Eisner v. Macomber,* 252 U. S. 189 (1920).

[2] *Koshland v. Helvering,* 298 U. S. 441 (1936); *Helvering v. Gowan,* 302 U. S. 238 (1937).

tax that must be paid upon sale of the stock. Thus, if a person paid $300 for a share of stock and subsequently the company had a 100 per cent nontaxable stock dividend, the cost price per share would be considered to be $150 a share. If one of the shares thereafter is sold for $180, a capital gains tax must be paid on the $30 gain. If only $200 had originally been paid for the stock, and one share was sold at $180 after the 100 per cent stock dividend had been paid, a capital gains tax would have to be paid on the per share profit of $80.

If the stock dividend is of the type that is taxable, then it will be taxed as ordinary income at its fair market value at the time the dividend is received. If the stock received is worth $150 a share (ex-dividends) then that amount is included in the ordinary income of the shareholders. If this stock is later sold for $180 a share, for example, $30 would be considered a capital gains and taxed as such. If any of the old shares on which the stock dividend was paid are sold, however, their cost value would still be the amount actually paid for them regardless of the fact that their value had been diluted by the stock dividend.

The savings effected by having a stock dividend taxable (when the stock is sold) at the capital gains rate rather than having a cash dividend taxable as ordinary income is appreciable for persons who are in the higher income tax brackets. A person with a taxable (ordinary) income of from $50,000 to $60,000 (for those filing a joint return the income bracket should be doubled) must pay a tax of 75 per cent on the top $10,000. Those with taxable incomes in excess of $200,000 must pay a tax of 91 per cent on all income over $200,000. But any profit made on the sale of a tax-free (at the time of its receipt) stock dividend is subject to a maximum tax of 25 per cent (assuming it is a long-term capital gain).

The 1954 Internal Revenue Code, however, gave some relief to taxpayers with respect to ordinary taxable dividends. The first $50 of dividends received from domestic corporations may be excluded in reporting earned income. Then after computing the tax on the total reportable income, a credit is allowed from the tax of an amount equivalent to 4 per cent of the reported dividends from domestic corporations. (The amount of the credit, however, cannot exceed 4 per cent of the total taxable income.) The relative advantage of the stock dividend over the cash dividend discussed above should, therefore, be modified accordingly.

FRACTIONAL SHARE WARRANTS. When a company pays a stock dividend of anything less than 100 per cent, the problem of fractional shares arises. For example, if a company paid a 10 per cent stock dividend, shareholders holding less than 10 shares would not be entitled to a whole share. Or if the number of shares held was not divisible by 10, such as for example, 25 shares, the shareholder would be entitled to 2½ shares. The share dividend certificate would be made out for the number of whole shares. In the example just given the certificate would be for 2 shares.

The right to fractional shares is usually handled in one of two ways. The company either gives the shareholders cash equivalent to the value of the fractional shares they are entitled to, or a *warrant,* which is often called *scrip,* is made out for the fractional shares. In the example just given the warrant would call for one-half of a share of stock. These warrants are made out to bearer and are transferable by delivery. They carry no voting rights and ordinarily are not entitled to any dividends or interest. It should be noted that these warrants are sometimes called *scrip,* but they should not be confused with the notes that are issued in connection with a *scrip dividend.*

Several things may be done with the warrants, and in some instances any of them could be used in a particular case depending upon the terms announced by the company. In some instances the company will redeem the warrants for cash. Or cash of a sufficient amount may be sent in along with the warrants to enable the holder to get a whole share of stock. Commonly a market for warrants is maintained, and in some instances this is done by the issuing company or its transfer agent. Thus, a person holding a warrant for one-half of a share might either sell his warrant, or he could buy another warrant for one-half of a share, and secure one whole share of stock. Usually a time limit, such as two or three years, is established for the exercise of the warrants; after that time they become void.

It should be noted that these *warrants* give the shareholders *rights* to fractional shares, but they are *not* certificates of fractional shares of stock. The latter are rarely issued since too much trouble and expense would be involved in handling their transfer for an indefinite period of time. Furthermore, dividends would have to be paid on them unless otherwise provided.

Stock Dividends Paid from Capital Surplus. Stock dividends may be paid from the retained earnings or from capital surplus. Some of the same principles governing the payment of cash dividends from capital surplus would apply with equal force to stock dividends, but in some instances a stock dividend, but not a cash dividend, would be recommended from certain types of capital surplus. If the surplus arises from the reappraisal upward of securities held as investments, it should not be capitalized through the payment of a stock dividend, since the market value of the securities may decline and accordingly the book value should then be marked down. If the amount representing the surplus has been invested in ordinary assets, the stock dividend would be warranted. It was pointed out above that in some states a stock dividend, but not a cash dividend, may be paid from the surplus arising from the revaluation of assets upward.

It is recommended that corporations inform their shareholders as to the source of the surplus from which stock dividends are paid. This is particularly true when the dividend is paid from capital surplus.

Pre-emptive Right to Stock Dividends. It will be recalled that shareholders have a pre-emptive right to subscribe to new shares in order to maintain their equity in the surplus and their degree of control. Such pre-emptive right would not apply to a nonvoting preferred stock which is limited both as to dividends and assets upon dissolution. But if a preferred stock is voting and has equal rights (in addition to the preference) with respect to dividends and assets upon dissolution, unless otherwise provided in the statutes of the state and the particular contract, the preferred would be entitled to a stock dividend along with the common. But since we have assumed the preferred to be participating with respect to dividends, the right to the stock dividend could be argued from the standpoint of the participation right. But suppose a corporation pays the regular cash dividend to the preferred and then attempts to pay a dividend of similar amount, but in stock, to the common shareholders. Would this be a violation of the pre-emptive right of the preferred? This question has not been settled by the courts.

A closer approach to reality would be to assume that the preferred stock is nonparticipating with respect to dividends either by expressed provisions of the contract or as a result of court decisions, but that it is voting and not restricted as to assets upon dissolution. We will further assume that all arrears have been paid on the stock, and that both the preferred and common have received their regular cash dividend for the year. The company now declares a special stock dividend to the common on the grounds that the preferred, being nonparticipating, is not entitled to the additional dividend. Can the preferred by proper injunction restrain the payment of the stock dividend to the common only?

If the stock dividend is paid only to the common, the degree of control possessed by the preferred stock would be lessened. Furthermore, upon dissolution of the company the common would get more in assets than if the stock dividend had not been paid. Some courts have held that the preferred stock should "participate" in such a stock dividend by virtue of its pre-emptive right. As a result of court cases such as this, some authorities have said that in the absence of provisions otherwise, preferred stock participates equally with the common in any dividends paid in addition to the regular dividends. Some courts have said the same. The great weight of authority is that preferred stock is not participating with respect to a cash dividend unless so provided in the contract.

The statutes of many of the states define or limit pre-emptive rights. Some provide that the pre-emptive right shall not apply in the following instances: if the shares are a different class from the ones under consideration; if the shares are not sold for cash; if the shares are issued as a dividend; and if the outstanding shares under consideration are limited as to dividend rate and liquidation price. Even if shares are entitled to the pre-emptive right so far as the law is concerned, the shareholders may waive such right.

READJUSTMENT OF CAPITAL ACCOUNT. When stock dividends are used rarely by a company, particularly when the amount of the dividend is relatively large in relation to the shares outstanding, the shareholder should look upon the procedure not as a dividend but rather as a readjustment in the capital stock account in order to reduce the market price of the stock, and/or reduce the earnings per share.

RESCISSION OF STOCK DIVIDENDS. Unlike the declaration of a cash dividend, the declaration of a stock dividend does not create a liability on the part of the corporation. It therefore follows that after declaration of the dividend, but before its payment, the directors could rescind their action and the shareholders could do nothing about it. This is true even if the shareholders have been called upon to authorize additional stock for the dividend.

NEW YORK STOCK EXCHANGE RULES ON STOCK DIVIDENDS. The New York Stock Exchange believes that the payment of regular stock dividends of a relatively small amount (or, those on a "continuing basis") are misleading to shareholders unless such stock dividends are paid from profits earned during the particular period and unless the amount represented by the dividend is transferred from the earned surplus to the capital stock or capital surplus account. To this end the Exchange, in 1953, adopted rules relating to the payment of such dividends.[3] If the stock dividend represents less than 25 per cent of the number of shares outstanding prior to the stock dividends (one new share for each four old shares would be a 25 per cent dividend), the Exchange will not approve the listing of the additional shares, (1) unless the company transfers from the earned surplus to the capital stock or capital surplus account an amount equal to the fair value of the shares, which should closely approximate the current market price of the stock adjusted to reflect the issuance of the new shares, and (2) unless the earned surplus for the particular period covered by the dividend is sufficient in amount to cover the aggregate fair value of the stock dividend.

The above stated rules *apply also to a stock split-up* if the number of new shares is less than 25 per cent of the number of shares outstanding at the time of the split-up. For companies whose stock is listed on the NYSE, the accounting procedure for stock split-ups will therefore be different from that described below if the split-up is of the type that falls under the NYSE rules. If the stock dividend or split-up comes under the NYSE rules and a cash dividend is also paid at the time, the earnings should be sufficient in amount to cover both the stock and the cash. The Exchange, however, believes that the split-up should be not less than 2 for 1, in which case the above stated NYSE rules would not be applicable.

If the stock dividend or stock split-up involves shares representing 100 per cent or more of the number of shares outstanding prior to the distribution, the NYSE rules or requirements stated above are not applicable. For stock distributions representing from 25 to 99 per cent of the number of shares outstanding, the presumption is that the NYSE rules are not applicable, but the particular circumstances present will be taken into account to determine the validity of the assumption.

Stock splits

NATURE OF STOCK SPLIT-UPS. *Stock split-ups*, or as they are sometimes called, *stock splits*, are not dividends at all, but their similarity to stock dividends warrants their inclusion in this chapter. As the name indicates, a stock split-up results in the replacement of the company's shares with a larger number of shares. But, unlike a stock dividend, the surplus account is not affected. Furthermore, the split-up does not increase the aggregate amount shown under the capital stock in the balance sheet. But the split-up does neces-

[3] New York Stock Exchange Company Manual, Sec. A 13.

sitate a reduction in the par value or stated value per share of the capital stock. If a company which has stock outstanding with a par value of, for example, $100, splits its stock 2 for 1, it will be necessary to reduce the par value per share from $100 to $50. A comparison of the relative effects on the balance sheet of a stock dividend and a stock split-up are shown below.

Before stock dividend or stock split-up

Capital stock (par value $100)	$1,000,000
Surplus	2,000,000
Total net worth	$3,000,000

After 100 per cent stock dividend

Capital stock (par value $100)	$2,000,000
Surplus	1,000,000
Total net worth	$3,000,000

After 2 for 1 split-up

Capital stock (par value $50)	$1,000,000
Surplus	2,000,000
Total net worth	$3,000,000

Since the surplus is not affected by the stock split-up, a company could conceivably have a stock split-up when no surplus existed, but it would be impossible to have a stock dividend under these circumstances. However, it is highly improbable that a split-up would occur if no surplus existed. A company may want to reduce the market price of its shares but still retain the advantage of showing the same surplus on the balance sheet. This could be accomplished with the split-up.

A stock dividend increases the number of shares on which future dividends will be paid, and at the same time lessens the surplus from which the dividend may be paid. If the same *rate* (expressed in percentage) of dividends is continued after a stock split-up, the future dividends would demand no more cash disbursements than before, and furthermore, the surplus from which such dividends may be paid is not reduced by virtue of the split-up. In other respects the stock dividend and stock split-up accomplish similar purposes. Since the par value or stated value of the stock must be reduced in event of a split-up, this will necessitate approval of the shareholders for a charter amendment (assuming in the case of no-par stock that the stated value is specified in the charter.[4]) But a stock dividend does not call for a charter amendment unless additional authorized shares are necessary for the payment of the dividend.

[4] If a $100 par stock is split 2 for 1, the issuing company usually sends the stockholders one new $50 par share for each old share held, and in addition sends him a $50 par "stamp" to be pasted over the $100 par designation on each old stock certificate.

As stated above in connection with stock dividends, if the split-up falls under the NYSE rules, the accounting for the split will be the same as for a stock dividend.

STOCK SPLITS AND TAXATION. Since stock split-ups do not result in any income to the shareholder, they are not taxable. For purposes of the capital gains tax upon the sale of the shares after a split-up, the original cost of the shares is apportioned to the new shares. For example, if $200 was paid for a share of stock and the company subsequently had a 2 for 1 split-up, the cost of the new shares would be considered to have been $100 for each share.

ADVANTAGES OF STOCK SPLITS. Following is a summary of the reasons for or advantages of a stock split-up. Since in most instances these same points apply to stock dividends, and were discussed in that connection, we will merely list the points.

1. The per-share earnings and dividends may be reduced.
2. The market price of the stock will be reduced.
3. The surplus of the company is not affected.

Shareholders may actually benefit from stock split-ups in the same way as stock dividends. That is, the split-up is interpreted as indicating that the management of the company is optimistic about the future, and although the market price of the stock may be depressed immediately after the split-up, it may tend to go back to its old price. If the dividends are continued at the same amount per share as before, the shareholder would get more in dividends. Stock splits were frequently used in the late 1920's and during the prosperous period following World War II.

REVERSE STOCK SPLIT-UPS. Many companies whose stock rose to relatively high prices in the prosperous 1920's, found that their stock fell to extremely low prices in the depression of the early 1930's. The split-ups, of course, resulted in the per share prices falling lower than otherwise would have been the case. In many instances the stock sold so low that it was in the "cat and dog" class. Many companies had acquired assets at inflated prices and the heavy depreciation charges were making a bad situation worse so far as earnings were concerned. To reduce the future depreciation charges it would be necessary to reduce the valuation of the assets. This would reduce the badly depleted surplus, or add to a deficit. To correct the situation many companies had a *"reverse stock split-up,"* that is, they would upon proper authorization call the old stock in and replace it with fewer shares. In this way the market price per share would be increased. But if two shares of $50 par, for example, would be replaced with one share of $100 par stock, the surplus of the company would not be affected. At the time the new shares were issued some companies did not change the par value per share. Many issued a fewer number of low par shares to take the place of no-par stock. This would add to the surplus and make possible the write off of some of the book valuations of the assets and thus permit lower depreciation charges.

Another factor accounting for the reverse stock split-ups was the stock transfer taxes. At the time of the depression many companies had a no-par stock outstanding. At that time both the federal and the New York State stock transfer tax treated each no-par share the same as $100 in par value. (This is no longer true of either transfer tax.) With the shares selling at extremely low prices, the transfer taxes from a percentage standpoint became a heavy burden on the person selling stock. A reverse stock split-up alleviated the situation. Also, as stated above, many corporations at the time of the split, changed their stock from no-par to a low par value. Ten shares of $10 par stock could be transferred for the same tax as one no-par share.

Questions

1. List the various kinds of dividends that may be paid by a corporation.
2. Distinguish between bond and scrip dividends. When would the payment of such dividends be justified?
3. Indicate how a 100 per cent stock dividend and a two-for-one stock split-up are similar and how they differ.
4. Indicate the various reasons why a corporation might pay a stock dividend.
5. If the object is to reduce the market price of the stock would you as a director vote for a stock dividend or a stock split-up? Give reasons for your answer.
6. Would you favor the payment of a regular stock dividend? Why or why not?
7. Indicate whether a stock dividend is taxable as income in the hands of the recipient stockholder. If the dividend is not taxable indicate how the capital gains or loss would be computed when the holder sold the stock.
8. In the long-run do you think that a stockholder has a good chance of gaining from the stock dividend or a stock split-up? Explain.
9. How do corporations handle the situation where in the case of a stock dividend the shareholder does not hold sufficient stock to obtain a whole share in dividends?
10. Would a nonparticipating preferred stock ever be entitled to share in a dividend paid in common stock even though it had received its preferential dividend for the year? Explain.

Problems

1. The following is a condensed balance sheet of the Smith Corp. as of Dec. 31, 19-1:

Assets		*Liabilities and Net Worth*	
Current Assets	$ 3,000,000	Liabilities	$ 1,000,000
Fixed Assets	8,000,000	Capital Stock	5,000,000
		Surplus	5,000,000
Total	$11,000,000	Total	$11,000,000

The par value of the stock is $50 per share, and it is selling in the market for its approximate book value. The company is contemplating an expansion program that will necessitate the raising of $2,000,000 through the sale of new stock to the public. Financial advisors have suggested that the new financing could be more successfully carried out if the offer price would be somewhat less than $100 per share. When the expansion program was considered by the directors, several of them favored a 100 per cent stock dividend before the sale of the new stock; others favored a 2-for-1 stock split-up. During the past 5 years the company has earned an average of 10 per cent on its net assets and has paid a regular dividend of $6 per share. (a) Could this proposed new stock issue be sold to the public without first offering it to the stockholders? Explain. (b) Why might it be desirable to offer the new stock to the public at less than $100 per share? (c) Why were the stock dividend and stock split-up proposed at the directors' meeting? (d) Explain why you as a director might favor the stock dividend instead of the split-up. (e) Explain why you as a director might favor the split-up instead of the stock dividend. (f) Would either the stock dividend or the split-up necessitate a charter amendment? Explain.

2. At the meeting of the directors of the Jones Corp. it was proposed that a scrip dividend be declared. Director Brown objected to this, saying that the paying of a scrip dividend was the same as declaring a cash dividend and not paying it; director Johnson objected on the ground that the declaring of such a dividend adversely affected the corporation in two ways: first, that it added to the liabilities, and second, that it also reduced the surplus of the company. (He stated that if a scrip dividend of $100,000 were declared, the liabilities would be increased $100,000, and the surplus reduced $100,000, thus affecting the company to the extent of $200,000.) (a) Under what conditions would you as a director vote for the declaration of a scrip dividend? (b) Criticize Mr. Brown's statement. (c) Criticize Mr. Johnson's statement.

Part VI

EXPANSION AND COMBINATION

Chapter 28

EXPANSION

Expansion the Rule. The United States is one of the newer countries among the nations of the world, but its commercial and industrial development has exceeded that of any other country. This has meant that in a relatively short span of time old businesses have had to expand, and new businesses to be formed. The population of the country has ever increased, and the standard of living of the people has been improving at the same time. It is sometimes said that a business must go forward to keep from going backward; it cannot stand still. Of course there are many business units, particularly in the services and merchandising, that tend to remain about the same size, but in the larger retail and wholesale organizations and the industrial world, expansion has been the rule.

The increase in the population and the improvement in the standard of living have called for the production and sale of more products. Companies that are already in the business in many instances have the production facilities, management, experience, and financial resources to expand their capacity to take care of the increased demand for goods far better than a new company that may come into the field. Expansion, therefore, of existing businesses in the United States has taken place at a rapid tempo.

With the increased demand for goods, the typical businessman wants to increase his production to take advantage of the additional sales possibilities. Larger-scale operations often result in decreased costs of one kind or another. In order to stay in business, competitors will find it necessary to expand their plant facilities and produce on a larger scale in order to reduce their costs to the point where they can sell their products in the competitive market. Furthermore, businessmen do not like to see their competitors enjoying the personal triumph that goes with bigness while they remain in obscurity.

Increasing costs both for labor and materials have also been a factor in expansion. These make it increasingly advantageous to obtain the economies of large-scale production. In many instances companies have expanded not only to increase the production and sales of their regular products, but in order to absorb the higher costs of operations, they have also taken on additional products and new lines of business. In times of prosperity and during war or defense periods, plant facilities are expanded rapidly to take care of the additional demand for goods. This results in a tremendous increase in plant capacity. When the extra demand has been satisfied and more or less normal times have returned, competition becomes increasingly keen.

Important Management Decision. The questions whether to expand, and the extent and direction of such expansion, are tremendously important for the management. Many businesses have passed out of existence or have been absorbed by their competitors because of failure to keep pace with other concerns. But perhaps an even greater number have failed because of unwarranted or unwise expansion. Studebaker, one of the leading wagon manufacturers, saw the handwriting on the wall, switched from wagons to automobiles and expanded plant facilities to take care of the increased demand for this new product. The expansion of General Motors, Ford and Chrysler in recent years, however, has resulted in a larger share of the market going to the Big Three. This has resulted in further combinations among the independents in an effort better to meet the competition. Sears, Roebuck and Co. realized that the automobile would bring better roads and the farmer would no longer have to rely on the mails for the purchase and delivery of goods. They accordingly started opening up retail stores in various communities throughout the country.

Expansion involves problems in all phases of business, such as purchasing, production, selling, management, and finance. The inability of any of these departments properly to handle their end of the expansion program may wreck the program and cause the business to fail. In the final analysis, the ability of management to cope with the problems arising from expansion are undoubtedly the most important. In fact, the failure of any of the various departments in an expansion program can be attributed to management.

Motives for Expansion. Following is a summary of typical motives for expansion.

1. *Desire for larger income.* In a capitalistic country such as ours the principal function of management is to make profits for

the owners. Managements that are able to pay the shareholders relatively large dividends need not have any fear of not being reelected or reappointed. Competition among executives for jobs, even in the higher echelons of management, is always present to a sufficient extent so that the executives must keep on their toes and give a good accounting of their stewardship.

In addition to keeping their jobs, many corporate executives have additional incentives to work toward the end of larger earnings for the company. In many companies the directors and officers have relatively large holdings of the company stock. Larger profits mean larger dividends. In some instances the executives hold options to purchase the company's stock at a set price. The higher the market price of the stock goes as a result of favorable earnings, the greater will be the value of the options and consequently the profit from the sale of the stock. Larger corporate profits often result in larger salaries to the officers. Also, in addition to salary, many officers get an annual bonus based on the company's earnings. Shareholders are also more willing to vote liberal pensions to officers if they are able to produce good earnings for the company.

Although several other reasons for expansion are listed below, it will be noted that in practically every instance the profit motive of all concerned is behind it.

2. *Competition.* It was stated above that competition in perhaps most lines of business is such that a particular company may have to expand to be able successfully to compete with other concerns in the same line of business. This obviously is another way of stating the profit motive.

3. *Lower costs.* The desire for lower costs could be interpreted to mean the same as larger profits. If expansion could bring about the production of a larger number of products at a decreasing cost per unit, that much more in profits may be earned. Or, the reduced costs may enable the company to reduce the selling price of the product, and this may result in additional profits from the increased volume of sales.

4. *Absorb competitors.* When competition gets too keen for a particular company it may attempt to buy out or combine with another company or companies. Life might be more pleasant and profits higher with less competition.

5. *Personal ambition* It is often difficult to determine just what makes some of the leading executives of our large corporations tick. Perhaps many of them do not know either. It is apparent that something besides money spurs them on. But just what? Business

leaders are human beings and like other people they want to be successful and command the esteem of their fellowmen. They get a kick out of being the head of a large business, and many of them like the feeling of having the final word in dealing with other people. The creative urge or a lust for power is present in many people. In some instances the businessman wants to become more important in order that he can climb socially and become a member of an élite business group or become acceptable to people in higher social strata.

It is not uncommon for top level executives to leave high-paying jobs in order to accept an important governmental post at a moderate salary. People sometimes will give up good business positions in order to engage in one of the professions, which pay much less for their services. Motives other than money may be the primary ones.

Perhaps we should not forget the executive's wife. In many cases she is the one who does the pushing. And her motive may be economic, but she may love riches mainly as a means to conspicuous consumption, because her highest ambition may be to belong to an élite and be envied by others.

ADVANTAGES OF LARGE-SCALE OPERATION. Some of the motives for expansion are similar to the advantages of expansion. But it is desirable to give a more detailed outline of the advantages. In this paragraph we have used the term "large-scale operation" instead of "expansion," but it is realized that expansion either of an existing unit or the combination of several units usually results in large-scale operation.

The following is a rather exhaustive list of advantages. And the case would be rare where all of these points applied to a particular situation. In many instances actually no advantages accrued from an expansion movement. It is believed that the points listed are self-explanatory, so no discussion will be given. The advantages can conveniently be classified under the following heads:

Purchasing:

1. Reduced costs due to large-scale buying
2. Possibility of obtaining more and cheaper credit
3. Buying from original sources and elimination of profit of middlemen
4. Control of sources of raw materials

Production:

1. Reduced costs due to large-scale production
2. Use of expensive labor-saving machinery

3. Economies of specialization
4. Use of technical experts
5. Stabilization of production
6. More effective utilization of by-products

Selling:

1. Lower selling costs
2. More effective use of salesmen
3. More effective use of advertising media
4. Possible elimination of middlemen
5. Saving in transportation costs
6. Possibility of foreign sales

Administration:

1. Affording better management
2. Better utilization of specialized experts
3. Management costs per unit of product may be less due to large sales volume
4. Better utilization of accounting and statistical methods and machines
5. Affording extensive research
6. Better methods and procedures which may result in better labor relations and smaller labor turnover

Finance:

1. Better credit
2. Raising funds through sale of securities to investment bankers and others
3. More effective control over credits and collections
4. More efficient use of money
5. Greater possibility of stabilized earnings and dividends
6. Ability to compete effectively with other companies
7. Ability to buy out competitors

Disadvantages of Large-Scale Operation. In spite of the economies of large-scale operation stated above, there are certain disadvantages of big business. In many cases the expansion proves disastrous and the company fails. Following are the possible disadvantages of large-scale operation. No attempt has been made to classify them.

1. The hoped-for economies of purchasing, producing, administration and financing may not be realized.
2. The management may not be able to cope with a large-scale business.
3. The personal element may be lost, or its effectiveness lessened.
4. Possibility of encountering public hostility due to large size.

5. Greater probability of regulation and intervention on the part of the government.
6. Possibility of more labor trouble.

Form of Expansion. In some instances a company, particularly a holding company, is large in size to begin with. But in most instances a company becomes large through expansion. There are various methods of expansion and there are several different ways to classify them. One is to classify the types of expansion into (1) internal, and (2) external.

When the original company enlarges its facilities without taking over or controlling other companies it is called internal expansion. This expansion may be financed from the retained earnings, or from the sale of securities.

If the expansion takes the form of buying the controlling stock interest in another company, or combining with it in some way, it is referred to as *external* expansion.

Internal expansion is not confined to the enlargement of the existing plant and facilities. Since the development of the atomic and hydrogen bombs, an increasing number of companies are giving serious attention to the decentralization of operations. If a company expands by the construction of plants scattered throughout the country, it is still classed as internal expansion.

Types of Expansion. Regardless of whether expansion is carried on internally or externally, the direction of the expansion may be one of several different types. The terms applied to these types are *horizontal, vertical* and *circular* expansion. When the expansion is effected through a combination of one type or another then these terms are applied to the type of combination.

Horizontal expansion. When the expansion takes the direction of acquiring more assets or other companies of a similar nature and in the same stage of production and distribution, in order to increase the production and sale of the original line of products, it is called *horizontal* expansion. If control of other companies is acquired in the process it is called "horizontal combination." The horizontal method is usually the way that most companies expand their operations. The motive behind it is, of course, the desire to make more profits. This may be brought about through decreasing costs resulting from large-scale operation. Advertising and selling may also be more effective with a larger volume of sales. In some instances the desire to control the market may be present. Greater stabilization of sales may result from a wider diversification of the sales territory. Typical examples of companies that have expanded their operations by this method are the following: American Tobacco Company, Chrysler Corporation, Colgate-Palmolive Company, National Dairy Products Corporation, and the Standard Oil companies.

Vertical expansion. When the expansion takes the direction of reaching back to the source of raw materials, or forward to the further processing of the products produced by the company, or sales of the finished product, it is called *vertical* expansion. When this is accomplished by the union with one or more companies it is called a "vertical combination." In some instances the term *integration* is used synonymously with "vertical expansion" or combination. Expanding in the direction of raw materials may be done to insure the source of the materials essential to the operation of the company, and in some instances the functions performed by the original supplier can be performed cheaper by the company itself. When plant facilities or companies are acquired to further process the company's products and distribute them to the public, better control of the market may be had. Whenever the expansion takes the direction of carrying on any additional step from the source of the raw materials to the ultimate sale of the products to consumers, economies may be effected which will lessen costs. If the functions of the various steps can be carried on at no greater cost than formerly, the profit of the middleman may be eliminated.

The United States Steel Corporation is a good example of a company that has expanded vertically. Through its subsidiaries it owns and operates mines, transportation systems, processing plants, manufacturing companies, and selling organizations. The General Motors Corporation has also expanded vertically through subsidiaries. The Ford Motor Company has done likewise, but the various processes are carried on by divisions of the company instead of subsidiaries. Richman Brothers Company, and the Singer Sewing Machine Company are examples of manufacturing companies that have acquired their own retail outlets.

As has been stated before, both horizontal and vertical expansion may be effected by extending the operations of the particular company or by combining with other companies. Also, either type of expansion may take place gradually over a period of time, or, particularly in the case of external expansion, it may all be accomplished at one time or several different times.

Circular expansion. When additional products or lines of products are taken on which are somewhat different from those being produced or sold, but involving the same channels of distribution, it is termed *circular* expansion. Similarly, when this is accomplished through a type of combination it is referred to as a "circular combination." The type of products involved in this type of expansion are said to be *complementary*, or supplementary, to the original line. The products are not directly competitive, but are sold through the same outlets. If a company selling ice takes on the sale of coal, or vice versa, it is referred to as circular expansion. Circular expansion resembles horizontal more than vertical expansion. It is undertaken primarily for the hoped-for economies in distribution.

A good example of circular expansion was the formation of the General Foods Corporation to effect a combination of companies selling food products. Included in the combination were the following companies: Calumet Baking Powder Company, Certo Corporation, Diamond Crystal Salt Company, Frosted Foods Corporation, Jell-O Company, Inc., La France Manufacturing Company, Log Cabin Products Company, Minute Tapioca Company, Inc., Richard Hellman, Inc., and Walter Baker and Company. In the hard goods industry the combination of the American Radiator Company and the Standard Sanitary Manufacturing Company to form the American Radiator & Standard Sanitary Corporation in order to offer a more complete line of building products, illustrates the circular combination. The General Motors Corporation can be classed not only as a vertical combination, but also a circular one, since it also involved the combination of companies producing other automobiles, at least some of which were sold through the same outlets.

PERIODS OF EXPANSION AND COMBINATION. Although many businesses are continuously expanding, there are several more or less pronounced periods when expansion has been accelerated. In many instances the expansion took the form of combinations, so these periods are commonly listed as periods of combination.

First period, 1885–1893. As would be expected, most expansion and combination movements begin after a recovery from a depression, and end with a panic, depression, or recession. The first period began about 1885, with the prosperous years following the depression, and ended abruptly with the panic of 1893. Following the Civil War the standardization of machines and equipment and the use of interchangeable parts made mass production more economical. Rapid strides made in the development of transportation and communications extended the markets for manufactured products. Businessmen were anxious to expand their facilities to take advantage of the greater production and sales possibilities.

The first combination to be active during this period was the Standard Oil trust which was first organized in 1879 (and revised in 1882). The personality behind this combination was John D. Rockefeller. The trust, as well as other forms of combinations, will be discussed in later chapters. Another early combination resulted in the formation of the American Sugar Refining Company in 1892.

Fearful of the effects that might result from these and other combinations, a number of the states enacted statutes to outlaw trusts. In 1890, Congress enacted the Sherman Anti-Trust Act. This legislation, however, did not immediately stop the formation of monopolies. The National Lead Company was formed later in 1890, and in 1892, the General Electric Company and the United States Rubber Company were formed. But the panic of 1893, and the ensuing depression rather than legislation, brought this first period of combination to an end.

In contrast to some of the later periods, the combinations formed during this first cycle were promoted by businessmen for the purpose of effecting economies in the production and distribution of goods and for the purpose of controlling the production and distribution of goods through monopolies.

Second period, 1897–1903. The depression which began in 1893 had completed its course by the autumn of 1896. The election of President McKinley, who was in sympathy with big business, over "Free Silver" Bryan, who was the apostle of the debtor class and the downtrodden, was interpreted as a sign of a revival in business prosperity. During the depression which had just ended, many businesses had experienced declining profits and increasing deficits, but a number of the large trusts had come through the period in relatively good shape. Exports were increasing faster than imports, farmers were prosperous, and earnings of business enterprises were increasing. Security prices began to rise and this enabled business to secure more money for expansion through the sale of additional securities. Although the Spanish-American War slowed up the expansion movement somewhat, the re-election of President McKinley in 1900 resulted in a renewal of the expansion and combination movement.

The following important companies (with dates of formation) were among the combinations formed during the second period: Otis Elevator Co. (1897), American Radiator Company (1899), Standard Sanitary Manufacturing Company (1899) (the latter two companies were consolidated in 1929, to form the American Radiator & Standard Sanitary Corporation), United States Steel Corporation (1901), Eastman Kodak Company (1901), and the American Can Company (1901).

During this second period of combinations the professional promoter and investment banker took the initiative in the formation of combinations. J. P. Morgan, who promoted the combination of a number of trusts into the United States Steel Corporation, was the outstanding promoter during this period. In some instances the bankers took over active management of the combinations. Investment bankers then, as now, made their money from the sale of securities. The organization of new companies or the formation of holding companies to acquire the securities of other companies called for the issuance, and in many instances the sale of additional securities. Thus the more securities they had to issue, the greater would be their profits. The "trust" form of organization had been used in the first period of combinations, but it later was outlawed by both legislation and court decisions. During the second period the holding company device, which had been specifically authorized by the statutes of New Jersey and some of the other states, was the favorite method of effecting the combinations.

The decline and end of this combination period in 1903 is accounted for by a number of reasons, chief among which were the following:

1. Stock market panic in 1901, which was precipitated by the corner in the stock of the Northern Pacific Railway
2. Decline in stock market activity during 1902
3. The profits made by the existing combinations disappointing
4. Unsuccessful promotion of the International Mercantile Marine Company in 1902, and the failure in the following year of the United States Shipbuilding Company, which had been in existence for only one year
5. Court decisions upholding the Sherman Anti-Trust Act
6. Because of the large number of existing combinations, fewer candidates for combination left
7. The panic of 1903.

Third period, 1919–1929. Holding companies, which had been so widely used in the combinations effected around the turn of the century, were thought to be immune from the Sherman Anti-Trust Act until the Supreme Court in 1904, held that the Northern Securities holding company constituted a monopoly and was in violation of the Sherman Anti-Trust Act.[1] This dampened the enthusiasm of promoters of combinations. Large public utility companies and systems started to be formed shortly after the turn of the century, and the interest of investment bankers and investors shifted from industrial combinations to public utilities. These factors in addition

[1] *Northern Securities Co., v. U. S.*, 193 U. S. 197 (1904).

to those stated above accounting for the cessation of combinations in 1903, are the reasons for the lull in the combination movement until World War I. Some important industries, such as automobiles, chemicals and chain stores, got started during these years, but there was no pronounced wave of industrial combinations. The General Motors Corporation was one of the important companies formed during this interval between the second and third combination periods.

With the ending of World War I in 1918, the third period of combinations got under way. This was the greatest combination era ever witnessed up to that time in the United States. Although in the previous periods combinations were limited to the railroad and industrial fields, this period embraced about every line of business, including amusement companies, financial institutions, and merchandising concerns. Following are the principal reasons accounting for this period of combinations.

1. The ending of World War I left many companies with excess capacity, and with falling prices businessmen looked about for ways of reducing costs and lessening competition. Taking over other companies or combining with them offered one solution. Although we encountered a business recession in 1921, the fall in prices accompanying it induced businessmen to give further thought to combination.
2. The higher wages paid to labor during and after the war enabled workmen to raise their standard of living. The increased demand for goods induced business expansion.
3. The purchase of government Liberty bonds during the war introduced thousands of people to securities buying. Due to higher wages, the rank and file of workmen had investable surpluses for the first time, and part of this was used to purchase corporate securities.
4. Higher corporate profits resulted in higher security prices. The public eagerly started buying stock on thin margins for speculative purposes.
5. The great demand for securities, particularly stocks, caused investment bankers to look about for a supply of still more securities to sell. The formation of combinations was an excuse for the issuance of more securities.
6. The courts became more lenient in the application of antitrust laws. Instead of saying that combinations in restraint of trade were illegal, they said that only those which were in "unreasonable" restraint were prohibited.
7. The national administration in Washington, D. C., was favorable toward the further development of large-scale business units.

Although trusts and the holding company device were the principal means of effecting combinations in the earlier periods, the third cycle made use of holding companies, mergers, consolidations, and every other form of combination. The investment banker, who was one of the types of promoters in the combination period which ended in 1903, occupied an even more important place in effecting combinations during this third period.

Many of the combinations which took place in the late 1920's were not effected for sound economic reasons. In many instances the only reason for their existence was the desire of investment bankers to make more money from the sale of securities. Businesses and business combinations became overextended. The same was true of credit. The stock market climbed to excessive heights not justified by the profits being earned or the dividends being paid. The stock market crash in the Autumn of 1929 brought to an end the greatest period of combinations we had ever witnessed.

Fourth period, 1940 to date. The excesses of the 1920's brought about one of the worst depressions that has ever occurred in this country. With declining sales and profits and depressed security prices, it is difficult to effect combinations. Furthermore, the administration in Washington changed, and became even hostile to big business.

After the recovery from the depression of the early 1930's and the recession of 1937, business began to enjoy prosperity again. Large governmental orders for defense materials offered a further impetus. With the preparedness program and the entry of the country into World War II in 1941, business began to hum again, and increased employment and wages resulted in a greater demand for goods. Again combinations were formed. Practically all of these have been in the industrial field. Among the principal motivating forces in the last combination period were (1) the relatively low common stock prices which prevailed at the beginning of the period, which facilitated their acquisition, (2) tax advantages derived from acquiring companies that had accumulated losses which could be used as an offset against profits of the acquiring company, and the tax free exchange of stock, (3) the increased market for goods necessitated additional plant facilities which in many instances could not be built because of wartime restrictions, (4) various other factors some of which were of importance in previous combination periods.

Since 1940, there have been two pronounced waves of combinations, the 1946-1947 period, and the one from 1954 to date. The most recent study of the combination movement was published by the Federal Trade Commission in 1955, which covered the period 1948–1954.[2] The study indicated that from the limited evidence available it appeared that "outside interests" played an important role in the combination movement. These included legal and economic consultants, banks, and investment bankers. The non-electrical machinery industry lead the field in numbers with 249 acquisitions of companies during the period. This was followed by the food products field which showed 243 instances of combinations. These two industries accounted for more than one-fourth of the total of 1,773 combinations in manufacturing and mining. The next five industries and the number of combinations, were as follows: chemical, 168; fabricated metals, 161; transportation equipment, 125; textiles and apparel, 117; and electrical machinery, 111. According to the study the five companies leading in the number of acquisitions and the specific number of other companies absorbed were as follows: Foremost Dairies, Inc., 48; Borden Co., 17; Olin-Mathieson Chemical Corp., 16; Food Machinery & Chemical Corp., 14; and H. K. Porter Co., 13.

Financial problems

Raising Capital for Expansion and Combination. It is usual in a book of this kind to list or discuss at this point the various ways in which new capital necessary for the expansion or combination may be raised. The various sources of capital and their relative advantages and disadvantages have been already discussed in various places throughout the book. The type and extent of the new financing depend, of course, upon the type of expansion or combination, and reference will also be made to financing when we later take up the various types of combinations. Now we shall discuss only some of the financial problems related to expansion and combination.

New Capital Needed. Internal expansion and some forms of external expansion require funds. The small company that cannot sell its securities through investment bankers will in most instances have to depend on retained earnings and depreciation "reserves" for expansion purposes. This means that expansion for this type of company will probably be relatively slow and therefore some time may elapse before the facilities can be greatly increased. Expansion based on the retained earnings, however, whether by a

[2] *Report on Corporate Mergers and Acquisitions,* Federal Trade Commission, U.S. Government Printing Office, Washington, D. C., May, 1955.

small or a large company, is a safe method to use. In recent years a number of companies have used relatively long-term bank loans and the sale-and-lease-back arrangement, to obtain funds for expansion.

The extent to which manufacturing and mining corporations in the United States depend upon depreciation and depletion reserves as a source of funds for expansion can be seen from Table 40 which is taken from an article by Professor Sergei P. Dobrovolsky in *The Journal of Finance*.[3] It will be noted that in most of the cycle periods the depreciation and depletion "reserves" furnished more funds for expansion purposes than did the "net retained earnings" (earnings left after taxes and dividends). It should also be noted that funds from these internal sources greatly exceeded the net amount received from security issues. From column (8) it can be seen that in six of the periods the funds from internal sources exceeded the amount expended for new plant and equipment. Both internal and external funds, of course, are used for expansion of plant and equipment and also for expansion of working capital.

Maintenance of Adequate Working Capital Position. The immediate reason that companies fail is the lack of cash. The real reasons for failure are all those factors which result in inadequate cash. The management of a company must keep close watch over the relationship between the current assets and the current liabilities. Although the current assets may increase, it may be accompanied by an even greater increase in the current liabilities; also, the current assets may be inflated with obsolete and overvalued inventory and uncollectible accounts.

It is a more or less normal process for a business to expand through an increase in sales. But the company may soon be hard pressed for cash and be unable to meet its accounts and notes payable, if the additional profits earned are invested in additional fixed assets. The mistake was the failure to realize that a permanent increase in the volume of sales necessitates additional working capital in the form of inventories to be tied up permanently in the business. Such companies may find their expansion programs to be disastrous, because they were financed out of needed working capital.

Avoidance of Excess Debt. The rate of interest that will have to be paid on bonds is usually less than the dividend rate that must be promised on the stock in order to raise capital for expansion purposes. Thus, in order to benefit from trading on the equity, a

3 "Capital Formation and Financing Trends in Manufacturing and Mining, 1900–1953," *The Journal of Finance*, May, 1955, p. 255.

company may prefer a bond to a stock issue. Unless the use to which the funds are put results in additional earnings, a company may find difficulty in meeting the bond interest, and the principal when it becomes due. Hoped-for profits from the expansion are not always realized. Furthermore, the increased maintenance and depreciation charges on the additional facilities add to the expense incurred by the company.

Another factor that may influence the company in deciding on a bond issue instead of a stock issue is the saving in income taxes. As we have shown before, bond interest is deductible before arriving at the net taxable income, but dividends on stock are a distribution of the profits after the taxes have been computed. Of course, a company should never issue bonds for tax saving purposes, unless the other circumstances are conducive for their sale.

Expansion takes place usually in a period of prosperity. In most instances interest rates are relatively high then, and thus the fixed charges may become a burden to the company.

Avoidance of Excess Stock Issues. A stock issue will not get a company into the trouble that may result from a bond issue. But an excessive amount of stock outstanding may produce a strain on the company to pay dividends. And the reduction of the dividend rate, or the passing of a dividend, adversely affects the company's credit and makes for poor stockholder relations.

Expansion usually occurs in a period of high prices. When the next depression hits, the maintenance and depreciation charges on the added facilities may prove to be burdensome, and the lower earnings make it difficult to maintain dividends.

Retention of Control. Large corporations that are controlled by the management through the proxy system need give little thought to the matter of control in deciding upon the means of financing expansion. But small- and medium-size companies often plan their financing so that there is little or no danger of losing control. When a company is controlled by an individual or a small group of persons, nonvoting preferred stock or bonds may be sold instead of common stock in order not to disrupt control. Even nonvoting preferred stock may not be issued because of the more or less necessity of including in the contract a provision giving it voting rights if dividends are in arrears for a specified number of quarterly periods.

In some instances the owners and managers of a company will hesitate to sell additional common stock to the public even if the amount sold is sufficiently small to enable the management to

TABLE 40

GROSS INTERNAL FINANCING, NEW SECURITY ISSUES, AND EXPENDITURES FOR NEW PLANT AND EQUIPMENT DURING CYCLES IN BUSINESS ACTIVITY, MINING AND MANUFACTURING CORPORATIONS, 1900–1953

*Business Cycle Period**	*Depreciation and Depletion (1)*	*Net Retained Profits (2)*	*Gross Internal Financing (1 + 2) (3)*	*Net Security Issues (4)*	*Gross Internal Financing Plus Net Security Issues (3 + 4) (5)*	*Expenditure for New Plant and Equipment (6)*	*Depreciation and Depletion*	*Gross Internal Financing*	*Gross Internal Financing Plus Net Security Issues*
							as a Percentage of New Plant and Equipment		
							(1 ÷ 6) (7)	*(3 ÷ 6) (8)*	*(5 ÷ 6) (9)*
	(average annual amounts† in million dollars)								
1900–1904	260	459	719	412	1,131	803	32.4	89.5	140.8
1904–1908	364	417	781	256	1,037	1,002	36.3	77.9	103.5
1908–1911	488	474	962	317	1,279	1,066	45.8	90.2	120.0
1911–1914	616	485	1,101	271	1,372	1,187	51.9	92.8	115.6
1914–1919	1,170	1,968	3,138	488	3,626	2,041	57.3	153.7	177.7
1919–1921	1,612	618	2,230	1,242	3,472	2,706	59.6	82.4	128.3
1921–1924	1,907	374	2,281	668	2,949	2,097	90.9	108.8	140.6
1924–1927	2,161	863	3,024	873	3,897	2,557	84.5	118.3	152.4
1927–1932	2,306	–988	1,318	587	1,906	2,285	100.9	57.7	83.4
1932–1938	1,889	–683	1,206	–75	1,131	1,763	107.1	68.4	64.2
1938–1946	2,763	2,002	4,765	206	4,971	3,171	87.1	150.3	156.8
1946–1949	4,146	5,687	9,833	1,935	11,767	8,382	49.5	117.3	140.4
1949–1953‡	6,424	4,645	11,069	2,128	13,197	10,308	62.3	107.4	128.0

* Based on National Bureau of Economic Research business cycle chronology.
† In computing averages, values for terminal years are weighted by one-half.
‡ Incomplete.

SOURCE:

Column 1. Based on data in Raymond W. Goldsmith's forthcoming *A Study of Saving in the United States* (Princeton University Press), Vol. I; *Statistics of Income*, Part 2 (Bureau of Internal Revenue); and *Survey of Current Business*, September, 1954, Dept. of Commerce, p. 5, Table 3.

Columns 2 and 4. S. Dobrovolsky, "Capital Formation and Financing Trends in Manufacturing and Mining, 1900–1953," *The Journal of Finance*, May, 1955, p. 258, Table 3.

Column 6. Data for all establishments for 1919–1929 from George Terborgh, "Estimated Expenditures for New Durable Goods, 1919–1938," *Federal Reserve Bulletin*, September, 1939, p. 732, Table 2; for 1930–1951 from *The Midyear Economic Report of the President, July, 1952*, p. 157, Table B-18 (a continuation of Terborgh's series); and for 1951 to 1953 from the *Survey of Current Business*, September, 1954, p. 4, Table 2, adjusted to an all-corporation level. The 1919–1953 series was extrapolated backward to 1900 using a weighted composite index based on the domestic consumption of construction materials and industrial machinery and equipment in William Howard Shaw, *Value of Commodity Output since 1869* (National Bureau of Economic Research, 1947), pp. 64–65 and 52–53, respectively, Table I-1.

retain control. The reason is that they do not want to be bothered with minority shareholders. The sale of additional common stock through the privileged subscription method, of course, would not alter control, but naturally it would necessitate additional investment on the part of the present owners.

It is obvious that the issuance of bonds for the purpose of retaining control would be an unwise act if in the circumstances the company should not be able to stand the fixed charges and additional debt.

TAX CONSIDERATIONS. It was pointed out above that the issuance of bonds rather than stock would reduce the income taxes that a company would have to pay. In some instances a sale or purchase of a business is prompted by tax considerations. A company may buy out another one at a relatively small price in order to write off against its profits the losses that have been incurred by the company which is purchased. Corporations can write off losses against the profits of the past three years (carryback), or against the profits of the next five years (carryover).

Opportunities also sometimes exist where owners of a small corporation may be desirous of selling or exchanging their shares for the purpose of lessening the estate taxes that would be levied against their estate upon their death. When shares of a company are not listed and have no market, upon death of the owner the tax appraisers may arrive at a fair value by capitalizing the past earnings or valuing the stock at the book figures. Either of these may result in a relatively high valuation for tax purposes. Anticipating this, the owners may seek opportunities of exchanging their shares for those of a large corporation whose shares are listed and have frequent sales that indicate their market value. Or, the owners of the small business may want to sell their shares for cash and pay the relatively smaller capital gains. In either case, the families of the owners would be in a better position to pay or to get the cash necessary to pay the estate taxes upon the death of the owners.

Questions

1. List the various motives that account for expansion of American business concerns. Which of these do you believe is the most important?
2. List the financial advantages of a large-scale operation.
3. What are the differences between internal and external expansion?
4. Indicate the difference between horizontal, vertical, and circular expansion or combination.

5. Under which of the three types of expansion or combination stated in Question 4 would you put the following companies: General Motors Corporation? United States Steel Corporation? General Foods Corporation?

6. Indicate the approximate years of the four periods of expansion and combination in the United States mentioned in the book.

7. Generally speaking, what type of companies can rely on retained earnings for expansion and which ones cannot do so?

8. If a company whose stock is widely held is in constant need of funds for expansion purposes, should it pay out a relatively large percentage of its earnings in dividends or retain a relatively large percentage? Explain.

9. Generally speaking, are there any limits to the size which a company may attain and still operate efficiently?

10. Indicate several of the financial problems that arise in connection with an expansion program.

Problems

1. The following information is available about the operations of the Standardized Part Co. for the year 19-1. The company sold 10,000,000 of its units for $1 each, on which it made a net profit before income taxes of 5 per cent on sales. Half of the sales price of the product was made up of materials cost. The unit labor cost was equal to 40 per cent of the materials cost, and the overhead costs were equal to 50 per cent of the labor costs. Administrative expenses were $500,000, and advertising and selling expenses made up the balance of the expenses. (Disregard income taxes in this problem.)

The sales manager of the company estimated that the sales volume (units) could be doubled if the selling price were reduced to $0.90 per unit. The president called in the department heads and had them prepare a budget for their respective departments based on this production schedule. It was found that the expenses would be as follows: unit materials cost reduced 10 per cent because of larger-scale buying; unit labor cost unchanged; overhead costs increased 50 per cent; administrative expenses increased 10 per cent; and advertising and selling expenses increased 50 per cent. In addition to these expenses, the company would have to pay annual interest of $120,000 on the money borrowed to acquire the additional equipment necessary to carry on this scale of operations. (Depreciation on the new equipment was considered in the increased overhead charges.)

The president then asked the sales manager to make an estimate of the price at which 30,000,000 units could be disposed of annually. This was reported back at $0.80 per unit. On this production schedule the budget committee gave the following estimate of costs: materials unit cost, $0.43; labor, $6,000,000; overhead, $3,000,000; administrative expenses, $600,000; advertising and selling expenses, $2,000,000; and interest expenses, $300,000. (a) Draw up an income statement for each of the three scales of operations. (b) As president of the company how many units would you order the production department to manufacture? (c) What would the total unit cost of the product be in each case? (d) If the product could be sold at $1 and the total unit cost was $0.96, how many units would have to be sold in order to make the same total net profit as was made in 19-1? (e) Should the company push production to the point where the unit cost of the product is least? Explain.

2. Classify the following as to type of combination: (a) A company making starting, lighting, and ignition equipment is merged into an automobile manufacturing company. (b) A bank stock holding company acquires all the stock, except qualifying directors' shares, of three banks. (c) A company making airplane motors buys out a company that makes airplane propellers. (d) A company that manufactures fighting planes buys up all the stock of a concern that makes small pleasure airplanes. (e) A coffee company, chocolate company, and a breakfast food company combine.

Chapter 29

COMBINATIONS

Combinations and the law

COMMON LAW. According to the early common law, all contracts in restraint of trade were void regardless of whether the restraint was *reasonable* or *unreasonable*. Thus, if a party to such an agreement broke it and the other parties brought action in damages against him, the courts would not lend themselves to the enforcement of something which they considered to be illegal, and would not, therefore, award damages. The courts and state and federal officials had no right to take the initiative and break up any such agreements. So long as the parties to the contract abided by its terms, the agreement or combination in restraint of trade continued. This constituted the inherent weakness of the common law in regard to agreements or combinations in restraint of trade.

COMBINATION OF CORPORATIONS IN RESTRAINT OF TRADE. Gentlemen's agreements and pools, which will be discussed later in the chapter, were weak forms of combinations and did not always prove effective, since the courts would do nothing to enforce the agreement in event one or more of the parties broke the contract. This weakness led to the trust form of combination. But the law found a way of getting at the trusts. In 1888, the attorney general of New York brought action against the North Sugar Refining Company to forfeit its charter on the grounds that its shareholders had participated in the formation of a trust. The court held that the act of the shareholders in turning over their shares to a board of trustees was really the act of the corporation itself. Such action, the court reasoned, was not in furtherance of the purposes for which the corporation had been formed, and was therefore, beyond the charter powers; and accordingly the charter could be forfeited by the state.[1] The court expressed a dictum that monopolies were in

[1] *People v. The North Sugar Refining Co.*, 121 N. Y. 582, p. 619 (1890).

restraint of trade, but the case was not decided on that question.

But the Supreme Court of Ohio went into the monopoly aspect further in the famous Standard Oil Case, which was decided in 1892.[2] The court agreed with the New York decision that the action of the shareholders was in fact the action of the corporation, and that the turning over of the shares to the trustees was wrong since it was beyond the purposes for which the company had been formed. But the Ohio court said further that such action created a monopoly and thus was contrary to public policy, and therefore void.

State Legislation. The opposition of the people to agreements in restraint of trade finally found expression through the enactment by various states of statutes or constitutional provisions prohibiting such agreements. Kansas, in March, 1889, was the first state to pass such legislation. Between then and July 2, 1890, when the Sherman Anti-Trust Act was passed by Congress, nineteen of the states had enacted statutes or adopted constitutional amendments opposing agreements in restraint of trade. By 1893, about half of the states and territories had taken similar action, and by 1900, a total of 31 states and territories had enacted such statutes or constitutional amendments or both.

The state legislation did not prove effective in breaking up agreements or combinations in restraint of trade. Some of the states did little to enforce the statutes. If one state prohibited a company from carrying on its business in that state, the concern would go to a more liberal state, or form a subsidiary in the particular state to carry on its business. Furthermore, the monopolies were usually effected by large corporations which carried on their business in many states, and across many state lines. In these cases there was little that a particular state could do to break up the combination.

The Sherman Anti-Trust Act of 1890. Because of the weakness of the common law and the ineffectiveness of the state legislation against agreements and combinations in restraint of trade, pressure was brought for Congress to enact legislation against agreements in restraint of trade and against monopolies. As stated above, many of the combinations carried on interstate commerce throughout the country, and the federal government through its Constitution had the power to regulate interstate commerce. After several unsuccessful attempts to get Congress to act, the Sherman Anti-Trust Act was passed by Congress and signed by President Harrison on July 2, 1890. But little was done by the government

[2] *State v. Standard Oil Co.*, 49 Ohio St. 137 (1892).

to enforce the Sherman Anti-Trust Act during the years immediately following its enactment.

LEADING CASES UNDER THE ACT. Among the first cases decided under the Sherman Act to reach the United States Supreme Court, and the first important one involving industrial combinations, was that of *United States v. E. C. Knight Company,*[3] which was decided in 1895. The Supreme Court, however, held that the combination was not in violation of the Sherman Act. The court admitted that the company had a monopoly in the manufacture of sugar, but it said that the Sherman Act referred to monopolies not in manufacturing, but rather to monopolies in *trade or commerce.*

The next important case to be decided by the United States Supreme Court under the Sherman Act was that of *United States v. Trans-Missouri Freight Association,*[4] which was decided in 1897. This case was of considerable importance at the time, because the court said that the Sherman Act applied to every contract in restraint of trade, and that it therefore was applicable to railroads, and also that the Act specified that all contracts in restraint of trade, whether they were reasonable or unreasonable, came under the prohibition of the Act.

The case of *Northern Securities Company v. United States,*[5] which was decided by the United States Supreme Court in 1904, was the first case tried under the Sherman Act which involved a holding company. Up until that time, it had been thought that the holding company form of combination (which will be discussed in Chapter 31) was out of the reach of the Act. This was true particularly after the Knight case decision, mentioned above. But the Supreme Court ruled that the Sherman Act did cover holding companies, and that the Northern Securities Company, which was a railroad holding company, was in violation of the Act, and that it had to be dissolved.

When the Standard Oil Trust was broken up, the trust returned the stock of the various companies to the holders of the trust certificates. Since the same group of people that formerly owned the trust certificates now again became the owners of the shares of the various companies, a type of community of interest resulted. In order to make a more effective form of combination, the principal shareholders of the companies formed the Standard Oil Company of New Jersey in 1899, and the shares of this company were

[3] 156 U. S. 1 (1895).
[4] 166 U. S. 290 (1897).
[5] 193 U. S. 197 (1904).

exchanged to the shareholders of the various companies for their shares.

Some years later the government brought suit against the New Jersey holding company contending that the Sherman Act had been violated because the combination had engaged in such practices as receiving rebates and discriminatory rates from the railroads, monopolizing control of pipe lines, cutting prices at local points in order to suppress competition, and other unfair competitive practices. The Supreme Court of the United States in a unanimous decision[6] handed down in 1911, held that the company had violated the Sherman Act, and ordered its dissolution. The importance of the Standard Oil case is due in part to the fact that the court set up the "rule of reason." This in effect modified the Sherman Act by judicial decree. The Act, as originally passed by Congress, stated that "every" contract or combination or conspiracy was illegal. The Court, in the Standard Oil case, interpreted the Act to state that every "unreasonable" contract or combination or conspiracy was illegal. This case marked a turning point in the enforcement of the Sherman Act as all later cases under the Act had to take into account the reasonableness of the combination. In spite of the "rule of reason" interpretation in this case, the Standard Oil Company of New Jersey was deemed an unreasonable combination and ordered dissolved. The Court did not clearly state whether it was the size of the combination alone or the abuse of the power accompanying that size which was unreasonable. This very important point was left to later decisions.

In 1911, the government brought action against the United States Steel Corporation on the grounds that it was violating the Sherman Act. Before the case was decided, World War I had begun, and since it was thought that if the company was ordered dissolved, the refinancing which would probably follow would interfere with the financing of the war, at the request of the government, the case was postponed. After the war ended, the action was resumed. The suit had originally been brought against the company because of its large size. But the court said that size alone did not mean that the company had violated the antitrust laws, and that so long as the company did not restrain trade or effect a monopoly, its activities were legal.[7]

A somewhat new philosophy was injected by the court in its decision since it indicated that the public interest would best be

[6] *Standard Oil Company of New Jersey v. United States,* 221 U. S. 1 (1911).
[7] *United States v. United States Steel Corporation,* 251 U. S. 417 (1920).

served by letting the company continue to exist. This virtually changed the court's "rule of reason," into a "rule of business expediency." The Court specifically stated that "the mere size of a corporation, or the existence of unexerted power unlawfully to restrain competition, does not of itself make such a corporation a violator of the Sherman Anti-Trust Act."[8] This decision that size alone is not the criterion for prosecution under the Sherman Act has been the subject of much controvery in recent years.

The Clayton Act of 1914. It had been felt for some time that the Sherman Act should be amended in order to clear up some uncertainties and to declare illegal certain practices which were not specifically mentioned in the Sherman Act. It was felt that if certain practices which led to monopoly were outlawed, the need for dealing with the monopolies after they were an accomplished fact would be reduced since earlier experience had shown the ineffectiveness of dissolving an accomplished monopoly or combination. In its review of the Sherman Act and its interpretation before preparing new antitrust legislation, the Congress had a chance to refute the "rule of reason" interpretation of the Supreme Court. By not doing so, Congress implicitly accepted the idea that only unreasonable contracts or combinations should be illegal. Instead of dealing with the idea of unreasonableness, Congress considered only certain practices which in themselves were considered unreasonable restraints of trade and which tended to reduce competition or lead to monopoly.

The agitation for strengthening the Sherman Act finally resulted in the enactment, in 1914, of the Clayton Act, and the Federal Trade Commission Act. The latter created the Federal Trade Commission to aid in the prevention and elimination of practices which are in restraint of trade. The Clayton Act was much longer than the Sherman Act, and contained more detailed provisions. Space will not permit a statement of all the various provisions of the Act, but the principal ones follow:

1. *Price discrimination.* Price discrimination was prohibited where its effect was substantially to lessen competition or where it tended to create a monopoly in any line of commerce. However, it was specifically provided in the Act that different prices could be charged where there were differences in grade, quality, or quantity of the commodity sold, or where there were differences in selling or transportation costs.

[8] *Ibid.*, p. 451.

2. *Tying contracts.* A "tying contract" refers to the situation where a company sells or leases its products only on condition that the purchaser agree not to buy or lease any of the products handled by a competitor. The Clayton Act specifically provides that such contracts are illegal where they substantially lessen competition or tend to create a monopoly in any line of commerce.

3. *Labor.* The government had previously prosecuted several labor organizations under the Sherman Act, although there had been considerable doubt whether labor was to be treated the same as other goods or commodities. The Clayton Act specifically states that the labor of a human being is not a commodity or article of commerce, and that nothing in the antitrust laws shall be construed as forbidding or making illegal nonprofit labor organizations.

4. *Intercorporate shareholding and holding companies.* Corporations engaged in commerce were forbidden to acquire the shares of another corporation engaged in commerce where the effect of such stock acquisition would substantially lessen competition between the companies, or restrain the commerce in any community, or tend to create a monopoly in any line of commerce. The act also specifically prohibited a corporation from acquiring the shares of two or more corporations if any of these situations resulted. It was specifically stated, however, that corporations could acquire shares of other companies as investments, and that they could organize and hold the shares of subsidiary corporations so long as competition was not lessened or a monopoly created.

5. *Interlocking directorates.* The Act under certain conditions prohibited a person from being a director in more than one bank or trust company. Concerning industrial corporations, the Act provided that no person could be a director in two or more corporations engaged in commerce, if any one of the corporations had capital, surplus, and undivided profits of more than $1,000,000, if the companies had been in competition, and if the elimination of competition by agreement between them would violate the antitrust laws.

The 1950 Legislation. Section 7 of the Clayton Act was so written that only monopoly combinations of corporations which were accomplished through the acquisition of stock in competing companies were illegal. For some time, the Federal Trade Commission had been complaining to Congress that this section had limited application. Instead of acquiring the stock of competing companies, businesses merely bought the assets of their competitors to accomplish the same objective and thus avoid prosecution under the Clayton Act. After considerable review of the Clayton Act and its interpretation, Congress passed an amendment in 1950 with the purpose of preventing corporations from acquiring another corporation by means of the acquisition of its assets, where under the present law it is prohibited from acquiring the stock of said corporation.[9]

Antitrust Exemptions. From time to time, Congress has seen fit to enact legislation which exempts certain types of agreements or combinations from the Sherman and Clayton Acts. The Webb-Pomerene Act, which was adopted in 1918, exempted from the Sherman Act those associations which are formed for the purpose of export trade, provided they do not restrain trade within the United States. The Capper-Volstead Act, passed in 1923, had as a purpose the exemption of certain actions of farm cooperative organizations from the antitrust acts. The Emergency Transportation Act of 1933 exempted certain types of railroad agreements from the antitrust laws. The National Industrial Recovery Act of 1933, which has since been declared unconstitutional by the Supreme Court, did the same for industrial corporations. The Agricultural Adjustment Act of 1933 exempted from the antitrust laws certain agreements providing for the marketing of agricultural products. Labor was first mentioned for exemption in the Clayton Act, but it was not until the Norris-LaGuardia Act of 1932, and the Wagner Act of 1935, that labor became completely exempt from Federal antitrust legislation.

Present Status of Combinations and the Law. While some business practices and certain mergers and combinations are clearly illegal under the present law and its interpretation, there is a wide area of action in which grave doubt exists concerning the legality or illegality. It is doubtful whether the law can ever be so clearly interpreted as to relieve all question regarding each individual action. A major problem today is that of size and monopoly. Is large size alone sufficient evidence of restraint of trade to be a violation of antitrust law? The Court has not given a clear-cut decision on this matter. In recent years, the government has brought action against certain large companies on the assumption that bigness was an indication of antitrust laws being violated. Some companies, particularly the Great Atlantic & Pacific Tea Company of America, successfully defended their position before the public through various advertising media. Some companies have successfully defended size in the courts while others have been unsuccessful.

[9] Public Law No. 899, Sec. 7, 81st Cong., 2d sess. (Dec. 29, 1950).

Considering the nature of the various antitrust laws and the court decisions that have been rendered under them, it is difficult to define the present attitude of the government and the courts toward large companies and combinations. Businessmen are also uncertain about how far they can go without the danger of their action being later declared illegal. The enforcement of the antitrust legislation has varied substantially with changes in the executive branch of the government. The entire problem of internal growth of corporations is very much unsettled by law. Corporations can grow internally as well as by absorbing competitors. Every large corporation today must keep in mind the effects of its actions on the competitive situation in its field if it wants to steer clear of antitrust prosecution. Even with constant guidance of good legal advice, corporations may perform some act which the government might consider a violation of antitrust legislation.

Forms of combinations

Various Forms of Combinations. Following is a list of the various forms of combinations which will be discussed in this and the succeeding chapters.

1. Gentlemen's agreements
2. Pools
3. Trusts
4. Communities of interest
5. Interlocking directorates
6. Trade associations
7. Leases
8. Purchase of assets
9. Mergers
10. Consolidations
11. Holding companies

Gentlemen's Agreements. The first form of arrangement which resulted in a type of combination was the *gentlemen's agreement.* This constituted the principal type of combination used in the period shortly after the Civil War and up until about 1875. Gentlemen's agreements were merely an oral agreement between the executives of two or more companies for the purpose of maintaining prices, restricting output, dividing the market, or about some other common policy. Being merely oral agreements, it is obvious that they were a weak, decentralized form of combination.

Agreements between companies are not in themselves necessarily illegal, but since these agreements concerned price maintenance, restriction of production, and limiting the market, they were illegal. But at the time they were used, there was not sufficient legislation for the governmental authorities or the courts to break them up, especially since they were more or less secret in nature. Reliance had to be placed on the "honor" of the individuals to carry out their agreements. The contracts carried no penalties for their violation. Even if they had, the contracts being illegal, no court would have enforced the penalties, and no legal action could be taken to enforce the contracts.

Gentlemen's agreements were used among railroads and in the industrial field, particularly in the oil and steel industries by the Standard Oil Companies and the United States Steel Corporation. The classical example of gentlemen's agreements were the famous "Gary dinners," although these took place between 1907 and 1911. The steel industry had overcapacity and when a depression came the various companies were inclined to cut prices in order to secure as much of the market as possible. Judge Elbert H. Gary, Chairman of the United States Steel Corporation, invited the leading executives of the steel companies to a dinner first in 1907, at which time he indicated what percentage of capacity of the entire steel industry could be sold at what price. He announced that his company would produce at only a stated percentage of capacity, and indicated the price it would charge for steel. The officials of the other companies were then called upon to state what policies their companies would follow. Almost invariably they would follow the lead set by Judge Gary.

Another example of gentlemen's agreements was the "Pittsburgh-plus" plan of setting the price of steel. In order to lessen competition, various steel companies throughout the country would agree to sell their steel at the Pittsburgh price plus the freight charges from Pittsburgh to the point of destination. This obviously would benefit the companies whose plants were in the Pittsburgh region.

Gentlemen's agreements were a weak form of combination, as they were illegal and could not be enforced. These factors plus the fact that later other more permanent and effective forms of combinations were devised, accounted for the relative decline in the importance of gentlemen's agreements.

Pools. Pools were similar to gentlemen's agreements and were formed for the same purposes, but they were somewhat more formal in nature and were usually reduced to writing. Penalties were usually provided for the violation of the agreement. But since the arrangements were illegal, the courts would not enforce the penalties or provide damages for the violation of the agreement. Usually, a central agency was set up for the administration of the pool. Combinations effected through the use of pools were prominent during the 1880's and 1890's.

Pools covered a wider ranger of activities than gentlemen's agreements. Following is a brief description of the different types of pools.

1. *Price and profit pools.* Some of the price pools were similar to gentlemen's agreements about prices. The famous Addyston pipe pool was formed by the Addyston Pipe and Steel Company and five other companies which manufactured pipe. Inquiries for bids from the territory covered by the pool received by the various companies were referred to a board set up by the companies. This board fixed the price that should be charged. The various companies would then compete against each other for the order and the one paying the largest bonus to the pool was awarded the order. The other companies were instructed to bid at higher prices than that set by the board in order that they would not get the contract. The bonus paid by the company which got the contract was divided up among the various companies according to the tonnage of their plants. The agreement listed a number of "reserved" cities from which only one particular specified company was allowed to bid on contracts. The Addyston pipe pool was broken up by a Supreme Court decision in 1899.[10]

2. *Output or traffic pools.* This type of pool was formed for the purpose of limiting the production of certain types of products and for the apportioning of the total output to the various companies which were members of the pool. The agreement would provide for fines for companies that exceeded their assigned quotas. Many of these pools also fixed the prices that could be charged for the products. Output pools were formed by the following industries in the years indicated: whiskey (1881), meat products (1885), gunpowder (1886), steel rails (1887), cotton bagging (1888), wire nails (1895), structural steel (1885), and wallpaper (1898).

Traffic pools among the railroads were similar in nature. Several railroads would agree to divide the traffic between two cities in an agreed ratio, and the roads would follow this procedure regardless of the road specified by the shipper.

3. *Market or territorial pools.* This type of pool divided the market among the members in some manner. The Addyston pipe

[10] *Addyston Pipe and Steel Company v. United States,* 175 U. S. 211 (1899).

pool mentioned above, was both a price and a market pool. Usually the market pools also fixed prices and limited production. In 1902, the American Tobacco Company entered into a pool arrangement with the Imperial Tobacco Company of England to divide the world market for tobacco products.

4. *Joint sales agency pools.* In this type the members agreed to turn over their entire output to the pool, which actually did the selling. Any independent sales by the member companies were subject to heavy fines. The Michigan Salt Association, which was formed in 1876, is one of the early examples. It handled the sale of most of the salt produced in Michigan. This pool was actually incorporated and was originally formed to operate for five years. It was renewed, however, several times and operated successfully for more than 25 years.

A more modern illustration of the sales agency pool is Appalachian Coals, Incorporated, which was formed in 1932, to serve as the exclusive selling agent of 134 coal-mining companies operating in eastern Kentucky, eastern Tennessee, southwestern Virginia, and southern West Virginia. Pools of this kind also usually have control over prices, terms of sale, and quality of the products produced and sold.

5. *Patent pools.* This kind of pool provides for the interchange of patents among the member companies. The company owning the patent may give licenses to the other companies for its use. In some instances the patent rights are assigned to a trustee, or a separate corporation, which licenses their use to the various companies. One example of this kind of pool was the so-called "bathtub trust," which was formed in 1910, and which controlled more than 80 per cent of the enamel ironware in the United States.

In 1919, the General Electric Company organized the Radio Corporation of America, and turned over to this company certain radio patents which it owned. Radio Corporation then acquired the assets and patents of the Marconi Telegraph Company of America, and entered into licensing agreements with a number of companies, including the American Telephone and Telegraph Company, the Western Electric Company, and Westinghouse Electric and Manufacturing Company. Radio Corporation was also made the sole distributor for vacuum tubes which were manufactured by these companies. Independent radio manufacturers complained that the charges made by Radio Corporation for the licensing of patents were excessive, and that the patent pool restricted competition in the industry. As a result of a number of court cases the companies in the pool agreed not to continue the exclusive rights to each other's patents. The agreements of the General Electric Company and the Westinghouse Electric and Manufacturing Company restricting their own right to make radio equipment were declared void, and these companies were compelled to dispose of their stock in Radio Corporation, and were prohibited from having any interlocking directorates with it.

6. *Export pools.* Although pools which restrict competition in the United States are illegal, special treatment is given those which may be formed for the purpose of carrying on foreign trade. Selling in foreign countries is expensive, and it can usually be done only by the larger companies which have adequate financial backing. Furthermore, competition with foreign companies for these markets is difficult because of the presence there of cartels, which are really a form of pool, which control production, fix prices, and divide the markets among the foreign companies.

The Webb-Pomerene Act specifically exempts from the Sherman and Clayton antitrust acts, pools formed for the sole purpose of engaging in the export trade. If any such pools, however, attempted to set prices or otherwise to restrict competition among the companies in the United States, they would be illegal. Most of the export pools which have been formed are of the price, or output, type, although some have been formed as sales agencies.

Trusts. The term "trust" is applied to a number of different situations. As pointed out when we were discussing the Massachusetts trust, it is applied to that form of organization, to trust companies, to voting trusts, and other forms of trust arrangements. It will be recalled that in the case of the voting trust, the stock of only *one* corporation is transferred to voting trustees. The word "trust" is also applied by many to any form of combination which is in restraint of trade. It is because the trust arrangement was one of the earliest and most effective forms of combination in restraint of trade, that the term is now often applied to any form of illegal combination. It is this old illegal form of trust that we are interested in at this point.

The *trust* was formed by the shareholders of two or more corporations transferring their shares, or the controlling shares, to a group of trustees. The trustees in turn gave the shareholders trust certificates to represent their shares. These trust certificates were transferable in the same manner as the stock. The trustees held the controlling stock interests in the various corporations and thus could elect the same people or part of the same people, to the boards of directors of these companies. Or if the same individuals were not elected to the boards, the trustees could still control the companies through the election of directors who would follow their dictates.

The gentlemen's agreements and pools were a loose form of combination and often lacked centralized control. They were more or less temporary in nature and the members could violate their agreement or withdraw at any time without a penalty for doing so. The trust, on the other hand, was fairly permanent and it gave absolute control of the various companies to the trustees. One of the earliest and largest trusts, and the model followed by a number of subsequent trusts was the Standard Oil Trust; so we will give a brief description of it.

The Standard Oil Trust was originally formed in 1879, but was revised in 1882. The following applies to the latter agreement. The trust was composed of the Standard Oil Company of Ohio and 39 other companies, some of which were corporations and some limited partnerships, and 46 individuals. Trust certificates with a par value of $100 were exchanged to the shareholders of the various corporations for their shares. Standard Oil companies were then organized in New York, Pennsylvania, and New Jersey, and the shares of these companies and the Standard Oil Company of Ohio were exchanged to the owners of the limited partnerships and the individuals for their properties. The shares received by these individuals were then transferred to the trustees for the trust certificates.

There were nine trustees and their terms were staggered so that after the trust got under way, three trustees would be elected each year for three-year terms. It was provided in the trust agreement that the trust would continue in operation until 21 years after the death of the last survivor of the original nine trustees. (The life of trusts, except nonprofit types, is limited in life both by the common law and statutes.) The agreement provided, however, that the trust could be dissolved after 1 year by the vote of 90 per cent of the trust certificates, or after 10 years by the vote of two-thirds of the certificates. The holders of the trust certificates could vote only on the matter of dissolution and the election of trustees. All voting rights on the stock of the various corporations held by the trustees were exercised by the trustees. Dividends paid on the corporate shares went to the trustees who in turn used the money, or at least part of it, for dividends on the trust certificates.

During the 10-year life of the Standard Oil Trust it acquired the shares of 78 additional companies, and it controlled about 90 per cent of the oil-refining capacity and pipe lines in the United States. This trust was broken up by a Supreme Court of Ohio case, decided in 1892.[11]

In addition to the Standard Oil Trust, the following important trusts, with dates of their formation, were formed: Cottonseed Oil Trust (1884), Linseed Oil Trust (1885), Whiskey Trust (1887), National Lead Trust (1887), and the Sugar Trust (1887).

COMMUNITIES OF INTEREST. When the policies of two or more companies, not otherwise combined or affiliated, can be influenced or controlled by a small group of persons who are members of the same family, or who hold controlling shares in the companies or otherwise dominate control, a *community of interest* is said to exist. This is, of course, an informal arrangement, but control over the companies may nevertheless be obtained the same as if the companies were combined in a more tangible way. Monopolies effected through the community of interest are often difficult to break up because the presence of this type of control is sometimes concealed since no outward evidences of combination appear, and there are no written agreements. When the community of interest is accompanied by interlocking directorates, which is oftentimes the case, evidences of the control appear on the surface.

INTERLOCKING DIRECTORATES. When one or more of the same persons serve on the board of directors of two or more corporations, it is referred to as *interlocking directorates.* This is sometimes listed as a type of community of interest, since the community of interest existing among a small group of people who own the controlling shares in several corporations often results in interlocking directorates. We are listing the latter as a special type of combination since a type of community of interest may exist without interlocking directorates, and also the latter arrangement cannot be kept secret.

The Clayton Act prohibits interlocking directorates in large national banks and large industrial corporations that compete with each other. The Banking Act of 1933 prohibited interlocking directorates in investment banks and commercial banks that are members of the Federal Reserve System.

TRADE ASSOCIATIONS. A *trade association* is a nonprofit organization formed to promote the mutual interests of individuals or companies engaged in the same line of business. It is a service organization, and does not engage in any business transactions on its own

[11] *State v. Standard Oil Co.,* 49 Ohio St., 137 (1892).

account. The name of the organization usually indicates the line of business which is carried on by the members. Trade associations carry on one or more of the following types of activities for their members: collection and dissemination of statistics concerning prices, production, and sales; standardization of accounting systems; credits and collection service; standardization and simplification; research; labor relations; public relations; mutual insurance; arranging conventions; publishing a trade magazine; lobbying; and legislative work.

The trade association differs from the other forms of combinations in that its activities usually are only indirectly related to the principal business carried on by the members, while the other combinations are formed for the primary purpose of fixing prices, limiting production, lessening competition, or effecting economies in connection with the primary purpose for which the businesses operate.

In some instances, however, trade associations have extended their scope of activities beyond those stated above. With an organization of the leading companies in the industry in existence, it is not surprising that it would be used to help the members in various ways. In some instances the association has been used as a means of limiting the production of the products or fixing prices, or restricting competition in other ways. When this has been brought to the attention of the courts, such activities have been held to be illegal.

Leases

Types of Leases. Leases may be classified in various ways. According to their duration, leases may be classified into (1) short term, and (2) long term; on the basis of the type of rental payments, as (1) fixed rent, and (2) variable rent; according to type of industry, as (1) industrial, (2) public utility, and (3) railroad; or according to the type or extent of the assets rented, as (1) ordinary real estate, (2) equipment, (3) entire assets of a company.

The reader is familiar with the arrangement of renting a retail storeroom, factory building, or warehouse, so nothing further will be said about this type of lease. In connection with our discussion of equipment obligations (in Chapter 10), the leasing of railroad equipment by the trustee to the road that was buying the rolling stock on the installment plan was discussed. Another type of the lease arrangement is that used by the International Business Machines Corporation and by the United Shoe Machinery Corporation, whereby companies wanting the use of the machines manufactured by these companies are compelled to rent them from the manufacturer.

Our interest here is not in the types of leases stated above, but rather in the long-term lease of all or a substantial part of the assets of other companies, as form for another type of combination—the subject we are now discussing.

Industrial Leases. Industrials have not used the lease method of combination to any great extent. Naturally they use the ordinary real estate lease and the equipment lease mentioned above. The extractive industries, however, such as mining, oil, and lumber, have made extensive use of leases to acquire lands that contained the minerals or lumber. Retail chain store organizations and theatre chains, however, have made considerable use of leases to acquire additional units throughout the country. Only occasionally do we see one industrial company acquiring the use of the entire assets of another through the lease method. When it has occurred, the leasing company has usually later acquired all or a substantial portion of the stock of the other company. The rights of the shareholders and bondholders of the leased company will be discussed after we have taken up railroad leases.

Public Utility Leases. Public utilities also have made little use of the lease method of combination. Natural gas companies, however, make use of it as stated above. Some utilities used the lease in the past, but later they acquired the stock of the leased companies and merged them into one of the companies comprising the utilities system. The holding company device, mergers and consolidations have been the methods used by the utilities to effect combinations.

Railroad Leases. Railroads have made extensive use of the lease method of combination. It was commonly used in the period from the middle 1870's to 1893, to acquire small lines and build them into large railroad systems. Since these leases were usually for a period of 99 years or more, many of them are still in operation today. About 15 per cent of the total railroad mileage in the United States is controlled through the use of leases.

Leases were being used among railroads before other forms of combinations, such as the holding company device, had been brought into existence. Furthermore, the cost of acquiring the assets or controlling shares of an entire railroad would be enormous. The lease enables a company to use the entire properties of another company without the outlay of any cash. The following discussion will pertain directly to railroad leases, but in some instances it would apply also to leases made by industrials or utilities.

Terms of the Lease. Practically all of the railroad leases in existence today provide for a fixed rent. The amount of the rent is determined after giving consideration to the taxes of the lessor (the company whose property is rented), interest on the bonds and dividends at a specified rate on the stock of the lessor, and any other fixed expenses that would have to be paid by the lessor. Since the latter gives up its independent earning power, it must rely on the rental payments to meet all of its obligations. All of the operating expenses of the lessor are paid by the lessee (the company that leases the property from the lessor). In most instances the dividends on the lessor's stock are paid directly by the lessee company.

When the variable rental has been used in the past the amount of the rent was based on one of the following: (1) the volume of interchanged traffic, (2) gross earnings of the leased lines, or (3) net earnings of the leased lines. In the case of mining companies the lessee usually must pay the lessor a stipulated sum for each ton of ore removed.

Acquiring the lines of other companies is somewhat similar to selling bonds and buying the property with the proceeds. The fixed rental payments covering the bond interest, dividends on the stock, and taxes, are comparable to the payment of interest on bonds that might have been issued by the company. But leasing the lines does not call for the repayment of a principal amount (although in most instances the lessor's bonds are guaranteed by the lessee) which would be necessary if the lines had been acquired from the proceeds of a bond issue. Another point of difference is that bonds would appear as a liability on the balance sheet of the company, but its obligation to pay the rent does not show up on the balance sheet. From what was said above, it is apparent that leasing the property of another company is another method of trading on the equity.

Rights of Lessor's Bondholders. The lease usually provides that the lessee must guarantee the payment of interest and principal on the bonds of the lessor. Thus, the bonds retain whatever lien they may have had on the property of the lessor, and in addition the guarantee of the lessee makes them in effect debenture bonds of the lessee.

Since the bonds issued by the lessor prior to the time the property is leased have a claim on the lessor's property senior to that granted to the lessee by the lease, the lessee will want to make sure that no default is made in the payment of interest and principal, when due, on the lessor's bonds. For this reason modern leases provide that the lessee will pay the interest directly to the lessor's bondholders, instead of giving the money to the lessor in the form of rent and depending upon it to pay the interest. The agreement will also provide that in event any of the lessor's bonds mature during the period covered by the lease, the lessor will turn over to the lessee a new issue of bonds to be used for refunding the old issue.

Rights of Lessor's Stockholders. Directors of a corporation are elected for the purpose of managing the properties of the company for the best interests of the shareholders. They therefore, cannot give up their responsibility and rent the corporate property without the consent of the shareholders. The statutes of practically all the states, however, provide for leasing the property if some specified percentage of the stock, such as a majority, two-thirds, or three-fourths, is obtained. The statutes of a number of the states also provide that shareholders who do not assent to the lease of the company's property are entitled to receive from the company a fair value for their shares.

It is necessary to obtain the approval of the Interstate Commerce Commission to effect a railroad lease. In some instances the public utilities commission of the particular state must approve any leases made by public utilities and railroads within the state.

As stated above, one of the provisions of the lease is that the lessee guarantees the dividends on the lessor's stock. Thus, in effect the shareholders of the lessor become creditors of the lessee with respect to the dividends on their stock.

Maintenance of Leased Properties. In the case of long-term leases of the kind we are here discussing, it is a matter of common law that the lessee shall make the necessary repairs in connection with the leased properties. The lease itself, however, usually specifically provides that the lessee will make all necessary repairs and otherwise maintain the property in operating condition, and that it shall carry proper insurance on the properties.

Additions and Improvements. It is also common law that any improvements or additions made to leased property by the tenant shall revert to the landlord upon termination of the lease. This, however, is not a serious matter to the lessee in most instances, because the lease may have, for example, 500 years yet to run. The great probability is that any improvements made to the property will have fully depreciated or become obsolete before that time.

Furthermore, most people, including corporate managers, are not too much concerned with what may happen 500 years from now.

The lessee may, however, be forced to give up the lease before its maturity. This, of course, would make the lessee liable for damages, but if it cannot pay the rental, and fails, there is little the lessor may be able to do about it. But as indicated above, any improvements in the property made by the lessee will benefit the lessor. In some of the old leases the agreement provided that upon termination of the lease the landlord would have to reimburse the tenant for the present value of the improvement. This, however, would probably be interpreted as meaning the termination of the lease at its maturity, rather than because of default by the lessee. Furthermore, it would probably be difficult to reach an agreement as to the value of the improvements. A more modern method is to provide in the agreement that new securities will be issued by the lessor to pay for the improvements at the time the improvements are made. Since the interest on the bonds or dividends on the stock will be guaranteed, and probably paid by the lessee, it amounts to an increase in the rental payments, but there is no immediate outlay of cash for the improvements.

Acquisition of Stock of Lessor. In some instances when a company is desirous of obtaining connections of one kind or another with some other company it may buy some of the latter's stock. The amount of stock acquired may be sufficient to give it some voice in the management of the other company. In order to get complete control over the use of the other company's property, the stock ownership may eventually result in a lease of the properties.

In some cases the lessee may own none of the lessor's stock at the time the lease is made, but gradually acquire controlling interests in the stock before termination of the lease. Many of the leases made years ago provide for fixed rentals of an amount that would be considered relatively low at the present time. Renewal of the lease may be possible only at a greatly increased rental payment. Anticipating this, the lessee may secretly buy up a sufficient amount of the stock of the lessor to give it control over that company. Then it could more or less dictate the terms of the lease renewal. In some instances the stock ownership has resulted in a merger of the lessor corporation into the lessee.

The income tax laws have in some cases been a factor in a merger. When the old leases were made, there were no income tax laws. After income taxes came into being the lease arrangement ran into difficulties. The lessor was required to pay income taxes on the rentals received. But the lease agreement contains no provisions relating to them. In a number of cases the government attached the rental payments to obtain the income taxes due from the lessor. This resulted in smaller dividends to the shareholders. Where the taxes were not paid, the courts have even held the shareholders of the lessor liable for them. In order to settle the matter, and at the same time eliminate the income taxes of the lessor, some companies have effected a merger.

EFFECT OF LEASE ON LESSOR. We have already indicated the effect of a lease on the security holders of the lessor. These and other advantages of the lease to the lessor are summarized below.

Advantages. The advantages of the lease to the lessor and its security holders are as follows:

1. A fixed income is assured regardless of the volume of business or the expenses incurred.
2. The bondholders benefit from the additional security of the general credit of the lessee.
3. The shareholders become general creditors of the lessee with respect to their dividends.

Disadvantages. The lease usually benefits the lessor otherwise it would not lease its properties. The following, however, are possible disadvantages:

1. The company gives up its independent control and earning power, and its future is thus dependent upon the lessee.
2. Future prosperity will not result in any direct benefit, except in the few instances where the rental payments are based on income or earnings.
3. The purchasing power of the money received by the shareholders may decline due to inflation.

EFFECT OF LEASE ON LESSEE. Some of the effects of the lease on the lessee have already been mentioned. These will be summarized now.

Advantages. The lessee takes the initiative in effecting a lease, so it would be expected that it would benefit from such an arrangement. The possible advantages are as follows:

1. Use of the property is obtained without the outlay of any funds or the issuance of additional securities.
2. Control over the properties may enable the entire system to benefit.

3. Future prosperity will benefit the company, particularly when the rental payment is fixed.
4. The company will tend to benefit from inflation.
5. The lease may be more easily disposed of in event of failure of the lessee, than an obligation to bondholders who might come into existence as a result of raising money to buy the properties as an alternative to the lease.
6. The obligation assumed under the lease does not show up as a liability on the balance sheet of the lessee. If bonds were issued to finance the purchase of the properties they would appear as a liability on the balance sheet.

Disadvantages. Some of the possible disadvantages of the lease to the lessee pertain to the acquisition of the property by any means, and others are comparisons with other methods of securing the use of the properties, as was true also of the advantages listed above.

1. The rental payments may become a burden if profitable use cannot be made of the properties, or if earnings in general decline.
2. Deflation would tend to harm the lessee.
3. Improvements made may revert to the lessor upon termination of the lease.
4. The taxes and fees to maintain the lessor as a separate company must be paid.
5. Separate reports of various kinds must be filed for both companies.
6. The leased property cannot be used by the lessee as direct security for bonds, although the leasehold may possibly be accepted as security.

Questions

1. What was the attitude of the common law with respect to combinations in restraint of trade? Could the common law break them up?

2. (a) Are all "trusts" illegal? Explain. (b) What were the early legal objections to the trust form of combination?

3. Indicate the important point in regard to the U. S. Supreme Court's attitude toward combinations that is contained in each of the following cases: the Knight Case, the Trans-Missouri Freight Association Case, the Standard Oil Company Case, and the United States Steel Corporation Case.

4. Indicate the principal provisions of the Clayton Act.

5. Explain what is meant by "tying contracts," and indicate whether or not they are legal.

6. Indicate what is meant by gentlemen's agreements in the field of business combinations and explain why they were in many instances ineffective.

7. What different kinds of pool combinations have been formed in the past. Why are they not used at the present time for domestic business?

8. What different types of "trusts" have been discussed in this course? Which kind are illegal?

9. What advantages did the "trusts" have over gentlemen's agreements and pools? What accounted for their dissolution?

10. What is meant by a community of interest? In what different ways may it be effected?

11. What is meant by "interlocking directorates?" When are they illegal?

12. How do trade associations differ from other forms of business combinations?

13. (a) What are the advantages to the lessee of the lease method of combination as compared to the outright purchase of the properties? (b) In what field have leases been a common method of combination? (c) What type of securities commonly arise in connection with a railroad lease?

14. Which, if any, of the forms of combinations discussed in this chapter have you studied in other courses? Which courses?

15. Try to recall as many situations as possible in this course thus far where the income tax consideration has been an important one in the making of business decisions.

Problems

1. The Standard Automobile Accessory Co. buys a number of its parts from other companies and assembles them for sale mainly to automobile manufacturing companies. One of its suppliers is the Acme Metal Company. The materials obtained from this company are so vital to the Standard Co. that the latter has given some consideration to the acquisition of some kind of control over the Acme Co. The Standard Co. does not have sufficient funds to buy the Metal Company, or to buy controlling interests in it. Because of several circumstances, it will not attempt to do any new financing. It has been suggested that the Standard Co. lease the Acme Co. under a long-term lease whereby the rental payments would be sufficient in amount to pay all the expenses of the Acme Co. and to allow a liberal dividend to its shareholders. List the possible advantages to the Standard Co. of the lease as compared to other methods of combination.

2. Mr. Atwood is a stockholder in the Jonesville Press which buys paper from the Meadville Paper Manufacturing Company, a company in which Mr. Atwood is both stockholder and a director. The Jonesville Press has asked him if he would accept a directorship in their company, but Mr. Atwood is afraid that to do so would be in violation of the antitrust laws. Do you think it would be in violation of these laws? Might any other type of objection be raised? What precaution could be taken against the latter?

Chapter 30

PURCHASE OF ASSETS, MERGERS, AND CONSOLIDATIONS

Purchase of assets

Meaning of Purchase of Assets. The term "purchase of assets" will be used here in a very special meaning. We are now interested in that purchase of assets which results in a form of combination of enterprises, and because of this, we have referred to the transaction as a "purchase of assets," rather than a "sale of assets." A better understanding of the meaning of the phrase can be had if we look at it from the standpoint of the selling corporation.

When a company acquires assets through the "sale of assets" method it is meant that it acquires assets that are not the ordinary stock-in-trade of the seller, and that all or a substantial part of the *total* assets of the seller are acquired. In looking up the law on this point it would be found under *sale of assets* rather than under "purchase of assets." A recent sale of assets that involved a considerable amount of money was the sale in July, 1955, of the assets of RKO Radio Pictures, Inc., (which company was controlled by Howard R. Hughes) to the General Tire & Rubber Co., for twenty-five million dollars.

Authorization for Purchase. The board of directors has the power to do all things necessary to carry out the purposes for which the corporation was formed. This includes the purchase of assets needed in the business or assets desired for expansion purposes. Thus only the board of directors of the purchasing corporation, and not the shareholders of the purchaser, need approve the purchase of assets. In some instances, however, when the sum to be expended for the assets is relatively large, or when the property is to be used for a purpose somewhat different from the business which is being carried on at the time, the directors may ask the stockholders for approval. But this is not legally necessary.

If the assets to be acquired, however, are to be used for a purpose not authorized in the charter, then, of course, stockholder approval must be obtained for a charter amendment. Also, if new stock is going to be exchanged for the property it may be necessary to get the stockholders to approve an increase in the authorized stock.

Authorization for Sale. The power given to the directors does not include that of selling all or a substantial part of the total assets of the company. Thus the selling corporation must not only have the sale of assets approved by the board of directors, but it must be approved also by the stockholders. At common law it was necessary to get the consent of all the shareholders for the sale of all or a substantial part of the total assets of a solvent corporation. Statutory provisions, however, have been adopted in most of the states which specify the percentage of the voting shares that would have to authorize the sale. This varies from a bare majority, to three-fourths of the shares. In some instances the statutes call for this qualified majority unless otherwise provided in the charter. But such statutes further provide that the proportion cannot be less than a majority. The statutes of Illinois, Maryland, New York, New Jersey, and Ohio, for example, require a two-thirds vote. If class voting is provided (each different class of stock voting separately) the approval of two-thirds of each class is necessary. In Ohio and a number of the other states, the charter may specify some other percentage, but it cannot be less than a majority. In some instances the preferred stock contract will call for approval by the preferred stock to a sale of the assets, even though it does not vote on ordinary matters. In the absence of such provision, however, a non-voting preferred stock would not have the right to vote on the sale of assets. In some states only a majority vote of the voting stock is necessary if the consideration to be received from the assets is cash, but a higher percentage, such as two-thirds, when the consideration is to be stock or other securities.

Rights of Dissenting Stockholders. The statutes of most of the states provide relief for shareholders who do not approve of the sale of assets. Even if the required vote authorizing the sale has been obtained, dissenting shareholders can demand that the corporation buy back their shares. This includes also shareholders whose stock is not entitled to vote. The statutes provide for a "fair cash value" for the shares. This is determined by negotiation between the corporation and the shareholders, and if no agreement can be reached, the law will provide for the appointment of independent appraisers, or for petition to the court for appointment of the appraisers. The usual provision is that the value of the shares shall be determined as of the day before the vote on the sale of assets took place. The shareholder usually has at least 20 days after the vote is taken to demand cash for his shares. The statutes prescribe that the corporation must pay the cash to the shareholders within a specified period of time, such as 30 days, after the fair cash value has been finally determined.

Since it is not known how many of the shareholders will dissent and demand cash for their shares, the directors in many instances reserve the right to cancel the sale of the assets until after the elapse of the period within which the shareholders have to register their dissent. Cancellation of the sale automatically terminates the right of the dissenting shareholders to the cash value of their shares.

At common law dissenting shareholders who demand the cash value for their shares virtually cease to be shareholders from the time they demand the cash, provided of course they do not properly withdraw the demand, or provided it is not canceled by the decision to not sell the assets. Thus dissenters would not be entitled to vote their shares, nor would they be entitled to dividends, or any other rights enjoyed by shareholders. The statutes of a number of the states have codified this rule, but some of them provide that if dividends are paid on the same class of shares as those held by dissenters, the amount of the dividend shall be added to the total amount to be paid for such shares by the corporation.

Rights of Creditors. Ordinarily, the creditors have no voice in the sale of assets, and unless special circumstances exist, they (creditors of the seller) have no claim against the assets acquired by the purchaser. If the creditors have a lien on the assets, however, this lien continues on the property after it has been acquired by the purchaser. If the assets are security for a mortgage bond issue which contains the after-acquired property clause, none of the other property of the purchaser will come under the lien of this issue because the *selling* company did not acquire any additional property. But if the purchasing company has such a bond issue outstanding, this issue would attach to the newly acquired property and take up a lien, junior only to the claim existing against the property at the time of its acquisition. From what has been said, it is apparent that the purchasing corporation acquires the new property *subject* to any existing mortgages. It does not *assume* the issue, unless it is so agreed, or unless the issuing company goes out of existence at the time the assets are sold.

General creditors of the selling company ordinarily have no right against the purchaser unless the former company is dissolved at the time and the creditors were not paid off. If the seller, however, was insolvent at the time of the sale, or if the sale caused it to become insolvent, the creditors could look to the purchaser for the satisfaction of their claims. This would be true also if the sale defrauded the creditors in any other manner. The Bulk Sales Act of most of the states, however, provides that the purchaser may be held liable if he failed to give appropriate notice of the purchase of the assets to the creditors.

What we have just stated always applies when the assets are sold for cash. If stock of the purchasing corporation instead of cash is given for the assets, and if the seller cannot secure the cash from this stock and if it has no other assets from which the creditors can be paid, the courts may hold that the purchaser is liable for the debts. If the seller is solvent, however, and remains in existence as a holding company, it is probable that the purchaser would not be liable for the debts of the seller even if stock had been exchanged for the assets. An example of the sale of assets for stock is that of the Adams Express Company. This company in 1918 sold all its assets to the American Railroad Express Company for the stock of the latter company. The Adams Express Company remained in existence and gradually shifted its investments into other shares, and today is one of the leading closed-end investment companies. (From the standpoint of the legal form of organization, it is a joint stock company.)

TAX CONSIDERATIONS. Many business transactions today are effected with tax matters in mind. If the assets are sold for cash, any profit arising from the sale would ordinarily be treated as a capital gain and taxed in the year in which the sale took place. If stock is received for the assets instead of cash, and if the transaction is properly carried out under the so-called "tax-free reorganization" sections of the law, no income or loss is reported at the time of sale, but a capital gain or loss would be taken at the time when the shares are sold.

The sale of part or all the assets may be done by the shareholders for the purpose of preventing forced sale of the business or the shares of the company to provide cash to pay the estate taxes upon death of the owners. Or, some of the cash may be distributed by means of gifts to reduce the size of the estate and thus the amount of estate taxes upon death of the owners.

ADVANTAGES. Since the purchase-of-assets method of combination is similar to the merger or consolidation, the advantages of the purchase of assets usually listed are in comparison with these other methods.

1. It was stated above that, except under the circumstances mentioned, the approval of only the shareholders of the selling company is necessary to effect a purchase of assets. Mergers and consolidations call for the approval of the shareholders of both affected companies.
2. The laws of some of the states do not permit their corporations to merge or consolidate with a corporation organized in another state.
3. Only the desired assets are acquired, whereas in a merger or consolidation all the property is involved.
4. It is usually easier to reach an agreement on the purchase price of specific assets than for the total business, which would be necessary for a merger or consolidation.
5. The liabilities of the selling company need not be assumed by the purchasing company, but in event of a merger or consolidation they must be assumed unless they have been paid off.
6. The tax advantages discussed above may be realized. The sale may also give rise to a capital loss.

Mergers

NATURE OF MERGER. A *merger* results when an existing company acquires all the assets and liabilities of another company, and the latter company passes out of existence. About two-thirds of the states have general statutes authorizing either mergers or consolidations or both. Several of them provide that the surviving or consolidated company shall be a domestic corporation. Usually mergers of railroads, public utilities and financial institutions cannot be accomplished under the general statutes. The procedure to be followed to effect a merger or consolidation is prescribed in the statutes.

Several points of difference between the sale of assets and a merger have been stated above. Another refers to the method of effecting the legal transfer of assets. In the case of sale of assets, title to the property is transferred by means of a deed or bill of sale, which is the usual way of transferring property, whereas in a merger the transfer is accomplished by the execution and filing of the merger agreement.

In some instances a company will sell all of its assets to another company and then dissolve. When this is done there is little difference between the sale of assets and a merger. But the procedure to be followed would be different.

STOCK ACQUISITION AN AID. In many instances a company will acquire a substantial stock interest in the company from which it expects to purchase assets, or which it expects to acquire by means of a merger. The approval of a designated percentage of the shares of the selling company is necessary to effect either a purchase of assets or a merger. Shares sufficient to give control may be acquired prior to negotiations for the actual sale or merger. Not only does this aid in getting the approval of the required amount of stock, but it may also lessen the amount to be paid to shareholders who dissent to the sale or merger. If all the stock is acquired, no problems can arise. In New York the statutes prescribe that in the case of ordinary business corporations, 95 per cent of the stock of the company to be merged must be acquired before a "merger" may take place.

ADVANTAGES OF MERGERS. Following are the principal advantages of the merger as a type of combination:

1. It results in the elimination of the merged company as a separate entity, and thus no corporate taxes must be paid on it.
2. There are no minority stock interests of other companies to deal with.
3. It is a permanent form of combination.
4. Management is centralized in the one company.
5. If properly handled, the shareholders of the merged company will not have to pay any taxes on the exchange of securities.
6. The statutes usually provide that the surviving company succeeds to all the rights and privileges of the companies that are merged into it.

SOME EXAMPLES. In some instances the sale of assets, merger and the holding company have all been used to form a combination. The General Motors Corporation is one example. Some of the present divisions of this company were acquired by means of a merger, while others were obtained by the purchase of assets. For example, in 1918 the General Motors Corporation exchanged its stock to the Chevrolet Motor Company for all its assets and business, except the General Motors shares held by it. Chevrolet then distributed the General Motors stock to its shareholders, and thereupon dissolved the company. Although accomplished through a purchase of assets, the effect was the same as a merger. As is the case with some of the other acquisitions, Chevrolet is operated as a separate division of General Motors, although it is not a corporate entity. Some units of General Motors, such as The General Motors Acceptance Corporation, are separately incorporated, with the General Motors Corporation owning the shares and thus acting as a holding company.

In 1937, the Kelvinator Corporation was merged into the Nash Motors Company, although at the time the name of the latter company was changed to the Nash-Kelvinator Corporation. The merger was effected by the exchange of 1⅜ shares of Nash-Kelvinator Corporation stock for each share of Kelvinator Corporation stock. The Kelvinator Corporation gave up its corporate charter although its business is being carried on under the name of the "Kelvinator Division."

In 1950, the Lima-Hamilton Corporation, manufacturers of locomotives and power shovels, was merged into the Baldwin Locomotive Works. The name of the latter company was at the same time changed to the Baldwin-Lima-Hamilton Corporation. The merger was accomplished by a share-for-share exchange. In order to effect an even exchange, however, the Baldwin company first formed the Baldwin Securities Corporation and transferred to it the shares which it held in the General Steel Castings Corporation, The Midvale Company, the Flannery Bolt Company, and also cash which was obtained from the sale of other securities. The shares of the Baldwin Securities Corporation were then paid as a property dividend to the shareholders of Baldwin Locomotive Works of record the day before the stock of the Lima-Hamilton Corporation was acquired. In 1954, the Consolidated Vultee Aircraft Corp. was merged into General Dynamics Corp., and in the following year the Stromberg-Carlson Co. was merged into General Dynamics Corp.

Consolidations

Nature of Consolidation. A *consolidation* results when a new company, formed for the particular purpose, takes over the assets and liabilities of two or more other companies, and the latter pass out of existence as separate entities. This is usually accomplished by the new company exchanging its shares with the shareholders of the other companies for their shares, and then canceling the latter shares upon dissolution of the companies.

It is apparent that although the merger and consolidation differ in some respects, they are very similar. In the case of a consolidation, two or more companies are fused ("merged" in a sense) into a new company, whereas the merger results from one or more companies being fused ("merged") into an already existing company.

Because the difference is more of form than of substance, the two methods of combination are often not distinguished. The term "merger" is commonly used to apply to the combination regardless of whether it is accomplished through a merger or a consolidation.[1]

If an existing company acquires the controlling stock interest in another company or companies, technically it is not referred to as either a merger or a consolidation, but rather it is a type of combination effected through the holding company device. Sometimes we refer to the companies as "parent" and "subsidiary."

The term "amalgamation" is sometimes used by textbook writers in this country to refer to what we have defined as a consolidation. It is an English word (from Greek and Arabic for alloy) and is used in Great Britain to refer to what we call a consolidation, and in some instances it is applied to other types of fusion, such as purchase of assets or merger. When the term is used it may be interpreted as meaning a consolidation unless it is evident that it refers to another form of combination.

Prepared by Stock Acquisition. Since the consent of the shareholders of the combining companies must be obtained for a consolidation, the same as for a merger, one company may buy up part of the stock of another company with which it wishes to consolidate. As in the case of a merger, this facilitates getting the proper shareholder consent and it reduces the number of potential dissenters.

Advantages of Consolidation. Following are the advantages of effecting a combination by means of consolidation:

1. The separate companies being consolidated lose their corporate identity, and thus no corporate taxes must be paid on them. The consolidated company, of course, must pay the corporate taxes. This advantage is also secured through merger.
2. Similar to the merger, there are no minority stock interests of other companies to deal with.
3. It is a permanent form of combination.
4. Management is centralized in one company.
5. If properly handled, no taxes will have to be paid by the shareholders in exchanging their shares.
6. The statutes usually provide that the consolidated corporation shall enjoy the rights, franchises and privileges possessed by the former constituent companies.

[1] The New York statutes use the term "consolidation" to apply to what we have defined as both a merger and a consolidation. The term "merger" is used there to apply only to the situation where the merging company owns at least 95 per cent of the stock of the other company. Merger under these circumstances can be accomplished merely by appropriate resolution by the board of directors of the merging company.

7. The consolidated corporation can start off with a clean slate. The old organizational and administrative setups are eliminated, and a completely new organization is effected.
8. The clash of selfish interests as to which company is to survive, which often arises in connection with a merger, is avoided.

SOME EXAMPLES. In some cases actually involving mergers, the combination appears on the surface to be a consolidation since the name of the merging company may be changed at the time the other companies are absorbed.

In 1945, a new company, called the Buffalo, Niagara Electric Corporation, was formed for the purpose of effecting a consolidation of the following companies: Buffalo Niagara Electric Corporation, Buffalo, Niagara & Eastern Power Corporation, Niagara, Lockport Power Company, and The Lockport & Newfane & Water Supply Company. In 1950, The Niagara Mohawk Power Corp. was formed to effect a consolidation of the Buffalo, Niagara Electric Corp., the N. Y. Power & Light Corp., and the Central N. Y. Power Corp. In 1955, the Sperry Rand Corporation was formed to effect a consolidation of the Sperry Corporation, and Remington Rand Inc.

Merger and consolidation procedures and problems

STATUTORY PROVISIONS. It was stated above that about two-thirds of the states have statutes authorizing mergers or consolidations or both. In many, if not most of the states, the procedure prescribed by the statutes is the same regardless of whether the combination is a merger or a consolidation. In some states only domestic corporations can combine, while others permit combinations of domestic and foreign corporations. In the latter case the consent of each state affected must be obtained. The statutes of some of the states permit combinations to take place only among companies that are engaged in the same or similar lines of business. Usually special provisions cover the combination of railroads, public utilities, and financial institutions.

Since the procedure to be followed is usually the same whether the combination is a merger or a consolidation, we will discuss the two forms together. If we use the term "merger" or "consolidation," it can be assumed that the same provisions would apply to the other form of combination. We will treat the two separately only when it is necessary to do so. The term "constituent company" will be used to refer to any of the companies which are parties to the merger or consolidation. In the case of a merger, one of the constituent companies continues as the "merged" company, although we may occasionally refer to it as the "consolidated" company. Technically, the latter term would apply only to the new company which is formed in a consolidation to take over the constituent companies.

Approval by Boards of Directors. Before a merger or consolidation may be effected it is necessary to get the approval of the boards of directors of all the constituent companies. A plan will have been worked out specifying the basis for the exchange of shares, the policies to be followed until the combination is effected, and in the case of a consolidation, the list of proposed directors and officers. The boards of the various companies will adopt resolutions approving the combination and calling for meetings of the shareholders of their respective companies to vote on the proposal.

Approval by Shareholders. Usually a special meeting of the shareholders of the various companies is called for the purpose of voting on the combination proposal. The statutes will prescribe the percentage vote required. Usually they call for a two-thirds vote of the shares entitled to vote on the matter, but the percentage varies among the states from a bare majority to three-fourths. Some of the statutes specify a two-thirds vote unless otherwise provided in the charter. In the latter instance, however, the law will state that the charter cannot provide for less than a majority. In some instances shares not entitled to vote on ordinary matters are entitled to vote on proposals for mergers and consolidations.

It will be noted that both mergers and consolidations require the affirmative vote of the shareholders of all the companies affected. It will be recalled that the sale-of-assets method of combination requires the consent of the shareholders of the selling company only, and not the approval of the shareholders of the purchasing corporation.

Merger or Consolidation Agreement. After the merger or consolidation has been approved by the shareholders, the appropriate corporate officers sign the merger or consolidation agreement, and it is filed in the required state office, which is usually the Secretary of State's office, where the original articles of incorporation were filed. If the agreement conforms to the law and the proper taxes and fees are paid, it will be approved, and the state will issue a certificate of merger or consolidation, which makes the combination complete. It is not necessary for the merged or constituent companies to issue bills of sale or execute deeds for the transfer of the corporate property. The merger or consolidation agreement accomplishes this.

The consolidated, or surviving company in the case of a merger, succeeds to all the rights, privileges, and liabilities of the constituent companies. Creditors' rights will be discussed further below.

RIGHTS OF DISSENTING SHAREHOLDERS. In the case of large corporations with thousands of shareholders, it is difficult to get all the shareholders to agree to the combination, or to the exchange of securities proposed in the plan. In some instances shareholders hold out for the sole purpose of attempting to get paid off at a high nuisance value. In some cases, of course, the shareholders of a particular company may not be given equitable treatment.

Regardless of the intent of the shareholders, they might bring an action in equity to enjoin the merger or consolidation on the ground that it is an *ultra vires* act, an illegal act, or that it was not properly authorized by the directors or the shareholders, or that the price is inadequate, or that the treatment of a particular class of stock is unfair. The matter then goes to the court and it may be some time before a decision is rendered. In some instances, of course, the court may decide in favor of the dissenting shareholders, and the combination will be blocked, or better treatment may have to be given the particular class of shareholders in order to effect the combination.

The other recourse for dissenting shareholders is to demand the fair cash value for their shares. The statutes authorizing the merger or consolidation will provide the procedure to be followed. In some states the shareholder must demand in writing from the corporation the cash for his shares before the vote on the combination has been taken, while in others no action need be taken until after the vote. After the vote has been taken the statutes will prescribe the number of days, usually 20, the shareholder has to make a written request to the surviving corporation for the cash value of his shares. The company has a period of time, usually 30 days after an agreement has been reached on the fair cash value of the shares, within which to make payment. If an agreement cannot be reached, the corporation or the shareholder has a specified period of time, such as four or six months, after the vote was taken, to petition the appropriate court to have a fair value for the stock determined. In a number of the states the dissenting shareholder may elect to ignore the procedure provided by the statutes for appraising the shares and bring action in a court of equity to recover the fair value of his shares.

The procedure prescribed for dissenting shares to secure the fair cash value for their shares is the same in many states regardless of whether it is a sale of assets or a combination effected through merger or consolidation. The statutes usually provide that shareholders who have petitioned in writing for the fair cash value for their shares shall cease to possess the rights of shareholders until and unless the combination plan is given up.

In order not to be forced to pay an excessive amount to dissenting shareholders, the merger or consolidation plan often provides that the combination will not be effective if shares in excess of a specified number dissent.

Rights of Creditors of Constituent Companies. In some instances the current assets, or part of them, are used to pay off the general unsecured creditors of some or all the constituent companies before the combination is effected. In that event only the fixed assets and fixed or long-term debt is taken over by the consolidated or surviving company. Also, the consolidated company may bring out a general consolidated mortgage bond issue for the purpose of refunding the bonds of the constituent companies.

Where the above procedure is not followed, the consolidated or surviving corporation would automatically assume all the debts, both secured and unsecured, of the constituent companies.

Bonds of the constituent companies which are secured by a lien on property retain that lien after the combination has taken place. They also assume the security of the general credit of the consolidated or surviving company. The rights of bondholders become complicated, however, when one or more of the bond issues contain the after-acquired property clause. The law relating to this has not been clearly worked out, but according to the authorities and a few court cases the following would appear to be the law in the absence of any provisions otherwise in the statutes or the contract.

If the combination takes place through a merger, any bonds containing the after-acquired property clause of the companies that lose their identity will not secure a lien on the property of any other such companies, nor will they secure a lien on the property of the surviving company. The reason is that these particular companies do not acquire any new property, but rather they themselves are acquired. The bonds, of course will retain whatever lien they had at the time of the merger, and in addition they will be secured by the general credit of the surviving company. But if the bonds of the surviving company which absorbs the property of the other constituent companies contain the after-acquired property clause, these bonds will obtain a lien on the property of the absorbed companies subject and secondary, of course, to any liens that were already on the properties at the time of acquisition.

When a consolidation, however, takes place any bonds of the constituent companies which contain the after-acquired property clause will not secure a lien on the property of any of the other companies. This follows because it is the consolidated company, and not the former constituent companies, that is acquiring the properties. For the same reason it would appear that property acquired by the consolidated company subsequent to the combination would not pass under the claim of the after-acquired property clause present in the bond issues of the constituent companies. Any liens on specific property possessed by the bondholders prior to the consolidation, however, continue after consolidation.

Open issues of bonds of companies that lose their identity in a combination are closed after the combination takes place. This is done as a practical matter. It is not clear, however, what the law would say on the point. But if a company loses its identity through the combination, which would be the case with all companies forming a consolidation, and all but one of the companies entering into a merger, it is difficult to see how another company could issue additional bonds under the particular indenture. Perhaps the legal question is not one of practical importance because it would undoubtedly be cheaper for the consolidated or surviving company to sell a large consolidated bond issue of its own rather than attempt to issue more bonds under the indenture of one of the former companies.

If any of the bonds of the companies that lose their identity are convertible into stock, in the absence of provision otherwise, the courts have usually held that the conversion right is extinguished by the merger or consolidation.

General creditors of the constituent companies become general creditors of the consolidated or surviving company. But the determination of the relative position of such creditors with respect to the assets of the former constituent companies is not always easy. Equity holds that the rights of creditors shall not be impaired in any way by a merger or consolidation. Furthermore, the courts have taken the position that the capital of a corporation is a "trust fund" for the benefit of creditors. The statutes authorizing mergers and consolidations also commonly state that the rights of creditors shall not be impaired by the combination. Courts of equity have accordingly held that both secured and unsecured creditors of a constituent company have a prior right to the assets of the old company ahead of either the secured or unsecured creditors of one of the other constituent companies to the combination, provided the specific assets can be identified. If they have been sold, then no such priority would exist. In any event, however, the secured creditors would have a senior claim to any property which specifically comes under their lien. As was stated above, the consolidated or surviving company assumes the debts of the constituent companies, and the general creditors of these companies can always sue at law to collect from the consolidated or surviving company.

Perhaps the above can be better understood by the following example. Let us assume that Companies *X* and *Y* have first mortgage bonds outstanding secured by Plant *X*, and Plant *Y*, respectively, and that they both have general creditors. These two companies are then consolidated into Company *Z*. The mortgage bonds of the constituent companies are secured by their respective claims against the plants, and in addition by the general credit of Company *Z*. The general creditors are secured by the general credit of Company *Z*. If a default occurs in the bonds issued by Company *X*, recourse could be had against Plant *X*, and against any property of Company *Z*, subject to any senior claims against Company *Z*. But if the property taken over from Company *Y* can be identified, both the bonds issued by Company *Y* and its general creditors will have to be satisfied before any of its former property can be applied toward the satisfaction of Company *X* bonds. If Company *Z* had sold the unpledged assets of former Company *Y*, then the general creditors of *Y* would not have any senior right to the cash obtained from the sale.

PROMOTION OF THE COMBINATION. The promotion of a merger or consolidation is somewhat similar to the promotion of a new company. Somebody has to think up the idea and do the spade work in connection with the proposed combination. It may be promoted by officials of the constituent companies, an investment banker, or a professional promoter. The merger is more likely to be promoted by the officials of one of the companies, particularly when there is an intercompany holding of stock, or if one family or small group of persons owns a substantial stock interest in the particular companies. This is sometimes referred to as an *inside* promotion or combination in contrast to one which is promoted by an investment banker or independent promoter, which is called an *outside* promotion. The consolidation is more apt to be originated by an investment banker than a merger since the former gives rise to a new issue of securities. Although the new securities, or at least part of them, will be exchanged for the old securities, some may be sold to the public to obtain cash in order to buy some of the old securities, to pay off the dissenters, or to furnish additional working capital for the consolidated company.

The intervention of the investment banker may help in other respects in addition to selling new securities. He may offer material aid to the companies in valuing their properties and suggesting the basis for the sale or exchange of securities. The judgment of the investment banker may be less prejudiced than that of the officials of the companies affected. His knowledge of the current market and its ability to absorb certain kinds of securities will be better than that of the company officers. The fact that the banker is behind the combination may result in its being more favorably accepted by the security holders. Besides, he may be better able to deal directly with dissenters than the officers.

In promoting a combination it is advisable to reduce to a minimum the possibility that a substantial number of shareholders will dissent to the plan. This calls for tact and skill on the part of the promoter. In many instances a substantial stock interest of the constituent companies is quietly bought up prior to an announcement of the proposed combination. The promotion will usually take one of two forms, the *option method* or the *bargaining method.*

OPTION METHOD. Under the *option method* the promoter deals with each of the companies separately. For a consideration which is usually cash, he buys from the particular company an option to purchase all its assets at a stipulated price within a stated period of time. If the option is not exercised by the expiration date it expires and the company retains the money paid for the option.

If options necessary to acquire the properties are obtained, the promoter, who may be an investment banker, will take the proper steps to form a syndicate of investment bankers who will undertake the raising of the money necessary to acquire the properties. When options are used, it is usual to form a new corporation to take over the properties. It is apparent that the use of options commonly accompanies the purchase of assets rather than a merger or consolidation. But since the constituent companies usually pass out of existence when the combination is completed, the result is the same as a consolidation. In some instances arrangements are made so that the securities of the company, rather than its assets, can be purchased with the options.

In view of the possible economies that may result from the combination, and the desire to have ample securities to offer to the other companies or to their security holders and to provide additional cash, arrangements are made to issue securities of the consolidated company in rather liberal amounts. Despite the fact that the options usually call for a cash consideration for the properties or the securities, it is usual to offer to exercise the options by the payment of securities of the consolidated company. The value of the securities offered is often in excess of the cash price specified in the option. If cash is demanded, then it is up to the syndicate to raise the necessary amount of money by the sale to the public of securities of the consolidated company. If a merger rather than a consolidation is undertaken, additional securities of the surviving company will be offered in exchange. These may also be underwritten by investment bankers.

The investment bankers may make an over-all profit on the total security issues of the consolidated company, and in addition an extra amount on all securities which they must sell to provide cash to buy the securities of the constituent companies. In addition, the bankers may obtain some of the securities of the consolidated company as part of their compensation. Part of the so-called profit, however, may represent compensation for maintaining a market in the securities of the consolidated company.

Bargaining Method. Mergers have been more common in recent years than consolidations, and usually the *bargaining method,* rather than the option method has been used to effect the combination. As the term suggests, under this method the promoter, who may be the president of a large company, approaches a smaller company, possibly through its president, and attempts to interest him and his company in combining with the large company probably through a merger, or possibly a consolidation. If the small company is interested, it may then be asked to furnish financial and other data about itself for the examination of the officials of the larger company. The officials of the small company will also want data on the larger company.

The examination and investigation of the companies may take a number of different forms. The accounting reports and statements are gone over thoroughly, and income statements and balance sheets are standardized in order that the data may be comparable. Special attention will be given to the method of valuing the assets on the books of the company, the depreciation policy, provision for bad debts, etc. Engineers may be sent in to inspect the physical condition of the plant and equipment, the efficiency of the production methods, and valuation of the physical properties. Experts will study the market for the company's product, the competitive situation, labor conditions, the management, and the future outlook.

When it has been established that a combination is possible or probable, a valuation of the worth of the respective companies must be made in order to know how much to pay for the properties, or to determine the basis for the exchange of securities, or to give those taking the initiative the information which is needed for bargaining.

Although the exact treatment given the various companies or their security holders will depend in part on the bargaining ability of the parties concerned, the price paid for the properties or the basis for the exchange of securities will tend to depend upon the relative worths of the companies. The relative values of the companies is usually arrived at by taking into consideration the value of the net tangible assets, the earnings record, and the market value of the securities. We will briefly discuss each of these factors.

VALUATION OF THE ASSETS. Any one of the following methods may be used to value the assets.

Reproduction cost. As the title indicates, this method of valuation is the cost of reproducing or duplicating the present properties at the present existing market prices. Since the cost figures would probably refer to new properties, due consideration must be given to the present deteriorated state of the existing properties in arriving at replacement values.

Substitution cost. The valuation by this method would be the cost (after giving due consideration to the deterioration in the present properties) of acquiring properties which would turn out the same quantity and quality of products and possess the same utility as the existing properties, but which might not be identical with the present properties.

Cost less depreciation. Under this method the worth of the properties is assumed to be the original cost less the depreciation. This eliminates write-ups and write-downs in the valuation, and gives no consideration to changing price levels. Attention should be given, however, to the depreciation policy followed by the company to determine if a sufficient amount has been charged off. One advantage or disadvantage, as the case may be, of this and the other two methods listed above, is that no consideration is given to intangible assets.

Book value. This method consists of merely valuing the assets at the figures at which they are carried on the balance sheet. When this procedure is followed due consideration must be given to the depreciation policy followed by the company, the valuation of inventories and accounts receivable, and any unusual write-ups or write-downs in the valuation of the properties. Intangible assets may also be valued at the book figures, or proper adjustment in the valuation may be made in view of the facts of the particular situation. The book value method has the advantage of being easy and quick to apply, it does not call for a field examination of the properties, and it is probably better understood by the security holders of the company than any other method. After giving consideration to proper adjustments, this method of valuing the assets is used more than any of the others listed above.

The current assets are commonly given special consideration in determining the worth of the total assets. Certainly there can be no question raised as to the valuation of the cash account. The book figure of the accounts receivable will also be fairly close to their actual worth. The same is true of marketable securities that are properly carried on the books. The inventory may not bring the book figure, but on the other hand since it will probably be carried at cost, the amount realized from it may exceed the book valuation. In most instances the current assets, after due consideration has been given to doubtful accounts and obsolete inventory, are commonly valued at the book figures.

The earnings of a company are often capitalized in order to arrive at the value of the assets, particularly the fixed assets, but this will be discussed under the heading of earnings, which follows.

Evaluation of the Earnings. Business property is worth what it will earn. Cost prices may have little relation to the value of business property unless that property can earn enough to justify the cost. But the future earnings of a company are unknown. Even though they could be estimated with a fair degree of accuracy, property cannot always be acquired at what it is estimated to be worth.

In the case of practically all combinations, weight is given to the probable future earnings, although in some instances book values may be given more consideration than they deserve, simply because those values must be paid in order to acquire the property. Since the future earnings are unknown, the past and present earnings, and the trend of the earnings, are used in estimating the probable future earnings. Certain adjustments, however, may have to be made in the earnings figures. For example, a small corporation, in order to lessen the amount of the corporate income tax, may pay out relatively large salaries to the officer-stockholder group, and small dividends on the stock. In larger companies the dividends may be relatively large in comparison with the salaries paid. The earnings figure is thus influenced by the policy followed in regard to salaries. In some instances, in order to arrive at comparable figures, the salaries are added back to the earnings.

Since the depreciation policies followed by the companies may vary widely, the charges made may be added to the earnings and then a similar rate of depreciation for all the companies may be subtracted. Adjustment may also have to be made in the earnings figure for any expenses, such as repairs, which have been charged to betterments, and any betterments or additions which have been charged to expense. Any nonrecurring profit or loss will also call for an adjustment in the earnings. One or more of the constituent companies may have bonds outstanding, and the earnings figure would be influenced by the interest charge. For that reason the earnings used in the computation may be the figure before deduction of interest charges. (It would also be before income taxes.)

The next problem is the determination of the period to be covered by the earnings. The current earnings and those of the immediate past are probably more indicative of the probable future earnings than the figures of some years past, but some unusual circumstances present may make the figures not typical. Furthermore, the seasonal nature of some businesses, or the way they may be affected by the business cycle would make it advisable to use a longer period of time. The earnings are, therefore, considered for a period varying from three to ten years, with five being used in many instances.

The earnings figure used may be a simple average for the period or it may be a weighted average, in order to give more emphasis to the recent experience. Let us assume that two companies show the following earnings record for the past five years:

	Earnings	
Year	*Company A*	*Company B*
19–1	$200,000	$470,000
19–2	250,000	380,000
19–3	300,000	300,000
19–4	400,000	250,000
19–5	450,000	200,000
Total	$1,600,000	$1,600,000

If we take a simple average of the above earnings we get average annual earnings of $320,000 for both companies. But, considering the trend of the earnings, it appears that Company *A's* future earnings would be greater than those of Company *B*. In order to give effect to the trend, for both companies, we might give a weight of 5 to the last year's earnings, 4 to the year previous, and so on, until the oldest year gets a weight of only 1. The weighted average annual earnings would be computed as follows:

	Company A		Company B	
19–1	1 × $200,000 =	$ 200,000	1 × $470,000 =	$ 470,000
19–2	2 × 250,000 =	500,000	2 × 380,000 =	760,000
19–3	3 × 300,000 =	900,000	3 × 300,000 =	900,000
19–4	4 × 400,000 =	1,600,000	4 × 250,000 =	1,000,000
19–5	5 × 450,000 =	2,250,000	5 × 200,000 =	1,000,000
Total	15	$5,450,000	15	$4,130,000

After assigning these weights to the earnings, we arrive at average annual earnings of $363,333 for Company *A* ($5,450,000 divided by 15), and $275,333 for Company *B* ($4,130,000 divided by 15). Thus, Company *A*'s weighted average earnings are nearly 32 per cent greater than those of Company *B*. If the value of the companies, or their assets, or shares are based on these earnings, it is thus apparent that Company *A* would be worth much more than Company *B*.

After getting the average earnings in one of the two ways stated above, the next problem is how to use these figures to arrive at a valuation of the companies, or their shares. This is usually done by the process of *capitalizing the earnings*. The nature of the business and the industry are taken into account, and a rate of return, on the invested capital typical of that business is determined. The greater the risk involved, the higher would be the rate of return used in the computation. It may be decided that a rate of, for example, 12½ per cent would be typical. (This is not high since, if the income taxes were 50 per cent, the earnings after taxes would be only 6¼ per cent. Furthermore, there is no assurance that 12½ per cent will be earned in the future.) We then let the average earnings, or estimated average earnings, equal this percentage, and proceed to find out what 100 per cent (the value of the business) equals. Applying this rate of 12½ per cent to the weighted average earnings in the example given above, we arrive at a valuation of $2,906,664 for Company *A* ($363,333 divided by .125), and a valuation of $2,202,664 for Company *B* ($275,333 divided by .125). (Or, the same result could be found by dividing 100% by 12½%, which gives us 8, and then multiplying the average earnings by the latter figure.)

VALUATION BY USE OF BOTH ASSETS AND EARNINGS. In some instances both the book value (or some other method of valuation) of the net assets and the capitalized earnings power are taken into consideration in determining the value of a company. The net tangible assets may be valued at the book value, and then that portion of the value, as determined by the capitalization of earnings, which is in excess of this is considered to be the valuation of the goodwill. For example, above we determined the value of Company *A* to be $2,906,664 by the process of capitalizing the weighted average earnings. If the book value of the net tangible assets was $2,500,000, then the goodwill might be valued at $406,664 ($2,906,664 less $2,500,000). For practical purposes this would probably be rounded off to $400,000.

If $2,906,664 in securities was given to Company *A* for its property, or given to *A*'s shareholders for their stock, the assets of the former *A* Company might be carried on the books of the consolidated company at this figure, or they may be carried at $2,500,000, the same valuation placed upon them by Company *A*, and the $406,664 (or, $400,000) may be carried as goodwill. Accountants usually object to carrying goodwill on the books unless it is purchased. In this case, however, it is really purchased. A legal question could also be raised whether the stock issued for the goodwill was fully paid. Since the total amount of stock indicated above had to be given to acquire the assets or shares of Company *A*, it would appear that all the stock issued by the consolidated company was fully paid. Despite what has just been said, it is probable that the assets would be carried at $2,906,664, and thus, the goodwill account would not appear on the books.

It was pointed out above, in connection with valuation based on assets, that in some instances when a combination is formed, the current assets are valued at their book value and the earnings are capitalized to determine the value of the fixed assets. This results in a somewhat inflated valuation since the earning power would represent not only the value of the fixed assets, but the current assets as well. But if the same method is used for the various constituent companies, they are all being treated alike. Furthermore, the offer of a liberal amount of securities is an inducement for the companies to come into the combination.

CAPITALIZING ADDITIONAL EARNINGS EXPECTED. Above we indicated that the goodwill as represented by the excess of the capitalized value of the earnings over the book value of the net assets, might be paid for in stock of the consolidated company. Usually when a combination is formed, the promoters expect not only to earn what the constituent companies had been earning before, but they expect or hope to earn more due to the economies of large-scale operations, lessening of competition, and perhaps better management. They may, therefore, capitalize these hoped-for earnings and accordingly issue much more in stock.

In the hypothetical example given above, the combined weighted average earnings of Companies *A* and *B* were $638,666 ($363,333 plus $275,333). If these earnings were capitalized on a 12½ per cent basis, stock amounting to $5,109,328 would be issued. If it was expected that the annual earnings would increase by $100,000 as a result of the combination, then on the same basis of capitalization, an additional $800,000 in stock might be issued ($100,000 divided by 12½ × 100). Part of this additional stock might go to the promoters and investment bankers as compensation, and the balance would go to Companies *A* and *B*, or their shareholders, as an added inducement to get them to come into the combination. If the promoters took 25 per cent of it, then $600,000 more could be distributed to the constituent companies. This might be divided between them according to the same ratio as the capitalized value of their weighted average earnings. Thus Company *A*, or its shareholders, would get an additional \$341,336 $\left(\frac{\$2{,}906{,}664}{\$5{,}109{,}328} \times \$600{,}000\right)$, and Company *B*, or its shareholders would get $258,664 more. The combined properties may then be carried on the books of the consolidated company at $5,909,328, instead of $5,109,328.

In the examples given above, we have always referred to the stock in terms of dollars. This would be appropriate if the stock had a par or stated value, and if in the above examples, the exchange of stock for property was dollar for dollar. If the consolidated company, however, wishes to begin business with a surplus on the books, it would be necessary to issue stock with a lower aggregate par or stated value than the valuation placed upon the assets acquired. In other words, for every $100 of property acquired, stock with an aggregate par or stated value of $75, for example, would be issued. The balance of $25 can then be carried to the surplus (capital surplus) account. The actual par or stated value per share could be $1, $50, $100, or any amount, and it would make no difference except in terms of the number of shares to be issued. As long as the division between the constituent companies is as stated above in dollar terms, it would make no actual difference to the shareholders, except possibly a psychological one.

Bonds and Preferred Stock. In the discussion above we have more or less assumed that the constituent companies had no bonds or preferred stocks outstanding, and that the consolidated company issued only common stock to effect the combination. If the constituent companies have bonds outstanding they would, unless provision was made otherwise, be assumed by the consolidated company. Or the consolidated company might issue its own bonds and attempt to get the bondholders to exchange their bonds for the new issue. The new issue may be underwritten, and the bankers, and eventually investors, may furnish the money to call in or buy in the bonds whose holders will not exchange them. A simple solution for the exchange of bonds, and one that is often followed, is to exchange them dollar for dollar, giving due consideration, however, to the face rate of interest, the maturity, and the price at which the bonds of the constituent companies are quoted in the market. It was pointed out above that the consolidated company may also sell bonds for the purpose of securing money to buy the properties of the constituent companies, or to provide additional working capital, or for future expansion purposes.

If the constituent companies have preferred stock outstanding, it is common practice to offer them a similar preferred stock of the consolidated company in exchange for their shares. This is on the assumption that the preferred stock is nonparticipating in respect to dividends, which is usually the case. If the constituent companies all have different types of preferred outstanding, the consolidated company would ordinarily not create as many different issues, but rather additional shares or a larger aggregate par or stated value would be issued to compensate for a company whose preferred stock had a higher dividend rate, or other relatively valuable features.

If the constituent companies have no preferred stock outstanding, the consolidated company may nevertheless issue preferred stock in connection with the combination. In some instances, particularly in the past, preferred stock was given for the net tangible assets at their book value, and common stock issued for the goodwill, in other words, for the excess of the capitalized value of the earnings over the book value of the net assets. In recent years, however, unless preferred stock must be given in exchange for preferred stock of the constituent companies, only common stock has usually been issued to the companies or to their shareholders.

When bonds and other liabilities are assumed by the consolidated company, the amounts of these liabilities are deducted from the total asset valuation in order to determine the asset value which is represented by the stock. If a constituent company has preferred stock outstanding for which preferred stock of the consolidated is given in exchange, the amount of the preferred is then deducted from the asset value to arrive at the value of the assets which is represented by common stock. This will be illustrated later in the chapter.

Valuation Based on Market Value of Stock. In some instances the amount that is given for the properties or the amount of stock that is exchanged for the stock of the constituent companies in a combination is based, or partly based, on the aggregate market value of the stock. This, of course, can be done only when the stock is listed or has a more or less active over-the-counter market. Assuming that the company does not have bonds or preferred stocks outstanding, the value of the net assets may be considered to be equivalent to the aggregate market price of the stock. This is found by multiplying the market price per share, by the number of shares outstanding.

The question will arise as to what date will be selected for the market value of the stock. Certainly the date should be far enough in the past so that the market prices of the stocks of the companies affected would not have discounted the combination or the possibility or probability of a combination. Because of factors which might influence the market price of the stock of a particular company on any one day, it might be advisable to take the average price of the stock over a specified period of time.

The relative market prices of the stocks of the constituent companies is given great weight by the shareholders. For example, if the combination takes the form of a merger, the shareholders of the surviving company will probably have to offer the shareholders of the other company or companies stock with an aggregate market price at least as great as the stock to be exchanged. Otherwise, these shareholders would probably not vote in favor of the merger, since they could get more by selling their shares in the market. In case of a consolidation, the market price of the shares being offered by the consolidated company will depend upon the value of the constituent companies. But if the consolidated company offers Company *X*, for example, one share for each $100 of the share market value, the shareholders of Company *Y* might also demand a share for each $100 worth of stock as measured by the market price.

Basing the ratio of exchange of stock on the market prices is realistic in that the market prices usually reflect the possible future earnings of the companies. The value of their properties, the prospects for the future, the management, and all or other factors of importance, are considered by the investor or speculator, and the combination of these factors is reflected in the market price of the stock. If anyone thinks the stock is worth more than the market price, he can always secure more shares at the market price or slightly higher. If he thinks the stock is not worth the market price, he can always sell it, or sell it short, at that price or slightly lower. In other words, from a going-concern standpoint, the relative market prices of the stocks of several companies probably reflect the possible future worth of the companies better than any other single factor, or possible combination of factors.

As stated above, basing the consideration received by the companies or their shareholders on the market price of the stock can be used only when a more or less active market for the stock exists. Even when this is present, certain allowances must be taken into account. For example, the constituent companies may have followed a different dividend policy in the past, and this would influence the relative prices of their stock. Although retained earnings increase the book value of the stock and increase the earning base of a company, in most instances a liberal dividend policy would reflect more favorably on the market price of the stock. The depreciation policies followed by the companies will also have to be investigated. If one of the companies is a close corporation, relatively large salaries may have been paid in order to lessen the corporation income tax. This would reduce the earnings and thus affect the market price of the stock.

In a preceding section we discussed capitalization of earnings as a basis for determining the value of the constituent companies. Actually there may be little difference between using that method and the one just described of basing it on the market value of the stock. The stock of similar companies under similar circumstances will tend to sell at about the same multiple of earnings. Thus, the results obtained from the two methods may be practically the same.

HYPOTHETICAL EXAMPLES. We shall now illustrate the exchange of securities under a consolidation with the following assumptions and hypothetical figures. We assume that, under the circumstances present, the condition of the assets and the relationship between the current assets and the fixed assets present no unusual problems. We will further assume that the capitalization of earnings, at the rate of 12½ per cent, would be a fair basis for valuing the companies. An abbreviated balance sheet, and the amount of the average annual earnings of Companies *A* and *B* will follow.

	Company A	*Company B*
Tangible assets (less current liabilities)	$2,200,000	$3,400,000
Bonds (5%)		$1,000,000
Preferred stock (6%, par value, $100)	1,000,000	
Common stock (par value $100)	1,000,000	2,000,000
Surplus	200,000	400,000
Total liabilities and net worth	$2,200,000	$3,400,000
Average annual earnings (before bond interest)	$300,000	$450,000

It is noted that the figure for the "tangible assets" is shown above. If any intangible assets appeared on the books they have been ignored here because, by capitalizing the earnings to determine the values of the companies, we are thereby giving effect to any value that might be represented by intangible assets. Any current liabilities have been subtracted from the gross assets. Either these liabilities would be paid off from the gross assets of the constituent companies before the consolidation actually took place, or the consolidated company would assume them.

Companies *A* and *B* are to be consolidated into Company *C*, which has been organized for that purpose. The easiest method of handling the bonds of Company *B*, would be for Company *C* to assume them. The alternative would be for Company *C* to issue its own bonds and attempt to get as many as possible of *B*'s bondholders to exchange their bonds for the bonds of Company *C*. Bondholders who do not want to exchange their bonds might be paid off in cash (assuming their bonds are callable) from the sale of *C* bonds to investment bankers. Company *C* will issue its own preferred stock, with similar rights, in exchange for the preferred stock of Company *A*.

Capitalizing the earnings on a 12½ per cent basis, would give a valuation of $2,400,000 for Company *A* ($300,000 divided by .125 × 100), and a valuation of $3,600,000 for Company *B* ($450,000 divided by .125 × 100). Since $1,000,000 of the value of Company *A* is represented by preferred stock, the common stock equity (on the basis of earnings) would therefore be worth $1,400,000. Similarly, subtracting the amount of Company *B*'s bonds from the total valuation would give a valuation of $2,600,000 for the common stock equity. Adding the common stock valuation of the two companies, gives a total value of $4,000,000. Company *C* will therefore issue common stock in the amount of $4,000,000 (par value $100), and $1,400,000 will be exchanged to the shareholders of Company *A* for their stock, and $2,600,000 will go to Company *B*'s shareholders for their shares. Thus Company *A*'s shareholders will get 1.4 shares of Company *C* stock for each share of Company *A* they held, and *B*'s shareholders will get 1.3 shares for each old share held. The balance sheet of Company *C* would appear as follows:

Company C

Tangible assets	$6,000,000
Bonds	$1,000,000
Preferred stock	1,000,000
Common stock	4,000,000
Total liabilities and net worth	$6,000,000

An alternative method of handling the items on the balance sheet would be to carry the tangible assets at the same valuations as used by Companies *A* and *B*, which would be $5,600,000, and then writing in goodwill of $400,000. One of the objections to the latter procedure would be the question whether the stock of $5,000,000 (preferred and common) was fully paid since it was exchanged for assets valued on the books at a net value of $4,600,000 (after subtracting the $1,000,000 in bonds). The above solution was stated first because of its simplicity. A criticism of this method, however, is that the surplus of the constituent companies has been capitalized, with the result that the new consolidated Company *C* is starting out without a surplus present on the books. This could easily be remedied by the issuance of no-par stock with a relatively low stated value, or par value stock with a lower par value. For example, Company *C* might still issue 40,000 shares of common and exchange it on the same basis as stated above, but the par value per share could be established at $50. On the balance sheet the common stock would then be carried at $2,000,000, and a surplus of $2,000,000 would be written in. This, of course, would be a type of capital surplus, and should be treated as such.

Questions

1. In the case of a combination effected through the "purchase of assets" is the approval of the shareholders of both the seller and the buyer necessary? Explain.
2. Are dissenting shareholders entitled to any relief when all or a substantial part of the corporation's assets are sold? Explain.
3. Explain the rights of creditors of both the selling and buying corporation with respect to the specific property which is sold.
4. Indicate the nature of the tax consideration that may be involved in connection with the sale of assets.
5. Look up the statutes of your state to ascertain how a merger or consolidation may be effected.
6. Distinguish between mergers and consolidations.

7. In order to effect a merger or consolidation is it necessary to get the approval of the board of directors and shareholders of all companies affected? Explain.

8. What rights, if any, are possessed by shareholders who dissent to a merger or consolidation?

9. Indicate the rights of both secured and unsecured creditors of the constituent companies when a merger or consolidation takes place.

10. Indicate how the value of the assets of the constituent companies might be arrived at when a merger or consolidation is effected.

11. Indicate specifically how the earnings of the constituent companies in a merger or consolidation might be evaluated.

12. Explain how bondholders of the constituent companies might be handled in a merger or consolidation.

13. State the advantages and disadvantages of determining the basis for the exchange of stock in a merger or consolidation by taking the aggregate of the market value of the stocks of the constituent companies.

14. In determining the valuation of assets for purposes of a merger or consolidation what weight should be given to any goodwill accounts on the books of the constituent companies? Explain.

15. Of the various methods of determining the values of the constituent companies entering into a merger or consolidation discussed in this chapter, which would you as an impartial adviser recommend? Why?

Problems

1. Two companies in the same industry, which started business some years ago, have now, because of the severity of competition, started negotiations for consolidation. They are both close corporations, and neither one has access to the financial records of the other. Each one, however, has the latest balance sheet of the other under the date of Dec. 31, 19-3, and the net profit of each for the past 3 years is publicly known. The data follow:

Balance Sheets
As of December 31, 19-3

	The Royal Co.	*The Empire Co.*
Cash	$ 5,000	$ 4,000
Receivables	60,000	20,000
Inventory	120,000	50,000
Fixed Assets	450,000	212,000
Good Will	20,000	0
Payables	25,000	6,000
Capital Stock	450,000	200,000
Surplus	180,000	80,000

Net Income
For the years indicated

19-1	$40,000	$15,000
19-2	30,000	35,000
19-3	20,000	40,000

The stock of each company has a par value of $100 per share. It is proposed that the Amalgamated Corp. be formed with no-par stock only and that this stock be issued to the shareholders of the Royal and Empire companies in exchange for their shares, and the latter two companies will then be dissolved. The following proposals have been made:

Plan A. Mr. Whitelake of the Royal Co. proposed that the Amalgamated Corp. issue 18,200 shares to be exchanged for the stock of the other two companies on the bases of their book values.

Plan B. Mr. Coventry, a director of the Empire Co., proposed that 18,000 shares of the Amalgamated Corp. be issued. The average earnings for the past 3 years were to be capitalized on a 10 per cent basis for the purpose of valuing the stock of the two companies.

(a) Criticize each of these plans. (b) How many shares would go to a stockholder holding one share in his respective company under each of the plans stated? (c) At what valuation should the assets and the stock be carried on the books under each of these plans? Explain. (d) Indicate a plan you would recommend and your reasons.

2. Neither of the plans stated above was acceptable to the directors of the other company; so Mr. Kingington, a financial expert, was called in for advice. His plan (Plan *C*) was to capitalize the weighted average earnings on a 10 per cent basis to determine the value of the fixed assets. In doing this he multiplied the 19-1 earnings by one, the 19-2 earnings by two, and the 19-3 earnings by three. The three figures thus obtained were added, and this result was divided by six. The figure thus obtained was capitalized at 10 per cent.

The current assets were valued at the *net* current asset book value. This latter figure was then added to the capitalized earnings figure and the result was considered the valuation of the company. The intangible assets were disregarded. Mr. Kingington recommended that the Amalgamated Corp. issue 16,728 shares of no-par stock. Since the stock of the two companies was closely held in large blocks, the problem of handling warrants for fractional shares would not be difficult. (a) State your opinion in regard to this plan. (b) How many shares would go to each company? (c) How many new shares would the holder of 100 old shares in his respective company receive? (Fractional warrants will take care of uneven amounts.) (d) At what figure would you carry the assets and the capital stock on the books of the Amalgamated Corp? Why?

Chapter 31

HOLDING COMPANIES

Importance of the Holding Company. The holding company device has perhaps been the easiest and cheapest, and at the same time one of the most effective ways, of forming combinations in the United States. It was used in the early railroad combinations; industrial companies made extensive use of it starting in the 1890's; and public utilities since the turn of the century have built up tremendous systems through its use.

Many of our largest combinations today operate under the holding company system. This is true in various types of industry—railroads, public utilities, and industrials. Hundreds of companies, representing an investment running into the billions, are controlled by a relatively small number of top holding companies.

The holding company device has promoted and encouraged speculative interest in stocks, and practices carried on under it have likewise been partly responsible for the stock market crash in 1929 and the ensuing depression. Some holding company systems have resulted in political abuses. The consuming public has at times suffered from the abuses resulting from the holding company system, and Congress, in 1935, found it necessary to regulate holding companies in the public utility field through the Public Utility Holding Company Act of 1935. Holding companies also have been the subject of legislation and court decisions on combinations in restraint of trade.

Nature of Holding Company. As the term is generally used, a holding company is one that owns sufficient voting stock of another company to have *working control* over it. Working control would ordinarily be assumed to be control over the election of a majority of the board of directors. Whether class voting or cumulative voting are permitted may influence the proportion of stock needed for control. The total amount of voting stock issued and the distribu-

Accounting Records and Reports. The Commission has set up rigid standardized accounting regulations for the holding company systems. Particular attention is given to provisions for depreciation and maintenance. The accounting regulations are designed to prevent the holding companies from "milking" the subsidiaries. The Commission may require annual, quarterly, and other periodic reports from registered holding companies. Both civil and criminal penalties are provided for false and misleading statements in accounts and reports.

Other Regulation. The Federal Power Act subjects electric utility companies transmitting and selling electric energy across state lines to regulation of the Federal Power Commission. Since this legislation does not refer directly to holding companies, and since it is concerned more with the operational aspects of the electric utility business, it has not been discussed here. In event of conflict between the regulation of electric utility companies under the Federal Power Commission, and that by the Securities and Exchange Commission under the Public Utility Holding Company Act of 1935, the latter prevails.

Railroad holding companies formed since June 16, 1933, are subject to control of the Interstate Commerce Commission, but those formed before that time are not so controlled. Bank holding companies are under the control of the Board of Governors of the Federal Reserve System. Air transport holding companies are regulated by the Civil Aeronautics Board. Holding companies in the industrial field are not subject to any special legislation. They, like ordinary companies are, of course, subject to the Securities Acts and to the antitrust laws.

Questions

1. What right, if any, does a corporation have to own shares in other corporations?
2. (a) What is meant by a holding company? (b) What different types of holding companies are found in business?
3. Indicate the advantages of forming a combination through the use of the holding company device as compared with a merger or consolidation.
4. What are the possible disadvantages to the parties concerned of using the holding company to effect a combination as compared with a merger or consolidation?
5. How much of the capitalization of an operating company is it necessary for a holding company to own in order to control the company? Explain.
6. Illustrate how the same effect as leverage results even when a holding company has no securities except common stock outstanding.

7. Illustrate how it is possible on a negligible amount of money to gain control of properties worth billions of dollars through the use of the holding company device.

8. Explain the nature of the abuses which have developed with the use of the holding company device. Have these been eliminated? Explain.

9. What are the principal provisions of the Public Utility Holding Company Act of 1935?

10. Some believe that holding companies are unnecessary, and that they should be abolished, and no new ones permitted. Do you agree? Explain.

Problems

1. Mr. A. Wizard has worked out a plan for the promotion of a number of utilities in South America. He wants to control all these utilities on a small amount of capital. His present plan calls for the construction of four utilities in each of four South American countries (a total of 16 companies). An intermediate holding company is to be formed in each of the countries to control each of the four utilities operating within that country, and a top holding company is to be organized to control the four intermediate holding companies.

The gross income of each of the operating companies is expected to be $20,000,000 annually, and profit before bond interest is paid is expected to be 8 per cent of the gross income. Sufficient operating company securities will be sold to construct the necessary plants, etc., and pay for the costs of selling all the securities, including those issued by the holding companies.

In determining the capitalization of the operating companies it has been decided that only one bond issue will be sold for each company and that the bond interest should be earned exactly four times. Common stock will be issued in an amount equal (in par value) to the bonds sold, and half of this common stock will be nonvoting. Preferred stock dividends will take only 20 per cent of the amount available for such dividends. The bonds of all the operating and holding companies will bear an interest rate of 5 per cent, and all the preferred stock issued will be 6 per cent nonparticipating and nonvoting. Two-thirds of the amount available for operating company common stock dividends will be paid as dividends on the common shares. All the stock of both operating and holding companies has a par value of $100 per share, and all the bonds, a face value of $1,000 each.

The intermediate holding companies will sell securities in an amount necessary to acquire a 50 per cent interest in the voting common stock of the operating companies. All securities of both operating and holding companies will be sold at their par value. The intermediate holding companies will issue the same amount of nonvoting common stock as voting common stock; preferred stock equal (in par value) to the common stock will be issued; and the amount of bonds issued will be equal to the common and preferred stock combined. The intermediate holding companies have no assets other than the stock of the operating companies. Their only income is the dividends paid by the operating companies, and all this is paid out to the security holders in the form of interest and dividends.

The top holding company owns only a 50 per cent interest in the voting stock of the intermediate holding companies. Its only income is the dividends paid by the intermediate holding companies, and all this is paid out to the security holders in the form of interest and dividends. The top holding company issues bonds, preferred stock and voting and nonvoting common stock in an amount necessary to acquire at par value the 50 per cent interest in the voting stock of the intermediate holding companies, and the amounts of these securities issued bear the same relation to its total capitalization as in the case of the intermediate holding companies. (a) Indicate the financial structure of an operating company, an intermediate holding company, and the top holding company. (b) Prepare an income statement for each type of company, showing the amount of dividends paid. (c) Assuming 50 per cent of the voting stock to be controlling interest, how much stock of the top holding company would Mr. Wizard have to have in order to control all the operating companies? Explain. What percentage dividend would he receive? (d) What were the earnings per share on the operating company's common stock? (e) If both the gross income and the expenses (other than interest) of the operating companies declined 10 per cent and they continued to pay out two-thirds of the amount available for common dividends, how much in dividends would Mr. Wizard receive based on part (c)? Assume that the capitalizations remained the same and that the holding companies continued their same dividend policies.

(In the foregoing problem the foreign taxes [assume no income taxes] and other expenses, except bond interest, of the holding companies are assumed to be paid by the operating companies in return for the managerial services furnished by the holding companies, and they are included in the expenses of the operating companies.)

2. Look up a "consolidated" balance sheet of a holding company system (in which the holding company owns no operating properties directly) in whatever source is available to you. (a) The property accounts of what companies appear on the statement? (b) Do the securities of the operating companies owned by the holding company appear as assets? Why or why not? (c) What consideration is given to the securities of operating companies which are not owned by the holding company?

Chapter 32

INVESTMENT COMPANIES

NATURE OF INVESTMENT COMPANIES. *Investment companies* are formed for the purpose of investing the proceeds of the sale of their own securities in the securities of other companies. The purpose of buying securities of other companies is investment rather than control, the latter being the objective of the holding company. The investment company, through the sale of its own shares, offers the investor a part ownership in the securities of a large number of other companies. In addition to this diversification, the investment company is in a better position, through its expert management, to decide what securities are the best to buy, and when to buy and sell them, than is the average investor.

Investment companies are sometimes called *investment trusts.* This is due to the fact that many of the early companies were formed under the Massachusetts trust form of organization. Some of those in existence today, such as the Massachusetts Investors Trust, are still operating under this form of organization. Most of them, however, are formed as corporations, and that perhaps is one of the reasons why they are now often referred to as investment "companies" rather than "trusts." Also the Investment Company Act of 1940, which will be discussed later in the chapter, calls them "companies." When the term "investment trust" is used, however, we should interpret it as referring to the type of company rather than the form of organization which is used. A few of the investment companies, such as the Adams Express Company, are formed and operating as joint stock associations. The form of organization under which the particular investment company is operating is of little interest to the investor.

EARLY HISTORY. Although the modern business type corporation originated in America, we must go abroad for the origin and development of investment companies. Wiesenberger[1] states that the origin can probably be traced to the Société Générale de Belgique, which was formed in 1822, by King William I of Belgium. Aside from this company and a few other isolated ones formed on the Continent, the real start of the organization of investment trusts began in Dundee, Scotland, in 1868, with the formation of the Foreign & Colonial Government Trust.[2] As the name would indicate this company was formed for the purpose of diminishing or diversifying the risk in the purchase of foreign and colonial government securities. Between 1868 and 1875, 15 investment companies were formed in Dundee.[3] One of the most successful of these was the Scottish-American Investment Company, which was formed in 1873.[4]

The early British trusts were fairly conservative. The emphasis was on income rather than capital appreciation. Diversification, particularly geographical diversification, was carried on to a considerable extent. Many of the securities purchased were those of the Commonwealth, or possessions, and foreign securities. Most of the companies had balanced portfolios, and they issued stock similar to our common and preferred stock, and debenture bonds. In many instances, however, founders' shares gave the organizers and managers a much larger return on their investment.

Early American Experience. The first investment company formed in the United States was the Boston Personal Property Trust, which was organized in Boston, in 1894.[5] This company is still in existence today. There were not many such companies formed in the United States, however, until the late 1920's. There was ample opportunity here for investors to buy the securities of operating companies which had possibilities of making greater profits for the investors than investing in the conservative investment companies.

In the late 1920's investment company formation began in earnest. Business was prosperous and stock prices were mounting. People were eager to purchase stocks with the hopes of making their profit through the sale at a higher price. Possible future earnings and dividends were projected ahead some years at the same

[1] Arthur Wiesenberger & Co., *Investment Companies* (15th ed.; New York, 1955), p. 19.

[2] Rudolph L. Weissman, *The Investment Company and the Investor* (New York: Harper & Bros., 1951), pp. 1, 3.

[3] *Ibid.*, p. 3.

[4] *Ibid.*

[5] Wiesenberger, *op. cit.*, p. 20.

trend that had been going on, and the existing prices of stocks were discounting this future possibility. People were talking about the New Era in which they expected things to keep booming indefinitely.

Investment bankers make their living through the sale of new securities. They promoted new companies and consolidated old ones in order to give rise to a new issue of securities which they could sell. When these possibilities were worked dry, they turned to the investment company idea. The bankers would form an investment company and sell the securities of this company to the public. They made their commission or profits on this sale. The proceeds from the sale would then be invested in the securities of other companies. In this way they capitalized on existing securities to sell new securities to the public. The bankers would also get a fee for managing the investment company.

The idea of investment companies was good—offering the small investor a wide diversification which he otherwise could not get, so-called expert management in the selection of the securities purchased, and the timing of the buying and selling. The shares of the investment companies, along with other types of companies, were in demand. In many instances investment bankers found it convenient to have an affiliated investment company because if they were unable directly to sell some corporate issue which they had taken over, they would merely dump it into the hands of the investment company and the latter would sell more securities to the public to secure the money to pay for it.

In addition to the weaknesses stated above, investment companies formed in the late 1920's were subject to the following criticisms. Many of them issued too high a percentage of senior securities. The selling and management fees were in many instances excessive. Inadequate information was given the investor relative to the methods of operation. Accounting methods were not standardized, and in many cases were subject to question. In many companies the reserves were inadequate to protect the company in event of a decline in security prices. Many of the companies were formed in the late 1920's when the prices of the securities they purchased were excessively high. When the stock market crash of 1929 came, terrific losses were taken by the holders of investment company shares. Of course, heavy losses were also taken by the owners of shares of other types of companies. But the weaknesses of investment company organization and operation began to show up at that time. We shall resume our discussion of the development of invest ment companies after we have considered the different types of companies.

Types of Investment Companies. There are several different ways of classifying investment companies. One is according to the form of organization used. This was discussed above, and is, as mentioned there, of minor importance. Another distinction is based on the nature of their portfolio. We will say more about this later. Still another method of classification, which we will discuss now, is according to the fundamental way in which they are set up for the sale, and in some instances for the repurchase, of their shares and the general operation of their business.

Face-amount installment certificate companies. Face-amount certificate companies contract with the investor for the sale to him on the installment plan of a certificate with a face or maturity value of a specified amount, such as $1,000. Payments are made in fixed amounts at specified dates over a period of from 10 to 15 years. Dividends are credited against the certificates, and these together with the installment payments build up the worth of the certificate to its face value at maturity. If cashed in before maturity, the certificates will have a surrender value, but during the first few years, when lapses are relatively high, there will either be no surrender value, or if there is one, it may be less than the investor has paid in. The investor pays a high selling cost for this installment type certificate, and it is not recommended for the average person. There are only a comparatively small number of these companies in existence in the United States, and nothing further will be said about them.

Another type of company similar to the above is the installment investment plan company. Like the face-amount company, it is of relatively minor importance. Later we will say something about the installment plans of open-end companies.

Unit or fixed or semi-fixed companies. The unit trust, or as it is sometimes called, the "fixed" trust was of some importance in the late 1920's and the early 1930's, but it is practically obsolete today. Under this plan a fixed group of securities or "unit" of securities was deposited by the sponsor with a bank or trust company, and against these, certificates of beneficial ownership in the unit of securities were sold to the public. The list of securities deposited remained "fixed," and could not be altered. In the case of the "semi-fixed" trusts, the management was given limited powers for the substitution of securities. According to the terms of the contract, the holder of the trust shares could convert them into cash equivalent to the value of his undivided portion of the securities deposited, or if he possessed sufficient certificates, he might convert them into a unit of deposited securities.

The *fixed trust* (more appropriate title since the certificates were not issued by a company) represented an effort to protect against poor management, and it was relatively popular for several years following the stock market crash in 1929. Naturally, it lacked the advantages of good management.

Closed-end companies. Closed-end companies are so called because they have a relatively fixed amount of securities outstanding. They may from time to time sell additional securities, the same as any other type corporation. Also they may occasionally purchase some of their securities in the market like other companies do. The shares issued by the larger closed-end companies are listed on the New York Stock Exchange, or other exchanges, and are bought and sold by investors through brokers the same as securities of ordinary corporations. The prices of these shares are therefore dependent upon the law of supply and demand, similar to other listed stocks. A few closed-end shares sell at a premium over their book value, but the great majority of them sell at substantial discounts below their book value.

Some of the closed-end companies issue preferred stock and bonds, in addition to common stock, while others confine themselves to the issuance of only common stock. Most of the closed-end companies invest in a broadly diversified list of common stocks.

The closed-end companies were patterned after the British companies. Practically all of the leading 29 closed-end companies in the country today were formed in the 1920's.[6] The largest closed-end company today is Tri-Continental Corporation, which was organized in 1929. The second-largest company is The Lehman Corporation which was formed in the same year. The shares of both of these companies are listed on the New York Stock Exchange. The assets (less current liabilities) of these companies at the beginning of 1956 were $278,027,599, and $233,362,650, respectively.

Open-end companies. The *open-end* investment companies stand ready at all times to sell new shares to investors and to buy back the shares outstanding. They are often called *mutual companies,* or *mutual funds.* Sales are made at the then existing book value of the shares plus a loading charge, which will be explained later. A few of the companies do not add a loading charge. They pur-

[6] Wiesenberger, *op. cit.,* p. 232.

chase the shares back usually at the existing book value. It is this constant sale and repurchase of the shares that distinguishes these companies from all others. The shares of the open-end companies are not listed on the stock exchanges. They are bought and sold through selling agents of the issuer or brokers who specialize in them, or they may be handled by ordinary brokers. Part of the loading charge goes to the broker. In some instances they are sold and bought directly by the issuing company.

The open-end companies, with a few exceptions, have only one class of stock outstanding. They do not issue preferred stock, nor do they sell bonds. The Investment Company Act of 1940, which will be discussed later in the chapter, forbids the creation of any new open-end companies with senior securities.

Although some of the open-end companies confine their investment portfolio to a list of common stocks of a particular industry, others have a broad diversified list of common stocks. Many of the open-ends have a balanced portfolio consisting of common stocks, preferred stocks, and bonds. Some of the open-end companies invest only in bonds, while others buy only preferred stocks.

The open-end company had its origin in the United States. The first open-end company to be formed was the Massachusetts Investors Trust, which was organized in Boston, in 1924. This company, which had assets (less current liabilities) of $957,467,000 on January 1, 1956, is also the largest investment company of any kind. This company invests practically all of its funds in the stocks of large, well-known companies. The largest balanced open-end company, and the second largest open-end investment company, is Investors Mutual, Inc., which was formed in 1940, by the Investors Diversified Services, Inc., of Minneapolis.

Investment companies, particularly the open-end companies, have had their greatest development since 1942. As noted in Table 41, the total assets of all investment companies increased from $1,044,114,000 in 1942, to a total of $9,036,609,000 at the beginning of 1956. This represents an increase of nearly 765 per cent. During this period the closed-end companies' assets increased from $557,264,000 to $1,199,085,000, or an increase of 115 per cent. But during the same time, the open-end companies' assets increased from $486,850,000 to $7,837,524,000, which is an increase of 1,510 per cent! Part of the net gain in assets has been due to the increase in stock prices, but in the case of the open-ends, particularly, it has resulted in large measure from the increase in the number of shares outstanding.

TABLE 41

GROWTH OF INVESTMENT COMPANY ASSETS, TOTAL ASSETS (END OF YEAR)

Year	*Open-End*	*Closed-End*	*Total*
1955	$7,837,524,000	$1,199,085,000	$9,036,609,000
1954	6,109,390,000	1,188,204,000	7,297,594,000
1953	4,146,061,000	928,458,000	5,074,519,000
1952	3,931,407,000	978,096,000	4,909,503,000
1951	3,129,629,000	942,459,000	4,072,088,000
1950	2,530,563,000	843,462,000	3,374,025,000
1948	1,505,762,000	744,728,000	2,250,449,000
1946	1,311,108,000	851,409,000	2,162,517,000
1944	882,191,000	739,021,000	1,621,202,000
1942	486,850,000	557,264,000	1,044,114,000
1940	447,959,000	613,589,000	1,061,548,000

SOURCE: Wiesenberger, *op. cit.*, 16th ed., 1956, p. 17.

In conclusion on our classification of investment companies it should be stated that both closed-end and open-end companies are classed under the head of *management investment companies.* This terminology results from the fact that in the case of both of these types of companies the management has full discretion in the selling or buying of securities for the portfolio. This is in contrast to the situation present in the unit or fixed investment trust.

CLASSIFIED ACCORDING TO NATURE OF PORTFOLIO. We indicated above that some investment companies diversify their portfolios more than others. The companies are sometimes classified as follows on the basis of their investments. (The word "fund" is more commonly used than "company" with this classification.)

Balanced fund. Balanced funds are found among the open-ends, but rarely among closed-ends. This type of fund has part of the investments in preferred stock and bonds as well as common stocks. In some instances government bonds and cash will form part of the portfolio. The average investor does not have sufficient capital to diversify between bonds and stocks. If he buys all stocks the risk is maximized, and he has no protection against deflation. If he buys nothing but bonds, his return will be relatively low, and he will have no protection against inflation. The balanced fund offers the small investor a part ownership in a wide list of both stocks and bonds. He thus is somewhat hedged against both inflation and deflation, his risk is less, and the average return should not be excessively low.

There is no law that governs the proportion of bonds and stocks. The management may tend to work out of stocks somewhat as the market advances, and buy more heavily in bonds. After a decline in the prices of stocks, the investment procedure may be reversed. As would be expected, the balanced fund is more conservative than a common stock fund. Balanced funds differ as to emphasis on income and appreciation. The following are among the leading balanced funds:

American Business Shares, Inc.
Boston Fund, Inc.
Eaton and Howard Balanced Fund
Investors Mutual, Inc.
Scudder, Stevens & Clark Fund
Wellington Fund, Inc.

Bond funds. There are several investment companies whose investment portfolios consist only of bonds. In some instances these are investment grade bonds, while others have more speculative ones. The securities offered by such companies have the advantages and disadvantages of purchasing bonds, but of course, the small investor can get a wide diversification and good management. The following are among the leading bond funds:

The Bond Fund of Boston, Inc.
Keystone Custodian Funds, B-1, B-2, B-3, and B-4.
Manhattan Bond Fund, Inc.

Preferred stock funds. There are a few investment companies specializing in the purchase of only preferred stock. Similar to the bond funds, the shares issued by these companies have the advantages and disadvantages of purchasing preferred stock, but like any other investment company, the investor gets the advantage of expert management and diversification. The following are among the leading funds of this kind:

Keystone Custodian Funds, K-1, and K-2.
National Securities Preferred Stock Series.

Diversified common stock funds. The majority of the investment companies come under the classification of diversified common stock funds. In some instances these companies will purchase some speculative bonds or preferred stocks, and in some cases a small amount of high-grade senior securities, but the great bulk of their investments consists of common stock. There is a wide variation, however, in the objective of the companies and the type of common stock which they purchase. Some, like Massachusetts Investors Trust, which is a conservative company, keep their funds fully invested in high-grade dividend paying stocks. This company stresses both dividend return and appreciation in the principal. Some, such as The Lehman Corporation, put more emphasis on "growth" possibilities and seek capital appreciation perhaps more than dividend returns. Keystone Custodian Funds S-4, specializes in speculative low-price shares that generally move faster, both ways, than the general market.

Among the leading diversified common stock funds are both open-end and closed-end companies. Following are among the leading companies.

Open-end

Dividend Shares, Inc.
Fidelity Fund, Inc.
Fundamental Investors, Inc.
Incorporated Investors
Keystone Custodian Funds, S-1, S-2, S-3, and S-4.
Loomis-Sayles Mutual Fund (principally common stock)
Massachusetts Investors Trust
State Street Investment Corporation[7]

Closed-end

The Adams Express Company
General American Investors Co., Inc.
The Lehman Corporation
Tri-Continental Corporation
U. S. & Foreign Securities Corporation

Funds specializing in one or more industries. Some of the investment companies specialize in the securities of companies within one industry, or within a few industries. Some of them are common stock funds, while others have a more balanced portfolio. Both closed-end and open-end companies are found in this classification. In some instances the particular company has several funds of a somewhat different character. Some of the companies, like Atlas Corporation, go in for "special situations" where they get controlling interests and exercise managerial rights. Following are among the leading companies in this classification. Both closed- and open-end companies are represented:

Atlas Corporation
Chemical Fund, Inc.
Diversified Funds, Inc.
Equity Corporation

[7] No new shares offered since 1944, so it is actually the same as a closed-end company.

Group Securities, Inc.
Newmont Mining Corporation
The United Corporation

Charges for Buying Shares. All except a few of the open-end investment companies charge a selling fee which is included in the price the investor pays for the shares. The typical open-end company computes the book value of its shares (net assets based on market price of investments divided by total shares outstanding), twice daily. The investment company shares will in most instances be offered to the investor at the book value plus the selling charge, or as it is commonly called, the "loading charge." Most companies have a loading charge of 7½ per cent of the selling price.

If a company has a loading charge of 7½ per cent, and its shares are offered at $20, it means that 7½ per cent of this, or $1.50, is the amount the investor is paying to the distributors of the shares. The book value of the shares would therefore be only $18.50. Some erroneously believe that a loading charge of 7½ per cent, means 7½ per cent of the book value. If $1.50 is charged when the book value is $18.50, the selling or loading charge is almost 8.11 per cent of the book value of the share. When the investment company's shares are sold through a wholesale distributor, he may get ⅓ of the loading charge, and the broker or retail seller will get ⅔ of it.

Investment companies will buy back their shares usually at the then existing book value. In the above example, it is apparent that the market price of the stock would have to rise $1.50 before the investor would be even with the board. Since the investor can sell the stock at its book value, that means the stock would have to go up approximately 8.11 per cent (not 7½ per cent). Also it should be noted that the inclusion of the loading charge in the selling price tends to cut down the yield to the investor since the yield will always be based on the purchase price of the stock.

If a person buys shares of an ordinary corporation, or a closed-end investment company, he does not have to pay a loading charge, but he will have to pay a broker's commission to buy the stock, and another broker's commission to sell it. A comparison of the relative costs of buying an open-end share and a closed-end share should, therefore, take that fact into consideration. The price of closed-end company shares depends, of course, on the market price as set by buyers and sellers, rather than on the book value. The amount of the broker's commissions depends upon the money value of the shares purchased and the shares sold. In most instances, where 100 or more shares are bought, the commission would average less than

1 per cent on each transaction. If less than 100 shares are purchased, the odd-lot differential must also be taken into consideration. For stocks selling at less than $40, the differential would be ⅛ of a point. If a person purchased 40 shares of a closed-end company's stock that was selling for $18.50 in the market, he would pay broker's commissions and odd-lot differentials totaling $16.20. The same amount would be paid if he sold the stock at the same price. Thus, the total buying and selling charges would be $32.40. This would be equivalent to a charge of $.81 a share, or approximately 4.4 per cent. This is only slightly more than half the cost of buying and selling shares of an open-end company.

Other things equal, the yield on the closed-end shares would tend to be more. In the above example, the purchaser of the closed-end shares would pay a total of $18.90½ a share. ($18.50 plus odd-lot differential and commissions of $.405.) The yield would be computed on that price, while in the case of the open-end company it would be computed on the purchase price of $20 a share.

Some open-end companies reduce the loading charge rate on large orders, or on sales made to fiduciaries. For example, some charge 7½ per cent on transactions of less than $25,000, and then a graded scale down until on sales of $50,000 or more, the charge is only 4 per cent. To fiduciaries the 4 per cent may be charged on sales of $25,000 and more.

Several of the open-end companies, however, do not include any loading or selling charge in the price of their shares. They sell the shares at the book value, and purchase them back also at the book value. Among the companies following this practice are the Loomis-Sayles Mutual Fund, Inc., Scudder, Stevens & Clark Common Stock Fund, Inc., and Scudder, Stevens & Clark Fund, Inc.

Market Price of Closed-End Companies. The prices of closed-end investment companies seek their own level in the market, and in the case of most companies this is normally at a discount of from 10 to 40 per cent or more from the book value. Although the open-ends are priced at book value plus a loading charge, people do not necessarily expect any correlation between the market value of ordinary stocks and their book value. But in the case of investment companies a more direct real relationship is logical. The market prices of corporate securities reflect the prospective earning power and dividends. The assets of the investment companies consist of these securities. And the shares issued by the investment company represent a fractional interest in these securities held in the portfolio. So some correlation should exist.

But why do the closed-ends usually sell at substantial discounts from the book value? Several reasons may account for this. In the first place, the investment company is not going to sell all the securities in its portfolio and distribute the proceeds to its shareholders. Also, some of the assets may be in low yielding investments such as government bonds, or held as cash waiting a favorable time for investment. Then too we must remember that the investment company will have to pay all of its expenses out of the income received before it can pay any dividends to its shareholders.

In some companies the leverage obtained from the issuance of bonds is so great that the earnings possibilities on the shares is appreciable, with the result that in good times the shares may sell at a premium over the book value. In some instances, such as the Lehman Corporation, the market appraises the management so high that the stock has in recent years been selling at a premium. This is a conservative, well-managed, nonleverage company. But the premiums resulting from high leverage are sometimes found among speculative companies.

TABLE 42

Discounts (Percentage Below Book Values) at Which Closed-End Investment Companies Were Selling at the End of Each Year, 1950–1955

Stock	*1955*	*1954*	*1953*	*1952*	*1951*	*1950*
Equity Corp.	51%	50%	53%	50%	44%	42%
Tri-Continental	48	35	45	40	47	43
U.S. & Foreign Securities	26	26	37	25	31	33
Pennroad Corp.	24	8	2	6	*	1
Adams Express	17	22	27	15	22	28
General American Investors	16	3	7	*	*	7
Newmont Mining	13	6	23	7	3	9
Lehman Corp.	12	*	3	*	*	*
Atlas Corp.	7	11	27	30	30	26

* Premium over book value.

Source: Wiesenberger, *op. cit.*, 16th ed., 1956, p. 242.

Since most of the closed-ends usually sell at a discount from the book value, the current yield should be higher than that obtained from an open-end company which is selling at its book value plus a selling charge. This is assuming other things such as the management, etc., are the same. Although the shares could be purchased at a discount, the capital gain arising from the sale of the shares might not be any greater since it would probably also be sold at a discount. If a share is selling at a greater discount than similarly situated closed-ends, then perhaps the future outlook for the particular company might not be favorable.

When a premium must be paid for a closed-end, it would tend to reduce the yield—other things being equal. But the presence of a premium is usually an indication that investors are willing to pay it to secure above-average management. The future dividends or capital gains might therefore justify the premium. Furthermore, a share purchased at a premium over the book value probably can also be sold at a premium.

MANAGEMENT FEES. The principal item in the operating expenses of investment companies is the fee paid to the management. In the typical company the management is paid an annual fee of ½ of 1 per cent of the average value of the net assets. This is usually computed quarterly. The other expenses include taxes, legal and auditing fees, and fees to the custodian of the portfolio, registrar, and transfer agents. The total expenses average usually from ⅔ to ¾ of 1 per cent of the net assets, or between 12 and 15 per cent of the annual cash income of the company.

If a person directly owns the securities of operating companies he will get 100 per cent of the dividends paid. But if he buys the shares of an investment company that owns these same securities, the investment company will get these dividends, and from them, it will have to pay the expenses stated above. The investor will receive whatever the investment company pays out in dividends. Usually this is substantially all of the income of the investment company after expenses have been paid and reserves have been set up.

It is sometimes argued that the investor would be better off to buy the shares of operating companies directly, rather than indirectly through the investment company, and thus receive 100 per cent of the dividends paid by the various companies whose shares are held. However, it should be realized that the average investor does not have sufficient capital to get the wide diversification that an investment company offers. Furthermore, he receives the advantage of expert management in the selection of the securities held by the investment company and in the timing of buying and selling. In some instances the so-called "expert management" has not been able to do much better than the performance of the stock averages, and some people have wondered at times whether the management was worth the price being paid for it.

A criticism of the type just made may, however, not be a fair one. An investor has no assurance that he would do as well as the performance of the stock averages. He might, for example, not buy stocks that moved the same way or as much as the stock averages. Furthermore, even if he had sufficient capital to buy the stocks that comprise one of the averages, he might trade in them with the result that any gains made might not be as much as if he had held the stocks and not traded.

Even though an investor can get diversification and expert management in buying the shares of investment companies, the performance of the various companies varies widely. The average person might not select the right company. But even if he does pick a good company, he might do the same thing that he would do if he were buying shares of operating companies directly—he might buy the investment company shares high, and sell them low. In other words, even though the investment company is being expertly managed, the individual investor still has to decide when he is going to buy and when he is going to sell the investment company shares.

Cumulative Investment Plans. In order to take the emotion out of stock buying, and thus obviate the possibility or probability of buying at relatively high prices, some people follow the procedure of investing a fixed amount of money in stocks at regular intervals of time. This is called *dollar averaging*, and was discussed earlier in the book (see p. 455). In recent years a number of the open-end investment companies have started a "cumulative investment program," or "systematic investment program," whereby a person can invest an initial amount, ranging from $50 to $250, and then invest a fixed amount, usually from $25 to $70 monthly or quarterly or some other specified regular period. Since the investment company's portfolio contains a wide list of securities of different companies, the investor gets diversification with the initial and the periodical purchases. Furthermore, the management of the investment company does the selection. Another advantage of this plan is that the investment company handles all the administration of the investment program. The investor is billed for the fixed amount at the periods specified. But the cumulative purchase of shares is optional with the investor—he is under no obligation to purchase any shares at any time.

Some companies will apply the entire amount of the periodic investment toward the purchase of their shares and fractional shares. Others will sell the maximum number of whole shares, and credit the investor's account with the balance, which will be used at the time of the next periodic investment in purchasing additional whole shares. Usually certificates representing the shares purchased are not sent to the investor unless he requests them, or until 100 shares have been accumulated. Most companies make it optional with the investor whether the dividends, either from regular income or from capital gains, are to be sent to him or credited directly to his account and used toward the purchase of additional shares. Most investors follow the latter procedure, which builds up the account faster, in the same way that compound interest works. Statements are regularly sent to the investor showing the status of his account.

Due to the risks of stock buying, whether it be in regular corporations or investment companies, a person should not put all his money into stocks, and a cumulative plan such as just described should not be substituted for a regular savings account in a financial institution. It should only supplement such an account.

Dollar averaging is subject to several shortcomings. In the first place, a person may have the necessary amount of money to carry out the program in good times, but when a depression hits he may have to discontinue it. If this occurs, the result may be that the shares are purchased only when stock prices are high. Another weakness, which is not a criticism of the plan but rather of the investor, is that a person may be tempted to buy more shares than the plan calls for when business conditions are good, and that is just the time stock prices are relatively high. Furthermore, during a depression the investor may get discouraged and, even though he may have the money, he may purchase a few shares only or none at all. This is the time stock prices are lowest, and if no shares are purchased, the investor forgoes the opportunity of accumulating many shares at relatively low prices.

A question may be raised when shares are to be sold when the dollar averaging plan is used. The plan itself provides for the continued purchase of shares on the theory that stock prices over a long period of years will continue upward, since they have done so in the past. If an investor attempts to sell out at what he believes are the peaks, he may eventually be back to the old practice of buying high and selling low.

THE INVESTMENT COMPANY ACT OF 1940. Due to the bad practices which had been followed by many investment companies, and as a result of a study made by the Securities and Exchange Commission, Congress, in 1940, enacted the Investment Company Act. Following are the principal features of the Act. (Face-amount certificate companies are subject to some other requirements not stated here.)

All investment companies are required to register as such with the Securities and Exchange Commission, which administers the Act. Investment companies must have a minimum capital of $100,000 before they can publicly sell shares. Open-end companies formed after the Act can issue only one class of securities—common stock. Closed-end companies can issue bonds and preferred stock, but any such bonds must be covered three times by the assets, and preferred stock must be covered twice. Only one class of bonds and one class of preferred stock may be issued by the closed-ends. Any preferred stock issued must be voting.

The registration statement that must be filed by the investment company with the Securities and Exchange Commission must contain a description of the company, the method of operation, and the investment policy it intends to follow. A statement of the investment policy must be included in the prospectus or other material given to prospective investors. Semiannual financial statements must be sent to the shareholders. When dividends are paid the shareholders must be informed what part, if any, represents capital gains or other special sources of income.

The Act provides that a majority of the board of directors or the board of trustees cannot be connected with the investment banking firm or brokers who handle the sale or purchase of the company's shares. At least 40 per cent of the directors must be persons who are not officers of the investment company or investment advisers of the company.

Investment companies formed after the adoption of the Act are prohibited from buying sufficient shares in other investment companies to obtain working control of the other companies.

The sale of new shares is subject to the provisions of the Securities Act of 1933. The Investment Company Act further regulates the sale of investment company securities. In practice this has been done largely by voluntary action through the National Association of Security Dealers, which is subject to the jurisdiction of the Securities and Exchange Commission.

Taxation of Investment Companies and Their Shares. Unless registered with the Internal Revenue Service as a "regulated investment company," an investment company would pay the same corporate taxes that are paid by any other type of corporation. That means that all of the interest income received, except that earned on tax-exempt bonds, must be reported. But in order to lessen the amount of double taxation, investment companies, like other corporations, are required to report only 15 per cent of the dividends received on the stock which they own. Capital gains, which are profits made on the sale of securities held in the portfolio, are reported as such. The tax rate on the long-term capital gains (made on securities held for more than six months) is 25 per cent.

The investor owning shares in a nonregulated investment company would pay the same income taxes that are paid by a shareholder of any other type of corporation. Some companies cannot qualify as a "regulated investment company," and are, therefore, taxed as any ordinary type of corporation because they do not pay a sufficient amount of their earnings out to the shareholders in the form of dividends. Other companies could qualify but wish to remain "nonregulated" in order to gain certain tax advantages for their shareholders arising from the incurring of capital losses from the sale of securities which have been acquired at relatively high prices.

The terms "nonregulated" and "regulated," as used above, are perhaps misleading. All investment companies are "regulated" by the Securities and Exchange Commission in the administration of the Investment Act of 1940. But when we use the term in connection with taxation, we are using it in a different sense. It is realized by the government that when investment companies are taxed as ordinary corporations, triple taxation to some extent results. That is, the ordinary corporation whose shares are owned by the investment company pays the corporate rate on its income. The investment company then must pay the corporation tax on the dividends (income) received on the shares of this corporation which it owns (subject, however, to the 85 per cent credit). Thus far, it is double taxation. Then the owner of the investment company shares would have to pay the personal income tax on the dividends received on his shares. Now we have triple taxation.

To lessen the tax burden, if an investment company, either open- or closed-end, can qualify, it may register with the Internal Revenue Service as a *regulated investment company.* One of the requirements for a regulated company is that it must pay out in dividends at least 90 per cent of its net income, exclusive of capital gains, for any taxable year. We will state the other requirements later. A regulated investment company does not have to pay any corporation income taxes on that portion of its income, whether obtained from ordinary income or capital gains, which is paid out in dividends to its shareholders. But it pays the regular corporate tax on the portion retained. (It is still allowed an 85 per cent credit on dividends received.) Any gains arising from the sale of securities are considered capital gains and are taxed as such (if not paid out in dividends).

The shareholder of the regulated investment company pays the regular personal income tax on the dividends received. Any part of the dividend which represents a capital gain, however, is taxed as a capital gain. (The maximum tax on a long-term capital gain at the present time is 25 per cent.) In some instances only a portion of the dividends received by a shareholder in a regulated investment company may be subject to the dividend exclusion and the dividend credit.[8]

In the past the *retained realized* long-term capital gains of a regulated investment company were in effect taxed twice—first when the company paid the tax upon realizing the gain, and second when the shareholder sold his investment company shares at the augmented value resulting from the capital gain. This double taxation was eliminated by an amendment to the law in 1956.[9] (Effective January 1, 1957.) As before, the company will pay the 25 per cent tax on realized retained long-term capital gains. The company will notify the shareholder as to the amount of the gain which is applicable to his shares, and he will report the capital gain on his personal tax form. The shareholder, however, can take credit for the tax which is paid by the company. (If the 25 per cent exceeds the amount of taxes that would be applicable to the particular shareholder's capital gains, figured at his top bracket rate, he can apply the balance of the credit against other gains, or he can apply for a refund.) The amount of the retained capital gain (less the 25 per cent tax paid by the company) is added to the cost basis of the stock for the purpose of determining capital gains or losses upon sale of the stock by the shareholder.

In addition to the requirement that at least 90 per cent of the ordinary earnings be paid out in dividends annually, the other qualifications for a regulated investment company are as follows. At least 90 per cent of the gross income for any taxable year must be from dividends, interest and gains from the sale of securities, but not more than 30 per cent of the gross income may be derived

[8] If the dividends *received* by the investment company constitute less than 75 per cent of its gross income (capital gains excluded), the portion that is entitled to the exclusion and credit may be computed as follows:

$$\frac{\text{Dividends received by investment company}}{\text{Investment company's gross income}} \times \text{Dividends received from investment company}$$

[9] Public Law 700, Sec. 852(b)(3)(D), July 11, 1956.

from gains on securities held for less than three months. Not more than 5 per cent of the company's assets may be invested in the securities of any one company, and not more than 10 per cent of the voting securities of any company may be acquired. Once a company has elected to be treated as a regulated investment company, it must continue the same status every year thereafter.

Questions

1. What is meant by an investment company? What other title or titles are sometimes used for them?
2. What was the first real period of development of investment companies in the United States? Were they as a class at first successful? Why or why not?
3. Indicate the various types of investment companies found in the United States today. Which is the most numerous? Why?
4. Distinguish between the open- and closed-end management investment companies. Which of these is the most numerous? Why?
5. Indicate clearly what determines the price an investor would pay for the stock of most open-end investment companies and the price he would get when he sells the stock.
6. (a) Look up the bid and ask prices of the following stocks as of a recent date: Eaton and Howard Balanced Fund, Incorporated Investors, Massachusetts Investors Trust, and Wellington Fund, Inc. Calculate what percentage of the book value of the stock of each company is added as a selling or loading charge (small purchase assumed). (b) Look up the book value of as recent date as available and the market price, of approximately the same date, of the following companies: Adams Express Co., General American Investors, Lehman Corporation, and Tri-Continental Corporation. At what percentage under or over the book values was each selling? If you purchased and sold 20 shares of any two of these stocks what would the total commissions be, expressed as a percentage of the book value for each stock? (c) What conclusions might you draw relative to open- and closed-end companies by a comparison of the answers to (a) and (b)?
7. Indicate the relative advantages of balanced funds and common stock funds.
8. How do you account for the tremendous increase in the assets of open-end companies during and after World War II?
9. Explain the nature of the cumulative investment plans offered by many of the open-end companies. Do you think they are a good thing for the average investor?
10. State the principal features of the Investment Company Act of 1940.
11. (a) What is meant by a "regulated" investment company? (b) Explain definitely how the income of a regulated investment company is taxed as compared with a nonregulated company. (c) How are the dividends from an investment company taxed in the hands of the recipient shareholders?
12. What are the advantages and disadvantages of buying investment company shares from the standpoint of the average investor?
13. Do you believe that investment companies will continue to grow in the United States? Explain.

Problems

1. (a) Explain the difference, if any, among the following: Corporation, Massachusetts trust, Investment company. (b) Explain the difference, if any, among the following: Financing company, Holding company, Investment company.

2. Assume that you purchased an open-end regulated investment company share for $20, and that the price included the customary loading charge of 7½ per cent. At the time you purchased the stock 40 per cent of its book value was made up of appreciation in the value of its portfolio. If the company sold these securities in which it had a book profit and distributed the long-term capital gain to its shareholders, how would you stand on your investment after you paid a 25 per cent tax on the capital gain?

Part VII

READJUSTMENT, REORGANIZATION, RECEIVERSHIP, AND DISSOLUTION

Chapter 33

RECAPITALIZATION, READJUSTMENT, AND FAILURE

DEFINITION. In the early part of the book we indicated that the capitalization of a corporation consisted of its bonds and stocks. In a general way, any change that is made in the amount or pattern of the securities may be thought of as "recapitalization," but this latter term is usually used with a more restricted meaning, as will be stated presently. The capitalization of a company may be affected by one or more of the following.

1. *New financing.* The capitalization of a company is increased when additional stocks or bonds are sold. The retirement of some of the stocks or bonds has, of course, the opposite effect on the capitalization. We have discussed these procedures at various places in the book, so nothing further will be said about them.

2. *Refinancing.* The term "refinancing" is ordinarily used to refer to the situation where one type of debt or securities is replaced by another form of debt or securities. If the operation is strictly "refinancing," no new money would come into the company. Refinancing may be classified as follows.

A. Funding. When a company retires a short-term debt by means of a long-term debt, the process is referred to as *funding* the debt. In some instances the creditors may agree to accept bonds in discharge of short-term notes. In other cases it will be necessary to sell the bonds to secure the money needed to retire the short-term debt. In many instances companies do not have sufficient funds on hand to meet their obligations, and a funding operation is often the course open to them. In some cases, however, the money is on hand, but is needed for some other purpose, such as expansion. Occasionally, a bond issue can be floated at a lower rate of interest than is being paid on the short-term debt, but when interest rates are relatively low, a higher rate will usually have to be paid on the longer-term debt.

B. Refunding. When a company issues a new bond issue to take the place of an old one, it is said to have *refunded* the debt. The refunding operation may take place at the time of maturity of the old issue, or if callable at the time, the old issue may be called in, or possibly the old bonds may be bought up on the market. It is common practice to offer the holders of the old bonds new ones in exchange, but in most instances part of the new issue will have to be sold to secure funds needed to retire some of the old issue.

Refunding may be done for any one of several reasons. In many instances it is the only method available for the payment of the old bonds. In some cases it is done because the new bonds can be floated at a lower rate of interest. Refunding is also sometimes done in order to eliminate some objectionable features present in the old issue.

C. Other Refinancing. Funding and refunding are not the only methods of refinancing. A company may, for example, retire a bond or preferred stock issue through the sale of additional common stock. As would be expected, this is done usually in a period of prosperity when a relatively high price may be secured for the stock. Such a procedure may prove to be beneficial to a company when a depression hits, since the preferred dividend or fixed charge would thereby be eliminated.

In some instances a preferred stock issue is replaced by a bond issue. This may result in a saving of financing charges since a company at any given time can usually sell bonds at a lower rate of interest than the dividend rate on the preferred stock. Furthermore a saving in income taxes is effected, since the bond interest is deductible before arriving at the earnings base on which the taxes are computed. In recent years there have been several instances of railroads having sold an issue of income bonds to replace a preferred stock issue in order to effect the tax savings. The refinancing may also take the form of substituting a new preferred stock issue with a lower rate of dividends than is being paid on the outstanding preferred issue.

3. *Recapitalization.* The sale of additional securities, the retirement of old securities, or refinancing, all mentioned above, are sometimes thought of as forms of recapitalization. But we will use here the term *recapitalization* in its more restricted sense to cover other changes in the form or amount of outstanding securities brought about by voluntary action on the part of the corporation

and its security holders. Some use the term in still a more restricted meaning to cover changes in the form or amount of only stock. Stock dividends and stock splits are examples of "recapitalization." Ordinarily a "recapitalization" brings no new money into the company.

4. *Readjustment.* In a very general way the term "readjustment" of the capital structure could be taken to mean any change in the form or amount of securities issued by a company. Usually, however, the sale of additional securities, or refinancing, discussed above, are not included. Some writers do not distinguish between "recapitalization" and "readjustment," and in the discussion which follows, we will not attempt to draw any exact distinction. When the two terms are distinguished, *recapitalization* is generally used to refer to such things as changes in the stock account due to stock dividends, stock splits, or the change of the par value, or the change from par to no-par or vice versa. Readjustment is then used to refer to more fundamental changes in the capital structure, other than from the sale of new securities, refinancing, and recapitalization. Such things as the lowering of the rate of interest on bonds with the consent of the bondholders, the extension of the maturity date of bonds, or other changes in the contractual features of a bond or preferred stock issue would be examples of "readjustment."

5. *Reorganization.* When a company goes through equity receivership or bankruptcy because of failure or threatened failure it is referred to as *reorganization.* This will be discussed in subsequent chapters. Recapitalizations and readjustments result from such procedures.

Common stock recapitalization and readjustment

VARIOUS METHODS. A recapitalization or readjustment may take place with respect to the common stock in one or more of the following ways:

1. Stock dividends
2. Stock split-ups
3. Reverse stock split-ups
4. Changes in the par value or stated value
5. Changes from par value to no-par value, or vice versa
6. Reclassification of the stock
7. Conversion of one type of security for another

STOCK DIVIDENDS, STOCK SPLIT-UPS, AND REVERSE STOCK SPLIT-UPS. Perhaps the most common way that common stock recapitalization takes place is through the stock dividend and the stock split-up. Since these, together with the reverse stock split-up, were discussed at some length in Chapter 27, the reader is referred to that chapter for the detail on these methods of recapitalization.

CHANGES IN THE PAR OR STATED VALUE. A stock split-up necessitates a change in the per-share par or stated value of the stock. For example, when the General Motors Corporation split its stock 2 for 1 in 1950, the par value per share of the stock was reduced from $10 to $5. In 1955, when the stock was again split, this time 3 for 1, the par value per share was reduced from $5 to $1⅔. A corporation, however, may reduce the par or stated value of its stock without increasing the number of shares outstanding. This would constitute a reduction in the stated capital and it would be necessary to follow the statutes carefully in order to prevent action against the company or its officers by the creditors. Any change in the per share par value requires consent of the requisite amount of stock for a charter amendment. A reduction in the per share stated value of no-par stock can be made by proper resolution by the board of directors, unless the stated value is specified in the charter, in which case a charter amendment would be necessary.

When the per-share par or stated value of stock is reduced without changing the number of shares outstanding, the surplus account would be credited with the aggregate amount by which the par or stated value was reduced. In fact, this is usually the reason why the stated capital is reduced. The write-down may have been undertaken in order to eliminate a deficit. Or it may have been advisable to increase the surplus. In some cases the write-down of the capital stock account is done in order to offset a corresponding revaluation downward in the goodwill or some of the tangible asset accounts.

A reduction in the per-share par value was formerly done for the purpose of lessening the transfer tax that must be paid by the seller of the stock. Prior to 1959, the federal stock transfer tax was 5¢ for each $100 of par or fraction thereof and 5¢ for each no-par share in event the stock sold for less than $20 a share. If the stock sold for $20 or more per share, the tax was 6¢ instead of 5¢. A reduction of the per share par value by 50 per cent, for example, would lessen the federal transfer tax by the same percentage (new rates on p. 454). The annual franchise tax would also be reduced by such action in those states where it is based on the par value of the stock.

Occasionally a corporation will increase the par value per share by charging surplus and crediting the stock account. In this respect it is similar to a stock dividend, but it differs in that the number of shares outstanding remains the same. It differs from a reverse stock split-up in that the number of shares outstanding is not reduced, and as just stated, the capital stock account is increased and the surplus reduced.

In addition to the reasons given above, changes in the par or stated value, or in the number of shares outstanding, may be undertaken in order to facilitate breaking up a company under the Public Utility Holding Company Act of 1935; to facilitate the exchange of securities in connection with a merger or consolidation; to lower the market price of the stock prior to the sale of additional shares; or to make it easier for shareholders to dispose of part or all of their interest in the company.

Changes from Par Value to No-Par Value or Vice Versa. As the various states enacted no-par stock laws, many corporations by appropriate charter amendment changed their stock from par to no-par in order to facilitate the issuance of additional stock and/or to obtain some of the other advantages of no-par stock which were discussed in Chapter 6. When the depression of the early 1930's arrived, accompanied by the drop in the prices of stocks, the transfer taxes became quite a burden on no-par stocks since, as was stated above, each no-par share was taxed the same as if it had a par value of $100. Because of this many corporations changed their no-par to a low par stock. If the share has a par value of $1, for example, 100 shares of it may be transferred for the same amount of federal transfer taxes as would be paid on one no-par share. In the meantime, New York State changed its laws to tax both par and no-par shares the same amount per share. In some states a low par stock company would pay less in franchise taxes since many of them tax a no-par share the same as if it had a par value of $100. Another reason for the change from a no-par to a low par share has been the fact that at the time the stock was originally issued the laws did not permit the issuance of shares with a lower par value than $100. A low par stock has many of the advantages that were originally claimed for no-par stock.

Reclassification of the Stock. By *reclassification* of the stock is usually meant the issuance of one class of stock to take the place of another class of stock. Thus common may be exchanged for preferred, or preferred may be changed for common. Or one class of preferred may be exchanged for several different issues of preferred that are outstanding. Such exchanges would be initiated by the board of directors, but the exchange would have to take place voluntarily on the part of the shareholders. If the preferred to be eliminated is callable, the call privilege may be exercised. But cash would have to be given the shareholder if he would not accept the other stock issue. The exchange of one class of stock for another would have to receive the requisite consent of the shareholders and probably a charter amendment would also be necessary.

Following are the principal reasons why a corporation may effect a reclassification of its stock:

1. To simplify the capital structure
2. To enable the shareholders to sell part or all of their holdings in the market
3. To facilitate the public offering of new stock
4. To strengthen the financial structure by eliminating senior securities
5. To reduce the outstanding voting stock
6. To comply with reorganization requirements under the Public Utility Holding Company Act of 1935

Conversion of One Type of Security for Another. Convertible bonds were discussed in Chapter 12. It will be recalled that conversion is usually from a bond or preferred stock to common stock. Conversion might be considered a type of recapitalization if we were to use the latter term in a broad way. Usually, however, it is not included since the change brought about by the conversion might cover a long period of time, and furthermore, conversion takes place at the option of the security holder and not of the issuing corporation.

Preferred stock recapitalization and readjustment

Methods and Reasons. Preferred stock recapitalization or adjustment may take place by any of the seven methods discussed above for common stock and for the same reasons. Relatively speaking, however, such changes in the preferred stock are made infrequently. Usually the action taken with respect to preferred stock would be one or more of the following:

1. Elimination of the preferred stock issue
2. Elimination of the accrued preferred dividends
3. Reduction of the dividend rate
4. Elimination of burdensome provisions in the preferred stock contract

Elimination of the Preferred Stock Issue. In our discussion of common stock above, it was pointed out that corporations sometimes wish to eliminate senior securities which have a senior right to the earnings in order to strengthen the financial structure and thus be better able to stand a period of reduced earnings. In some instances common stock is offered in exchange for the preferred. In some cases the preferred is bought up in the market either from the proceeds of the sale of additional common stock or from retained earnings. When a corporation has a number of different issues of preferred outstanding it may offer the various classes a new issue of preferred as a means of simplifying the stock structure.

In some instances a company will retire a preferred stock issue through the exchange or sale of bonds. The reasons for this are because the rate of interest on the bonds is usually lower than the dividend rate on the stock, and the interest will reduce the income taxes since it can be deducted before arriving at net taxable income.

Elimination of the Accrued Preferred Dividends. When a stock carries a preferential rate of dividends, the courts interpret this to mean that the dividend must be paid in any year before dividends can be paid on the common. And if the dividends are not paid in any particular year, they accrue into subsequent years, and these arrears must be paid before anything can be paid on the common. In other words, the preferred stock is held to be cumulative, unless it is specifically made noncumulative in the contract. Aside from this legal point, preferred stock is commonly specifically made cumulative by the terms of the contract.

When the preferred dividends have been accruing for a number of years, the issuing corporation is adversely affected in a number of ways. The mere presence of the accumulation is evidence that the earnings have probably been low or nonexistent, and that the working capital position of the company is weak. The accrued dividends only make a bad situation worse. The company will probably find that no additional preferred stock can be sold, and also since the possibility for dividends on the common is usually remote, it will also probably not be able to sell any common stock. Furthermore, the stock, both preferred and common, will probably be selling in the market at a relatively low price. All of this will also adversely affect the company's credit, and it may find borrowing either impossible, or the rate of interest that would have to be paid on a loan, if obtainable, would probably be prohibitive.

Although preferred stock is commonly made nonvoting by the terms of the contract, it is usual to provide that the preferred will come into voting power if dividends are in arrears for a specified number of dividend periods. The contract may merely provide that the stock shall then vote the same as the common, which is usually one vote per share, or it may be stated that the preferred stock, voting as a class, can elect from one up to a majority of the board of directors. Accrued dividends on the preferred may, therefore, jeopardize the management position of the common shareholders.

For the reasons stated above, a corporation is usually anxious to eliminate in some way large accumulations on the preferred. Naturally, the common shareholders are of the same frame of mind. The preferred shareholders themselves may realize that their chances of receiving the cash dividends in the future are rather slim. Various methods of eliminating the preferred arrears have been used, but they usually take one or more of the following forms.

The simplest method is that of offering common stock to the preferred shareholders for the accrued dividends. But since the success of the plan depends upon the acceptance by the preferred shareholders, this might not meet with their approval. In some instances they are given new preferred stock for the accumulation. Or, the plan may call for a combination of new preferred and some common stock. The new preferred may be of the same class as that outstanding, or it may be either junior or senior to it. As an added inducement, a sinking fund may be provided for the new stock, and it may be made convertible into common. In some instances no new stock is offered, but the company attempts to get the shareholders to agree to some change in the contractual features of their old stock in exchange for the cancellation of the accrued dividends. This may take the form of a higher rate of dividends, the addition of a redemption fund, making the stock convertible into common, or giving certain participation rights to the preferred shareholders. In some cases a company will offer the preferred shareholders a new issue of preferred in exchange for their old stock and the accrued dividends.

In rare instances bonds are given in payment of the arrears. The wisdom of the latter action is subject to some question, since the burden of meeting the interest on the bonds and the principal at maturity, may merely compound the situation. In some instances the preferred shareholders are asked to accept part of the arrears in stock, either common or preferred, and then the balance is offered in cash, if such a procedure is possible.

The company must always give consideration to the feasibility of the plan. Although it will try to clear up the arrears by giving the least possible, enough must be offered to induce the preferred shareholders to accept the settlement. The par or market value of the securities offered may be practically the same amount as the accrued dividends, although in some instances since it is realized that the full amount of the dividend would probably never be paid in cash, the market value of the securities offered may be less than the amount of the accumulated dividends.

In the early part of the chapter we indicated that "funding" a debt meant changing it from a short-term to a long-term debt. When an accumulated preferred dividend is canceled by issuing stock or bonds for it or making some of the other compromise settlements stated above, it is stated by some writers that the arrears are thereby "funded."

REDUCTION OF THE DIVIDEND RATE. A preferred stock recapitalization or readjustment is sometimes made for the purpose of lowering the rate of dividends. As the credit of a company improves, other things being equal, a preferred stock issue could be floated at a lower dividend rate. Also, as interest rates in general decline, the rate that would have to be paid on new preferred stock is usually also lessened. A material saving can sometimes be effected by a company calling in its old preferred stock and replacing it with an issue bearing a lower rate of dividends. Many of the shareholders will accept the new stock in exchange since their alternative would be to accept the call price in cash. If the stock is not callable, it may be purchased in the market, but this would ordinarily not involve any savings since a relatively high price would have to be paid for the stock.

If the preferred stock is noncallable, it may be difficult to get the shareholders to consent to an exchange for shares bearing a lower rate of dividends. In some instances added inducements, such as making the new issue convertible, will result in a successful exchange. In some states charter amendments may be made to reduce the rate of dividends. Care should be taken to secure the requisite vote of the shareholders to effect such a change. Furthermore, dissenters will have to be dealt with in the manner specified by the statutes.

Some companies have issued a new preferred bearing a lower rate of dividends in return for both the old stock and the dividends that have accrued on it. In some of these cases part of the accumulated dividend was paid in cash.

ELIMINATION OF BURDENSOME PROVISIONS IN THE CONTRACT. In order to secure approval for a preferred stock issue, or in order to sell it, it may be necessary to place certain restrictions in the preferred stock contract. The amount of debt that may be incurred, or the amount of preferred stock that may be issued, are in some instances limited by the contract. Or the provision may take the form of requiring the maintenance of certain ratios before dividends can be paid on the common. In some instances it is necessary to provide redemption funds for the retirement of the preferred.

When some provision such as those stated above prove to be burdensome or impractical, the corporation may want to eliminate it. If the stock is callable, this privilege may be exercised and the undesirable feature can be eliminated by canceling the stock issue. The shareholders may be asked to accept a new preferred stock, which does not contain the undesirable feature, in exchange for their shares. If the new stock is not acceptable to them, the company will secure the money necessary to exercise the call feature by selling the new preferred stock, or possibly additional common stock, in the market.

Procedure for Preferred Stock Recapitalization. We have stated above in several places that preferred stock recapitalizations or readjustments are often effected by exercising the call feature in the preferred issue. When the stock is not callable, it is more difficult. In some states the laws consider that the rights under which the stock was issued constitute vested rights and cannot be changed without the consent of the particular stockholder. Some states will not permit the elimination of accrued dividends. The statutes in some of the states, such as New York, provide that changes in the preferred stock contract may be made if they are approved by a two-thirds vote of the shares affected by the change. It is usual for the statutes to provide further that any shareholder who does not agree to the change can secure a fair cash value for his shares. This is true of the New York law.

Debt readjustment

Types of Debt Readjustments. In the early part of the chapter it was indicated that the part of the capitalization made up by bonds would be altered by selling new issues, retiring old ones, and by funding and refunding operations. We are now interested in other methods of readjustment in the bonded indebtedness. It should be kept in mind that we are still considering readjustments that take place for companies that have not failed. Subsequent chapters will deal with readjustments that follow failure. It must be admitted, however, that some of the readjustments which are here listed are accomplished to prevent a company from failing. Following are the objectives of a debt or bond readjustment.

1. Extension of maturity
2. Reduction of interest rate
3. Reduction of principal
4. Elimination of burdensome provisions in the bond indenture

Extension of Maturity. Corporations may be able to operate successfully and pay the interest on the bonds when due, but sometimes they have insufficient cash to meet the principal on a large bond issue that may be coming due. The market may be such that a new issue of bonds could not be sold. Judging from all the facts available at the time, it may appear probable that after a few more years the company may become able to meet the bonds, or to put out a refunding issue. If the bondholders pursued their strict legal rights, they could force the company into receivership or bankruptcy. But this might be harmful not only to the company, but to the bondholders themselves. If the company appears to have good management, and that time alone is what is needed, the management may sell the bondholders on an extension in the maturity of their bonds.

The success of an extension depends upon the company getting the assent of an appreciable number of the bondholders. The management usually realizes its inability to meet the principal amount some time in advance of the maturity date. Leading bondholders, such as insurance companies and other institutional holders, are consulted in an effort to obtain their consent and in the hope that this might influence the other bondholders. Bondholders who do not agree to the extension can force the company to pay off their bonds at maturity, or otherwise they can force legal action which may lead to receivership or bankruptcy. Usually, however, the average bondholder knows little about his legal rights, and lacks the organization and the money necessary to instigate legal action. It is therefore common for the typical bondholder to go along with the others in an extension of the maturity of the bonds.

As an inducement to the extension, the issuing company may add some features to the maturing bond issue, such as a sinking fund, making the issue convertible, agreeing to restrict dividends on the common stock during the extension period, agreeing not to issue any senior obligations, or offering a bonus in stock or cash.

Reduction of Interest Rate. Where it appears that the rate of interest contracted for in the bond issue is too high for the company, and that this situation will probably prevail in the future, the company management may be successful in getting the approval of most of the bondholders to reduce the rate of interest. In some cases the fixed rate is lowered, and the payment of the difference between this and the original rate is made contingent on earnings.

In order to induce the bondholders to agree to a reduction in the rate of interest the company may add some of the features stated above in connection with the agreement for an extension. A bondholder cannot be forced to accept the lower interest rate. The company would have to pay dissenters the original rate, otherwise they could force the company into receivership or bankruptcy.

In some instances a company has sufficient cash to pay off part of the amount due and it asks that the bondholders agree to extend the maturity of the remaining part of the principal.

REDUCTION OF PRINCIPAL. In rare instances a company will ask the bondholders to reduce the principal amount that is owed. When this is done, however, it is usually in effect a composition settlement. In some cases the bondholders are offered part in cash and the balance in the form of other securities.

ELIMINATION OF BURDENSOME PROVISIONS IN THE BOND INDENTURE. Companies may find that certain provisions in the bond indenture are burdensome or impractical, similar to the situation discussed above in connection with preferred stock, and ask that the bondholders release the company from such provisions. For example, the company may want to postpone the payment of interest which is about due, or postpone a sinking fund installment or eliminate entirely the requirement for a sinking fund. When the company is unable to obtain financing by any other method, the bondholders may be asked to subordinate their liens to a new issue which is being proposed. Or the company may want certain assets securing a bond issue released from the lien in order to pledge them for a new issue of bonds.

In order to obtain such concessions, the company may find it necessary to add some of the inducements to the bond issue like those stated above in connection with the extension of maturity.

APPROVAL OF BONDHOLDERS NECESSARY FOR CHANGES. The bond indenture should be consulted to determine whether the terms of the bond contract can be altered, and if so, the requisite vote of the bondholders necessary to accomplish it. Even where a substantial vote of the bondholders approves an extension of the maturity or a reduction in the interest rate, any bondholder can still demand that the company live up to the original contract. If this is not done, the bondholder has a legal right against the company to compel it to abide by the terms of the contract, or force receivership or bankruptcy on the company.

It is usual, however, for the bond indenture to provide that changes may be made in provisions of the indenture upon the approval of a specified percentage of the bonds, usually from 66⅔ to 75 per cent.

Failure

WHY STUDY FAILURE. It is customary in a book of this kind to discuss the subject of business failure. Our interest, of course, is not in the failures themselves, but rather in the events leading toward failure, and the causes of failure. An understanding of these factors is of importance in formulating procedures and policies that may prevent failure. We are interested in failure also in order to study and discuss methods of reorganizing companies which have gone on the rocks.

MEANING OF "FAILURE." The term "failure" has different meanings to different people. It may also be used by the same person in different ways. The term "insolvency," which also has different interpretations, is sometimes used interchangeably with the word "failure," and at other times a distinction is made between the two terms. We will not attempt to give an exact definition of these words, since no generally accepted meaning has been formulated. But we will attempt to explain how the terms are commonly used.

Economic failure. It is generally stated that a business is an *economic failure* when it is unable to earn a satisfactory return on the investment of the owners after giving effect to the degree of risk involved. From an economic standpoint, therefore, it must be apparent that many companies are economic failures. Many firms during their early life fail to earn a satisfactory return on the investment. In fact many of them operate at losses from time to time, but the state of their working capital is such that they are able to continue in business. But we would not classify them as economic failures unless, over a long period of time, they failed to have adequate earnings.

Since most people do not use the term "failure" to mean *economic failure,* it is not common to refer to an economic failure as an actual failure. So long as the capital represents the owner's contribution and not borrowed capital, a company may not earn an adequate return, but if it pays its bills as they become due, the company may remain in business for years. Many small retail establishments are economic failures. In many instances they do not even return a satisfactory wage to the proprietor and his family who may work in the store, but as long as the debts are paid, the business can continue to operate. From what has been said it should be apparent that when we use the term "failure" we will not be referring to an "economic failure."

Financial failure. Many businesses at various times have debts coming due that cause considerable loss of sleep on the part of the owners or managers. They may have a special sale for the purpose of getting cash immediately to pay the debts. Or, perhaps a bank loan may be obtained. If the need is for long-term funds, a stock issue, or a bond issue may be arranged. In some instances assets other than the stock-in-trade may be liquidated in order to obtain funds. But as long as the funds are obtained and the debts are paid, we would not classify the business as a financial failure.

As the term is generally used, *financial failure* occurs when the business is unable to pay its debts. The business may thereupon liquidate and close its doors, or some cooperative arrangement may be worked out to keep the business going, or it may go through a drastic reorganization. Some writers state that financial failure occurs when some loss falls on the creditors—regardless of whether or not the business is terminated. Some use the term "legal failure" to mean the same as *financial failure,* but others apply it to the situation where the failure has been confirmed or adjudicated by the court, and a receiver or trustee has been appointed, or the business has been declared bankrupt. When we use the term "failure" hereafter we will be referring to *financial failure,* that is, the inability to meet debts as they become due.

We pointed out above that a concern may operate as an economic failure for a number of years without actually failing (financial failure). It is likewise true that a company may be earning a satisfactory return on its investment, in other words it is not an economic failure, but the inability of the company to meet a bank loan or a maturing bond issue may cause it to fail actually (from a financial point of view).

Insolvency. The term "insolvency" is often used to apply to the situation where a business is unable to meet its debts as they fall due. In other words, the same meaning as *financial failure.* From a statutory standpoint, however, *insolvency* applies to the situation where the assets, at a fair valuation, are insufficient to pay the debts. This is the way the term is defined in the Bankruptcy Act. We will use the latter meaning, particularly when the term is applied to a particular company or individual that is a bankrupt or about to become one.

When prices of property and securities decline, many companies would be unable to pay all their obligations if they were forced to liquidate. In other words, from the statutory viewpoint they are insolvent. But so long as they can meet their debts as they come due, they are not regarded by businessmen as being a failure or insolvent. Likewise, a company's total assets may exceed its debts; in other words the company is not insolvent, but it may fail (using the term in its financial sense) because of inability to meet a bond maturity.

Since 1900, an average of 74 out of every 10,000 firms listed in Dun & Bradstreet Reference Book failed with loss to creditors each year.[1] Since 1941, however, the average annual failures has been only 24 out of 10,000.[2] It should be noted that in published figures on failures, usually only those which fail with loss to creditors are recorded in the statistics.

Real vs. Apparent Causes of Failure. The immediate reason for practically all failures is the inability to pay debts. In other words, the reason is lack of cash or its equivalent. But this is merely a superficial sign. The real reasons for failure are those underlying factors which result in the weak working capital position. It is in these underlying causes that we are interested.

Although we do not consider a company to have failed until it is unable to meet its debts, or is forced to undergo some compromise settlement with its creditors, or is reorganized or closes its doors, the factors causing the failure may have been at work for many years. It is therefore often difficult to determine the real cause of the failure. Furthermore, there may be a number of different factors which caused the failure. Also one causal factor may have led to another. One weak situation may have necessitated action which possibly would not have been taken if the particular situation had not been present.

Management Chief Cause of Failure. There can be no doubt that the most important single cause of failure of most business enterprises is incompetent and inefficient management. In fact, during the same period a number of companies will be operating under similar circumstances, but some will fail and others will survive. If we were to trace back the real cause of the failures we could probably attribute it to the managements. Below will be listed a number of causes of failure, but it is realized that in perhaps

[1] "The Failure Record Through June, 1955," Dun & Bradstreet, Inc., New York, 1955.

[2] *Ibid.*

most instances the particular cause would not have resulted in failure if the management had been on its toes and had insured against the calamity or had taken the proper steps to prevent or to correct the shortcomings before it was too late. Thus in discussing the various causes of failure it is understood that the real factor underlying the apparent cause given may have been incompetent management, although we are not going to repeat this in every case.

In many instances the individuals entrusted with running a business do not have the mental or physical capacity properly to manage the concern. Or they may be very capable, but they lack the necessary experience, and the business fails before they are able to acquire sufficient experience. The officers or owners may not apply themselves diligently to their duties because of too many outside activities. Occasionally a man will wreck a business because he tries to do too much work. Failures sometimes result from dishonesty of the company officials.

While we are on the subject of management, it should perhaps be mentioned that many businessmen succeed despite themselves. During a period of rising prices and increased prosperity many businesses are able to show large profits despite the fact that the management may be inexperienced and inefficient. But when a reversal in business occurs, these are the businesses that will probably fall by the wayside.

Causes of Failure. There are about as many causes of failure listed as there are books dealing with the subject. The length of the classification depends upon how minutely the causes are listed.

The causes of failure are usually classified as "external" or "internal," depending on whether they arise outside or inside the business. We will follow that procedure. Since this is a book on finance, we will separate the financial causes from the other internal factors. In the following classification management is included as an internal cause, but because of what has already been said, we will not further discuss it.

I. *External causes*
  1. Excessive competition
  2. The general business cycle
  3. Change in public demand
  4. Governmental acts
  5. Adverse acts of labor
  6. Acts of God

II. *Internal causes*
  A. Nonfinancial
    1. Poor over-all management

2. Unwise promotion
3. Unwise expansion
4. Inefficient purchasing
5. Inefficient production
6. Inefficient selling
7. Overextension of inventories

B. Financial
1. Poor management
2. Excessive fixed charges
3. Excessive funded debt
4. Excessive floating debt
5. Overextension of credit
6. Unwise dividend policy
7. Inadequate maintenance and depreciation

External causes of failure

Excessive Competition. Competition is often cited as the reason for failure of many concerns. The managements of the defunct companies particularly are inclined to give that as a reason. Normal competition, however, usually helps to keep businessmen on their toes and in many instances is a healthy factor. The mere fact that the cause of failure is attributed to competition in itself may be more or less a confession that other companies have been more successful in pricing policies, selling, or service rendered. When the competition, however, gets to the cutthroat stage where price wars are being waged by the large strong companies against the smaller and financially weaker concerns, then it can be ruinous. In some instances combinations that are violating the antitrust laws make it difficult for other companies to successfully compete with them.

In the past many businessmen have found that one way of eliminating some of the competition is to combine with your competitor. This has been an important factor behind many of the large combinations which we have today.

The Business Cycle. A recession or depression is often given as the reason for many failures. It is true that most businesses are adversely affected by falling prices, a drop in sales, and slow collections, and many of them fail as an immediate result of some or all of these factors. In some instances the failure of one or more other companies will result in the failure of a particular company. It must, however, be admitted that if a company is strong financially, has liberal reserves, good management, and makes a useful product which can be sold at a fair price, it has good chances of surviving a depression.

TABLE 43

WHY BUSINESSES FAIL

(per cent)

Apparent Causes	*Manu-facturers*	*Whole-salers*	*Retailers*	*Construc-tion*	*Com-mercial Services*	*Total*
Neglect	3.8	5.1	5.1	5.3	3.7	4.8
Bad habits	0.6	1.2	1.2	1.8	0.7	1.2
Poor health	2.8	2.7	2.8	2.4	1.4	2.6
Marital difficulties	0.3	0.6	0.5	0.6	0.7	0.5
Other	0.1	0.6	0.6	0.5	0.9	0.5
Fraud	2.3	3.3	2.2	1.4	1.2	2.1
Misleading name	..	0.1	0.1	0.1	..	0.1
False financial statement	0.3	0.5	0.5	0.3	0.2	0.4
Premeditated overbuy	0.1	0.2	0.1	..	..	0.1
Irregular disposal of assets	1.6	2.5	1.2	0.8	0.6	1.3
Other	0.3	..	0.3	0.2	0.4	0.2
Inexperience	91.4	89.7	91.1	91.5	93.0	91.3
Inadequate sales	50.2	48.5	48.9	30.7	47.2	46.7
Heavy operating expenses	7.4	5.4	4.5	17.7	7.9	7.1
Receivables difficulties	13.4	18.3	5.5	16.0	5.6	9.8
Inventory difficulties	5.9	11.1	11.7	1.2	1.4	8.3
Excessive fixed assets	12.8	2.9	11.9	6.6	17.7	9.1
Poor location	0.5	0.7	5.6	0.4	2.0	3.1
Competitive weakness	17.0	19.1	22.3	26.1	22.2	21.4
Other	5.1	3.7	2.8	9.0	4.2	4.3
Disaster	2.2	1.6	1.2	1.0	1.2	1.4
Fire	1.3	0.6	0.7	0.1	0.7	0.7
Flood	0.2	0.3	0.1	0.1	..	0.1
Burglary	0.1	0.1	0.1	..	..	0.1
Employees' fraud	0.1	0.3	..	0.1	..	0.1
Strike	0.3	..	0.1	0.4	0.1	0.1
Other	0.2	0.3	0.2	0.3	0.4	0.3
Reasons unknown	0.3	0.3	0.4	0.8	0.9	0.4

While the percentages in the broad categories of apparent causes of failures (Neglect, Fraud, Inexperience, and so on) add to 100 per cent, the sum of the specific causes may exceed the total for the category because some failures are attributed to a combination of specific causes. Based on opinions of informed creditors and information in Dun & Bradstreet's Credit Reports for the year 1955. Used with permission of Dun & Bradstreet, Inc.

CHANGE IN PUBLIC DEMAND. A business can be successful only when it sells a product or service which the public wants and can afford to buy. As advances are made in the arts and sciences, and research results in the creation of new products which the public prefers to the old products, a company that continues to manufacture only the obsolete product is doomed to failure.

We have seen the automobile replace the horse, but not all carriage or wagon manufacturers failed. Those who changed their line of products to answer the public demand remained in existence. The automobile, airplane, and pipeline have made it difficult for the railroads, but most of them are still successful today. Television has made inroads on the demand for radio, but the radio manufacturers and networks that have added television are keeping pace with the public. Television has also produced adverse effects on the movie industry, but the companies which lead in the introduction of improved techniques and better quality pictures at reasonable cost will undoubtedly survive.

Many companies constantly carry on research so that they might be able to lead in the introduction of new and better products. As the public demand changes, the better managed companies usually change their production to conform to what is wanted. Even if a company is successfully producing and selling a particular product or products, it may take on additional products so that if the demand shifts, it will be prepared with a well-balanced line of products.

Governmental Acts. The enactment of certain laws, particularly federal statutes, and some court decisions occasionally result in the failure of certain companies. The enactment, in 1918, of the 18th Amendment to the Constitution resulted in the failure of many concerns in the beer and liquor industries. The lowering or elimination of protective tariffs sometimes affects an industry so much that many companies may fail. Business taxes have in some cases caused a failure. The chain store taxes that exist in some states are an example. An undistributed profits tax, such as existed for several years in the 1930's, can result in the distribution of so large a percentage of the earnings that no adequate reserves are built up to enable a company to weather a severe depression.

In war times or periods of emergency certain governmental restrictions may cause some companies to fail because of their inability to get raw materials for the manufacture of their products. Price and wage regulations may also work severe hardship on some concerns.

Where the success of a particular company has been due to the possession of certain patents, the expiration of such rights or the granting of patents to a competitor may result in failure of a concern.

ADVERSE ACTS OF LABOR. In recent years the demands of some labor unions have resulted in the failure of business concerns. Unreasonable wages may result in such excessive costs that it becomes impossible for the company to compete in the market. This is true particularly with small companies and those where the labor costs comprise a relatively large percentage of the total cost of the product. In some instances prolonged strikes in plants supplying the raw materials used by a particular company may force that company to close its doors. A sound labor relations policy and program is essential for modern business. The management should be fair to labor and labor should do likewise.

ACTS OF GOD. Certain fortuitous factors, which the law terms "acts of God," are the cause of some failures. These include fires, earthquakes, tornadoes, explosions, and floods. Although management cannot prevent the occurrence of all catastrophes, danger can often be lessened by the selection of a proper location or by watchfulness. Also the financial loss from some of these calamities may be eliminated if proper insurance against some losses is maintained. Insurance against all sorts of losses, however, would be too costly.

Even though adequate insurance is carried, if a company's properties are destroyed by some of these forces, it may take a considerable period of time to rebuild the facilities. In the meantime the company loses the profits that it otherwise would have been enjoying. Furthermore, the former customers will have to secure new suppliers, and many of them will probably continue to do business with these other concerns.

Internal causes of failure—Nonfinancial

UNWISE PROMOTION. We are turning now from the external causes of failure to the nonfinancial internal ones. Poor management is undoubtedly the principal internal cause of failure, but this factor was already discussed at some length above. Some concerns start business under such conditions that they are almost certain to fail. Adequate consideration should be given to the nature of the product to be manufactured, or service to be rendered; the costs should be well worked out and pricing and the market should be known; due attention should be given to the location, source of raw materials, and labor. Then two important requisites are always needed for success: good management and adequate finances.

UNWISE EXPANSION. Many companies are successful as long as they operate as a small or medium-sized concern, but fail when they expand their production, sales, and plant facilities. This may be accounted for by many reasons. In some instances the management is unable to cope with the problems that arise from large-scale operations or the market may not be able to absorb the output. In some instances the expansion is made when prices are too high, or the financing may have been too expensive. In some instances the expansion takes the form of branching out into other lines with which the management is not familiar.

Some businesses run into the law of diminishing returns; as the number of units of output increases, the costs per unit may become more. This may result from inadequacy of plant and equipment, or from the inefficiencies accompanying large-scale operation. But even though the unit costs rise, if the additional sales result in larger total profits, production will be pushed upward to get the maximum profits.

INEFFICIENT PURCHASING. In some instances a company does not have adequate funds on hand to take advantage of discounts offered on purchases. This may prove to be disastrous particularly when the discounts are relatively large. Other companies will be taking the discounts and therefore will be in a position to undersell those companies which do not take the discounts. When raw materials are scarce, such as in war times, a small company, or one that does not have good connections with war material suppliers, may have considerable difficulty getting materials and may actually be forced out of business as a result.

INEFFICIENT PRODUCTION. Inefficient production may result in such high costs that a particular company may not be able to sell its products in competition with lower-cost producers. In some instances this results from inadequate or obsolete machinery and equipment. In some cases not enough of the production is mechanized and as a result direct labor comprises too high a percentage of the total cost of the product. Or the trouble may be inadequate foreman supervision, poor lighting, too high a labor turnover, excessive waste, improper inspection, or a host of other internal factors in the production department.

INEFFICIENT SELLING. American industry is noted for its emphasis on advertising and selling. Materials well purchased and produced mean nothing until and unless they are sold. Considerable emphasis must therefore be put on the proper selling in order to make money. Efficient selling calls for proper advertising, the careful selection and training of salesmen, adequate supervision of the salesmen, and a proper knowledge of the market and potential market.

Inadequacy in any of these factors may cause a company to fail. In some instances the sales department greatly overestimates the future sales and the production department produces more than can be sold. The large amount of money tied up in inventory may result in failure of the company, particularly if prices in general should decline. In some cases a good product is manufactured at a fair cost, but inadequate advertising or the use of improper channels of distribution may result in the product remaining on the shelves. As a result the company may fail.

Overextension of Inventories. Overextension of inventories is the immediate cause of many companies failing, particularly in the merchandising field. Some of the causes of failure stated above, such as the general business cycle, or the improper estimate of sales, may result in the accumulation of excessive inventories, but failures resulting from excessive inventories sometimes occur when it cannot be blamed on the sales department or the business cycle. This is such a common cause of failure that we wanted to list it separately.

Funds tied up in inventory commonly come from working capital sources. When too much is invested in such assets, the company will be hard pressed for cash. Such a situation can easily cause failure.

Internal causes of failure—Financial

Poor Financial Management. Although management as a cause of failure was discussed above, we were there referring to management in general. Perhaps most of the internal financial causes of failure can be attributed to weak financial management. A fundamental error of having too much of the capitalization in bonds, and too little in stock, can easily wreck a company. Incorrectly estimating the capital needs can do likewise. Improper terms of sale and slack collection policies can cause considerable trouble. The selection of the wrong type of securities to sell at a particular time, or the improper timing of a security sale can be disastrous to a business. Unwise dividend policies, and inadequate maintenance and depreciation can eventually cause a company to fail. Some of these are listed below as separate causes of failure. We wanted to emphasize at this point, that probably most of them could be traced back to poor financial planning. If the management is not acquainted with the problems of raising of funds through the issuance of securities, it should consult investment bankers.

Excessive Fixed Charges. The presence of too large an amount of bonds outstanding can result in such excess that the company is unable to meet the charges, and failure results. Many railroads have failed because of this. In some instances the companies probably could have met the principal of the bonds at maturity, or possibly refunded the obligation, but the immediate inability to pay the fixed charges resulted in failure. Bond issues should be sold only when the company can see its way clear in the future to meet the obligations imposed upon it by the issue. In some instances unforeseeable circumstances arise which result in less earnings than contemplated. Conservative financial planning would take such a possibility into consideration.

Excessive Funded Debt. In some instances a company can successfully meet its current fixed charges, but the inability to meet a large bond maturity causes it to fail. It is easy to say that the management should have been anticipating the bond maturity and provided for it. In many cases, however, the earnings are inadequate to provide the funds, and other sources of capital may have been exhausted. A company might not really be insolvent, that is, its assets may exceed its liabilities, but the working capital position may be so weak that it is unable to provide the funds to meet the bonds, and failure results.

Bonds ordinarily provide a cheaper method of financing than issuing stock, and also the tax saving is material. But from the standpoint of safety, common stock remains the ideal type of instrument to issue. It is still considered good financing to issue the weakest form of security first. Once a bond issue is outstanding constant attention should be given to its retirement. Excessive bond issues sometimes are present from the inception of the business, while in other instances they come about from expansion.

Excessive Floating Debt. By "floating debt" is meant the current liabilities. Aside from the possibility of a real estate mortgage, this is the only kind of debt that practically all small companies have outstanding. The floating debt is usually owed to either banks or to trade creditors, or to both.

Many businessmen attempt to finance their working capital needs, or at least part of them, through their trade creditors or the bank. Those that start out on a shoestring necessarily have to do this. Although the turnover of inventory will eventually bring in cash, at least part of this cash, if not all, must be reinvested in raw materials. Furthermore, some accounts receivable will probably always be on the books. Also, a minimum cash balance must be maintained. A certain amount of the working capital will thus be in reality fixed capital. Therefore, the minimum working capital needs should be financed with long-term capital. If stock cannot be sold to provide it, then the owners should put in this minimum working capital out of their own funds. If current sources are relied upon for the minimum working capital, it may result in failure of the company.

Most failures result immediately from the lack of cash coupled with too much current debt. If profits are not earned, this is an inevitable result. But it sometimes occurs because a business is prosperous. It is a normal desire of businesses to want to expand their sales. If a company attempts to expand its sales volume without the addition of any new capital in the business, unless it had ample cash resources to begin, financial difficulties probably will be encountered. The additional working capital investment will drain the cash, and the current liabilities will pile up. Failure can result from such a situation.

Some companies make the mistake of attempting not only to finance the additional sales out of working capital, but they make a bad situation worse by committing themselves for the additional fixed assets without bringing any new fixed capital into the business. Unless the cash reserves are large, or the profit margin great, or both, such a procedure can easily lead to failure.

The sales volume tends to expand during the recovery period following a depression. Prices are usually rising then, and although the cost of raw materials increases, the company profits from the increase in the value of the inventories on hand. More money is being collected from the additional sales, and collection policies tend to become more lax. Furthermore, the company usually becomes more liberal in the granting of credit. When the reaction sets in, and it is detected by the management, purchases should be restricted and the granting of credit should be tightened. Thus, cash should tend to accumulate during such a period. But commonly the reverse situation occurs. New purchases are not reduced, and liberal credit may still be in order. This is often due to the inability of the management to foresee what is happening. Collections slow up and creditors start pressing for what is owed to them. This coupled with inability to sell, commonly results in a tight cash situation, and can bring on failure.

Overextension of Credit. The tendency to overextend credit during a period of prosperity was discussed above. The credit policy should be such that sales are encouraged to the point that the profits remaining after bad debt losses are at a maximum. In addition to the setting of proper terms of sale, and the selection of credit risks, a proper collection policy should be in effect. Many companies fail because of their inability to collect what is owed them. In some instances the failure of the company's debtor will cause the particular company to fail. For that reason, too much credit should not be granted one individual or one company. A company's credit and collection policy should constantly be under review, not only to determine if it fits the particular customer, but also to see if it fits the particular period of the business cycle. The failure to tighten up on the extension of credit during the later stages of a period of prosperity is a common cause of failure.

Unwise Dividend Policy. Shareholders of publicly-owned corporations (large corporations with many shareholders) usually expect dividends to be paid on their stock. Corporations that are constantly expanding from the sale of securities realize that the market for their securities will be improved if they maintain a regular and rather liberal dividend policy. Some companies, whose earnings are fairly regular, can safely follow a regular and liberal dividend policy.

Many companies, particularly small ones, cannot sell new securities in the market. In order to finance expansion such companies must retain a relatively large portion of their earnings. Companies whose profits fluctuate widely should also retain a rather large percentage of their earnings to act as a buffer in those years when profits are small or nonexistent.

Many companies do not reduce their dividend rate even in the face of declining profits. Some pay dividends out of accumulated surplus even when deficits for the particular period exist. Some companies may be justified in following such a policy, but the great majority of them are not in a financial position to follow this course of action. In some instances liberal dividends are paid right up to the time that failure is admitted. And in many of these cases it would appear that if the dividends had not been paid the company could have prevented the failure. Such a policy is followed usually in order to cover up a weak financial position in the hope that help can be obtained.

In some instances too liberal a dividend policy is followed because of putting too much emphasis on the profit as shown in the income statement, or the surplus as displayed in the balance sheet, and not enough on the cash or working capital position of the company. It is well-known that the profit figure or the surplus may be greatly overstated because of erroneous accounting practices. But even when the accounting statements are correct, it should always be kept in mind that there is not necessarily any connection between the net profits or surplus figure and the cash account. Even if there is abundant cash, due consideration should be given to the amount of the liabilities and when they become due. Many companies are constantly expanding their plant facilities through depreciation reserves and retained profits. The accumulated surplus is thus sunk into fixed assets. It is not in such form that a cash dividend could be paid from it. Actually the fact that a large surplus has been invested in fixed assets might necessitate the retention of even more money in the business in order that proper insurance and repairs on the additional property may be maintained.

Inadequate Maintenance and Depreciation. In some instances too liberal a dividend policy results at least in part from the fact that a company undercharges maintenance and depreciation. Dividends may thus have been paid partly from capital rather than from profits. A long continued policy of this kind will result in the eventual wearing out of the property, and no cash will be available with which to replace it.

To stay in business it is necessary to keep the properties in proper repair. Adequate provision should constantly be made during the life of the property to replace it when it is no longer of any use to the company. The charging off of depreciation properly charges the particular period with the depreciation expense, but the setting up of a reserve account does not in itself provide the cash with which to replace the property. It is the duty of management to see to it that the company secures cash to replace the worn-out or obsolete property.

During a period of inflation companies find that to replace a particular piece of equipment may require upwards of twice the original cost. Depreciation charges and depreciation reserves are usually calculated on the original cost basis. Thus, even if cash or its equivalent equal to the depreciation reserve is available for the replacement of equipment, the new equipment may require twice that amount. It is the function of management to take this into account and provide the necessary amount of cash for the replacement of the properties.

Questions

1. Distinguish between the following terms: refinancing, refunding, recapitalization, readjustment in the capital structure, and reorganization.
2. Indicate the various ways in which a recapitalization or readjustment in the common stock may occur.
3. (a) What advantages might result from changing a no-par stock into a low par stock? (b) What advantages might result from changing a par stock into a no-par stock?
4. (a) Do accrued dividends on preferred stock constitute a debt of the corporation? Explain. (b) What drawbacks to the corporation might result from a large accumulation of dividends on the preferred stock? (c) What are some practical ways of eliminating the accumulated preferred dividends without actually paying the dividend? (d) Must the consent of the preferred stockholders be obtained in order to alter their contractual rights? Explain.
5. What are the various types of debt readjustment that may take place without receivership or reorganization?
6. (a) Does a bondholder have any right against the issuing corporation if changes are made in the terms of the bonds without his consent? (b) Does the indenture ever provide that changes in the contract may be made with the approval of a designated percentage of the bondholders? Would this apply to changes in the rate of interest?
7. Consult the statutes or court decisions of your state to determine if accrued dividends on preferred stock can be eliminated by the vote of a designated percentage of the stock.
8. Why may a write-down in the book value of the fixed assets accompany a recapitalization or readjustment in the capital stock account?
9. If a readjustment in the capital stock account results in a surplus taking the place of a deficit, can such a surplus be used as a source of dividend payment? Explain.
10. Explain how a period of prosperity and inflation might have the same effect on a corporation as a reduction in the bonded indebtedness during normal times.
11. Indicate how the widespread stock ownership and use of the proxy system of voting makes it relatively easy in many instances to effect stock recapitalizations and readjustments.
12. (a) Distinguish between economic failures and financial failures. (b) Distinguish between the terms "failure" and "insolvency."
13. Indicate how a company might be considered insolvent but not a financial failure, and vice versa.
14. Indicate what is meant by the distinction between the real and the apparent causes of failure.
15. (a) What is the most frequent cause of failure? (b) List the *financial* causes of failure.
16. Competition is often cited as the cause of failure. When this is done is competition usually the real cause? Explain.
17. Excessive taxation is sometimes given as a cause of failure. Explain how this could or could not be the cause of failure.
18. Aside from the question of taxes, do governmental acts ever cause failure of business concerns? Explain.

19. Some company owners have liquidated their businesses because they said that the wage demands on the part of the labor unions was such that they could no longer operate at a profit. Have you any suggestions as to what might be done in a situation of this kind to prevent liquidation of the business?

20. The operation of the business cycle is oftentimes given as the reason for failure of business concerns. Do you believe that this is more of an apparent cause rather than a real cause? Can the probable future trend of business be predicted now any better than 25 or 30 years ago? Explain.

Problems

1. The following is a balance sheet of the Acme Machine Tool Co. as of Dec. 31, 19-1:

Assets		*Liabilities and Net Worth*	
Cash	$ 10,000	Notes Payable	$ 400,000
Receivables	250,000	Accounts Payable	50,000
Inventory	810,000	Accrued Dividends	700,000
Fixed Assets	5,600,000	Preferred Stock	2,000,000
		Common Stock	3,000,000
		Surplus	520,000
Total	$6,670,000	Total	$6,670,000

The following is a condensed income statement for the year ending Dec. 31, 19-1:

Sales	$10,000,000
Cost of sales,etc.	9,575,000
Operating Profit	425,000
Interest Expense	28,000
Net Profit	$397,000

The preferred stock is 7 per cent cumulative and nonparticipating. The interest expense was for the annual interest paid on the notes. The latter were issued 4 years ago to finance the construction of one of the plant buildings that had been destroyed by fire and was uninsured. (Insurance is now carried on all the properties.) These notes are closely held and mature in one year. All the stock of the company has a par value of $100 per share and is closely held.

The company was hard hit by a recent depression, and the accrued dividends represent 5 years' accumulation on the preferred stock. During the late months of the present year the company received a great number of orders for machine tools from armament manufacturers and other industries. Because of the time required for "tooling up," none of these orders had been filled.

The plant facilities are wholly inadequate to take care of present orders, and if additional plant capacity were acquired at the present time a large number of additional orders would be forthcoming. The president wanted to issue $2,000,000 more in common stock to finance a new plant, but the treasurer of the company told him that they could not do this successfully until they had a financial "housecleaning," which, he said, any first-year finance student could tell was needed by taking one look at the balance sheet.

(a) Indicate specifically what you think the treasurer meant. (b) If you were called in by the company for advice, indicate specifically what you would recommend to improve the present financial condition of the company. (c) If your plan, stated in part (b), would not be acceptable to the particular class or classes affected, what would be your second plan?

2. The following are the balance sheets of the *A*, *B*, *C*, and *D* companies as of June 30, 19-1, when stock prices were lower than they had been for many years:

Balance Sheets
(in thousands)

	Co. A	*Co. B*	*Co. C*	*Co. D*
Cash	$ 5	$ 10	$ 0	$ 5
Receivables	50	80	40	50
Inventory	200	400	180	300
Fixed Assets	1,000	3,500	1,600	800
Total	$1,255	$3,990	$1,820	$1,155
Current Liabilities	$ 800	$ 20	$ 20	$ 5
Fixed Liabilities	0	1,000	0	0
Capital Stock	300	2,000	2,000	1,000
Surplus	155	970	–200*	150
Total	$1,255	$3,990	$1,820	$1,155

* Deficit

Company *A* has been able to meet obligations to date. Its current liabilities represent notes which come due July 31, 19-1. The directors considered selling all the assets to pay off the notes. In an independent appraisal it was found that the gross assets would bring only $650,000.

Company *B* has been earning 9 per cent on its capital stock for the past three years. Its fixed liabilities represent bonds which came due June 30, 19-1, and which the company was unable to pay off or make other provisions for settlement.

Company *C* has been earning 7 per cent on its stock for the past three years. There has been no occasion to have an appraisal made of the corporate property. All obligations have been paid when due.

Company *D* enjoyed large earnings before the depression, but earnings fell off materially in the two years previous, and in the first six months of 19-1 the company suffered a deficit. It has, however, met all obligations when they fell due. The company's stock was selling in the market for $30 a share at the date of the above balance sheet. The par of the stock is $100. It is to be noted that the stock was selling for an amount which was less than the net current asset value of the company. There has been no occasion for an appraisal of the property.

(a) Indicate in the case of each company whether it is insolvent or a financial failure and the reasons why it is or is not. (b) Indicate whether you think any of the companies should dissolve, and state your reasons.

Chapter 34

COMPROMISES, RECEIVERSHIP, AND REORGANIZATION

Compromises

COMPROMISE SETTLEMENT DESIRABLE. In many instances of failure creditors will lose less if some kind of a compromise settlement can be worked out between them and the owners or managers. Forced liquidation of a business results in the sale of the assets at sacrifice prices. Both the creditors and owners may lose less if the business is allowed to continue in operation.

If the business should be reorganized, it may also be to the advantage of both the owners and creditors to avoid legal or judicial reorganization. When a reorganization takes place through equity receivership or the Bankruptcy Act it is costly and time consuming. Every effort should be made to work out some kind of an understanding for the rehabilitation or liquidation of the business without resorting to court action. Under the latter, the referees, trustees, and lawyers may benefit more than the business and its creditors.

In Chapter 33, a number of compromise procedures that might be followed by a company which had failed or was about to fail were discussed. Some of the procedures explained in that chapter, such as recapitalizations resulting from stock dividends or stock split-ups, ordinarily have no relation to business failure; while others, such as a reduction in bond interest rates, may be effected for the purpose of preventing failure. In the first part of the present chapter we will be concerned with readjustments or compromise settlements which are more drastic than recapitalizations, and which are a result of failure or threatened failure. Later we will discuss the still more drastic procedure of reorganization under equity receivership or under the Bankruptcy Act.

EXTENSIONS. Some types of extension were discussed in Chapter 33, but they were primarily extensions in the maturity of bonds.

Extensions are also possible of short-term notes or accounts payable. A new note with a longer maturity may be issued to replace an existing note, or the due date on an account may be extended. In some cases, notes may be given to replace accounts that are due or past due.

For reasons already given, it might be to the advantage of creditors to grant the debtor a little extra time to pay his debts rather than attempt to force him to pay by legal action. An extension is more probable when the business is small or the number of creditors not large, when the management appears to be sound, and the financial trouble only temporary.

The success of an extension depends upon agreement of all the creditors. Since he has a legal right to receive payment, any creditor who does not agree to the extension can sue and receive judgment against the debtor and then levy on the business property for the satisfaction of his claim. This may force receivership or bankruptcy. In some instances when several of the small creditors will not agree to the extension plan, they will be bought out by the larger creditors. Larger creditors recognize that it is to their advantage to make some arrangement and keep the business in operation. Smaller creditors might realize this too, but may feel that they can benefit by being dissenters if they believe the larger creditors will buy them out. One of the disadvantages of extension is that it is not final in law unless *all* parties agree. This is one reason why extensions are difficult to effect.

Composition. A composition settlement is a common-law arrangement whereby the creditors agree among themselves and with the debtor to accept less than the full amount of their claims in discharge of the debts. Like an extension, a composition is used when the creditors believe they will in the long run get more out of the debtor than if they immediately forced liquidation or receivership or reorganization. But unlike the situation where extensions are made, the debtor is in a more drastic financial position and probably has an excess of liabilities over assets. Compositions are often used in the merchandising field. A reason for their prevalence in this field is that the creditors want to see the debtor remain in business so that they may sell him additional goods in the future.

Like the extension, the composition settlement can ordinarily be used only when the business is relatively small, and when there are not many creditors. In order to effect a composition there must be at least two creditors entering into the agreement. As a practical matter it is desirable that all the creditors join in. A composition, however, may be worked out by only part of the creditors, such as the unsecured creditors, for example. Creditors not entering into the agreement could proceed against the debtor in the regular way, but those agreeing to the composition would be held to their agreement, even though they got less than the other creditors. To be successful, however, agreement of all should be obtained. Those not agreeing may still force the debtor into bankruptcy.

Commonly, the composition settlement does not provide for complete payment in cash of the agreed amount at the time of the composition. Sometimes the entire payment is deferred for the future. In other cases part of the settlement is made in cash and the balance is represented by installment notes that mature at a later date.

The above applies to common-law compositions. Under the Bankruptcy Act, compositions, which are called "arrangements," may be worked out for compositions under court supervision. But this applies only to corporations with unsecured debt. Unlike the common-law composition, the arrangement is binding on all the unsecured creditors after it has been approved by a majority of each class of creditors and by the court. The Act provides for similar arrangements for individuals and unincorporated concerns. Arrangements are discussed further in the following chapter.

Assignments. Small concerns are sometimes liquidated through an *assignment* of the assets for the benefit of the creditors. This may be done under either the common law or the statutes of the particular state. Under common law, the assignment is not recorded, and the administration of the assets is under the supervision of the creditors rather than the court.

If one or more of the creditors take aggressive action ahead of the other creditors, the debtor may effect an assignment so that all the creditors will be treated equally. The debtor may prefer assignment to equity receivership or bankruptcy because less publicity is involved and because his future credit rating may suffer less. Creditors prefer assignment over procedures under the Bankruptcy Act because of lower costs and faster settlement. Usually the creditors receive a larger percentage of their claims under an assignment than through bankruptcy proceedings because more time is available to find good buyers for assets, a foreclosure sale is not necessary, and court and legal costs are substantially reduced.

The procedure is for the debtor to assign the assets to a trustee, who is referred to as the "assignee." The assignee is often one of the creditors or a group of creditors. In other cases he may be a disinterested third party. The assignee administers and sells the property in an orderly fashion, and distributes the proceeds to the creditors proportionately according to the amount of their claims.

As a practical matter it is usually necessary for all the creditors to be satisfied with the assignment. Since the Bankruptcy Act provides that an assignment constitutes an "act of bankruptcy," any creditor not agreeing to the assignment can file a petition in bankruptcy. The Federal Bankruptcy Act takes precedence over the state laws on the subject. It is for this reason that the assignment is rarely used today. Since the concern may end up in bankruptcy, it would be better in those instances where this appears probable, to dispense with the assignment and start action under the Bankruptcy Act. If the costs of bankruptcy are to be incurred in the future anyway, there is no point in adding the costs and time of an attempted assignment.

Creditors' Committee Management. Many companies found themselves in financial difficulty in the depression period of 1920–21 due to large inventories which had been accumulated at high prices and, in many instances, financed through bank loans. When the depression hit, sales dropped, prices fell, and collections became slow. Many companies were unable to pay their debts and faced failure, receivership, or bankruptcy. In many instances there were no inherent defects in the organization or management, and in time they could bring themselves out of the difficulty. In the meantime, they were in financial difficulty which had to be settled in some fashion to avoid the shortcomings of legal reorganization or liquidation. It was at this time that the creditors' committee plan of management and reorganization came into being.

The management and a committee representing the creditors would enter into an agreement whereby management of the particular company was turned over to the creditors' committee. In some instances the committee would hire a business expert to run the business. In some cases an officer of the company was appointed. The committee was usually composed of some of the principal creditors who were thought to be good business managers. Commonly bank creditors were represented on the committee. Existing creditors were in many instances asked to extend the maturity of their loans and to subordinate them in favor of new financing which was necessary. The new money was supplied either by the principal old creditors, or from new sources.

Although the creditors' committee would determine policies, part or all of the old company officers and directors were allowed to remain. In some instances involving corporations, a voting trust arrangement was set up giving the creditors' committee the power to elect the directors. After the old debts were paid the management was returned to the old officers and directors. If a reorganization appeared necessary, the creditors' committee would formulate the plan; or if liquidation was indicated, the committee in some instances supervised it.

It was thought that the creditors' committee arrangement would avoid the unfavorable publicity that accompanies receivership or bankruptcy, be less costly than going through legal proceedings, and that better management might result. On the other hand, creditors' committees had no authority to set aside unprofitable contracts as may be done under receivership or bankruptcy, they could not set aside questionable claims, and they were powerless to prevent a creditor from throwing the debtor into receivership or bankruptcy. These weaknesses, plus the fact that the Bankruptcy Act was amended in 1933 to facilitate the reorganization of businesses, account for the fact that creditors' committee management was relatively less important during the depression of the early 1930's.

The National Association of Credit Men has been active in advocating friendly reorganizations to prevent the more costly and time consuming bankruptcy proceedings. This organization has throughout the country approved adjustment bureaus on its list which are able and willing to assist with friendly adjustments. The creditors' committee may work through one of these adjustment bureaus. The latter will also aid in cases involving extensions and assignments.

Receivership

Reasons for Receivership. In many instances a friendly arrangement cannot be worked out for the continuation, reorganization, or liquidation of a business. This is particularly true when the concern is large and has a large number of creditors. Creditors who have a lien on the company property, such as mortgage bondholders, might take steps to foreclose their liens and thereby, when it is to their advantage, leave the company stripped of its most valuable assets. Or some of the unsecured creditors might be impatient with the other creditors and with the debtor, and take aggressive action ahead of the other creditors by suing and obtaining judgment against the debtor. With the judgment, they then get a lien on the company property. They may then have the sheriff seize and sell the property for the satisfaction of the claim.

Forced sale of the kind just mentioned usually results in the property being sold for a relatively small percentage of its book value. Furthermore, creditors who have reduced their claims to judgments and liens are entitled to 100 cents on the dollar before the other creditors get anything. This procedure obviously results in liquidation or partial liquidation of the company. Not only are the assets sold at sacrifice prices, but the going-concern value of the company is destroyed. Also, liquidation of the company may work a hardship on the customers or consumers who can no longer buy the products or services of the company. Liquidation would, of course, also throw the employees out of work.

The primary purpose of receivership is to place the company under the protection of the court so that creditors possessing judgments and liens cannot foreclose and seize the company property. In the meantime, under the protection of the court, some equitable solution to the company's problem may be worked out, and it may be allowed to continue in business even though a reorganization may be necessary.

Because of changes which have been made in the Bankruptcy Act, beginning in 1933, which permit reorganization in addition to liquidation, companies now select the bankruptcy proceedings rather than receivership in practically all instances when financial difficulties force them to do so. Receivership is still used occasionally under circumstances of financial difficulty, but it is more likely to be used when there is some other need for court jurisdiction, such as dispute among the shareholders over the election of a board of directors, or when the company officers are charged with fraud. Since receivership following financial difficulties is more involved than when it results from other causes, in the following discussion we will assume that the receivership is brought about by financial troubles.

Equity Receivership Procedure. Since receivership is an equitable rather than a legal action, petition for the appointment of a receiver comes under the equity courts. That is why it is referred to as *equity receivership*. The receiver may be appointed by either a state or a federal court, depending upon where the petition is filed. Federal rules are uniform and have been more carefully worked out than those in most of the states. Furthermore, when the property of the company is located in several states, it is better to have the federal court administer the property. A receiver appointed by a state court would have jurisdiction over only that property which is located within the state. Separate receivers would have to be appointed in the other states. When federal action is taken, if the property is located in more than one federal court district, ancillary (auxiliary) receivership action will be taken in the other districts. This usually results in the appointment of the same receiver.

The receiver appointed may be a lawyer in whom the court has confidence, or it may be an official of the company. Quite often both are appointed as co-receivers. The lawyer would be familiar with the many legal problems and procedures involved, while the company official would be experienced in the company's affairs.

A creditor might on his own initiative file a petition for the appointment of a receiver. But in most instances, in order to prevent the foreclosure of any liens, the corporate management itself would initiate the action by arranging with a "friendly" creditor to file the petition. In order to get federal court jurisdiction, the claim of the creditor would have to be in excess of $3,000. Since actions between citizens of different states can originate in the federal courts, the creditor would be a citizen of a state other than the one in which the corporation was organized. When the corporation itself initiates the action, it is called a voluntary receivership. When a creditor or group of creditors initiate the action, it is called *involuntary receivership*. Voluntary receivership is much more common than involuntary.

The creditor will file a complaint that the corporation is unable to meet its debts as they mature, that some of the creditors have secured judgments against the company or are about to secure judgments, and that if a receiver is not appointed the creditors would seize the assets with resultant losses to all. At the same time, the corporation files an answer admitting the allegations and asks that a receiver be appointed. A court hearing will then be held and, if the court believes that a receiver is needed, one will be appointed.

Powers and Duties of Receiver. Receivership places the property under the jurisdiction of the court, and the receiver is the agent of the court appointed to administer the property. The court order may define the duties and powers of the receiver in a very general way, or they may be specified in detail. Major actions on the part of the receiver will be taken only upon court order, although the order may follow requests made by the receiver. Generally the powers and duties of the receiver are as follows:

1. *Receive and conserve the assets of the company.* The primary function of the receiver is to take over the assets of the company for the purpose of keeping them intact. The receiver serves

during the period in which some plan of reorganization is being worked out. He is supposed to see to it that as much of the property as possible be still available at the time the receivership is vacated. He prevents the payment of any of the assets to old creditors. In this way, certain creditors cannot benefit at the expense of others by being paid off while others are trying to work out some kind of settlement. One reason for receivership is the prevention of foreclosure of liens in order that all assets be available for continued operation or for payment to all creditors after a solution to the particular problem is worked out.

2. *Manage and operate the company.* In most instances, the best way to conserve the assets is to continue to operate the company. Continued operation may help change the assets into more liquid form as well as maintain customers and suppliers for future operation.

Under receivership the receiver becomes the chief executive of the company. He may decide, however, to retain the principal officers of the company in order to obtain the benefits of their past experience. In some instances, the old management may not be directly responsible for the condition of the company. In fact, as stated before, the receiver appointed by the court may be one of the company's officers. The receiver may also hire experts to help him in the operation of the business.

The receiver will take in the money from operations and apply it to the operating expenses. It is his duty also to collect the debts owed the company. Funds, if available, may also upon court order be applied toward the debts owed by the company. Since the company is in financial difficulties the receiver might find it difficult to obtain sufficient supplies or enough employees to operate the company efficiently. For this reason the court may provide that all claims incurred under receivership shall have a prior right to the income and assets of the company.

3. *Raise new money.* Regardless of what may have been the fundamental or underlying cause of the failure of the company, the immediate cause is always the lack of cash. In an attempt to prevent failure, the management will have used all the available funds, and all possible new sources of funds will have been exhausted. Furthermore, in an effort to prevent failure, cash will have been used only for the most pressing needs. Thus, the property may be in a rundown condition because of inadequate maintenance, needed supplies and new equipment may not have been purchased,

and creditors may be pressing for the payment of their overdue claims.

The receiver will have the use of any money that the company earns during receivership, and that which is available as a result of not paying the interest charges on the company's bonds, or rents on leased property. But commonly this will not furnish enough funds to meet the needed requirements. From what has already been said, it is obvious that in view of the financial condition of the company, new money could not be obtained from the sale of stock, or borrowed in the ordinary way. The court may therefore authorize the issuance of *receiver's certificates.*

Although receiver's certificates are considered to be obligations of the receiver, they are his obligations in an official rather than personal capacity. The certificates, like other obligations of the company, must be repaid from the property of the company. If the assets of the company are not sufficient to satisfy the obligations, the receiver has no personal liability for them. The claim or lien of the receiver's certificates is specified by the court. As a practical matter it will be necessary to give them sufficient priority over other obligations of the company in order that they may be sold. Commonly this means that they will be placed ahead of all defaulted obligations, but not necessarily ahead of some or all of the obligations in which default has not occurred. In some instances, it will be necessary to place them ahead of the first mortgage bonds.

In the case of a reorganization, receiver's certificates may be paid off from the proceeds of the sale of new securities, or in part or entirely from the assessments made upon shareholders. In some instances, however, the financial affairs have been so bad that receiver's certificate holders have been forced to take senior bonds of the reorganized company rather than receiving payment when due.

4. *Validate claims and handle payments.* As has been stated before, the appointment of a receiver throws a cloak of protection over the company property and prevents any creditor from foreclosing his lien. When creditors file their claims it will be up to the receiver, subject to approval by the court, to determine which, and to what extent, they are valid. In paying any claims, the current expenses of receivership will be taken care of first. Any balance of funds may be used to pay certain earlier creditors as designated by the court. The court, for example, after giving consideration to the priority of liens, may authorize the payment of bond interest, to the extent that it is earned. These payments would be handled

by the receiver. It should be emphasized here that it is not the position of the receiver to establish or approve the plan of reorganization or to set up compositions or extension. This work is done by the creditors themselves. The receiver merely validates claims and handles any payments provided for by the court during the period in which he is responsible for the property.

5. *Action on company contracts.* It is an important function and duty of the receiver to examine all contracts and leases made by the company with the view toward determining their profitableness. One of the objectives of receivership is to restore the company to efficient operations. If it develops that the company has taken some leases of property or given guaranties with respect to subsidiaries or their securities, in which the benefits received are less than the amount the company is paying out on the lease or guaranty, the receiver will ask the court that these agreements be canceled. This, of course, is an important objective that could never be accomplished by the company without the benefit of the courts.

The other party to the contract, however, may file a claim in the final reorganization for any damages sustained by him as a result of the cancellation of the contract. But for the claim to be recognized it will be necessary for him to prove that he had been harmed by the cancellation.

6. *Report on the condition of the company.* It is the duty of the receiver to report to the court the condition of affairs of the company. This report does not make suggestions for disposition of property or any plan of reorganization, or settlement of claims. It merely discusses the value of the property and the future possible results of operations. The final report can be made only after the company has been under the receiver's jurisdiction sufficiently long for him to have arrived at a final conclusion in regard to the company property and prospects. This report is of great value to the court since the latter will, on the basis of the contents of the report, decide what action shall be taken in regard to the company.

Receivership Compared with Compromise Settlements. Receivership has certain advantages over compromise settlements. One of these is that cooperation of the creditors and their agreement to receivership are not required. Under receivership, claims of creditors are properly evaluated and validated. In receivership, new money may be raised through the issuance of receiver's certificates. Receivership permits operation of the company until sufficient time has elapsed to determine what is wrong with the company and what is needed. In the meantime, creditors cannot foreclose their liens.

Receivership, however, publicly acknowledges to the world that the company has failed. If the company gets back on its feet, much goodwill and credit will have been destroyed by such action. Receivership is the most costly and time-consuming method of reorganizing or liquidating a company. After we have considered reorganization resulting from receivership, further shortcomings will be mentioned.

PROCEDURE FOLLOWING RECEIVERSHIP. Although receivership may last many years, it is merely a temporary action pending the determination of the final solution to the problem. One of the following three courses of action will be taken following the lifting of receivership:

1. *Rehabilitation.* In rare instances the financial difficulties are resolved under receivership, and the company is returned to its owners in a solvent condition. Since receiverships usually follow serious financial trouble, this is a rare case.

2. *Liquidation.* If the company cannot be rehabilitated and also cannot be reorganized, and if the company is not a public utility, it may be decided that the situation is hopeless, and the court may order liquidation.

3. *Reorganization.* In most instances the two extremes stated above are not followed, but rather the company is reorganized and continues in business. The procedure in such a reorganization is indicated below.

Reorganization following receivership

Since equity receivership is less commonly used today than before 1933 for companies that are in financial difficulty, we will only briefly describe the procedure of reorganization which follows equity receivership. In the following chapter we will discuss reorganization under the Bankruptcy Act in more detail. It should be noted, however, that an understanding of equity receivership reorganizations is essential for a proper understanding of reorganization under the Bankruptcy Act, due to the fact that this statute contains the following:

> The court shall have and may exercise all the powers, not inconsistent with the provisions of this chapter, which a court of the United States would have if it had appointed a receiver in equity of the property of the debtor on the ground of insolvency or inability to meet its debts as they mature.[1]

[1] Bankruptcy Act, Chap. X, Sec. 115.

Meaning of Reorganization. We have already discussed recapitalizations, adjustments, compromise settlements, and receiverships. In some instances we used the word "reorganization," without defining what was meant by the term. There is no exact definition of the word, and it is used by different people to mean different things. Some use the term to mean any recasting of the financial structure because of failure or threatened failure; that would include some of the recapitalizations and adjustments and compromise settlements discussed above. The term has also been used in a more restricted way to apply to only those instances in which a new company is formed to take over the properties of the old company through a court sale following receivership. Some authors use the term "reconstruction" when a new company is not formed after a major realignment of interests.

Usually the term "reorganization" is not used when the readjustment called for is minor in nature. In other words, we will not apply it to those situations which were included under recapitalizations, readjustments, and compromise settlements. But when financial difficulties are so serious in nature that adjustments of this kind cannot successfully be made, and it is necessary to recast the financial structure through receivership or the Bankruptcy Act, we will then use the term "reorganization."

Reorganization Procedure. The various classes of security holders have antagonistic positions in a reorganization since the settlement given one class may be at the expense of another class. The management, due to their election by the shareholders or at least by shareholders' proxies, and also because they are usually important shareholders in the company, will probably look after the interests of the shareholders, particularly the common shareholders, more than the interests of the creditors. Some of the large bondholders, or the investment bankers who handled the particular bond issue, may take the initiative and form a committee for the protection of that particular class of creditors. Other classes of creditors will also probably form protective committees. In some instances several different groups will compete with each other to represent the interests of a class of creditors.

Each of the protective committees makes a call for the deposit of securities representing the class of security holders the committee was set up to protect. The deposit of securities gives the committee authority to represent the security holders. Some of the deposit agreements make it exceedingly difficult for the security holders to pull out. In some instances they can do so only after they have paid their pro rata share of the committee expense.

The various committees cannot hope to effect a reorganization plan themselves. Thus, representatives of the various committees form a *reorganization committee* for the purpose of formulating a suitable plan of reorganization. Also on the reorganization committee may be some of the top officers of the company, and possibly a representative of an investment banking firm that is to sell any new securities to be issued. Several of the individuals may be designated as "managers" of the reorganization committee. This committee will try to effect some feasible plan. With the protective committees representing divergent interests, they will be asked to compromise on many points.

When a plan has been worked out, the protective committees will ask that various security holders sign a *ratification* agreement, which binds them to the plan. Those not agreeing can usually ask for a return of their securities. If all of the security holders would agree to the plan, it could be put into immediate operation without the necessity of a court sale of the properties. But such one hundred per cent agreement would rarely be possible. Before the court will approve a reorganization plan it will be necessary to get a substantial majority of the various classes of security holders to agree to the plan. The court is interested primarily in the satisfaction of all those with legal claims against the company. Any creditor dissatisfied with the proposed plan will have to receive equitable treatment before the court will approve the plan.

After having arrived at a value of the corporate property, the court will establish an *upset price*. This is the minimum price acceptable by the court for the corporate properties. At the time and place specified by the court the public sale of the properties will take place. The reorganization committee uses the securities which have been deposited with the protective committee as part of the consideration to be used in bidding on the properties. The court will also specify the minimum amount that must be paid in cash by the committee. The reorganization committee, through its control of the securities, will probably be the only bidder at the sale and will pay for the property by turning in the securities it controls plus the required amount of cash. From a legal standpoint, the sale represents a foreclosure of all the liens possessed by the securities held by the reorganization committee as well as those possessed by other creditors.

The sale price of the property establishes the equity of security holders who do not agree to the plan. Let us assume that a corporation had outstanding a $10,000,000 first mortgage bond, a $5,000,000 second mortgage bond issue, and a $5,000,000 debenture bond issue. We will furthermore assume that the corporate properties are sold for $15,000,000, the amount established as the upset price. Of this amount $10,000,000 is paid for properties securing the mortgages and $5,000,000 for other properties. The first and second mortgage and debenture bondholders who agreed to the reorganization would get whatever the plan called for. Dissenting first mortgage bondholders, however, would be entitled to 100 cents on the dollar since the pledged property brought this amount. Dissenting holders of the second mortgage bonds and of the debentures would get 50 cents on the dollar. These payments would be based on the legal order of claims. In a situation of this kind the reorganization plan would probably call for the agreeing first mortgage bondholders receiving new first mortgage bonds similar to those they already possessed, while the second mortgage bondholders and debenture holders might have been asked to accept income bonds, or undergo some other type of sacrifice.

The upset price should be sufficiently high to allow the dissenters a fair value for their securities, but not so high as to prevent the sale of the properties. In some instances where there is no bidder, the court is forced to lower the upset price. The upset price must be low enough to cause the reorganization committee to submit a bid since they are often the only bidders. The committee will submit a bid only if it feels that the price paid for the properties would be low enough to permit profitable operation in the future.

Upon court sale of the properties, the reorganization committee buys the properties and turns them over to a new corporation which is formed for the purpose. Usually the name of the new company is similar to that of the old one. The old corporation and its securities pass out of existence, and the new securities are distributed to those who agreed to the reorganization plan.

Reorganizations commonly call for new cash. This is needed to pay off dissenters, retire receiver's certificates, pay reorganization expenses, and to provide new working capital for the reorganized company. A major problem of the reorganization committee is the raising of this needed new cash. One of the best ways is through assessment of present interested parties. The stockholders of the company may be asked to pay in a certain amount of cash if they wish to maintain any interest in the new company. Even creditors may be assessed in certain instances. Sometimes new securities are sold by the reorganized company to obtain needed cash. In this event, old security holders are generally the major parties interested in the new securities. New securities are often offered on a rights basis to old security holders. Where possible, investment bankers are brought in to underwrite the new issues. The bankers agree to take over all of the new issue not taken by old security holders. An agreement of this type by an investment banking firm assures the success of the sale of securities. In some cases, investment bankers may agree to stand all assessments not paid by dissenters to the plan in return for the rights of these dissenters in the new company.

SHORTCOMINGS OF EQUITY REORGANIZATIONS. Equity receiverships and reorganizations have been largely superseded by reorganization under the Bankruptcy Act. Following are the more important shortcomings of reorganization under the equity courts which have led to increased use of reorganization under the Bankruptcy Act.

1. *Cost.* Equity receiverships and reorganizations are the most costly of the various methods of readjustment or reorganization. The procedure followed must conform to the law, and lawyers play an active part in the work. Fees collected by them are sometimes grossly out of proportion to the services rendered. The protective committees also often collect excessive compensation. Court costs must be paid along with receiver's fees and all his expenses.

2. *Time consuming.* Equity receiverships and reorganizations are long drawn-out affairs, which, of course, adds to their cost. Some companies have been in the receiver's hands for a quarter of a century, or longer, and then after emerging from one, they may sink back again into another protracted receivership. For example, the Pittsburgh, Shawmut and Northern Railroad Co. had been in receivership for forty-two years prior to the sale of its properties in 1947.

3. *Appointment of ancillary receivers.* We stated above that if the receiver is appointed by the state court, receivership proceedings will have to be started in the various states in which the corporate property is located. This is costly and complicates the procedure of receivership. When action is brought in the federal court, ancillary actions will be necessary in the other federal court districts in which the property is located. Although the same receiver may be appointed by the other districts, in some instances different ones are appointed. This divides the responsibility, and in some instances results in the particular receiver favoring local creditors.

4. *Little control over protective committees.* The protective committees are formed through the initiative taken by some of the

creditors, shareholders, or investment bankers. Although they are supposed to represent the particular group of security holders whose securities they received on deposit, in some instances the management of the corporation controls them. In some cases the committees appear to be more interested in the fees and expenses they collect than in protecting the security holders.

5. *Court has little control over reorganization plan.* The reorganization plan is drawn up by the reorganization committee. This committee may be dominated by one class of creditors, or it may be controlled by the common shareholders. Whoever controls this important committee may receive preferential treatment in the final plan. This lack of control on the part of the court over the formulation of the reorganization is sometimes mentioned as the most serious objection to equity reorganizations.

6. *Court lacks authority to replace liens.* Aside from giving priority to those who grant credit for the receivership expenses, and the giving of some priority to receiver's certificates, the court lacks the authority to subordinate any liens in favor of new creditors. This makes it impossible to secure any new funds except through the issuance of receiver's certificates. Where agreement on the part of all classes of security holders cannot be obtained, which is the usual situation, it is necessary to have a judicial sale of the property in order to freeze out certain security holders, and to force equitable settlement on others.

7. *Problem of dissenters.* Dissenters can destroy any plan set up by the reorganization committee regardless of its fairness or reasonableness. The court has no authority to force dissenters to agree to any plan. They are entitled to their payment or they can force bankruptcy regardless of long-range advantages of reorganization to themselves as well as to other creditors. Paying off dissenters in equity receivership reorganizations places a cash burden on the reorganized company at a time when it is already short of cash for operations and other needs.

Questions

1. Is the consent of all creditors necessary to effect an extension in the maturity of a debt? Explain.

2. (a) Indicate the situation under which a composition settlement might be effected. (b) Is 100 per cent agreement necessary to effect such a settlement? Explain.

3. (a) Indicate the circumstances under which an assignment for the benefit of creditors might be successfully used. (b) If this action is taken could the debtor be thrown into bankruptcy? Explain.

4. (a) Indicate the circumstances under which creditors' committee management and reorganization might be accomplished. (b) What are the relative advantages and disadvantages of this form of reorganization as compared with reorganization following receivership or trusteeship under the Bankruptcy Act?

5. Indicate the procedure for placing a company in the hands of a receiver in equity.

6. What is usually the primary reason of a company voluntarily applying for receivership?

7. Indicate what is accomplished while a company is in the hands of a receiver?

8. Indicate the procedure followed under receivership pointing toward the final reorganization of the company.

9. (a) Under whose authority are receivers' certificates issued? (b) What determines the lien possessed by receivers' certificates?

10. What are the relative advantages and disadvantages of equity receiverships as compared with the other forms of adjustments previously discussed?

11. What three courses of action might be taken by a company that is in receivership?

12. Explain the meaning of the term "reorganization" as used in this chapter to distinguish this form of reconstruction from the other types previously described?

13. Indicate what is meant by the "upset price," who establishes it, and what is accomplished by setting such a price.

14. What treatment is given dissenters in a reorganization following court sale of the company's properties?

15. Why are equity receiverships now rarely resorted to in case of the financial failure of business concerns?

Problems

1. The Hopewell Manufacturing Co. presented the following balance sheet as of Dec. 31, 19-1:

Assets		*Liabilities and Net Worth*	
Cash	$ 5,000	Accounts Payable	$ 150,000
Receivables	110,000	Notes Payable	300,000
Inventory	685,000	Accrued Taxes	50,000
Machinery	1,500,000	First Mortgage	1,000,000
Plant	5,000,000	Second Mortgage	1,000,000
Deficit	200,000	Debenture Bonds	1,000,000
		Common Stock	3,000,000
		Preferred Stock	1,000,000
Total	$7,500,000	Total	$7,500,000

The notes bear interest at the rate of 7 per cent. The interest rates of the bond issues are as follows: First, 5 per cent; Second, 6 per cent; Debentures, 7 per cent. The capital stock has a par value of $100 per share. The inventory valuation should be discounted about 10 per cent, and it is probable that 3 per cent of the accounts receivable are uncollectible. The notes come due June 30, 19-2; the first mortgage bonds are due Dec. 31, 19-1; the second mortgage bonds mature Dec. 31, 19-4; and the debentures come due Dec. 31,

19-2. The preferred stock is 7 per cent cumulative, but the dividends on this stock have not been paid for the past 4 years.

The company was very successful many years ago. The debentures were issued some years ago to get money for expansion purposes. The mortgages were later sold to secure funds to acquire another plant. The company was hard hit in the deflation period but came back fairly well in the following prosperous period. But the company has never recovered from the depression. Earnings before interest charges for the past 2 years have averaged only $80,000. Interest was paid in part in these years from the sale of some real estate that the company owned in the business section of the city.

The company manufactures two products, similar in nature, which are purchased by consumers. It started out manufacturing product A, which is high grade and expensive. When the public later demanded a cheaper product, the president of the company, who has served in that capacity since the company was formed, refused to lower the quality of his product. Later he was forced to give in, and he started manufacturing product B under a different trade name. He has, however, insisted on still making product A, although the losses suffered on this product have had to be borne by the profit made on product B. List in general the things that should be done in an attempt to put this company back on its feet as a successful business enterprise.

2. The following question relates to the Hopewell Manufacturing Co. mentioned in Problem 1. Do you think the company should be reconstructed through creditors' committee, or consent operation? Give reasons for your answer.

Chapter 35

REORGANIZATION UNDER THE BANKRUPTCY ACT

History of Bankruptcy Laws. The first bankruptcy laws were enacted by the Romans as early as 313 B.C. The first statute of this kind in England came in 1542, but this law was for the benefit of creditors and not debtors. It was not until 1705 that provision was made in the English law for the discharge of the debtor from his obligations under bankruptcy proceedings.

At the time of the formation of the federal government in the United States there was considerable difference of opinion whether the right to enact bankruptcy laws should be delegated to the federal government or retained by the various states. Those favoring the federal government finally won. The first federal statute was adopted in 1800, but it lasted only two years. Several other federal statutes enacted subsequently were of short duration. Finally the federal government, in 1898, enacted the Bankruptcy Act, which with its amendments is still the law of the land today.

The Bankruptcy Act of 1898 provided for the liquidation, and not the reorganization, of an insolvent company. Due to the public necessity for the services rendered by railroads and public utilities, they were exempt from the Bankruptcy Act. When the financial difficulties of these types of companies reached the stage where something had to be done, they applied for, or had a creditor bring action for, appointment of a receiver in equity, and then were subsequently reorganized in the manner briefly described in the preceding chapter. Although other types of corporations could avail themselves of the bankruptcy law, many of these companies resorted to equity receivership and reorganization rather than bankruptcy which could lead only to liquidation.

Due to the shortcomings of equity receivership and reorganization, Congress, in 1933, amended the Bankruptcy Act, through the enactment of Section 77, to permit railroads to *reorganize* under the *Bankruptcy Act.* In 1934, Section 77B was added to the Act to permit all other types of corporations to *reorganize* under the Bankruptcy Act. In 1938, Section 77B was supplanted by the Chandler Act, which is sometimes referred to as Chapters X and XI of the Bankruptcy Act. Chapter XI was designed for the reorganization of small concerns with only bank and merchandise creditors, while Chapter X pertains to larger corporations which have securities outstanding. We will first discuss Chapter X, then briefly indicate how Section 77 pertaining to railroads differs from this (the Mahaffie Act will be discussed in this connection), and then we will state the principal features of Chapter XI concerning arrangements.

It should be kept in mind that we are discussing *reorganizations* under the Bankruptcy Act. Corporations undergoing such action are referred to in the law as "debtors," and not "bankrupts." After discussing reorganization at some length we will briefly consider liquidation under the Bankruptcy Act, which before 1933, was the only action possible under this statute.

Much of what is said in relation to reorganization under Chapter X, will apply with equal force to the reorganization of railroads under Section 77. Also equity receivership and equity reorganization and reorganization under Section 77 and Chapter X are similar in respect to the events leading up to such actions, the objectives to be accomplished in the reorganization, the formation of protective committees, some of the court procedure, etc.

INITIATING ACTION UNDER CHAPTER X. Reorganization under Chapter X (Chandler Act) may be accomplished by any corporation other than a railroad, bank, building and loan (savings and loan) association, or municipal corporation. The company may voluntarily instigate the proceedings, or involuntary proceedings may be started by three or more creditors whose claims against the company aggregate $5,000 or more, or by a trustee under the indenture of a bond issue (provided the bonds represent a fixed and agreed sum). When the company files a voluntary petition it must be stated that the company is insolvent or unable to pay its debts as they mature. When involuntary action is brought the petition must show that the company was adjudged a bankrupt, or that a "proceeding to foreclose a mortgage" or similar action had been undertaken. The petition, which is filed in a federal court, must state why reorganization cannot be accomplished under Chapter XI (dealing with "arrangements"), and other matters provided in the law. If the petition conforms to law, the judge must approve it. If it is contested, the judge must satisfy himself as to the allegations presented in the petition before approval.

APPOINTMENT OF TRUSTEE. After the petition has been approved, the judge must appoint a trustee, or trustees, to conduct the necessary business of the company. If the liabilities of the company amount to $250,000 or more, the judge must appoint a "disinterested" trustee. In order to qualify as a disinterested party, a trustee cannot be (a) a stockholder or creditor of the company, (b) an underwriter of any of the company's outstanding securities, or an underwriter of any of the company's securities within a period of five years prior to the filing of the petition, (c) director, officer, attorney or employee of the company, or underwriter or attorney of an underwriter of the company at the time, or within two years prior to the filing of the petition, or (d) any other person directly or indirectly connected with the company or underwriter and who might have an interest materially adverse to the interests of any class of creditors or shareholders.[1] In addition to the disinterested trustee, the judge may appoint a director, officer, or employee of the company as a co-trustee. When the total indebtedness is less than $250,000, the judge may appoint a disinterested trustee or he may at his discretion allow the company to continue in possession of its property.

DUTIES OF THE TRUSTEE. The trustee in bankruptcy has more duties to perform, and plays a much more active part in the reorganization of the company than the receiver in equity. In addition to running the business in a manner similar to the receiver in equity, Chapter X of the Bankruptcy Act states that the trustee shall perform the following duties.

1. Collect the essential information in regard to the company's financial position, condition of its property, operation of the business, and the desirability of continuing the operations, and report the findings to the judge, the stockholders, creditors, and the Securities and Exchange Commission.
2. Investigate the past conduct of the officers and directors and report to the judge any evidence of fraud, mismanagement, or irregularities. This information is of value in determining whether any action should be taken against them, and also whether these officers and directors should be left in their positions.

[1] The "disinterested" trustee requirement was added to the law by Chapter X. Under the old Section 77B the trustee could be an interested party or one who was friendly with the management or underwriters. The charge was made that many such trustees favored the management and the change in the law was made in order to overcome this possibility.

3. Invite the various classes of creditors, bondholders, and shareholders to submit to him plans for the reorganization of the company.
4. Preparation of a reorganization plan and the filing of it with the court within the time limit set by a judge. If a reorganization is not recommended a report must be filed setting forth the reasons.

It will be recalled that under equity receivership the receiver has nothing to do with the reorganization plan. It is formulated by the reorganization committee. That was one of the principal weaknesses of such reorganizations. In a reorganization under Chapter X of the Bankruptcy Act, the trustee is charged with the drawing up of the reorganization plan. Since the trustee is the agent of the court, it follows that the latter will supervise the reorganization procedure.

PROTECTIVE COMMITTEES. Protective committees, and in some instances a "reorganization" committee, are used in reorganizations under Chapter X, but they are under court control, and have less power and authority than under equity receivership reorganization. Chapter X provides that the court may require full disclosure of the lists of stockholders and bondholders, so that interested parties may proceed to form protective committees. Under equity proceedings the management and investment bankers had the inside track in regard to such lists. Under Chapter X the amount of the compensation of the committees, the lawyers, depositaries, and reorganization managers may be fixed by the court.

The members of the protective committees or the reorganization committee may formulate a plan for the reorganization and submit it to the trustee. Although each class of security holders will be interested in getting the most for its particular class of securities, it is realized that an inequitable plan would be unacceptable to the trustee and to the court. It will be recalled that under Chapter X the trustee, and not the committees, is charged with the duty of drawing up the reorganization plan.

WORK PRELIMINARY TO PLAN. Before a reorganization plan can be formulated it is necessary to know what caused the company to fail. The reorganization plan should take the cause of failure into consideration in an attempt to prevent such occurrence in the future. It is also necessary to know the nature of the company's assets and liabilities and to determine whether adjustments in the books will be needed to bring them in line with the actual condition. A complete audit should be made by independent accountants. The books may carry intangible assets, such as goodwill and patent rights, at greatly exaggerated values. Other property accounts, particularly inventory and accounts receivable, may also be on the books at inflated values. The accounting for depreciation, depletion, and obsolescence should be critically reviewed.

Engineering reports on the condition of the physical plant are needed. Much of the machinery or equipment may be found to be in need of repairs or replacement because of physical deterioration or obsolescence. A study of the debtor's industry and its relative place in that industry are needed in order to determine the desirability of continued operation by the company. Estimates should be made of the amount of money needed to bring the physical equipment up to the proper standard to enable the company successfully to compete with others in the field. It should be remembered that practically all companies are hard pressed for cash before failure. What funds are available will be used on the more pressing claims, and maintenance and replacement of machinery and equipment will be neglected.

Intensive legal work must be done. The various contracts and leases made by the company should be searchingly examined to determine their legality and profitableness. In some instances it is necessary to investigate a complicated system of subsidiaries and intercorporate holdings of securities.

From the examination of the company it should be possible to determine what are the profitable and unprofitable units. The relative position of the various liens will be determined, and from this it will be possible to arrive at some conclusion on the sacrifices which must be made by any class of security holders. Considerable weight is given to the ability of the company's earnings to meet the fixed charges. From the study it will also be possible to determine the amount of new money which should be necessary for the reorganization.

MANDATORY PROVISIONS OF REORGANIZATION PLAN. Chapter X provides that certain provisions shall be in every reorganization plan, and specifies others that may be included. The following are included in the mandatory provisions.

1. Provisions calling for the payment of all costs and expenses of administration and other allowances approved by the court.
2. Provisions for the rejection of any executory contract except contracts in the public authority.
3. Provisions in the charter prohibiting the issuance of nonvoting stock, and insuring equitable distribution of voting power among the various classes of stock. Where preferred stock is made non-

voting, adequate provisions must be made for the election of directors representing them in event of default in their dividends.

4. Adequate provisions relating to the execution of the reorganization plan, including any sale of the corporate property, merger with one or more corporations, or other procedure for the carrying out of the plan.
5. Certain provisions for changes must be listed in the plan if they are to take effect. All alterations or modifications in the rights of any class of creditors or stockholders, either through the issuance of new securities or otherwise, must be spelled out. A list of any creditors or shareholders or any class of creditors or shareholders which will not be affected by the plan must be included along with any provisions relating to these individuals or groups. All claims which are to be paid in full in cash must be specifically listed in any reorganization plan.
6. Provisions relating to the treatment of any class of creditors where the required two-thirds majority assent to the plan is not obtained.

Objectives To Be Accomplished in Reorganization. Due to different circumstances, the exact nature of the reorganization plan varies with every reorganization. The purpose of the reorganization is to eliminate whatever is wrong and get the company back on its feet as a going concern. In most instances, however, failure results from several causes that are common to many businesses. The principal objectives to be accomplished will be briefly stated under the headings listed below. Although we are now discussing reorganizations under Chapter X, the objectives to be stated would apply with equal force to reorganizations under any other procedure.

1. Correct any managerial defects. In many instances, managerial inefficiencies have at least been a contributory cause of failure. In some instances failure can be placed directly at the door of the management. If this is the only thing wrong, the reorganization can be effected rather quickly by the appointment of new management. But in most instances it is not so simple. Chapter X specifically provides that the judge, before approving the reorganization plan, shall be satisfied that the new management appointed, or the old management that may be continuing in office, shall be consistent with the investors' interests and with public policy.
2. Reduction of fixed charges. Railroads and public utilities are formed with a relatively large percentage of their capitalization in the form of bonds. The immediate cause of failure of many of these types of businesses is the inability to pay the fixed charges. One of the objectives to be accomplished therefore is the reduction in the amount of the fixed charges. This may be done by the

reduction in the rate of interest, or a reduction in the principal amount of bonded indebtedness, or both. It is also done in some instances by the issuance of income bonds to take the place of some of the ordinary bonds. Industrial corporations often fail without having any bonds outstanding. In the reorganization of some of these companies they may emerge with a bond issue and fixed charges.

3. Reduction of floating debt. Industrial corporations commonly fail because of too large a debt owed to banks or trade creditors. The objective then is to reduce this debt or extend the time when it becomes due. In some instances where extensions, composition settlements, or arrangements cannot be effected, the plan may call for the issuance of bonds to the creditors.
4. Collection of new money. As we have stated several times before, all companies that fail are in need of cash. Expenses of reorganization must be paid, the property must be put in proper repair, and new equipment must be purchased. In addition it will be necessary to raise some money to make proper settlement with those who have a claim against the company and who do not agree to the reorganization, or in the case of reorganization under Chapter X, those belonging to a class of creditor in which a two-thirds majority assent to the plan is not obtained. This money may come in part from the assessment or sale of securities to the old security holders, or the sale of securities to the public through investment bankers.

Treatment of interested parties

To carry out the above stated objectives, we will now indicate briefly how the various classes of creditors or shareholders are affected.

Preferred Creditors. Under the Bankruptcy Act the claim of the United States, or a state or political subdivision thereof, for taxes is entitled to priority. Certain employees to whom wages were due within three months before legal bankruptcy proceedings were started are entitled to preference up to $600 each. Expenses and debts incurred by a receiver in equity or a trustee in bankruptcy also receive preferred treatment. In the case of public service corporations, creditors who supplied goods or services to the company within a period up to six months prior to the time bankruptcy proceedings were started may also be given preferred status.

Creditors having a preferred status are usually paid off during receivership or during the period the property is under the jurisdiction of the bankruptcy court. If not, the reorganization plan makes provision for their payment.

RECEIVER'S AND TRUSTEE'S CERTIFICATES. *Trustee's certificates* are issued in reorganization under Chapter X in the same manner and for the same reason that receiver's certificates are issued under equity receivership. As has been stated before, the relative standing of the certificates depends upon the lien given them by the court. If they are given a claim prior to the first mortgage bonds, then they would rank immediately after the preferred creditors listed above. They are commonly paid off from the proceeds of the sale of new securities or from assessments made on the old security holders. In some instances, however, they are not paid off in cash at the time, but are given prior lien bonds of the reorganized company. There have been a few cases where the holders of such certificates have been forced to make sacrifices.

OTHER CREDITORS. Generally speaking, the secured bonds of a company would receive better treatment in the reorganization than the unsecured obligations. Their actual treatment would depend upon the exact nature of their lien, and the value to the company of the property which constitutes their security. If the earnings of the company are such that the property which constitutes their security appears capable of earning the interest on the bonds, then no sacrifices will be asked of these secured bondholders. If a new company is formed, they will be given new bonds similar to their old ones, par for par. Such bonds would be said to be "undisturbed" or "unaffected." Since simplification of the capital structure is often attempted in a reorganization, one large new issue of open-end bonds might be exchanged for several different undisturbed issues. The security behind the new issue would probably be greater than that of any of the separate old issues. Where the company would not be expected to earn enough to pay the interest on the old senior bonds, they would have to undergo sacrifices similar to those for junior bonds (see below).

If the company has been earning enough to pay the interest on the senior bonds secured by strategic property but not enough to cover the total interest on senior bonds on less important property or junior liens on strategic property, then sacrifices would be expected in the case of the latter two types of bonds. The actual treatment accorded any security holders depends in part on the bargaining power of the particular protective committee, but in general it tends to represent their actual worth as measured by the earning power of the particular property which constitutes the security for the bond issue. For example, if the property behind a second mortgage, or the less strategic property behind a first mortgage bond, is capable of earning enough to pay half the interest on the particular bonds, then the reorganization plan may provide that new bonds, similar to the old, will be given to the extent of 50 per cent of the face value of the old bonds, with preferred stock possibly making up the other 50 per cent. In some instances these bondholders may be given income bonds, or they may be asked to accept a new issue of bonds bearing a lower rate of interest than was being paid on the old bonds.

Greater sacrifices must be made by bondholders who are junior to those stated above. Where the worth of the properties is less than the amount of the first and second mortgage, bonds having a claim junior to these, and debenture bonds, may be asked to exchange their bonds for stock. Or, they may be asked to stand an assessment of, for example, 20 per cent of the face value of their bonds, for which they will receive a junior bond. In order to induce them to pay this assessment, or buy the new securities, they may also be offered some stock in addition.

After reorganization the company would not want to be faced with large bond maturities within a few years. This could probably force them back into receivership or bankruptcy. Thus even though a particular bond issue might be undisturbed in a reorganization, the new bonds exchanged for the old may have a maturity much farther in the future.

General unsecured creditors theoretically are on equal standing with the debenture bondholders. Actually, however, the debenture bondholders might come out better because through their protective committee they may have been better bargainers than the general creditors. Where the corporate property is worth no more than the amount represented by the senior claims, the general creditors may be given the "opportunity" to buy new securities, in some instances junior bonds. They may also be offered some stock free as an inducement to buy the other securities.

In the case of some industrial reorganizations where there are no bonds outstanding, the general creditors may be given bonds for their claims. In such cases the reason for the failure is usually the inability to pay off the large floating debt as it became due. The solution here would therefore be to fund the debt and thus extend the maturities some distance into the future.

When income bonds and preferred stock are offered to old security holders, sinking funds are often provided in the contract as an added inducement. It is realized that such funds might improve the market for the securities in the future. Furthermore, the financial structure would be improved by the retirement of senior securities. In some instances the income bonds and preferred stock will be convertible into common stock, or they may carry warrants entitling the holders thereof to buy the common stock at prices stated in the contract. In this way old security holders, who have been asked to undergo sacrifices, will be able to benefit from any success that may be experienced by the company in the future.

The reorganization plan should provide for a capitalization that will enable the company to meet the bond interest even in bad years. Average earnings should also be sufficient to meet the interest on income bonds. In some instances the income bonds carry a low cumulative or fixed rate, and an additional "contingent" rate. Or, the interest may accumulate for only a limited number of years, such as three years. The company should see its way clear eventually to pay dividends on any preferred stock that may be issued, but in many instances, since the preferred dividends do not constitute a fixed charge, preferred stock may be issued in rather liberal amounts.

Leases and Rental Contracts. Under Chapter X of the Bankruptcy Act, pending the reorganization of the company, the trustee may continue paying rentals for the lease of property, or he may refuse to pay them. In the latter case the owner of the property is entitled to a fair value for the use of the properties during the period the trustee has charge of them. In the case of rejected leases the owners in the reorganization can claim the amount of overdue rent, plus an amount not to exceed three year's rent from the time the property was returned to the owner or when he took possession. Under Section 77, railroads may also break leases and the owner of the property can come in as a creditor. The measure of damages is determined, however, by taking the present worth of the difference between the rent specified in the contract and a fair rent, for the period of the contract. Whether or not guaranties of interest and principal on bonds and dividends on stock, which arose in connection with a lease, are continued generally depends upon the disposition made of the lease. In most instances, when the lease is valuable to the leasing company, the guaranties will be continued in the reorganization.

Stockholders. Stockholders are often referred to as the residual owners of a company. In an ordinary liquidation all creditors would have to receive 100 cents on the dollar of their claims, both for principal and interest, before the shareholders would be entitled to anything. If the preferred stock is given a preference as to assets in event of liquidation, which is the usual situation, then anything left after the payment of creditors would be applied first toward the preferred until they had received the liquidating price. As a matter of academic interest it should be stated that anything remaining after this would be applied to the common stock. Actually, of course, liquidation usually brings less than the amount needed to pay creditors, and as a result, the shareholders, both preferred and common, receive nothing.

In an equity reorganization the courts have more or less followed the reasoning of the procedure indicated above for liquidation, with some modifications. It is referred to as the "absolute priority rule." If the property of the company is worth less than the amount of claims outstanding, the stock interest, both preferred and common, is wiped out, and they receive nothing in the reorganization.

According to Chapter X of the Bankruptcy Act, all classes of security holders must be given consideration in the reorganization plan. But this does not mean that the old stock interest cannot be eliminated. In some instances the preferred stockholders are given common stock and the old common stock is eliminated. In some instances the preferred stockholders are given a combination of both preferred stock and common stock. In some cases, the preferred stockholders are "assessed" a designated amount of dollars per share for which they are given a new bond equal in par value to the amount of the assessment, and then they are also given a certain amount of either new preferred or common shares. The common shareholders may be "assessed" a proportionately larger amount, and may also be given a proportionately smaller amount of new common stock. At the time of reorganization this common stock would normally be worthless, but it could gain value in the future as it has the residual claim in the reorganized company.

Shareholders, of course, cannot be compelled to pay assessments. But if they do not do so, their old stock interest is wiped out, and they receive nothing in the reorganization. When they are "assessed," it amounts to giving them the "opportunity" to buy new securities in the company. Since, however, they are usually given stock in the new company, many shareholders feel that paying the assessment results in their not only buying new securities in the company, but also in the retention of their stock interest in the company. Perhaps the shareholder should realize that under these circumstances his old equity is gone, and now he is merely being asked to buy new securities in the company. In some instances, however, the reorganized company gets back on its feet, and the stock may assume an appreciable market value sometime in the future. The bonds that are sold with the assessment are sometimes senior to those which the old bondholders, or some of them, have had to accept in exchange for their old bonds.

The new money that is needed in the reorganization may come in part from assessments of the kind just mentioned. Under the old reorganizations following equity receiverships it was oftentimes absolutely necessary to secure an appreciable amount of new money since part of it had to be used to pay off those security holders who had an equity left in the company, but who would not agree to the reorganization plan. Where the required majorities have approved the plan under Chapter X of the Bankruptcy Act, as will be discussed later in the chapter, the plan is binding on all the other security holders of the same class and, therefore, less payment would be necessary. For that reason, assessments are not so common now as formerly.

In some reorganizations the common shareholders are merely given warrants entitling them to purchase stock at a price in excess of the probable market value at the time. Although the warrants may not have a theoretical value at that time, they may actually sell in the market at a price which reflects the anticipated future rise in the price of the stock.

In many instances where the failure cannot be attributed directly to management, the old company officials may be needed to manage the reorganized company. Usually the management holds a substantial common stock interest in the company. If the common shareholders were offered nothing in the reorganization, the old officials might be lost to the company. It might be argued that they could be induced to stay with the company with an offer of large salaries. But with high tax rates, salary offers are not much of an inducement. Since any gain on the sale of stock would be reported as a capital gain on which a much lower tax would be paid, giving them stock, or warrants to purchase stock, would increase the probability of the old management staying with the company.

Chapter X procedures

Use of Voting Trust. The voting trust is often used in connection with a reorganization. In many instances the management is responsible at least in part for the failure of the company. Since the company officials are usually large shareholders, where an exchange of stock is effected in a reorganization, the old officials would probably, through their stock holdings, again be in immediate control of the reorganized company. The court may feel that adequate protection to the creditors might not result from this situation.

Aside from this point, another undesirable situation might result. Following reorganization the stock would probably sell for a relatively low price in the market since there would be little or no equity behind it. Thus it would be comparatively easy for some outside group to buy up control of the company for a relatively small amount of money before the company could get back on its feet.

In order to prevent situations of the kind just mentioned, the court may decide that the voting stock of the reorganized company should be placed in the hands of a voting trust for a designated period of years. The court will appoint trustees to hold and vote the stock. Voting trust certificates, rather than the stock itself, will be distributed to the security holders. But regardless of who the voting trust certificates may be given to, or regardless of who may acquire them in the market, the control of the company, through the election of directors, is in the hands of the trustees of the voting trust. In this way continuity of the management may be had until the company can get back on its feet, and the purposes of reorganization are accomplished.

Underwriting New Securities. As previously stated, the reorganization may call for the sale of new securities to the public, or an ordinary sale of new securities to old security holders, or the sale to them through an assessment. In the case of large companies, it is usual to have the sale of new securities, either to the public or to old security holders, underwritten by investment bankers. The latter will then take up any securities that remain unsold. Where shareholders fail to stand the assessment and buy the new securities along with the exchange of stock, the bankers will pay the assessment and get the new securities, and in addition will get any new stock offered the old shareholders. If warrants were being offered under these circumstances, they would be entitled to those not taken up by the shareholders.

Hearing on Reorganization Plan. We have been concerned at some length with the practical and legal considerations that go into the formulation of the reorganization plan. We will now return to the steps provided for in Chapter X of the Bankruptcy Act.

Within the time specified by the court, the trustee will submit the reorganization plan to the court. A hearing will then be held at which time the creditors or shareholders may present objections to the plan, amendments to it, or they may present reorganization plans of their own.

Role of the Securities and Exchange Commission. Chapter X provides that if the indebtedness of the company exceeds $3,000,000, the judge must request an advisory report from the Securities and Exchange Commission before he can approve or disapprove the plan. If the indebtedness is less than this amount, it is optional with the judge whether he will present the plan to the SEC. The report of the SEC, if requested, must be filed with the court within the time specified, or the SEC must indicate that it will not file a report, before the judge can take any action on the plan.

By this request the SEC becomes a party to the reorganization. It will make a searching examination of the company's position, and will be represented at all hearings. It will work with the protective committees and consult with their lawyers. Furthermore, the Commission will attempt to prevent the compensation of the protective committees from being excessive.

The Commission will then file a report with the judge indicating its recommendations with respect to the reorganization plans. It should be made clear, however, that the Commission acts in an advisory capacity only. The judge can follow the suggestions of the Commission, or he may ignore them entirely. As a practical matter, however, the Commission is in a position to give sound advice, and the judge usually is anxious to secure its recommendations.

In the case of public utilities doing an intrastate business the approval of the plan by the state regulatory commission may be necessary.

Approval of Plan by Court. After receiving the report of the SEC, if requested, the judge will enter an order approving one or more of the plans presented by the trustees, or others. In so doing the judge will make sure that the plan, (1) conforms to the requirements of the Bankruptcy Act, (2) that it is fair and equitable to the various classes of creditors and shareholders, and (3) that it is feasible and practical.

The judge then sets a time within which the creditors and shareholders affected by the plan may accept it. Those who are undisturbed in the reorganization, and those whose equity is wiped out, are not required to act. The judge will indicate into which class the particular creditors and shareholders are to be put. This is important since they vote on the plan by class.

Approval by Creditors and Shareholders. Following approval of a plan or plans by the court, the trustee is required to send to all those affected by the plan—(1) a summary of the plan or plans approved by the court, (2) the opinion of the judge approving the plan or plans, (3) the report, if any, filed by the SEC, or a summary thereof, and (4) any other material which the judge deems desirable for the creditors or shareholders.

The voting by the security holders is done under the supervision of the trustee. When *two-thirds in amount* of each class of creditors has voted in favor of the plan, and these acceptances in writing are filed with the court, the plan is binding on *all* creditors of that class, regardless of whether they voted or how they voted on the plan. If the company is insolvent, the shareholders have no vote on the plan, but if it is solvent, the approval of the plan by a majority in amount of each class of stock will make the terms binding on all the other shareholders in that class.

FINAL APPROVAL BY COURT. After the necessary favorable vote on the reorganization plan has been accomplished and this information is filed with the court, the latter will call a hearing to consider final confirmation of the plan. After the court is satisfied as to the validity of the plan, it will finally approve it and issue a final decree, (1) discharging the company from its debts and terminating the rights of shareholders, except as provided in the plan, (2) discharging the trustee, (3) making such other provisions as may be equitable, and (4) closing the estate. The judge may also specify that not sooner than five years thereafter, holders of old securities who shall not have surrendered their old securities shall not be entitled to the new securities. Any securities or cash remaining unclaimed shall thereupon become the property of the company or its successor.

RECEIVERSHIP UNDER CHAPTER X COMPARED WITH EQUITY RECEIVERSHIP. The major change in receivership under the Bankruptcy Act has to do with the problem of dissenters. Under equity receivership, dissenters can demand their full payment. In this way, some creditors can benefit at the expense of others who take a long range rehabilitation point of view. Under the Chandler Act, dissenters may be bound by the actions of others of their class. The law takes away certain rights of creditors to demand their legal claim in bankruptcy. Since Chapter X states that all of a class of creditors will be bound by a reorganization plan if two thirds of that class agree, certain safeguards for fairness are written into the Act. Under equity receivership, all the court looked for was approval of the plan by interested parties. In Chapter X reorganizations, the plan must be approved by two thirds of each class of creditor and one half of each class of owner with equity, but in addition, it must be approved originally by the Trustee and must also be approved by the court after a recommendation from the SEC. In Bankruptcy Act reorganizations, the court, trustee, and SEC consider the proposed plans on their fairness to interested parties as well as on the satisfaction of those parties. The Chandler Act prevents a small group of dissenters from holding up reorganization. It also usually reduces the need for payment of cash to dissenters; thus allowing the new corporation to get a better start with less new cash required.

Advantages of Reorganization Under Bankruptcy Act. We pointed out earlier in the chapter that the Bankruptcy Act was amended to permit reorganizations in order to overcome the defects in reorganizations following equity receivership. The study leading to these amendments was made by the Securities and Exchange Commission. Following are the principal advantages of reorganization under the Bankruptcy Act. These apply with equal force to reorganization of railroads under Section 77, which will be briefly discussed later in the chapter, and to other types of corporations under Chapter XI.

1. *Foreclosure sale eliminated.* It will be recalled that in reorganizations following equity receiverships, if 100 per cent agreement could not be obtained among the security holders, a court sale of the property was necessary in order to freeze out those whose equity was gone, and to establish a basis for settling with those who did not agree to the plan. Under the Bankruptcy Act, when the required two-thirds approval of each class of creditors, and a majority approval of each interested class of stock is obtained, the reorganization plan is made binding on all the security holders. This eliminates the necessity of court sale.

2. *Ancillary receiverships eliminated.* It will be recalled that when action is brought for the appointment of a receiver in a federal court, if some of the property of the company is located in other court districts, it will be necessary to bring ancillary receivership actions for the appointment of receivers in the various court districts. This procedure is costly and may prove to be burdensome. Under the Bankruptcy Act, the one trustee (or co-trustees) is all that is necessary.

3. *Protective committees under the supervision of the court.* Under equity reorganizations the management or bankers having access to the lists of security holders in some instances were able to form protective committees for their own protection before others could get in touch with the creditors and other security holders.

Also in many instances the management was able to control the committees and thus control the reorganization committee. Under the Bankruptcy Act, lists of security holders must be made public. Furthermore, the activities of the protective committees are under the supervision of the court, and in some instances also of the Securities and Exchange Commission.

4. *Reorganizations accomplished in less time.* Under equity proceedings receiverships often dragged out over a long period of years. The procedure provided under the Bankruptcy Act shortens the time of court jurisdiction.

5. *Reorganization plan formulated by trustees.* Under equity receiverships reorganization plans were drawn up by the reorganization committee, which represented the various protective committees. Often the plan favored one class of security holders over other classes. Under the Bankruptcy Act the independent trustee is charged with the duty of formulating the plan. He, of course, may get suggestions and plans from the security holders and in some instances from the Securities and Exchange Commission, but the final plan must be presented by the trustee. Furthermore, the final plan must be approved by the court after it has been satisfied that the plan meets all the requirements of the Act, is fair to the various classes of creditors and shareholders, and is feasible and practical.

6. *Reduction of problem of dissenters and reduced new cash needs.* These points were discussed under the comparison of Chapter X reorganizations with equity receivership proceedings.

Reorganizations other than Chapter X

ARRANGEMENTS UNDER CHAPTER XI. In addition to Chapter X, the Chandler Act amendments to the Bankruptcy Act in 1938 also added Chapter XI. This latter legislation is designed for the adjustment of smaller companies with only unsecured debts, whose financial difficulties have not reached a drastic situation. Like the other part of the Chandler Act, this chapter applies only to corporations other than railroads. Chapter XI provides for an "arrangement" rather than a complete reorganization of the company. According to the law, an *arrangement* is a "plan of a debtor for the settlement, satisfaction, or extension of the time of payment of his unsecured debts." As stated in the previous chapter an arrangement is similar to a composition settlement or extension, except that it is carried out under the Bankruptcy statutes and has the approval of the courts.

Only the debtor corporation can petition for an arrangement. The petition must state either that the company is insolvent or that it is unable to meet its debts as they become due. The amounts owed to creditors and the plan which the company proposes for the settlement or extension of the debts are included in the petition. If the court deems it necessary, a receiver will be appointed for the company. If a trustee in bankruptcy has already been appointed, he may continue his functions. If no receiver or trustee is appointed, the debtor company will continue in possession of its property. The court may in its judgment appoint an appraiser to examine the property.

The court then calls a meeting of the creditors and other interested parties. The notice of the meeting also includes a summary of the financial position of the company and the arrangement plan proposed by the company. At the meeting the judge hears witnesses, receives proofs of claims and allows or disallows them, examines the debtor company, and if they are willing, receives the acceptances of the creditors to the arrangement.

If the arrangement is accepted by all the creditors at this first meeting, the court will confirm the plan. If 100 per cent agreement cannot be obtained at this meeting, the court will not confirm the arrangement until it has been accepted in writing by a majority of the creditors representing a majority in amount of the claims (or if they are divided into classes, a majority in number and amount of each class of creditors). The debtor company must pay into the court any money or securities to be distributed to the creditors in accordance with the plan before the court will give its final confirmation. With the approval indicated above, the plan becomes binding on all the creditors regardless of whether they voted for the arrangement.

If the required approval of the creditors cannot be obtained, the court may dismiss the action and direct that proceedings be instigated against the company under other provisions of the Bankruptcy Act. It will be recalled that before the court will approve a petition for reorganization under Chapter X, it must be shown that relief cannot be obtained under Chapter XI.

Railroad Reorganizations Under Section 77. Most of our discussion of reorganizations under the Bankruptcy Act concerned industrials and public utilities, which come under Chapter X of the Bankruptcy Act (Chandler Act). Railroad reorganization is governed by Section 77 of the Bankruptcy Act. The general procedure in railroad reorganization is somewhat similar to that discussed above for other types of corporations, so we will merely indicate the major differences.

The petition to the court can be made voluntarily by the railroad with the approval of the Interstate Commerce Commission, or by creditors with claims aggregating 5 per cent or more of the total indebtedness of the company. If the petition is approved, the court will appoint the trustee who must be approved by the Interstate Commerce Commission.

The reorganization plan may be presented by the company, the trustee, or 10 per cent in amount of any class of creditors or shareholders. These plans are presented, not to the court, but directly to the Interstate Commerce Commission. The latter holds hearings on the plans and then files a report indicating its acceptance of one of the plans, or it may formulate its own plan of reorganization. Hearings are then held on this plan and the Commission files the final report with the court. If the court rejects the plan it is referred back to the Commission and the same procedure as before takes place.

Upon approval of the final plan by the court, the Interstate Commerce Commission will conduct the voting on the plan by the various classes of security holders. To make the plan effective it must be approved by two thirds in amount of each class of creditors, and if the company is solvent, a majority in amount of each class of shareholders. (If insolvent, approval by the shareholders is not necessary.) But even if less than these majorities vote in favor of the plan, the court may nevertheless approve the plan if it conforms to the requirements of the law, and it is thought that fair and equitable treatment is given to those rejecting the plan, and that the rejection is not reasonably justified. After confirmation by the court the plan is put into operation under the supervision of the Interstate Commerce Commission.

From what has been said, it is obvious that the Interstate Commerce Commission, rather than the trustee, has the principal responsibility for the reorganization plan. Furthermore, all fees of trustees and protective committees and other reorganization expenses must be approved by the Commission.

THE MAHAFFIE ACT. Despite the advantages of reorganization of railroads under Section 77 as compared with that following equity receivership, it is nevertheless costly and time consuming. In an effort to facilitate reorganizations of certain kinds, Congress in 1948 enacted the Mahaffie Act, which added Section 20b to the Interstate Commerce Act.

The Mahaffie Act provides for the voluntary recapitalization or readjustment of the funded indebtedness of railroads without going through the lengthy and costly reorganization procedure under Section 77. Under this new legislation the company may, with the permission of the Interstate Commerce Commission and the required approval of the security holders affected, alter any provision of a mortgage, indenture, charter or other instrument of any class of securities. Before submitting the proposed alterations to the security holders, the Commission must hold public hearings and make sure that the proposed alterations are (1) within the provisions of the law, (2) in the public interest, (3) in the best interests of the railroad, each class of shareholders, and each class of security holders involved, and (4) not adverse to the interests of any class of creditors not affected by the alterations.

After approval by the Commission, the plan is submitted to each class of security holders which is affected by the proposed alterations. To make the plan effective it is necessary to secure the approval of at least 75 per cent in amount of each class of security holders affected by the proposed alterations.

It should be noted that readjustments under the Mahaffie Act cannot be instigated by the general unsecured creditors, nor can their rights be altered in any respect under this legislation.

Questions

1. (a) Does the Bankruptcy Act provide for liquidation or reorganization of a company? Explain. (b) When was reorganization under the Bankruptcy Act first possible?
2. What types of corporation cannot be reorganized under Chapter X?
3. Indicate the procedure for having a trustee appointed under Chapter X.
4. Indicate the procedure followed under Chapter X to effect a reorganization.
5. Indicate in general the relative treatment accorded various classes of creditors in a reorganization under Chapter X.
6. What are the usual objectives to be accomplished in a reorganization?
7. Indicate in general the treatment given shareholders in a reorganization.
8. Compare reorganization under Chapter X of the Bankruptcy Act and under the equity courts.
9. (a) Explain what part, if any, is played by the Securities and Exchange Commission in a reorganization under Chapter X. (b) What advantages may be secured by reorganizing under Chapter X?
10. How does the reorganization of railroads under Section 77 differ from the reorganization of industrial companies under Chapter X?

11. Indicate the procedure for effecting an "arrangement" under Chapter XI of the Bankruptcy Act.

12. Indicate how a reorganization might be effected under the Mahaffie Act.

Problems

1. The following questions relate to the Hopewell Manufacturing Co. mentioned in the problem in Chap. 34. It is assumed that the company went into receivership; that 100 per cent agreement could not be obtained from the security holders; and that a court sale was necessary. Assume, further, that the taxes due have been paid off from the collection of accounts receivable; that there are no preferred general creditors; and that the security holders follow their strict legal rights. (a) At what figure do you think the "upset" price should be set? Why? (b) If the court sale takes place at the upset price stated by you in part (a), indicate how much will be received by each class of security holders. (c) If the average earnings were $110,000, at what figure do you think the property would sell? (d) If the property were bought at court sale for $1,500,000, how much on the dollar would be received by each class of security holders?

2. Assume that the Hopewell Manufacturing Co. is undergoing reorganization under Chapter X of the Bankruptcy Act and that the reorganization plan should give consideration to the collection of new capital through the assessment of security holders. Assume that the average earnings for the past 3 years have been $90,000; that the taxes have been paid off; that there are no preferred general creditors; and that the property is considered to be worth about $1,667,000. Draw up a reorganization plan for this company indicating the treatment that you would recommend for the various classes of security holders.

Chapter 36

DISSOLUTION, LIQUIDATION, AND BANKRUPTCY

Dissolution and Liquidation Contrasted. Thus far in the book we have been concerned with the organization, financing, financial administration, combination, and reorganization of corporations. The final phase in the life of any concern is dissolution and liquidation. In the chapters immediately preceding we have discussed the reorganization of corporate failures. Now we will briefly discuss the dissolution and liquidation of corporations, regardless of whether or not they are brought about by financial failure. The latter part of the chapter will be concerned with the termination of the business through bankruptcy proceedings. But first we should distinguish between "dissolution" and "liquidation."

The term "dissolution" means the legal termination of the life of the corporation. The charter of the company is surrendered and all the rights, powers, and duties conferred upon the corporation by the statutes and the charter are brought to an end. To dissolve a corporation properly it is necessary to follow in detail the procedure prescribed in the statutes of the state of its formation.

In contrast to dissolution, "liquidation" refers to the winding up of the business affairs of the corporation, the conversion of the assets into cash and the distribution of the cash to the proper creditors and security holders. In some instances the company will accept securities of other companies in payment for its assets, and then it will liquidate by distributing these securities to its own security holders.

In many instances involving failures, corporations are dissolved and liquidated at the same time. But this does not necessarily have to take place. A corporation that has failed may go through a reorganization and give up its old charter (thus being dissolved), but continue in business with a new corporate structure. In such a case it cannot be said that the business was liquidated. A company may liquidate by distributing its assets to its owners, but remain in existence as a corporate shell. Thus it was not dissolved.

Termination without failure

Reasons for Voluntary Dissolution or Liquidation. In most instances a company is liquidated because it is insolvent, is unable to pay its debts, or is unable to earn a satisfactory return. In some cases, however, the business is terminated due to other reasons. These reasons are as follows:

1. *Desire of owners to retire from business.* In the case of small close corporations, the owner-managers may be old and wish to retire from active business operations. They may sell the business in its entirety, or sell the assets piecemeal, distribute the cash to themselves, and dissolve the corporation.

2. *Liquidation prompted by excessive taxation and regulation.* There have been some instances where the owners have become indignant over what they believed to be excessive federal taxation or restrictions during defense or war times, and as a result have liquidated their businesses.

3. *Dissolution to lessen taxes.* When corporate tax rates are increased and excess profit taxes are imposed or the rates increased, a number of close corporations will dissolve the corporation and continue the business as a partnership in order to lessen the amount of taxes that must be paid. Double taxation for shareholders results from the fact that the corporation income is taxed, and then the same income (aside from the dividend exclusion and credit) is taxed again when it is distributed to the shareholders in the form of dividends. Furthermore, only corporations have been subject to the excess profits tax when it was in existence. Another factor which made the partnership form of organization more advantageous from a tax standpoint than formerly was the split-income provision for husband and wife which was put into the law in 1948. It should be noted that we are here speaking of dissolution of a corporation, and not liquidation of the business.

4. *Inordinate labor demands.* In some instances in recent years owners have liquidated their business because of unwise demands on the part of labor unions for wages in excess of what could be paid by the business.

5. *Liquidation due to decreasing profits.* Sometimes the decision to liquidate a business is made because the company's profit trend

is downward. The product manufactured may be of inferior quality compared with that made by other companies. Or large companies may be able to undersell the particular company. The concern may not be insolvent, or unable to pay its debts. It may merely be evident that insolvency or failure may result from continued operations, and the decision is made to liquidate.

6. *Exhaustion of resources.* Wasting asset companies such as mines, quarries, and oil and lumber companies are constantly depleting their assets as operations continue. There may be no more minerals or other assets to acquire in their particular region. When the assets are exhausted, the company may pay a liquidating dividend to the shareholders and dissolve. If depletion charges have been made, the company should have cash or its equivalent on hand equal to the original cost of the minerals to distribute. Or if it is not contemplated that the depletion reserve will be reinvested in new assets, the company may during the period of operations have paid dividends that represented in part liquidating dividends. In this event there would be relatively small liquidating dividends to pay upon dissolution of the company.

7. *Simplification of corporate structures.* In some instances in the process of expanding or absorbing other companies a large company or combination may have a number of different corporations operating properties. This may facilitate the management and operation of the combination, but in some instances it becomes unduly complex. Furthermore, separate taxes will have to be paid by all the corporations. In some instances a saving in taxes can be effected by the dissolution of some of the corporate entities. Here again it should be observed that we are discussing dissolution rather than liquidation.

8. *Dissolution Under Public Utility Holding Company Act.* This and the following reason for dissolution are not necessarily representative of voluntary dissolution, but since some discretion may be exercised by the company, and also since the dissolutions result from causes other than financial failure, they are listed under this heading.

The Public Utility Holding Company Act of 1935 requires the dissolution of certain electric and gas holding companies which are not necessary for a single integrated system. The plan for paying creditors and shareholders of the dissolved company must be approved by the Securities and Exchange Commission. In some instances the securities of the holding company are sold and the cash proceeds distributed to the security holders. In other cases dissolution takes place through the distribution of securities held by the holding company to its own security holders. Sometimes, assets sufficient in amount to pay off the creditors are sold, and the shareholders of the holding company receive the subsidiaries' shares.

Bondholders' claims are usually recognized at their face or involuntary liquidation value, rather than at a call or voluntary liquidation value, since the dissolution is considered to be involuntary. Preferred stock has not been accorded the strict priority treatment over common stock that it would receive in event of reorganization. Even though the worth of the corporate assets are less than that needed to pay the preferred in its entirety, the common shareholders may nevertheless be given some of the company's assets. This has resulted from the fact that the treatment accorded the two classes of stock has been based on the relative investment worths of the two classes of shares from a going-concern standpoint.

Another departure from the ordinary treatment of security holders is for the Securities and Exchange Commission to allow the public holders of securities better treatment than that accorded the same classes of securities which are held by the holding company. This has grown out of the theory that the holding company should not take advantage of its position to take precedence over the individual investor. This principle has been set forth by the United States Supreme Court in the "Deep Rock" case.[1]

9. *Dissolution resulting from antitrust laws.* In some instances dissolution of companies has resulted from a court decision or a consent decree when the company or combination has been found in violation of the antitrust laws.

Procedure of Voluntary Dissolution. We indicated above that dissolution is a statutory procedure and can be accomplished only by following the steps prescribed by the statutes. These statutes vary among the states, but the following is typical.

1. *Vote by shareholders.* In some states the voluntary proceedings may be initiated by the written approval of all the shareholders. If a meeting is called for the purpose of voting on the dissolution, the notice may have to be sent to all the shareholders, regardless of whether or not they possess voting rights. The usual vote required is two thirds of the voting power. In some states it is provided that this shall be the vote required unless otherwise specified in the charter, but in no case can it be less than a majority of

[1] Taylor v. Standard Gas and Electric Co., 306 U.S. 307 (1939).

the votes. In some states the vote by the shareholders follows the adoption of a resolution to dissolve by the board of directors.

2. *Filing of certificate.* The officers or shareholders then file a certificate of dissolution or statement of intent to dissolve with the proper state official, usually the secretary of state.

3. *Notice of dissolution.* All the shareholders and creditors are advised of the dissolution by the appropriate corporate officials.

4. *Liquidating agents.* The board of directors or trustees appointed by the shareholders may act as liquidating agents.

5. *Sale of property and distribution of proceeds.* The liquidating agents then proceed to sell the property in accordance with the statutes, pay the creditors off according to the degree of their claims, and any balance left is distributed to the shareholders. If preferred shareholders are entitled to a designated preference in event of voluntary dissolution, then this amount must be paid them before the common are entitled to anything. Ordinarily, the preferred is by contract entitled to the liquidation price plus accrued dividends before the common get anything. This is usually interpreted as a contract for the return of capital, and the preferred would be entitled to such accrued dividends even though they had not been earned by the company.

When the preferred is by contract entitled to a preferential amount ahead of the common in event of dissolution, and there are assets left in excess of the amount needed to pay the common its par or stated value, a serious question can be raised whether the preferred stock should participate with the common in the distribution of this excess. A similar question has been raised with respect to dividends from a going-concern standpoint. In the judgment of the author, and this is supported by some court decisions, although there are some of the contrary opinion, the giving to the preferred a preference as to assets upon dissolution should impliedly limit the stock to that preference. In other words, it would get the preferential amount and any excess of assets remaining should go to the common stock. If the preferred does not have a stated preference as to assets upon dissolution, then the preferred and common share and share alike. In other words, the preferred then would have no preference as to assets, but it would be equally participating with the common. In other situations the exact terms of the contract would govern.

The reason we do not have more decisions relating to the respective rights of the preferred and common upon dissolution is that usually the creditors take so much of the proceeds of the sale of the property, that there is little or nothing for the stockholders to share.

6. *Surrender of stock certificates.* In some states the statutes provide that upon receipt of the final liquidating dividend, the shareholders shall surrender their stock certificates for cancellation.

7. *Certificate of dissolution.* Some statutes prescribe that after the final winding up of the affairs have occurred, articles of dissolution must be filed, and the state will then issue a certificate of dissolution which officially extinguishes the corporation.

DISSOLUTION INITIATED BY STATE. The charter of a corporation is a contract between the state and the corporation as well as between the corporation and its shareholders. Since the state, through its laws, creates the corporation, it can also by its laws dissolve it. Following are the reasons why a state may dissolve a corporation.

1. *Revocation by legislature.* When special charters by the legislature are permitted, they may contain a clause giving the legislature the power to dissolve the corporation. This could also be done by the legislature if the constitution or statutes of the state gave it this power. If such power is not given, the legislature has no authority to dissolve a corporation unless it has violated the contract or the laws of the state.

2. *Dissolution based on contingency.* The statutes in some of the states provide that certain acts or their omission on the part of the corporation will dissolve it. For example, in Illinois, unless the corporation begins business within one year from the date of the approval of its certificate of incorporation, the certificate shall be deemed to be revoked. The statutes of a number of the states provide that a corporation may be dissolved in event it fails to pay the taxes that are due the particular state.

3. *Dissolution from misuse or nonuse.* In some of the states the statutes provide that if the corporation misuses its rights and privileges, such as the doing of *ultra vires* acts, the state might bring action in the courts to dissolve the corporation. The nonuse of the corporate franchise may also give rise to court action to dissolve the company. This is similar to point 2 above except that in the one case the nonuse automatically cancels the charter, whereas in the other instances it merely gives the state the right to bring court action to revoke it.

4. *Dissolution due to expiration of charter.* In some states the life of a corporation is limited, and the duration must be stated in

the charter. In most of these states, however, the life may be extended by taking the proper action. But if this is not done, the life of the corporation automatically terminates at the end of the period stated in the charter. In many of the states the life can be perpetual, and this is assumed, unless otherwise stated in the charter.

PARTIAL LIQUIDATION. In some instances a corporation will undergo merely partial liquidation, and therefore will not dissolve. For one reason or another the securities of the company may be selling in the market at a relatively low price. If the company nevertheless has adequate working capital it might take advantage of the situation and use part of its cash, or convert some of its assets into cash, and retire part of the bonds that may be outstanding. This would tend to strengthen the capital structure of the company.

If no bonds are outstanding, or if they have all been retired, the company might buy back part or all of any preferred stock that may be outstanding. If there are both bonds and preferred stock outstanding, care should be exercised if any of the preferred stock is purchased before the bonds are retired. Otherwise, if the company fails as a result of such use of its cash, or if it is unable to meet any of its obligations, the company officials may be accused of giving preference to the preferred shareholders over its creditors. A company might also buy back part of its common stock, but should follow the same precautions.

Even if the securities of a corporation are not selling at a relatively low price in the market, if surplus cash is on hand, perhaps some of the senior securities should be retired either by their purchase in the market, the exercise of any call feature, or the asking for tenders from the security holders.

Termination following failure

FRIENDLY LIQUIDATION. In the case of small concerns with a relatively small number of creditors, it may be possible to have a friendly liquidation following failure. If all the creditors agree, the debtor company may be left in charge of its properties and its officers may proceed with an orderly liquidation of these properties, and the application of the proceeds on the debts owed.

If the management is honest and fairly efficient, and the creditors have confidence in them, this may prove to be the most satisfactory method of dissolution since it eliminates all the expenses of court action and may consume much less time than some of the judicial proceedings.

Compositions and Assignments. Composition settlement and assignments were discussed in Chapter 34, and are included here merely for the sake of completeness. Such settlements also are of a friendly character since if 100 per cent agreement cannot be obtained, dissenters, if not bought off, could throw the concern into receivership or bankruptcy. These settlements may be arranged privately or through an adjustment bureau sponsored by the National Association of Credit Men.

Liquidation Following Receivership. In Chapter 34 we discussed equity receivership. There it was pointed out that the outcome of receivership might be the rehabilitation or reorganization of the corporation, but that if neither of these was possible, the court might, except in the case of public service companies, order the liquidation of the corporation. Also in event of an attempted reorganization under Chapter X, if the required agreement of the security holders cannot be obtained, action may be brought for liquidation through bankruptcy proceedings.

Bankruptcy

Meaning of "Bankruptcy." In the preceding chapter we discussed the Bankruptcy Act in relation to the reorganization of corporations. It will be recalled that we stated that reorganization under the Bankruptcy Act was first made possible in 1933, by the enactment of Section 77. Later, Section 77B, and then in 1938, its substitute the Chandler Act, was added to the law. All these provisions related to reorganization. Up to 1933, the Bankruptcy Act provided only for the *liquidation,* rather than reorganization, of companies and the relief of individual debtors. The Bankruptcy Act still contains these provisions pertaining to individuals and companies, and it is with these provisions that we will now be concerned. When a company is undergoing reorganization under Section 77 or the Chandler Act, it is referred to in the law as a *debtor* company, but when it is undergoing liquidation under the Act it is called a *bankrupt.* Bankruptcy means that debts cannot be paid and that a court procedure is necessary for the discharge of the debtor's remaining debts and for the proper settlement of obligations with available assets. Bankruptcy is a last resort measure to obtain a discharge for the debtor and a fair treatment of creditors after all other possibilities have disappeared.

Purpose of Bankruptcy. Bankruptcy proceedings may be to the advantage of both the debtor and the creditor. If a person fails, not only may all his assets be exhausted by the creditors, but they may get deficiency judgments against him for the balance of whatever may be owed. If the debtor attempts to continue in business, or to start in anew, he can get nowhere because his old creditors may attach his property. Thus he may be prevented from ever getting back on his feet. Through bankruptcy proceedings, although his assets will be taken to apply to the debts, he is discharged from the balance still owed. This permits him to re-enter business or accumulate other property free from interference from his old creditors.

From the standpoint of the creditors, a debtor may conceal part of his property that should go to them. Or certain creditors may be preferred over others with the result that some will get more than they are entitled to while others will get less. Furthermore, the method of liquidation may be such that less will be available for the creditors. If bankruptcy proceedings are begun, all the assets of the debtor must be reported under the penalty of criminal action. The assets will be sold in an orderly fashion, and the creditors will be paid off according to their legal rights and preferences.

If a debtor goes through bankruptcy, he is prevented from doing so again within a period of six years. The bankruptcy laws apply to both individuals and corporations.

Initiating the Action. Bankruptcy proceedings may be started voluntarily by the debtor or involuntarily by the creditors. Any person or corporation, except a railroad, moneyed, or municipal corporation, may initiate a *voluntary* bankruptcy proceeding by filing a petition in the federal court stating that he is unable to meet his debts and asking that he be declared a bankrupt. In the case of corporations, the petition is filed by the board of directors.

Bankruptcy proceedings are usually not started, particularly voluntarily, unless all hope of a friendly settlement, extension, composition settlement, possibly creditors committee reorganization, or reorganization under equity receivership or the Bankruptcy Act, is abandoned.

Involuntary action can be brought by creditors against any person, partnership, or corporation owing debts of $1,000 or over, except railroad, moneyed, or municipal corporations, and wage earners and farmers. If there are 12 or more creditors, the petition must be filed by three or more of the creditors having claims aggregating $500 or more above any specific security for their claims. If there are less than 12 creditors, the petition may be filed by one creditor having claims of $500 or more in excess of any specific security. The petition must state that the debtor is totally insolvent and that an *act of bankruptcy* has been committed within four months from the time the petition is filed. Insolvency is defined by the statute to mean that the total assets, at a fair valuation, are insufficient to pay the debts.

ACTS OF BANKRUPTCY. Voluntary bankruptcy proceedings may be instituted without the debtor committing an act of bankruptcy, but as stated above, it is necessary that an act of bankruptcy be committed within four months from the time the petition was filed before involuntary action may be had. A creditor can ordinarily force a debtor to commit an act of bankruptcy by obtaining a lien against his property, if the debt involved is not satisfied within 30 days. A simplified statement of these acts follows:

1. Transferring, concealing, or removing any property with intent to hinder, delay, or defraud creditors
2. Transferring any property to one or more creditors with intent to prefer them over other creditors
3. Permitting any creditor to obtain a lien on the property through legal proceedings and not vacating or discharging the lien within 30 days
4. Making a general assignment for the benefit of creditors
5. Permitting or suffering either voluntarily or involuntarily the appointment of a receiver or trustee while insolvent or unable to pay the debts as they became due
6. Admitting in writing inability to pay the debts and expressing a willingness to be adjudged a bankrupt

FURTHER PROCEDURE. If the petition for bankruptcy has been filed voluntarily by the debtor, the action cannot be disputed, and the court will immediately adjudicate him a bankrupt. If it is an involuntary action, the debtor will be served with a subpoena and a copy of the petition. A hearing will be held and the court will then either dismiss the action because of lack of evidence that the debtor is insolvent and has committed an act of bankruptcy, or the court will adjudicate him a bankrupt.

At any time between the filing of the petition and the selection of a trustee, if the court deems it necessary, it may appoint a *receiver in bankruptcy* to take charge of the bankrupt's property and run the business until the petition is dismissed or a trustee selected. The functions and duties of this receiver are similar to those of a receiver in equity, except that he ordinarily serves for a shorter period of time.

The court will assign one or more *referees* to administer the case. A referee is a judicial officer who is appointed by the court for a term of years to administer bankruptcy cases. He may be working on several different cases in the same circuit at the same time. The referee acts practically as the judge in the case. He usually, however, does not have authority to discharge the bankrupt, and his actions are at all times subject to review of the court.

The referee will call a meeting of the creditors at which time their claims are proved and the bankrupt's position is examined. The creditors will be given the opportunity of selecting one or three *trustees* to take over the corporate property. In some instances the receiver is appointed a trustee. The trustee must receive the approval of the referee or the court, and he is considered an officer of the court. If the creditors do not select a trustee, the referee or court will appoint one. Title to all the bankrupt's property passes to the trustee, and it is his duty to collect all the property of the bankrupt, convert it into cash, pay the dividends (the term used in the law) declared by the referee, to the creditors, and render the required reports to the referee.

PRIORITY OF CLAIMS. Since the property of the bankrupt will bring an amount insufficient to pay off all the creditors' claims, it is of importance to know the order of priority under bankruptcy. The statute specifies the following order of priority:

1. The actual and necessary expenses of preserving the bankrupt estate—this includes filing fees, cost of recovering transferred or concealed property, and other administrative costs
2. Wages due workmen or servants of the bankrupt, earned within three months before filing of the petition for bankruptcy, but not to exceed $600 a person
3. Reasonable costs of creditors resulting in refusal, revocation, or setting aside an arrangement, a bankrupt's discharge, or conviction of a person for an offense under the statute
4. Taxes due the United States, a state, county, district, or municipality
5. Secured creditors with respect to the amount received from the specific security
6. Rent owed a landlord, and accrued within three months prior to the bankruptcy
7. General, or unsecured creditors, such as debenture bondholders and trade and bank creditors and balances, if any, owed secured creditors after they have received the proceeds from the sale of the specific pledged property

Debts Not Affected by Discharge. A discharge in bankruptcy discharges only those debts which are incurred before bankruptcy, and only those that are provable. Unless the following debts, however, are paid off in closing the estate, they are not discharged through bankruptcy.

1. Taxes due the United States, or a subdivision thereof
2. Liabilities for obtaining property under false pretenses or for willful and malicious injuries to the person or property of another, or for alimony due or to become due, or for support of wife or child
3. Debts that are not scheduled in time for proof, if known to the bankrupt, unless the creditors had knowledge of the bankruptcy proceedings
4. Debts created by the bankrupt's fraud, embezzlement, or misappropriation while acting as an officer or in any fiduciary capacity
5. Wages due workmen or servants, which have been earned within three months prior to the bankruptcy proceedings
6. Money received from an employee and retained to secure faithful performance by the employee of his contract

Bankrupt's Exemptions. The various states have statutes which exempt certain property of debtors from seizure by judicial process. The type of property exempt, its value, and who may claim the exemptions are specified in the law. In many of the states a *homestead* exemption up to a specified amount is permitted. In some states *personal property* such as household furniture and articles, tools, and clothing up to a specified value are exempt. Although the Bankruptcy Act is a federal statute, the exemptions allowable by the law of the particular state will be observed if the proper procedure is followed. Generally, exemptions apply only to individuals, not to corporations.

When preparing his schedules of property the bankrupt should claim his exemptions. The trustee will set aside this property or amount which is claimed as an exemption and report it to the referee. If the bankrupt agrees, the exempt property may be sold along with the other property, and the exemption will be allowed out of the proceeds obtained.

In some states a debtor can waive his right to certain exemptions, or he may lose them by failure to make proper claim when filing his schedules. In other states, however, it is considered contrary to public policy and therefore void, for a debtor to waive his exemptions. This grows out of the fact that the exemptions are of the nature of tools and clothing that will be needed by the bankrupt in earning a living, or household articles or the home which are not only for the benefit of the bankrupt, but also for the benefit of his wife and family.

ADVANTAGES OF BANKRUPTCY. The advantages of bankruptcy are the same as the reasons for bankruptcy laws stated earlier in the chapter. They are repeated here as a summary. If bankruptcy was not possible, a debtor might use his assets to pay some creditors, and the others would get little or nothing, although they might be on an equal footing with the repaid creditors. Or, the debtor might continue in business, even though he is running into debt further each day, until all the assets are exhausted, and there is little or nothing left for the creditors. Through bankruptcy the property or business of the bankrupt is placed under the control of the court and it cannot be dissipated. Furthermore, the creditors will be paid off in the order of their legal priority.

From the standpoint of the debtor, bankruptcy discharges him from any amounts owing to creditors after the property has been exhausted. This enables him to acquire property or a business in the future without interference from earlier creditors. He thus is given another chance to make good. In a few instances bankrupts have later become successful and paid off all the debts that were discharged in bankruptcy, even though they had no legal obligation to do so. If the property had been taken by the creditors without bankruptcy proceedings, probably the debtor would never have been able to get started in business again because the creditors would attach his property immediately for their deficiency judgments.

SHORTCOMINGS OF BANKRUPTCY. In some instances bankruptcy has been used by unscrupulous persons as a means of getting out of paying their just debts. Honest individuals in the same circumstances would probably not petition for bankruptcy, but rather would continue in business in an effort to pay their debts. In some instances debtors will conceal property in one way or another, and thus be discharged from their debts and still retain some of their property. The Bankruptcy Act is federal law, and the intentional concealment of property is a federal offense for which a person may be punished by imprisonment for a period not exceeding 5 years, or fined not to exceed $5,000, or both.

The expenses of bankruptcy proceedings are extremely high. In a great many cases all the property of the bankrupt is consumed by these expenses, and the creditors get nothing. Almost any type of judicial proceeding is costly. The forced liquidation resulting from the proceedings is also another factor in accounting for the relatively small amounts that are received by the creditors.

In some instances the creditors suffer because of the fact that the receivers, trustees, referees, and attorneys are appointed because of political favors. Since they are appointed either by the court, or with court approval, they are usually lawyers. The latter may not be poor businessmen, but the fact that a person is a lawyer is no assurance that he is a good economist or businessman. Every means available should be used to effect a settlement before bankruptcy proceedings are started.

Questions

1. (a) Distinguish between liquidation and dissolution. (b) How can a company liquidate without dissolving?
2. List the reasons why a company might liquidate and dissolve even if it did not fail or was about to fail.
3. Consult the statutes of your state to determine the procedure prescribed for the dissolution of a corporation.
4. For what reasons may a state initiate dissolution proceedings against a corporation?
5. Distinguish between voluntary and involuntary bankruptcy and state the ways that such actions may be initiated.
6. Indicate what is meant by an act of bankruptcy and give a list of such actions.
7. What debts are not discharged by bankruptcy?
8. Can all of a person's property be used to apply toward his debts under bankruptcy? Explain.
9. What advantages to the debtor might result from dissolution following bankruptcy rather than without such legal action?
10. (a) Can bankruptcy be taken by both individuals and corporations? (b) Can a person go through bankruptcy more than once? Explain.

Problems

1. The following questions relate to Problem 2, Chapter 33. (a) Do you believe that any of the companies should go through bankruptcy and dissolve? Explain. (b) Do you believe any of the companies should be reorganized under the Bankruptcy Act? Explain. (c) Do you believe that any of the companies could get along without the necessity for reorganization or liquidation? Explain.
2. If the company or companies that you recommended bankruptcy and dissolution for in the above question were unincorporated, would you be more inclined or less inclined to recommend bankruptcy and dissolution? Explain.

SELECTED READINGS

Accounting Trends and Techniques. New York: American Institute of Accountants. Published annually.

AMERICAN BANKERS' ASSOCIATION COMMITTEE ON CONSUMER CREDIT. *Instalment Loans to Small Business.* New York: The Association, 1947.

AMERICAN INSTITUTE OF ACCOUNTANTS. *A Program of Financial Planning and Controls.* (Financial Management Series, No. 103.) New York: The Association, 1953.

———. *Accounting Trends and Techniques in Published Annual Reports,* 7th ed. New York: The Institute, 1953.

AMERICAN MANAGEMENT ASSOCIATION. *Executive Compensations: Company Policies and Practices.* (Financial Management Series, No. 97.) New York: The Association, 1951.

ATKINS, W. E., EDWARDS, G. W., and MOULTON, H. G. *The Regulation of the Security Markets.* Washington: The Brookings Institution, 1946.

BACH, G. L. *Economics: An Introduction to Analysis and Policy.* Englewood Cliffs, N.J.: Prentice-Hall, Inc., 1954.

BADGER, RALPH E., and GUTHMANN, HARRY G. *Investment, Principles and Practices,* 4th ed. Englewood Cliffs, N.J.: Prentice-Hall, Inc., 1951.

BAIN, J. S. *Pricing, Distribution, and Employment,* rev. ed. New York: Henry Holt & Co., Inc., 1953.

BAKER, J. C. *Directors and Their Functions.* Boston: Harvard University, Graduate School of Business Administration, Division of Research, 1945.

BALLANTINE, H. W. *Ballantine on Corporations,* rev. ed. Chicago: Callaghan & Co., Inc., 1946.

BALLANTINE, H. W., and JENNINGS, R. W. (eds.). *Students Corporation Law Service.* Englewood Cliffs, N.J.: Prentice-Hall, Inc., 1950.

BARNES, LEO. *Your Buying Guide to Mutual Funds and Investment Companies.* Larchmont, N.Y.: American Research Council, 1956.

———. *Your Investments.* Larchmont, N.Y.: American Research Council. Published annually.

BECKMAN, THEODORE N., and BARTELS, ROBERT. *Credits and Collections in Theory and Practice,* 6th ed. New York: McGraw-Hill Book Co., Inc., 1955.

BELLEMORE, DOUGLAS H. *Investments: Principles and Practice.* New York: B. C. Forbes & Co., Inc., 1953.

BELLEMORE, DOUGLAS H., and IRONS, WALTER H. *Commercial Credit and Collection Practice,* 2d ed. New York: The Ronald Press Co., 1957.

BENSON, P. A., and NORTH, N. L. *Real Estate Principles and Practices.* Englewood Cliffs, N.J.: Prentice-Hall, Inc., 1954.

BERGH, LOUIS O., and CONYNGTON, THOMAS. *Business Law,* 5th ed. New York: The Ronald Press Co., 1956.

BERLE, A. A., JR. "Protection of Non-Voting Stock," *Harvard Business Review* (April, 1926), 257-65.

———. "Receivership," *Encyclopedia of the Social Sciences,* XIII, 149-53.

———. *The Twentieth Century Capitalist Revolution.* New York: Harcourt, Brace & Co., Inc., 1954.

BERLE, A. A., JR., and WARREN, W. C. *Cases and Materials on the Law of Business Organizations (Corporations),* Part II. Brooklyn: The Foundation Press, Inc., 1948.

BLACK, KENNETH, JR. *Group Annuities.* Philadelphia: University of Pennsylvania Press, 1955.

BOARD OF GOVERNORS OF THE FEDERAL RESERVE SYSTEM. *Sales Finance Companies.* (Release G 20.) Washington, D.C.: Government Printing Office, March 13, 1953.

BOGEN, JULES I. (ed.). *Financial Handbook,* 3d ed. New York: The Ronald Press Co., 1948.

BOGEN, JULES I. "Investment Banking," *Encyclopedia of the Social Sciences,* VIII, 268-77.

BOLTON, H. A., and EITEMAN, WILFORD J. *Investment Advice for Professional Men.* Ann Arbor, Mich.: Masterco Press, 1951.

BONBRIGHT, J. C., and MEANS, G. C. *The Holding Company.* New York: McGraw-Hill Book Co., Inc., 1932.

———. "Holding Companies." *Encyclopedia of the Social Sciences,* VII, 403-9.

BONNEVILLE, JOSEPH H., and DEWEY, LLOYD E. *Organizing and Financing Business,* 5th ed. Englewood Cliffs, N.J.: Prentice-Hall, Inc., 1952.

BOSLAND, C. C. *Corporate Finance and Regulation.* New York: The Ronald Press Co., 1949.

BRADLEY, JOSEPH F. "Accounting Aspects of Protective Provisions in Industrial Preferred Stocks," *Accounting Review* (October, 1948), 385-90.

———. *Fundamentals of Corporation Finance.* New York: Rinehart & Co., Inc., 1953.

BROWN, E. C. *Effects of Taxation: Depreciation Adjustments for Price Changes.* Boston: Harvard University, Graduate School of Business Administration, 1952.

BRYANT, WILLIS R. *Mortgage Lending, Fundamentals and Practices.* New York: McGraw-Hill Book Co., Inc., 1956.

BURTCHETT, FLOYD F., and HICKS, CLIFFORD M. *Corporation Finance,* rev. ed. New York: Harper & Bros., 1948.

CASEY, W. J., and LASSER, J. K. *Executive Pay Plans: A Research Study.* New York: Business Reports, Inc., 1951.

CHANDLER, LESTER V. *The Economics of Money and Banking,* rev. ed. New York: Harper & Bros., 1953.

CHAPIN, ALBERT F. *Credit and Collection Principles and Practice,* 6th ed. New York: McGraw-Hill Book Co., Inc., 1953.

CHERRINGTON, H. V. *The Investor and the Securities Act.* Washington, D.C.: American Council on Public Affairs, 1942.

———. *Business Organization and Finance.* New York: The Ronald Press Co., 1948.

CHURCHILL, B. C. "Size Characteristics of Business Population," *Survey of Current Business* (May, 1954), 15-24.

CISSEL, ROBERT, and CISSEL, HELEN. *Mathematics of Finance.* Boston: Houghton Mifflin Co., 1956.

CLENDENIN, JOHN C. *Introduction to Investments,* rev. ed. New York: McGraw-Hill Book Co., Inc., 1955.

COOPER, ROBERT V. *Investments for Professional People.* New York: The Macmillan Co., 1952.

Corporation Course. Englewood Cliffs, N.J.: Prentice-Hall, Inc., 1950.

Corporation Manual. New York: United States Corporation Co. Published annually.

CRANE, J. A. *Handbook of the Law of Partnership and Other Unincorporated Associations,* 2d ed. St. Paul, Minn.: West Publishing Co., 1952.

Credit Manual of Commercial Laws. New York: National Association of Credit Men. Published annually.

DAUTEN, CARL A. *Business Finance,* 2d ed. Englewood Cliffs, N.J.: Prentice-Hall, Inc., 1956.

DAVIS, RALPH C. *The Fundamentals of Top Management.* New York: Harper & Bros., 1951.

———. *Industrial Organization and Management,* 3d ed. New York: Harper & Bros., 1957.

DEWING, ARTHUR S. *The Financial Policy of Corporations,* 5th ed. New York: The Ronald Press Co., 1953.

DICE, CHARLES A., and EITEMAN, WILFORD J. *The Stock Market,* 3d ed. New York: McGraw-Hill Book Co., Inc., 1952.

DILLAVOU, ESSEL R., and HOWARD, CHARLES G., *Principles of Business Law,* 6th ed. Englewood Cliffs, N.J.: Prentice-Hall, Inc., 1957.

"Dividend Rights of Non-Cumulative Preferred Stock." *Yale Law Journal* (February, 1952), 245-52.

DOBROVOLSKY, S. P. *Corporate Income Retention 1915-1943.* New York: National Bureau of Economic Research, Inc., 1951.

DODD, E. M., and BILLYOU, DEFOREST. *Cases and Materials on Corporate Reorganization.* Brooklyn: The Foundation Press, Inc., 1950.

DORIS, LILLIAN (ed.). *Corporate Treasurer's and Controller's Handbook.* Englewood Cliffs, N.J.: Prentice-Hall, Inc., 1950.

———. *Business Finance Handbook.* Englewood Cliffs, N.J.: Prentice-Hall, Inc., 1953.

DORIS, LILLIAN, and FRIEDMAN, E. J. *Corporate Secretary's Manual and Guide,* rev. ed. Englewood Cliffs, N.J.: Prentice-Hall, Inc., 1949.

DOUGLAS, W. O. *Democracy and Finance.* New Haven: Yale University Press, 1940.

———. "Bankruptcy," *Encyclopedia of the Social Sciences,* II, 449-54.

DOWRIE, GEORGE W., and FULLER, DOUGLAS R. *Investments,* 2d ed. New York: John Wiley & Sons, Inc., 1950.

DRUCKER, P. F. *Concept of the Corporation.* New York: The John Day Co., Inc., 1946.

DUE, JOHN F. *Intermediate Economic Analysis,* 3d ed. Homewood, Ill.: Richard D. Irwin, Inc., 1956.

EITEMAN, WILFORD J., and DAVISSON, CHARLES N. *The Lease as a Financing and Selling Device.* Ann Arbor, Mich.: Bureau of Business Research, University of Michigan, 1951.

ENGEL, LOUIS. *How To Buy Stocks.* Boston: Little, Brown & Co., 1953.

EPSTEIN, RALPH C. *How To Invest Your Money.* New York: The Ronald Press Co., 1955.

Ettinger, R. P., and Golieb, D. E. *Credits and Collections,* 3d ed. Englewood Cliffs, N.J.: Prentice-Hall, Inc., 1949.

Federal Tax Course. Englewood Cliffs, N.J.: Prentice-Hall, Inc. Latest year.

Fergusson, D. A. "Recent Developments in Preferred Stock Financing," *Journal of Finance* (September, 1952), 447-62.

Finney, H. A., and Miller, H. E. *Principles of Accounting, Advanced,* 4th ed. Englewood Cliffs, N.J.: Prentice-Hall, Inc., 1952.

———. *Principles of Accounting, Introductory,* 4th ed. Englewood Cliffs, N.J.: Prentice-Hall, Inc., 1953.

Fisher, E. M. *Urban Real Estate Markets: Characteristics and Financing.* New York: National Bureau of Economic Research, 1951.

Foster, Major B., Rogers, Raymond, Bogen, Jules I., and Nadler, Marcus. *Money and Banking,* 4th ed. Englewood Cliffs, N.J.: Prentice-Hall, Inc., 1953.

Foulke, R. A. *Financial Guides to Healthy Business Management.* New York: Dun & Bradstreet, Inc., 1951.

———. *Practical Financial Statement Analysis,* 3d ed. New York: McGraw-Hill Book Co., Inc., 1953.

Friedrich, A. A. "Stocks and Stock Ownership," *Encyclopedia of the Social Sciences,* XIV, 403-7.

Friend, Irwin. *Activity on the Over-the-Counter Markets.* Philadelphia: University of Pennsylvania Press, 1951.

Gerstenberg, Charles W. *Financial Organization and Management,* 3d ed. Englewood Cliffs, N.J.: Prentice-Hall, Inc., 1951.

Gordon, Leland J. *Economics for Consumers,* 2d ed. New York: American Book Co., 1950.

Gordon, R. A. *Business Leadership in the Large Corporation.* Washington, D.C.: The Brookings Institution, 1945.

Graham, Benjamin. *The Intelligent Investor,* rev. ed. New York: Harper & Bros., 1954.

Graham, Benjamin, and Dodd, David L. *Security Analysis,* 3d ed. New York: McGraw-Hill Book Co., Inc., 1951.

Grange, W. J. *Corporation Law for Officers and Directors.* New York: The Ronald Press Co., 1940.

Grodinsky, Julius. *Investments.* New York: The Ronald Press Co., 1953.

Guthmann, H. G. *Analysis of Financial Statements,* 4th ed. Englewood Cliffs, N.J.: Prentice-Hall, Inc., 1953.

Guthmann, H. G., and Dougall, Herbert E. *Corporate Financial Policy,* 3d ed. Englewood Cliffs, N.J.: Prentice-Hall, Inc., 1955.

Hayes, Douglas A. *Appraisal and Management of Securities.* New York: The Macmillan Co., 1956.

Heckert, J. Brooks, and Willson, James D. *Controllership.* New York: The Ronald Press Co., 1952.

Hickman, W. Braddock. *The Volume of Corporate Bond Financing Since 1900.* National Bureau of Economic Research, Inc. Princeton, N.J.: Princeton University Press, 1953.

Hoagland, Henry E. *Corporation Finance,* 3d ed. New York: McGraw-Hill Book Co., Inc., 1947.

———. *Real Estate Finance.* Homewood, Ill.: Richard D. Irwin, Inc., 1954.

Holzman, Robert S. *Corporate Reorganizations,* 2d ed. New York: The Ronald Press Co., 1955; rev. printing, 1956.

Homan, P. T., and Watkins, M. W. "Trusts," *Encyclopedia of the Social Sciences,* XV, 111-21.

How to Invest Wisely. Great Barrington, Mass.: American Institute for Economic Research. Latest edition.

Howard, Bion B., and Upton, Miller. *Introduction to Business Finance.* New York: McGraw-Hill Book Co., Inc., 1953.

Husband, William H., and Dockeray, James C. *Modern Corporation Finance,* 4th ed. Homewood, Ill.: Richard D. Irwin, Inc., 1957.

Investment Bankers Association of America. *Fundamentals of Investment Banking.* Englewood Cliffs, N.J.: Prentice-Hall, Inc., 1949.

Jacoby, N. H., and Saulnier, R. J. *Term Lending to Business.* New York: National Bureau of Economic Research, Inc., 1942.

———. *Business Finance and Banking.* New York: National Bureau of Economic Research, Inc., 1947.

———. *Financing Inventory on Field Warehouse Receipts.* New York: National Bureau of Economic Research, Inc., 1944.

Jacoby, N. H., and Weston, J. F. "Factors Influencing Managerial Decisions in Determining Forms of Business Financing: An Exploratory Study," *Conference on Research in Business Finance.* New York: National Bureau of Economic Research, Inc., 1952.

James, Clifford. *Economics, Basic Problems and Analysis.* Englewood Cliffs, N.J.: Prentice-Hall, Inc., 1951.

Johnson, R. W. "Subordinated Debentures: Debt That Serves as Equity," *Journal of Finance* (March, 1955), 1-16.

Jome, Hiram L. *Corporation Finance.* New York: Henry Holt & Co., Inc., 1948.

Jordan, David F., and Dougall, Herbert E. *Investments,* 6th ed. Englewood Cliffs, N.J.: Prentice-Hall, Inc., 1952.

Kamm, Jacob O. *Economics of Investment.* New York: American Book Co., 1951.

———. *Investor's Handbook.* Cleveland: The World Publishing Co., 1954.

———. *Making Profits in the Stock Market.* Cleveland: The World Publishing Co., 1952.

Kaplan, A. D. H. *Big Enterprise in a Competitive System.* Washington, D.C.: The Brookings Institution, 1954.

Karrenbrock, W. E., and Simons, Harry. *Intermediate Accounting,* 2d ed. Cincinnati: South-Western Publishing Co., 1954.

Kennedy, R. D., and McMullen, S. Y. *Financial Statements,* rev. ed. Homewood, Ill.: Richard D. Irwin, Inc., 1952.

Kimmel, L. H. *Share Ownership in the United States.* Washington, D.C.: The Brookings Institution, 1952.

Koch, A. R. *The Financing of Large Corporations 1920-1939.* New York: National Bureau of Economic Research, Inc., 1943.

Leavitt, D. A. *The Voting Trust.* New York: Columbia University Press, 1941.

Leffler, George L. *The Stock Market,* 2d ed. New York: The Ronald Press Co., 1957.

Lilienthal, D. E. *Big Business: A New Era.* New York: Harper & Bros., 1953.

Loeb, Gerald M. *The Battle for Investment Survival.* New York: Hurry House Publishers, 1954.

LUSK, HAROLD F. *Business Law, Principles and Cases,* 5th ed. Homewood, Ill.: Richard D. Irwin, Inc., 1955.

McCORMICK, E. T. *Understanding the Securities Act and the SEC.* New York: American Book Co., 1948.

MANN, EVERETT J. *You Can Make Money on the Stock Market.* New York: The Macmillan Co., 1955.

MASTELLER, KENNETH C. *How to Avoid Financial Tangles.* Great Barrington, Mass.: American Institute for Economic Research. Latest edition.

MAURER, HERRYMON. *Great Enterprise: Growth and Behavior of the Big Corporation.* New York: The Macmillan Co., 1955.

MAYER, MARTIN. *Wall Street: Men and Money.* New York: Harper & Bros., 1955.

MERRITT, ROBERT D. *Financial Independence Through Common Stocks.* New York: Simon & Schuster, Inc., 1954.

NADLER, MARCUS, HELLER, S., and SHIPMAN, S. S. *The Money Market and Its Institutions.* New York: The Ronald Press Co., 1955.

NATIONAL ASSOCIATION OF MANUFACTURERS. *Financing Small Business.* New York: The Association, 1946.

———. *Major Tendencies in Business Finance.* New York: The Association, 1953.

NATIONAL BUREAU OF ECONOMIC RESEARCH. *Conference on Research in Business Finance.* (Special Conference Series, No. 3.) New York: The Bureau, 1952.

———. *Regularization of Business Investment.* Princeton, N.J.: Princeton University Press, 1954.

NATIONAL INDUSTRIAL CONFERENCE BOARD, INC. *Employee Stock Purchase Plans in the United States.* New York, 1928.

———. *Employee Stock Purchase Plans and the Stock Market Crisis of 1929.* New York, 1930.

———. *Prevailing Practices Regarding Corporation Directors.* New York, 1939.

———. *Employee Savings and Investment Plans.* (Studies in Personnel Policy, No. 133.) New York, 1943.

———. *Compensation and Duties of Corporate Directors.* (Studies in Business Policy, No. 16.) New York, 1946.

———. *Profit Sharing for Executives.* (Studies in Personnel Policy, No. 90.) New York, 1948.

———. *Executive Stock Ownership Plans.* (Studies in Personnel Policy, No. 120.) New York, 1951.

———. *The Duties of Financial Executives.* (Studies in Business Policy, No. 56.) New York, 1952.

———. *Stock Ownership Plans for Workers.* (Studies in Personnel Policy, No. 132.) New York, 1953.

———. *The Corporate Directorship.* (Studies in Business Policy, No. 63.) New York, 1953.

NEW YORK STOCK EXCHANGE. *Stock Ownership Plans for Employees.* New York, 1953.

———. *1956 Census of Shareowners.* New York, 1956.

OWENS, R. N. *Business Organization and Combination,* 4th ed. Englewood Cliffs, N.J.: Prentice-Hall, Inc., 1951.

Partnership or Corporation Under Today's Tax Rates. New York: Research Institute of America, Inc., 1955.

Paton, W. A. *Advanced Accounting.* New York: The Macmillan Co., 1947.
———. *Essentials of Accounting,* rev. ed. New York: The Macmillan Co., 1949.
Paton, W. A., and Paton, W. A., Jr. *Asset Accounting.* New York: The Macmillan Co., 1952.
———. *Corporation Accounts and Statements.* New York: The Macmillan Co., 1955.
Phelps, C. W. *The Role of the Sales Finance Companies in the American Economy.* Baltimore: Commercial Credit Co., 1952.
———. *Instalment Sales Financing: Its Services to The Dealer.* Baltimore: Commercial Credit Co., 1953.
———. *Financing the Instalment Purchases of the American Family.* Baltimore: Commercial Credit Co., 1954.
———. *Using Instalment Credit.* Baltimore: Commercial Credit Co., 1955.
———. *The Role of Factoring in Modern Business Finance.* Baltimore: Commercial Credit Co., 1956.
Pickett, Ralph R., and Ketchum, Marshall D. *Investment Principles and Policy.* New York: Harper & Bros., 1954.
Pilcher, C. James. *Raising Capital With Convertible Securities.* Ann Arbor, Mich.: Bureau of Business Research, University of Michigan, 1955.
Plum, Lester V., and Humphrey, Joseph H., Jr. *Investment Analysis and Management.* Homewood, Ill.: Richard D. Irwin, Inc., 1951.
Prather, Charles L. *Financing Business Firms.* Homewood, Ill.: Richard D. Irwin, Inc., 1955.
Prime, John H. *Investment Analysis,* 2d ed. Englewood Cliffs, N.J.: Prentice-Hall, Inc., 1952.
Prochnow, Hebrert V. (ed.). *American Financial Institutions.* Englewood Cliffs, N.J.: Prentice-Hall, Inc., 1951.
Prochnow, Herbert V., and Foulke, R. A. *Practical Bank Credit,* 2d ed. Englewood Cliffs, N.J.: Prentice-Hall, Inc., 1950.
Purdy, W. L., and Others. *Corporate Concentration and Public Policy,* 2d ed. Englewood Cliffs, N.J.: Prentice-Hall, Inc., 1952.
Rappaport, Louis H. *S E C Accounting Practice and Procedure.* New York: The Ronald Press Co., 1956.
Robbins, Sidney M. *Managing Securities.* Boston: Houghton Mifflin Co., 1954.
Robnett, R. H., Hill, T. M., and Beckett, J. A. *Accounting, A Management Approach.* Homewood, Ill.: Richard D. Irwin, Inc., 1951.
Rodkey, R. G. *Preferred Stocks as Long-Term Investments.* Ann Arbor, Mich.: University of Michigan, 1932.
Rohrlich, Chester. *Organizing Corporate and Other Business Enterprises,* rev. ed. Albany: Matthew Bender & Co., Inc., 1953.
Ryals, Stanley D., and Cox, David F. *Investment Trust and Funds.* Great Barrington, Mass.: American Institute for Economic Research. Latest edition.
Sanders, T. H. *Annual Reports to Stockholders, Employees, and the Public.* Boston: Harvard University, Graduate School of Business Administration, 1949.
Saulnier, R. J., and Jacoby, N. H. *Accounts Receivable Financing.* New York: National Bureau of Economic Research, Inc., 1943.
———. *Financing Equipment for Commercial and Industrial Enterprises.* New York: National Bureau for Economic Research, Inc., 1944.

Sauvain, Harry C. *Investment Management.* Englewood Cliffs, N.J.: Prentice-Hall, Inc., 1953.

Schultz, B. E. *The Securities Market and How it Works.* New York: Harper & Bros., 1946.

Seidman, W. S. *Finance Companies and Factors.* New York: National Conference of Commercial Receivables Cos., Inc., 1949.

Shaffner, F. I. *The Problem of Investment.* New York: John Wiley & Sons, Inc., 1936.

Shaw, E. S. *Money, Income, and Monetary Policy.* Homewood, Ill.: Richard D. Irwin, Inc., 1950.

Shultz, W. J., and Reinhart, H. *Credit and Collection Management,* 2d ed. Englewood Cliffs, N.J.: Prentice-Hall, Inc., 1954.

Small Business Administration. *Bank–SBA Participation Loan Plans.* Washington, D.C.: Small Business Administration, February, 1956.

Smith, C. A., and Ashburne, J. G. *Financial and Administrative Accounting.* New York: McGraw-Hill Book Co., Inc., 1955.

Spellman, H. S. *A Treatise on the Principles of Law Governing Corporate Directors.* Englewood Cliffs, N.J.: Prentice-Hall, Inc., 1931.

Steiner, W. H., and Shapiro, Eli. *Money and Banking,* 3d ed. New York: Henry Holt & Co., Inc., 1953.

Stevens, R. S. *Handbook on the Law of Private Corporations,* 2d ed. St. Paul, Minn.: West Publishing Co., 1949.

Stevens, W. H. S. "Rights of Non-Cumulative Preferred Stockholders," *Columbia Law Review* (December, 1934), 1439-61.

———. "The Discretion of Directors in the Distribution of Non-Cumulative Preferred Dividends," *Georgetown Law Journal* (January, 1936), 371-96.

———. "Stockholders' Participation in Profits," *Journal of Business of the University of Chicago* (April, 1936), 114-32; (July, 1936), 210-30.

———. "Stockholders' Participation in Assets in Dissolution," *Journal of Business of the University of Chicago* (January, 1937), 46-73.

———. "Voting Rights of Capital Stock and Shareholders," *Journal of Business of the University of Chicago* (October, 1938), 311-48.

Stocking, G. W., and Watkins, M. W. *Monopoly and Free Enterprise.* New York: Twentieth Century Fund, 1951.

Stokes, M. L., and Arlt, Carl T. *Money, Banking, and the Financial System.* New York: The Ronald Press Co., 1955.

Taylor, W. Bayard, and Graner, Frank M. *Financial Policies of Business Enterprise,* 2d ed. New York: Appleton-Century-Crofts, Inc., 1956.

Thomas, Rollin G. *Our Modern Banking and Monetary System.* Englewood Cliffs, N.J.: Prentice-Hall, Inc., 1950.

Tomlinson, Lucile. *Practical Formulas for Successful Investing.* New York: Wilfred Funk, Inc., 1953.

Twentieth Century Fund, Inc. *The Security Markets.* New York, 1935.

Votaw, Dow. *Legal Aspects of Business Administration.* Englewood Cliffs, N.J.: Prentice-Hall, Inc., 1956.

Waterman, M. H., Eiteman, W. J., and Others. *Essays on Business Finance,* 2d ed. Ann Arbor, Mich.: Masterco Press, 1953.

Weimer, Arthur M., and Hoyt, Homer. *Principles of Real Estate,* 3d ed. New York: The Ronald Press Co., 1954.

Weissman, R. I. *The Investment Company and the Investor.* New York: Harper & Bros., 1951.

WESTON, J. F. *The Role of Mergers in the Growth of Large Firms.* Berkeley, Calif.: University of California Press, 1953.

———. "The Finance Function," *Journal of Finance* (September, 1954), 265-82.

WHITTLESEY, CHARLES R. *Principles and Practices of Money and Banking,* rev. ed. New York: The Macmillan Co., 1954.

WIESENBERGER, ARTHUR. *Investment Companies.* New York: Arthur Weisenberger & Co. Published annually.

WILHELM, DONALD, JR. *Credit Sources for Small Business.* [Economic (Small Business) Series, No. 46.] Washington, D.C.: Department of Commerce, 1945.

WILLIAMS, C. M. *Cumulative Voting for Directors.* Boston: Harvard University, Graduate School of Business Administration, 1951.

WILLMORE, THOMAS F. *A Lifetime Investment Program.* New York: Harper & Bros., 1954.

WINN, WILLIS. *Factors Affecting Long-Run Growth of Over-the-Counter Markets.* Philadelphia: University of Pennsylvania Press, 1954.

WIXON, RUFUS (ed.) and KELL, WALTER G. (staff ed.) *Accountants' Handbook,* 4th ed., New York: The Ronald Press Co., 1956.

INDEX